Persuasions of the
Witch's Craft

Persuasions of the Witch's Craft

Ritual Magic in Contemporary England

T. M. LUHRMANN

Harvard University Press
Cambridge, Massachusetts

First Harvard University Press paperback edition, 1991

Library of Congress Cataloging-in-Publication Data

Luhrmann, T. M. (Tanya M.), 1959–
  Persuasions of the witch's craft: ritual magic in contemporary
England / T. M. Luhrmann.
      p.   cm.
  Bibliography: p.
  Includes index.
  ISBN 0-674-66323-3 (alk. paper) (cloth)
  ISBN 0-674-66324-1 (paper)
  1. Witchcraft — England — History — 20th century.   2. Magic — England —
History — 20th century.   3. England — Religion — 20th century.
  I. Title.
BF1581.L84   1989   88-33382
133.4'3'0942 — dc19   CIP

For my parents

Contents

Part V Belief and action

Acknowledgements

THIS book owes a great deal to other people, and it is a pleasure to thank them for their kindness and concern. Its roots lie in a doctoral thesis in social anthropology, although the fruition has been quite different than the nature of those roots might have suggested. Three people in particular saw the thesis emerge, read drafts of the book, and have guided me from the very early stages of the research. Stephen Hugh-Jones supervised the thesis: he gave generously of his time and insight, and helped me to fashion scattered intuitions into a coherent whole; Ernest Gellner, who took over the supervision during Stephen's sabbatical, always pressed me to see the broader picture, and to be bolder in my claims; Geoffrey Lloyd spent many hours in conversation with me about the nature of magic, and inspired my interests in many of the issues described within. Gilbert Lewis and John Skorupski examined the thesis on which the book is based – John Skorupski also read the book for the publishers – and each made pertinent and productive remarks which have helped to shape this final product. Alan Macfarlane helped me to think about the nature of witchcraft and its practitioners; Sarah Harrison actually introduced me to my first witch, through friends of a friend's friend. Vincent Crapanzano read the draft for the publisher, and made very helpful comments. Paul Seabright read a draft of the book, and pointed out when the paragraphs became tendentious. Conversations with Pascal Boyer helped me to see the issues of part two more clearly. Shelley Burtt read the thesis and the book and helped me to put them both in order; she, more than anyone else, has taught me how to write – the clumsiness that remains is my own. John Geanakopolos read the draft, made acute comments, and tolerated me when the sentences misbehaved. I am most grateful to my family, who gave me the support and the courage I needed to approach my questions through an unconventional route.

The magicians I met and came to know as friends were welcoming and supportive even when I was at my most frustrating. Beth and Enoch in particular, but also Emily, Angel, and the Companions of the Glittering Sword; Simon and the Hornsey group; Gareth Knight and those at Greystone; the myriad of people I met in pubs and rituals – I learned far more from them, about human relations, about self-awareness, and about friendship, than I could begin to express. I am deeply grateful to them.

I would also like to thank those whose financial generosity has made this effort possible. The Wenner Gren foundation supported the fieldwork, as did the Richards Fund and the Wyse Fund of Cambridge University, and the National Science Foundation in the United States supported the graduate study itself. Christ's College elected me to a Research Fellowship during which time the thesis was completed and the book actually written. Without this support, the work may never have been done; without the grace and scholarly encouragement with which Christ's surrounded me, it certainly would have been done less well.

The author and publisher would like to thank the following for their kind permission to reproduce figures: Wolfe van Brussel for figs 12, 13; Century Hutchinson Publishing Group Limited for figs 8, 9; Hermetic Research Trust for fig. 14; Marc Edmund Jones Estate for fig. 7, from Marc Jones *How to Learn Astrology* (Shambhala Publications, Inc., Boston, 1978, p. 103); Samuel Weiser, Inc., York Beach, ME for fig. 1, from Edred Thorsson *Futhark: A Handbook of Rune Magic* (1984, p. 8).

Finally, the author and publisher would like to thank the following for their kind permission to reproduce plates: Ruth Bayer for 11, 12, 13, 14, 15, 16, 17; Bodleian Library, Oxford for 6, from Robert Fludd *Utriusque Cosmi Maioris scilicet et Minoris Metaphysica, Physica Atque Technica Historia In duo Volumina secundum Cosmi differentiam divisa . . . Tomus Primus De Macrocosmi Historia* (Oppenheim, Johann Theodore de Bry, 1617, pp. 4–5); Janet and Colin Bord for 18, 19; Mary Evans Picture Library for 2, 3, 5 from Robert Fludd *Tomus Secundus De Supernaturali, Naturali, Praeternaturali Et Contranaturali Microcosmi historia, in Tractatus tres distributa* (Oppenheim, Johann Theodore de Bry, 1619, p. 275) and 7, 8; Fay Godwin for 20; Mansell Collection for 1; Museum der Bildenden Künste, Leipzig for 4; Cheska Potter for 9, 10.

T. M. Luhrmann
Christ's College, Cambridge

Persuasions of the
Witch's Craft

PART I

Speaking with a different rhythm: magicians in the modern world

1

What makes magic reasonable?

WILLIAM has been witch, kabbalistic initiate and solitary magician. He was born into a prosperous English family between the two World Wars. He was an only child. His father died soon after he was born, and as a young boy he was raised by his mother and aunt. He remembers that it was a strict but loving household. Rather shy by nature, he seems to have led a conventional and retiring life, first in private schools and then at Cambridge. He graduated with a classics degree, and took a comfortable job in the Foreign Office in London.

In the sixties, when new therapies, values and lifestyles appeared like apples in the market, William came across a popular psychological technique for controlling one's dreams and decided to experiment. For a while he went to sleep each night determined to 'visit', while dreaming, a friend he knew in a distant town. He always failed. One night, in the twilight between sleep and awareness, he heard a voice saying 'sacrifice to Zeus'. He decided that this was a voice of guidance, possibly the voice of God, and that if he followed the instructions his dream experiments might work.

So William set off for Silbury Hill, to sacrifice to Zeus at dawn. Silbury Hill is an ancient mound near one of Britain's most impressive stone circles. It is a drive of several hours from London. He arrived before dawn and clambered to the top of the grassy hill. To his pleasure, he lit the fire with the first match. He then sacrificed a steak. The Athenian divines traditionally were given meat. His classical education helped him with the invocation. When he got back to London he broke his fast – apart from the charred beef heart he had also sacrificed and eaten on the hill – and went to sleep, and dreamt that a sword was being forged for him with a blade the colours of the rainbow. The next night, he dreamt easily of visiting his friend. It was his first step into magic.

'These people wholly worship the devil, and often times have conference with him, which appeareth unto them in most ugly and monstrous shape.'[1] Something like an anthropology emerged in Hakluyt's sixteenth-century collection of voyagers' tales, rich with anecdotes of the spice and silk trade, of explorations of the torrid Americas and the frozen Russian wastelands, of

---

[1] David (1981: 563).

poison-darting Native American Indians and guru-worshipping Indians.
Savages fascinated early modern Europe, as counterpoint to an encrusted
civilization. Lafitau and Rousseau were among many who saw in 'natural man'
the way to understand and criticize themselves. Anthropology was fully born
only later, in the colonial heyday of a society which needed to assimilate
different cultures while maintaining its own hegemony.[2] As a discipline it has
progressed through many phases: grand theories of speculative evolution,
attacks upon the complacency of biological determinism, sweeping attempts to
understand the nature of Mind. In all these phases, anthropologists have
focused on the distant and more primitive, and claimed that through their very
exoticism, the near and apparently more complex might be better understood.

The world has changed for anthropology. The primitive societies are slowly
vanishing, and the foreign governments have become more wary of inquisitive
intruders. Ever more anthropologists are turning inward to study their own
society. But they have tended to focus on the immediate problems of urban life:
ethnicity, acculturation, religious revitalization. Few have continued to ask
traditional anthropological questions, to look for the exotic and learn from it
about the familiar. This study looks at ordinary middle-class English people
who become immersed in a netherworld of magic and ritual, and asks a classic
anthropological question: why do they practise magic when, according to
observers, the magic doesn't work?

In England several thousand people – possibly far more – practise magic as a
serious activity, and as members of organized groups.[3] They are not conjurors,
hired to produce rabbits at children's birthday parties. Their magic involves a
ritual practice based upon ideas about strange forces and the powers of the
mind. These are people who don long robes and perform rituals in which they
invoke old gods to alter their present reality. They read tarot cards and cast
astrological charts and may feel more holy on Beltane than on Good Friday. It
would be incorrect to think of them as 'only playing' at their magic, or as joining
their groups for the same social reasons that lead many people into
Freemasonry. Many of them take this magic as both a religion and a pragmatic

[2] Pertinent references on the emergence of anthropology include: Hodgen (1964), Pagden
(1982), Berkhofer (1978), Burrow (1966).
[3] This figure is an educated guess, based on the percentage of occultists I met who had taken
correspondence courses (about a third) and the number of people who had taken the major
correspondence courses (about four thousand; but some of those lived abroad, and many of them
had only ordered the course, or taken the first lesson or so and then dropped it, and so the
significant figure is probably closer to one thousand. Thrice that figure is three thousand). By most
standards this is an extremely conservative estimate. Figures given by occultists range from 80,000
witches (Farrar and Farrar 1981) to 6000–10,000 'Chaos Magickians' (Chris Bray, who runs the
Sorcerer's Apprentice course, gave this figure on 7.5.87). All these numbers seem grossly inflated
to me. Nevertheless, because groups are secretive and fluid, there is no way to estimate numbers
with accuracy. Moreover, there is a great range of involvement, from the casually interested to the
practitioner who spends nearly every evening in a magical group meeting. By 'serious activity', I
mean someone who belongs to a group which meets regularly: my prototype is a coven, a small
group of people who call themselves witches. Such groups, as will be seen, often take a year to join
and can be quite stable. There are many people who are very interested in magic who are not
members of such groups.

result-producing practice, and some of them have practised it regularly, in organized groups, for over a quarter of a century.

In the United States the number of participants is impressive. Adler's reliable report of paganism in the United States – not quite the same thing as magic, but close[4] – suggests that there may be 80,000 self-identified pagans or members of Wicca [modern witchcraft] in America.[5] Starhawk's *Spiral Dance* (1979), a manual for witches we shall encounter frequently in these pages, sold 50,000 copies between 1979 and 1985.[6] 1985 saw at least fifty major American festivals with a pagan focus, attended by hundreds or thousands of people. Some 40,000 people have taken part of a correspondence course offered by an organization called the Church and School of Wiccan.[7] There are hundreds and hundreds of groups, stores, journals, and events.

To return to England, the focus of this book, these numbers scarcely indicate the wider popular sympathy. There, interest in the occult has ballooned during the last two decades. The largest mail order occult store, The Sorcerer's Apprentice, has over 25,000 customers who have placed at least two orders with them over the last thirteen years. Many of these regular customers buy once a month; most, the proprietor said, buy at least once a year. The store turns over between 800 and 1000 items each week – books, magical robes, incenses – and employs ten people full time.[8] Their catalogues advertise crystal balls and talismans the way other catalogues offer exercycles.

CANDLEMAGIC STARTER KIT: Code P132. Basic outfit introduces you to traditional candlemagic property. 12 × 8″ asstd. candles; candle-oil; 4 candleholders; tapers and book. Have all you need to get to grips with potent form of magic. 19 items! Book shows how to work a variety of candlemagic rituals.

WAX IMAGE DOLLS: Code P63. Cure sickness, capture love, heal and hate with image dolls. Made from traditional formulae incorporating natural wax, herbs. By making an image you can work magic on that person perpetually. 6″ male or female dolls supplied ready to be personalized. Doll prepared with all accumulators, herbs, essences, ready to go. Natural wax colour. Some shamans keep shelffuls of dolls to control all their acquaintances.[9]

Mysteries, the largest shop for occult items in London, also caters to the wider range of alternative, self-development, spiritualist interests. They opened in

[4] Paganism is the loose title for people who practise a nature-oriented religion which usually involves magic. Many of the groups discussed in this book are Christian, and explicitly not pagan. In fact, I use the term 'pagan' to identify certain sorts of nature-worshipping groups which do not initiate their members into a closed fraternity. There is a significant difference between American and English practices in their symbolism and conception of their practice, but Adler speaks about roughly the same category of magic-oriented practitioners and provides a useful comparison.

[5] Adler (1986: 418). J. Gordon Melton conducted a survey of self-identified pagans in the States in the early 1980s and asked them if they owned a copy of a certain book, *The Golden Dawn*, of which no more than 15,000 copies had been printed. The book is more or less a staple on the magical bookshelf. Melton extrapolated a figure of 40,000 from his response.

[6] Adler (1986: 419).

[7] Adler (1986: 423).

[8] Conversation with the proprietor, Chris Bray, on 7 May 1987. My sense is that Bray is a businessman and that the figures are probably accurate.

[9] 1987 Sorcerer's Apprentice mail-order form.

1982; trade doubled every six months for several years, and they have expanded
to three times their original quarters. They see two to three hundred customers
a day.[10] The Aquarian Press, a popular printing press committed to publishing
magical material, some of it quite arcane,[11] has so far published 10,000 copies
of a beginner's book on magic: Marian Green's *Magic for the Aquarian Age*. The
1987 *Quest List of Esoteric Sources* cites some forty British suppliers of occult
goods, and about a hundred British 'esoteric' magazines, journals and
newsletters: for example, *The Pictish Shaman*, *The Moonstone*, *The Cauldron*. One
of these magazines, *Prediction*, has a circulation of 32,000 and is sold by major
newsagents. 'By the quantitative indices of books published and organizations
founded, there can be little doubt that public interest in the occult has grown
rapidly since the mid-sixties.'[12]

The groups I am discussing are only part of the multifarious occult. Modern
magic is a mixture of many different activities and ideas: paganism, astrology,
mysticism, the range of alternative therapies, even kabbalism – a Jewish
mysticism grafted onto Christian magical practice in the Renaissance. People
practise as individuals or as members of groups which come and go in a
fluctuating population, although some groups have stayed intact for decades.
The groups are astonishingly diverse. But there is a working definition of the
practices, or at least the ones I saw. Practitioners think of themselves as, or as
inspired by, the witches, wizards, druids, kabbalists, shamans, of mostly
European lore, and they perform rituals and create ritual groups in which they
invoke ancient deities with symbols taken from Sir James Frazer, Thomas

[10] Conversation with the proprietor, 7 May 1987.

[11] For example, they publish unusual texts from the late nineteenth century, when a well-known
magical group was founded, and from the Elizabethan era, another period of great interest to
magicians. These texts have included an obscure text by John Dee (*The Heptarchia Mystica*, ed. by R.
Turner, 1986), the letters of a not-very-well-known member of the nineteenth-century group, who
happened to be interested in alchemy (*The Alchemist of the Golden Dawn: the letters of the Revd. W. A.
Ayton to F. L. Gardner and Others 1886–1905*, ed. by E. Howe, 1985), the Masonic encyclopaedia
written by an earlier contributor to the formation of the nineteenth-century group: some of its
entries are unusual for a Masonic work, and this is due to the author's magical interests (*The Royal
Masonic Cyclopedia*, by Kenneth Mackenzie, intro. by J. Hamill and R. A. Gilbert, 1987). It is
somewhat extraordinary that a popular market exists for these texts, but clearly it does. The first
impression tends to run between three and four thousand copies for major books.

[12] Galbreath (1983: 20). Galbreath is speaking of America, but uses sources that indicate
concomitant English growth. It should be noted that some cast doubt on the notion of an occult
revival. Jo Logan, *Prediction*'s editor, certainly agrees that media coverage of magic and witchcraft
has increased dramatically in recent years, but thinks that the number of practitioners has remained
more constant: previously, people were more secretive (7 May 1987). Chris Bray, the archmage
behind the Sorcerer's Apprentice, also says that there are far more 'dabblers' these days, but no
more 'serious' occultists (7 May 1987). Academic doubt has been poured on the question of whether
the occult has been 'revived' by Galbreath 1983: he questions what counts as a revival, and whether
there hasn't always been a public interest in the quirky. There is no doubt some truth in these
caveats and qualifications. However, I find it highly unlikely that there were as many magicians in
the 1950s as there are today. One reason is that far fewer people knew about the occult as
something to do, whether they did it seriously or not, and another is that the risk of getting involved
was higher and more inhibiting, because the social cost of public knowledge of involvement was
greater. In any event, contemporary interest is considerable. In America, even the Pentagon seems
not unaffected. In 1984 it was reported that the Pentagon had spent millions on investigating
extrasensory phenomena in the name of national security (*The New York Times* 10 January 1984).

Bulfinch, E. Wallis Budge and Jessie Weston. They identify with the mystical religions of Eleusis, Orphism, Mithraism, even of Richard Rolle and Julian of Norwich. And they have two marked characteristics. First, they tolerate a surprising spiritual diversity. Central to the ethos is the notion that any path to a religion is a path to a spiritual reality, and whatever symbols and images one chooses are valid. Groups and their practices are creative, syncretic, their rites often an amalgam of Egyptian headress, Celtic invocation and Greek imagery. The only dogma, they say, is that there is no dogma, and feminist witches, kabbalistic Christians and neo-Nordic shamans socialize well together. Second, they practise what they call magic. They often describe themselves as magicians, perform what they call magical rites, and talk as if they expected those rites to have effects. Not all people involved in these groups would use the term 'magic' to explain their activities. I use the term as a convenient shorthand, because they all practice what most of them call magic, even if they do not immediately think of themselves as 'magicians' but as kabbalists, witches and the like.

While I am interested in the reasons behind the current 'revival' of witchcraft, or the explanation of why some people, rather than others, have become involved in practice, an even more interesting question concerns the process that allows people to accept outlandish, apparently irrational beliefs. 'Belief' is a difficult term, and I shall try to avoid it until the final chapters. But the question is how people come to make certain assertions and to act as if they were true. Magicians are ordinary, well-educated, usually middle-class people. They are not psychotically deluded, and they are not driven to practise by socio-economic desperation. By some process, when they get involved with magic – whatever the reasons that sparked their interest – they learn to find it eminently sensible. They learn to accept its core concept: that mind affects matter, and that in special circumstances, like ritual, the trained imagination can alter the physical world. Many non-magicians find that theory fatuous or false. But the Janus face of the outsider's bafflement and the insider's nonchalance is not unique to magic. Modern magicians are interesting because they are a flamboyant example of a very common process: that when people get involved in an activity they develop ways of interpreting which make that activity meaningful even though it may seem foolish to the uninvolved.

Understanding how someone comes to find magic persuasive is, roughly, the same problem as understanding how someone can become a priest in a community of unbelievers. More generally, it is the problem of describing what happens as an undergraduate turns into a lawyer: the way she alters her perceptions, interpretations and ideas as she grows older. The youth has one set of habits for interpreting events, and these habits may evolve into a quite different set for the adult. In many cases, the later set is less common to outsiders. An atheist may not understand what a college friend is talking about after he becomes a priest. A literary critic learns to be sensitive to ways of conceptualizing the written word that the historian may find meaningless. The real issue is not that magicians become comfortable practising an irrational activity, but that when someone becomes a specialist, he finds his practice progressively more persuasive through the very process of interpreting and making sense of his involvement; this changing understanding may become progressively more opaque to outsiders. Magic makes the issues particularly clear because magical practice is hard to confirm empirically and is socially unsupported, and so the challenges to finding it persuasive, one might think, are particularly strong.

Magicians raise another question. They maintain their jobs as civil servants, businessmen and computer analysts. If anything, they become more effective at their jobs. Yet they rarely suggest that their clients use magic in their transactions, and they rarely confuse the magical circle with, for example, a foreign policy affair. All people move between different parts of their lives with ease – anthropologist and father, politician and grandmother, executive and socialite. Social theorists have ways of referring to the phenomenon that one acts like a mother when mothering and like a banker while banking: we talk about different discourses, frames of reference, social roles, and the like. There seem to be distinctive ways of talking, acting and – one suspects – thinking in different situations. But how this happens and what it involves is still unclear. Magic presents this problem in particularly sharp outline because the contrast between the role of wizard and computer scientist seems so extreme.

Why do people find magic persuasive? This, the main theme of the book, has been a central problem in social anthropology since the earliest days of the discipline. It arose because magical rituals seem to be intended to do things which, observers say, they cannot possibly achieve. How do practitioners continue to practise in the face of constant failure? They perform rituals which seem to be about producing an effect, to the anthropologist the rituals cannot possibly produce that effect, and yet the indigenous natives perform the rituals generation after generation. Explaining this puzzle has been the major task of the anthropology of religion, for at the bottom of the puzzle, at its inmost core, lies the issue of how people believe in a god whose existence cannot be proven to an unbeliever's satisfaction.[13]

There have been two major approaches to this problem in the anthropological literature on primitive societies, and though there have been efforts to overturn them, their assumptions still underlie much anthropological thought. Either, it is said, the ritualists are making claims by their rituals, and the claims happen to be false and one's task is to explain the perpetuation of the falsehood, or the ritualists are not making claims at all, and one's task is to explain what it is that they are doing.[14] That is, either they really believe that magical theory is correct

---

[13] One might also say that a central task in sociology has been to explain how the elimination of magic was ever possible, and how it was that Western society moved into its rational mode. This is the task that Max Weber undertook in his *Sociology of Religion*.

[14] There is a third explanation: that magic works. Or, more specifically, that the peculiar states and practices associated with ritual practice are associated with extrasensory events, and that these events – or at least the states – may well exist. There has been some serious, worthwhile literature on this subject, usually associated with shamanic practice: Winkleman (1982), Noll (1985), Prince (1982), Bourguignon (1974), Harner (1980); there are also some hesitant remarks in Hallpike (1979).

and they are just deluded – they are forced to cling to their beliefs because the beliefs explain the world (Frazer), or because they have no others (Horton), or because they are not psychologically developed enough to see their falsehood (Hallpike), or because they never have to confront their contradictions (Evans-Pritchard) – or, on the other hand, the rituals really have nothing to do with magical theory at all, and it is the observer who is deluded when he thinks that they do. According to this view, rituals are performed because they have certain social effects (functionalists), or they help to order an otherwise incoherent reality (structuralists), or they poetically, aesthetically, devotionally, express (symbolists). Basic to these approaches are two preconceptions about the way to understand magic and ritual.

The first preconception is that magic, and ritual with an intentional goal, is based upon a theory, upon which the ritualist acts to achieve certain goals. At its most explicit, this assumption takes shape as a direct comparison between scientific theory and indigenous practice, with an elaborate sketch of the intricate theoretical permutations in the traditional preliterate religion. Primitive man becomes an amateur scientist. A more common version is the implicit assumption in much anthropological writing that in order to describe ritual, the anthropologist must produce the premises and logical associations which, if adopted, would make that ritual the act of a reasonable person. Often the description is cast as if these were premises held by all individuals and acted upon intentionally and consciously in every rite. The Durkheimian legacy presented magic as the individual's manipulation of religious ideas. The magician extracted a theory from collective ritual action, and consciously exploited it for personal advantage. While this interpretation may be no longer widely held, there remains a sense that magic demands an intellectual explanation, that action which seems so irrational can only come about because actors hold different, elaborate and relatively coherent theories about the physical world.

The second preconception is that ritual should be understood in relation to the social system: how it supports, maintains or expresses the cultural order. In the forties and fifties, when functionalism dominated the disciplinary ethos, fieldworkers assumed that rituals were performed because they served some general cultural end. The anthropologist's burden was to determine and explain the rite's effective function: it impressed moral principles upon ascendent rulers, healed communal tension of those embarking upon dangerous but communally necessary enterprises. Anthropologists then took linguistics and communication as their analytic lodestone and saw rituals as semiotic signifiers which presented social truths to their individual participants. Symbolism was a compelling echo of the cultural norm. Under the more recent sway of literary criticism and interpretative anthropology, rituals are treated like opaque symbols in a cultural text. The anthropologist teases out the associations and implications of the symbolism which make it pertinent, a prism refracting social essence. In analysing magic, the tendency has been to focus upon the non-magical ends which the rite might serve; the primitive magician essentially became poet, therapist and social engineer. The cognitive or psychological impact of ritual on the individual, irrespective of cultural issues, was not often directly confronted.

Neither of these approaches struck me as valid. People seemed far fuzzier than that, less coherent and theory conscious than they often think they are, and yet more theory- or at least idea-dependent than many anthropologists would have them be. I decided to explore a field situation which would highlight these inadequacies, and to chart the messy, complex way in which people come to hold what we call beliefs.

I chose my subject carefully. To cast the issues sharply I decided to do fieldwork in a society which was familiar to me but also very different from my own, and in which I could work in my mother tongue. I am American, and I had lived in England – in Cambridge – for two years before I began the fieldwork in earnest. I was comfortable, then, in England, but very aware than its society was unlike America's. This may have made me more observant; certainly it eased entry into the field, if only because it freed me from the shackles of caste that the English accent can place upon its users. And it meant that I could come to know people easily, and have in-depth conversations on highly complex topics from quite early on in the study.

I became interested in modern magic because these particular people seemed to pose difficulties for the standard interpretations of magic. Modern magicians are sophisticated, educated people. They know a way of explaining nature – science – which has been remarkably successful in its explanation and remarkably antagonistic towards ritualistic magic. They do not come from a background which accepts magic easily and their rites are novel creations: their magic cannot be explained as some burden of the past. They are clearly equipped with the mental equipment to think non-magically. Yet an extended acquaintance with them reveals that it would be specious to assert that they do not mean to achieve results by their practice, that they only perform rituals to think new thoughts or to express some otherwise inexpressible emotion. Modern magicians could neither be excused from their magical belief because of their inferior education, nor could they be said not to have theories or beliefs at all, to be doing something quite different – and aesthetically or sociologically respectable – with their practice.

From a combination of extensive participation, socializing, formal and informal interviews I began to understand how these people came to find their magical practice engaging. There seemed to be something of a paradox: people entered magic with the dim notion that it involved a different, and science-like, theory of reality. They soon got involved with a range of spiritual and emotional experience to which the ideas were largely irrelevant, and they came to treat their practice like a religion – in that they spoke of gods and spiritual experience – rather than like a theory-laden science, and to value it more for its spiritual, symbolic experiences than for the truth of its magical theory. They defended the theory nevertheless: new intellectual habits made it seem more reasonable, and, more important, that theory, or rather those ideas, legitimized the rich experiences that had become so important to their lives. Through magic, magicians' perception of their world – what they noticed and experienced – altered, and the way they interpreted these perceptions altered. They did not always recognize that their manner of observing and responding has changed. But the end-product was that the business of engaging in magic became reasonable and straight-forward to its practitioners, the practice became emotionally important to them, and when challenged they usually defended magical ideas with force, even though they might have a fuzzy sense of the theory and might change their arguments to suit their questioners.

The goal of this book is to describe the process by which this happens, and the particular experiences, linguistic transformations, analytic mutations, and intellectual strategies which seem central to the transformation. Certain behaviours – particular verbal patterns, non-verbal emotional and physiological responses – emerged from each magician's involvement with the practice. It seemed that if one wanted to understand how magical involvement became gripping, one had to describe those patterns and responses carefully: what they were; how they emerged; how they influenced each other. In the book's first part I tell the ethnographic story of my fieldwork: whom I encountered, what they did, and how they described themselves. Then, in the rest of the book, I move on to describe these particular behaviours.

Upon analysis it seemed to me that these behaviours fell naturally into three categories pertinent to the magician's involvement with his practice. The book is divided into parts on that basis. First, there were certain shifts in the basic perception and analysis of events. When a ritual was performed, the performer began to notice subsequent events in a way that allowed her to conclude that the rite had been successful. The very way magicians observed and analysed action would change, in a manner favourable to the interpretations they wanted to make. They learned to identify certain categories of events as 'evidence' for the success of a ritual, criteria so loose that most rituals could be called successful but tight enough so that some would be said to 'fail'. They acquired the basic knowledge – common knowledge – and basic assumptions, sometimes explicitly articulated, other times implied, which affected the way they noticed and could observe the events around them. Salience was redefined. The existence of this bias is a well-known phenomenon, but it has not been ethnographically well documented and described. Nor has there been much awareness of a surprising fact: that people can be convinced that they are carefully testing a theory despite their palpable failure to do so. These changes in intellectual habits form the subject of part two.

Second, there were basic experiential changes which seemed particularly important to the participants. In part these were simply psychological or emotional. Magicians began to meditate and to 'visualize', and began to have spiritual, emotional and physical experiences which they found moving. Some of these experiences were specific physiological experiences which often arose from particular practices – out-of-body phenomena, or the relaxation engendered by meditative technique. Others were subtler shifts, of emotional or psychological mood, that evolved as the individual became more deeply enmeshed with the activity. Certain linguistic styles and the emergence of vivid symbolism seemed integrally connected to these new experiences; they were associated with what magicians called new ways of 'knowing' – a phrase they used to imply emotional, rather than cognitive, awareness. These experiential changes, and the way magicians describe them in terms of new ways of knowing and understanding, are the subject of part three.

Third, there seemed to be common intellectual strategies to handle the disjunction between involvement in magic and in what magicians called science, or the scientific way of understanding. Whether or not magical ideas are incompatible with, say, the teachings of a university faculty of physics is not at issue. What is important is the perception that they are not. Magicians seemed to feel that the larger society around them assumed the incompatibility. That magicians felt uneasy about practising magic was clear: that they resorted to particular strategies to reduce their uneasiness was quite interesting. In the fourth part I describe these rationalizations and compare them to the rationalizations of another activity which feels similarly threatened – Christianity. The form of the rationalizations seems striking: people offer several justifications for their beliefs in a manner which allows them to waver, asserting commitment in one context, avoiding it in another. This seems to be a common strategy in this doubt-ridden, self-conscious world.

I turn finally to the way these different elements work together, a process I call 'interpretive drift': the slow shift in someone's manner of interpreting events, making sense of experiences, and responding to the world. People do not enter magic with a set of clear cut beliefs which they take to their rituals and test with detachment. Nor is their practice mere poetry, a new language to express their feelings. Rather, there seems to be a slow, mutual evolution of interpretation and experience, rationalized in a manner which allows the practitioner to practise. The striking feature, I found, was how *ad hoc*, how seemingly unmotivated, this transformation became. Magicians did not deliberately change the way they thought about the world. Becoming involved in magic is exciting, and as the neophyte read about the practice and talked to other practitioners he picked up intellectual habits which made the magic seem sensible and realistic. He acquired new ways of identifying events as significant, of drawing connections between events, with new, complex knowledge in which events could be put into context. At the same time his involvement embraced rich phenomenological experience which he found deeply important, experience labelled and understood within the practice but not outside. Hard to abstract, hard to verbalize, these dynamic experiences became part of the business of engaging in magic, and they made the magic real for its participants, because they gave content to its ideas. To protect his involvement, the magician engaged in a range of 'patch-up job' arguments which allowed his commitment without violating his scepticism. The rationalizations again were *ad hoc* and not necessarily coherent, but they served the purpose of justifying and reinforcing involvement.

The other striking feature of the process was the centrality of play. Magic gives magicians the opportunity to play – a serious play, but nevertheless a rule-defined, separate context in which they identify with their imaginative conceptions, and act out the fantasies and visions of another world. They find their increased capacity for play a great resource, and indeed through this play there are real psychotherapeutic benefits from the practice. And there is a remarkable extension of this play structure into the realm of belief. The ideas and theories of magical practice are for magicians both assertions about the real world, and 'let's pretend' fantasies about strange powers, wizards, even dragons. Magicians treat these ideas and theories sometimes as factual assertions, sometimes as fantasy, without necessarily defining to themselves where they stand. It is as if they were playing with belief – and yet they take themselves seriously, act on the results of their divinations, talk about the implications of their ideas. What this really means is that they are not very concerned about the objective 'truth' of their beliefs – a nonchalance at variance with modern ideals of rationality. That magicians are aware of this variance, and that they take steps to explain it, is one of the most interesting features of this material.

The broad question at the theoretical centre of this inquiry is the nature of rationality and irrationality, and the basic form of human cognition. It is an issue so large as to be nearly unmanageable. Yet the drive to know why it is that people do what they do, and how they can possibly do it, lies behind most anthropological endeavour. Anthropology, like philosophy, asks the loose, ambitious questions about human understanding. Unlike philosophy anthropology does not try to develop a coherent language to describe these human features by introspection. The point of the discipline is to describe observable human action, choosing its subjects carefully to challenge the comfortable assumptions Western intellectuals often hold about human thought. One of our most comfortable assumptions is of the rational human, of our purposeful, effective action and our logically consistent ideas and motivations. Most people will consciously acknowledge this to be an unnatural ideal. Nevertheless faith in one's own basic rationality has a strong hold on this culture, and the way in which we are not rational is not well-understood. What we must explore are the ways in which people systematically depart from some clean-shaven rational ideal, the way in which their interpretative techniques depend on things which might seem irrelevant, the ways imagination shapes understanding. The purpose of this book is to examine a case in which apparently irrational beliefs are held by apparently rational people, and to identify the elements which seem important to explaining how they do so.

A new cross-disciplinary field has slowly emerged in the last few decades. 'Cognitive science' concerns the old, fundamental philosophical questions about human understanding: the nature of perception, memory, mental imagery, how people reason. Such questions used to be ignored by more empirical fields, rejected as contentless or ill-defined. Now several fields of inquiry are focusing on these studies of mental activity, more basic than the cultural and more general than the neurochemical, to try to gain some clearer notion of the nature of our mental life. Howard Gardner names six: psychology, artificial intelligence, neuroscience, linguistics, philosophy and anthropology. Each provides different models and explanations for different features of our complex mental process. Each uses different methods and strives for different goals. Nevertheless, projects in these separate fields have converged upon topics like memory and rationality, with a growing awareness of multi-disciplinary effort.[15]

Anthropology's contribution is to provide careful accounts of human behaviour in its natural environment, under the influence of very different cultures. The idealized conception of participant observation as the pass to privileged understanding has undergone a sophisticated critique in recent years. Fieldwork, it is now understood, does not grant a blanket awareness of the hearts and minds of the fieldworker's chosen society, as if he were a woolly sponge. The fieldworker cannot learn what 'they' 'believe': nor can she ever really know what really occurs in the mind of any one individual. Fieldwork consists, instead, of a series of conversations, as flexible, tendentious, and idiosyncratic as conversations between individuals often are. And the fieldworker is to some extent caught in an intellectual trap not of his own making: to tell the story of an experience, one must distort, simplify, symbolize, compress the complex holism of daily life into a plot.

For all the occasional pretentiousness of this new criticism within anthropology, the educated awareness is one of anthropology's greatest strengths. The criticism draws attention to the difficulties of gleaning knowledge about society from conversations with individuals. The patchy communication embodied in fieldwork has implications not only for the anthropologist's state of knowledge, but for cognition more generally. Given the limitations of conversation, given that people say such varied, incomplete and heterogeneous things about ritual, those very facts should be a central focus in analysing how and why people become willing to argue for a certain point of view. The fieldwork encounter presents the anthropologist with the multiple interactions, subjective responses, and intersubjective creativity that tend to disappear from the clarity of a structured interview. The challenge is to illuminate the complicated ambiguity without reducing it, to describe carefully the complexity of fieldwork conversations while assuming as little as possible about the beliefs, attitudes or other mental baggage of the conversationalists. It is an attempt to describe psychological activity without imputing a particular psychology to the people concerned.

Much of human experience is not verbalized. The new criticism in anthropology stresses the ethnographer's subjectivity, and some recent ethnographers have illustrated the insight gained through complete community participation. Someone who only converses will lose the richness of her interlocutor's life. And often human experience is stimulated in similar ways by

[15] Gardner (1987).

similar activity. Being deprived of food in an initiation ceremony, undergoing group-led imaginative 'journeys', dancing until exhausted in a group ritual – all these have a significant subjective impact upon the participants, and some features of the subjective response to each will be common to many. One must be careful not to generalize from the subjective to the collective. But to some extent, the anthropologist who genuinely participates in a cultural practice can take himself as a subject. One cannot have access to the inner reaches of those to whom one talks; one can have partial access to one's own, and through that involvement at least begin to understand what some of the others may have been experiencing. That can provide some awareness of the psychological landscape in which certain assertions are made – again without resorting to unwarranted assumptions about mental actions. Introspection is a dangerous tool because it lends itself to self-delusion. Yet to talk about cognition and emotion at a level more insightful than mere behaviourism, introspection is a necessary tool, though one to be used with caution.

Anthropology is the naturalist's trade: you sit and watch and learn from the species in its natural environment. Ethnographies concerned with fundamental philosophical problems like rationality do their work through the description of a particular example in detail. Description demands model-building and models always distort; there is no clear window on a different culture. However, the attempt to build an account sensitive to interpretive limitations may provide a powerful understanding of the phenomenon. The task before me here is to depict the manner in which becoming a specialist changes the way someone interprets events and becomes partly unable to communicate to an outsider. I have tried to present a description which categorizes the types of conversations and subjective feelings that I observed and in which I engaged: the explanations people gave in my presence, the particular experience of rituals which was described to me and which I felt, and the arguments presented to me to justify the practice. Through that broad account it seemed to me that certain features of what one wants to call belief emerged, and that these were not what we normally stereotype belief to be. It also seemed to me that these modern magicians were asserting claims about their magic in a remarkably ambiguous manner; they were almost self-consciously playing with their understanding of the truth. I hope that the ethnography might help to make the viability of various philosophical or psychological theories clearer to members of those fields; it may contribute to a more general awareness of the nature of human understanding.

This is a work of psychological anthropology, in which the subject is the mercurial complexity of belief. My observations have been varied and multi-dimensional. The tools to help elucidate them have been similarly diverse. I have looked to recent work in cognitive psychology, philosophy, cognitive dissonance theory, to psychoanalysis and psychotherapy. This is in many ways a theoretical jumble, but I would defend the multiplicity. Psychological anthropology is not defined by a particular theoretical approach from within psychology, nor should it be. Like cognitive science, it too is a relatively new, or new-old, endeavour,[16] and like cognitive science it must hold that a variety of frameworks are needed properly to describe its subject. Psychological anthropologists focus on the conceptual play in the interstices between individual and society, and the multi-faceted nature of their subject demands the use of different approaches developed in mainstream psychology. If, through the dependence on these different tools, psychological anthropology can develop general models to describe human understanding observed in its natural environment, its contribution will be considerable. The subdiscipline is one of the most exciting in contemporary anthropology.

Whether the claims that magical rituals can alter physical reality are true or not is beside the point of the present essay. Most of the remarks which people tend to make as belief-statements – asserting that a president is the best of all possible presidents, asserting that the Shroud of Turin bears the marks of Christ's body, asserting that a certain university is a superior university – are not obviously true. People become persuaded of these ideas, and speak as if they were true. Sometimes individuals have thought deeply before championing such claims, sometimes such views are unjustly attributed to them by others. Very intelligent, thoughtful people often find themselves on different sides of an argument. Many if not all such arguments are undecidable, in the sense that people go on arguing about them indefinitely, often convinced that they themselves are in the right, often armed with 'evidence' that their interlocutors understand differently. Neither here nor elsewhere in the book shall I consider the question of whether the rituals might work, and whether the strange forces and abilities spoken of in magic might actually exist. Magical ideas are not incontestably true; neither are they incontestably false, just as libertarianism and Christianity are not necessarily the true, or even the best, perspective on reality. Intelligent, reasonable people hold different views about the subjects. The anthropologist's challenge is to identify the factors which allow them to do so, without intruding his or her own opinion. The interesting problem is how different people can find different claims persuasive, not whether those claims are ultimately correct.

Before turning to the main body of the material I should mention some methodological limitations. Putting oneself in a position to watch imposes certain constraints. If, as an anthropologist, I wanted to understand what it was to be an insider, I had to be an insider. And that meant no microphone, no note-taking, no questionnaires. Very, very occasionally, I taped a conversation. But I was fortunate, because magicians themselves made recordings – of ritual reports, or discussions that superseded rituals – and some of these I was allowed to borrow. I was fortunate also in the wealth of material that a technologically advanced society makes available: where Richards describes the

---

[16] Psychological anthropology as the study of the different psychological cast of different cultures or the application of psychoanalytic concepts to different societies, emerged alongside psychoanalysis itself. This newer emerging form of psychological anthropology characterized by such authors as Crapanzano (1978), Obeyesekere (1981), Whitehead (1987), has a different agenda of concerns.

strain of writing down ritual procedure in smoke-filled Bemba huts, I was handed xeroxed notes for most of the rituals I watched. However, my fieldnotes of conversations could not be as detailed as one assumes that those of more traditional anthropologists must be. Mostly, I remembered a Simonidian skeleton of interesting points during the evening, jotted down the outline on my midnight return, and wrote up an account of each evening – no more than five typed pages – during the morning after.

The point of the study was to understand how an outsider like me, and all magicians were once outsiders, could come to treat apparently outrageous claims as sensible topics for discussion. Very early on in the study I realized that the new subjective experiences involved in learning to practice magic were crucial to an individual's decision to become further involved. I decided that I would understand magic best if I did what people did to become magicians. I moved to London in July 1983, as the following chapter details, and I read magical books, took magical courses, did magical exercises, and became initiated into practising magical groups. I wrote and led rituals and made my own magical robe. I learnt how to read tarot cards and to argue about the interpretation of astrological charts. For fourteen months I spent nearly every evening with magicians. I talked to a good many people in magic, and came to know some of them well.

I am one of the few anthropologists who could not be distinguished from their field. I am white, middle-class, and intellectual. So are the people with whom I spent time. During the research I was in my mid-twenties, a young woman like many others in the practice. I was honest about my enterprise, but my intention was to fit in, to dispel outsider status, and I was rather relieved when people forgot what I had so carefully told them. But as a result I collected little systematic information on magicians' backgrounds. I saw no obvious patterns and thought it foolish to damage my acceptance by passing out questionnaires which only asserted my outsider status and would not begin to touch the things I thought important: what it felt like to have a tarot reading, how magicians argued for their practice, what they meant when they said that they 'saw' the Goddess. I did not see a complete or representative set of magicians – I cannot speak for all Samoans, let alone their fathers – but I did gain considerable participatory insight into the way some people found magic compelling.[17] In any event, the question of what factors predisposed people to

---

[17] I did in fact have a sociological predecessor: he passed out questionnaires, asked direct questions, acted like an authoritative sociologist and got himself heartily despised. When he finished his report, an occult journal printed a series of rude letters with these addenda [the sociologist's name has been changed]: 'Kim Booze, who is currently employed as a lavatory assistant at the Ziperoo Private Cinema and Massage Parlour in Soho, has NO CONNECTION WHATEVER with Bob Smith, who has just completed a five-year study of English witchcraft . . . Ben Raunch, who is currently recovering from a severe depressive breakdown in Friern Barnet mental hospital, has NO CONNECTION WHATEVER with Bob Smith, who has just completed a five-year study of English witchcraft'. In the first letter, Kim Booze had concluded, on the basis of careful observation of the trees in his garden, that trees do not grow. In the second, Ben Raunch had concluded, on the basis of similarly careful observation, that it was impossible to have sex and be English simultaneously (*Aquarian Arrow* 2: 10–11).

begin practising magic seemed less intriguing than the effect which entering magic had upon their manner of understanding events.

Magic. The word has many echoes. I am no witch, no wizard, though I have been initiated as though I were. There were personal reasons for finding the intellectual problem so compelling; there always are. I was an imaginative child, a first child, an only child until seven, and I lived in the world my books carved out for me: Tolkien, Lloyd Alexander's *Mabinogian*, the *Odyssey*, stories of Black Raven, Hunting Bear and Winnie the Pooh. By the time I was ten I had developed a secret fictional character, a child with a silver circlet, and before I slept each night I told myself stories in which he was the central actor and in which novels and television became the basis for his scripts. The nightly stories became almost sacred inner worlds. Perhaps my shyness made the romance more central than it might have been. But I have always been troubled and intrigued by the intensity: I always wanted to make sense of the vividness of my own daydreaming. I was enchanted by the imaginings, and yet I always knew, when I was a child, that the make-believe was never real. I never have and do not now 'believe' in magic. But the summer after I left college, I came across a teach-yourself guide to witchcraft, a book that told you how to draw a magical circle and what to say to cast a spell. I was hooked. These witches were recreating a childhood world, enchanting adulthood, and their involvement offered me a means to come to intellectual terms with my past.

2

Initiation ritual: my introduction to the field

NOW, if I wanted to get involved in magic, I would go to an occult bookstore and look at the notices and index cards pinned to the shelves. Beth's occult workshop is advertised in London's Atlantis bookstore, as is the Green Circle, two groups I later came to join. Or I would look in the back pages of *Prediction* magazine, the monthly journal with a circulation of 32,000. *Prediction* is the casual occultist's delight: articles about the tarot, palmistry, vibrations, and so forth. Pitched to a general audience, it lacks the idiosyncrasy of many smaller publications and it places more emphasis on the 'scientific' proof of these activities because its authors write to persuade the unpersuaded of the occult's validity. It has a free personal column at the back, and every month it carries one or two advertisements like these:

INTERESTED in basic Craft, old religion, tarot, astrology, the power of herbs, etc. We are hoping to start a serious discussion group within the Bucks, Herts area, with a view to a working community in basic Craft. Write Box no. EXXX enclosing SAE (April 1984).

A recently formed occult group has vacancies for new members. The group is led by experienced occultists who follow traditional and modern practices aimed at self-development and discovery. Hemel Hempstead area. Enclose SAE to Box no. EXXX (January 1985).

COVEN, Leicester-based, teaching the basics of occultism and Wicca, wishes to open its circle to new members. Free correspondence course for all postal members. Personal contact assured. Box no. EXXX (March 1985).

LONE witch, 5.6.65 [birthdate provided for rough astrological chart], wishing to contact/meet other witches in Cumnock/Ayrshire area to join a genuine working group or start fresh one. Also, witches/pagans through British Isles. No left-hand workers.[1] [name and address provided] (September 1985).

Prediction is glossy and popular. I know people who have advertised here, and others who have followed the leads listed. But it's thought 'bad form' to do so: the good groups, the 'real' groups, are said never to let their names appear here. If you are good, the folklore says, you never need to advertise.[2]

---

[1] This term means 'no black magic'; as in many cultures, the left-hand is associated with evil. My impression is that both magicians and non-magicians think that there is more Satanism than there is.

[2] This tendency is sometimes taken to extremes. I knew a couple who were trying to attract others to their coven, and almost refused to talk about, let alone advertise, the group. Recruitment technique seemed limited to spells. However, the coven did slowly expand.

In the 1950s and 1960s, few practitioners had published books on magic, and people used to come in to magic through the popular press sensationalism intended to prove the corrupted depravity of such groups. One member of the coven I joined, initiated over twenty-five years ago, saw a journalistic essay and 'something clicked. I used a magnifying glass to get the address of the photo of the house, and wrote to her'. That coven's high priest, also initiated over twenty-five years ago, saw a sensationalistic piece and wrote off to the paper in support of a group of people 'who seemed quite reasonable, doing their own thing, but brutally treated by the press'. The newspaper passed his letter on to the people, who invited him over for an afternoon. 'I loved it. It felt like coming home.' The more publicly known witches are often somewhat despised by the more private practitioners because they have few qualms about appearing in the more popular press, but it is sometimes said that they do a service in bringing witchcraft to the attention of the public. As one witch told me, 'if one out of every thousand readers decides to learn something more, the article's done good'.

These days more people become magicians through magicians' own literature rather than through sensationalistic journalism. Most experienced magicians are known through their writings. Books are expected from very senior practitioners. Such books describe what magic is about, what this magician does and thinks about the world, and what steps the reader should take to become involved. Some are published by small presses, with tiny circulations,[3] but they sell quickly in occult bookstores. When such books present themselves as manuals – particularly within a branch of magic known as the 'Western Mysteries' – they often have an address printed at the back: 'anyone wishing to pursue courses of study along the lines laid down herein are [sic] invited to contact the publishers [address given], who will be pleased to advise about groups, courses or teachers known to them who are specializing in this field'.[4]

But at the time I began my fieldwork I was uneasy about following these leads. I knew about the notices in Atlantis, but I felt chary of calling up a random group and I felt, even then, that the more someone advertised the less interesting they were likely to be. In any event I was fortunate. I met the friend of a friend's friend, who introduced me to another friend, and she told me to call a woman called Beth[5] who she said was involved in witchcraft. I sent off a

---

[3] As mentioned, Aquarian's first publication run tends to be around three to four thousand books for major publications. There are far smaller presses, however: the Mouse That Spins (published out of a basement; it seems now to be defunct); Helios Books; Magnum Opus Hermetics Sourceworks (this publishes Renaissance and Rosicrucian texts, however). Other manuals are published more widely. Matthews and Matthews, *The Western Way*, was published by Arkana, an imprint of Routledge and Kegan Paul (1985), Starhawk *The Spiral Dance* was published by Harper and Row (1979), King and Skinner *Techniques of High Magic* was published by Destiny Books (1976), and so forth.

[4] Knight, *Practical Guide to Qabalistic Symbolism* (1965).

[5] All participants' names are pseudonymous. Most magicians use pseudonyms in their dealings with the public; when these are well-known (e.g. 'Gareth Knight') I have used them instead of inventing new ones. Sometimes personal details have been disguised.

postcard introducing myself and mentioning an interest in witchcraft and phoned. Beth suggested we meet at an upcoming 'Quest' conference.

This connection was a stroke of considerable luck. Beth was sane, balanced, and warm. She was also deeply involved with many different varieties of magical practice, as I would later learn. She and her partner ran the oldest coven in England, having inherited it from the man who essentially created witchcraft as it is practised in this century. They were also involved in one of the most serious of kabbalistic 'Western Mysteries' groups, and led another more casual, *ad hoc* group. Beth's partner Enoch was as dynamic as she, and had been involved in magic for even longer; he had in fact introduced her to it. The two of them inspired much respect and loyalty in the circle of fifty or so magicians whose lives they touched directly. Becoming involved with them was perhaps the best possible route into serious, long-term magical practice; it was also the founding, for me, of a cherished friendship.

The sixteenth annual Quest Conference met in Russell Square on a Saturday, on 5 March 1983. About a hundred people came, as many as the hall could hold; I learned later that it had been advertised in occult journals and newsletters, and that it was something of an annual 'event'. In fact it was one of the longest running magical events. There have been magical groups in Britain throughout the twentieth century, but the great variety of meetings and lectures open to the public began to emerge only in the early seventies. At the conference, speakers began at 11:30 a.m. and continued until 7:00 p.m. There were folksongs and a talk on 'hermetic music', the mystical, alchemical significance of the eight-tone octave; there was a talk on 'village witchcraft', by a practitioner; and a panel discussion on magic by five of its respected practitioners. Most of them, I later learned, were more or less famous in the field – a limited field, to be sure, but nevertheless not an easy achievement. The meeting had been organized by someone called Marian Green, a woman who had been on the occult scene for years and whose skill lay in presenting magic as down-to-earth and sensible. She herself was down-to-earth and sensible, a healthy, hearty woman in her forties.

I met Beth over the lunch break – a handsome, leonine woman who seemed in her forties but was in fact older. She pointed out that the last person to try to study this modern London magic had passed out questionnaires and offended everyone, a remark which initially dampened me. Beth was half-hidden behind the incenses and books and magazines of a display stall – these conferences often have occult suppliers on the side – and I watched people come up and buy dragonsblood, benzoin, and pamphlets on 'herbs, incense and candle magic'. Eventually she invited me to a weekly workshop. Later in the day, at the end of the afternoon, a young woman stood up and announced a 'Green Circle' meeting on dreams, and offered to give information to those who were interested. I went over and gave my name and was told the house to go to. 'It's at Gertrude's.' 'Gertrude who?' 'Last names aren't important.'

The dream meeting took place before the workshop. I took the train to London and was picked up at an Underground station by two women who had been introduced to me while buying dragonsblood incense. They spent some ten pounds sterling on incense and other materials: they explained that they were 'setting up'. In the car, they talked obscurely about 'meetings' and warned me to be careful before I got involved in anything. Our destination was an intellectual's house in Tufnell Park, slightly rundown but stuffed with books, plants, a heavy wooden desk. There were twenty or so people crowded into the outer room, and Gertrude – a severe, fortyish German woman with kind manners and, when it appeared, a lovely smile – served tea and cookies. Marian Green told us about dreaming: that dreams were significant, mostly as a key to your own psyche, and that you could control them by a technique called 'lucid' dreaming. The essential idea behind this is that one can be conscious that one is dreaming while in the dream itself, and so manipulate it for more personally satisfying ends. It seems to be a possibly effective psychological technique.

It was a remarkable evening. The first thing I noticed was how pleasant the room was, the second, how ordinary the people were – a biochemistry graduate student, a banker, a down-and-out rock musician, none of whom I would have avoided at a party. Their ages ranged from twenty-five to seventy. Not all seemed from the same background, though most seemed middle class. The rock musician showed me his watch, which had stopped, and said that it often stopped in 'this sort' of atmosphere: in fact, his twelve-hour digital had once showed thirteen. He seemed sincere. At the meeting's end a wiry blonde came up to me, asked me if it was true that I was interested in magic – she apparently knew the women who had given me a lift – shrieked when I said yes, and announced that I looked like a moon priestess. I had already noticed that Helga was one of the more flamboyant people in the room. She had a magical group, it transpired, and the woman who was meant to be its moon priestess had disappeared. Literally: the police had been involved and a local paper headline had already expressed its outrage at this victim of a black magic coven. Helga suggested that I come around to meet people – 'to make sure that it works' – some nights later. Memories of obscure mutterings notwithstanding, we set a date for the following Wednesday.

Helga more or less ran a collective house in a once grand section of Tufnell Park. She ran it quite well, though with noise. And despite her occasionally strident tones, she had a mature, level-headed understanding of people's motivations. She had come from Holland some years ago, already deeply interested in the occult: the first thing she had done was to search out the most notorious witch in England and be initiated by an acolyte. That had been several years ago. Now, in her thirties, she had become obsessed with the Nordic gods and her Germanic past. Through the year I would see her change. She began to speak of herself as a Volva or Valkyrie, dreamt of sacrificing herself to Wotan (Odin), and worshipped the Aesir, the blond and blue-eyed Nordic gods. And, seemingly as a result, she became progressively more self-confident, and more socially secure. Helga was quite good as a magical group leader, and as a house-leader: both of those organizations were supposedly democratic and egalitarian, and she managed the difficult task of establishing such a group without asserting her leadership. Many people in the magical group had some difficulty with her personal style, although they respected her formidable knowledge of the runes. By the end of my stay she had developed a considerable reputation for her rune-knowledge – the magical, mystical nature of the old Germanic alphabet – and began teaching and publishing with success.[6]

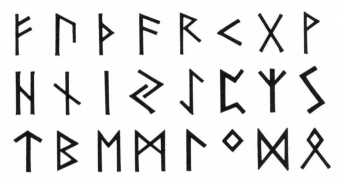

Figure 1   Runes were ideographic and phonetic signs used by the Germanic peoples to represent their language; it seems likely that they were thought to have magical powers. The Elder Futhark, the 24 runes represented above, was the first codification of the letter runes. It was in use roughly between 200 BC and AD 800.

On Wednesday I met Eliot, Helga's partner, and William, whom I had already seen at the dream meeting. Eliot had a kind face. He was also one of the most impressive ritual performers I came to know. He had already been a witch for twenty years, and he and Helga had a coven (a witches' group) of their own in tandem with this other magical group. He was a factory engineer, although difficulties in the company had left him unemployed some years before retirement. William was a computer scientist-cum-astrologer, slightly older. He had worked with Enoch (Beth's partner) when they created a company in the mid-seventies, and stayed with it until it bankrupted. He was a Cambridge man: not only that, but from my college. When we met it was like being interviewed for a shared apartment: delicate grilling underneath the civility. When I left the

[6] There is a growing interest in a magic which draws its symbology from the old Germanic and Icelandic tales, and the corpus of Norse mythology. This is called 'Odinism' (I would describe it as a version of 'ad hoc' ritual magic in the classification that shortly follows). I knew of two or three groups of practitioners in London during my fieldwork period. These groups also seemed to have a political nature, and some practitioners seemed to consider themselves to be involved in a political magic, with overtones of the National Front. Because of these overtones, most of the practitioners I met were wary of Odinist groups – sometimes quite unfairly (see Alder, 1986: 273–282 for comments on the American groups). However, there was a growing general interest in the runes, the old Germanic alphabet, which could be used for divination, meditation and magical ritual in a manner similar to the tarot. One popular text was *Futhark: A Handbook of Rune Magic* (Thorsson, 1984).

flat I still had relatively little sense of what joining a magical group involved.[7] But they liked me, and I liked them.

So I came into the Glittering Sword.[8] As in the dream group, I found its first meeting both surprisingly normal, and bewildering. There were about twelve people, who seemed quite ordinary – including the two women of the muttered warnings. We did nothing more than drink tea and eat biscuits. But there was talk of the 'temple' and the 'power' and of sacrifices to Isis. I gathered that the first ritual that the group would do was a sacrifice to Isis, and that most members were relatively new to magic, but that others were quite experienced. My appearance precipitated an argument, because one of the women who had given me a lift thought that she had been promised the role of the moon priestess when the previous priestess disappeared. After considerable discussion – people apologized to me for the fuss which I had unwittingly caused – it was settled that I should not be the moon. Instead, I would be the sacrifice.

My sacrificial role was not determined until the second meeting. I arrived early that afternoon at Helga's collective to make the robe I was told I would need. Helga first asked me whether I was making the gown only for the ritual. When I said that I was not (I assumed that I would use it in other rituals) she let me go ahead, but warned me that Gertrude had phoned that afternoon to say that she was very unhappy with my presence in the group.

When we had settled down with tea at that evening's meeting, Helga rang a bell, and asked whether anyone would like to speak. Gertrude then said that she felt strongly about my presence in the group, and that she objected to my presence on rational and irrational grounds. First, I was unreliable (I had missed a meeting, a schedule conflict I had explained in the first meeting): a magical group is 'like a family', she said, and it needs to trust and rely upon its members. Then, when I had rung to enquire about the dream meeting, I had talked to her lover, and not to her, when she was in fact the leader of the group. There were already too many people in the dream group, and she would have vetoed my attempt to join. At this point several people broke in, saying that they had not known that the dream group even had a leader. Gertrude became upset and explained that it had been her idea, since November (it was now April). But then she moved on to the irrational grounds. She said that she had seen Thomas (her lover) talk to me for a while in the previous meeting, and that things were rough between the two of them, which was their problem but that I had been a catalyst for an argument. I offered to say something at this point – I had been oblivious of any flirtation at the previous meeting – but was turned aside for a moment; a bit later on, I said that I would like to get to know her, that we might get on, and she burst into tears and said yes, in different circumstances.

---

[7] The conception of this group had been formed some years earlier, and some people had become members, but little had occurred until this much larger group had been recruited.

[8] This was not the actual name of the group, though it was similar. In general, the correct name is used or not mentioned apart from a slightly misleading geographical location, as many of the groups have a public interface with the world.

At this point there was a spirited defence of me by several people about the social innocence of the conversation, which had been about Thomas' recent trip to the States: was Gertrude really upset that Thomas had left her to travel in the States? and so forth. Then Helga threw up her hands and said that she had the solution: Gertrude, Thomas and I had problems to work out, and we could best address them by taking the central roles in the Isis ritual: Isis, her priest, and the sacrifice. This was instantly hailed as an excellent solution. Someone pointed out that we should still work things out on the physical 'plane', but that the 'astral plane' was also important, and that such a rite would be good magic. Gertrude (who was new to magic) said that she could not take the responsibility (Isis was the major ritual role). Helga announced that it was a gift, from her, because Helga had previously been chosen to be Isis. People started to talk about how difficult it was to receive gifts. Eventually, weeks later, we did the ritual, and my first session of ritual participant-observation was spent face down on the floor. Gertrude and I stayed in the temple afterwards to talk about her anxieties and her fears of abandonment, a talk which seemed cathartic. My entries into other groups were less tortuous.

The Glittering Sword had evolved out of another general meeting like the dream group (both were 'Green Circle' general meetings), this one on ritual. Initially it was Eliot's idea. He had been in a ritual group before which had dissolved, and he wanted to recreate something like it. Apart from Helga, William, and Eliot there were nine other members, some of whom I recognized from the Quest conference and from the dream meeting. Emily was a tough, lower middle-class woman in her twenties who had been to art college but now worked as a betting agent, an occupation she had taken up to pay off a bank overdraft some years ago but now thought of leaving to return to art. Angel was a Courtauld student, also in her late twenties, now in museum conservation work. Like Emily she was a committed feminist, and I learned that they had a joint group about something called the 'Women's Mysteries'. There were two women (of the offered ride) who were secretaries in their fifties. One spoke of herself as a Cockney; the other had a not dissimilar accent. I was right to guess that they were relatively new to magic; previously, they had been involved with spiritualism, crystal healing and activities on the alternative-healing outskirts of occult practice. I knew that they had just joined Helga's coven, and I was struck by their care in not mentioning the coven within the Glittering Sword meetings, though most members knew of their affiliation: a lesson in the etiquette of secrecy. There was Gertrude, the German woman (a translator) who had hosted the dream group, and her Oxonian lover (an author), and a thirty-plus graduate student in the sciences. There was a young Austrian woman who had met Helga some years earlier in the library's occult section, and had over the years become a close friend. She was training as a photographer. And there was another man from my Cambridge college (he had not known that William had also been its student) a friend of the Oxonian, a technical writer who was famous within these circles for an odd but intelligent magical book of mixed cynicism and romance.

We met biweekly at the collective. We would gather, have tea, and change into magical robes which each of us had made according to a simple pattern. Then, around nine p.m., the lights would be dimmed and we would sit in meditation. Eventually someone would stand up, and we would solemnly file down to the basement. There was a special room in the basement called a 'temple', a cave-like room some twelve-feet square, low-ceilinged and ringed with a cement ridge that served as seats. There were strange symbols on the walls and a hollow on one side filled with statuettes. During rituals the room was lit only by candles – most rituals use only candlelight – and the incense lent a permanent tangy sweetness to the air. The room was shielded from an outer room by dark curtains. Once downstairs, we sat again in meditation outside the temple before standing to light our candle from the single flame before the temple door, and we would then pass through the curtain, to stand silent in a circle while the companions assembled.

Whenever we had a meeting, the programme was nearly always the same: tea, a change into robes, silent meditation, the descent to the temple door, more meditation, then entry into the temple. To begin the ritual, any ritual, we 'opened' the temple by ritually creating a 'magic circle' around the temple's edge and declaring that the temple was then 'open to the forces'. That ten-minute ritual had been written by William, and bore witness to his classical training. 'Zephyros, Lord of the soft west wind, we bid thee welcome . . .'. The opening was complemented at the evening's end by a 'closing' to 'ground' the force and 'banish' the magical circle. Rituals, meat of the evening, were written by different members of the group. Sometimes they were single, isolated performances. William, for example, wrote the ritual invoking the goddess Isis for the first full group meeting. There was also a requiem for a member's relative. But most of the rituals were parts of sequences. For the most part, these rituals were not really meant to 'do' anything. The idea was to see if we could summon a magical force, and that if we summoned it properly, it would dispense beneficence through the channels appropriate to its nature. For example, Isis, goddess of the watery Nile, brings emotional depth, and sun-god Apollo brings earthly strength and power.

These gentle rituals seemed far removed from the spirit-conjuring invocations I had anticipated from a magical group. But they also seemed tame – albeit beautiful – to the participants. In discussions, members of the Glittering Sword talked about being in 'training'. They said that we were learning to work together as a group, and to alter our awareness as a group. Even in the beginning they spoke of the ritual's effects: 'rituals always have consequences'. But conversation rarely focused on these consequences. One series of rituals was more power-oriented, for we worked through the planets, starting with the underworld and doing moon, earth, Mars, Saturn and so forth. In modern magical practice the planets are said to have distinctive types of 'energy': Mars is aggressive and bellicose (martial), Mercury sparkly and unpredictable (mercurial). If one performs a ritual about the moon, moon-related events – emotion, inspiration, dreams – should come one's way. These rituals we did collectively, so that each individual contributed something to the evening, and somewhat more attention was paid to the question of the ritual's 'results'. Eventually, I was told, we should be good enough to do some 'real' power rituals.

After some time the Glittering Sword disintegrated, partly due to attrition and partly through internal social friction. Three people moved; one of the couples split up; another member decided that she was over-committed (she was a member of many magical groups) and would have to drop the group.[9] One of the secretaries seemed to have difficulty with the younger Helga, and the two secretaries left the Glittering Sword in February 1984 and the coven soon after. Conscious of the dwindling membership, the group sought new members. Helga, passionately interested in Nordic mythology, took eagerly to anyone who shared her interest. She introduced an English friend in July 1984, sixteen months after I had joined the group in its early days. Alas, he was well-meaning, but young and slightly arrogant, and he announced that it was his personal responsibility to redeem the German nation from the atrocities they had committed in the war, an ethical responsibility unappreciated by the strong-minded German translator. The afternoon became somewhat Wagnerian, and in the aftermath of the conversation, we decided to abandon further plans to meet.

Around the time I joined the Glittering Sword, I also began going to the occult workshop to which Beth had invited me. This was a Monday night 'exercise class'. It was more or less open: all you needed to do was to write to Beth's postal box number for the street address, and you could get her box number from the ad in the occult bookstore, from the magazine her partner published, or from many other sources. Many people came through friends, however: after a few months, they might ask for contact with the 'real' secret inner groups whose members, they knew, were also present. And people came back, and back. Perhaps fifteen people came, on average, each Monday night. Nine of them might be old-timers. Eliot came, and Helga, and William; for a time Emily and Angel attended. There were a couple of witches of maybe ten years' standing, sometimes an initiate of a more solemn kabbalistic fraternity, and so on. And there were often new people. Harold used to wander into Atlantis, and he had taken down the phone number given for the Green Circle – an advertised contact number for interested outsiders. He kept it for a while. Finally he did a tarot reading about whether to use it. The reading described 'great change', and Harold dialled. He was passed to Emily, who was initially uncomfortable with him – he was quite supportive of women, but enjoyed teasing forthright feminists – but she thought that he was decent, despite the teasing. Through Emily, he met William, who told him about Beth's group. He

---

[9] She decided which group to drop by 'dowsing', letting a pendulum swing over the different names of the groups. I was impressed by this, because I had not thought that she would want to drop this particular group. On reflection, it may be that she felt that this group was not as enjoyable as the others. However, the interesting point is that these different groups did matter to her and she seemed willing to let the decision about her participation be taken by apparently arbitrary means.

and Beth and Enoch got on very well – again, it 'clicked' – and eighteen months later he was initiated into their coven, which was a secret society never discussed in the informal Monday night meetings.

The workshop was always a warm, happy evening, almost child-like in its innocence. People said that they came because they liked the imaginative involvement: they also came because of Beth, whose soothing but authoritative personality put people at ease. We would meet for tea at eightish and go into the living room half an hour later. There was a ten minute exercise session to 'loosen up'. Then followed the serious business of the evening, the imaginative exercises. The lights were cut. Beth took over as narrator, and we would imagine that we were a tree, or sparkling water, or a tarot card, or a cat, with dreamy, soothing music. The following paraphrases the imaginative sequence she often described:

You are floating . . . the air is good and clean . . . you find yourself upon a tiny cloud, in the middle of a clear blue sky. You are floating . . . see a waterfall of golden effervescent light before us . . . feel yourself absorbing its golden, radiant energy, revitalizing yourself. Feel the golden light focusing on some area of the body which you find painful . . . the light circles it, healing it . . . Feel the healing light penetrate to every part of your body, activating your natural recuperation powers . . . And now feel the cloud slowly come down, and, with a gentle bump, you have landed in the room . . .

The highlight of the evening was a pathworking, a dream-like story read out slowly so that listeners could visualize the images it described. ('You see before you a full clear moon – as you watch, a shaft of light descends from it'.) Pathworking is a central technique in magic and it is the subject of a later chapter, where examples of the pathworking style are given. The workshop was described as a magical gathering, an occult gathering, because it taught the techniques of visualization and meditation which are central to the practice.

And the year wore on. I became involved with many different groups, many different activities. I was initiated at least four times in secretive groups, and joined many others in their rituals. I probably participated in about a hundred rituals, and I attended hundreds of organized meetings and casual social events.

3

Journey to Aquarius: the sociological context of magical groups

BEFORE moving into a detailed discussion a general overview might be useful. Magical practice is not well-defined: there is a great range of enthusiasm, from those who casually read tarot cards to those who belong to several different groups and spend several evenings a week in magical activities. It is extremely difficult to identify the nature of this wide population: the secrecy of the practising groups and the rapidity of their change, the anonymity of the mail-order service that supplies so many thousands of customers – these factors make it nearly impossible to characterize the interested population. *Prediction* magazine apparently sells to members of both sexes, and to all ages and professions.[1] Nevertheless one can probably say that practitioners are on the whole middle class urbanites. Certainly the opportunity for involvement in groups is greater in London, and most of those I met were middle class, or came from middle-class backgrounds. For the most part, they tended to be lower middle or middle rather than upper middle, although there were exceptions even to this generalization. But they were not, in general, inhabitants of wealthy, chic Hampstead. They lived in Hornsey, Tufnell Park, Wood Green, Turnpike Lane, Hackney – places perhaps now being gentrified, but still accessible to those with relatively limited means. I met some working-class practitioners, though not many, and one type of magic – chaos magic – appealed to 'heavy metal' motorcyclists without means. Their involvement, however, was different in kind than most of the groups discussed here.

That the groups are primarily city-based is predictable. The greater concentration of people in urban areas favours the creation of practising groups: there is a larger sympathetic audience, more choice to tempt the individual, and more opportunity to create new groups if an old one should fall apart. Moreover, it genuinely facilitates involvement to be near an occult supplier, with a continual supply of books to browse through and buy. Mail-order services do ameliorate the difficulties of limited access to material, but one must know that the supplier exists. There are many practitioners, some deeply involved, who are not urban-dwellers: some of them became interested

---

[1] This information comes from its editor. Apparently the magazine was sold primarily to women some thirty years ago. The change may be due to a general broadening of interest in the occult or to the change in the magazine's content, which placed far more emphasis on spiritualism at that point.

in magic and paganism, and moved to the country as a result. Urban or otherwise, their professions range widely, from Eton schoolboy to Glasgow working-class runaway, from postdoctoral fellow in biochemistry to exhibiting artist, from higher civil servant to factory engineer.[2]

In whatever form magicians practise magic, they situate it within what is proclaimed the 'New Age'. This is a broad cultural ideology, a development of the countercultural sixties, which privileges holistic medicine, 'intuitive sciences' like astrology and tarot, ecological and anti-nuclear political issues, and alternative therapies, medicines and philosophers. The 'New Age' has become a widely accepted catch-phrase for this matrix of concerns: there are 'New Age' medicines, music, meditation tapes, and 'New Age' centres which offer classes in herbalism and Akido. Another name for this set of interests and attitudes is 'Aquarian'. Talk about the 'New Age' or Aquarian Age is utopian and idealistic: when it arrives, people will work together, there will be neither hierarchy nor loss of individuality, and science will be used for constructive purposes only.[3] This ideology is far more widespread than the occult, or at least the use of the word 'occult', and magical practitioners often see themselves within its terms. The following excerpt appeared in an article in *Quest* magazine, one of the largest and longest-running of occult journals. The article, by 'Moonwalker' – probably the editor, Marian Green – is called 'Preparing for Aquarius':

> Although astrologers tell us that the real Aquarian Age will not start until well into the next century it seems very obvious that many of the currents of the New Age are already with us . . . If you are a magician, and particularly if you are a witch, [you] should be working with the Great Mother of Earth to preserve the wilderness, restore the forests, refertilise the land . . . Some strong thoughts aimed at the Minister of the Environment will do for a start . . . Everyone would be healthier if they ate natural foods, in season. Health is an area in which every one should take care and consideration. It is your body, your personal gift from the gods . . . Find time every day to enter into meditation . . .[4]

This is standard magical-Aquarian fare: environmental, political concerns acted upon with magical techniques, with an emphasis on natural foods, good health and personal stability.

One feature of the New Age experience is the festival, a gathering to sell incense and musical tapes, to advertise groups or therapies, and to offer lectures and workshops to the public. In 1983 I attended the Aquarian Festival (an annual event now run by *Prediction* and called the Prediction festival). This was a very magic-oriented New Age festival; when I attended the Mind and Body festival a year later, most of the stalls hawked health food and aerobic sports equipment. However, the Aquarian Festival might illustrate the corner that magic occupies in this milieu. The festival was organized in 1978 as an annual

---

[2] A later section discusses the personality characteristics they sometimes share.

[3] Some writers (particularly those involved with 'deep ecology') identify the Aquarian Age with a technocratic conspiracy. When the term 'Aquarian' or 'New Age' is applied by people who attach the label to themselves, it has the described utopian implications.

[4] *Quest* (September 1987: 23).

event by someone who simply wrote to people whom she thought might want to display their wares. The reason? 'It's time to take a stand, and show people that we support the earth', she said. The March 1983 festival was held in Wandsworth Town Hall, on the outskirts of London. Over Saturday and Sunday three thousand tickets were sold, at £1.20 a head. One year, attendance exceeded five thousand, but it had declined. 'There are too many other similar festivals now. People don't feel that they *have* to come.'

Wandsworth Town Hall has two floors. The ground floor was set aside for some thirty tarot readers, crystal ball gazers and the like. Many of the readers make their living by travelling between festivals and psychic centres, charging five to ten pounds for a session. The upper floor (the main attraction) held the stalls, the lecture halls and the (vegetarian) cafeteria. Merchants played electronic meditation music. Competing incense sellers burnt their wares. Crystals and chimes and pendants dangled in the light. A Hare Krishna group chanted for a while. There were fifty-eight stalls in all; they paid an average of ninety pounds for their space and many of them made a profit. Fifteen dealt with natural healing and herbal medicine; eight concerned eastern arts and philosophies; five were political, such as the El Salvador Solidarity campaign. The remaining thirty stalls displayed the range of western occultism – staffs were sold by Dusty Miller and the Traditional Cudgel Craftsmen, the store Magistra, run by a witch, offered silver pentacles, crystal balls, and useful manuals; various 'earth mysteries' societies distributed pamphlets on leylines. The International Order of Kabbalists advertised its lodge meetings and the Hornsey group left leaflets discreetly at the entrance. The lecture halls held sessions on witchcraft as a spiritual alternative, on a Graeco-Roman fertility religion – 'these initiation mysteries concerned the polarity of male and female and the transformation of consciousness onto a trancendental and deathless level' – and an occultist's panel on a general discussion of the New Age. It was an amalgam of spirituality, health fads and politics, in which magic was a particular variant of an alternative to the mainstream.

Many people interested in magic will go to these festivals, attend the lectures, buy a 'New Age' music cassette or a tarot pack, and meet friends. Some of them, probably after several years at that level of interest, decide to contact a group they know to be practising magic, either through the festival (though few groups advertise overtly there), or through the occult magazines, the notices in bookstores, or at a friend's suggestion. Or they decide to start a group themselves, using the books and manuals available. These groups differ greatly. Some are long-standing fraternities which demand that the applicant take a year-long home-study course before they enter. Some are volatile societies organized by an enthusiast. Some are small groups of supposedly family-like closeness which seem remarkably long-lived. A newcomer interested in joining a group might have a variety of careers within it, depending upon the stability of the group he enters and his compatibility with its members. Some people join one group and remain with it for twenty years; others join a group they find that they dislike, or the group splinters, and the individual lets years pass before joining anything again. Or he may join several groups – a study group, and then a workshop, a coven and an Isis-oriented fellowship. Magical practice is a loosely interconnected community which, for the individual, need not depend on any one particular group. It is a floating, ill-defined collection of people, practices and organizations.[5]

Despite this diversity, some factors distinguish the different groups, and for heuristic purposes one can impose a crude typology upon them. Magicians practice in roughly four sorts of organizations: the Western Mysteries, *ad hoc* ritual magic (like the Glittering Sword), witchcraft, and non-initiated paganism (like Beth's occult workshop). These are not tidy categories, and I use the word 'magician' to describe practitioners of all four. Groups which are true to type, however, are markedly different from others in their symbolism, their structure, and their self-conception. The following pages describe them in some depth, but the chart presents some key terms associated with each.

witchcraft	**Western Mysteries**
covens	fraternities
high priestesses	adepts
goddess-oriented	'contacts'
moon (Diana) and stag god	kabbalah
nudity	formal robes
	home study courses

***ad hoc* ritual magic**	**non-initiated paganism**
self-created	study groups
Celtic, Nordic, Egyptian	earth-worship
independent	general gatherings in pubs and parks
the Glittering Sword	

Witchcraft 'covens' are small groups, run by high priestesses, which claim to practise a pre-Christian nature religion. Western Mysteries fraternities are run by 'adepts': in the rituals they are meant to have access to spiritual 'contacts' who guide them in solemn ceremonies. *Ad hoc* ritual magic groups are organized outside of witchcraft or a Western Mysteries lineage, sometimes around a particular mythological theme. Non-initiated paganism includes study groups, lecture courses, workshops, and general gatherings in London parks to welcome in the spring. They are all interested in ritual, and they all talk about magic.

The secrecy and grass-roots independence of magical practice means that it is difficult to be sure of any portrait of the durability and interconnectedness of the various groups. However, there are several reasons for confidence in the representative nature of the groups which I encountered and the network

---

[5] See, for example, Jorgensen and Jorgensen (1982); they studied a collection of tarot users, and concluded – contrary to some theorists – that the occult is a loose community, composed of people who are not primarily ex-hippies, and who show little sign of serious socio-economic deprivation or psychological instability.

between them. My primary contacts were with two people who had been deeply involved in many types of magic for over twenty years; I had the benefit of their sense of magic's development, and the gossip that passed through about other magicians. I met nearly all, and came to know most, of the public figures who wrote the books and manuals and who organized the public (or semi-public) courses and gatherings. One individual made a great effort to contact practitioners across London and throughout Great Britain; I knew her well, read her network newspaper, and went to the open meetings she sponsored. Through these people I became aware of the different 'types' of magic. Two of these types are particularly important: witchcraft and the Western Mysteries. I purposefully joined the oldest of the current witchcraft groups, and one of the best respected of the Western Mysteries groups. Through these networks, I met people, learned their impressions of the sorts of magic practised, and tried to find people from that sort of group. As well as making an effort to meet the better-known practitioners, I approached less famous people who spoke at the festivals and followed up conversations with those I met at casual gatherings. I tried to meet the new people at an open meeting. I frequented 'psychic centres' where tarot readers handled clients, and I went to the open, informal meetings advertised in the occult bookshop. I became part of a complex, dense network in London which kept doubling back upon itself: I would meet someone independently, who turned out to have been initiated by someone I knew and whose name was known to other people I also knew. I was familiar with groups in the centre of this network and at its edge, and I chose the groups I entered carefully, so that I had experience with long-time practitioners and with newcomers. I am sure that no matter what my point of entry had been, if I had started in London I would have ended up in contact with many of the people I know now.

However, there are two significant uncertainties in my knowledge of practising groups. First, while I was fairly sure of my knowledge of witchcraft and the Western Mysteries, I was less secure about my knowledge of *ad hoc* groups like the Glittering Sword, simply because they could be organized independently of any network. As I learned of progressively more groups, it seemed that my experience in the few I joined was fairly typical of the rest, but I cannot be sure. By the nature of the fieldwork, I was more likely to hear rumours of a group which had been maintained for several years rather than those which emerged and fizzled, and I have less sense of how many short-lived groups arise. Second, I had little experience with Crowley-type, 'chaos' magic. These are *ad hoc* groups organized around a sexual, somewhat violent ideology which take their inspiration from Aleister Crowley. Crowley was a brilliant man with a peculiar spiritual bent and a certain literary talent, and his works have influenced much of modern magic. The people who were my primary contacts performed his 'Gnostic Mass' four times yearly to an invited 'congregation' – the rite symbolically enacts a 'mystical marriage' – and through this means they would hear gossip about other groups interested in Crowley. In London, I knew of no such groups then practising, although there were

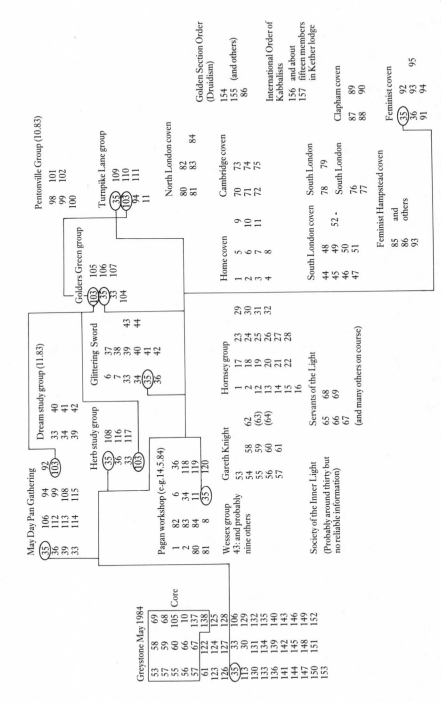

Figure 2 Relations of some groups in May 1984. Each number refers to one particular individual. Black lines define examples of overlapping membership. The author is not included in the diagram.

rumours of one formed as I left. However, there were a number of groups around Leeds who used literature from the mail-order suppliers, the Sorcerer's Apprentice. This type of magic, described later, may well attract those from less economically successful backgrounds. Certainly I knew of black leather-jacketed motorcyclists whose 'heavy metal' music made reference to Crowley and who seemed interested enough in magic to buy some books. However, I am not sure how much they practise and in what style.

By May 1984, I knew several hundred people involved in various magical gatherings. The figures below describe their interconnections: figure 2 identifies the people with whom I was familiar, figures 3 and 4, for clarity, identify the groups themselves and the people who will be most commonly encountered in the descriptions below.

The striking feature of the figures is the density of overlap in *ad hoc* magical groups and the comparative isolation of many of the covens and the Western Mysteries fraternities. This is partly because those two types of groups tend to be more sustaining and self-perpetuating: *ad hoc* groups are formed by one or more energetic people who cull the study groups for prospective members. They actively sought members, and people sometimes joined several. The covens and the Western Mysteries groups tend to be more difficult to enter. The common parlance was that you were never asked to join one of these groups; any coven or Western Mysteries lodge that had to ask you to join could not be worthy of its magical salt. The newcomer had to take the initiative herself, and initial contact would only catalyse the year-long correspondence course or series of social contacts that led up to initiation.

The other significant feature is the multiple involvement of some of the

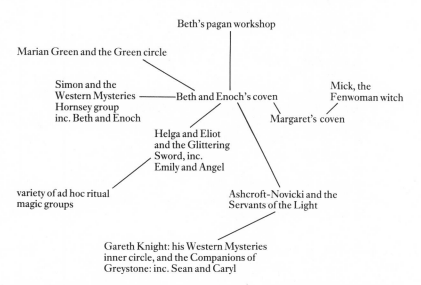

Figure 3   Some of the frequently mentioned groups. A connected line indicates friendship.

BETH: high priestess in coven, member of Hornsey group, member of *ad hoc* ritual group, runs pagan workshop. Has never attended Greystone.

ENOCH: high priest in Beth's coven, member of Hornsey group, member of *ad hoc* ritual magic group.

MARGARET: friend of Beth and Enoch, and of Mick; high priestess of coven; edits pagan magazine.

MARIAN GREEN: organizes network of magicians, involved in several *ad hoc* groups, friend of Beth and Enoch and of Gareth Knight; has attended Greystone.

SIMON: adept of Hornsey group; knows Beth and Enoch; knows Knight only from 'student' days in the Society of the Inner Light.

HELGA: helped organize the Glittering Sword; ran coven; very involved in the 'Nordic' tradition.

ELIOT: helped organize the Glittering Sword and coven; then became member of Beth's coven; was initiated in witchcraft (like Enoch and Robert) over twenty-five years ago.

ROBERT: member of Beth's coven; member of several *ad hoc* ritual magic groups; initiated as a witch into the Gardnerian coven over thirty years ago.

WILLIAM: helped to organize the Glittering Sword; once a member of Beth's coven; involved with several *ad hoc* ritual magic groups.

EMILY: feminist, involved with Women's Mysteries and several *ad hoc* groups, including the Glittering Sword.

ANGEL: feminist, involved with Women's Mysteries and several *ad hoc* groups, including the Glittering Sword.

ASHCROFT-NOVICKI: adept of the Servants of the Light. Knows Beth and Enoch (but not very well). Used to work with Knight, but now is more independent.

GARETH KNIGHT: adept of his inner circle and of Greystone; knows Ashcroft-Novicki and Simon, but not many others on this list.

SEAN: once a witch, now very involved with the Western Mysteries, and with Ashcroft-Novicki and Knight.

CARYL: once a witch, now very involved with the Western Mysteries, and with Ashcroft-Novicki and Knight. She and Sean have an enormous library of books about magic and mythology.

MICK: calls herself a witch but is a member of no group. She lives in an isolated Cambridgeshire village.

Figure 4   The people.

individuals. Some people seemed to be involved with a wide range of activities, until nearly every evening could be devoted to magic. Their multiple involvement illustrates one of the important elements of the practice: being involved in magic is a general enterprise, not best defined as the practice of joining one particular group but as a practice whose ends can be met by joining some group, more than one group, even no group at all. Different groups argue about the importance and correctness of their own persuasion, and they often felt that belonging to more than one group muddied one's symbolic, spiritual waters. But in the end, as many people told me, 'all paths are the same path'. People would be 'around' the magical world for years, sometimes part of a group and sometimes not, a consequence of the stability and nature of the group as much as of their own inclination to join. These people would still be defined as 'magicians'. The result of this understanding of magical practice is that it is difficult to estimate the drop-out rate, the ease with which practitioners leave their practice. After the Glittering Sword broke up, some members were left without a group: within two years, nearly all had joined some other magical organization.

These magical groups have, in general, different degrees of stability, notably because they have distinctive mechanisms for perpetuating the practice. Gerald Gardner, the man who created witchcraft in its modern form, was creating a practice which he wanted to expand. It was integral to the nature of a coven that it remain small – covens were meant to be small, intimate societies – and so Gardner, and later witches, were interested in propagating covens. Witches speak of an amoeba-like fissioning wherein one or two members leave the group to set up a coven on their own. They call this 'hiving off'. They are often aware of the history of their own coven, and proud of the groups that their coven has spawned. Some witches even give a special name to a high priestess that has spawned three or more groups.[6] Western Mysteries groups, on the other hand, are not amoeba-like. Their fraternities can, in theory, be quite large, and they pay more attention to hierarchy within the group than to the creation of new groups. Fraternity structure tends to be formal and elaborate, and when a junior member of leadership calibre ascends too far up the hierarchy he will leave. As it became clear that the various founders of current Western Mystery fraternities had seniority and leadership skills, they left the core organization to found their own groups. These days the leaders of the five groups have little contact, though their students know each other well. Two students (Sean and Caryl) of one group, with ties to another, have recently written their own text for magical practice and show signs of branching off themselves.[7] *Ad hoc* ritual magic groups have no such in built procedure – there is no pre-existent group from which they come – and they tend to dissolve under internal conflict. With fewer barriers to joining, members know each

---

[6] Farrar and Farrar (1984: 266).

[7] One could say that witches follow a Hadza-type hunter-gatherer model and the Western Mysteries a more lineage-dominated Lugbara-type African model of splitting and separation.

other less well and are less committed to the group's continuity, and as a result even in the best of circumstances they tend to be unstable.

Consider the history of the coven into which I was initiated. It had survived considerable internal conflict over forty years because whenever dissension became too great, a new coven 'hived off' from the old one, and there was a standard procedure of passing the high priestessship from one woman to another. Beth had taken over only in the mid seventies, over ten years after she had first joined the group. She was comfortable and familiar with all the members, and they with her. Several members of what was then a fairly small coven (perhaps six or seven members) decided to establish a large magical group, primarily for training purposes and to see if they could handle large, dramatic rituals. They gave it a romantic name and held fortnightly meetings. Partly through this more open group of fifteen to twenty people, they encountered people who were eager to join and seemed suitable for the coven, and that expanded by three or four. But relations in the *ad hoc* group became very tense, partly because two young girls each began having tumultous affairs with other members of the group. The open group collapsed from internal social tension after only about a year, but the coven persisted. Covens have a flexible, stable structure while *ad hoc* ritual groups easily splinter and need to be created from scratch each time.

We turn now to the description of the particular groups. They emerge from a historical context, however, and a brief history may give some perspective on their nature.

RECENT HISTORY

Most modern magical groups ultimately descend from a late nineteenth-century group called the Hermetic Order of the Golden Dawn, formed in 1887 by three dissident freemasons during the heyday of spiritualism and psychical research. This was a time of optimism, of social confidence, of awareness of the multifarious complexity of cultures. Victorian England was a strange mixture of technological progress and romantic yearning, and magic was an odd but filial offspring.

Many Victorians felt the tension between science and religion keenly. God's kingdom was slowly being conquered by scientific progress, and the optimism of the industrial revolution. Technological advance and the scientific ideology that accompanied it undermined religious faith and the trust in God's truth. Darwinian argument, though fiercely contested, did so markedly. Direct rejections of this ideology were not welcome. One of the most poignant figures of this period is the elder Gosse, who argued that God had placed the fossils in the soil to tempt mankind's belief with evolution's heresy, and was ridiculed. Gosse was a Plymouth Brethren preacher and a distinguished biologist, a Fellow of the Royal Society. He was torn by the need to reconcile the blasphemous theories of the one with the fervour of the other, and although his resolution was laughable to most, his anguish was not uncommon.[8]

Theosophy and interest in psychic research became popular as attempted reconciliations. Theosophy was claimed to be Tibetan spiritual teaching which was truly scientific and deeply spiritual.[9] As its founder proclaimed, 'by combining science with religion, the existence of God and immortality of man's spirit may be demonstrated like a problem of Euclid'.[10] Theosophy spoke of spiritual existence almost as a type of substance, and conveyed the sense that through learning one could make contact with the divine and alter one's own nature and possibly the world around one. The important feature was that it was a spiritual science: spiritual essence was affirmed to be a part of reality, often hidden from the mundane, which could be comprehended through philosophical training.

Psychical research was another attempt to maintain religious understanding with scentific honour. Frederic Myers reported this conversation with the society's first president of the Society for Psychical Research: 'In a starlight walk which I shall not forget . . . I asked him, almost with trembling, whether he thought that when Tradition, Intuition, Metaphysic had failed to solve the problem of the universe, there was still a chance that from any observable phenomena – ghosts, spirits, whatsoever there might be – some valid knowledge might be drawn as to a world unseen' . . . 'We caught together', he went on to say, 'the distant hope that Science might in our own age make sufficient progress to open the spiritual gateway which she had been thought to close'.[11] The plea had much appeal. The early membership of the Society for Psychical Research was remarkably distinguished: Tennyson, Ruskin, Gladstone, Balfour, William James, numerous Fellows of the Royal Society, and others distinguished in the academic and political world. Its first president, in 1882, was Sidgwick, one of the leading English philosophers.[12]

The early part of the century had seen the emergence of a literary romanticism in which religious questing was redescribed within the natural world, a 'natural supernaturalism' in which spiritual yearning took nature rather than God as its object. Romantic writers 'undertook, whatever their religious creed or lack of creed, to save traditional concepts, schemes and values which had

---

[8] Gosse (1983 [1907]); also see F. M. Turner (1974) for an account of the anxieties between religion and science in this period.

[9] The Theosophical Society was founded in New York in 1875, and rapidly gain·ed nternational acclaim. Madame Blavatsky and Colonel Olcott, its astonishing leaders, arrived in London (via Bombay) in 1884, when the British branch of the Theosophical Society had long been established. Its emphasis on Indian philosophy did not universally appeal – nor did the scandals of fraud and corruption – and Anna Kingsford (once a theosophist) founded the Hermetic Society in 1884 as a forum for her mixture of Christianity, Renaissance magic, Eastern mysticism, and late Victorian feminism (Oppenheim 1985: 187). See Gilbert (1983a: 21–3); and Oppenheim (1985: 158–203).

[10] Blavatsky (1887: I:vi).

[11] Quoted in Gauld (1968: 103). In 1903 this student would write a 'scientific' tract on psychic research: it has been called the 'last great manifesto of English Romanticism'. See Turner (1974: 108).

[12] Oppenheim (1985: 135). Other useful work on this intriguing period includes: Gauld (1968), Turner (1974), Haynes (1982), Brandon (1983).

been based on the relation of the Creator to his creature and creation, but to reformulate them within the prevailing two-term system of subject and object, ego and non-ego, the human mind or consciousness and its transactions with nature'.[13] That period was also witness to the burgeoning of chivalric imagery. In 1839 one hundred thousand people came to watch thirteen knights joust at Eglinton castle, a medieval extravaganza costing thousands and thousands of pounds.[14] William Morris and Dante Gabriel Rossetti painted Jane Morris into a reincarnate Guinivere and mixed socialism with medieval fantasy, and English public schoolboys became knights-errant of the cricket ground. Indeed the chivalric imagery ran throughout the self-referential mythology of the public schools. For example, in 1876 an article in the *Marburlian* remarked that 'a truly chivalrous football player . . . was never yet guilty of lying, or deceit, or meanness, whether of word or action'.[15]

In the course of the century the growing awareness of other cultures and societies brought about an interest in the religious concepts of other nations, and in the possibility of understanding their own society through comparison to others. The archaeological excavation of ancient Egypt alerted popular interest to the grandeur of ancient, preclassical civilization while colonial rule fed fantasies of mystical knowledge in the East. Some scholars argue that comparative mythology and anthropology were developed to order the cultural complexity[16] and the public sought the roots of its civilization in folklore and folk culture, with Max Muller's theory of myth as the disease of language and Herder's discovery of the national soul hidden in a folktale.[17] Comparative religion became popular drawing room conversation, and the accepted possibility that exotic religions were simply different conceptualizations of a common human dilemma and a common quest enabled such enterprises as theosophy to flourish.

The magic of the Hermetic Order of the Golden Dawn, founded in 1887, appealed to romanticism, to the interest in comparative religion, and to those who demanded a scientific framework for their spirituality. Its Masonic founders claimed to find an old, encoded Rosicrucian document which led them to a long-hidden society of secret rites and power.[18] They pored over medieval and kabbalistic magical texts in the British Library for arcane symbols. They invested elaborate ceremonial with Greek and Egyptian imagery and

[13] Abrams (1971: 13).

[14] Girouard (1981: 87–110); this work on late English 'chivalry' provides a rich account of some of the currents guiding the interest in folklore, anthropology and magic.

[15] Quoted in Girouard (1981: 169).

[16] See Burrow (1966).

[17] This period was witness to a fierce debate over the nature and origin of mythology between Muller and Lang and to the emergence of interest in Celtic ancestry, Herder's and Wagner's interest in Germanic mythology, and a general rise in the appreciation and importance of national folklore and myth.

[18] The founders – Westcott, Woodman and Mathers – emerged out of a magically-oriented masonic group called the Societas Rosicruciana in Anglia. Its members included Bulwer Lytton, who had published an occult novel, *Zanoni*, in 1842, and became Grand Patron of the society in 1871. Lytton, and possibly other members of the society, made contact with the French occultist Eliphas Levi; this influence was undoubtedly important in the emergence of full-blown English occultism.

chivalric myth. The official papers of the society – most of which are ritual texts – fill fat volumes with a daunting compendium of this lore.[19] And they claimed to use the imagination scientifically, to contact the spiritual world and work with it as a sort of technology to produce physical effects. By the time internal dissension split the group in 1903 there had been perhaps 400 initiates in the four temples in London, Weston-Super-Mare, Bradford and Edinburgh. They came from the upper and middle classes and from the literary world: Arthur Machen, Victorian novelist; Florence Farr, actor and Bernard Shaw's lover; Mina Bergson, the philosopher's sister;. A. E. Waite, mystical scholar; alchemist clergymen and ceremonial scientists. W. B. Yeats was the most famous initiate and his involvement was considerable – he ran the London temple in 1900–1. He also initiated Maud Gonne. Aleister Crowley and he remain its most famous initiates, garlic and sapphire of the membership.[20]

The Golden Dawn split and reassembled, and was severed and reformed, producing several groups that became far more Christian and morally high-flown. The most important of these was the Society of the Inner Light, formed in 1922 by a woman considered by many magicians as the finest occultist of this century: Dion Fortune. The leaders of current Western Mysteries groups were trained by her order, or by those whom her order had trained. Witchcraft grew up independently, in the forties and fifties, though the man who wrote its modern rituals was influenced by Golden Dawn practice. The other practising groups emerged even later, mostly in the seventies and eighties, out of the literature that the Western Mysteries and the witchcraft produced. Pagans and *ad hoc* magicians are often people who have purchased books about magical practice from occult bookstores, and created groups without the formal training and lineal descent that witchcraft or the Western Mysteries would offer them. Now, witchcraft covens are created independently, using the books published by witches (and other magicians) which contain information on how to create a practising group. The growth of these groups is in part a publishing phenomenon: when the books became available, people could set up independent groups on their own. The Golden Dawn does stand at the apical origin of them all, if only through its literature, but few now owe more than romantic allegiance to its practice. All magicians know of its existence; many of them have read its books. But the solemn ceremony seems arcane and tired now, fantasies of the antiquarian mind. The following pages describe witchcraft, the Western Mysteries, *ad hoc* ritual magic, paganism and Satanism (or the lack thereof). Each is introduced with an atmospheric vignette, intended to give a sense of the practice itself. Then, we turn to the practitioners: their nature and their literature.

[19] Regardie (1970).
[20] The classic study of the Golden Dawn is Howe (1972); Gilbert (1983a) is also useful, and Gilbert has edited some of the writings of early members which are quite interesting (Gilbert, 1983b and 1983c); other papers can be found in King (1972), who has written a lively, if not entirely reliable, history of magic in the last hundred years. The original Golden Dawn papers have primarily been collected in Regardie (1970). There have been a number of works which touch upon Yeats' involvement with the Golden Dawn; among the more detailed are Hough (1984), Harper (1974); the works of Kathleen Raine should also be consulted.

4

The goat and the gazelle: witchcraft

*   *   *   *

F
ULL moon, November 1984. In a witches' coven in northeast London, members have gathered from as far away as Bath, Leicester and Scotland to attend the meeting at the full moon. We drink tea until nine – in London, most rituals follow tea – and then change and go into the other room. The sitting room has been transformed. The furniture has been removed, and a twelve foot chalk circle drawn on the carpet. It will be brushed out in the morning. Four candlesticks stake out the corners of the room, casting shadows from the stag's antlers on the wall. The antlers sit next to a sheaf of wheat, subtle sexual symbolism. In spring and summer there are flowers everywhere. The altar in the centre of the circle is a chest which seems ancient. On top an equally ancient box holds incense in different drawers. On it, flowers and herbs surround a carved wooden Pan; a Minoan goddess figure sits on the altar itself amid a litter of ritual knives and tools.

The high priestess begins by drawing the magic circle in the air above the chalk, which she does with piety, saying 'let this be a boundary between the world of gods and that of men'. This imaginary circle is then treated as real throughout the evening. To leave the circle you slash it in the air and redraw it when you return. The chalk circle is always drawn with the ritual knife; the cakes, wine and the dancing always move in a clockwise direction. These rules are part of what makes it a witches' circle and they are scrupulously observed. On this evening a coven member wanted us to 'do' something for a friend's sick baby. Someone made a model of the baby and put it on the altar, at the Minoan goddess' feet. We held hands in a circle around the altar and then began to run, chanting a set phrase. When the circle was running at its peak the high priestess suddenly stopped. Everyone shut their eyes, raised their hands, and visualized the prearranged image: in this case it was Mary, the woman who wanted the spell, the 'link' between us and the unknown child. We could have 'worked' without the model baby, but it served as a 'focus' for the concentration. Witches of folklore made clay and waxen effigies over which they uttered imprecations – so we made effigies and kept a packet of plasticene in the altar for the purpose. By springtime, Mary reported, the child had recovered, and she thanked us for the help.

*   *   *   *

Modern witchcraft was essentially created in the forties – at least in its current form – by a civil servant, Gerald Gardner, who was probably inspired by Margaret Murray's historical account of witchcraft as an organized pre-Christian fertility religion branded devil-worship by the demonologists, and more generally by the rise of interest in anthropology and folklore.[1] Gardner had met Aleister Crowley, knew of the Golden Dawn, and may have been a Freemason. (Indeed his rituals show Crowleyian and Masonic influence.[2]) In the early fifties, Gardner published fictitious ethnographies of supposedly contemporaneous witches who practised the ancient, secret rites of their agrarian ancestors and worshipped the earth goddess and her consort in ceremonies beneath the full moon.[3] He claimed to have been initiated into one of these groups, hidden from watchful authorities since the 'burning times'.[4] In his eyes, witchcraft was an ancient magico-religious cult, secretly practised, peculiarly suited to the Celtic race. Witches had ancient knowledge and powers, handed down through the generations. And unlike the rest of an alienated society, they were happy and content. This paragraph gives the flavour of his romanticism:

Instead of the great sabbats with perhaps a thousand or more attendents [the coven] became a small meeting in private houses, probably a dozen or so according to the size of the room. The numbers being few, they were no longer able to gain power, to rise to the hyperaesthetic state by means of hundreds of wild dancers shrieking wildly, and they had

---

[1] In *Witchcult in Western Europe* (1921), Murray argued – much influenced by Frazer – that an organized pre-Christian fertility cult lay behind the witchcraft persecutions. The religion centred on the cycle of the seasons and their crops, and deity was incarnate in a horned male god, who had a female form, Diana. Murray proposed that the male god had superseded the female deity, and that the Inquisition had twisted the symbolism into a cult of devil-worship. Murray described her researches as anthropological, and compared witches to shamans: just as shamans understand themselves to leave their bodies, so witches believed themselves to leave their bodies to 'fly' – when they participate in certain rituals. It was a commendable approach, because it interpreted the witchtrials as concerning genuine popular belief – not as the collective delusion historians often assumed.

Other influential books in the development of modern witchcraft were Leland (1899) *Gospel of Aradia*; Frazer (1890; the twelve volumes were slowly published, and the abridged volume appeared in 1922, when Frazer's influence was at its peak – Cohn (1975: 107) *The Golden Bough*; Evans-Wentz (1911) *The Fairy Faith in Celtic Countries*; and later, Graves' (1968; first edition 1948) *The White Goddess*.

[2] There seems to be no hard evidence that Gardner actually was a Mason. However, there are some striking similarities in ritual structure between the two practices: an initiatory hierarchy of three 'degrees' (Masonry of course has many higher degrees in addition to the three basic ones); an initiation ceremony in which an initiate is presented blindfolded, with a garter around one leg, then presented to the different directional quarters, and presented with the 'weapons' or 'tools' of what is known as the 'Craft'.

[3] He claimed that he had only published then because of the repeal of the Witchcraft Laws in 1951, which proclaimed the practice of witchcraft illegal. They were replaced by the Fraudulent Mediums Act. See Farrar and Farrar (1984: 277).

[4] Gardner may well have been initiated into a practising group. He claimed that he had been initiated in 1939 by one Dorothy Clutterbuck. Some members of the group I joined had actually known him, and one at least – the most senior member – was persuaded that the group had existed, and that 'Old Dorothy' was not a fictitious character. Gardner talked about her, he said, as if she had been alive. Valiente, Gardner's close associate, was also persuaded of this woman's reality, and searched for the traces of her in county records. She produced evidence of a Dorothy Clutterbuck born and buried at a suitable time, in suitable places. See appendix in Farrar and Farrar (1984: 283–300). However, there is no reason to suppose that if such a group existed, it necessarily pre-dated the publication of Murray's book.

to use other secret methods to induce this state. This came easily to the descendents of the heath, but not to the people of non-Celtic race. Some knowledge and power had survived, as many of the families had intermarried, and in time their powers grew, and in out of the way places the cult survived. The fact that they were happy gave them a reason to struggle on. It is from these people that the surviving witch families probably descend. They know that their fathers and grandfathers belonged, and had spoken to them of meetings about the time of Waterloo, when it was an old cult, thought to exist from all time. Though the persecution had died down from want of fuel, they realized that their only chance to be left alone was to remain unknown and this is as true today as it was five hundred years ago.[5]

The invention of tradition is an intriguing topic: why is it that history should grant such authority, even in so rational an age? Witches speak of a secretive tradition, hidden for centuries from the Church's fierce eye, passed down in families until the present generation. There is no reason that such claims could not be true, but there is very little evidence to support them. The most sympathetic scholarship that speaks of an organized, pre-Christian witchcraft has very shaky foundations[6] – although there is more recently work that suggests that there were at least shared fantasies about membership in witch-related societies.[7] But those accused of witchcraft in early modern Europe were very likely innocent of any practice.[8]

[5] Gardner (1954: 46).

[6] While the attempt to examine the sixteenth and seventeenth century witchcraft persecutions as the product of popular belief was laudable, Murray took the apparent beliefs of the accused for their actual practice, and she drew her evidence from literary accounts of trials and from confessions exacted under torture. Certainly many confessions attest to the existence of sabbats, flying and the like, and there were those who believed that they were witches and confessed freely. However, there is little evidence to indicate the existence of an organized pagan fertility cult. Macfarlane, for example, found no evidence for an underground pagan religion in his thorough study of witchcraft prosecutions in Essex, nor did the language of the prosecutions include descriptions of the sabbat, the diabolic contract, and so forth (1970: 10). Thomas, drawing on a formidable knowledge of the period, concludes that 'in England there can be little doubt that there was never a "witch-cult" of the type envisaged by contemporary demonologists or their modern disciples' (1971: 516). The 'Murrayite thesis' is rarely taken seriously, in its full form, today.

[7] The relative ease with which people confessed to practice in itself indicates a widespread popular belief in witchcraft: whatever political purpose the persecution may have served, it depended upon common folk belief. In addition, there seems to have been popular medieval European belief in a Diana (Herodias, Holda) figure, who travelled through the night accompanied by souls of the dead and by female devotees. These 'ladies of the night' visited households with benevolent care; there were also beliefs of 'night-witches', cannibalistic women who devoured babies (Cohn, 1975: 206–19). Ginzburg presents evidence from late sixteenth-century Friuli of a belief in the 'benandanti', 'good walkers', who left their bodies at night and, armed with fennel stalks, set out to battle witches over the crops, the livestock, or other desired goods. This fantasy seems to have its roots in a pre-Christianity fertility religion. However, it is not clear that the benandanti ever met in the flesh, or that the fantasy was anything but that. 'On the basis of the available documents, the existence or non-existence of an organized set of witches in fifteenth- to seventeenth-century Europe seems to be indeterminate' (Ginzburg, 1983: xiv). Further evidence of a pre-Christian belief in witchcraft is given by Le Roy Ladurie (1987).

[8] Explanations of the 'witchcraft craze' of early modern Europe are rife. Accounts include: Trevor-Roper (1956), Cohn (1975), Thomas (1971), Macfarlane (1970), Henningsen (1980), Ginzburg (1983), Larner (1981, 1984), Estes (1983), Le Roy Ladurie (1987), Ben-Yehuda (1980). Accounts of the Salem trials include Boyer and Nissenbaum (1974) and Demos (1982). The corpus of this work is one of the best illustrations of the complex causality of any particular historical events, for the different accounts – admittedly handling different events in varied contexts – point to

Witches have ambivalent attitudes towards their history, as a later chapter details. They share, however, a common vision of their past, differing only on whether this past is myth or legend. Many of them say that the truth of the vision is unimportant: it is the vision itself, with its evocative pull, that matters. The basic account – given by someone who describes it as a myth – is this:

Witchcraft is a religion that dates back to paleolithic times, to the worship of the god of the hunt and the goddess of fertility. One can see remnants of it in cave paintings and in the figurines of goddesses that are many thousands of years old. This early religion was universal. The names changed from place to place but the basic deities were the same.

When Christianity came to Europe, its inroads were slow. Kings and nobles were converted first, but many folk continued to worship in both religions. Dwellers in rural areas, the 'Pagans' and 'Heathens', kept to the old ways. Churches were built on the sacred sites of the old religion. The names of the festivals were changed but the dates were kept. The old rites continued in folk festivals, and for many centuries Christian policy was one of slow cooptation.

During the times of persecution the Church took the god of the Old Religion and – as is the habit with conquerors – turned him into the Christian devil. The Old Religion was forced underground, its only records set forth, in distorted form, by its enemies. Small families kept the religion alive and in 1951, after the Witchcraft Laws in England were repealed, it began to surface again . . .[9]

It is indeed an evocative tale, with secrecy and martyrdom and hidden powers, and whether or not witches describe it as actual history they are moved by its affect.

Witchcraft is meant to be a revival, or re-emergence, of an ancient nature-religion, the most ancient of religions, in which the earth was worshipped as a woman under different names and guises throughout the inhabited world. She was Astarte, Inanna, Isis, Cerridwen – names that ring echoes in archaeological

the interdependency of psychological fantasy, small-scale social tension, and larger political and economic developments: the fear of a being who subverts the fertility of body and land, with unrestrained perverted sexuality, the cannibalistic, incestuous 'bad mother'; the child-rearing customs particular to a given society; the availability of criminal proceedings which made prosecutions available; the rise of a commercial ethic, a new individualism and the demise of the small face-to-face community; the collapse of a magic-like Catholicism for a stern, unforgiving Protestantism and the rise of a post-Galenic medicine, able to differentiate between the natural and non-natural cause for a disease; the political tensions within a given community; and then, Reformation and Counter-Reformation tensions, the rise and tenure of a notion of the 'godly state' in which Christianity held political significance. This blend of personally salient fantasy, cognitive shift, and political ideology probably precipitated the outbreak of witchcraft fear as Europe crossed the boundary from early modernism into secularized nation-states, heightening and creating social tension in its wake. But it is a phenomenon with many explanations and many causes, a typically messy transformation.

The accounts of African witchcraft are as numerous, but tend to be more homogeneous in their explanation, pointing primarily to witchcraft's role in relieving social tension – a social 'strain gauge', as one author puts it. Nevertheless, authors sometimes mention the psychodynamic elements of witchcraft fantasy, and point to some of the larger political elements of a rash of witchcraft accusations. The primary collections of essays, which include papers or book-excerpts from most of the scholars in the area, include: Marwick (1970), Douglas (1970), Middleton and Winter (1963), and Middleton (1967).

[9] Adler (1986: 45–6).

texts. She was the Great Goddess whose rites Frazer and Neumann – and Apuleius – recorded in rich detail. Witches are people who read their books and try to create, for themselves, the tone and feeling of an early humanity, worshipping a nature they understand as vital, powerful and mysterious. They visit the stone circles and pre-Christian sites, and become amateur scholars of the pagan traditions behind the Easter egg and the Yule log.

Above all, witches try to 'connect' with the world around them. Witchcraft, they say, is about the tactile, intuitive understanding of the turn of the seasons, the song of the birds; it is the awareness of all things as holy, and that, as is said, there is no part of us that is not of the gods.[10] One witch suggests a simple exercise to begin to glimpse the nature of the practice:

> Perhaps the best way to begin to understand the power behind the simple word *witch* is to enter the circle . . . Do it, perhaps, on a full moon, in a park or in the clearing of a wood. You don't need any of the tools you will read about in books on the Craft. You need no special clothes, or lack of them. Perhaps you might make up a chant, a string of names of gods and goddesses who were loved or familiar to you from childhood myths, a simple string of names for earth and moon and stars, easily repeatable like a mantra.
>
> And perhaps, as you say those familiar names and feel the earth and the air, the moon appears a bit closer, and perhaps the wind rustling the leaves suddenly seems in rhythm with your own breathing. Or perhaps the chant seems louder and all the other sounds far away. Or perhaps the woods seem strangely noisy. Or unspeakably still. And perhaps the clear line that separates you from bird and tree and small lizards seems to melt. Whatever else, your relationship to the world of living nature changes. The Witch is the change of definitions and relationships.[11]

The Goddess, the personification of nature, is witchcraft's central concept. Each witch has an individual understanding of the Goddess, which changes considerably over time. However, simply to orient the reader I will summarize the accounts which I have heard and have read in the literature. The Goddess is multi-faceted, ever-changing – nature and nature's transformations. She is Artemis, virgin huntress, the crescent moon and the morning's freshness; Selene, Aphrodite and Demeter, in the full bloom of the earth's fertility; Hecate and axe-bearing Cerridwen, the crone who destroys, the dying forests which make room for new growth. The constant theme of the Goddess is cyclicity and transformation: the spinning Fates, the weaving spider, Aphrodite who each year arises virgin from the sea, Isis who swells and floods and diminishes as the Nile. Every face of the Goddess is a different goddess, and yet also the same, in a different aspect, and there are different goddesses for different years and seasons of one's life.

The Goddess is very different from the Judaeo-Christian god. She is in the world, of the world, the very being of the world. 'People often ask me whether I *believe* in the Goddess. I reply, "Do you believe in rocks?" '[12]Yet she is also an

---

[10] This is a phrase taken from Crowley's Gnostic Mass (1929: 345–61). It sometimes appears in witchcraft rituals or in writings about the practice.

[11] Adler (1986: 43–4).

[12] Starhawk (1979: 77).

entity, a metaphor for nature to whom one can talk. 'I relate to the Goddess, every day, in one way or another. I have a little chitchat with Mommy.'[13] Witches have talked to me about the 'duality' of their religious understanding, that on the one hand the Goddess merely personifies the natural world in myth and imagery, and that on the other hand the Goddess is there as someone to guide you, punish you, reward you, someone who becomes the central figure in your private universe. I suspect that for practitioners there is a natural slippage from metaphor to extant being, that it is difficult – particularly in a Judaeo-Christian society – genuinely to treat a deity-figure as only a metaphor, regardless of how the religion is rationalized.[14] The figure becomes a deity, who cares for you.

Gardner began initiating people into groups called 'covens' which were run by women called 'high priestesses'. Covens bred other covens; people wandered into the bookstore, bought his books and then others, and created their own covens. By now there are many types of witchcraft: Gardnerian, Alexandrian, feminist, 'traditional' and so forth, named for their founders or their political ideals. Feminist covens usually only initiate women and they usually think of themselves as involved with a particularly female type of spirituality. Groups stemming from Gardner are called 'Gardnerian'. Alexandrian witchcraft derives from Alex Sanders' more ceremonial version of Gardnerian witchcraft. Sanders was a charismatic man who deliberately attracted the attention of the gutterpress and became a public figure in the late sixties. Some of those who read the sensationalistic exposés and watched the television interviews were drawn to witchcraft, and Sanders initiated hundreds of applicants, sometimes on the evening they applied. Traditional witches supposedly carry on the age-old traditions of their families: whether by chance or otherwise, I met none who could substantiate their claim to an inherited ritual practice.

Covens vary widely in their style and custom, but there is a common core of practice. They meet on (or near) days dictated by the sky: the solstices and equinoxes and the 'quarter days' between them, most of them fire-festivals in the Frazerian past: Beltane (1 May), Lammas (1 August), Halloween (31 October), Candlemas (2 February). These are the days to perform seasonal rituals, in which witches celebrate the passage of the longest days and the summer's harvest. Covens also meet on the full moons – most witches are quite aware of the moon's phases – on which they perform spells, rituals with a specific intention, to cure Jane's cold or to get Richard a job. Seasonal ritual meetings are called 'sabbats', the full moon meetings, 'esbats'.[15] Membership usually ranges between three and thirteen members, and members think of themselves – or ideally think of themselves – as 'family'. In my experience, it

---

[13] Witch, Z. Budapest, quoted in Adler (1986: 105).

[14] Gombrich's (1971) study of Sinhalese Buddhism draws a related conclusion, that devotees tend to treat the Buddha-figure as a god, not – as doctrine would have it – an enlightened man.

[15] The terms are probably drawn from Margaret Murray, although 'esbat' appears in a sixteenth-century French manuscript (Le Roy Ladurie, 1987: 7). 'Sabbat' is a standard demonologist's term.

usually took about a year of casual acquaintance before someone would be initiated.[16] The process took so long because people felt it important that a group should be socially very comfortable with each other, and – crucially – that one could trust all members of the group. As a result, covens tended to be somewhat socially homogeneous.[17] In the more 'traditional' covens, there are three 'degrees'. First degree initiates are novices, and in their initiation they were anointed 'witch' and shown the witches' weapons.[18] Second degree initiates usually take their new status after a year. The initiation gives them the authority to start their own coven. It consists in 'meeting' death – the initiate acts the part of death if he is male; if she is female, she meets death and accepts him. The intended lesson of the ritual is that the willingness to lose the self gives one control over it, and over the transformations of life and death. Third degree initiation is not taken for years. It is essentially a rite of mystical sexuality, though it is sometimes 'symbolic' rather than 'actual'. It is always performed in privacy, with only the two initiates present.[19] Behind the initiation lies the idea that one becomes the Goddess or God in one of their most powerful manifestations, the two dynamic elements of the duality that creates the world.

Witchcraft is a secretive otherworld, and more than other magical practices it is rich in symbolic, special items. Initiates have dark-handled knives they call 'athames', which are the principal tools and symbols of their powers: they have special cups and platters and incense burners, sometimes even special whips to 'purify' each other before the rite begins. There is always an altar, usually strewn with herbs and incense, with a statue of the Goddess, and there are always candles at the four directions, for in all magical practice the four directions (east, south, west, north) represent the four ancient elements (air, fire, water, earth) which in turn represent different sorts of 'energies' (thought; will power; emotion; material stability).[20] Then, another symbol of the secrecy and violation of convention, most covens work in the nude. This is ostensibly a sign of freedom, but probably stems from the evocative association of witchcraft and sexuality, and a utopian vision of a paradisial past. There are no orgies, little

[16] I was fortunate: there was a feeling in the group I joined that my time in the country might be limited, and certainly that my stay in London was relatively brief (fifteen months). In consequence I was initiated only six months after my initial contact with the members.

[17] This may be an exaggeration. Social ease with the applicant was clearly pertinent to the coven's decision to initiate someone, and personality style seemed more crucial than socio-economic standing. I knew an applicant turned down by one coven, despite the fact that he was of a similar age and background as most of the members, and despite the fact that their coven needed more men to have an even balance of the sexes – which is thought desirable. This was probably because he seemed too independent to the high priestess; there was at least some personality conflict between them.

[18] As already mentioned, this portion of the ritual resembles the first-degree initiation in Freemasonry.

[19] The role and nature of this 'third degree' initiation has been, not surprisingly, a source of some controversy within witchcraft, and different participants have differing views about whether it should be 'actual' or 'symbolic' or held at all.

[20] Air, earth, water and fire were recognized constitutive elements in the ancient world and their role and nature was a matter of considerable debate. The attribution of directional definition and human capacity may be a later accretion.

eroticism, and in fact little behaviour that would be different if clothes were being worn. That witches dance around in the nude probably is part of the attractive fantasy that draws outsiders into the practice, but the fantasy is a piece with the paganism and not the source of salacious sexuality. Or at least, that seemed to be the case with the five covens I met.

I was initiated into the oldest of these witches' groups, a coven which has remained intact for more than forty years. It was once Gardner's own coven, the coven in which he participated, and three of the current members were initiated under his care. It pleases the anthropologist's heart that there are traces of ancestor worship: the pentacle, the magical platter which holds the communion 'mooncakes', was Gardner's own, and we used his goddess statue in the circle.

The coven had thirteen members while I was there. Four of them (three men and one woman) had been initiated over twenty-five years ago and were in their fifties: an ex-Cambridge computer consultant, who flew around the world lecturing to computer professionals; a computer software analyst, high priest for the last twenty years; a teacher; an ex-Oxford university lecturer. The high priestess was initiated twenty years ago and was a professional psychologist. Another woman, in her forties, had been initiated some ten years previously. She joined the group when her own coven disbanded; another man in his fifties also came from that coven. He was an electronic engineer in the music industry. By the time I had been in the group several months, Helga and Eliot's coven had disbanded (this was the coven associated with the Glittering Sword) and Helga at any rate preferred to think of herself as a Nordic Volva rather than as a Celtic witch. So she abandoned witchcraft altogether, though she became deeply engaged in the other magical practice, and Eliot and another member of his coven, the young Austrian who was also in the Glittering Sword, joined the group. The rest of the younger generation included a woman in her thirties who was a professional artist but spent most of her time then raising a young child. Another member was a middle-level manager of a large business. He was in his late thirties and was my 'psychic twin': we were both initiated into the group on the same night. Another man, thirtyish, managed a large housing estate. The computer consultant and the teacher had been married twenty-five years, the high priest and high priestess had lived together for twenty. Four other members had partners who did not belong to the group, but two of them belonged to other magical groups. Three members of the group were married to or closely related to university lecturers – but this was an unusually intellectual group.

This coven, then, had a wide age range and was primarily composed of middle-class intellectuals, many of whose lovers were not members of the group. This was not particularly standard: another coven with whom this group had contact had nine members, all of whom were within ten years of age, and it included three married couples and three single individuals. A Cambridge coven had a similarly great age span, and as wide a range of professions. But one in Clapham was entirely upper working class, and its members were within about fifteen years of age. For the meetings, the group relied upon a standard

ritual text. Gardner (with the help of Doreen Valiente, now an elder
stateswoman in what is called the 'Craft') had created a handbook of ritual
practice called the 'Book of Shadows', which had supposedly been copied by
each initiate through the ages. ('Beltane special objects: jug of wine,
earthenware chalice, wreaths of ivy . . . High priestess in east, high priest at altar
with jug of wine and earthenware chalice . . .') The group performed these rites
as written, year in and year out: they were fully aware that Gardner had written
them (with help) but felt that as the original coven, they had a responsibility to
tradition. In fact, some of them had been re-written by the high priest, because
Gardner's versions were so simple: he felt, however, that he should treat them
as Gardner's, and never mentioned the authorship.

The seasonal rituals were remarkable because in them, the priestess is meant
to incarnate the Goddess. This is done through a ritual commonly known as
'drawing down the moon'. The high priestess' ritual partner is called the 'high
priest', and he stands opposite her in the circle and invokes her as the Goddess;
and as Goddess, she delivers what is known as the 'Charge', the closest parallel
to a liturgy within the Craft. Gardner's Book of Shadows has been published
and annotated by two witches, and it includes this text.

The high priest: Listen to the words of the great Mother; she who of old was called
among men Artemis, Astarte, Athene, Dione, Melusine, Aphrodite, Cerridwen,
Dana, Arianhod, Isis, Bride, and by many other names.

The high priestess: Whenever ye have need of anything, once in the month, and better it
be when the moon is full, then shall ye assemble in some secret place and adore the
spirit of me, who am Queen of all witches. There shall ye assemble, ye who are fain to
learn all sorcery, yet who have not won its deepest secrets; to these will I teach things
that are yet unknown. And ye shall be free from slavery; and as a sign that ye be really
free, ye shall be naked in your rites; and ye shall dance, sing, feast make music and
love, all in my praise. For mine is the ecstacy of the spirit, and mine is also joy on
earth; for my law is love unto all beings. Keep pure your highest ideal; strive ever
towards it; let naught stop you or turn you aside. For mine is the secret door which
opens up the Land of Youth, and mine is the cup of the wine of life, and the Cauldron
of Cerridwen, which is the Holy Grail of immortality. I am the gracious Goddess, who
gives the gift of joy unto the heart of man. Upon earth, I give the knowledge of the
spirit eternal; and beyond death, I give peace, and freedom, and reunion with those
who have gone before. Nor do I demand sacrifice; for behold, I am the mother of all
living, and my love is poured out upon the earth.

The high priest: Hear ye the words of the Star Goddess; she in the dust of whose feet
are the hosts of heaven, and whose body encircles the universe.

The high priestess: I who am the beauty of the green earth, and the white Moon among
the stars, and the mystery of the waters, and the desire of the heart of man, call unto
thy soul. Arise and come unto me. For I am the soul of nature, who gives life to the
universe. From me all things proceed, and unto me all things must return; and before
my face, beloved of Gods and men, let thine innermost divine self be enfolded in the
rapture of the infinite. Let me worship be with the heart that rejoiceth; for behold all
acts of love and pleasure are my rituals. And therefore let there be beauty and
strength, power and compassion, honour and humility, mirth and reverence within
you. And thou who thinkest to seek for me, know that seeking and yearning shall avail

thee not unless thou knowest the mystery; that if that which thou seekest thou findest not within thee, thou wilt never find it without thee. For behold, I have been with thee from the beginning; and I am that which is attained at the end of desire.[21]

The nature-imagery, the romantic poetry, the freedom – this is the style of language commonly heard within these ritual circles. The point of this speech is that every woman can be Goddess. Every man, too, can be god. In some Gardnerian rituals – like Halloween – the high priestess invokes the stag god in her priest, and he gives similar speeches.

When the coven I joined performed spells, no ritual form was pre-scribed because no spell was identical to any other. The idea behind the spell was that a coven could raise energy by calling on their members' own power, and that this energy could be concentrated within the magical circle, as a 'cone of power', and directed towards its source by collective imagination. The first step in a spell was always to chant or meditate in order to change the state of consciousness and so have access to one's own power, and then to focus the imagination on some real or imagined visual representation of the power's goal. The most common technique was to run in a circle, hands held, all eyes on the central altar candle, chanting what was supposedly an old Basque witches' chant:[22]

> Eko, eko, azarak
> Eko, eko, zamilak
> Eko, eko, Cernunnos
> Eko, eko, Aradia[23]

Then, the circle running at its peak, the group suddenly stopped, held its linked hands high, shut its eyes and concentrated on a pre-arranged image.

Sometimes we prefixed the evening with a longer chant, the 'Witches' Rune':

> Darksome night and shining moon
> East, then South, then West, then North;
> Hearken to the Witches' Rune –
> Here we come to call ye forth!
> Earth and water, air and fire,
> Wand and pentacle and sword,
> Work ye unto our desire,
> Hearken ye unto our word!
> Cords and censer, scourge and knife,
> Powers of the witch's blade –
> Waken all ye unto life,
> Come ye as the charm is made!
> Queen of Heaven, Queen of Hell,
> Horned hunter of the night –
> Lend your power unto the spell,
> And work our will by magic rite!

[21] Farrar and Farrar (1981: 42–3).
[22] Pennethorne Hughes corroborates this attribution, but it is not clear that other historians would substantiate the claim.
[23] Farrar and Farrar (1984: 17).

> By all the power of land and sea,
> By all the might of moon and sun –
> As we do will, so mote it be;
> Chant the spell, and be it done![24]

The tone of the poem captures much about witchcraft; the special 'weapons' with special powers, the earthly power and goddess power used within the spell, the dependence of the spell upon the witches' will.

Most of the coven meetings I attended in England – in all I saw the rituals of some six Gardnerian-inspired groups – were similar in style. However, there were also feminist covens, a type of witchcraft relatively rare in England but quite important in the States. Witchcraft appeals to feminists for a number of reasons. Witches are meant to worship a female deity rather than a male patriarch, and to worship her as she was worshipped by all people before the monotheistic religions held sway: as the moon, the earth, the sheaf of wheat. Members of feminist covens talk about witchcraft and its understanding of cyclic transformation, of birth, growth and decay, as a 'woman's spirituality', and the only spirituality in which women are proud to menstruate, to make love, and to give birth. These women (and sometimes also men[25]) are often also compelled by the desire to reclaim the word 'witch', which they see as the male's fearful rejection of a woman too beautiful, too sexual, or past the years of fertility. The witches of European witch-craze fantasies were either beautiful young temptresses or hags.

Feminist covens emphasize creativity and collectivity, values commonly found in that political perspective, and their rituals are often quite different from those in Gardnerian groups. Perhaps I could offer an example, although in this example the women did not explicitly describe themselves as 'witches' but as participating in 'women's mysteries'.

On Halloween 1983 I joined a group of some fifteen women on top of a barrow in Kent. One of the women had been delegated to draw up a rough outline of the ritual, and before we left for the barrow she held a meeting in which she announced that she had 'cobbled together something from Starhawk and Z Budapest [two feminist witchcraft manual authors]'. (Someone shouted, 'don't put yourself down'.) She explained the structure of the rite as it stood and then asked for suggestions. Someone had brought a pot of red ochre and patchouli oil which she wanted to use, and someone else suggested that we use it to purify each other. Then it was suggested that we 'do' the elements first, and people volunteered for each directional quarter. The person who had chosen earth asked if the hostess had any maize flour which she could use. We talked about the purpose of the rite. The meeting was like many other feminist organization meetings: long on equality, emotional honesty and earthiness, short on speed.

---

[24] Farrar (1971: 20).

[25] There was at least one group of this ilk that was mixed: they would probably argue for the importance of integrating the male divine principle into a goddess-centred religion, and so justify the men's presence in a context usually focused on 'women's mysteries'.

When we arrived on the barrow some hours later, we walked round in a circle. Four women invoked the elements, at the different directions, with their own spontaneously chosen words. It was an impressive midnight: leafless trees stark against a dark sky, some wind, an empty countryside with a bull in the nearby field. Then one woman took the pot of red ochre and drew a circle on the cheek of the woman to her left, saying, 'may this protect you on Halloween night', and the pot passed around the circle. Then the woman who had drafted the ritual read an invocation to Hecate more or less taken from Starhawk, copied out in a looseleaf binder with a pentacle laminated on the front:

This is the night when the veil that divides the worlds is thin. It is the New Year in the time of the year's death, when the harvest is gathered and the fields lie fallow. The gates of life and death are opened; the dead walk, and to the living is revealed the Mystery: that every ending is but a new beginning. We meet in time out of time, everywhere and nowhere, here and there, to greet the Death which is also Life, and the triple Goddess who is the cycle of rebirth.

Someone lit a fire in a dustbin lid (the cauldron was too heavy to carry from London) and each of us then invited the women that we knew, living or dead, to be present. We then chanted, the chant also taken from Starhawk, in which we passed around incense and each person said, 'x lives, x passes, x dies' – x being anger, failure, blindness, and so forth. The chorus was: 'it is the cold of the night, it is the dark'. Then someone held up a pomegranate (this was found in both Starhawk and Z Budapest) and said, 'behold, I show you the fruit of life'. She stabbed it and said, 'which is death' and passed it around the circle, and each woman put a seed in the mouth of the woman to her left, saying, 'taste of the seeds of death'. Then that woman held up an apple – 'I show you the fruit of death and lo' – here she sliced it sideways, to show the five pointed star at its centre – 'it contains the five pointed star of life'. The apple was passed around the circle, each woman feeding her neighbour as before and saying, 'taste of the fruit of life'. Then we passed a chalice of wine and some bread, saying 'may you never be hungry', pulled out masks and sparklers, and danced around and over the fire. Many of these actions required unrehearsed, unpremeditated participation from all members present, unlike the Gardnerian coven, where those not doing the ritual simply watch until they are called to worship or to take communion (members often take turns in performing the rituals, though). There was also the sense that the group had written some of the ritual together, and that some of the ritual was spontaneous.

There are also 'solo' witches, individuals who call themselves witches even though they have never been initiated and have no formal tie to a coven. I met a number of these women (they were always women). One had an organization she called 'Spook Enterprises' and sold candles shaped like cats and like Isis. Another called herself a witch but had never been initiated, although she was well-established in the pagan world. Another, the speaker at the 1983 Quest conference, gave talks on 'village witchcraft': on inquiry, it appeared that she had been born in Kent, and was an ex-Girtonian.[26]

[26] Girton is the oldest women's college at Cambridge.

Mick, the woman of this sort whom I knew best, owned a Jacobean cottage where she lived alone on the edge of the Fens, the desolate drained farmland outside Cambridge. She managed a chicken farm. She told me that she discovered her powers at the age of ten, when she 'cursed' her math teacher and he promptly broke his leg in two places. It was clear that witchcraft was integral to her sense of self, and she took it seriously, albeit with theatre. She called her cottage 'Broomstick Cottage', kept ten cats and had a cast iron cauldron near the fire place. In the corner of the cottage she had a small statue of Pan on an altar, alongside a ritual knife stained with her own blood. Many of the villagers knew her and in Cambridge I heard of the 'Fen witch' from at least four different sources. Once, when I was sitting in her garden (her Elizabethan herb garden), two little boys cycled past. One shouted to the other, '*that's* where the witch lives!' Mick got 'collected' for her personality, she told me: people seem to think it exotic to have a witch to supper. And this may have been one of the reasons she cherished her claims. She was a very funny, sociable woman, always the centre of a party, but a bit lonely, I think, and a bit romantic: witchcraft served a different function for her than fervent Christianity might have done, but like all religions, the witchcraft reduced the loneliness, lent charm to the bleak landscape, and gave her a social role.

There is a certain feel to witchcraft, a humour and an enthusiasm, often missing in other groups. Witchcraft combines the ideal and the mundane. It blends spiritual intensity and romanticism with the lovable, paunchy flaws of the flesh. Fantasies of elfin unicorns side comfortably with bawdy Pans. The high priest of the coven I joined described this as 'the goat and the gazelle': 'all witches have a little of each'. Part of this is the practice itself. People can look slightly ridiculous standing around naked in someone's living room. One needs a sense of humour in order to tolerate the practice, as well as enough romanticism to take it seriously. And witches are perhaps the only magicians who incorporate humour into their practice. Their central invocation, the declamation of the priestess-turned-goddess, calls for 'mirth and reverence'. Laughter often rings within the circle, though rarely in the rites. One high priestess spontaneously explained to me that 'being alive is really rather funny. Wicca [another name for witchcraft] is the only religion that captures this'.

5

Meditations on the Tree of Life: the Western Mysteries

*   *   *   *

S PRING equinox, 1985. A terraced house in dilapidated but respectable Hornsey shares walls and a clinging trellis rose with its neighbours. It is entirely unmarked on the outside. The owners, a Western Mysteries group, moved here quite recently – the temple at the other house was too small for the expanding membership – and furnishings have the raw propriety of recent decoration. The carpet is thick and the furniture spare but quietly antique. In the front room the watercolour shows white horses emerging from the breaking waves.

The 'brethren' arrive perhaps half an hour before the ritual begins and change quickly into cowled black gowns. Precisely ten minutes before the hour – the pattern was set twelve, thirteen years ago – we file upstairs. The temple is exactly square. They rebuilt it when they moved in, and hung heavy drapes across the windows. No natural light has entered the chamber since it was built, and little else but candle light is ever used. 'Etheric forms dissipate quickly beneath strong light', I was told. In ritual, particles of incense cast a hazy filter in the light from four thick candles.

The officers arrive in the temple five minutes after the brethren, and take their seats on high thrones. The adept, the officiating magus, then enters and the keeper of the portal locks the door. The adept walks three times around the room and purifies it 'by the power vested in me in another place . . .'. He takes his seat upon the eastern throne. Unlike the brethren he is robed in scarlet, with a scarlet Egyptian nemyss (the Pharaonic headdress). The other officers, too, wear nemysses, but the brethren pull hoods over their faces to hide their features.

Spring equinox is the most important date in the Western Mysteries calendar, which has meetings on the equinoxes, solstices, and often at more frequent weekly or monthly intervals. Members say that it marks the turning of the magical tides. The purpose of the meeting is to hook the fraternity into these tides; the larger purpose, rarely explicit in the rite itself, is to provide a 'priesthood' to the unknown, unseen powers who work to hasten human evolution. Rituals may also have a more specific goal: to reduce the conflict in a city, or to 'bring the power in' at an ancient site. The first part of all rituals in Hornsey involves invocations set in Gothic script and read from tall volumes placed before each officer. 'I now declare this temple contacted on the tides of the Lesser Mysteries.' The readings are intended to announce to the beings on that other magical plane that there are now willing and able servants for their present use. Then the ritual focuses on the participants, to transform their elemental being so that they might be fitted to be servants, channels for the gods. 'Now let us go upon an inner journey . . . We find ourselves upon the shore. It is high tide. Before us stands a bonfire of driftwood and as the sun sinks below the horizon our leader plunges a brand into its depths . . . When we reach the top of the conical grassy hill we see that there are seats of stone. Take your seat . . . We have called Maat, goddess of truth. She is here . . . Now we see Whitehall . . . We will build the feather of Maat above it. See the feather clearly: it is crystalline . . . as we walk down the conical grassy hill we turn and look back at our stone temple. But now it seems dim, hazy; it is as the eternal light of this earthly temple, and you find as you look around you that you have returned to this earth and this plane.' The brethren shift and open their eyes. The ritual has ended.

*   *   *   *

After the Golden Dawn, the large nineteenth-century magical order, collapsed in 1903, it was remoulded as the Stella Matutina and it was into this group that one of the most influential twentieth-century magicians, Dion Fortune, was initiated in 1919.[1] In 1922 Fortune founded the Society of the Inner Light. This society is still active today, and at least five fraternities have descended from it: the society itself (the SIL), the Gareth Knight group, the Wessex group, the Hornsey group, and the Servants of the Light (the SOL). The last four descendants were each founded in the seventies by individuals who were SIL students in the fifties. The Servants of the Light (SOL) first emerged as a training school led by someone trained in the SIL. It is now run by one of his students. Supposedly – although I have not located any of the members – there is also an organization called the Hermetic Order of the Cubic Stone.

These groups call themselves the 'Western Mysteries'. They do so because they see themselves as the continuation of the mystery traditions of the West: of Egypt,[2] of Eleusis, of Mithraism, Druidism, and Renaissance Hermetic-kabbalistic magic. Witches, too, understand themselves as part of the long tradition of mystery religions in the West, but their sympathy has a different quality, more drawn by the earthy, instinctual shaman than by the ethereal monk. The Western Mysteries is a far more intellectual engagement than witchcraft: magicians say that witchcraft comes from the guts and loins, but that the Western Mysteries come from the head.[3] A Mysteries initiate is likely to take John Dee, rather than a shaman or wise-woman, for his inspiration – Dee

---

[1] 'Dion Fortune' was the pen name created from her magical motto, Deo, non Fortuna: her baptismal name was Violet Firth. King and Sutherland (1982) offer a brief history of Dion Fortune; more sympathetic, more detailed, is Richardson (1987).

[2] Egypt is seen as source of the Western Mystery tradition. Its true source, however, is commonly ascribed to Atlantis and to Lemuria, which is the name of Atlantis' predecessor.

[3] A good fictional description of the Western Mysteries ethos can be found in the fiction of Peter Valentine Timlett, who was once a member of Fortune's fraternity.

was an Elizabethan scholar, possibly Shakespeare's model for Prospero,[4] who wrote an influential introduction to Euclid's *Elements*, owned the largest library in England, and developed an extremely complex alchemical magical practice which he thought to have magical effects.[5]

The basic conception behind the Western Mysteries is that the universe has evolved into complex collections of entities with different degrees of material and spiritual existence. There are different 'planes' of existence, of which the material is merely the lowest. After death, it is thought, the human soul does not die, but reincarnates, in a long process in which each incarnation teaches the soul progressively more about its obligations and responsibilities. Eventually, the individual evolves to the point in which reincarnation would only 'inhibit' its development. Most of these highly developed souls leave this world for another, but some remain in contact with the earth, to guide those that are willing to help in the progress of human evolution.[6] These of course are the initiates, who have deliberately chosen to hasten their own evolutionary progress by bearing more responsibility for the race itself.

The ethos in a Western Mysteries group – it is called a fraternity or lodge – is of a disciplined service, almost an asceticism in the interests of the wider society. Practitioners describe themselves as 'in service': they are the 'spiritual commandos', a 'secret band of do-gooders' who stand guard over a naive humanity. Fictional accounts by their members present them as silent watchers behind closed doors who protect a society which barely knows of their existence. One author's ideal portrait of the student who 'commits' himself to the work reads thus:

Eventually there may come a time when the student wishes to dedicate himself definitely to the work of the group . . . Before making the unreserved dedication he is free to give as much to the work as he thinks fit. After it the work has to come first, before everything. Few realize the implication of this though many are keen to do it. It is a way for the very few.[7]

The student becomes a 'priest' (the imagery is classical, not Catholic), a channel for the unseen forces, and commits himself to the 'work' which is the regeneration of himself and of the planet. 'Generally speaking, the function of the advanced initiate is to act as a pioneer in the march of human evolution'.[8]

This work takes place through individual initiation and group ritual. Like all magical practices, the Western Mysteries lay great stress upon learning to meditate and to visualize, but the techniques are particularly important in these fraternities because it is thought that the group's 'contact' communicates through the practitioner's imagination during ritual or meditation. As a result, Western Mysteries initiates were the most serious meditators I encountered among

[4] Yates (1975b: 95).
[5] French (1972); Yates (1972); Dee's major alchemical, mystical tract is the *Monas Hieroglyphica*, trans. Josten (1964).
[6] See particularly Fortune (1966).
[7] Knight (1975: 265).
[8] Knight (1975: 265).

magicians, and many of them seemed quite skilled at the difficult art of moving into another state of consciousness during meditation. The point of the meditation was to try to pick up energies, communications or symbols that were pertinent to the ritual task at hand: one group leader described this to me as becoming a 'radio receiver'. You had to have a clear channel, and you had to receive and broadcast well. Some of this reception involved picking up a 'contact's' communication. Some of it involved using many symbols to access forces and energies which simply were in the world, and could be manipulated. The symbols which you picked up indicated that you should do rituals to 'project' certain types of 'energies' into the race's 'group soul'. In the ritual, you would use symbols as a 'channel' to allow the energy to pour in through the magician and out into the world in a specified manner.

Initiates had a specialized vocabulary about their meditations: they talked about being on the 'inner', about 'doing work'. The 'inner' was a shorthand for 'inner plane', a 'level' of spiritual reality on which you could interact with beings too ethereal for the material world – in practice, one was on the inner while dreaming, meditating, and doing rituals. 'Doing work' meant meditation on certain symbols, usually at the group leader's request, and reporting the thoughts and images that arose in that time. The group leader would study his initiates' reports, and if several people had had similar meditations, or if one of the meditations had seemed particularly important, she might interpret this as a communication from the contact, and base the group's ritual work upon it. For example, the group might be 'working' on the underworld, reading and meditating and talking about death, the dark, the Furies, Charon, and the like. If, in their meditations, many had strong impressions of, say, Cerebus and Anubis – canine guardians at the gates of hell – the leader might conclude that the group should do a ritual using a dog-symbol. She would suppose that only the contacts really knew why the ritual had to be done, but she might think that the ritual had to do with revitalizing a nation somehow unconsciously wounded by recent death or conflict.

The interesting part of this enterprise, to an observer, is how realistic the practice becomes, and yet how vague – how explicitly vague – the actual concepts and reference remain.[9] Most of the practitioners I met were not committed to any theory of the earth's evolution; they did not know what a contact really was; they did not suppose that their minds were as clear as telephones, to transmit communication from the sky. Theories of evolution were presented as guesses – 'the best we can do right now' – to formulate the conviction that there are external beings who are trying to guide rituals which have some effect upon other people. Even more ambiguous, it was never clear what counted as a contact's voice, and what did not. Whatever came through the meditator's mind was said to be filtered by the personality of the meditator and cloaked in his personal symbolism, and initiates thought themselves as

---

[9] Richardson (1985) provides the 'magical records' of two of Fortune's senior initiates in the Society of the Inner Light, 1937–39. This is a quite interesting portrait of the degree of reality which these 'workings' can attain.

having to grasp somewhat blindly at the possible significance beneath the megalomania and neuroses which smothered cryptic information. However, the sense of reality about the meditations, and about the external inspiration for their symbolism, became very strong. Caryl, a librarian in her thirties, is an excellent example of long acquaintance with the 'Mysteries'. She uses the standard vocabulary freely; the first time I met her, over breakfast at the December 1983 Greystone meeting, she was remarking (casually) that she had been 'called' to do 'work' in the north, but that she didn't have the money for it. 'They'll have to get someone else.' By this she meant that during her meditations, she had a very strong feeling that a ritual should be done in the north, and that external, powerful beings had chosen her to do it. But she could allow herself not to follow these 'commands' for financial reasons. She explained that those on the 'inner' – the Inner Plane Adepti – were last on earth so long ago that they had little awareness of the practicalities.

The first task as a member of such a group is to fashion oneself into a fit instrument for the greater powers to use, to straighten out the neurotic wrinkles which will warp the meditating and ritually concentrating mind. Practitioners often speak of such groups as 'hothouses', and neophytes are warned – as indeed they are in every branch of magic, and for more or less the same reason – that their life will fall into turmoil upon initiation, for the contacts – or the Goddess, or whomever – will shake up the settled patterns that have prevented further individual growth.

The leaders of these groups, those who have gone through years of training and have risen in the ranks, are remarkable people. They are called 'adepts'. While I knew only two of them at all well – Gareth Knight and Simon, leader of the Hornsey group – those two impressed me. They conveyed the impression that all their actions were guided by a trained intuition. They also both seemed remarkably vital: their eyes were bright, they always seemed alert, and so forth. I suspect that these qualities are the consequence of long meditative experience; these are often characteristics of holy men. Whatever the cause, Western Mysteries magicians treat adepts as a breed apart from other men and women. Very few people are widely regarded as adepts, or at least have groups of loyal followers that regard them as such. (For example, Beth and Enoch, the leaders of the oldest Gardnerian group and also deeply involved in the Western Mysteries, did not think of themselves as adepts despite their seniority.) Such men and women are almost venerated by their followers. They are treated as lovably fallible humans, but their words are treasured, their simple actions carefully examined. A member of Gareth Knight's group, for example, said that meeting with Gareth Knight, 'a person like that', can be quite intense even in the most casual of circumstances. 'I remember one time when we were just washing up, and the stuff was just pouring out of him in waves.'

The people who join these adept-led groups must want to combine personal power with service under the command of others. They must like the idea of a disciplined course of study, and they must be willing to tolerate a fairly strict hierarchy: it is assumed that the adepts are without question more 'advanced' and rightfully authoritative. It is not that easy to become an initiate: usually a candidate must take a home study course in magical technique and symbolism which requires daily study for at least a year, and then must pass an interview. (The anonymity of the course, however, assures that there is somewhat less social homogeneity in the Western Mysteries than in witchcraft). They must also be able to tolerate the conventional – not obviously a magician's need. A leaflet for the SIL declares: 'An old tradition was that nobody should be accepted for initiation until he had fulfilled all the duties of citizenship – which included solvency, the bringing up and launching into the world of children, and contribution to civic life ... the principles underlying this tradition still operate'.[10] The Society announces in its booklet that members must be practising Christians, and that they may not be, or have been at any time in the past, homosexuals or drug-takers.

In fact the groups often tend to be Christian, which may not be surprising in light of their conventional values. They have a very different concept of power than do most witches: whereas witches feel that they generate power from within their own body, Western Mysteries initiates understand themselves to draw in power, aided by the contacts, from a higher spiritual realm, and to channel it out to a physical reality as if their own material bodies brought the force to earth. Indeed they explain ritual performance as necessary because unless the force is 'grounded', it will dissipate without effect. Christ, in these terms, is the ultimate magical talisman: the physical incarnation of the highest divine, which sent a spiritual shockwave through the world. Western Mysteries initiates often see all religions as working towards the same end, but conceptualize Christianity as the most mature and accurate understanding of divine action. I know practitioners who have had visions of Christ, or intense experiences of Christian love flooding in upon them during meditation. Although they read many of the same books that witches read and fill their rituals with many of the same pagan, mythical themes, their primary symbolism is formed by the kabbalah, and most of the magical work and the training course is based on kabbalistic principles.

The kabbalah is part of the Jewish mystical tradition, but in the fifteenth century it was adopted by scholarly Christian magicians to purify and empower a gentle Hermetic practice.[11] When the nineteenth-century pundits perused the old magical manuscripts, it was the kabbalah that seemed to hold the secrets of magical knowledge. It became the basis of Golden Dawn rites, and has so come down to modern practice. These days the kabbalah is an integral part of magical practice – at least in the Western Mysteries, which descended from that nineteenth century group. Practitioners learn to meditate on the different sephiroth and their interconnections, and to understand them as representing

[10] 'Concerning Membership', received from the Secretary 4.4.84.
[11] Gersholm Scholem is the authoritative scholar of the Judaic kabbalah; see Scholem (1941) and (1974). The account of the kabbalah's incorporation into Christian magic in the Renaissance, by Pico della Mirandola who took his nine hundred theses to Rome in 1486, is given by Yates (1964). Pico's hopes that the incorporation of the kabbalah would ease the Church's antagonism to natural magic proved optimistic.

different 'energies' of one's life. The kabbalah can be quite dauntingly complex: that is part of its appeal, for it offers intricate ways of understanding and interrelating different events, feelings and fantasy.

In the Western Mysteries, the kabbalah is presented as a complex glyph to 'map' the descent of spirit into matter. Ten different 'sephiroth' represent different stages of the descent, and different types of 'energies', or ways of being. These are interconnected by twenty-two different 'paths' – the Hebrew letters – and magicians sometimes refer to the thirty-two paths of the 'Tree of Life', to include the sephiroth. The paths between the sephiroth are identified with tarot cards, and the sephiroth themselves associated with planetary forces. Each sephiroth is understood to symbolize some form of human experience: Malkuth, the lowest, is man's physical nature, while Yesod, the next highest, is his imaginative, psychic awareness, and also his sexual dynamism. Practitioners meditate upon the different sephiroth and often do 'pathworkings' (imaginative narratives visualized in a meditative state)[12] from one sephirah to another. The magical explanation for the kabbalah's use is that it maps the entirety of world being. Fortune says, in her manual on the 'mystical qabalah'[13]

Each symbol upon the tree represents a cosmic force or factor. When the mind concentrates upon it, it comes into touch with that force; in other words, a surface channel, a channel in consciousness, has been made between the conscious mind of the individual and a particular factor in the world-soul, and through this channel the waters of the ocean pour into the lagoon [the individual soul]. The aspirant who uses the Tree [the kabbalah] as his meditation-symbol establishes point by point the union between his soul and the world soul. This results in a tremendous access of energy to the individual soul; it is this which endows it with Magical Power.[14]

The idea behind Fortune's quotation is that the kabbalah is a complex symbolism that is intimately bound within the many spiritual and material dimensions of the world. If one is familiar with the kabbalistic intricacies, one can use them to influence the forces that act upon human beings and natural events. These forces are described by the kabbalistic glyph, and are psychological in tone: forces of spiritual kingship, of sexuality, of earthiness, of intellectuality, and so forth. If the magician is like a radio, the kabbalah is the mechanism both of receiver and transmitter, and can be used to garner chosen frequencies and broadcast them at will.[15] Figure 5 illustrates the basic symbolic knowledge that the beginning Western Mysteries practitioner learns about what is called 'The Tree of Life'.

To an outsider it may seem surprising that these groups are so proper, given the tiara of unconventional eccentricity which magic wears. The implicit conservativism emerges clearly in practitioners' attitudes about homosexuality.

[12] See chapter 14.
[13] 'Kabbalah' has several spellings: kabbalah, cabala, qabala. The last is often used by magicians. I have chosen to systematically use Scholem's transliteration.
[14] Fortune (1935: 18).
[15] This understanding of kabbalistic magic is not wildly different from that understood in the Renaissance Hermetic-kabbalistic magic, although the metaphor of a radio is clearly a recent exegetical aid. See Yates (1964); also in this book chapter 19.

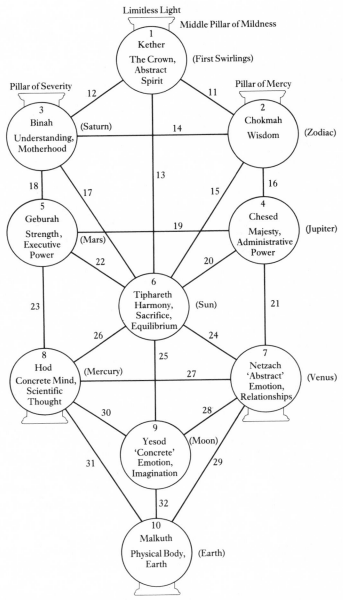

Figure 5 The kabbalah is extremely complex, and the diagram only begins to map its associations. As a whole, the glyph portrays the descent of divinity into matter, following the sequential path of the numbered sephiroth. Each sephirah is associated with a particular sort of human or divine experience, and with a planet: it is also associated with archangels, god-names, colours, titles and so forth, although these are not depicted. The vertical dimensions are described as 'pillars': the 'middle pillar' is the path of harmony and balance, and the student often sets himself the goal of rising up 'through' the middle pillar in meditation. The student will also imaginatively 'travel' between the sephiroth on the 'paths', which are associated with the 22 major arcana of the tarot trumps.

TITLE: Malkuth, the Kingdom. (Hebrew spelling: מלכות : Mem, Lamed, Kaph, Vau, Tau.)

MAGICAL IMAGE: A young woman, crowned and throned.

SITUATION ON THE TREE: At the base of the Pillar of Equilibrium.

YETZIRATIC TEXT: The Tenth Path is called the Resplendent Intelligence because it is exalted above every head and sits upon the Throne of Binah. It illuminates the splendours of all the Lights, and causes an influence to emanate from the Prince of Countenances, the Angel of Kether.

TITLES GIVEN TO MALKUTH: The Gate. The Gate of Death. The Gate of the Shadow of Death. The Gate of Tears. The Gate of Justice. The Gate of Prayer. The Gate of the Daughter of the Mighty Ones. The Gate of the Garden of Eden. The Inferior Mother. Malkah, the Queen. Kallah, the Bride. The Virgin.

GOD-NAME: Adonai Malekh or Adonai ha Aretz.

ARCHANGEL: Sandalphon.

CHOIR OF ANGELS: Ashim, Souls of Fire.

MUNDANE CHAKRA: Cholem ha Yesodoth, Sphere of the Elements.

SPIRITUAL EXPERIENCE: Vision of the Holy Guardian Angel.

VIRTUE: Discrimination.

VICE: Avarice. Inertia.

CORRESPONDENCE IN THE MICROCOSM: The feet. The anus.

SYMBOLS: Altar of the double cube. The Equal-armed cross. The magic circle. The triangle of art.

TAROT CARDS: The four Tens.
      TEN OF WANDS: Oppression.
      TEN OF CUPS: Perfected Success.
      TEN OF SWORDS: Ruin.
      TEN OF PENTACLES: Wealth.

COLOUR IN ATZILUTH: Yellow.
   "   "   BRIAH: Citrine, olive, russet, and black.
   "   "   YETZIRAH: Citrine, olive, russet, and black, flecked with gold.
   "   "   ASSIAH: Black, rayed with yellow.

Figure 6   To indicate the complexity of associations to the kabbalah, and the magician's parasitic use of the Judaic texts from which it stems, the following chart on the associations to the sepirah Malkuth is presented. The chart is taken from the basic text on the kabbalah, by Dion Fortune, and in that book precedes the chapter on that sephirah.

For example, in 1978 a small furore broke out because at a general gathering of established members of the Western Mysteries and others (another Quest conference) one of the leaders announced that she would consider accepting homosexuals into a magical group. The occult journal *Aquarian Arrow* carried this statement:[16]

Two members of the [Hornsey] group attended the 'Aquarian Age' symposium held in London on May 13th [1978]. During this meeting it was publically stated by the leader of one group that she approved of working publically with homosexuals. The [Hornsey] group wishes to dissociate itself from such a viewpoint. Further, it considers that any genuinely contacted fraternity could not countenance working with sexual deviants of any sort. The reasons for this should be plain to any properly trained occultist. It is reasonable to conclude, therefore, that of the other 'leaders' and delegates present, there were none who were genuinely contacted on to the Western Mysteries.[17]

The journal also carried a rather prim rejoinder from the woman who had made the initial comment:

I have unwittingly caused bad feeling over a subject raised FOR DISCUSSION ONLY at a recent London meeting. In fairness to myself I feel that it was reported to you a little out of context . . . I have great faith in the power of occult training and its balancing effect on human nature and it seems to me that it could be of great use in these circumstances . . .[18]

These views about homosexuality are always explained as the result of the theory of magic: ritual tries to create a human 'battery' for magical force, and it uses the 'inevitable' attraction between male and female to provide the 'opposite charges'. (The views also demonstrate the worst insult that can be thrown against a Western Mysteries group – that it is not 'contacted'.) 'I have nothing against homosexuals' a member of the Hornsey group confided in me on a drive home. 'But you can't work magic with a homosexual. Homosexuals just can't create a current.'

I myself joined the Hornsey group. I knew the Gareth Knight group fairly well, and I knew different members of the SIL, SOL and the Wessex group. I settled on the Hornsey group because it seemed quite secretive and traditional, a real 'inner sanctum', and it was led by an adept who was one of the two or three most highly respected magicians in the subculture. This was where, if anywhere, the 'real' and most secretive magic went on, and I wanted to see it happen.

I did not find it easy, initially, to join the fraternity. Again I was fortunate, both in my contacts and in Cambridge's proximity to London. I had begun to understand the importance of this secretive kabbalistic magic by October or November 1983, six months after the Quest conference. I heard of the Hornsey group a bit later, and wrote off to them in December, explaining my project and

---

[16] The journal also independently criticized the entire affair for its hide-bound view of homosexuality.

[17] *Aquarian Arrow* 3: 10.

[18] *Aquarian Arrow* 3: 13.

requesting an interview. The secretary replied, saying that it would not be possible for me to join the group while my academic interests were entwined with the personal. Nevertheless we met and talked; some weeks later we met again. Enoch and Beth, who were in the group though they'd told me nothing of it, vouched for me. I was briefly introduced to Simon, the leader. By the summer I was allowed to begin the nine-month study course. I was due back in Cambridge in that October, and it was only because I could eventually commute to the rituals that it made sense to embark upon the coursework.

I started the course and did my daily half hour lesson for the nine months, and learned much about meditation, visualization and magic. I met no further members: I simply corresponded with my anonymous supervisor every two weeks, sending in lessons which were then marked or commented upon. By February 1985 I finished the course. I was interviewed at a café in the Liverpool Street railway station by two ordinary-looking middle-aged women with cardigans and brooches. They warned me not to get inflated ideas of my magical prowess, and that magic was all service and self-exploration. They asked me how I had become interested in magic and what I could offer to the group, what books I had read and whether I knew how I'd choose if I had to choose between the Gardnerian coven I had joined and the Western Mysteries fraternity (I said that I didn't know, and they replied that, considering my ignorance, this was fair.) They said that membership in two magical groups was rare for someone in this group, because magical groups demanded so much commitment in time and emotional energy.[19]

I was told to present myself at a certain address in Hornsey at 7.40 p.m. exactly, with a black robe made to certain specifications, black slippers and a long white cord. I hovered on the street corner for a few minutes when I arrived, and presented myself on the moment. The door was opened by one of the women who had interviewed me. She conducted me upstairs to a small room to change and meditate. She told me that when she returned, she would be robed and in office. When she returned, in black, with a black Egyptian headress, she conducted me upstairs and blindfolded me, and knocked to announce my entrance. When the blindfold was removed some time later, the room did look impressive. Twenty or so brethren ringed the room, their faces shadowed by their hoods and gowns. The light was murky with the smoke of incense. The suspense and mystery, the months of solitary study on the course, the drama of the smoky blackness, had worked their effect: I was awed and elated.

As in basic Freemasonry the Hornsey lodge confers three degrees. First degree meetings, which all attend, are held about once a month, and the meetings of the second and third degree between them. These rituals have abstract, morally lofty goals and use their imagination to effect general goals: the revitalization of a city, the restoration of peace, the integration of a paganism

---

[19] As we have seen this was not necessarily the case, although few of the members of that group had joined other groups. The perceived reasons for not joining two groups is that it can confuse the initiate's concentration upon one's group's symbols, and that it can distort the 'group mind', the identity of the group on the inner or astral plane, which is 'built' by group concentration.

and Christianity. Members enter the temple softly and sit in a circle, trying to visualize the images described and will them to have impact. Usually, prospective members meet no member until they have completed the course. They are then interviewed, often in an anonymous railway station café, and told to appear at a certain address on a particular date, exactly on time. The whole enterprise is over-protected with secrecy.

The Hornsey group included three civil servants among its approximately thirty members. There was also a university lecturer (the adept, Simon; he lectures on computers); a homoeopathist; a senior secretary at a major bank; a less senior secretary; a therapist; a nurse; a psychologist; an actress, then turned proof-reader; another actress; a graduate; a school teacher; two librarians; a computer software analyst; a Borough Council employee; a mature student (and mother); other mothers; a retired woman; and an electrician. Their ages ranged from twenty-five to early sixties. Ten of them had been with the group since it began thirteen years ago and the others had joined along the way. There had been some, but not many, drop-outs. This, perhaps, is the consequence of a lengthy study course. Gareth Knight told me that seventy per cent of the students would drop a study course before the first year was finished, but 'if they stay with you through the first year, you have them for life'. The Gareth Knight group, a small band of ten to fifteen, ranged as widely among the professions. One member was a saddler; another – an ex-hippie – taught educationally subnormal schoolchildren; one was an actor, now involved with television but once a member of the Royal Shakespeare Company; another was a builder; another, the headmaster of a comprehensive school; two were students; another was a New York lawyer (he joined in England, before he left for New York); and so on.

The Gareth Knight group also initiates its members into a secretive inner group after a study course, this one five years in length (the student can be initiated after a year or so). But Knight is seen as an innovator, a revolutionary, because in addition to his group he holds an open annual May weekend at Greystone, a converted manor house in Wiltshire. This is daring, because it breaks the bonds of secrecy and rigid hierarchy. Over eight years these courses have evolved into two days of 'lectures' followed by a ritual at the end. The weekends have become an established feature of the relatively small but quite dedicated group of ritual magicians. Some witches attend, as well as some *ad hoc* magicians and pagans and even some members of other Western Mysteries fraternities. Though expensive they are nearly always fully booked to or beyond the maximum of fifty, and pressure encouraged Knight to present additional weekends in December 1983 and 1984. Many of the participants are magicians of seniority and status and most of them return; in May 1984, forty of the fifty-six had attended previously. One man flies from Nigeria every spring. In December 1983 and 1984 three people flew for the weekend from North America; in May 1985 there were four. Those present meet a greater concentration of senior magicians than at any other time during the rest of the year. The Sunday ritual (and indeed, the whole weekend) is usually described as important and serious, and after the magical ritual people wander about slightly dazed, and disappear early to sleep.[20]

The structure of rituals at Greystone differ somewhat, but not markedly, from those of the Hornsey group. Let me, then, give three short excerpts of the hour-long ritual performed at Greystone in 1981. It is called the Ritual of the Catechism of the Grail. It contains many of the standard elements of all Western Mysteries. These include: an introductory 'meditation', or 'inner journey'; and a question-and-answer interchange between the adept, at the east, and the other ritual officers at the south, west and north. At the end of the ritual, the adept serves wine from the Grail-like chalice. The basic conception is that this ritual form allows magical force to pour into the magical circle, like water into a cup, and that it is concentrated there and then released in ways that the collective imagination specifies. The important feature to notice, however, is the mixture of fairy-tale enchantment and spiritual solemnity.

WEST: I invite you to come with me upon an inner journey. Therefore close your eyes, and sinking deeply into meditation, visualize the scenes described.

We are in the centre of a wide plain. Above us are the deeps of the night sky. The Pole Star is above our heads to the North. About it circles the Great Bear, called in these latitudes Arthur's Wain. The starry belt of the zodiac circles the earth. We are assembled in the name and under the protection of the Mysteries of Albion, and when we pass within the Veil, one will meet us, who is the Arch-image of our island race, whence are these islands called Merlin's enclosure.

In the darkness within the circle there rises a dark tower of impenetrable thorn. Yet even as we watch it becomes light green and then white with the opening blossoms of May. We stand in wonder about the shining white tower and pray for the inspiration that will give use entry and guidance. This is the hawthorn tower of Merlin and Nimue. In the silence, whoever has ears to hear, may perhaps perceive the low clear call of Merlin to all who are worthy to serve his Mysteries.

At the base of the tower we detect a movement and a rustling. From a narrow archway opening appears an Elemental guardian, tall and light green and gold, with an angular body and unhuman features. It stands sentinel and beckons us to pass through the narrow door to the Tower of the Mysteries.

Be ye conscious of the deepest aspiration of why you are here as you pass before its scrutiny.

Within the tower is a circle of stones. Great trilithons as old as time, that contain the secrets of the pattern of the universe. At the cardinal points of East and West and North four great high seats are raised, at which sit the Officers of the Four Quarters.

(some pages later: this following segment is repeated, with different symbols, in the other quarters).

OFFICERS CIRCUMAMBULATE THREE TIMES DEOSIL [SUNWISE, TO THE LEFT].

EAST: Who sits at the Southern Gate?

---

[20] The Servants of the Light was slightly different. This organization was instituted in the late seventies as a correspondence course – another lengthy course, five years in duration. Inner group members had no formal fraternity, and some of them attended the Greystone weekend and worked magical rituals with the people there. But recently their leader held a series of semi-secretive gatherings at a place similar to Greystone; from this, a closed fraternity may develop.

SOUTH: Arthur, son of the Pendragon and a Princess of Atlantis, King of the Land of Logres.

EAST: Why so situated?

SOUTH: To guard that gate.

EAST: What is the principle of your office?

SOUTH: The active inspiration of the peoples of the Land of Logres, that leads them to the following of their destiny.

EAST: What is the symbol of your office?

SOUTH: The sword Excalibur, drawn from the Lake, flashing like a thousand suns.

EAST: What does the flashing sword signify?

SOUTH: It cuts and hews the way. Its steel is mined from the deeps of earth and it is forged by fire through the brain and skill of man to become the weapon of achievement, whether in the form of sword, tool, lancet, artefact or plough share.

EAST: Let the sword be placed upon the altar, to indicate that the powers of your office are functioning in this place.

(some pages later: this describes the purpose of the rite)

EAST: We are met this day to celebrate the catechism of the Grail . . . Let all present, as the questions are asked, seek deeply within for an answer.

There will be a pause before each answer is given to enable each one present to formulate the question for themselves, and to await an answer from within. Even when no answer seems to be received, whether in pictures, words, or mental realization, there will, even so, be a contacting with the inner principles so invoked. In the waters of consciousness the greater stillness may reveal the profoundest depths of awareness. Likewise, a pause will follow each answer so that each one present may allow it to drop, like a precious stone, into the deep well of the mind.

Let us invoke the inner offices of the Quarters . . .

Solemn, chivalric, intellectually elaborate within the rite itself – as the Charge was the distillation of witchcraft, so this rite indicates much about the Western Mysteries. These magicians have invested serious purpose into stories now surviving as children's tales, and they see them rich with esoteric meaning. There is an almost mystical sense of the land, and the spirit of the land, and the responsibility to those who people it. And to the participants, steeped in the Grail legend and its magical interpretation, sure that the power is flowing, the rite can seem profound.

6

Space between the worlds: *ad hoc* ritual magic

* * * *

SCRIPT for the initiation ceremony for the Pentonville group (the leader put this on the altar table to guide him as he spoke)

18 October 1983

1 Lesser Banishing ritual (kabbalistic cross, pentacles at elements, invocation of archangels, kabbalistic cross).
2 Greetings to the four lords. 'Welcome, name, element, direction. Be our guide, be our guest'. [Taped on each of four walls: Raphael, east, air; Michael, south, fire; Gabriel, west, water; Auriel, earth, north].
3 Invocation of the Holy Guardian Angels.
4 To each person:
   Q: 'Why do you come to this place'?
   A: I come seeking light and knowledge.
   Q: 'Do you come of your own free and true will'?
   A: I do.
   'Then repeat after me these words. I, x, will work with the light, and I ask to be guided along my true path to become one with the light'. 'I welcome you to the light and to this group'. High priest, high priestess kisses seeker on cheek.
5 Consecration of chalice. Mix: bread (body), salt (mind), wine (blood), water (spirit). Each to take and drink. Say: 'I will help and share with each of my brothers and sisters in times of pain and joy, and help them in their journey to light'.
6 Request by high priestess. 'I call upon thee great ones of light to give thine aid to our brother Charles to find a place to live in with the rooms necessary for all he needs and wants. We ask that this is brought about in the next two weeks and for as long as he needs it. All those present do wish and will this to happen in the name of light. I give thee thanks. Amen.'
7 Thank Holy Guardian Angels.
8 Thank Great Ones.
9 Thank Lords.
10 Lesser Banishing ritual to close.

* * * *

There are many other magical practitioners, however, who are not of the Western Mysteries lineage, nor do they call themselves witches. These people have often run across some books on magic, taken a course, or attended a study group or series of lectures, and they set out to form their own group. Some will pick themes, and centre their rituals around such texts as *Practical Egyptian Magic*, or around Celtic or Greek mythology. There is, for instance, an organization called The Fellowship of Isis, with six thousand members[1] (by post) world-wide. Its members receive a newsletter, which always includes a ritual about Isis – an invitation, a seasonal celebration, and so forth. Members can be consecrated priest or priestess of Isis in a formal ritual in Ireland, the founders' home, or they can create groups – 'temples' – independently, using the rituals in the newsletters. However, the temples of the Fellowship of Isis have far more guidance than most of these groups. The majority of the groups of this sort that I knew had decided to form a group, wrote their own rituals, and chose the structure of the practice. I call these groups '*ad hoc* ritual magic', and use the category to include groups which are sufficiently elaborate to initiate themselves as members of an established companionship.

Creativity is a curious gift, perhaps best expressed within constraints. The members of these groups are quite creative: members each write the equivalent of hour-long, one-act plays. They design elaborate settings and costumes, and theatrically perform varied dramatic roles. They collectively participate in drafting other rituals; they choose names and mottos and emblems. Many of them experience their involvement as a creative effloresence, and talk about the rediscovery of long-dormant poetic, artistic talents. But they develop their talents with a loose collage of pieces of magical manuals, previous rituals and myths. Their creativity lies in the pastiche of cultural symbols and myths from different periods and places, through which their own ideas emerge.

The Glittering Sword, the group run by Helga and Eliot, performed two ritual sequences, the first on the Grail legend and the second on the planets. Emily organized the first of these ritual sequences, on the Grail legend. Each of us picked the name of an Arthurian knight, and then a quest, from a hat – only instead of being a hat it was a small incense pot – and each was then responsible for writing a ritual. We performed these sequentially in the fortnightly meetings. I picked Percival, Parsifal, and a white horse as my quest, and like the others I went first to Mallory to start my reading. The idea was to do enough research to know something of your subject and then to write an evocative ritual loosely based upon the subject's themes. Evocation was far more important than scholarly exactitude. Most members had read many standard works on magical ritual: they 'knew' what a ritual was and had little difficulty producing one. They wrote the way a trained dancer choreographs on a certain subject: the subject is the inspiration, the focus is the dance, and despite compositional freedom certain moves and patterns tend to reappear. Many things fed into this understanding of what made good ritual: the books they read, the courses they took, their own magical experience. This ritual creativity is not so different from the minister's choice of hymns and sermons. There are always hymns and sermons on a Sunday morning, but they are always different. The point to

[1] On 31 March 1986 the membership total was 6174, in 57 countries (the predominating countries were Great Britain, the United States, and Nigeria). *Isian News* No. 40 (1986).

remember is that in this magic, it is as if members of the Anglican pews took turns writing the Sunday service and could choose Mary, Luke, or John instead of Jesus if they preferred.

Once written the ritual was treated as if it were a theatrical performance. The ritual's author would choose officers for the speaking parts and hand them xerox copies of the script. Sometimes he would even rehearse them, days in advance, for the evening of the performance. The following script was written by Eliot on Gawain and Avalon. In it, Eliot adapts the original account. Gawain refuses to choose whether his espoused wife should be beautiful only during the day (for other people) or during the night (for himself alone) and because he refuses to choose for her, he breaks the spell that binds her. Eliot incorporates his understanding of the Goddess (Demeter, Isis, Cerridwen) whom he takes to represent all women; as such she becomes the mystical centre of the Celtic religion: Avalon.

All the Glittering Sword seated after the Celtic opening. Then Gawain goes to the centre of the temple and kneels, holding sword. Avalon retreats behind veil.
Music: first section of dance.
Two priestesses (maidens) arise and circle the temple and Gawain in a dance step.
Music stops: priestesses in front of Gawain on either side.
Dark maiden: 'Sir Gawain, wilt thou choose but one of us, the dark or the fair, the night or the day'.
Fair maiden: 'Gawain, if thy choice is upon me, then shall beauty and joy be known in the bright sunlight and all the peoples shall rejoice in my radiance'.
Dark maiden: 'Sir Knight, if thy choice be upon me, then in the hours of darkness thou alone shalt see my beauty and manifold are the sublime mysteries that to thee alone will be revealed'.
Gawain: 'My ladies, the fair and the dark: I cannot choose, for in very truth, I may not, for ye are both that which a noble knight would seek; ye are priestesses who bear true knowledge of gentleness and intelligence, the deeper secrets of love and shadowy enchantments, the quiet paths under the moon. No, the choice is not mine to make, and I am not worthy of it. Still yet do I understand that not all men see the loveliness of your kind, those whose eyes are blinded to the fair, unseeing to the dark, and many, fearful of both'.

Pause

Fair maiden: 'Sir, does thou but know it? Thou hast chosen'.
Dark maiden: 'Gawain, kneel not before us, for at last for thee, the spell is broken'.

Bell

Gawain arises. The maidens salute him.
Dark maiden: 'Now shall we bring thee a third, without whom we are not complete'.
Fair maiden: 'We will journey far beyond the veil to bring to thee, she who ruled in Avalon'.
Maidens go to temple veil.
Dark maiden: 'Come thou, O Queen of the moon and tides'.
Fair maiden: 'Be thou present among us.'
Second section of music. Allow a few beats before parting the veil. Then maidens greet Avalon before moving with music to eventually confront Gawain.
Music ends. Gawain again kneels.

Avalon: 'Sir knight, long have I dreamed that thou wouldst come this way, darkly though
thou seest the path; the path that leads to Avalon. This Avalon contains many things
not understood by mortal man, Avalon wherein was forged the mighty sword of
Logres, wielded by the Guardians of this land against our ancient enemy. It is here
that thou shall fulfil thy testing. Yet many of your race do hesitate to come my way; are
they so fearful of me? I who embrace all womankind, feeling their pain of sorrow, their
laughter and their tears; their joy is my joy and my birth was of their creation; my life is
their love!

   Is my aspect so terrible and so hideous that mankind dare not seek my face? Have I
offended thee, O Man, that ye may not come to lie in my bosom? What great sorrow
holds ye that ye canst not reach forth and hold my hands? Did I not give to thee my
daughter? Hast thou not heard her in the high song of summer or ever in the waves
against a distant shore?

   Come: come ye, O man, the four gates of Avalon shall open wide for ye who enter
with pure hearts and love, come, come yea, for the light of the grail shall guide your
steps and at the end ye may drink deep of this cup'.
Silence.

Third section of music. The three maidens dance until its end when they shall kneel, the
arms and hands to form a chalice.

Pause
Bell by music master

All return to seats for Celtic close.

The remarkable aspect of this ritual is the knightly language, closer to
William Morris than to Mallory, and the divergence between the original tale
and the ritual form. I rarely heard such archaic forms in ritual, although it suits
the rite quite well (or at least, it suits common cultural conceptions of Arthurian
language). I have never elsewhere heard 'Avalon' understood as a person, or as
eternal woman. Avalon is a place, the mystical heartland of Celtic Britain, and
while a magical novel recently described Avalon as home of the Celtic priestess,[2]
the idea of personifying the land was quite unusual. Eliot also read a moral,
emotional lesson into the Gawain tale: that men want to own or display women
because they fear them, and that the true test of manhood is to accept women in
their own right. He blends that lesson with imagery of the Goddess of the moon
and tides, and associates it with the hidden grail whose emblem is the chalice.

   There is probably little point in sketching the genesis of creativity: when
Lowes did so with Coleridge the lesson after many pages was only that poetic
genius consists in creative bricolage, bits of the old assembled and reshaped in
unexpected forms.[3] But there is a point to illustrating that magical practice,
particularly in an *ad hoc* magical group, encourages this creativity, but that it
does so within a context which seems to be traditional. The ritual simply seems
to be more satisfying if it suggests ancient times and rites. Anthropologists share
the intuition that rituals are age-old and traditional, though some are sensitive
that the 'traditional' aspect of many rites is more a commitment to the ritual's

   [2] Bradley (1982).
   [3] Lowes (1927).

time-honoured nature than an indication of actual authenticity.[4] In modern magic, as one might expect, the awareness and pride in personal creativity is strong. Nevertheless, there is still an attempt to create with elements of previous myths and rituals.

I knew many of these groups. I was initiated into the Glittering Sword when it was being formed in March 1983. For a short time I was also part of a magical group organized by utter novices (the Pentonville group). I regularly saw members of two other groups (the Golders Green group and Turnpike Lane group) which were mostly novice, but had some experienced members, and I knew most members of (and knew countless stories about) another group (the Muswell Hill group) run by Beth and Enoch. I also met, was interviewed by, or was told of at least five other groups in London (one now defunct): near Walthamstow, Sudbury, Hendon, Notting Hill Gate and Earl's Court. There was some overlapping membership. The Turnpike Lane group, for example, was organized by some members of both the Glittering Sword and the Golders Green group, because they felt that they should teach others as they had been taught. Those groups which I knew were politically leftwing and socially countercultural, but this may have been an accident of my sample.

The Pentonville group was quite different from the Glittering Sword, that well-run, well-integrated group of relatively successful, stable people. This was distinctly a group of the down-and-out and the unstable, the only such group that I encountered. I first was told about it by John, a poor student at the Acton Polytechnic. There were six of us: myself; John; Charles, the leader, a nervous, unstable squatter in a council flat who read tarot cards for cash at the now defunct Camden New Age Psychic Centre and who told me that his brother was a diplomat; Pat and Kevin, a working-class couple with tattoos and punk hair; and Francesca, a lovely young wanderer who had been involved with what seemed like every religious group in London and Glasgow and whose working-class father used to beat her before she ran away. All members were recruited out of the Camden New Age Psychic Centre. This centre had been established during my fieldwork period in what had been a large warehouse on the Camden High Street. A changing population of around fifteen tarot card readers, crystal ball gazers, and other diviners and spiritual healers spent their weekdays there, offering divination and healing at around five pounds per session. For a while I used to go down there one or two afternoons a week to chat to the readers and to learn how to read the tarot. John sold books for one of the tarot readers; Francesca had consulted Charles, who suggested the group to her; and Pat and Ken had also, I believe, first met Charles through the centre. The rhetoric they used was not uncommon. The reason to join a magical group, Charles said, was to make contact with the divine light within and to meet the higher light. But he

---

[4] Richards (1956) points to this in her study of Bemba initiation ritual: the song or dance may vary from year to year; it is the conviction that it is the same that matters. A similar issue of personal creativity within the performance of traditional song emerges in oral formulaic poetry (Lord 1960). The song is said to be sung as it always is, though it may be radically different from an earlier performance; the difference is attributable to a particular singer, who is said to be good or bad.

himself did rituals for quite specific ends. The first we did was both to introduce the fraternity to the 'light' and to find him a permanent home. And he advised Pat – who complained that there was something 'nasty' in the house 'which definitely caused the armchair to move' to use the Lesser Banishing Ritual (a major ritual in the Golden Dawn handbook of ritual practice) to get rid of it.

The Muswell Hill group was run by Beth and Enoch (they of the Gardnerian coven and the Hornsey group; they were, as I have mentioned, quite important in the magical subculture and involved in more groups than most participants). This group had been active in the late seventies, had fractured, and was being reformed as I left London. Beth and Enoch called it an 'art magic' group. Initially it had been organized as a 'training' group, with an emphasis on the theatre of ritual rather than upon its goal-oriented impact. Beth and Enoch felt that a successful ritual, 'real' magic, required skillfully performed ritual and performers highly trained in their use of meditation and concentration within a ritual context. This group was intended to provide basic training along these lines. The sorts of rituals performed, then, were less important than the skill with which they were enacted. Members wrote their own rituals – once, they each wrote one titled by a different colour – and the magical 'power' was rarely directed to a given end. Beth's 'Yellow Ritual' dramatized a myth of the birth of the universe, and its central characters were the void, the universe, and the logos. The final speech by the void – adapted from a published text on the Egyptian goddess of the night sky, Nuit – gives the sense of the group's ritual style:

I am she who has no beginning and no end; the Mother of all beyond space and time. She from whom all things proceed and to whom all things must return . . . I hold within me the aeons of time and the immensity of space, and they are as nothing. Yet I am also within the atom and the neutron, and I am lost within their vastness . . . Laugh, my children: I am too great for solemnity. Join in my laughter, which is the music of the constellations.

This was a ritual designed primarily to enable the participants to understand aspects of the incomprehensible unknown and aspects of themselves as human. It had no specific goal, though its practitioners would probably say that it had an effect – that some force was generated, focused and released.

The Golders Green group and the Turnpike Lane group were formed, at different times, from people involved either with the Green Circle or with its associated study course in 'Natural Magic'. The Green Circle (as described) was a loose network of individuals in magic, particularly 'pagan' magic – magic with an explicitly religious orientation which found its gods in nature. The study course was unusual. The author and teacher, Marion Green, had been a member of a Western Mysteries group for a while, and had trained under an established figure of that world, but her course did not claim to be a Western Mysteries course. It did not use the kabbalah, and it did not present itself as the outer court of an inner, practising group. Rather, it presented itself as a very beginner level year-long course which focused on 'natural magic' – how to interact, magically, with the natural world. Green formed the Golders Green group by writing to reasonably advanced students on her course and asking them whether they would be interested in participating. Perhaps eight were initiated. The Turnpike Lane group, of about the same size, was organized by one of her students with later students and some others who attended Green Circle meetings and showed interest. These groups met every two to four weeks and tended to do rituals concerning the planets or the ancient elements (fire, water, earth, air). As in other groups, the rituals were described essentially as training rituals, the intentions were unclear, and there was no assumption that any one person had unusual and advanced contact with the non-physical powers.

All of these groups, bootstrap organizations, had different degrees of formality and elaboration. They all used magical robes – in the Pentonville group, I was sternly told to take off everything beneath my robe, so that the power would flow – and all used special spaces, although some groups simply moved furniture out of the room to make it a proper 'temple'. The Muswell Hill group had rehearsals, special dancers and special music; the Glittering Sword had a less elaborate opening ritual, but a more elaborate setting. In all cases, the time and effort invested in the practice was considerable. Members rarely talked about the rituals themselves as a religion, although they would think of magic as a form of mystery religion, but they took the rites seriously. No member I met ever described their practice as a 'hobby'.

7

The Old Ways: non-initiated paganism

* * * *

LAMMAS (1 August), 1983. We finished eating in darkness, and collected the rubbish in polythene bags. Then Beth took us into the stone circle high above the Cotswold plains. We walked sunwise in the circle and tried to imagine ourselves as priests and priestesses, pulsing with intuitive knowledge of the stones. We knelt and pressed our palms against the soil, to feel the dormant, vital 'power' in the earth, and we tried to feel earth power flowing through us like electric force. Then we lay down and looked upwards at the sky. We thought of the distant power of the sky, and then we imagined the two powers intermingling, ourselves its conduits, small mediators of the mighty earth and heavens. Then we stood up. 'The Lady Artemis invites you to watch as the night sky takes her in his arms.' We watched, in the northwest corner, as the crescent slowly sank into the trees.

Returning to the centre we softly described the stone circle as perhaps it had been, or ought to have been, two thousand years ago. 'I see small fires, animals, children.' 'The priests are on the outskirts. They are men of the margin, lone watchers in the night. But the community is whole.' Comments were wistful, nostalgic, not precise; they made utopia of a squalid neolithic era. 'It was a time when all work had meaning.'

We lit a fire in the cauldron and danced around it to the cassette, the taped music feeble and incongruent. But after the folk reels the night seemed warmer. Then we had the ritual. Part guided imagination, part religious evocation, the theme was the estrangement of earth and sky, feeling divorced from reason. 'We stand between Earth and Heaven and are of both; our roots are in the earth and we reach, aspiring, to the sky.' We lit the quarter candles, and walked around the circle, to make 'space between the worlds'. We hummed, a soft, low hum, which became stronger and louder. At the peak of the humming we suddenly stopped. 'And in the days when the planet was young there arose between the lord of light and the mistress of the darkness a misunderstanding, and the lord withdrew from the lady, to his isolation in the sky.' We mimed the earth mother ascending from her slumbering depths. We drew the sky father down from his icy heights. 'Come, father of fire, sheath your sword in the womb of time . . . awaken the mother with your kiss of wine.' We passed a silver chalice with ruby wine and broke off pieces of the bread. Communion marks the ritual's end.

* * * *

Non-initiated paganism is a catch-all category for the meetings and rituals I attended which were not limited to initiated members. 'Pagan' is a much-used term, both within and without the boundary of modern magic. To magical practitioners, the term implies a polytheistic nature religion whose deities are meant to be personifications of nature, often as they were found within the ancient pantheons. Many modern urbanites use the term, without any thought of magic, to describe their religious attitudes to nature and their sense of Judaeo-Christianity's limitations. Many magicians describe the activities of their small, initiated groups as paganism. (All witches, for example, are pagans – although some might also include Christianity in their purview.[1]) However, all the study groups, meetings and casual, non-initiated rituals I attended were distinctly pagan: their point was to understand and to develop their paganism, and since that was the overarching philosophy of the practice it seems suitable to use the word to identify their doings.

The Green Circle has already been mentioned. It was created in 1982 by Marion Green, a central figure in this world: for years she organized its only 'conference' (the Quest Conference) and her journal *Quest*, founded in 1970, is one of the most established. The Green Circle was intended to be a network of pagan magicians which would enable people – particularly interested newcomers – to meet each other. Members were encouraged to organize local groups, and a newsletter circulated to keep these different groups in touch. Green said that by December 1983 there were five hundred members in the United Kingdom (there was a one pound subscription fee and a list of who had paid it) and some thirty regional groups. The number of active members may well have been lower. In London there was a fair bit of activity. There was a monthly social meeting, in a Wood Green pub or in the Royal Festival Hall café, so that new members could meet others. It seemed to attract ten to fifteen people each time, of which at least one would be completely new. In November 1983 the London newsletter listed six groups: a dream study group and a herb study group in north London (I was a member of both of these), each with about seven people; a weekly West London group, whose numbers were not indicated; a Southeast London/North Kent group of ten to twenty members (I attended one meeting and one outing); a weekly Thames Valley group of uncertain numbers; a monthly Surrey group of twenty to thirty members. These groups cast themselves as 'study groups'. Members met to explore a given topic (a kabbalistic sephirah, the tarot, magical theory). In north London, there were also less regular meetings organized in the name of the Green Circle: several on divination (in Hampstead, near the Finchley Road); one on the kabbalah, in Willesden Green. The Glittering Sword, of course, had evolved out of a Green Circle study group meeting on ritual.

These study groups were a common feature of the magic. The practice, in

---

[1] Among the more well known witches who also accept Christianity are Lois Bourne, author of an autobiography titled *Witch Amongst Us*, and Aidan Kelly, chronicler of Gardner's creativity and modern witchcraft historian, who decided after years of practice that the concept of the Goddess actually derives from the Virgin (Adler, 1986: 174).

any form, demands a considerable degree of knowledge of mythology and symbolism, and the development of the different skills of meditation and visualization. Becoming involved in magic also needs acculturation, for the very idea of performing magic is alien to educated urbanites. Most practitioners attended study groups to learn about the practice. These study groups were far more active, however, than seminars or lecturers would be. They often had a quasi-religious air about them. Beth's occult workshop, for example, was explicitly a weekly forum to train people in meditative and imaginative techniques. But all the pathworkings were about gods – we invoked Thoth and Isis, visited Demeter's temple, watched Hephaestus at his forge, danced with the lords of light at the beginning of creation. Beth thought that it did not matter whether you thought that you were involved in a psychological exercise or in religious worship.

These groups make you comfortable with magic, put you at ease with its concepts, and begin to encourage you to immerse yourself in the rich symbolism that the practice provides. As I met the Glittering Sword I began attending the Dream Group, remnant of that first large Green Circle session on dreams where I first met Helga. All seven of its members were also in the Glittering Sword, so it was something of a font of gossip, but the focus was on the dreams and on the deteriorating relations between the German woman and the Oxonian in whose house the meetings were still held. Magic involves symbolism and the interpretation of symbolism and the point of the meetings was to discuss the meaning of dreams. We kept dream diaries, recording dreams as we woke up from sleep. Two people would tell their dreams each evening, and the group would discuss their symbolism – the significance for the person, and their significance in the psychological or cultural world at large. This extract from my fieldnotes for 7 June 1983 illustrates the sessions [participants took notes on the dreams as a basis for discussion].[2] Only five members were present:

William described his dream: an Australian stamp with an image of Angel seated on a throne, tall, golden and queenly, with a child on her lap. To gloss the dream, William explained that he had collected stamps between the ages of eight and eighteen. After the dream he went to a stamp store and found a stamp from Victoria which matched the dream, which he said he might have seen before.

He explained that he saw the woman as a Tipareth figure: throughout his description of this and the previous dreams he stressed that the dreams were closely linked to the kabbalistic Tree of Life. The child he saw as Crowley's crowned and conquering child, and he also pointed out that the visual image of the child in the dream was of his sister-in-law's baby: he had a photograph of himself holding that baby in the same way that the woman was holding the baby in the dream, the way that the Virgin held her child. He thought that the photograph was the visual model for a dream with more complex significance.

The Australian stamp represented Queen Victoria, whom he saw as a matriarchal

---

[2] My fieldnotes were particularly elaborate – and accurate – on this occasion because we took notes in the group to help us remember the dreams as the dreamer told them.

figure. Already, before the dream, he had thought of Tiphareth as a matriarchal sephirah. The Queen is also the Virgin Mary, he said, and – 'I'm sure that anyone would agree with me' – the Virgin belongs at Tiphareth on the Tree of Life. The Australian element he linked with Prince Charles and Lady Di's tour of Australia at the time – and after pulling out two postcards of Queen Victoria, he whipped out a postcard of the Royal Couple and child. To him, he said, in his fantasy life, they represented the chance for the restoration of the Golden Age. Angel pointed out that Di is Diana – a pagan goddess, and that his name was also the name of the royal child. William looked stunned, and said he'd never thought of that.

William then reported two other dreams. The second was a dream of a sentence: 'The pagan goddess is only the Virgin Mary northeast through west to south'. He explained this on the Tree of life, marking out an arc which cut out Binah. He then remarked on the Hamlet quotation: 'I am but mad north-northwest.' Third was the same dream as the throned Madonna dream, but instead of Angel the woman on the throne was Elizabeth of York (whose picture he first saw on a box of matches and with which he was very familiar). Elizabeth of York was the wife of Henry VII: their marriage marked the end of thirty years of civil war.

William's interpretation of the sequence: The baby is the new self he is looking for: it is William himself. Also the baby is somehow Angel as well – partly because Angel had, some weeks previously, told a striking story of the birth of her sister's child. In fact he kept trying to relate the dream to Angel all evening, trying to show what significance it had for her. Gertrude at one point said, didn't he think that the dream was more connected to *his* experience? He responded that in fact since it was so archetypal, it was more significant than being related to him alone. That some dreams were personal, but that others had larger implications. And he thought that it was important that 'the dream had chosen' Angel, because Angel was both someone he didn't know very well, and someone who was appropriate for that role. Also, the dream had the look of a tarot card, he said: the high priestess or the empress. He had a strong feeling about the high priestess concerning it. At this point he realized that it had occurred shortly after the Isis ritual, and said 'Yes! It's Isis, too.'

Angel gave a long, involved explanation – quite coherent – almost a lecture on the triple aspect of the Goddess as maid, mother and crone, and how the dream included all of them. She saw it as a dream of integration between paganism and Christianity. She called it a three-fold integration, and used the image of interlocking pentacles. She also mentioned that the maid and crone are autonomous, but the mother is not. [One underlying dynamic in all this was a blossoming friendship between William and Angel, Platonic but emotionally intense.]

Gertrude gave a kabbalistic explanation which was quite good and complex; her partner drew out an elaborate astrological interpretation which left all others far behind – he is extremely comfortable in that arcane symbology – and focused on the significance of the second dream. I talked about the truth beneath the appearance: colour dream despite the black and white stamp, paganism beneath the Christianity, politics beneath the marriages.

We turn to the hermeneutic style of magical practice later: here the important point is the complexity and order of William's symbolism. He dreams in and interprets with kabbalah, Greek mythology, English history, philatelism, Crowley, witch-like paganism, Christianity, and he has little difficulty weaving all of them together to provide an elaborate, delineated description of an event.

One of the notable characteristics of his interpretations is its psychoanalytic feel: William is deliberately using the dreams to understand his personal unconscious feelings and desires. Yet the introspection is distinctly limited. Rather than exploring these feelings directly in the group, we tended to focus upon the general features of the symbolism. That is, William dreamt of a baby, and interpreted this as an expression of his personal needs to form himself anew. But he did not discuss any of the personal background which led him to have those feelings, nor did the group press him for any such explanation. Instead, the discussion focused upon the nature of the Goddess, and thus, on the possibility of the dream's realization, for the Goddess is the symbol of change and transformation. The other striking characteristic is that William was also perfectly ready to interpret his dream as revealing objective truths about the world – that, for example, it was a message for Angel, communicated from some other source than himself.

You learn things from such a group – beyond understanding the members' remarkable familiarity and ease with kabbalah, tarot, and astrology – because you begin to dream in its symbols. Your dreams become more ordered and symbolic when under constant scrutiny, you remember them more clearly when you train yourself to reach for your notebook the moment you awake, their complex interconnections with other symbols and experiences appear more readily to your mind. I have no doubt that this group, and others like it, significantly altered my personal dream and fantasy experience during the year.

There were also casual rituals in London parks and stone circles to celebrate the earth. In 1984 a network of these self-designated pagans met under the rubric of PAN (Pagans Against Nukes). PAN was the name of an organization in Reading which mingled spiritual reverence for the earth with the political commitment to keep nuclear weapons off it. It was one of several politically oriented pagan groups.[3] In their journal, *The Pipes of Pan*, their manifesto reads: 'Pagans Against Nukes (PAN) is an activist organization dedicated to the banishment of a nuclear technology from our Earth, and the re-establishment of a culture that lives in harmony with her. We seek to co-ordinate all pagans, of whatever land or tradition, in political and magical work to achieve this end, that the Earth be Greened Anew.'[4] The PAN group in Reading organized a number of events – among them, a week long camping celebration of the summer solstice at Sherwood Forest (for about a hundred people). Similar gatherings are held elsewhere (e.g. the Cambridge Autumn Equinox group organized a large bonfire and pagan gathering for about thirty people in 1983).

My contact with PAN came through small ritual meetings organized by its London representatives. During my time in London, two or three people associated with PAN would inform a diffuse network that there would be a gathering in a London park, usually around one of the traditional festivals. On

---

[3] In America many groups think of themselves as having a political orientation. Many think of their feminist orientation in itself as a political commitment; beyond that, some consider magic to be a political tool. Starhawk wrote an entire book on political magic, *Dreaming the Dark* (1982). Adler (1986) also describes some self-consciously political magic activity.

[4] *Pipes of Pan*, No. 15, Beltane, 1984.

one Lammas (August 1) forty of us dedicated summer fruit to the goddess while we stood in a circle on Highgate Hill (this is not the ritual of the vignette). At the summer solstice ten of us danced around a tiny fire in Alexandra Park. On May Day, fourteen of us met on Hampstead Heath at dawn to walk in a spiral towards a tumulus in the grey morning light. Once there we stood in a circle. Each used his or her own words to 'invite' the earth goddess and her consort to be present. We stood in silence; we danced in a circle and chanted; we broke bread and poured a libation to the earth. Then we hung ribbons on a tree and ran around the living Maypole. Having been passed by several joggers, we were then joined by six policemen, with one policecar and one policetruck. They were polite, but seemed to anticipate being burnt in wicker baskets.

Throughout all these groups, there was the sense that we were relearning the 'old ways', that there were ways of communicating and experiencing with each other and with the earth that had been lost. Whether through the meditations or pathworkings taught in the study groups, the invocations to the Goddess in the London parks, or the explorations of stone circles and ancient pre-Christian sites, practitioners felt that they were 'returning' to an earlier way of being, more intuitive, more psychic, more in touch with their minds and bodies. 'Those who walk [this path] must learn to think differently to the rest of warring humanity, must indeed relearn all that we have forgotten from the Beginning, the Foretime, when living *was* life, was creation, was nature, was God.'[5]

SATANISM

I never encountered anything remotely resembling Satanism, though there were rumours of a Satanic cult in California and occasional stories of a cat sacrificed in Highgate cemetery. Indeed, magicians seem very concerned about morality. They talk about black magic; they usually tell you that there are black magicians elsewhere and stress that they, by contrast, are very white. Inevitably there are unstable individuals who lay claim to evil powers, but in my fieldwork I met no-one of that ilk who was not personally isolated and obviously mentally disturbed, and there were enough of those. Throughout my work I met no group, nor any stable individual, who actually seemed to engage in practices which other magicians – or indeed, the wider public – would call 'black'. Black magic seemed to be a myth, and the talk about it seemed to be part of a general determination to be as morally virtuous as possible.

The magical concern about morality seems to serve two purposes. On the one hand, it suggests that the elusive forces are real, powerful and significant by emphasizing the increased responsibility of the magician: if black magic is prohibited, it must be because it has an effect. 'If you are a hedonist or anarchistically inclined, *give up the idea* [of Egyptian magic] *completely*. This magical discipline abides very strictly by cosmic law.'[6] The negative sanction

---

[5] Matthews and Matthews (1986: 239).
[6] Hope (1984: 129).

implies a positive power. On the other hand, the concern might provide a worthy intention in the face of the possibility of practical failure. If individuals imagine themselves to be moral magicians, their good intentions may reinforce their belief in their efficacy.[7] For example, I attended open meetings (another Green Circle gathering) at a pub, where the intention was to have newcomers meet other interested people. Once, a young woman showed up and announced that she wanted a curse to kill her boyfriend. She was clearly unstable; she also seemed quite clearly interested in the spell. Nobody would talk to her about the specifics of magical ritual. In fact, someone tried to explain that magic was not that sort of enterprise, and then became embarrassed at her behaviour when she went on with her demand. However, I was struck by the conversation in the car on the way home later. I was travelling with people who were fairly new to the practice and I knew that at least some of them had doubts about its efficacy. They were nevertheless delighted that no-one had spoken to this woman about the techniques in magic, and they seemed to be somewhat more confident about magic's power, and their own possibilities as magicians.

Nevertheless, magic is often perceived as weird and dangerous by the general public, and one cannot understand the magician's practice without paying attention to the curious cultural associations it evokes. My sense is that magicians are slightly horrified by others' perceptions, but also secretly pleased. Certainly, many of the general cultural perceptions make magicians seem very powerful indeed.

In Britain, most of the country's forty-three dioceses have priests with a special responsibility for exorcism. The Christian Exorcism Study Group was established in 1972 to run seminars for the increasing number of clergymen who are interested in exorcism and the paranormal.[8] I spoke with two clergymen at the start of my project, and both warned me against Satanism and devil worship: 'there's definitely a lot of it about'. They both gave accounts of being approached by people who claimed to be possessed, or who had been involved with a coven or with voodoo[9] and were terrified. Both warned me that in 'dabbling' with the occult, some evil influence might enter my life. In 1985 Father Dominic Walker, of the Christian Exorcism Study Group, said that he counsels about two hundred occult 'casualties' each year. 'This week I had a family with two members in a coven, too scared to leave it as they were afraid of being cursed. What was a reasonably happy family two years ago is now frightened and in debt. Another family which had joined a major Satanist group had to move away and change their identity, they were so deeply involved and in such fear.'[10] In 1982, there was a Cambridgeshire scandal because schools

---

[7] See Luhrmann (1986) for a discussion of morality in magic.

[8] *Guardian*, 28.2.83.

[9] Voodoo is practiced in London. However, it seems to be accepted by people of a different cultural background than the middle class Englishman. Certainly I encountered no one involved in both voodoo and the modern magic I have described, except in one instance in which a West Indian woman approached a reasonably well known witch in order to ask for her help against a voodoo curse.

[10] *Guardian*, 6.3.85.

began to celebrate Halloween American-style, with pumpkins and cutouts of ghosts and skeletons. One John Porter of Swavesey kept his six-year-old daughter at home to protect her from the discussion of evil spirits. 'In the Old Testament it clearly says that all witchcraft and all consultation with familiars and spirits is abhorrent to the Lord. People try to describe Halloween as fun but its basis is in darkness. I believe if people thought about it they would realize how dangerous a game it is.' Mr Porter was thought by many to have extreme views, but the reality of black magic was reiterated by the other members of the church.[11] In 1986 Derry Mainwaring-Knight was arraigned for raising money from wealthy Christians to free him, he said, from the clutches of a Satanic group. Mrs Susan Sainsbury, wife of the Member of Parliament whose family created the successful supermarket chain, contributed nearly £80,000. Lord Hampton paid £37,000 for a white Rolls Royce and £2783 for a car telephone, all in the name of freedom from Satan. Mainwaring-Knight had approached a vicar about his need to escape from the aforementioned clutches; the vicar had prayed to God and concluded that money should be raised to buy and destroy the Satanic regalia which Mainwaring-Knight claimed bound him to the devil. In all, some £216,000 were raised, from a fairly small number of people. Mainwaring-Knight was eventually convicted of having raised the money under false pretences and spending it on women and fast cars. But the most astonishing feature of the case was the ease with which the wealthy reached into their pockets to drive the devil away.

Certainly the wider culture plays upon imagery of sex and Satanism. Heavy metal rock groups use Satanic imagery, and the motorcycle gangs who follow them often keep chains and magical knives, magical books and other accoutrements of the practice. One album by a popular group, Iron Maiden, is called *The Number of the Beast*, homage to Aleister Crowley. The album cover gives the Biblical quotation from Revelation (XIII: 18) and displays demons, fires and souls burning in hell. The lyrics are about imprisonment and death by hanging; they speak of the Children of the Damned and the rape of the American Indian's land. Part of the title lyric is worth quoting:

> Torches blazed and sacred chants were praised
> as they start to cry hands held to the sky
> In the night the fires burning bright
> the ritual has begun Satan's work is done
> 666 the number of the beast
> Sacrifice is going on tonight
>
> This can't go on I must inform the law
> Can this be real or some crazy dream
> but I feel drawn to the evil chanting hordes
> they seem to mesmerise me . . . can't avoid their eyes
> 666 the number of the beast
> 666 the one for you and me

[11] *Cambridge Evening News*, 23.10.82.

I'm coming back I will return
And I'll possess your body and I'll make you burn
I have the fire I have the force
I have the power to make my evil take its course

It is a bizarre mixture of sex, Satanism, science fiction and paganism.[12] The imagery also emerges in disconcerting cultural forms. In 1983 a store called 'Beasts – Clothing for the Living Dead' opened in the countercultural chicness of Camden Lock. The clothes were black, sensuous and fitted with chains, crosses, studs and coffins. 'I find it very sad that the modern reaction to death is that it should be ignored as long as possible and eventually brushed aside as an inconvenience', the designer remarked. 'We need to get away from the fear and back to a healthy respect for death and the dead.'[13]

At the same time, there are progressively more sympathetic pieces in the popular press. 'Witchcraft . . . *Wicked* witchcraft?' reads the title of one article in *Living*.[14] The piece talked about 'Wicca, the ancient pagan religion of the British Isles . . . White witches undergo a three-year training to attain knowledge and "powers" which they then use to heal people.' The *Sunday Times* interviewed an artist-witch with a chatty, friendly discussion of her skills. 'The power of witchcraft, of course, is in the believing, and Una Woodruff, who has been concocting magic potions and casting spells for most of her thirty-two years, is remarkably persuasive about her powers.'[15] The *Boston Globe* carried an article on 'Witches: They're Casting a Positive Image'. 'Witches, Erinna Northwind is explaining, are not evil, Satan worshipping people. In fact, she says, "Good witches make good neighbors".'[16]

It is unclear what this coverage means for those who practise magic. I suspect that many practitioners enjoy the sense that their neighbours would be shocked

---

[12] Occasionally there are news reports of murders in which some Satanic motivation seems to be seen. A New York murder involved angel dust and Satanism, and the homicide chief investigating the murder blamed 'rock videos that glorify Satanic ritual'.

> According to investigators, Kasso stabbed Lauwers in revenge for stealing ten bags of hallucinogenic 'angel dust' – then turned it into a ritual mutilation. 'They built a roaring fire in a field near the woods', he said. As he was being dragged away to the field, Lauwers reportedly sat up and said, 'I love you Mom', [Lt.] Dunn said. Dunn added: 'They were chanting while they did this. Just before they killed him, they forced him to say, "I love Satan" . . . A crow cawed just then, and Kasso thought it was the devil telling him it was time for Lauwers to die. So he stabbed him multiple times again.' *New York Post*, 7.7.84

Such cases are rare, but they happen. In 1983, two boys pleaded guilty to criminal damage when they beheaded a family's pet goat to get its blood to drink in a ritual, and to acquire its horns. 'When he was interviewed Hughes was said to have stated that he had selected the goat for slaughter because it reminded him of a picture of a devil-woman with cloven feet, goat's head and long, curly horns' (*Times*, 1.3.83).

These incidents are rare, and the magicians described in the body of my text would describe the criminals as deranged fools. Nevertheless, these reports contribute to the public perception of magic, a perception compounded by occasional exposes in the more popular presses that present the existence of these groups as evil, sex-crazed Satanism oozing through the land.

[13] *Time Out*, 3–9.11.83.
[14] *Living*, 6.84, pp. 14–18.
[15] *Sunday Times*, 21.8.83.
[16] *Boston Globe*, 24.3.84.

at their involvement. They also probably enjoy the more supportive articles – witches are unusual, these articles say, but moral and even rather creative. Certainly the complex image helps to pre-select the type of person who chooses to enter magic. The following chapter turns to the people who are drawn to this varied practice with its odd, conflicting public image.

8

The 'child within': a portrait of the practitioners

INDIVIDUAL psychology and culture interact like oblique mirrors. The collective should not be understood as psychodynamics writ large; nor can the psychological significance of an individual's involvement in some activity be dismissed on the grounds that the activity is a collective enterprise. Modern magic is not a direct expression of the unconscious fantasy and conflict of its practitioners. Nor are those who practise it an arbitrary sample of the population. They find magic fascinating, sufficiently so that they are willing to explore it at considerable length and at possible risk to their reputation. In some manner the themes and concepts of the practice speak to them. Something in their personal makeup draws them to the practice, though different desires motivate different individuals. And regardless of their inspiration, most will be affected by the imaginative context of the practice.

To illustrate this alchemy of personal psychological conflict and thematic content, this chapter depicts the psychological themes latent in the practice, and then the personality traits that many of the magicians share. The thematic concerns within the practice are most clearly expressed through its literature. Most magicians read certain novels avidly. In many cases their enthusiasm for the literature actually led them into practice. Understanding the novels, then, is a necessary prelude to understanding the practice. In the same way, grasping the themes of the practical teaching literature is a prerequisite to comprehending the context in which an interested reader decides to make an effort to find and enter a practising group. We turn first, then, to the novels; then to a central theme in the practical literature, and finally to the people who find these themes impressive.

Ultimately, magic is presented as a romantic morality, a clash between good and evil in which nobility lies in the abdication of superhuman power. The novels are all about dramatic battles between two forces in which the protagonist is invested with power and responsibility to right a wrong, and learns to handle that power maturely, and they conclude with the acceptance of the mundane, slightly mucky human world. They are dramas of power and human limitations, the promise of omnipotence and the morality which must constrain any human ambition. And thus their magic is a tamed romanticism, flamboyant fantasies reconstituted into human aspiration. The practical teaching texts describe an underworld or darkness which must be confronted, entered and accepted before personal power can be gained: the abyss whose negotiation confers adepthood. The notion of the Goddess within the practical literature is a vision of continuity between chaos and order, destruction and creativity, in which the way to personal empowerment and selfhood leads through the valley of dissolution. The themes which emerge from this creative amalgam of different myths, stories and symbols are about the nature of power: of the value of losing it to regain it, of the knowledge to control it. Those who become magicians are compelled by these portrayals. They often seem to be people self-sufficient within a withdrawn, subjective fantasy world who are conflicted about their own desire to have impact within the larger social world, and the romantic fantasy constitutes for them some sort of resolution, perhaps as therapy, perhaps as escape. It is as if the magic dramatized the psychodynamic tension of early childhood – the terror of dissolution, the negotiation of the power relations between the powerful other and oneself, the need for autonomy – and characterized its resolution as mature adulthood.

THE NOVELS

I felt that magical practice taught me to read again the way I had read books at the age of ten, with an uncritical absorption in the characters. The educated reader asks whether Joyce has successfully portrayed human mundanity. The child simply enjoys Narnia. Magical books encourage an embracing, dream-like absorption, a dissociated daydream of dragons, powers and higher realms. This sense of imaginative absorption, quite apart from any themes which it encompasses, is one of the most striking elements of the magical fiction. Magical practice attempts to elicit this uncritical imaginative absorption in ritual, a suspension of judgmental, reality-testing criticism, and the novels use a dream-like prose intended to encourage this state. I would like to convey this extraordinary dreaminess, but it is not a quality that is easily described. Therefore, I have interspersed anthropological prose with literary passages. Out of context they may seem quite odd. However, they should evoke the mysterious, romantic simplicity on which the literature depends, and they may convey the startlingly clear moral dicta which form the background of the tales.

I have chosen the works of five authors for my purpose: J. R. R. Tolkien's *Lord of the Rings*, Ursula LeGuin's *Earthsea Trilogy*, Marion Zimmer Bradley's *Mists of Avalon*, Dion Fortune's *Sea Priestess* and *Moon Magic*, and Dennis Wheatley's *The Devil Rides Out*. These are probably the novels most magicians would choose as the most important fictional works about magic. Most magicians have read them: many use their characters, plots and language in their rites and meditations. Most of them say that they loved these books, or that these novels were what excited them about the idea of practising magic. Only the first two, and possibly the last, are well known by the general population. Bradley's retelling of the Arthurian romance was only a transient bestseller, steeped with practical experience of modern witchcraft, and Fortune wrote for magicians, who take the books as fictionalized ideals. When I made my first forays into magic, I was directed towards her novels as the best way to understand the practice. Wheatley paints seething evil outdone by noble good; he is Gothic in the extreme, but many magicians make their first acquaintance with magic through his books.

At the heart of these novels lies the notion of an ancient power, older than man, amoral, pagan, primordial. Tolkien writes of a Middle-earth with a history that stretches back to time beyond memory, when the earth was untainted. 'It was not called the Old Forest without reason, for it was indeed ancient, a survivor of vast forgotten worlds, and in it there lived, ageing no quicker than the hills, the fathers of the fathers of trees, remembering times when they were lords.'[1] Some powers are beyond evil and before evil. 'Nothing is evil in the beginning. Even Sauron was not so.'[2] Other early powers sully the earth with evil.

There agelong she had dwelt, an evil thing in spider form, even such as old had lived in the land of the Elves and in the West that is now under the Sea, such as Beren fought in the mountains of Terror in Doriath, and so came to Luthien upon the green sword amid the hemlocks in the moonlight long ago. How Shelob came there, flying from ruin, no tale tells, for out of the Dark Years few tales have come. But still she was there, who was there before Sauron, and before the first stone of Baradun; and she served none but herself . . .[3]

These are powers that obey no laws. They are unto themselves. Against them the protagonist-magician is shown to be a mere human, with certain powers but ultimately a trinket in the lap of time. 'I am a Mage, what you call a sorcerer. I have certain arts and powers, that's true. It's also true that here in the place of the Old Powers, my strength is very little and my crafts don't avail me.'[4] That is Sparrowhawk, wizard of LeGuin's *Earthsea*. The contrast between the oldest of powers and human power appears in all these novels, and they allow the novels to describe all human power as limited, like the humans who wield it. Magic may involve harnessing ancient powers, but in the end, they are far more mighty than those who try to master them.

[And in the storm] I saw the sea-gods come, moving with an irresistible momentum, not rising into the airs as the riders rose, but deep in their own element, unhasty, unresting; for the power of the sea is in the weight of the waters and not in the wind-blown crests. These Great Ones rose with the tide, and like the tide, nothing might withstand them. Their faces were vast and calm; they were the rulers of the great waters and in their realm their word was law. By their grace and not otherwise life moved on the surface or lived at the tide-mark, and only those might live who knew this.

And I saw with clear eyes the folly of men who thought that they might master the sea. For only by the grace of the sea-gods does man live upon the face of the land, for if they gathered themselves together in wrath they could drown the earth. And I saw that man's life is spun out like a thread between irresistible forces that with a breath could destroy him, but that nevertheless, from them he draws strength.

---

[1] Tolkien (1965: 1: 181).   [2] Tolkien (1965: 2: 351).   [3] Tolkien (1965: 3: 422).
                                     [4] Le Guin (1979: 249).

For there is in the earth a reservoir of elemental force, just as there is a fountain of life beyond the stars, and from the violence of the sea the violence of man's own nature draws its energy even as he draws breath from the air, for all things are but one thing in the last analysis and there is no part of us that is not of the gods. (Fortune *The Sea Priestess*) [5]

In these novels, intellectual knowledge is the route to control what power can be summoned. The wizard knows, controls and summons, and he usually does so by a name. On the island of Roke boys are trained to be wizards, and they spend hours with the Master Namer, who commands them to learn lists of names by day, before the ink of his writing vanishes at midnight. 'It was cold and half dark and always silent there, except for the scratching of the Master's pen and the sighs, maybe, of a student who must learn before midnight the name of every cape, point, bay, sound, inlet, channel, harbour, shallows, reef and rock of the shores of Losnow, a little islet of the Pelnish sea.' [6] Naming is often associated with magic: there is the sense that a name gives power over its object. 'Ged sighed sometimes, but he did not complain. He saw that in this dusty and fathomless matter of naming the true name of every place, thing and being, the power he wanted lay like a jewel at the bottom of a deep well. For magic consists in this, the true naming of a thing.' [7]

Wheatley also sees knowledge as power, but his books are full of weighty tomes and arcane invocations. *The Devil Rides Out* is the clash of Good and Evil within the decadence of international wealth, James Bond on the astral plane. The aristocratic De Richelieu is the good, forced to draw upon forgotten, youthful studies to save a friend from Satanic clutches. 'With trembling lips he began to mutter strange sentences of Persian, Greek and Hebrew, dimly remembered from his studies of the past – calling – calling – urgently upon the Power of Light for goodness and protection.' [8] Saved from that danger but wary of his ignorance, the Duke spends some hours in the British Museum, deep in the study of 'some old key works'. As a result he is able to draw a protective barrier around his companions to shield them from harm. 'He then chalked in, with careful spacing around the rim of the inner circle, the powerful exorcism . . . and, after reference to an old book which he had brought with him, drew certain curious and ancient symbols in the valleys and mounts of the microcosm of stars . . .'. [9] Wheatley's book is full of these accounts of strange, forgotten symbols. Secret words are the key to wealth and the domination of human minds. The moral, of course, is that true humanity involves the understanding to resist the temptations of power.

The Master Hand looked at the jewel that glittered on Ged's hand, bright as the prize of a dragon's hoard. The old Master murmured one word, 'Tolk', and there lay the pebble, no jewel but a rough grey bit of rock. The Master took it and held it out on his own hand. 'This is a rock; *tolk* in the True Speech', he said, looking mildly up at Ged now. 'A bit of the stone of which Roke Island is made, a little bit of the dry land on which men live. It is

---

[5] Fortune (1957: 165–6). [6] Le Guin (1979: 50). [7] Le Guin (1979: 50).
[8] Wheatley (1934: 39). [9] Wheatley (1934: 61).

itself. It is part of the world. By the Illusion-Change you can make it look like a diamond – or a flower or a fly or an eye or a flame – .' The rock flickered from shape to shape as he named them, and returned to rock. 'But that is mere seeming. Illusion fools the beholder's sense; it makes him see and hear and feel that the thing is changed. But it does not change the thing. To change this rock into a jewel, you must change its true name. And to do that, my son, even to so small a scrap of the world, is to change the world. It can be done. Indeed it can be done. It is the art of the Master Changer, and you will learn it, when you are ready to learn it. But you must not change one thing, one grain of sand, until you know what good and evil will follow on the act. The world is in balance, in Equilibrium. A wizard's power of Changing and Summoning can shake the balance of the world. It is dangerous, that power. It must follow knowledge, and serve need. To light a candle is to cast a shadow ...' (LeGuin *The Earthsea Trilogy*)[10]

The novels also talk about another form of knowledge, intuition. Sometimes this is psychic – gained through some other means than the five senses – and sometimes merely a deep attunement to the world around one. In magic, the unconscious is not treated as a random, frightening source of subjectivity. Magicians redefine the apparent randomness of instincts and emotions as a knowledge, a matter of sensing, intuiting, feeling the interconnections of the world. Priestesses gaze into fires and crystal to read the symbols revealed to them there. Bradley's priestesses of Avalon communicate without words, see the future in pools of still water, are visited with sudden visions clothed in symbolic garb. Fortune's heroine is touched in her sleep, awoken by unsought understanding, and driven by insights only partly articulated. It is the mark of a good priestess to trust her responses and dreams and to understand when they serve as knowledge and when they are only the personal fantasies of a tired soul. The priestess has intellectual knowledge in her head but an intuitive understanding of the earth in her veins. The apparently chaotic irrational does not control us; it itself becomes the means of control, by providing an understanding of the natural world.

There was no sleep for me that night. Alone, I walked in the garden till dawn, and I knew already, shaking with terror, what must be done. I did not know how, or whether, alone, I could do what I had begun, but as I had been made priestess so many years ago and renounced it, so must I retrace my steps alone. This night I had been given a great grace; but I knew there would be no more signs for me and no help given until I had made myself, alone, unaided, again the priestess I had been trained to be.

I bore still on my brow, faded beneath that housewifely coif Uriens would have me wear, the sign of her grace, but that would not help me now. Gazing at the fading stars, I did not know whether or no the rising sun would surprise me at its vigil; the sun tides had not run in my blood for half a lifetime, and I no longer knew the precise place on the eastern horizon where I could turn to salute the sun at its rising. I knew not, anymore, even how the moon-tides ran with the cycles of my body ... so far had I come from the training of Avalon. Alone, with no more than a fading memory, I must somehow recapture all the things I had once known as part of myself ... I learned again to count sun tides from equinox to solstice and back to equinox again ... count them painfully on

[10] Le Guin (1979: 48).

my fingers like a child or a novice priestess; it was years before I could feel them running in my blood again, or know to a hairline's difference where on the horizon moon or sun would rise or set for the salutations I learned again to make. Again, late at night while the household lay sleeping round me, I would study the stars, letting their influence move in my blood as they wheeled and swung around me until I became only a pivot point on the motionless earth, center of the whirling dance around and above me, the spiral movement of the seasons. I rose early and slept late so that I might find hours to range into the hills, on a pretext of seeking root and herb for medicines, and there I sought out the old lines of force, tracing them from standing stone to hammer pool . . . (Bradley *The Mists of Avalon*)[11]

True knowledge, deep understanding, is, however, understood to be self-knowledge. All of these novels involve some testing of the protagonist, facing the soul's essence at the edge of the world, beyond pain. In LeGuin's novels, for example, the wizard Sparrowhawk loosed an evil spirit on the world when he tried to summon a woman from the dead to show off to his peers. The being chased him through the world until he himself turned and hunted, and beyond the reaches of the world he faced it and called it by his own name, and conquered it. Here wisdom is the knowledge to know oneself, and to know one's limits and those of mankind.

Who am I – though I have the power to do it – to punish and reward, playing with men's destinies? . . . If there were a king over us all again, and he sought counsel of a mage as in days of old, and I were that mage, I would say to him: My lord, do nothing, because it is righteous, or praiseworthy, or noble to do so; do nothing because it seems good to do so; do only that which you must do, and what you cannot do in any other way.[12]

And this, after all, is Tolkien: a ring which grants all power which must therefore be destroyed. Frodo is the anti-hero: someone chosen by fate to act because he must, in a land of magic and enchantments. It is Aragorn, not Gandalf, who keeps his power at the end of the trilogy, and his strength is a human strength, of human limitations. His humanity, of course, is romantically appealing. 'Tall as the sea-kings of old, he stood over all that were near; ancient of days he seemed and yet in his flower of manhood; and wisdom sat upon his brow, and strength and healing were in his hands, and there was a light about him.'[13]

In these books, childhood gems, magic is grand deeds and valour and wisdom, but it is also power in the hands of those who know when not to use it, strength in the hands of those who know how to be weak. Tolkien, LeGuin, and Wheatley write tales of battle against an evil. In them the morals are clearly painted, and the magic's purpose gives the story point. Fortune and Bradley speak more of the way of the magic – the sensitivity to the intuitions, the knowledge of the shadows and hidden things, the sense of service to a greater being whose nature is not clear. For them all, the poignancy in magic lies in the human contact with greater powers or other beings, and the possibility of the greater than human within the limited human frame. The novels are romantic,

---

[11] Bradley (1982: 679–80).   [12] Le Guin (1979: 362).   [13] Tolkien (1965: 3: 304).

in that they depict grand themes of destiny and self-determination within a relatively simple moral universe. In some cases this simplicity becomes more complex. Bradley's novel, for example, hinges on the conflicting loyalties of friendship and divine command which are never resolved. But for the most part the human is projected as an actor on a divine stage, and reaccepts his human limitations after justly vanquishing the enemy.

CHAOS AND CONTROL IN THE PRACTICAL LITERATURE

The theme that dominates the practical manuals of magical literature is the primordial goddess, the abyss or the chaos into which the magician must relinquish himself. Chaos is repeatedly stressed as the prerequisite of power: control of your life and your world arise through the courage to release what command you possess.

> I was of the cult of the Black Isis, which is very different from that of the green-robed Goddess of Nature to whom the women prayed for children. They represent her with a human face, or horned like a cow; but the Black Isis is the Veiled Isis, upon whose face none may look and live, and because I represent Her, I too went veiled and cloaked . . . Some equate the Black Isis with Kali, and say that She is evil; but I do not think She is, unless one counts elemental force as evil, which I do not. She is indeed the Breaker in Pieces, but then She sets free. She is also most ancient Life, and people fear the primordial as they fear nothing else . . . I broke Wilfred, and he rose like a phoenix, reborn from the ashes of his dead life, and knew Great Isis. I slew him and I gave him birth. That is not evil, unless you reckon pain as evil, and I do not; for pain brings power, and destruction is freedom.[14]

The most challenging concept in magic is this darkness: the deep, the destructive, the angry, primordial, irrational. There is no clear parcelling out of the issues here, and all participants intellectualize them differently. The dark has no representative, definitive description in the literature. But this is the stuff that you fear, whatever you fear, the depth you are afraid to dive into: the fetid feminine, the chthonic unconscious, the sea. 'The dark: all that we are afraid of, all that we don't want to see – fear, anger, sex, grief, death, the unknown'.[15] Again, it is a romantic conception of an evil, an unconscious or a chaos which is radically opposed to that which is good, and the point made by the literature is that one must experience and accept that otherness because it is, in the end, of a piece with the good. Magic, magicians say, is about plunging into the terror of the abyss, and through this acquiring strength.

The three ways (at least) to understand this chaotic darkness reflect three different sorts of magical practice, but they are intermingled and entwined. Most practitioners see darkness as an aspect of the 'Goddess', who (or which) is a spiritual embodiment, or interpretation, of natural process. But they also conceptualize darkness in two other ways, as the 'abyss' in kabbalah, or as the

---

[14] Fortune (1956: 42).   [15] Starhawk (1982: xiv).

'chaos' in something called 'Chaos magick'. Each of these conceptualizations takes the major task of the magician to be willing submission to the destruction as a means of gaining strength through the transformation it brings.

Many magicians – all those who call themselves witches, or pagans, but also many others – see themselves as involved with an earth goddess, venerated under many names in all early societies. As described earlier, she is nature, and nature's change. The world is the Goddess, and we are in the world, and for all things in this world there is a time and season. The Goddess is cyclicity and transformation, rise and fall, waxing and waning. She embodies the knowledge that out of every destruction there comes creation, and from all creation follows death.

The nature of the Goddess is never single. Whenever She appears, she embodies both poles of the duality – life in death, death in life. She has a thousand names, a thousand aspects. She is the milk cow, the weaving spider, the honeybee with its piercing sting. She is the bird of the spirit and the sow that eats its own young. The snake that sheds its skin and is renewed; the cat that sees in the dark; the dog that sings to the moon – all are Her. She is the light and the darkness, the patronness of love and death, who makes manifest *all* possibilities. She brings both comfort and pain . . .[16]

For magicians, this transformation is usually modelled through the changes of the moon, in its three aspects: Artemis, virgin huntress, unpossessed and independent, free and fierce, the youth of all beginnings; Selene, lover and mother, passionate and nurturing, sexually uninhibited, life-giver, who brings into fruition through maturity; Hecate, crone, the destroyer, the devourer, who eats what must be eaten and who grimly claims what is her own. The above quotation was taken from the teach-yourself manual which introduced me to this study. The author sets these meditative exercises for the neophyte witch:

Visualize a silver crescent moon, curving to the right. She is the power of beginning, of growth and generation. She is wild and untamed, like ideas and plans before they are tempered by reality. She is the blank page, the unplowed-field. Feel your own hidden possibilities and latent potentials; your power to begin and grow. See her as a silver-haired girl running freely through the forest under the slim moon. She is Virgin, eternally unpenetrated, belonging to no one but herself. Call her name 'Nimuë!' and feel her power within you . . .

Visualize a round full moon. She is the Mother, the power of fruition. She nourishes what the New Moon has begun. See her open arms, her full breasts, her womb burgeoning with life. Feel your own power to nurture, to give, to make manifest what is possible. She is the sexual woman; her pleasure in union is the moving force that sustains all life. Feel the power in your own pleasure, in orgasm. Her color is the red of blood, which is life. Call her name 'Mari!' and feel your own ability to love . . .

Visualize a waning crescent, curving to the left, surrounded by a dark sky. She is the Old Woman, the Crone who has passed menopause, the power of ending, of death. All things must end to fulfil their beginnings. The grain that was planted must be cut down. The blank page must be destroyed, for the work to be written. Life feeds on death – death

---

[16] Starhawk (1979: 80).

leads on to life, and in that knowledge lies wisdom. The Crone is the Wise Woman, infinitely old. Feel your own age, the wisdom of evolution stored in every cell of your body. Know your own power to end, to lose as well as gain, to destroy what is stagnant and decayed. See the Crone cloaked in black under the waning moon; call her name 'Anu!' and feel her power in your own death.[17]

The Goddess is dissolution. The very nature of the concept entails the interconnectedness of all things. We are not separate from the world, magicians say. We are of the world, not autonomous individuals but connected wholes, connected with webs, meanings, vulnerabilities that shared yield greater strength. 'There is nothing to be saved *from*, no struggle of life *against* the universe, no God outside the world to be feared and obeyed; only the Goddess, the Mother, the turning spiral . . . each of us her own star, her Child, her lover, her beloved, her Self.'[18] Only connect, but the style is rather different from Forster's. In magic's understanding, the credo is that while we are all uniquely different, the important lessons come through letting go of that frightened separation from the world and other people. A lone marcher is a fool but ten thousand marchers can begin to stop a war. Joy and freedom only come through becoming one with others. Goddess worship is said to melt defensive, rigid selves into the amorphous ambiguity of the universe.

The dissolution is more frightening, though, than gentle happy liberalism. The Goddess as Crone eats and destroys. Some writers claim that this destruction is an essential part of femininity which most women have repressed. Femininity is not sugared sweetness, they say, but the madness of the raging tiger, the mother bear's fury, Kali child-eater and Clytemnestra man-slayer, M$_{the}$a, the Furies and the witches on their blasted heath. When I was in London a book on the Goddess was passed from hand to hand among some of the women. Called *Descent to the Goddess*, it focused on the most ancient of the Persephone tales, the Sumerian myth of Erishkigal and Innana, written on clay tablets in the third millennium BC.

In the Sumerian poem Inanna decides to go into the underworld; she 'set her heart from highest heaven on earth's deepest ground', 'abandoned heaven, abandoned earth – to the Netherworld she descended.' As a precaution, she instructs Ninshubur, her trusted female executive, to appeal to the father gods for help in securing her release if she does not return within three days.

At the first gate to the Netherworld, Inanna is stopped and asked to declare herself. The gatekeeper informs Erishkigal, queen of the Great Below, that Inanna, 'Queen of Heaven, of the place where the sun rises', asks for admission to the 'land of no return' to witness the funeral of Gugalanna, husband of Erishkigal. Erishkigal becomes furious, and insists that the upper-world goddess be treated according to the laws and rites for anyone entering her kingdom – that she be brought 'naked and bowed low.'

The gatekeeper follows orders. He removes one piece of Inanna's magnificent regalia at each of the seven gates. 'Crouched and stripped bare', as the Sumerians were laid in the grave, Inanna is judged by the seven judges. Erishkigal kills her. Her corpse is hung on a peg, where it turns into a side of green, rotting meat. After three days, when Inanna

---

[17] Starhawk (1979: 78–9).   [18] Starhawk (1979: 14–15).

fails to return, her assistant Ninshubur sets in motion her instructions to rouse the people and gods with dirge drum and lamenting.

Ninshubur goes to Enlil, the highest god of sky and earth, and to Nanna, the moon god and Inanna's father. Both refuse to meddle in the exacting ways of the underworld. Finally Enki, the god of waters and wisdom, hear Ninshubur's pleas and rescues Inanna, using two little mourners he creates from the dirt under his fingernail. They slip unnoticed into the Netherworld, carrying the food and water of life with which Enki provides them, and they secure Inanna's release by commiserating with Erishkigal, who is now groaning – over the dead, or with her own birth pangs. She is so grateful for the empathy that she finally hands over Inanna's corpse. Restored to life, Inanna is reminded that she will need to send a substitute to take her place. Demons to seize this scapegoat surround her as she returns through the seven gates and reclaims her vestments.

The last part of the myth involves the search for her substitute. Inanna does not hand over anyone who mourned for her. But finally she comes upon her primary consort, Dumuzi (later called Tammuz), who sits enjoying himself on his throne. Inanna looks on him with the same eyes of death Erishkigal had set upon her, and the demons seize him. Dumuzi flees with the help of Utu, who is the sun god and Inanna's brother. Utu transforms him into a snake to permit escape. In a related poem, Dumuzi dreams of his downfall. He goes to his sister, Geshtinna, who helps him to interpret his dream and urges him to flee. When flight proves useless, she shelters him and finally offers to sacrifice herself in his stead. Inanna decrees that they shall divide the fate and spend half a year each in the underworld. The final poem ends with the words:

> Inanna placed Dumuzi in the hands of the eternal.
> Holy Erishkigal! Sweet is your praise![19]

Persephone, Inanna: their names run like ore throughout magical practice. Magical rituals and writings make much of this theme of voluntary descent, destruction and rebirth, transformation and return. The destructive underworld must not be feared and shunned, but entered. Some magicians feel that because this is a neglected part of a woman's spirituality, Goddess worship is the only religion in which women are truly themselves. Women, they explain, face the whirlpools of pain and emotion created by their fluctuating hormones. They tend to be, for better or worse, particularly aware of emotional bonds with surrounding others, and they tend to be more aware of the havoc one's unconscious can wreak when ignored. They understand the need to face emotion. But the concept of facing one's fears directly is also a generally lauded cultural theme. Only when the hunted becomes the hunter can he claim victory: the hunted seeks tired refuge in escape, as did LeGuin's Sparrowhawk. Only those who face death willingly can master it.

The kabbalistic conception presents darkness as the Abyss. The Western Mysteries use the kabbalah as their symbolic, mystical system to describe the descent of spiritual life into matter and its incarnation therein. The human being is a creature of earth, Malkuth, and he must attempt to ascend through meditation along the interconnected paths of the 'tree of life' until his entry into Kether, Godhead. The Western Mystery schools teach that this mystical

---

[19] Perera (1981: 9–10).

account of descent, struggle and rebirth is found in all mystery religions. The Eleusinian mysteries, Orphic mysteries, Celtic mysteries, Mithraic mysteries – all are said to involve the destruction and recreation of the soul. 'Above all it is in the Orphic mysteries that we first come to terms with this perilous descent into darkness and re-emergence against primal light. The suffering of Orpheus, who loses Eurydice (through fear, first pitfall of all mystery knowledge) and is then dismembered by the Maenads, is a paradigm of the suffering and rebirth of the sleeping soul. As a descendant of Dionysius, Orpheus is the intellectual image of a demigod raised to deity by his sufferings in the underworld: a perfect symbol for all who follow the path of the Mysteries.'[20] You must go down to go up. The initiate of the kabbalah must meditate on the different symbols, and then ultimately face the dismemberment and transformation of the Abyss which is the nature of the deep initiation.

What then are the experiences of this second Dark Night of the Soul? In a phrase, they could be described as a 'sense of utter desolation'. All the expansion of awareness and feeling of at-one-ment that is possible to the soul with Tiphareth consciousness is suddenly annihilated and the soul seems empty, alone, without God and without the love of fellow men. This is an automatic experience once a certain stage of the path is reached . . . Such a high level of purification, of course, leads the soul straight to God, or Kether. It is, in fact, a final purification.[21]

Again, it is a descent into one's own self, a kind of dissolution and death, and out of it, rebirth.

Chaos magic offers the third version of this chaotic dissolution. Chaos magic is a less innocent magic, the Crowley-oriented magic of heavy metal music and adolescent boys. The basic idea behind it is that we are locked rigidly within conventions: to escape them we must break them, and destruction yields power. 'We have endured (but so far SURVIVED!) years of conditioning and repression and to break free from this protective but limiting shell is an act of courage and perhaps for some of us, an act of desperation.'[22] 'The chaotic aspect of new aeon magic is psychological anarchy . . . The aim is to produce inspiration and enlightenment through disordering our belief structures.'[23] The universe *is* chaos, *is* confusion: we who are able to face the whirling abyss directly can transcend it and unite with it to effectuate our will. This can be a noble, romantic vision, an aesthetic vision of romantic decadence.

But the fantasy often has a bizarre, bleak form. The indubitable logic of the philosophy presses the role of violence, murder, sexual degradation: the most stringent regulations should yield greatest power when violated.

Energy is liberated when an individual breaks through rules of conditioning with some glorious act of disobedience or blasphemy. This energy strengthens the spirit and gives courage for further acts of insurrection.

Put a brick through your television, explore sexualities which are unusual to you. Do something you normally feel to be utterly revolting. You are free to do anything no

---

[20] Matthews and Matthews (1986: 24).   [21] Knight (1965: 147; 149).
[22] Wilde (n.d.a: i).   [23] Carrol (n.d.b: 4).

matter how extreme so long as it will not restrict your own or somebody else's future freedom of action.[24]

For most magicians such practices are mere fantasy. They read the literature, form their groups, and if they are of this ilk engage in philosophical discussions of such practice. Humankind cannot bear very much reality, as the poet said. The romantic brutality of the chaos magician takes place largely in his head. I met at least one group engaged in this sort of practice in London. They reminded me of boys boasting of wild sexual exploits: far too well behaved and nervous to kiss a girl they claimed they should have raped. It is a difficult, sophisticated philosophy, however, and in the literally minded or the unstable it can yield unhappy results.[25]

The key notion in all three of these chaoses – the primordial Goddess, the Abyss, the Chaos – is that to enter the chaos is to empower oneself. The notion that one grows through facing what one fears is common enough. The more subtle notion, that the deepest fears are in the psyche and it is these which one must control through confrontation, is the keystone of the therapeutic arch. In the psychoanalytic 'talking cure', for example, the aim is that the patient confront emotions and experiences so powerful and frightening that at first he cannot bear to recognize them directly. When he does, through the sessions, they are mastered and, in theory, he is cured. Jungian analysis demands that one probe one's deepest fears. When, in your dreams, you have crawled down into the very basement of the dream-house that is your ego, and have found the cave beneath it, and descended the ladder and picked up the skull at its foot, then you have mastered your shadow, and, again in theory, the cure is complete.[26] Scientology shares a similar vision: the subject is a 'thetan', a spiritual being for which all things are possible, attached to a body whose major drawback is its irrational mass of confusions called the 'Bank'. The bank is full of knotty life experiences which prevent the thetan from acting out his perfect rationality. When these knots, 'engrams', are articulated in 'confronts' – where another person asks questions to draw them out – they disappear, and the person with his Bank drained dry becomes a 'Clear'.[27]

What is special in magic is the conception of the chaos and the manner of its mastery. Many of the most important rituals deal directly with death and the underworld. For example, witches are initiated into a 'second degree' when

[24] Carroll, (n.d.a: 38).

[25] In 1987 I was called to advise on a murder in which the murderer seemed to have been influenced by chaos magic. He did not perform a premeditated ritual, but it is probably true that if he had not been reading these books, the murder would not have occurred. The books did not cause the murder: they simply gave a somewhat unstable psyche a sense of power in which murder beame a reasonable type of action.

By 7.5.87 the Sorcerer's Apprentice had sold nearly 3000 of Wilde's *Grimoire of Chaos Magick*, the book often cited as the basic manual. Bray estimated that six to ten thousand chaos magicians were found throughout the country. Of all Sorcerer's Apprentice material, 35–40 per cent sold concerned witchcraft, 35–40 per cent kabbalah and hermetic magic, and 25–30 per cent chaos magic.

[26] See Jung (1965).

[27] See Whitehead (1987).

their high priestess feels that they are knowledgeable and experienced: the initiation is meant to carry with it the authority to found one's own coven. This authority is symbolized in a ritual called the 'descent of the Goddess', a Persephone tale about the Goddess' descent into the underworld, death's courtship and their marriage, and her eventual return. (Initiates take the role suitable to their gender.) 'To be reborn you must die and be ready for a new body; and to die you must be born; and without love you may not be born; and this is all the Magics.'[28] The books written by magicians, or read by them, use the imagery of the dark, or of the dark Goddess, and speak of the dark's incorporation as essential to establishing integrated personal wholeness. The author of the witchcraft meditations about the moon has written a book called *Dreaming the Dark* about power: to ignore the dark, she says, is to have 'power-over', and oppress out of fear, but to go through the dark is to have 'power-from-within', and to be truly strong. 'She [Joy, a fellow witch in a trance] lets go. She dissolves. She leaps into the dark – into her very fear of dissolving – and recovers, instead, an ease, a comfort, a sense of being at home in the body, a sense of rightness in her being.'[29] Rituals in the Western Mysteries proclaim that magic is the process of 'regeneration'. It achieves this, according to the philosophy, only by taking you into the abyss to allow self transformation to occur. And Chaos magic says that power comes through shattering, because it gives one the power and freedom to act.

Some of these themes emerge in a character that in ways summarizes magic's complex attitudes to power, dissolution and control: Pan, Greek god of nature and instinct. Pan is a central figure in magic, particularly so in witchcraft but also for other practitioners: Fortune, most famous of Western Mysteries initiates, thought Pan the key to human nature. In modern magic, Pan becomes a potent symbol in ritual and worship, and he is an ambiguous, ambivalent character. He is ribald, earthy bawdiness, the god of untamed bodily instinct. He is also a god of power, of the power of the dance, of Bacchic frenzy, of the unthinking panic that sweeps the crowd into action. Pan is to do with the guts, not with the heart or head. Pan is the god of death, for death is a bodily matter, and Pan is the horned god, whom witches say was recast as the devil when Christianity established its hegemony in a pagan Europe. Pan is power because he escapes control, because no social rules constrain him, and he is the laughing, mocking god of wine and dance. His instinctual energy is the magician's harnessed power. In one of Fortune's novels, the protagonist is described as a vital human and a potentially powerful magician because she has a Pan-like aspect to her.

It was as if there were two sides to her [the protagonist] – the extreme fastidiousness that gave her the appreciation of the finer nuances of the most sophisticated culture and that made her make of life an art; and another side, a side that made her kin to the Maenads who followed Dionysius and tore fawns to pieces in their mystical frenzy; and, even baser, the women who crept out of the medieval walled towns at night to go to the

---

[28] Farrar and Farrar (1984: 30).   [29] Starhawk (1982: 69).

witches' sabbath and 'kiss the buttocks of the goat'. This side of life horrified her; and yet, denied it, life seemed savourless.[30]

In Pan, magicians identify the dissolution of the Goddess with instinctual release, and claim that potentially frightening mixture of sex-frenzy-and-death as human, something to accept and incorporate. Pan is the god of the coven altar, with the ambivalent overtones of devil-worship, death, and sweet lovers in the springtime. In ways magic's complex thematic set is like Mikhail Bakhtin's medieval carnival – a condoned flaunting of the social order, filled with laughter and bodily imagery, which asserts power in the real world through the creation of a fantastic one. Even more, this is a romantic fantasy of the heights of ecstasy and the depths of despair, a religious yearning to submerge oneself in nature and to accept and by accepting, transform, the demonic force within one.

Controlling the chaotic unconscious by plunging into the dissolution, a romantic fantasy of the primordial blended with an ambivalent sense of its power – these are themes that emerge in the books a magician reads and in the practices he follows. The relationship of mythological theme and follower is always ambiguous. Whether specifically drawn to these themes through their own psychological needs or not, these concepts begin to shape the magician's imagination. Through her practice she begins to think of what it means to confront death, or what a woman's spirituality might be. But there do seem to be some common psychodynamic tendencies among the magicians I met.

PORTRAIT OF THE PRACTITIONERS

Most sociological accounts would suggest that people join marginal groups out of socio-economic frustration.[31] This claim is patently false in magic. These participants come from the middle class; if any profession predominates, it is the computer industry. The people drawn to magic often become practitioners through browsing in occult bookstores and then following up the groups, study sessions and open meetings advertised on index cards pinned to their shelves. They also tend to be sane, if by that one means a person capable of successfully holding a job and participating in a 'normal' social life. I met few people that I thought less sane, in this ordinary language sense, than those I met in my social or professional life.[32] Magical practice does attract the mentally unstable, but

---

[30] Fortune (1960: 211).

[31] Standard sociological texts explain recruitment to cults, sects and marginal groups as the consequence of relative deprivation of some sort. Beckford (1975) has an excellent discussion of these theories; they include Troelstch (1912), Niebuhr (1929), Glock (1964), Runciman (1966), Demerath and Hammond (1969). Simple economic deprivation, however, will not explain the practice of these middle class magicians, nor will simple personality disorder theories (as in Lofland and Stark 1965). More recent discussions of marginal religions, by Beckford (1975) and Barker (1984), stress a combination of risk-free problem-solving, developing friendships within the group, and creative satisfaction as the factors which propel people towards committed membership of such groups, an account which seems more apposite to modern magic.

[32] Jorgensen and Jorgensen (1982) corroborate both the socio-economic stability and the relative sanity of these groups.

the process of selection – the extensive social interaction, the lengthy correspondence course – means that relatively few of them are accepted. By the crude standards of admission to inpatient hospital care for mental illness, there may be a higher than average tendency towards mental instability. Out of the fifty people I knew well, at least four had periods of marked instability in the course of three years, and three of them ended up in hospitalization. In England, in 1984, 409 from every 100,000 head of population were admitted into mental hospitals, a rate of roughly one in two hundred and fifty per year as contrasted to the one in fifty per year I noticed among magicians.[33] However, this magical sample is extremely small. Not only is it small, but three of those four people were members of the same self-selected, socially homogeneous witchcraft group and had been initiated many years ago, under very different social circumstances from those that influence recent practitioners.[34]

My impression – based on close involvement with fifty people and passing acquaintance with perhaps two hundred more – is that magicians often do have certain personality traits. The sort of person who takes the relatively dramatic step of initiating contact with magicians and then enjoys the practice well enough to continue with it, may well be imaginative, self-absorbed, reasonably intellectual, spiritually inclined, and emotionally intense. He also may be rebellious and interested in power, possibly dreamy or socially ill at ease. He may be concerned on some level with issues of control – controlling himself, or the world, or the two in tandem. This is a descriptive, not a causal, account. The basic point is that magicians are middle-class people of a particular, and not uncommon, temperamental cast – not people with similar socio-economic profiles.[35]

[33] Department of Health and Social Security Statistics for England 1984. Booklet 1: Table A1.1.

[34] It is not clear to me how magical involvement affects those who do have breakdowns. In February 1984, I saw, from the edges of a domestic crisis, a magician develop a full blown manic psychosis. In the first few weeks of his illness he covered reams of paper with magical insights and messages from higher realms, and thought himself, for a while, a channel for great powers. And for him, the high was probably heightened by his everyday longing to be a great magician. After a while the ravings and his insistent refusal to let the rest of the household sleep forced his partner to hospitalize him. In several weeks he returned home, and regained chlorpromazine-free normality some months later. Perhaps the magic independently added to the psychotic seclusion of his world and made the breakdown more dramatic; perhaps a breakdown made likely by his emotional past had been mitigated by the fantasy control one learns in magic, and had been aided by the self-therapy skills which the magician can develop.

[35] G. G. Scott studied a group of Californian witches. She describes them as follows: 'anti-establishment tribalism [witchcraft] appeals to those who typically rebel against the impersonal bureaucratic character of modern life, who blame the system for their problems, and who want a warm, supportive environment, often because they lack close family ties. Typically, they reject structure and mainstream values and seek, instead, a nurturing group that espouses alternate values and offers extensive personal freedom. They seek magical practice as a way to manipulate the system' (Scott 1980: 126). She also asserts that witchcraft appeals to the young and the 'hip', with its countercultural focus, that witches often came from Catholic backgrounds, that many practitioners had already sought alternative systems of politics or communal living, and that the groups often appealed to those who lacked a sense of power. This characterization is probably valid for Scott's group; it seems too countercultural – too Californian – to fit the London magicians.

One American study suggests that the women drawn to feminist groups were raised with a home life which valued traditional women's roles but who now have non-traditional, achievement-oriented careers. The author suggests that the witchcraft provides a means to alleviate the tension

There is no 'average' magician. Some magicians, however, seemed to make remarks about their personal lives that I often heard from others. Peter often did so. To make the account concrete, I shall describe him.

Peter

When I knew Peter, he was an initiate of a magical fraternity in northern London, the Hornsey group, and attended meetings there every three weeks. He had been a witch, for a while. Three years after I first met him, he moved from London in order to afford a house on his own. He found no magical groups in this town, though he still seemed interested in joining one. In the meantime he was exploring psychosynthesis, a therapeutic technique, inspired by Jungian analytic psychology, which utilizes theatrical dramatic enactment of specific traumas and general human emotions and experiences. The technique has a considerable appeal for many magicians, and I met a number who were engaged in its study with an eye to becoming a therapist or teacher.

Peter strikes me as an unusual blend of a shy, withdrawn dreamer and a flamboyant rebel. He never had a girlfriend when I knew him, and he was quiet, almost formal, in a meeting. When I first spoke with him we exchanged only pleasantries, and I took him for a timid executive. As I came to talk with him at greater length – he came to Beth's workshop, and then joined the Hornsey group – I learned with surprise that he was an excellent dancer, that he led dance workshops, and saw later, at parties, that he became the cynosure on the dance floor. He told me that he had an 'exhibitionist streak' and that he liked to 'go wild' at costume parties. He liked to think of himself as daring and unconventional, as challenging some idealized constrictive mores, and he liked to be singled out as different. I was startled by his attitude towards me. Whereas many magicians made efforts to show me how normal their magic was, he seemed curious about the salacious, unsalubrious features I had encountered – as if he wanted to be told that his practice was deviant and dangerous, even though his own involvement was markedly tame. Peter also seemed to have a capacity for intense imaginative absorption. Certainly his creative urge was strong. He told me that he liked to write, and that magic had helped him free the expressiveness his job had dampened. Already, he told me after coming to the workshop, he had begun to scribble short stories on the train. But his creativity had a solipsistic quality. When he came back from a holiday to Crete, rather than describing the sights he told me about a long solitary walk in which

---

between their childhood values and their current occupations (Van Blerkom 1985). Again, I am not sure that this could be said of the contemporary English feminist coven.

Another study of American witches (Kirkpatrick 1984) found them politically motivated: the value-oriented practice to match their norm-oriented political concerns. The author provides a considerable amount of information on feminist witches and on the nuclear-centred pagan movements, based partly on the literature and partly upon interviews with twenty-seven witches. He finds them surprisingly poor; far poorer than the average American, but his figures or sample may be skewed; certainly most of his interviewees were involved in artistic, philanthropic activities, and these middle-class pursuits provide little in the way of financial support.

he was able to feel as if he were in a dream, and in which colours, sounds and sight had become sensually rich. He was proud and pleased about this experience, more so than about any other event during the vacation, and he had written pages about it in his diary. And yet, Peter had gone on holiday as part of a group package. He liked the group packages, and always chose them: they provided friends and parties. So he specifically went with a group for the gregarious socializing, but made an effort to break away for long solitary periods. In some ways this is like the dynamic of a magical meeting: people go to lengths to join together in magical ritual, in which they spend most of their time in solitary fantasy.

Peter is now forty. He is a not-too-smallish cog in the behemoth of government machinery, a reasonably senior civil servant. He likes his job and feels that he has power in it. But he has fantasies of even great power, about being a direct advisor to the Prime Minister, a sort of Merlin to a contemporary Arthur. 'Not, perhaps, to this one [Margaret Thatcher]. But a later one'. This is a striking fantasy. Peter wants to 'do' something, to be important and effective in the world at large, but he also wants to be in service to some greater being. He would rather be counsellor than king. And he has certainly chosen a safe, sober profession for his energy. Almost no job in England so effectively conjures up an image of bored respectability.

Peter became involved in magic through Rudolf Steiner. In late adolescence he went through a period of religious exploration. He wanted religious involvement, and toured the different services that temples and churches offered. He read about Zen Buddhism and flirted with Russian Orthodoxy. But he was never drawn to any of the cults. He says that he abhors gurus, and he denied that his search was like the seeker who wanders from group to group with the same desperation and weathervane change of public commitment as those who become English Sikhs and Moonies. The wandering probably emerged to reconcile intellectual understanding and emotional need. Intellectual coherency matters to him. He is certainly bright – he went to a state school and then to one of the better universities, where he got a good degree – but it is more that he has a philosophical bent, and likes to analyse, and explain. When he came across Steiner in his period of searching, it made a tremendous impact on him, because it seemed to make sense of 'religion in a modern world'. Rudolf Steiner's books are a mixture of mysticism, meditation, imagination and evolutionary science. They claim to present a scientific account of spiritual experience, and they argue that the child must learn to be creative before he learns to reason. In other words, Steiner justifies religion through its creativity despite its apparent irrationality. Peter, I suspect, is an intellectual with intense emotions, and his questing seems the result of his attempt to meet the emotional need which has been frustrated by his intellectual tangles. Steiner seems to have enabled him to justify his creative spirituality.

Peter himself gives two reasons for his involvement with magic. He believes, he says, in the practical efficacy of group meditation for intervening in society. He also believes, like many magicians, in the value of ritual for therapy and life-enhancement, a conviction affirmed by his Jungian work, encounter groups, 'psychosynthesis' training, and so forth. He also finds it exciting. He likes its secrecy and the cloak-and-daggerish air it has, and it makes him feel more daring than his civil service colleagues. It makes him feel effective, because the magical group is 'working' on Britain's 'group soul'. 'You can work on the streets', he told me, 'but you can also work on other people's consciousness'. It is, as it were, civil service in a different form. In fact he complained that the people and the practice seemed too ordinary. He had expected more drama, more daring, more acting out of fantasies. But he did feel that the magic had been psychotherapeutic, that it has improved his self-esteem, made his dreams more vivid and his spiritual and imaginative life more intense, and enhanced his creativity.

Peter shares many of his basic emotional tendencies with other magicians. Modern magic, by its nature, involves a private imaginative absorption alongside a concern with self-control or control of the world around one. It is almost as if the practice encourages a regression to an earlier childhood state. In that state dreams, fantasies and personal emotion seem all-encompassing and to gain maturity is to negotiate a relationship with the world around one, to be independent of one's mother, to learn that one can control one's fantasies rather than be controlled by them. Certainly managing an intense fantasy life is the central issue in magical practice. The prescription to submerge yourself in the dark, bad mother, accepting dissolution within her as a means of personal integration rings changes on these childhood themes. The child fears loss and separation, and may split the love and hatred towards the mother. Magic dramatizes a split between good and evil, good mother and bad mother, and announces that they are one and that one must accept them both to be powerful. The magician-as-child is exhorted to merge himself with the mother he fears, to experience the frightening dissolution of ego boundaries, and told that through this process he will emerge stronger and more mature. It is as if magical practice returns the practitioner to the early stages of negotiating the boundaries between imaginative solipsism and the social, physical world.

Magicians themselves freely draw the comparison between magician and child. This is a period of imaginative creativity and play, of exploration and self-discovery. Magicians repeatedly described themselves as having a 'child-like wonder' at the world, a continual surprise at the diversity of nature, and they talk about the need for and value of playful fantasy. In Beth's occult workshop, in the coven, in the study groups and trips to the stone circles, people often mentioned their need to be childlike, to marvel at nature and to re-experience an imaginative intensity they had lost. Magic is meant to release the child within and return us to the gentle humour of being human. Witches, as one says, 'have never lost the simple wonder and curiosity of small children'.[36] Adler's personal experience seems common to many practitioners. She identifies powerful childhood fantasy as her own route into practice. At twelve, studying the Greek myths in school, 'in my deepest and most secret moments I daydreamed that I

[36] Adler (1986: 382) referring to another practitioner.

had become those beings, feeling what it would be like to be Artemis or Athena. I acted out the old myths and created new ones, in fantasy and private play'. As she grew up, the experience 'became a strangely discarded part of youthful fantasy. No one told me directly, "People don't worship the Greek gods anymore, much less attempt to become them through ritual and fantasy", but the messages around me were clear enough'.[37] Adler had been raised in a family of agnostics, and embarked upon an adolescent religious search through Catholic masses, Quaker meetings, synagogues and churches. 'Today it seems to me that I thirsted for the power and richness of those original experiences, though I found only beliefs and dogmas that seemed irrelevant or even contradictory to them.'[38] Her first encounter with witchcraft was emotionally powerful because it 'had simply given me *permission* to accept a part of my own psyche that I had denied for years'.[39] In other words, magic allowed her to re-experience powerful childhood emotions in a way that other religions had not been able to do.

I saw in many of the people with whom I spoke a curious quality of what seemed like innocence, of absorption in stories, music, flowers, the details of the natural world. Sometimes there was some remoteness from the meaty reality of local politics and current events. One witch told me that 'I don't think that I've ever really been in the real world as most people understand it. I think I've always been in a much more magical, mythical world than most people. I'm just that sort of person. I think that anyone who's creative is a bit like that anyway. [What does that mean?] It's a bit difficult explaining things. Either you know about it, or you don't . . . The real continuity in the world was always the continuity of my ideas, creative ideas in particular. Either the latest project I was involved in, or the latest poem I was writing. So, the real passage of time was a subjective one, and the real passage of time need to be got together *around* this subjective time.' In other words, she felt self-contained within an imaginative inner world, absorbed in subjective experience, a narcissistic reality distanced from the pragmatics of the world around her. She may be right to say that all creative people live within a subjective bubble. But it certainly seems true that people who become magicians find the subjective universe of the imagination to be deeply significant.

At the same time many magicians seem to express a concern with control, in the sense of self-mastery and mastery over the environment. Different practitioners experience the psychodynamics in different ways. But magic is about power, about controlling and dominating and being dominated or being in service to a higher form, and issues of power are often highly charged in these practitioners' lives. The witch of the disconnected world explicitly spoke of her need to be in control of her world, and in college she was aggressive and physical. As we shall see, magicians specifically train themselves to be in control of their dreams, their fantasies, their emotions. Yet while magical practice appears to advocate control over one's self and world, many people I talked to

---

[37] Adler (1986: 15–16).   [38] Adler (1979: 16–17).   [39] Adler (1979: 20).

seemed to feel controlled by external events. One man, an intelligent ex-Cantabrigian who had taught at Harrow for several years and then became a technical writer, told me that he felt himself a leaf, blown by the press of events. He thought, he said, that life was a sort of mechanism in which he was a passive participant. Ritual worked as a mechanism as well; you could choose to go through it to effect some change. Astrology explains the circumstances which govern the outcome of one's action, and he was deeply immersed in studying astrological trends and movements. Conversations with him continually return to the stars: you will feel this way, he would say, because Saturn is transiting your natal Mercury, her confidence blossomed when Jupiter aligned with her natal Mars. Astrology, for him, explained all events as occurring independently of his volition. And yet he enjoyed magical practice partly because he felt that it gave him an impact on his world.

Taken together, the themes of the magical literature and the personality characteristics the magicians display suggest that part of magic's appeal lies in its direct confrontation of powerful unconscious feelings and their translation into romantic imagery. The emotions most often alluded to are those of rage, and the fear and desire of dissolution: fear of the rage and desire for union with nature, the mother, the mystical whole. These are primitive feelings of early childhood, when issues of separation and independence involve powerful currents. The child feels helpless, struggling for autonomy, desiring both to dominate and to be absorbed within the powerful maternal being without. These themes are prominent in magic, with its central notion of the raging or chaotic mother who destroys and its pronounced demand to accept the destruction of the self by merging with the other – and emerging as a more mature adult. The fictionalized magician faces an evil enemy and triumphs: the wisdom he learns is that human power, perhaps adult self-control, is better than the superhuman power of the wizard. Repeatedly, the psychodynamic issues spin around the extreme passions of love and anger, the good and the evil, the extrahuman power of the magicians, and the wisdom that true strength is merely human power.

Magic casts these issues in the paradoxical clarity of myth, usually of a particular kind. The enemy is well-defined. There is the dragon, the destructive mother, the bottomless abyss, Sauron. These images of darkness turn out often to be intertwined with good, but they nevertheless present clear templates for the projection of primitive feelings. Indeed magicians often refer to the imagery as 'archetypal', imagery that characterizes basic human fantasy and experience: the conquering hero, the wise old man, the destructive hag. Powerful feelings are dramatized upon a romantic battlefield of good and evil, portrayed as a struggle which is eventually resolved. There are the heights; there are depths; there is the human mediation which gains its power through coming to terms with both. Perhaps they are the projection of helplessness and its perceived source; one element in magic's appeal is that it gives power to those who feel frustrated.

Some of those who choose to practise magic no doubt use the fantasy as escapist release. And indeed, many outsiders reject magicians' fiction because it seems to them psychologically too simple. However, many who practise magic seem capable of using these imaginative themes constructively. Magicians tend by temperament to be particularly absorbed within an inner subjective world, and to be concerned with issues of controlling it, themselves, and the outside world. They may be peculiarly able to utilize this imagery because they are particularly inclined to invest imaginative fantasy with emotional depth. They do connect the magical imagery with powerful feelings, as we shall shortly see, and for some it profoundly affects their lives. The combination of their own psychic self-absorption and the almost stark drama of the magical imagery seems to be deeply appealing.

Beyond these psychodynamic tendencies there are two not uncommon background elements of the magician's profile. The first is that perhaps one or two out of every ten magicians I met had something to do with computers.[40] Computer people are notorious science fiction readers and Dungeons and Dragons players.[41] Why this should be true is unclear, but several possible explanations present themselves. Perhaps the most important is that both magic and computer science involve creating a world defined by chosen rules, and playing within their limits. Both in magic and in computer science words and symbols have a power which most secular, modern endeavours deny them. Those drawn to the symbol-rich rule-governed world of computer science may be attracted by magic. A Massachusetts Institute of Technology sociologist who published an extensive study of these computer 'hackers', speaks of 'an affinity between the aesthetic of building a large computer program, with its tree-like structure, its subprograms and sub-subprograms, and making one's way through a highly structured, constructed world of mazes and magic and secret, hidden rooms'.[42] One reason that the fantasy games designed for the computer may be so appealing may be because of the complexity of the rules. Another explanation is the sense of mastery and power when the machine obeys your dictates, which may feel like the mastery of magic. One well-known science-fiction fantasy writer describes the life of a man who was once a Chinese imperial black dragon and is now embroiled in a Silicon Valley computer scandal. In the course of the story another character tells him this:

---

[40] This was corroborated by Adler's 1985 questionnaire, which was distributed at pagan festivals to 450 people; 195 were returned. 16 per cent of the respondents were computer programmers, systems analysts and software developers, and an additional 5 per cent worked in technical fields.

[41] Dungeons and Dragons is a fantasy role-playing game developed primarily by Gary Gygax (registered trademark TSR Hobbies, Inc.) in which a person takes on the characteristics of a certain character, like a warrior, wizard, thief and so forth. The character is numerically defined by certain attributes of a particular score: for example, strength 17, dexterity 11, intelligence 9. It encounters challenges and characters to which its response is partly governed by the roll of the dice. The Dungeon Master, the leader of the game, usually arranges these challenges. The important point is that players choose many of the parameters of the game – there is no board, players can choose their own abilities – and the imagery and scenery is taken from Tolkienesque science fiction: there are Viking-like fighters, trolls, sorcerers, and so forth. There are twenty or so particular variants of the rules for expert players, and there have been millions of sales.

[42] Turkle (1984: 84).

Everyone wants to be a wizard. Every engineer, that is. Goes with unicorns and dragons: but with technical people it's particularly wizards – a secret fantasy that lies behind all the pin diagrams . . . they think that because they can design a pc board and it's right and it works, that everything they do or believe is going to be just that right . . . Secret ways. Secret knowledge. Not bound by ordinary rules.[43]

The wizard commands the material world, breaking the laws which seem to bind it. Something in that imagery may appeal to the computer programmer. In Turkle's words, 'most hackers are young men for whom at a very early age mastery became highly charged, emotional, coloured by a particular desire for perfection and focused in the triumph over things'.[44] Yet another explanation – more unsatisfactory because more general – may lie in the strange social world which the computer buff inhabits, an inverted world of late night fantasy when the layman leaves the computer centre and the buffs, who run their machine-costly programs then, take over. For some it is an isolated, curiously unmixed society, with its own computer-peppered language, populated by people often markedly uneasy in larger social groups. Turkle describes many students involved with computers as feeling ugly and unsociable, and she points out that every year MIT has a competition to choose 'the Ugliest Man on Campus'. For these people the fantasy world might provide some form of escapism into a solipsistic world. There is, however, a much simpler explanation of the preponderance of computer-related magicians which relies on none of these sterotypic images of the computer devotee. Many magicians become computer programmers because they need a job. They are often people who are not driven by a career choice; they are often bright. The natural arena to which such a person might turn for a well-paid job, particularly in England, is the computer industry.

The second background factor is that magicians sometimes come from families in which strange claims are drawn from spirituality or in which religious intensity intermingles with rebellion. Perhaps two or three out of every ten magicians had a Catholic upbringing, or Pentacostalist parents, or a father with books on spiritualism and magic on the shelf. In her study of American witchcraft Scott found that witches were more likely than not to be Catholic in origin; she attributes this, however, to the ritual pageantry and group orientation of Catholicism.[45] However, this impression may be incorrect. Adler's survey of American pagans – in which she included witches, druids, and so on – discovered that their religious backgrounds closely mirrored the national religious profile.[46] For various reasons they become disenchanted with the religion of their past and become involved with magic.

Magic's practitioners are difficult to characterize; one reason for this is that the nature of the groups which practise magic are so varied that demands of the particular group do not limit the sorts of people involved. Some magical groups have hierarchical structures, some are anarchic. Some are deeply Christian (they see their magic as enhancing their Christian devotion), others see

[43] MacAvoy (1983: 118).   [44] Turkle (1984: 201).   [45] Scott (1980: 127).
[46] Adler (1986: 444).

themselves as radical agnostics. The type of group ranges so widely that one could not predict the sort of person who might be drawn to enter them. One might, for instance, assume that all who become Moonies could tolerate authority, for theirs is an authoritative religion, demanding public renunciation of a previous lifestyle. But in magic, with its varied societies, these generalizations are not possible.

Margaret

Here, as an example that will primarily speak for itself, I would like to introduce Margaret. Like Peter, Margaret is rebellious, spiritual, intelligent and intense. She is interested in psychology and therapy; she is very imaginative; she talks about power and control. She explains her involvement as arising out of emotional, political and philosophical concerns similar to those sketched above, and she illustrates the way these themes emerge in one practitioner's experience.

All witches, being human, have idiosyncratic life trajectories. Margaret was one of Britain's first female lorry drivers, and is becoming one of its public witches. She is smarter and more highly educated than many witches, but she is not unusual in being smart and highly educated. She has also opted for unpressured, unconventional jobs, again not that common but hardly unusual in this world of alternative ways of being.

Margaret came up to Cambridge in the early seventies to take a philosophy degree. She was good at the difficult symbolic logic she called philosophy's real challenge. But halfway through university, coursework bowed to adolescent rebellion, and she missed the first class honours she had hoped for. She went off to graduate school in Canada, but did not like the program and found the thesis overwhelming – for interesting reasons: the doctoral thesis was about irrationality, and she explained that she could not cope with the irrational within the academy. She came back to England in search, she said, of the irrational roots of her own being, and in search of her 'women's mysteries'. And she became a lorry driver, and then a witch, and now makes a living as a psychological counsellor and astrologer, two separate jobs.

Margaret is the sort of person one trusts instinctively. She is a strong, big-boned woman with auburn hair, and in repose her face has a sculpted beauty. It is also a tense face, slightly rigid, somewhat unsure of itself. In the following discussion, she describes how witchcraft helped her to understand herself and to give herself a greater sense of confidence and coherence. In particular, she talks about chaos and letting go, and a strength which comes through confronting one's fears and weaknesses.

'. . . I've known about mind over matter all my life. I've always been a person with a strong will, and when you're like that your body follows your mind. That's what drew me to philosophy. Philosophy was an attempt to be very down to earth and to be rational and powerful in intellectual terms. But there was always another side. When I was fourteen I read Goethe – Faust – and that really gripped me, that story. What really interested me was that he was doing something secret, something that was frowned on, and that he was looking for the truth behind appearances. The pact with the devil didn't grab me very much, that was just old-fashioned and superstitious. But the interesting thing was that there was this man who had devoured all of the available knowledge of his day and he saw that in personal terms it had got him practically nowhere.

'. . . Nietzsche is just the opposite. Nietzsche said that the strong will was simply the domination of all your drives by one single drive, or set of drives, so that you have all your drives and instincts, and what we mean by strength of will has nothing to do with the intellect, and standing apart and being cut off and all that rubbish. It's knowing precisely what you want to know and directing all your energies precisely towards that end. I read Nietzsche at twenty, and it sounded very sensible to me. It's a very affirmative philosophy. And that led me directly into a world rather different from that which I'd lived before, which had been very ascetic, very withdrawn . . .

'. . . It seemed that through the way of the passions you could actually get a different sort of power which didn't cut out the rest of your life. And you could enjoy it. So I tried that. And that's when the witch power really started coming through, when the ecstacy and the inspiration came through in a big way. Before it had been a few nights spent quietly in my room. But after I read Nietzsche I was trying out everything I hadn't tried before. Getting drunk, smoking dope, really throwing myself into dope in a big way. Being very physical, very sporty and hardy. Lots of physical activity. Burned up a lot of energy. And it was after that that I came across some of the books on Greek religion. Again, it's philosophy – Jane Ellen Harrison's *Prolegomena to the Study of Greek Religion*, Esther Harding's *Women Mysteries* – and I suddenly realized that this was very much to do with being a woman. Which was rather nice, because of course as a woman before I'd been very ambivalent about being a woman. It seemed to be a second class status, and it made me very uncomfortable. And this said to me that the new thing I'd found was actually a gift *because* I was a woman, and that was *so* valuable. It was such a confirmation . . .

'. . . You see, it's easier for women to be in touch with that physical, animal power, and that animal power keeps the world going. It's not your personal power, it's the power you're given by nature. Nature is the power. It's the common ground that you have with other women and with the earth itself. And with the heavens. And with the cycles of the earth and heavens, and the planets, and the whole rhythm of the cosmos. Women are very rhythmic. In the old days, I used to think that that was a terrible thing. One was flaky, one was unstable, one was unreliable. Proper people – that is, men – were constant, with a firm will, a firm purpose, were unified, were one person. That's a lot of bullshit. If you identify yourself so strongly with just one nature, then what happens to the rest of the world? You end up with enemies, or people who embody your opposite nature. If you think that you are logical, rational, a cool character, the logician type I was keen on for a while, then you get surrounded by people who are chaotic, crazy, hysterical, sort of out of it, and they mess up your life for you. But that's because they just respond to your own unconscious. If you accept that you sometimes go between the two, you end up not being hysterical, but being creative. Not being un-together, but being aware of many things, as well as having a good mind. And it all fits in with the periodicity of the earth. And the blood mysteries of women, the menstrual mysteries, and the birth mysteries . . .

'Menstruation is the time of the greatest witchpower for any woman. That's when women have their car accidents, go in for ghosts, cause poltergeists – it's just the power going haywire. Poltergeists are often associated with menstruating women. When a person's cut off from that power – if you naturally have it, if you're naturally a robust sort of charismatic individual, and you try to deny the power, it will hurt you, and it will hurt those around you. It will go amok. Can't get rid of it. You've got to accept it and use it. And as women we're particularly in touch with that power and ancient cultures had whole mysteries related to the cycles and experiences of women. We're nearer the earth, we're nearer the heavens as well. We're nearer the ground of nature, as well as being able to be estatic and inspired. So that was a very exciting thing for me.

'. . . I began researching on the so-called pre-Socratics, or, all the other philosophers apart from Socrates, so pre-, para-, and post-. And those guys just blew my mind. It fitted in with the Jane Ellen Harrison stuff, it fitted in with Esther Harding, it was a whole different philosophy which worked from the irrational as well as the rational. It was seeking to find a balance between rationality and irrationality, and both are sacred. The thesis was about medieval logic, really; I just became interested in the pre-Socratics because my supervisor was an expert on them. Medieval modal logic. Not what's true or false, the way we think of it in this century, with our two-valued logic, our black and white mathematics, but the way in which things are true and false. And in the middle ages, people were actually researching that. And they came up with some stuff which blew my mind. There was far more depth here than I could actually handle. I knew that I couldn't handle it, that you can't actually reduce it to modern jargon. For me it was a sort of bridge between the rational and the irrational mind, and I just knew that I had to find out an awful lot more about this irrationality. I came back to England to explore the ancient mysteries, the female mysteries.

'. . . I'd taken my Heavy Goods Vehicle license in the meantime. So I thought to myself, what the hell. We just had the Equal Opportunities Act go through. What the hell? Let's have a bit of fun, I'll go and be a lorry driver. So I went from teaching symbolic logic and Wagner criticism and writing poetry and getting heavily into the ancient mysteries – I'd made contact with some witches by then. The Pagan Front. Liked those people. Seemed really sincere, good white witches. Also with a thing called the Fellowship of Ishtar. Ishtar is the Babylonian goddess of love and war, which sounded exactly my themes. The sort of person I am. In fact I found it radically incoherent. They were just loonies, as far as I could see at that time. So I dropped them like a ton of hot bricks. But I was reading . . . I was practising magic and going around talking about witchcraft to all and sundry and saying what a wonderful thing it was. I wasn't in a coven, but I'd do it myself. There are enough books telling you how to do elementary spells.

'. . . In Etruscan mythology, it's only through the earth that you reach the heavens. You have to go down to go up. In psychoanalysis, in Jungian therapy, a person is whole, isn't complete, isn't mature until they've been down. And when they come up, their brightness, their optimism, their lightness has a different quality. They've found their centre. And that's quite different than just being a jolly person. And it's quite different from giving in to depression. You have to go down to go up. Now, witchcraft works at the bottom there, it grounds you, and the witches I've known since I was initiated into the Craft, later, after I left lorry driving, are the most sensible, down to earth people. They're not your airy fairy occultists, those spaced out people are rare. I don't know many people in magic who are disturbed and obviously unhappy. I think that those who are disturbed actually settle down through the Craft. It's so incredibly sensible . . .'

Plate 1   The Four Witches *(1497), an engraving by Albrecht Dürer. Modern witches are often familiar with this picture. I have been told that the different headdresses illustrate the diversity of socio-economic classes of the practitioners, and that nudity — these days, without headdresses — enforces a basic democracy by literally stripping away the signs of social differentiation.*

Plate 2 The devil and the coquette. Der Ritter vom Turn, *Augsburg, 1498. The devil, here not hoofed but clawed and horned, became the prime mover in early modern conceptions of magical practice. Here he is portrayed in the coquette's mirror; his buttocks emerge as a focal point for demonological symbology.*

Plate 3 The Abomination of the Sorcerers, *a seventeenth-century engraving by Jasper, illustrates the demonologist's mixture of learned ritual magic and rural witchcraft in popular conception in this period. The floor displays the circles, insignia and grimoires of Hermetic-kabbalistic magic; yet the women are witches, possessed of a cauldron, and associated with the incendiarism of the burning house. Around the women are presumably the evil spirits they have conjured.*

Plate 4 Love's Enchantment, *Flemish school, 1670–80. It is not entirely clear that this woman is a witch, although she is working magic. Modern witches sometimes present this picture as a piece of historical evidence, not only for the real existence of witches in early modern Europe but for their proclivity towards 'working' in the nude.*

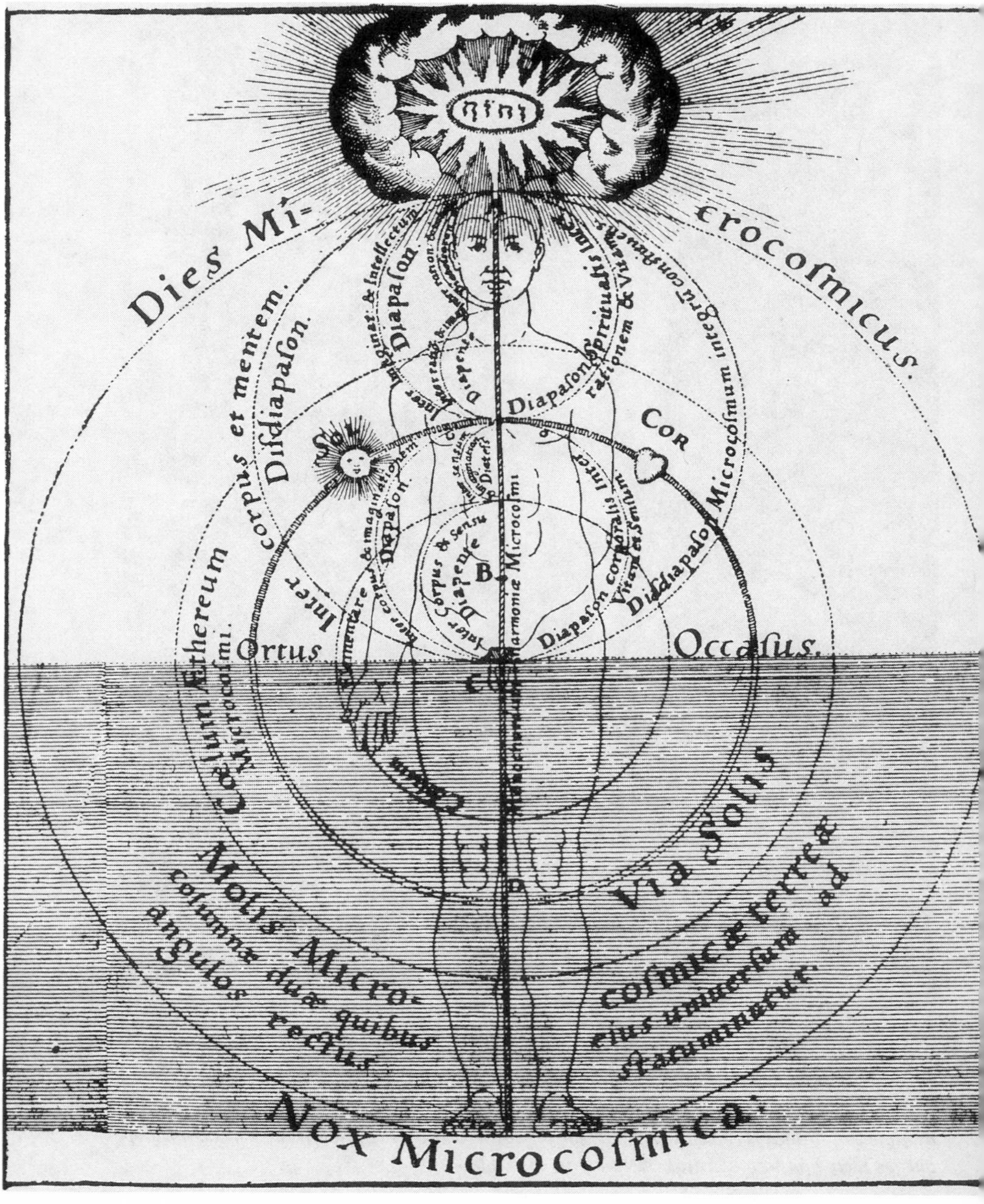
Dies Mi=
crocoſmicus.
Inter corpus et mentem.
Diſdiapaſon.
Diapaſon
Sol
Cor
B.
Ortus
Occaſus.
Cœlum Æthereum
Microcoſmi.
Via Solis
Motus Micro-
columnæ duæ quibus
angulos rectus
coſmicæ terræ
eius uniuerſum ad
ſtatuminetur.
Nox Microcoſmica.

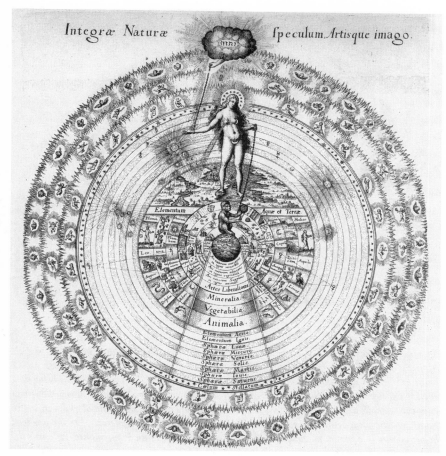

Plates 5 and 6   Robert Fludd was among the most interesting of the seventeenth-century magical philosophers. A Paracelsian physician with a Renaissance intellectual apetite, he wrote encyclopaedic treatises which attempted to systematize all knowledge within an Hermetic-kabbalistic framework. That is, he combined a practical knowledge of nature with a Neoplatonic conception of a universe defined by a hierarchy of spiritual beings. Central to this concept was the idea that man replicated as microcosm the macrocosmic complexity of the universe, which existed as three worlds – earthly, celestial and divine. Plate 5 diagrams this microcosmic mirroring. The interlaced circles of head, chest and body – intellect, imagination and sense – represent the three worlds, as do the three concentric circles marked empyreum, aethereum, and elementaire. The strong central line represents the spiritus mundi which extends from God to the earth, and is of both. Plate 6 is possibly the most comprehensive of Fludd's cosmic designs. The universe is subdivided into a hierarchy of divine, planetary and elemental spheres, dominated by Nature as a virgin, chained to God. Chained to her in turn is Art – the ape of nature – born of human ingenuity. The point to emphasize in both these engravings is the intricate intellectual complexity of the philosophy behind them.

Plate 7   The Sabbatic Goat forms the frontispiece for the second volume of Éliphas Lévi's (Alphonse Louis Constant) Dogme et Rituel de la Haute Magie *(1856). The book had a significant impact upon the development of modern English magic. Lévi describes this being as a magical androgyne, with 'Solve' inscribed upon the right arm and 'Coagula' upon the left to recall the symbolic architects of the Second Temple who bore a sword in one hand and a trowel in the other – the point being that nature simultaneously destroys and regenerates. On the forehead the pentagram, a common magical symbol, represents (for Lévi) man as microcosm, reflecting the macrocosmic universe, and signifying the integration of 'astral energy' within the material body. The creature is winged, presumably to indicate its spiritual nature, and it bears Hermes' caduceus, representing not only the magical philosophy of Hermes Trismegistus but also that controlled intertwining of opposite forces which Lévi calls the secret of the permanence of power. Magical power for him derives from the balanced use of magic forces. The paired crescent moons presumably also represent this balanced opposition, as do the hands in blessing.*

Plate 8   Aleister Crowley (1875–1947) was the black sheep of modern magical practice. Brilliant, flamboyant, unstable and sexually perverse, he produced lyric poetry and philosophy that inspire some people and horrify others. W. Somerset Maugham's The Magician *(1908) was loosely modelled upon him.*

Plate 9   Silbury Hill, an ancient Wiltshire mound, is often treated by magicians as sacred, and as a place of the Goddess. The artist depicts her conception of this primordial earth goddess, force emanating from her genitalia, hands and head. The third eye indicates her connection with intuition and instinct. These strong images of female power draw many women into magical practice.

Plate 10   This is the same artist's depiction of the God, the horned hunter who is the consort of the Goddess. Connected with the birth and the death of the harvest, he is shown with winter – or death – on his right and spring on his left.

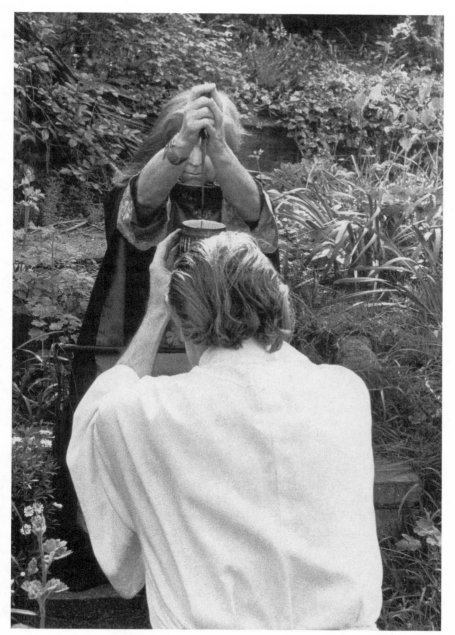

Plate 11   In the witchcraft ceremony which consecrates the wine, the priestess holds the dagger – the athame – and lowers it into a chalice of red wine held by the priest. The symbolically pertinent feature is that the male holds the feminine symbol and the female the masculine, to indicate that sexual polarities can be reversed on a 'higher plane'.

Plates 12, 13, 14   Crowley's 'Gnostic Mass' is an elaborate ritual about the male and female elements of divinity. In plate 12, the priestess, in 'Isis' pose, speaks as Nuit, and as the mystic, veiled essence of the feminine: 'For one kiss wilt thou then be willing to give all; but whoso gives one particle of dust shall lose all in that hour . . . I am the blue-lidded daughter of Sunset. I am the naked brilliance of the voluptuous night sky. To me! To me!' In plate 13, unveiled, she holds the lance given to her by the priest, who then adores her. Her crown, plate 14, is called the Isis crown. It bears the horns of Hathor, Egyptian cow-goddess, and a crystal sphere which suggests infinity and magical clairvoyance. The symbolism is elaborate and inordinate care is given to the ritual enactment.

Plate 15   The witchcraft altar displays some of the canonical tools of the practice; the four ancient elements represented by the chalice (water), the salt (earth), and the censer (air and fire); the pentacle or pantacle, also representing earth, used to hold the communion 'mooncakes'; the communion wine; the altar candle; and the witch's personal 'weapons' – the white-handled knife (a utilitarian instrument), the athame or black-handled knife (the most important symbol of the witch's power), the magical wand, the scourge (used for self-purification), and the sword (used for initiation).

Plate 16   Most witchcraft altars display images of the Goddess and the God. These two capture the nature of the revered deities well: the Minoan statuette is the primordial, primitive earth goddess, and the God is represented by Pan, horned god of bodily instincts.

Plate 17   Some witchcraft rituals use a priest to represent the horned god during some of the rites. Many covens have a 'god-headdress' which the priest wears as the stag god.

Plate 18 Witchcraft rituals often take place in the nude. When weather permits, covens sometimes hunt for quiet forested areas where they can do what witches are supposed to do: dance naked around a bonfire. This picture was taken in Lough Leane, Co. Kerry, Ireland, in 1981.

Plates 19 and 20   The actual function of the circles of standing stone, such as Stonehenge (plate 19) and Callanish (plate 20), is not clear. They may have had astronomical, ritual and political significance. Modern magicians see them as places of great spiritual power, as holy and awe-inspiring.

PART II

Listening to the Goddess: new ways to pay attention to the world

9

Introduction: the magician's changing intellectual habits

OW can a magician take his ideas seriously? Part of the answer is that the very process of learning to be a magician elicits systematic changes in the way that the magician interprets events. Interpretation depends upon a complex set of assumptions, biases, conceptual frames, knowledge, heuristics and attributive tendencies – intellectual habits in paying attention, in organizing what one notices, and in remembering it. The exact nature of this interpretive process is not well-understood, though it is the subject of considerable debate. Indeed, it is the subject of several disciplines and theoretical schools within them. Anthropology, of course: but also philosophy, linguistics, cognitive psychology with its current concerns with attribution theory, episodic and semantic memory formation, evolutionary epistemology, script theory, the nature of conceptual categories, and the like – all these have stakes at the gambling table of experimental and theoretical work on interpretation. The anthropological challenge is to identify the characteristic features of the interpretive process, and the value of this material on modern magic is that it allows the observer to observe what changes occur as the magician enters magic and begins to interpret his practice as effective.

There seem to be three outstanding changes in intellectual habits. The magician learns what events count as evidence that the ritual has worked, and begins to find new patterns in sets of events, to see connections where previously he has only seen coincidence. Then, he acquires the knowledge shared by fellow practitioners – their common knowledge – which gives a depth and complexity to his practice, and allows him to discriminate between events in new ways, armed with these new categories and distinctions. Finally, he begins to use a battery of new assumptions – some of them explicitly formulated, others implicit in the conversation – which alter the types of remarks he takes for granted and does not question. The cumulative effect is as if the magician acquires new spectacles, with a different focus on the buzzing confusion of Jamesian reality, and slowly, gradually, steadily, begins to adjust to the new perspective on events.

For the most part, these different interpretations of the outsider and the practitioner do not arise from the peculiarities of magic, but from the process of becoming knowledgeable, good at something in particular. I would argue that the rift between magician and non-practitioner is carved out by the very process of becoming a specialist in a particular kind of activity. Becoming a specialist often makes an activity seem sensible. The specialist learns a new way of paying attention to, making sense of and commenting upon her world. The important point is that the significant features of becoming a specialist can be identified. There are new ways to define evidence which offer grounds to the expert that the non-specialist cannot see, and ways to order events so that the specialist sees coherence where the non-specialist sees only chaos; there is a body of specialist knowledge which gives discrimination and depth to the specialist's interpretations; there is a semi-explicit philosophy which creates the assumptions which frame most conversation.

Most of the learning involved in becoming a specialist is not self-consciously verbalized; it is an unacknowledged accretion of knowledge and assumptions, ways of seeing and ways of making sense. People are often innocent of the changes in their own style of perceiving events, interpreting their actions, and organizing their memories. Many of these changes creep in slowly as the neophyte becomes a skilled hand at practice. The new ways of noticing, encoding, remembering, perceiving, not only alter the way events are observed, but also affect which ideas and theories seem plausible. To the long-term practitioner, magical theory seems more or less coherent, ordered, and rational. The magician argues about premises, debates the wisdom of certain actions, evaluates the evidence for his claims with care. He feels and behaves as if he acts according to a falsifiable system of whose validity he is slowly becoming persuaded. He may feel as if he has a keen, discriminating eye to judge his rituals and their effects.[1]

The striking observation is that in the course of practising magic the magic comes to seem eminently reasonable to the magicians, and that rather than realizing that their intellectual habits have changed they feel that they have discovered that the ideas behind magic are objectively true. To the non-practitioner, the magician's claims are woolly and ambiguous, undermined through the very attempt to protect them from disconfirmation. The practitioner seems to believe steadfastly in a theory for which everything could

---

[1] A constantly reiterated theme of cognitive psychology over the last fifty years (but particularly in the last two decades) has been that the mental activities such as perceiving, remembering, understanding, knowing, are active, constructive processes. The mind is not a blank passive slate. It structures its world. Bartlett (1932) is an apical ancestor of this approach: recent exemplars include Schank and Abelson, Neisser, Lakoff, Kahneman and Tversky, Johnson-Laird, Fodor, Rumelhart, and much of the work on visual perception, mental imagery and categorization (see Gardner, 1987 for a summary). As Neisser says, 'seeing, hearing and remembering are all acts of *construction*, which may make more or less use of stimulus formation depending upon the circumstances' (1967: 3). The investigatory problem is how someone perceives an event, and frames a problem. This chapter provides a skeletal account of three types of constructive features (macro-level features) which alter as outsiders become magicians. Another common theme (e.g. D'Andrade, 1981; Lave, 1986) is that the ease with which one reasons about certain events, or in certain ways, depends upon familiarity, not upon some transcendent ability to reason – an important observation, because the inability of preliterate Africans to perform well on experimenter's task of syllogistic reasoning has been taken by some to indicate their cognitive inferiority. Part of reasoning depends upon being taught to reason with familiar content, in familiar contexts. Magical training makes the unfamiliar context seem natural and persuasive.

be taken as proof and which nothing could disconfirm, a theory riddled with dubious remarks and meaningless statements. But as magicians become involved with the practice, their intellectual habits change, and what they think of as the theory of magic begins to seem both testable and true.

Why do they stay with it? What motivates magicians to continue the learning process that gradually shifts these ingrained habits of thinking about their world? The real lesson of these intellectual changes is that magicians find them illuminating, and the fact that they are illuminating makes the practice and its theory seem effective. By illuminating, I mean that the magician is able to give a rich distinction-filled description of the events which surround his rituals, and that this rich description is both exciting and intellectually challenging because it gives complex structure to life's disordered whole. This description may give a sense of discovery and confirmation, which may give the sense that the theory has been 'tested'. But practitioners do not in fact go to great lengths to treat their rituals like experiments, to tabulate the results and judge the hypotheses. To describe some theory as falsifiable – the fiercest test for a science – there must be a clear-cut set of hypotheses which are tested against empirical events and rejected should the test repeatedly fail.[2] In magic, that elaborate set of hypotheses is rarely present, let alone subjected to scientific test. There is a more or less coherent body of ideas, which will be described below, but different magicians develop it differently, talk about it in different ways, and pay more or less attention to it. Sometimes they play with the ideas, elaborating them or arguing about them, but more commonly they ignore the subject of magical theory unless it is deliberately introduced. But as they learn more about magic and as their sense of satisfaction increases, the very features which make it illuminating prevent them from seeing its weaknesses.

Before exploring this interpretive shift, however, I should explain more clearly the body of ideas which magicians find persuasive, the position, as it were, to which they shift.

THE IDEAS BEHIND MAGICAL PRACTICE

Modern magic rests upon the idea that thought can affect matter without the intervention of the thinker's acts. The first step in the reasoning is to argue that the two, thought and matter, are essentially one. Knight, the Greystone adept, writes scathingly of Descartes' 'arbitrary assumptions', and states that:

The most glaring assumption upon which all modern science is based (except perhaps in certain areas of advanced atomic physics) is that there is an absolute dichotomy between mind and matter, between subjective and objective, between the observer and the phenomenon observed. It is, in fact, no more than a useful fiction.[3]

---

[2] Falsification is more complex than this is made to sound. The necessary feature of any falsification, however, is the conception of a hypothesis that could be overturned by experiment. Magicians often feel as if they are 'testing' a hypothesis, but an examination of the way in which they argue illustrates that they do not really treat their magic in a manner that at all resembles this. The question of falsification is discussed later in the section.

[3] Knight (1981b II: 20).

This may be an inaccurate characterization of modern science; Knight, however, means something more subversive than the neurophysiological base of mental activity. In his view, the distinction between 'inner' and 'outer', imagination and physical reality, is mere illusion. 'We have to grasp the fact that the underlying reality of things is not matter – or any equivalent base external from ourselves – but is an immaterial relationship.'[4] When one imagines, that imaginative act – in itself, as a mental image, regardless of its behavioural compulsion – can affect what we think of as an unrelated 'material' reality.

Magicians use this conception of dynamic interconnectedness to describe the physical world as the sort of thing that imagination and desire can affect. The magician's world is an interdependent whole, a web of which no strand is autonomous. Mind and body, galaxy and atom, sensation and stimulus, are intimately bound. 'Witchcraft strongly imbues the view that all things are interdependent and interrelated.'[5] Individual objects are not fixed but fluctuating, constantly responding to their surroundings, bundles of relationships, rather than settled points. To treat objects as isolated and unique is a Western distortion in magicians' eyes. The distortion may be useful for scientific analysis, but it fails to understand the object's essence. One manual speaks of:

the world view that sees things not as fixed objects, but as swirls of energy. The physical world is formed by that energy as stalagtites [sic] are formed by dripping water. If we cause a change in the energy patterns, they in turn will cause a change in the physical world – just as, if we change the course of an underground river, new series of stalagtites will be formed in new veins of rock.[6]

The idea of magic emerges naturally from a philosophy of a world in interacting flux. If all the universe co-exists in delicate balance, minor variations should produce substantial change. Like a lever, a small magical spell can shift the world.

One could forge a magical theory solely from that account of flux. But magicians also often speak of forces or energies which are not generally recognized by science. Some of these forces or energies are called 'psychic'. Most magicians – all I have encountered – accept the existence of parapsychological effects: communicating without speech or sight, moving objects without touch, sensing the future or the past. Magicians commonly accept that psychic ability, like the ability to play the violin, is distributed differently by nature, but they assert that all people can improve their skill with practice. The concept of magic implies that psychical effects can occur – they are but another example of an interwoven world – and magicians talk about working on the 'psychic plane' during rituals, of using 'psychic intuition', of trying to 'contract' someone else's mind. Psychic ability itself is not that highly valued: magicians are often disdainful of mediums, on the grounds that mediums are passive vessels while the magician actively directs and intervenes. And magicians often distinguish between the psychic ability and magical

[4] Knight (1981a I: 11).   [5] Starhawk (1979: 11).   [6] Starhawk (1979: 112).

efficacy, the difference being that between a radio receiver and the radio station producing its waves. Nevertheless, a parapsychological vocabulary helps magicians to speak of unusual, scientifically imperceptible forces. Magicians also talk of other forces, powers or currents, which pervade the universe and can be generated or directed by the knowledgeable. These are often described as if they were electro-magnetic currents, but the analogy is loose. The basic idea is that the forces are both part of the world, accessible by human effort, and yet somehow not like more familiar forces like gravity. A member of the coven I joined explained that:

> The spiritual 'currents' postulated in magic and witchcraft are 'immanent' because they are within our subconscious minds, but not bound by our body's space and time limitations. They are both part of us, yet universal, and thus link us in a telepathic way to equivalent levels of other people's sub-conscious.[7]

These forces are rather badly defined but they are thought to exist, and to be elicited and directed in magical rituals. It is as if magicians think of themselves as creating an electrical storm in rituals, and dispensing bolts of lightning to chosen targets.

So magicians tend to conceptualize reality as a dynamic flux shot through with subtle forces and unknown energies. What they call their magical 'technology' – the mechanism by which their magic works – involves an account of the 'correspondences' between reality's different bits. Different planets, gems, numbers, symbols, and so forth are grouped together as a set, and any given set is associated with particular ways of being, types of force or energy. Mars is associated with red, dragonsblood and aggressive anger. To draw another into love, you might wear a robe of rose and amber, burn benzoin incense, light seven candles while invoking Venus, and concentrate upon your desire. Contemporary magicians devote considerable time to mastering common correspondences and drawing up their own lists of the patterned associations. They read countless books and take courses and talk to others about the most suitable incense for Jupiter. 'Of this gathering of correspondences there can be no end, for the whole cosmos in all its planes corresponds in endless sequences.'[8]

However, today's magicians tend to have quite different opinions about the role that these associations play. Some think of them as real connections which the magician must use to manipulate the power; others interpret them as a symbolic language which the magician learns as a means to help him concentrate upon his goals. The magician may also argue only for the latter notion but act as if the former is correct. Most magicians would finally agree that the primary use of ritual and its paraphenalia of correspondences is as an aid to concentration. It is commonplace for the magician to say that the ritual is a 'prop'.

---

[7] This was Robert, who has written an extensive account of the proper understanding of magic.
[8] Fortune (1935: 65).

A spell is a symbolic act done in an altered state of consciousness, in order to cause a desired change. To cast a spell is to project energy through a symbol. But the symbols are too often mistaken for the spell. 'Burn a green candle to attract money', we are told. The candle itself, however, does nothing – it is merely a lens, an object of focus, a mnemonic device, the 'thing' that embodies our idea. Props may be useful, but it is the mind that works magic.[9]

Magicians tend to act as if the rules and symbols of ritual are terribly important, but they will often make remarks that emphasize the irrelevance of the 'props' and the importance of the concentration those props are meant to induce.

It is the mind that works magic. Modern magic holds that thought affects the world directly – even though it is patently obvious that most of the time it does not, without action. The magical idea is that mind affects matter in very special circumstances, namely when the magician frees himself from the shackles of everyday awareness and focuses his entire being on obtaining his goal. The ordinary analytic mind, it is said, cannot work magic. One must sink down into the lower realms of instinct and psychism, where primary desire mingles with vivid fantasy. Then one must represent the goal in the imagination, and focus on that image with total concentration and intense desire. Rituals help this to happen. They change the circumstances so that the appropriate concentration can occur.

Magic is ultimately the conception that mind alters matter when mind in all its complexities – conscious, unconscious, with emotion, desire and imagination – focuses completely upon a particular goal. One witch writes of 'the four cornerstones of magic from which the whole mysterious edifice of witchcraft arises . . . a virulent imagination, a will of fire, rock-hard faith, and a flair for secrecy'.[10] Know what you want, know that you can get it, and focus on it utterly (the secrecy is to protect oneself from being distracted by mockery). Like shamans, mystics and religious devotees throughout the world, magicians use various techniques to alter their sense of consciousness, to shake off their sense of the everyday and to stimulate their emotions. When strong emotions are directed to magical goals in an altered state of mind, magic is possible. Thought affects the world when it is intensely concentrated, fuelled by great desire. Magical practice is the attempt to train the mind and find the means through which such concentration can occur.

When I talk of the magician's 'claims', and of magical ideas, I mean first of all the general commitment to the efficacy of ritual, in this more than psychological sense (i.e., the ritual did more than psychologically boost the ritualist), and second that the commitment is usually coincident with some version of the account given here. To some extent I have inferred these ideas from scattered passages in magicians' own writings. Some magicians, however, explicitly try to order and explain these concepts as a theory in the books they write for newcomers. In one such book, entitled *Techniques of High Magic: A Manual of Self-Initiation*, the authors list 'four fundamental theoretical assumptions' of magic:

[9] Starhawk (1979: 110).   [10] Huson (1970: 22).

1 That the universe of the physical scientist is only a part, and by no means the most important part, of total reality.
2 That human will power is a real force, capable of being trained and concentrated, and that the disciplined will is capable of changing its environment and producing supernormal effects.
3 That this will power must be directed by the imagination.
4 That the universe is not a mixture of chance factors and influences, but an ordered system of correspondences, and that the understanding of the pattern of correspondences enables the occultist to use them for his own purposes, good or ill.[11]

The tenets are an ordering of the ideas expressed above. Not all magicians would accept them as they are baldly stated, but they tend to be accepted in some form by most practitioners. The following pages discuss the intellectual attitudes or habits associated with the person who wants to treat them as valid.

[11] King and Skinner (1976: 9–10).

10

Drinking from Cerridwen's cauldron: learning to see the evidence

I MAGINE there to have been a ritual. A witch's uncle has lost his job in Austria. The coven asks her about him: what he is like, the sort of job he needs. She passes around his photograph. The group decides to do a 'run-round' for him, a chanting dance. Then they will visualize a tree, firmly rooted in the soil, healthy and growing, and they will visualize the energy going towards him through Ann, the member of the group who knows him. Or take a ritual with a vaguer goal, one from the Glittering Sword. It is Emily's turn to lead that evening, and she has written a ritual about the sea, with Celtic symbolism. For half an hour, an hour, we visualize images of the sea. We imagine that we are led to the heart of the sea, into its beribboned inner chamber, and there we meet Cerridwen, who gives us strength. We drink from Cerridwen's cauldron as voices chant around us. What needs to happen to show that the magic 'worked'?

If magic is meant to be an activity with real forces and practical effects, magicians need evidence to find their efforts laudable and their theory well-grounded. The rituals often have specific goals, to get houses, health or jobs; they almost always have *some* goal, like gaining strength or revitalizing humanity, however indefinite the goal might be. In any case, ritualists repeatedly affirm that any ritual, done properly, should have some impact. The question, then, is how magicians identify that impact, and how they cope with what must be frequent failure to meet their goals.

The rough answer is that they learn to notice events and to explain events in such a way that the rituals can be said to have worked. Magicians usually begin their practice with considerable scepticism and even if they never entirely lose their sceptical eye they tend to be persuaded that the rituals have been effective and that something like magical power exists. This involves learning to find evidence that the rites have worked, and magicians do so by learning to observe new aspects of events and new patterns in sets of events. They learn, almost, to see a new world – two dangerous metaphors – because they significantly alter the way they pay attention to – and then remember – events associated with magical practice. They even may generate some of the feelings and responses which magical ideas suggest will result from the practice. And over time, these new perceptual skills become more persuasive, the evidence seems ever more concrete, as the practitioners gain a history of successful, satisfying rituals. One could say that magicians alter their attribution of 'casual propensity', the tendency to interpret causal ambiguity in particular ways. Faced with explaining an event as caused either by ritual or by coincidence, magicians tend to become comfortable with attributing the event to the power of magic.[1]

Magicians acquire certain criteria which allow them to evaluate any ritual's effect. They also do evaluate certain rituals as failing, so the criteria seem stringent: the criteria seem to set standards which not all rituals can meet. Magicians learn to discriminate between good evidence and bad evidence, then, and they acquire a history of distinguishing 'successful' rites from 'failures'. They also manage to maintain a sense of the possibility of falsification. That is, they often practice rituals with the feeling that they are 'testing' a 'theory' of magic against the world, that they would abandon the theory if no proof were found, but that the world gives them empirical evidence of the theory's rightness. The pages below illustrate that magicians maintain this sense of testing a testable theory through some very common human tendencies: certain mnemonic and attributional inclinations, the distorting influence of bias, and the endogeneity of experimenter-produced evidence. These tendencies take advantage of the loopholes in an experimental methodology which are inevitable when any complex theory is being tested.

The interesting aspect of this evidence-defining process is that it seems, to an outside observer, that magicians have ways of claiming any ritual to be effective and ways of explaining any failure away, but to insiders, to those becoming magicians, it seems as if they have tested a theory sceptically, and found it good. This is not because they have deliberately drawn up defined hypotheses and tabulated the results of their ritual enactments: quite the contrary. Magicians do not think through their understanding of magic in axiomatic detail, nor do they test their concepts with anything like Popperian care. Nobody does. Even Popper described his account of stringent falsification as a rational reconstruction, the scientist's ideal but not necessarily his practice. Indeed, magicians end up feeling confident about magic's efficacy, despite the ambiguities about its effects, because of the inherent difficulties in confirming a complex theory and the advantage human bias takes of those same difficulties.

Falsification is a knotty problem. Popper's manifesto announced that falsifiable science subjected hypotheses to empirical experiments, and when tests failed to meet the experimental prediction, the hypothesis was abandoned.

---

[1] The question of how and why people attribute particular causes to particular events is a matter of considerable controversy in cognitive psychology. 'Attribution theory' is a branch of that discipline, which seeks to understand commonsense explanation by identifying crucial parameters which provide information (e.g. Hewstone, 1983; Jaspars *et al.*, 1983 for a summary of recent work). Some authors in that field (particularly Kelley) treat humans as lay scientists, disinterestedly able to attend to the available information; others point to systematic distortion in an individual's perception of the available information, that the way individuals attend to immediately available information depends strongly upon prior impressions (e.g. Nisbet *et al.*, 1982). Schank and Abelson discuss casual propensity in the context of 'scripts': scripted understanding of what events 'go together' (1977: 32–5). Magical practice makes the practitioners more likely to interpret an event as being the result of a ritual. The following pages identify some of the analytic alterations which make this possible, and the subsequent chapters describe the experiential involvement which may create a tendency towards bias.

There were, he admitted, 'conventualist' strategies to avoid the hypothesis-destroying with honour: one could add *ad hoc* hypotheses to the tested theory, modify ostensive definitions, adopt a sceptical attitude to the technical competence of the experiment or experimenter. 'The only way to avoid conventualism is by taking a *decision*: the decision not to apply its method'[2]. But no scientist behaves like a crudely dogmatic Popperian, a fact which led Lakatos to develop a 'sophisticated falsificationism' to describe, as he said, a Kuhnian Gestalt-switch without removing his Popperian spectacles. (Lakatos actually identified several Popperian accounts of falsification, only one of which was dogmatic and suggested the absolute empiricism popularly associated with Popper's name; sophisticated falsification was also a version embedded in Popper's text. Popper was far from a crudely dogmatic positivistic Popperian himself.) Lakatos also offered a rational reconstruction of science, as a battlefield of competing research programmes which maintain an inner core of hypotheses unchallenged by the researchers (the 'positive heuristic') but which test and revise a belt of auxiliary hypotheses to maintain continuous growth, theoretical fertility and predictive success in the discipline. No-one abandons a theory, Lakatos emphasized, just because one experiment goes wrong.[3]

Even in its strictest formulation, the experimenter's dependence upon falsification can be only an attitude, because there are always other logical ways to explain experimental failure, and attitudes have an ambiguous relation to action. Magicians do allow human psychological proclivities to influence them in ways which are supposedly checked in formal experimental procedures. They also often explain failure in ways common to conventualist strategy, usually on the basis of faulty technique. However, they often think of themselves as subjecting hypotheses to tests, and they often find that their 'hypotheses' are not disconfirmed – primarily because the difficulty of magical technique allows them to define evidence quite broadly. Sometimes they interpret a ritual as failing, and conclude that one particular idea about how to conduct a rite is incorrect, and they revise it. They might still maintain an attitude of being willing to subject hypotheses to tests. Magicians are not blind,

---

[2] Popper (1959: 82).

[3] The bulk of Lakatos' well-known essay on this subject describes experimental research in which unsuccessful experiments do not falsify, in which falsifying 'crucial' experiments are identified as many as twenty years after the fact (e.g. the Michelson-Morley experiment) and in which the multiple interpretation of experimental results and the competitive revision of auxiliary hypotheses forms the major focus of scientific work.

The sense in which magicians resemble these ideal scientists of Lakatos is not clear, for they do espouse 'auxiliary' theories of ritual and tarot-card use (although 'theory' is not a word I would choose to use), and different interpretations of astrological analysis (for example, there are different systems, much debated, to plot the 'houses' in the astrological chart). To an observer these sub-theories do not seem to sustain Lakatos's requirement of 'continuous growth'. He rules such theories as Marxism and psychoanalysis out of his definition of science on the grounds that even though they revise their auxiliary theories in the wake of new facts, they do so without anticipating others. 'What *novel* fact has Marxism *predicted* since, say, 1917?' (1970: 176). New types of magic do appear, are practised, and disappear in favour of others (e.g. chaos magic). Outsiders to magic would argue that it is clear that one brand of magic is obviously not superior to another brand and that nothing like continuous growth takes place; some insiders might well assert the fertile superiority of one particular theory of magic to another.

believing fools: that they conclude that magic is effective speaks more to the ambiguity of interpretation, than to their gullibility or the truth of their ideas. This is also a problem of induction – not whether induction can be validated as a reliable scientific technique (a philosophical chestnut) but why certain characteristics are privileged over others in forming generalizations (a more recent chestnut, discussed by Goodman)[4] and, particularly, how people generalize from a small number of examples, ignoring statistical information about the probability of ritual success over a series of rituals. Magicians often feel quite confident that magical theory is valid, on the basis of a string of successes. The question is what elements feed into that inductive certainty.

Let me turn first to the mnemonic and attributional inclinations which influence the evaluation of the ritual. One point is almost obvious: that the newcomer remembers the one dramatic cure, and forgets the ten that did not really work. The more striking an event, the more firmly it becomes embedded in episodic memory – a theme well established in the literature on memory formation.[5] Dramatic stories are recollected and recounted while ambiguous outcomes fade into the murky past. The coven I joined, for example, never tabulated any results of the two or three spells it performed each month. Participants occasionally inquired after someone for whom we had 'worked', and when the spell seemed effective the story was eagerly told. The cumulative effect of these stories is impressive: as a magician, you are told incident upon incident in which the rites apparently effected change. The psychological pattern is to remember the dramatic incidents, and to induce from those incidents remembered rather than the host of more ambigious incidents in which they were embedded that magical ritual produces non-coincidental results.[6]

[4] Goodman (1983).

[5] The literature distinguishes between 'episodic' memory, memory of singular events, and 'semantic' memory, organized by some underlying structure. One's first visit to a foreign conference, an unusual and striking event, would be remembered as an episode; further visits are likely to add to a semantic knowledge of the various airports in the world. The less striking an event is, the more quickly it may fade from memory unless anchored by a semantic organizing grid (Tulving, 1983; Neisser, 1982).

[6] Russell once remarked that 'popular induction depends upon the emotional interest of the instances, not upon their number' (1927: 269; quoted by Nisbet et al. in Kahneman *et al.*, 1982). Many cognitive psychologists have argued that bias significantly affects inductive activity: people are not rational, information-processing animals (e.g. Nisbet *et al.*, 1982). The body of work on 'cognitive dissonance' (discussed in part 4) points to the emotional pressure which people bring to bear upon intellectual perception. Tversky and Kahenman offer a different explanation. They describe the 'limited number of heuristic principles which reduce the complex task of assessing probabilities and predicting value to simple judgemental operations' (1982: 3). People are bad at induction, not so much because they are emotionally biased, but because they rely upon certain well-established intellectual 'short-cuts' which produce systematic and predictable failures when faced with certain problems. These limitations are quite intriguing: they include representativeness – the probability that 'a' is 'b' is judged by the degree that 'a' resembles the stereotype for 'b', not on the basis of the underlying probability that 'a' is 'b'; availability – the frequency of a class or the likelihood of an event is assessed by the ease with which it is brought to mind; and adjustments and anchoring – people estimate outcomes from an initial value, and then correct (1982: 3–22). The expectation of a result, the tendency to ignore statistical information, the importance of magic to the ritual-result-watching magician – all these will influence the magician's tendency to interpret the rite as effective.

For example, in 1986 Robert, the most senior member of the coven I joined, sent me a list of nine effective workings which had helped to persuade him that magical forces, in the most literal sense, existed and could be affected by human action. His first two examples occur in 1958. The second one illustrates the sort of incident that the magician remembers, and his reasoning about its impact.

Case 2: Healing Françoise. November 1958–January 1959.

Background: In October 1958 I took a week's vacation to visit the Brussels World Fair. On the last day, I met a twenty-two year old Belgian girl, Françoise, at lunch and we spent the afternoon visiting the Fair together. She told me that she was epileptic and had had particularly serious fits three years earlier, which had deprived her of her intellectual ability and memory. But she didn't care: she was frozen in a happy acceptance of whatever life brought. Her doctor had just prescribed a new drug for her, but so far it had had no effect. I commiserated, and we parted after exchanging addresses.

It was not until later that it occurred to me that with my – admittedly rudimentary [Robert was fairly newly initiated into witchcraft] – knowledge of sorcery I ought to do better than that. So I wrote to her guardedly explaining that I engaged with friends in spiritual healing experiments. 'We are not very good at it, and I cannot promise any results. But you will come to no harm: the worst that can happen is that nothing changes in your state of health.' If she was interested, she should send us a recent photograph and a lock of hair (as psychic links), cooperate by praying to the Virgin Mary (she was Roman Catholic and said that she had been doing so already) and keep us informed of her progress. She gladly gave her consent and sent us the requested psychic links.

The workings: We performed our first healing ritual on Françoise at Halloween, on Saturday 1 November. She reported that she had 'unfrozen': her intellectual memory was returning, but she had lots of minor epileptic fits and spent hours weeping uncontrollably. So we repeated the ritual at our next regular meeting on Saturday 29 November.

The following weekend some of us were visiting two group members at their home in Chichester. On the Saturday evening (6 December) we decided on an impromptu magical meeting and we performed a third healing ritual on Françoise, with myself as usual as the energy 'transmitter'. During that working, I felt unseen forces telling me in effect: 'Your message has been received and understood. Now leave the rest to us: You can do no more'.

The outcome: Françoise's next letter reported a tremendous inflow of energy: she had signed on to two evening classes, was going out every night, was looking for a job. This continued in January, and then suddenly her letters ceased.

At Whitsun 1959, I was due to attend the annual get-together of the College of Europe alumni in Bruges, and wrote to Françoise to ask her if I could visit her. She sent me a welcoming invitation to spend the previous weekend with her family, and she came with her mother to meet me off the mailboat in Ostend. The mother expressed her great pleasure in meeting the man who had 'healed Françoise'.

I asked since when she had been healed. 'Oh, since my accident.' 'What accident?' 'Oh, didn't you know? On my way back from a party on the 31 January with a man who had drunk too much, we had a head on collision, and I went flying through the windscreen. I was in hospital for a couple of weeks and have still got the scars where the glass cut me (she showed them to me). But since then I have felt quite normal and had no more fits.'

On my return from England, I checked with a medical member of our group who said that it was quite common for epilepsy to be cured by a sudden shock. Unfortunately, I then lost touch with Françoise and don't know whether the cure lasted. She was close to falling in love with me, and the only alternative was to marry her or let the acquaintance fade.

Analysis: This story leaves room for plenty of alternative explanations. Convinced materialists would say that Françoise owed her healing to the accident, and that given the standard of Belgian driving in the days before licences were required in that country, she was likely to be involved in such an accident sooner or later. As for her emotional unfreezing three months earlier, it was due either to the new drug her doctor had just prescribed for her, or to the psychological encouragement of having attracted the interest of an eligible young man.

A Roman Catholic believer would say that any miraculous element in her cure would be due to her praying to the Virgin Mary.

However, had I not been an initiated sorcerer, I would not have written to Françoise and offered our group's spiritual healing help. She thus would not have received the psychological encouragement to unfreeze emotionally, and start on her round of feverish intellectual and social activity. Without her feverish socializing, she would not have put herself in the position of being thrown through the windscreen of a drunk Belgian driver, and receive the shock that cured her epilepsy.

The unseen powers of the magical circle left another discreet signature for the discerning eye: Françoise's accident occurred at Full Moon on the pagan festival of Candlemas, an exact quarter year of thirteen weeks after my first healing working for her on Halloween. And who knows that my 'accidental' meeting of Françoise at the Brussels World Fair was not in itself an answer to her earlier prayers to the Virgin Mary?

In this account, the ritual goal was very clear and it seemed to be clearly achieved. The magician worried about the possibly 'coincidental' nature of the outcome, but pointed to the startlingly unusual elements – the magical pertinence of the accident's date, the feeling of confidence after the ritual – which would make the outcome seem non-coincidental. What he was sure of is that the goal of the ritual unambiguously came to pass (at least, it was reported to do so in unambiguous terms). This he remembered twenty-seven years later, and identified as evidence – nine dramatic cases out of hundreds of rituals across a span of twenty-seven years – that his workings have had effect. When I spoke to magicians about the effect of their practice, not one listed a total number of rituals performed out of which some percentage had achieved a goal. They responded as Robert had done, describing one or two dramatic events which had persuaded them of the ritual's possible efficacy.

The related attributional phenomenon is that it is extremely difficult to call an event coincidental if it seems uncanny and if some putative cause could explain it. People prefer to give causal explanations. Tarot card readings or the interpretations of astrological charts are excellent examples of this process. The reader gives a complex, rich description of the querent's emotional state, of her health and her relations to other people. The reader gives so much information – and such ambiguous information – that it is almost inevitable that the querent would find *some* uncanny coincidence in the reading. The reading is based on a highly specific, contingent collection of symbols which only have meaning according to a contested theory. Yet faced with one particular uncanny insight it is hard to remember that some random uncanny insight was extremely likely. The natural response is to think that the contested theory must be correct. For instance, when I met my first magicians they immediately drew up my astrological chart to find out what I was like. The following parapgraph is but one out of a five page text:

Sun in mercury a very impressionable and 'feminine' sign – being also in fifth house suggests that this is creatively expressed (e.g. as artistic sensibility) or expressed in love affairs. Sun's rulers are Jupiter and Neptune: Jupiter in Sagittarius would like to colour the receptive Pisces nature with a studious, philosophic streak – seeking meanings and patterns: Neptune in Scorpio would like to explore the deepest emotional levels. Jupiter in the second house suggests that the studious nature is linked with a feeling of material security – to understand is to feel secure.

The interpretation had a daunting amount of highly specific information taken from the unique constellation of my chart. No one else, practically speaking, shares the exact arrangement of planets which forms my chart, and the reading should be unique. And the interpretation managed to identify feelings which, at times, I have felt, and character traits which to some extent I possess. When the chart was done for me I 'knew' intellectually that – given that the interpretation runs on in this way for five pages – it would be extremely unlikely that, whatever it said, I would not see myself on some of its pages. Nevertheless, I was struck by how difficult it was to pass off the reading as a coincidence. I *wanted* to see the reading as an insight; it was exciting and fun to think that it might be correct. People strive for order. They find it difficult really to accept the existence of coincidence, if only because there is creative pleasure in drawing connections between events, in making interpretations.[7]

The distorting effect of bias is particularly clear in the use of the criteria to evaluate a rite's success, and of the advantage taken of the methodological loopholes. Magicians learn criteria by which to judge the rites' effects, as all experimenters and critics learn criteria to evaluate a performance. But in order to provide a description of the nature of supporting evidence, what 'counts' as evidence, which is broad enough to fit all cases, their criteria must be broad enough to allow the enthusiast to extract a verdict of success from any rite. This is particularly true when the magician (or any experimenter) is able to

---

[7] Part of the critique of conceptualizing people as rational logicians has been that people tend to make causal attributions on the basis of their stereotype of the actors, rather than on the basis of statistical likelihood. As above, Tversky and Kahneman argue that people ignore underlying statistical base-rates. More generally, the tendency to identify a causal connection between sequential events is strong (e.g. Johnson-Laird and Wason 1977: 437–8). Shweder argues that 'correlation and contingency are relatively complex concepts that are not spontaneously available to human thought'. People tend, instead, to rely upon resemblance to estimate correlation, and to seek 'symbolic and meaningful connection (resemblances) between events' (1977: 447).

distinguish between the ideas of the magic – the claims that mind affects matter and that rituals, done properly, have actual effects – and its technique. According to magical ideas, you only see magic's effects if your technique is sufficiently developed to manipulate the forces and interconnections of the shifting world. As a result, there must be ways to identify the presence of magical force even if the technique is faulty, which allows a wide range of ambiguous evidence, and ways to explain failure that do not challenge the basic concepts of the practice, but only its technique. This strategy is sometimes described as secondary elaboration, or the invocation of auxiliary hypotheses: a dodge to avoid rejecting the theoretical hypothesis even when the experiment designed to test it seems to have failed.[8]

It must first be said, at the risk of banality, that the successful outcome of a ritual is not uncommon. Many spells are aimed at healing, and inevitably, these spells have a certain success rate, particularly when the patient knows of the magical working. It is said that the spell is more likely to work if the patient knows of the working. The newcomer is told that when the hoped-for outcome appears, she must take it as a sign of magic's efficacy, even if she could explain the result as coincidence. One guide says:

[The magician] may well seriously work a ritual, offer the right incenses, wear the appropriate colour and jewels, but the outcome of his working will not be miraculous, it will look like a coincidence, a bit of luck that things turned out as he wished. Because he knows that he has done the work and because he has achieved similar results [in the past], he will recognize that coincidence as being the outcome of his working – he will have faith brought about by experience in his methods in the past and he will *know* that his magic has worked.[9]

The new magician learns that what she previously would have called coincidence, she must learn to recognize as the calculated consequence of her magic. (It is identifying coincidence as cause with a vengeance.) Rituals often have goals which are fulfilled. The author reminds her readership that when this happens, it is because the ritual has brought about that end, and not because of felicitous coincidence. The witch was delighted when her Austrian uncle got 'exactly' the job he needed, and she thanked us for the help.

But the aims of rites and spells are not always so well defined, and not always clearly achieved. Magicians also look for evidence of magic's efficacy through what I shall call 'lateral' effects, coincidences associated with the symbolism of the ritual's actual performance. If you perform a ritual using water symbolism,

[8] Evans-Pritchard lists twenty-two reasons to explain 'why the Azande do not perceive the futility of their magic' (1937: 475) – the magic is meant to attack mystical powers and 'since its action transcends experience it cannot easily be contradicted by experience' (1937: 475); it is intellectually coherent, explaining all events in its terms; scepticism applies to particular magicians and medicines, not the general theory, etc. (1937: 475–8). Tylor also provides a variety of explanations for the failure of practitioners to perceived that their magical theory is false. More scathing about the practitioner – 'at once dupe and cheat, [the magician] combines the energy of an unbeliever with the cunning of a hypocrite' (1871: I: 134) – Tylor describes the 'tricks' used to protect the magic, and the ease with which evidence for success can be found (1871: 134–6).
[9] Green (1971: 4).

you expect water – as tears, emotions, even burst pipes – to emerge in your life in the subsequent weeks. These events are understood as the tag end of power released through symbolic 'gateways' in ritual. They dramatically broaden the range of rituals which can be thought to have worked because with this evidence the magician does not need to achieve her ritual goal in order to assert that magical power was present. Magical power may have been raised, she may say, but it was either misdirected or insufficiently strong for the job.

For example, a December 1983 Greystone ritual used mirrors and candles in a ritual centred on heavenly forces. Subsequently, in a lecture during March, Knight announced that he had recently learned that on that same December afternoon thousands of protestors had surrounded the Greenham Common airbase with mirrors, the idea being that they were reflecting the evil back into the base, forcing the guards to see themselves. Knight presented this detail to indicate that something had been 'right' at Greystone. At the time of the ritual, he had just had the feeling that he ought to use mirrors. Now he thought that perhaps he had been guided by a higher source. And he thought that this indicated that great power must have been generated in the rite. The feminist witch who had attended the ritual with me and the subsequent lecture was delighted. She had had no idea he was unaware of the Greenham Common action; in fact she had rather thought that he had been borrowing their ideas without acknowledgement. On the strength of his account, she decided to attend Knight's next Greystone meeting even though she disapproved of his Christianity. In May 1983 the Greystone ritual had been about the sea. It was a warm, sunny weekend, the participants told me, and they thought it significant that the pipes burst and flooded someone out of her room.

The same reasoning can also find partial success in apparent failure, as when some event occurs that seems associated with the ritual, even if it is not its goal. A man works a ritual for a new house. No house is forthcoming, but a packet of advertising leaflets on home maintenance arrives in the post a week later. This is reported with mixed pride and self-mockery – the rite worked, but not quite with the intended results. The symbolic channels got blocked or tangled up, magicians explain, and the power came through in a funny way. The coven I joined told the story of a spell performed to make a member pregnant. Another woman had stood with her in the magical circle, and describes herself as trying very hard to visualize, willing the spell to work. The woman for whom the spell was cast remains childless. But the second woman's toddler, born some ten months after the ritual, is sometimes introduced with the story.

Let me provide another, longer, example. This taped excerpt is from a discussion group in the Western Mysteries. Martha explains that she used some incense associated with Aphrodite to liven up a party, thinking that the incense would infuse a benevolent, sexy feeling in to the room. She had a pleasant party – but the only people who came were beautiful women. Magicians find the story funny because Aphrodite, famous as a goddess of beautiful women, had provided the beauty but had neglected to summon up any men to appreciate it. Enoch follows her account with a similar tale. The moral of these stories, in magicians' eyes, is that you can never be sure quite how the ritual will work, because you can never be quite sure through which symbolic channels the power will flow.

Martha: There's *much* more to this whole thing, as I said before, than I even begin to dream of. But also something occurred to me which I thought was a good analogue of why one might not like to mess about with ritual, and that was that once I thought I'd like to jolly up a party, with incense, before the party, you see. And I was aware that planetary incense was, you know, fairly serious business, so I was very careful. I was concerned not to choose one which might have unfortunate results in any respect. So I burnt the incense to Venus, for the party. . .

Enoch: You thought it would be trouble free? This is the lady who at seventeen wondered why she'd got a body (laughter).

Martha: Fourteen. Seventeen was when I resolved it. So I burnt this incense, and then the party started, and everything was fine. And I don't know whether I noticed that there was anything odd about it until two things happened, and it all fell into place. And one thing was that I opened to door to a guy who lived two doors away, and he said 'Hi', you know, and then – 'I've never seen so many pretty women in my life!' And shortly after that this woman came up to me and said, 'Where are all those men you invited?' So that was what happened, and you know, it was fairly uncomfortable for some people. And I'd done my normal thing, which was just to invite people, and it always works out. But there was an enormous preponderance of very good-looking women, and just very few men. So what it was is that I had an intention there, and the intention was fulfilled, but there were other results, which I hadn't taken into account.

Philip: What was your intention?

Martha: My intention was that the party should be pleasant and successful, and it was. But there were – riders, other factors – that I hadn't taken into account, and that's been almost my – proviso, about magic at all. Since I discovered magic existed I thought, well, don't touch it, you know, until you can see what's going on.

Enoch: That is a very salutary story. I will risk capping it. It's a tale that comes from way back, before I was an initiate in the Mysteries and thereby had somewhat more elbow room than one has after taking the oaths of the Mysteries. We were entertaining my boss. What we wanted him to do was to invest a whole lot of money, or get a whole lot of money invested, in a project. We didn't actually want him to give us the money; we knew what we wanted, we wanted it for something, and it was something very idealistic, too, a revolutionary management exploration, things like this. So it wasn't entirely a black magical approach, but it was a bit grey. And we thought, we wanted this guy in the right mood and we wanted him invested in the right things, so what'll we do? We'll invite him to dinner and make the whole damn thing a Jupiter ritual, and so we're going to have blue and purple things everywhere [blue, purple and the number four are associated with Jupiter, ruler of business success], we're going to have fourfold things everywhere, we're going to have blue candles, we're going to have the whole damn place enthused with Jupiter music and Jupiter colour and Jupiter smell, Jupiter incense, Jupiter everything. This guy comes along. He's a little guy, very much an establishment figure, sort of – English, upper class, university educated. City type. But unorthodox, with it. I mean, he was a wild man in that sort of universe. Unpredictable, imaginative, Liberal MP, Liberal candidate, Liberal Party man. Terribly progressive and experimental attitude towards everything, and not above playing ducks and drakes with the stock exchange to get what he wanted. Anyway he came along and had dinner and talked the hind leg off a donkey, which he always did, and no-one got a word in edgeways, which they never did anyway. And we never got around to talking about our thing. And he went away all fired up and quite happy and we sort of collapsed among all these horrible bits of cigar ash and blue napkins and blue candle ends, the whole place sort of smelling like stale mastic, and we said what was all that about? We never got around to talking about our thing. And *two* days later the guy said to me, you know I've been thinking, I think I'd like to get out of all this business and join the church. (Laughter: Jupiter is also associated with religious power). I never heard him say the same thing before or since. And this is what happened, the whole Chesed-Jupiter [Chesed is the kabbalistic symbol associated with Jupiter] had gone straight in and hit him on that middle, on that wavelength, and he suddenly found he'd got this buried ambition that he'd never noticed for ages, 'I would really like to get into the Church'. Remember this? (to Beth).

Beth: Um. He wanted to be a bishop.

Enoch: He wanted to be a bishop. We'd actually been a bit naughty, by working magic without telling him, by putting him in this incredible Chesed atmosphere, this is what happened. We thought, well, if you ever wanted your knuckles rapped by the inner plane, they just rapped them. The joke was on you.[10]

Magicians become adept at this pattern-making, at seeing order in complexity. They look for such patterns, and the patterns become fodder for jokes, interpretations, acceptable stories. 'That 200 foot waterspout was the biggest materialization I've ever had' (a member of the Gareth Knight group, reminiscing); 'she did a Saturn ritual when she first joined the group, and it really did her in – lost her job, nearly broke off the affair, the works' (Emily, describing a member of the Green Circle). Both of these quotations refer to the aftermath of rituals. In the first case, someone performed a ritual and later saw a waterspout – to him, it was the manifestation of left-over magical force which took that material form. In the second, someone rather innocently performed a Saturn ritual and afterwards lost her job, and a magician uses this to warn of the dangers of doing ritual without carefully thinking of the results. As a would-be lover scans his beloved for signs of interest, so the magician scans the circumstances for the signs of her magic's effect.

Human behaviour, some philosophers say, is best described by showing, rather than generalizing with abstractions. Let me offer yet another account. One witch who talked about power with me used this example:

I know one man who's a witch who's a computer programmer, he's in computers, and he came round to my house and we had a talk about this or that, and something happened, and I suddenly had the feeling that this bloke was getting irritated. And my immediate reaction to that, being the sort of person I am, was 'stuff that. Do your own thing'. And I could feel some sort of energy rising. Then he went off to the loo, and he came back, looking sheepish, with the handle in his hand, and he said, 'oh dear, look at what's happened, it's fallen apart in my hand'. He'd pulled the handle off. And the first I thought was, 'oh you fart, you're just not expressing your aggression, why don't you come out with it, and argue with me directly, whatever the hell it's about'. It just seemed

---

[10] The 'inner plane' is here used to identify the magical 'contacts' which guide this Western Mysteries group. Section four includes an account of the role and nature of this metaphor.

to me that he was angry and he'd just displaced it. This Freudian stuff. I suddenly had a thought – I said, 'Does this happen to you often?' 'It's funny you should say that. Yes. I'm an expert at mending other people's things, but I never break my own'. 'Ah', I said, 'you know you're a witch?' '*Oh*', he said. 'Do you crash computers?' 'It's funny you should say that. I don't know how much longer I'll keep this job'. And just the sheer animal power – it was tied up with frustration and anger, when it's frustrated, it goes haywire. And so he was one of the men who actually has that power. And he wasn't channelling it, and it went haywire.

His action 'made sense' because the witch – Margaret, the lorry driver – could see it as fitting a pattern, which tallied with a fairly clear understanding of magical force, and it served as evidence in support of that understanding.

Endogeneity rears up as well from the split between concept (or theory) and techniques and the necessary breadth of what counts as evidence. Magicians look for the magical power's impact in the magician's personal experience of ritual, for she is described as the conduit of power and as a result she should feel its force. This follows from the split between idea and technique because whether and how you feel the power indicates your skill in channelling the force. If the ritual performer feels no power, it can indicate that she is still incompetent, that the ritual's leader performed badly – or that the magical hypothesis is invalid. If she does feel the power, it means that magical force exists, whether or not the ritual leader and the participants are skilled enough to carry the force through to effect the ritual's goal. People's responses in ritual are so varied that the evidence for the power's impact is quite widely defined. If magicians want to find evidence for the rite's success they can do so by this means. One suspects that if a hypothesis – or a speculative idea – is hard to confirm directly, the burden of proof is shifted on to personal experience, much as the proof of a transcendent deity is often shifted onto personal revelation, for the proof is much easier to find, and more convincing when it occurs.

Magicians report a gamut of emotional, spiritual and physiological responses in ritual, and they attribute these experiences to the presence of power in the rite. Magicians will 'feel' the power flowing, 'feel' the current run around the circle. They often assert that they *know* whether rituals raise any power because they can sense power intuitively during the ritual – regardless of any external consequences which the rite was meant to yield. Magical power is also thought to be the sort of thing that requires training to handle properly, and some of the magician's responses are attributed to inadequate training for the experience.

One reported experience is an altered identity. At a Greystone ritual where, it was said, there was much power, the adept told me that he felt in his circumambulation as if he had become Father Time himself, the spear which he held, a pendulum of some eternal clock. Magical novels present that experience as possession; 'it was possible to bring the soul to single-pointed focus by adoration and dedication . . . when this took place, the god came down and possessed the worshippers, and the power of the god shone out from him like a lamp'.[11] People do, at moments, feel themselves to be an incarnation of

[11] Fortune (1957: 173).

the gods. 'I carried Isis for a while when I was doing some work for someone' (Servants of the Light supervisor); 'I *was* a Valkyrie, Wodan was there, could you tell?' (Helga); 'I felt for a moment as if I had expanded as the Goddess herself, that I was eternal and encircled the universe' (officer's report, Greystone 1981).

Others simply describe 'not being there', of feeling their personalities vanish so that they become a channel, a vehicle, for the force. During the 1984 Greystone ritual, one officer described herself as 'flying', 'I felt as if my feet would leave the ground'. She said that she is 'not there' when the ritual is good: she becomes a 'channel' for the forces. For William, founding member of the Glittering Sword, the difference between powerful and powerless ritual was whether he was 'doing' or 'being done'. When he was 'doing', the ritual hadn't taken over. It was 'empty'. When the rite was good, it felt as if something was acting through him and that he himself was absent. In such rituals his normal sense of space and time alters, and he knows that the only things of consequence lie within the confines of the rite. A witchcraft priest told me that 'when it [the ritual] works, then my personality – me, Paul – steps aside, and someone else takes over'.

Witches in particular use the word 'shamanism' to describe how much they can alter in a rite. By this they mean that their spirits or souls leave their bodies, and either travel in the world, or allow their bodies to be occupied by some divine being. The witch priestess is said to become the Goddess, the priest the God, in a ritual of 'drawing down' the moon or horned hunter.[12] Helga was a witchcraft high priestess before she abandoned the religion to work specifically with the Nordic gods. She calls herself a shaman, and feels that the power rushes in and submerges her normal self within the rite. She also 'travels' in her 'shamanic body' to find information for healing or protection. The high priestess of the coven I joined finds the witchcraft power 'raw, shamanistic'. As the Goddess in a ceremony, she feels expanded, increased, transformed, as though the 'power' pushed her normal self aside. 'I am lifted up and out of myself, flowing with the forces.' For some practitioners, these descriptions have a precise neurophysiological correlate: 'out-of-body' experiences are actual psychological events with a delineable epidemiology.[13] This, I suspect, is true at times for Helga. Magicians try to induce out-of-body experiences – one method is to gaze with great concentration at a geometric form (a 'tattwa') or a

---

[12] E.g. Adler (1986).

[13] Most individuals having out-of-body experiences, either deliberately induced or unintended, will feel as if their 'spirit' or 'soul' rushes out of the centre of their forehead, and that they see their 'material' body lying beneath them before they then move off. Autoscopy (the *doppelgänger* effect) is discussed by psychiatrist Grostein in Friedman and Faguet (1982: 67–79); it 'seems to follow from migraine, epilepsy and central nervous system affectations of the temporo-occipito-parietal lobes of either hemisphere; may occur in dissociated states such as in hysteria, borderline and psychotic states, and drug-induced states; and is also a variant in normal personalities that are easily prone to imaginative visualization and audition' (1982: 73–80). It is also reported in near-death experiences. The classic occult source for out-of-body states is Muldoon and Carrington (1929). A recent detailed discussion, with a wealth of information (it does, however, focus on the possible objective reality of the out-of-body trip) can be found in Blackmore (1981).

tarot card image so that it expands, and then imagine stepping through it.[14] Occasionally, but not often, they experience such a state during ritual.

Spiritual experiences also count as evidence. Sometimes these seem to be genuine mystical experiences, particularly in the cases of adepts or those with great experience. But, like out-of-body experiences, responses of such intensity are rare. More common are feelings of an awareness of spiritual love, or the sense of unity with others. One of Knight's students stayed with magic because in one of his home study lessons 'I went out onto the inner planes and just felt all this love coming'. The junior priest at a Gnostic Mass told me that he understood why the priest took communion for the officers as a whole: that the five officers formed a single body, a living organism, with a merged and corporate mind.

Other responses that magicians take to confirm the efficacy of a rite are more specifically emotional. In particularly important rituals, and in initiations, participants sometimes leave the room in tears.[15] Magicians reminisce about emotionally bruising rituals the way marathon runners talk about Heartbreak Hill. At my own initiation into the Glittering Sword a co-initiate dissolved in tears before her oath of dedication. At the December 1983 Greystone ritual an officer walked out weeping and a novice burst into tears. 'The power is always slightly unbalanced when there are untrained people present', an experienced participant explained. 'Someone must bear the brunt.' Earlier in the year (Greystone May 1983) a ritual had been 'dangerous', 'difficult', 'important'. Participants spoke repeatedly of being hurt, confused, in turmoil at its finish. Another of Knight's students acts professionally, and thought as a novice that ritual 'would be easy, just like acting, learning to say the lines'. But 'Boy, I was wrong'. After being Arthur in the 1981 Greystone ritual, he spent two days in emotional exhaustion. 'I didn't understand until then what it meant to bring down an archetype, to take that responsibility.'

Those experiences – the sense of an altered identity, the sense of channelling, of not being there, the mysticism or sense of love or unity, the emotional collapse into tears – seem psychological or spiritual in nature. Associated physiological experiences include nausea, a 'tingling' or buzzing sensation, and a change in body temperature. Change of temperature is particularly common. 'When I'm working you can fry an egg on my skin', one Craft high priestess told me. 'When the power goes – zip – I'm frozen.' But some of Knight's students get very cold. I made myself a thin gown as ritual garb when I joined my first ritual magic group in the spring, and asked whether I should make a different one for winter. 'Don't worry' I was sagely advised. 'You always get hot in ritual.'

A buzzing sensation is said to indicate the onset of power. 'I can always tell if the ritual is going to work, if I'll raise power, by the tingling in my fingers when I begin', a witch told me. Knight knew that the May 1984 Greystone ritual would

---

[14] E.g. King and Skinner (1976: 54–9); Brennan (1971: 26–35).
[15] There are rarely tears in the ritual itself; that would be a violation of the disciplined self-control magical practice supposedly engenders.

be powerful by the atmosphere in the room after the pathworking on Saturday night: 'the air is electric, tingling with energy'. Perhaps related to this, there is an intense excitement associated with magic. Magical power is 'like being absorbed in a good novel, or like being sexually turned on' according to one of Knight's students. A member of the Golders Green group said that 'magic is tremendously exciting. It's like being in love. The colours are richer, the air is fresher, the world is electric and alive.'

There is nausea. At the May 1984 Greystone ritual at least several participants felt nauseous, the result, they said, of the power. An experienced magician explained that 'it's from rising quickly on the planes before you're used to it'. One of them lost the nausea when the power was 'dissipated'. She is a feminist witch to whom Christianity is anathema. When the imagery turned from the Celtic to the Christian the power 'went'. She had not seen the crystal cross atop a coiled dragon, as Knight had described; her dragon slept beneath a white-blossomed apple tree. She thought that if only Knight had used *that* imagery the power would have been 'properly' directed. Another friend 'felt' the power until the Christian imagery appeared; after that, she says, she has no recollection of the rite.

Magicians accept the variation in ritual response as an inevitable feature of training, experience and idiosyncracy. After performing perhaps his thirtieth Gnostic Mass the high priest ruefully concluded that he could never anticipate someone's sense of the evening. 'Sometimes you think it's barely adequate and you're told its the best you've done, sometimes you think it was tremendously powerful and the others shrug their shoulders.' Everyone has their own internal magical landscape, everyone responds in different ways. The acting priestess or magus hopes that all participants find powerful the ritual in which she or he has also found great power. Power is meant to have an objective correlate. But its presence is difficult to detect. In using immediate experience to judge the rite at the time, the variety and fallibility of human experience is consciously recognized.

So in rituals magicians are not themselves; they get sick or weepy or want to fly; they can feel a halcyon oneness with Isis and their neighbour an unutterable sadness. Yet all states are said to testify to the power of the rite. The interesting thing about these experiences is not so much that they are the consequences of ritual experience – they are very real results of intense imaginative stimulation within a highly charged emotional and spiritual context – but that these experiences are used to legitimate the ritual as 'good' ritual. And the result is that to those who experience them, they seem to be irrefutable proof of the power's presence. At the same time, the sceptical outsider might perhaps rightly believe that the motivation to feel such effects should produce those effects, regardless of the magic's truth. The experiences are not the explicit goal of the rites: 'thrills and spills are the by-products of magic, not its aim', Knight says. But they serve an important function to magicians, because they indicate the magic's reality regardless of its results.

Three types of biases allow certain events to be interpreted as evidence for magic's success: the mnemonic, attributional inclinations, the criterial freedom created by the distinction between theory and practice, and the endogenous experimenter's effects. One might imagine that any ritual could be interpreted as producing effects. But idea of evidence loses all usefulness if there is nothing which is not evidence, and no experiment which ever fails. Not all rituals are said to be powerful, and not all rituals achieve their goals. There do need to be ways of explaining dramatic failure, as when the subject of the healing spell dies. And some rituals are clearly going to seem as if they have involved more power than others, the way some horoscope predictions seem uncannily accurate and others barely appropriate, even to those who always want to see meaning in the stars. Magicians need an account of varying success, and such an account demands a notion of failure by which the success can be defined. Again, the explanations tend to take advantage of the split between technique and conceptual framework. Failure is attributed to faulty technique, not to fragile theory. This accounts for practical disaster without challenging the basic validity of magical ideas. It is as if a biologist explained that the experiment failed because the beaker broke, not because the theory it was meant to test is incorrect. As a result, the theory appears to remain falsifiable while allowing any disconfirming instances to be explained away.

A ritual is said to fail either when a specific goal is obviously not obtained – you do a ritual to help a friend obtain a job, and a year later he commits suicide from despair, still unemployed – or when members of the group 'feel' that there was no power. The only way to tell if power is present while performing a ritual is to feel, sense or intuit it. Sometimes, for various reasons, group members say that they did not feel the power's presence, and they then need to explain that lack. (The reasons can include social tension within the group, or the exhaustion of group members, among other reasons.) The technical faults which lead to failure tend to fall into certain categories.

First, magicians set high standards for the performance of their ritual, and explain ritual failure as the failure to live up to them. Regardless of whether the ritual techniques are seen as important in themselves, or as merely the means to concentrate the mind, the ideal portrait of the truly powerful magician is almost impossible to emulate. 'The Magician must be in control of the whole of his nature; every constituent element in his being must be developed under Will to the topmost pitch of perfection.'[16] The magician is a superhuman creature, absolutely in control of himself. Even his unconscious responses become signals which he can search for information. Consider this fictional portrait of a true adept:

the strange, impassive countenance, exaggerating with its flickering shadows the deep lines of the parchment skin . . . the eyes, deep set and glittering, were those of a hawk . . . Veronica knew that this man was not an Asiatic, any more than he was a Westerner; he was absolutely detached. He gave the impression of tremendous power, utterly impersonal, completely under control.[17]

[16] Regardie (1969: 36).   [17] Fortune (1957: 252).

Such a person concentrates mind and will utterly, allowing no intrusion. He probably could work powerful magic. But he cannot, really, exist in the flesh, although the real adepts are understood by some adherents as a close approximation.

In an ideal world, magical rituals would be performed by a group of highly trained practitioners – people resembling the adept just described, a person trained for years, indeed lifetimes, under careful supervision. In grubby reality, rituals are performed by relative newcomers. Indeed, veterans of ten years standing are called newcomers, and of course many practitioners are newer still. Magicians usually regard themselves as undertrained and undeveloped, and they attribute their less than dramatic impact on their environment to their technical limitations. For example, nine months after Maria began a home study course on magic, she was beginning to experience slight shifts in her state of mind and in her perceptions. She was still frustrated by 'scrying', a practice where the magician is meant to look into a pool of water, or a dark glass, and see images appear. On her course, this is taught by looking at an object and then trying to reproduce visually the object elsewhere. 'Months of staring at my palm and then staring at the wall, trying to *see* – not imagine – it against the wall.' She attributed her failure to inexperience, not to the unlikelihood of images actually appearing on walls, and to her own struggle in coming to terms with magic's validity. 'I fought the whole way.' Still, she looked back wonderingly at how much she'd changed from the days when she considered taking the Natural Magic course. 'I said, I have twelve pounds to chuck away. That was my understanding of magic. Twelve pounds to throw away.'

In addition, rituals themselves have standards of perfection. The ritual chamber should be exactly square, hermetically sealed, the altar carefully arranged. Everything must be just so. Simon, the leader of the Hornsey group, had the group entirely reconstruct the upper floor of the house they had bought, so that there was a room which was a perfect cube. Once built, no natural light ever entered the room (the only light was a tiny bulb, for cleaning). Simon spoke to the group once about precision in ritual.

8 p.m., on the dot, is very important, and what it generates on the inner is a sort of jewel. If anything's out of place it's as if the various lines making up the jewel don't meet, so that it looks like a badly arranged computer game . . . The whole thing is rhythm, totally. Later on, in higher power ritual, rhythm is absolutely vital in the ritual, in the form of the ritual furnishing, in the outer form of the temple, the officers, the complementary aspects of officers and the work that the officers are doing.

Precision and exactitude are everything, Simon asserts. You must know exactly what you are doing, and why; you must perform every action with a conscious awareness and in a state of utter control. If the ritual asks you to pick up the altar candle and present it to the east, you must know exactly how and why you turn, how many steps you take, the arc of the circle you make by stretching out your hand, and exactly why you are doing that action. The Hornsey group has some thirty members, six of whom have been members for thirteen years of weekly meetings. They think of themselves as raw novices. With such high standards, the impression is not surprising.

The second common explanation of failure is the magician's weakness of will. Failure to believe that the spell will work causes the spell to fail.[18] This is an old explanation of failure: Agrippa says that 'he who works in magic must be of a constant belief, be credulous, and not at all doubt of the obtaining the effect'.[19] I once visited a particular coven as a guest and participated in a spell to alleviate a friend's suffering in the aftermath of a hospitalization. Those present thought that the spell had failed. Months later, in an angry reaction to a draft of some chapters of my doctoral thesis in which I had remarked that 'my sceptical view of parapsychological effects remains largely unaltered', the high priestess of that meeting responded: 'This is an interesting point of view in that it would be impossible for you to participate in producing such effects while in your capacity as an observer. You might find the parapsychological literature on experimenter effects of interest'.[20] My lack of conviction was used to interpret the perceived failure of the spell – even though they were unaware of that lack while performing it. Faith in your power is part of your magical will – the determination that your magic will succeed. A magical will is like a thing of steel, they say. One must temper it, keep it sharp and powerful, use it as a weapon and never as a toy. If it is weak, the spell will fail. The high priest of the coven I joined was horrified when a confirmed smoker made a magical vow never to smoke again, because if the vow was broken, his magical will would be damaged.

Third, technique itself may be defined as misconceived. This is rather important because failure in this way particularly supports the self-image of magic as a testable technology. A magician will be said to have used the wrong invocation, to have chosen an inauspicious day for a ritual, to have blocked the flow of power at a crucial time. And the debate about what exactly went wrong may actually strengthen a magician's commitment to his craft.

The best example comes from a ritual I myself did not attend. (I was told then that I was too much of a novice.) It became an item on the gossip-and-rumour circuit for weeks afterwards, and I talked to many of its forty-odd

---

[18] There is a name invoking this phenomenon in the literature on psychical research: the Batcheldor effect, which asserts that the experimenter's disbelief will inhibit the experimental subject's performance. See Long (1985), Winkleman (1982) and Batcheldor (1966, 1982/1984). The more persuasive version of this thesis is that psychic ability, whatever it is and if it exists, cannot be displayed at will.

[19] Barrett (1967 [1801]: 97). Quoted without acknowledgement.

[20] Fieldwork in a literate, sophisticated society poses particular difficulties. I was indistinguishable from the magicians, and there was some misunderstanding of my purpose (although I had discussed the project specifically with the letter-writer). The letter was written by a high priestess of a coven who was outraged by the tone of draft chapters of my doctoral thesis which I had shown around (she thought it too clinical; my Cambridge supervisor criticized them for insufficient objectivity). Other members of her coven disagreed with her judgement of my moral venality, and the group split, and became two covens. It may have been that I was only the catalyst which brought underlying tensions to the surface: this is what all onlookers told me, but that style of de-personalized explanation was extremely common in these groups. In any event, this was one of the most unfortunate consequences of my study, and I deeply regret the discomfort which it caused.

participants. The May 1983 ritual at Greystone has become legend within its circuit; to have participated confers something like occult adulthood. Some fifty people participated in what was meant to be the culmination of a series of seven annual rituals. Its intent was to bring the underworld forces into earthly cooperation, to change the destructive tension between earth and underworld into constructive union. This may seem vague: what it meant is that before the weekend, participants read about a dark goddess, about hell, and meditated on how to transform that destructive energy into happier forms.

The ritual involved imagery about Atlantis, about releasing the souls held beneath the sea in its collapse. Many of those present at the ritual said that it was singularly the most upsetting rite in which they had participated. They spoke of leaving the room in confusion, of rushing outside after a ritual to link arms around a tree. There was a general sense that something had gone wrong. What seems to have happened is this. Two high level magicians, considered by the others to be adepts, worked together as they had done in all previous occasions. Knight, as usual, was responsible for designing the ritual action. Normally, he and his (female) partner would sit facing opposite each other, with ritual officers on either side. But this year, Knight placed his wife in the centre of the foursome. And the displaced partner explained: 'but the magical flow won't go through living bodies . . . [Knight's wife] was going on about her impressions when suddenly I got a strong contact . . . I told it, go back, go back, we're not ready yet. And it got furious . . . At one point, Knight leant around his wife and said, 'Are you all right, Augusta?' Something in me snapped. You don't use Christian names in a magical ceremony . . . I let this thing loose, and it walloped Knight. He rocked slightly. Then it picked me up and strode down the corridor with me until it left.' She collapsed, apparently gasping and shaking, clutching the wall. Chief officers rarely stalk out of the room in rituals. The observers must have found it quite upsetting.

I was tempted to attribute Augusta's explanation (delivered in the British Museum tea room) to a wounded ego, but regardless of its cause it was clear that she had had a vivid experience of thwarted spiritual possession during the ritual. She also felt that the experience had initiated her (on the 'inner') into a higher grade of practice. The failure hardly challenged her acceptance of the general concepts of magic. Quite the reverse. She concluded that Knight was not as good a magus as she had thought, but she gained a far deeper respect for the practice itself, and a greater confidence in her own powers.

Failure can also be understood in terms of the difficulty of the goal. Magic, it is said, works in ambiguity, in fluctuating situations where the outcome is not determined. 'Your ambition is to become a witch, not God, and it would be wise to bear in mind that there is a difference'.[21] One's power is limited. Efficacy depends upon propitious circumstances:

Casting a spell is like sailing a boat. We must take into account the currents – which are our own unconscious motivations, our desires and emotions, our patterns of action, and

---

[21] Huson (1970: 25)

the cumulative results of all our past actions. The currents are also the broader social, economic and political forces that surround us. The winds that fill our sails are the forces of time and climate and season; the tides of the planets, the moon and the sun. Sometimes all the forces are with us; we simply open our sail and run before the wind. At other times, the wind may run against the current, or both run counter to our direction, and we may be forced to tack back and forth, or furl the sail and wait.[22]

If the 'currents' – the way things are – are not moving in a suitable direction, the author says, the spell will fail. 'No magic spell will work unless channels are open in the material world.'[23] The proviso that 'magic does not break the laws of nature'[24] is repeated again and again: even more, magic does not alter things which are fixed, but only those in flux. If events are amenable to alteration, then the magic may have its way.

How is it possible for the magician to retain his faith in the face of constant failure? The succinct answer is that failure is perceived to be far from constant, and it is easily explained within the terms of the theory. Success is easy to establish: the goal of the ritual is often met by the natural process of healing; the freedom to use symbolically associated events and personal experience as evidence allows the magician to interpret almost any ritual as at least successfully raising magical power. Failure, when identified, is ascribed to the particular magician – and her belief, goal, or technique – rather than to her general 'theory'. The standards of successful practice are so high that they are impossible to meet. Magic is said to work in situations of flux, not fixed reality. And some failure of ritual is needed to support the image of magic as a testable activity, so that the occasional dramatic non-achievement of a ritual goal need never damage a conviction of magic's efficacy. Magicians do not confront the spectre of constant failure. They banish it. And because these explanations focus on technique, they appear to be more or less independent of the organized ideas of the practice. That is, they appear to suggest that the ideas are consistently tested and not disconfirmed. If the only failure occurs when the beaker is broken, the failed experiment never disconfirms the theory.

The intriguing aspect of the magician's development of this evidence-seeking skill is that practitioners usually feel that they are being discriminating. They have criteria that could conceivably allow them to interpret any ritual as effective, and a way of explaining away the failure of any rite. This would seem to make nonsense of any account of testing, which requires at least the possibility of failure. But because criteria do exist, because magicians identify unsuccessful rites as well as successful ones, and because failure always remains a possibility, the magician is often satisfied that he has tested some theory to that theory's favour. The tendencies which seem to warp his perception of the rite's effects – the mnemonic and attributional inclinations, criterial freedom, the endogeneous creation of experimenter-produced evidence – seem to arise very naturally, from common human tendencies and from the loopholes in complex methodology.

---

[22] Starhawk (1979: 113). [23] Starhawk (1979: 113).
[24] Farrar and Farrar (1984: 110).

It is not, after all, surprising that magicians sometimes think of themselves as stern, successful experimentalists. They do have a history of 'experimental' success, in that they see considerable evidence for the efficacy of their rites. When a ritual goal is met, it is undeniably met, and magicians are no different from anyone else in remembering notable success. When the magician is struck by a remarkable coincidence, it is hard to blame contingency rather than cause when a putative cause goes begging. Personal experiences of a tarot reading or a ritual are often dramatic and persuasive, and by their uniqueness – they seem unusual, striking, remarkable – they remain in the memory, and call for explanation. Magicians also assert their unwillingness to accept magical interpretations without examination. In no group was I ever asked to make an assertion of belief: the basic attitude was that you took nothing on faith, but you experimented with the practice, and eventually you would conclude on the basis of personal practice, that the magical ideas were probably correct. This attitude is constantly reiterated: 'In my fifteen years of contact with these groups I was never asked to *believe* in anything.'[25] Manuals commonly press the need for scepticism before intellectual commitment: 'I do not offer [this model of how spells work] as "proof" that magic works – nor do I want to convince anyone to drop their doubts. (Sceptics make better magicians.)'[26] 'As an occultist I am committed to a number of beliefs which you probably do not share . . . Now, nearing the end of the book, I propose to give this esotericism full play for a little while. Whether you accept a word of it is a matter for yourself.'[27] Many magicians retain some of the scepticism. But most of them could cite startling 'synchronicities'[28], lateral effects, dramatic cures, insightful tarot card readings. They acted and spoke as if their practice had persuaded them of the merit in the magic out of a position of initial scepticism. And yet – it was not so much that the ideas were being *tested*, but that they were being *used*.

In the process magicians develop a particular style of marking certain events in experience's flow as significant, and remembering them as important and related to other events. A friend's fight has a new significance after a Mars ritual, with Mars' bellicose associations, and rather than sinking out of existence into the forest mulch of memory, the fight becomes a significant, noticeable item, a *capiton* to anchor memory's shifting nexus. Magicians begin to pay attention in different ways, to different things, motivated by the desire for confirmation but with no aim of self-deceit. And because the apparent successes of past ritual confer confidence in future rituals, pattern-drawing is self-perpetuating. The desire to find ritual effects presents a hermeneutic challenge: magicians become skilled interpreters of symbolic association, and learn to anticipate these unfolding patterns in their lives.

[25] Adler (1979: 20).   [26] Starhawk (1979: 112).   [27] Brennan (1979: 101).
[28] 'Synchronicities', as the term is used in modern magic, are two events which happen more or less at the same time, which have no direct causal connection, but arise because of some common underlying cause. If a magician chose an arbitrary date for a conference on, say menstruation and the moon, and the date turned out to be astrologically significant, this would be called a 'synchronicity'. The one event did not cause the other, but they were interconnected in some larger plan. The term is borrowed from Jung.

Since Simonides reconstructed the list of dinner guests crushed under fallen rubble by remembering the order in which they sat around the table, people have been aware that what you remember depends on particular mental activities. Simonides – and Cicero, Matteo Ricci, and Giordano Bruno – practised the classical art of memory, in which the subject to be memorized was associated with a visual pattern.[29] The study of memory has produced complex, debated results, but nevertheless it seems clear that people remember selectively, that dramatic incidents are more memorable than others, and that the selective memory is often structured by a 'script' or pattern. Certainly people seem to remember information pertinent to their own activity. 'Everybody who is skilled at anything necessarily has a good memory for whatever information that activity demands.'[30] Magicians become skilled at magic. They learn to mark certain incidents as significant and memorable, and to do so in a manner that persuades them that when they have performed rituals, the rituals have worked, and thus that the practice, and the ideas behind it, are valid.

[29] Yates (1966) is the most detailed account of the classical art of memory; Spence (1983) provides an intriguing account of one of its practitioners.

[30] Neisser (1982: 17).

11

Astrology and the tarot: acquiring common knowledge

L IKE most specialists, magicians have a rich body of knowledge at their command. And as the new understanding of evidence changes the magician's way of seeing patterns and connections between events, acquiring this knowledge changes the magician's ability to discriminate between events, the models he uses to associate one event to another, and the interest he takes in a subject. This new knowledge substantially contributes to his drift away from some previous interpretive manner, some other way of making sense of his world, to which non-magicians do not have access.

When magicians become magicians, when they read magician's books, arrange and perform rituals and talk about them afterwards, they acquire a vast amount of knowledge. They learn about mythology, about astrology, kabbalah and tarot, about seventeenth century Gaelic cures. They learn about the moon, and when it waxes and wanes, with which gods it is associated: these are the facts, the information, the content of learning. I call this 'knowledge' because it is learnt, and because what is learnt is conventionally accepted as knowledge among magicians. This is slightly tricky, because the type of convention and the nature of empirical 'truth' to which it appeals is ambiguous. Many non-magicians, for instance, would not countenance magic as a body of justified true belief. Moreover, that silver is associated with the moon is a piece of magical knowledge, but different magicians have different conceptions of 'the moon' – it is a deity, a planet, a concept, a sort of psychic energy – and what it means to be 'associated with' it.

The ambiguity is part of my point. This knowledge, common knowledge, consists in the sort of remark you can make to a group which they easily accept as valid – and do not necessarily analyse. Clifford Geertz describes common sense as what the mind filled with presuppositions concludes.[1] Common

---

[1] Geertz (1983: 84). This is not to say that there is not a commonsense-ness to the business of being a magician. In ways, what this chapter describes is the emergence of a type of commonsense particular to magic – the sort of practical, taken-for-granted, down-to-earth judgements about events. The purpose of this part is to describe some of the intellectual parameters which alter as magic becomes commonsensical for them, as it starts to play a role in people's evaluation of their lives. The implication of this treatment of specialist knowledge as a type of commonsense is also an implication of Geertz's essay. The unsystematized thinking characteristic of commonsense in Geertz's sense is also characteristic of people engaged in specialist disciplines: the speciality may have an articulated systematization (this is more true of a speciality like biochemistry than of magic), but (again to differing extents) people may think in a commonsense way within the boundaries of the discipline.

knowledge, which is a little different, is part of the packing of the presupposition-filled mind, not a set of theoretical assumptions or conclusions, but a set of more or less common terms of reference. This common knowledge is not so much a body of precise facts which all magicians know and assume that other magicians also know, but something fuzzier: information, associations and symbols taken for granted in a conversation. It is not as if the magician acquires one lump set of shared information that all magicians possess. Rather, it is common to encounter certain types of information in conversations and in magician's books, and the conversations seem to assume that this information does not need elaborate explanation.

Ambiguous as the common knowledge might be, it is quite crucial for magicians, for it provides them with the tools for insight. Much of this common knowledge consists in organized sets of symbols, myths, and ideas: the tarot, astrology, the classical myths. These complex sets allow their users to distinguish between two people, or events or thoughts: she is like the tarot's Empress, calm and fecund, he has the mercurial temperament of a Hermes. Learning this knowledge is part of what makes the magic so exciting, for the new magician gains mastery over these complex sets, develops skill in using them and talking about them with others, and most significantly is able to illuminate areas of his own life with their subtlety. Memories of loss and transition become Persephone-like trials, menstrual pains become Erishkigaal's challenge. Magicians argue together with the pleasurable grasp of complex detail, as participants debate over Saturn's effect on Uranus and the implications of a newly discovered planet-like mass for astrological analysis. Common knowledge provides the ground for ordinary intellectual creativity, a language to describe events that other magicians will understand, and a way of characterizing events which make them rich and complex for their participants. Consider the following description of a Western Mysteries initiation:

Enoch: Let's talk over some salient points first. In general there seemed to be an awful lot of activity in the north, in the east as well to some extent but principally in the north. We had in the north a certain inertial resistant force and also, as far as we can tell, the presence of an awful lot of helpful inner plane activity. We had a Master Serapis knocking about, and we had also an influence left over from some work done earlier in the lodge, which the new initiate was not aware of. Perhaps it's a good time to point out, for her benefit, that it just so happened that earlier on that day we were asked by the Greater Mysteries to lend them our room so that they could do a requiem for one of their own people who'd just – left. I think 'passed on' is the right term. I loath the term, I won't use it. She'd gone, you know – left. Shuffled off this mortal coil at the age of ninety-three, after a long and inevitably involved life in the Mysteries, because people who get involved in the Mysteries inevitably have an involved life, it goes on and on and it won't stop. Anyway, it finally escaped and they decided to do a requiem and they said, can we please use your temple? And we said, yes you can use our temple, of course you can use our temple, you know, we think you're terrific. (Laughter).

The shared understanding that rituals involve non-material entities, that different 'energies' accumulate at the different directions, that death is only the name for a complex transition into another form of being – all this provides the ground on which a detailed description can be built. Jokes rely on shared knowledge and assumptions: Enoch's joke is funny because the unrepentant schoolboy adulation caricatures – without deriding – the solemn respect which initiates gives to these highly evolved spiritual guardians.

One consequence of this specialist's common knowledge, perhaps evident from the quotation, is that magic involves statements which are meaningless to outsiders but quite debatable to those inside. For example, 'blue is a good colour for success'. Magicians happily argue over whether business prosperity is more properly associated with Mercury (orange) or with Jupiter (blue). They discuss whether the witches' altar should stand in the middle of the circle or at its side. They argue within the boundaries of magical ideas; the value of talking about astrology sinks out of sight as a questionable problem. Outsiders miss the reference, even the structure, of the debate. The interested newcomer, tentatively prepared to accept the explicit ideas, learns to argue with the experienced, and in learning, slowly finds, by trial and error, the structure which gives it content.[2] This structure of course comprises many elements – the assumptions and associations within the conversation as well as the fact that the terms of the conversation refer to knowledge unknown to the uninitiated. These different elements are difficult to disentangle: one could probably argue that they are not separable. But the gap between the magician's and the non-magician's common knowledge makes the magician's unintelligibility particularly clear.

The sort of common knowledge background that lies behind statements like 'silver is a good colour for inspiration' includes many elements. Such a statement often hinges on the assumption that ritual actions produce results. But leaving that assumption aside, the statement rests on certain 'facts', or on fact-like knowledge of the conventional system of symbolic correspondences. 'Conventional' of course means established within this group, the 'common knowledge' of the magical subculture. Magicians know a good deal about

---

[2] Hacking (1982) and Taylor (1982) both discuss ways in which certain styles of reasoning, or ways of talking about events, create historical and cultural divides. Taylor's concern is primarily to distinguish between the 'rich' concept of rationality which describes a contemporary, science-dominated community, and an attunement-oriented pre-scientific world-view, redolent of symbolic sympathies. He discusses the incompatibility of these two, and even defines them as incommensurable, but does not conclude that the incommensurability of a different way of talking about events means that an interpreter is precluded from understanding them both. Hacking goes farther: the translation of a sentence – this is short for 'understanding' or 'intelligibility' – depends on having certain ways to reason about it. He concludes that to some extent one cannot compare alternative systems of reasoning. Without addressing that final assertion, one can ask what would denote a 'style' of reasoning – an issue Hacking skates over quickly (1982: 49–51). One obvious part of the style of reasoning is common knowledge, the references that make a magician's conversation not only confusing but unintelligible to the outsider. Common knowledge is not difficult for an outsider to obtain, after some work. Other elements are the pattern-finding, evidence-defining tendencies, and the assumptions hidden in the practice, though these are not all that the term 'style' might include. As a tight philosophical concept, 'style' faces some difficulties. But were one to want to flesh it out, these would be some of its characteristics.

various conceptions of magic, about various magicians, about bits of myth and folklore associated with Halloween, toads and Aleister Crowley. They also more or less agree that various divinatory systems work (or at least that they offer important insights), and they tend to know a fair amount about astrology, kabbalah and tarot, and about the existence of – if not the nature of – the I Ching, the runes, and palmistry. But what it is to know these matters is a complex issue, for it involves gaining access to information, knowing where it is stored, and knowing how to use it. Here I shall discuss, briefly, two common magical involvements, tarot and astrology, with which most magicians are quite comfortable. And for most magicians, the remark about silver would draw from at least those two areas.

All magicians know something about astrology. This is not of course unusual: a good many people know something about astrology. Every year more newspapers carry horoscopes, more books on astrology are printed and sold in ordinary bookshops. England even has a dial-the-stars number, your horoscope at the end of a push button phone.[3] But many horoscope watchers know little beyond the general characteristics of their own personal birth sign. A non-magical Piscean might know that Pisceans are poetic, imaginative people, but lack much sense of what Cancerians are meant to be. Magicians usually know a little more.[4]

Astrology assumes that the position of planets at the hour of your birth will have a significant impact on your personality and upon the direction and outcome of your life. Astrologers draw up 'charts' which describe the position of planets in the sky at the exact moment of your birth in relation to a band of constellations (the zodiacal signs) and to the horizon.[5] Each planet, sign, and house (the sky is divided into a discrete number of areas called 'houses', determined by the rising sun[6]) is associated with certain characteristics. The 'real' meaning of any particular element of the chart, however, arises only in relation to its other elements. The planet Jupiter, for example, generally concerns worldly success and material satisfaction. An astrologer might say that if Jupiter were found in the second house, realm of domestic affairs, it would mean that your lodgings would always be handsome, whereas if it were found in the ninth house, realm of worldly relations, it might betoken fame. Each of these interpretations, however, would be affected by other planets with which the planet was 'aspected' (with which, in other words, it forms an arithmetically neat geometric relationship), and by the chart as a whole. As a result, interpretations can grow exceedingly complex, and chart interpretations often

---

[3] This is a British Telecom service. It is not operable at all times.

[4] Astrology is a practice with a long past indeed. The Mayans, Chaldeans, Babylonians – until relatively recently, astrology was not distinct from astronomy, and the sky loomed large to those in the pre-electric world. Cumont (1960 [1912]) provides a succinct account of the early astrologer-astronomers.

[5] There are many reference books on astrology. One basic, if rather ancient, one is M. E. Jones (1977 [1941]).

[6] There are at least two methods of determining the astrological houses, but the basic conception of the house is the division of the sky by directional coordinates.

run on for twenty pages. And any particular interpretation is always qualified with the understanding that it is always partial and may be wrong, for it is impossible to consider any chart in its full complexity.

It may be useful to provide a sense of this complexity. Liz Greene is a well known, well-respected author often read by magicians. This passage, on Saturn, is excerpted from a book entirely devoted to that planet and its effects.

No interpretation of Saturn by sign, house or aspect can be complete, of course, since it is necessary to synthesize these elements and align them with the combination of Sun, Moon and Ascendant first of all, corresponding with the individual's conscious expression, his unconscious or instinctual reactions, and his behavioral patterns. These isolated factors in combination with Saturn become the spinal column of the natal chart from the point of view of character. They will in a very concise manner shed light on what the individual wants (the Sun), what he needs (the Moon), the style in which he goes about getting these things (the Ascendant), and the thing within the man which

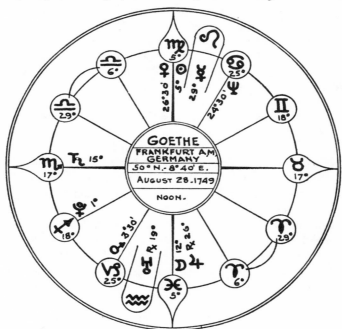

Figure 7   The astrologer who cast this chart points to its 'water-sign' emphasis: Neptune in Cancer, Saturn in Scorpio and the moon in Pisces. These planets form a geometric relationship known as a 'grand trine'. In astrology water is an indication of emotional, diffuse, poetic, universal concerns. A grand trine in water signs is evidence of 'a particularly intensive struggle for universal harmony'. Neptune is the key to the chart, according to the astrologer, because of its relationship to the other planets. 'The planet, which indicates the extreme sense of social obligation in any life, is here found in the self-centred sign Cancer, giving every benefit from Cancer's emphasis on inner growth, and in the eighth house, where the rulership of regeneration, self-reconstitution and rediscovery is a clear indication of the special creative quality which Goethe exhibited in writing Faust'.

causes him either to fail or to be dissatisfied once he has achieved his Desire (Saturn). This is, of course, grossly simplified, and entire volumes could be filled on all the known meanings of the Moon alone; however, from this relationship of four factors – and every trinity must in the end be integrated by a fourth factor, a psychological as well as an esoteric law – we may gain insight into the meat of the individual struggle towards greater consciousness indicated on every birth chart. There is no chart which does not contain Saturn, however dignified and admirably aspected he may be, and there is no life without struggle.[7]

Greene's book provides descriptions of Saturn's influence and interaction with other planets and with the houses of the astrological chart. Saturn is struggle, restriction, the teacher and the disciplinarian, but the individual's experience of and response to limitations will be unique, and uniquely represented in his chart. The astrologer has a quite considerable quantity of data to work with, and many books to consult; the learned astrologer has read many books indeed, and speaks knowledgeably upon the complexity of these planetary interactions. Yet even at his most knowledgeable he can, like the psychoanalyst, still claim that the personality expressed in any one chart is overdetermined and under-interpreted.

Less than half the magicians I knew could draw up an astrological chart, a task which requires a certain amount of arithmetical plotting and whose technique is relatively difficult to pick up casually from conversations about the topic. Most, however, could make stabs at interpreting a chart, and nearly all would know the various associations of planets and zodiacal signs – the former because they are part of the essential working tools of magic, the latter because they come up all the time in conversation. 'Be warned – she's a Leo squared' (the high priestess of my coven joking about another woman); 'it's my Virgoan moon that makes me obsessed with food' (Angel, a member of the Glittering Sword). The planets are the core of the correspondences with which magic is filled. Astrological charts are sufficiently important that as soon as I appeared on the occult scene, my astrological chart was drawn up separately by at least three people and discussed extensively as an indication of my character and my ability to embark upon the project I had outlined.

That the sun is associated with benevolence, Saturn with rigidity and gloom – these are the sorts of things most magicians know through their conversations and their participation in ritual. They also learn, and this is crucial, where to look up further associations, 'correspondences', so that they can make use of them in ritual. These reference texts are not always – even often – teaching manuals: one of the most famous, Crowley's *777* is simply a collation of lists. Other examples include Fortune's *Mystical Qabalah*, Highfield's *Book of Celestial Images*, Knight's *A Practical Guide to Qabalistic Symbolism*, Williams's *Herbs, Incense and Candle Magic*. Some general manuals include excellent reference sources, as Budapest *The Holy Book of Women's Mysteries*, Huson *Mastering Witchcraft*, King and Skinner *Techniques of High Magic*. Starhawk appends a 'Table of Correspondences' to her text. For the moon, she lists these attributes:

[7] Greene (1976: 15–16).

MOON

Rules: women; cycles; birth; generations; inspiration; poetry; emotions; travel, especially by water; the sea and tides; fertility; rain; intuition; psychic ability; secrets.

new or crescent moon: the Maiden, birth and initiation, virginity, beginnings, the hunt.

full moon: the Mother, growth, fulfilment, sexuality, maturation, nurturing, love.

waning or dark moon: the Crone, the woman past menopause, old age, deep secrets, wisdom, divination, prophecy, death and resurrection, endings.

day: Monday
element: water
colour: new   white or silver
       full   red or green
       waning   black
sign of the zodiac: Cancer
tone: ti
letter: s
number: 3 or 9
jewel: moonstone, pearl, quartz, rock crystal.
kabbalistic sphere: 9 Yesod – Foundation.
angel: Gabriel
incense: bay leaf, ginseng, jasmine, myrtle or poppy.
plants: banana, cabbage, chickweed, cucumber, leafy vegetables, lotus, melons, mushrooms, myrtle, opium poppy, pumpkin, purslane, sea holly, seaweed, watercress, wild rose, winter green.
tree: willow
animal: hare, elephant, cat.
goddesses: Artemis, Brigit, Brizo, Cerridwen, Diana, Hathor, Isis, Hecate, Levanah, Lunah, Mari, Nimue, Pasiphaë, Phoebe, Selene, Anna.
    new   Artemis, Nimuë
    full   Diana, Hecate
    waning   Hecate, Anna
gods: Atlas, Khnosu, Sin.
And for Jupiter:

JUPITER

Rules: leadership, politics, power, honour, royalty, public acclaim, responsibility, wealth, business, success.

day: Thursday
element: air, fire
colour: deep purple, royal blue
signs: Sagittarius
tone: so, A
letter: d
number: 5 or 4
metal: tin
jewel: amethyst, chrysolite, sapphire, or turquoise
kabbalistic sphere: 4 Chesed – Mercy
angel: Tzadkiel
incense: cedar, nutmeg

plants: agrimony, anise, ash, balm, betony, blood root, borage, cinquefoil, clover, dandelion, hyssop, linden, mint, mistletoe, nutmeg, sage.
tree: oak, olive or terebinth
animal: unicorn
goddesses: Isis, Hera, Juno, Themis
gods: Bel, Eurymedon, Jupiter, Marduk, Thor, Zeus.[8]

Different magicians will know some, but not all, of these associations before they turn to the text, and they will find some, but not all, of them useful. Perhaps I might take myself as an example. As an anthropologist of magic I have read a great many magical books, but I have read them for their tone and not their content, and I have not referred to them extensively for ritual use. Thus my knowledge of the moon, say, might not be dramatically unusual for a first-year initiate. When I looked at the above list at the end of my year's research, I had known, through reading and conversation, that the moon was to do with women, intuition, water, and the secretive, mystical, psychical mind. I knew of the tripartite division of the moon and its associations; this is one of the first things I learnt in magic. I had known of the moon's association with water, with Monday, with nine, three, silver and purple and with the kabbalistic Yesod. The connection of red and green to the full moon was new to me; I suspect Starhawk of 'discovering' this association through her meditation. I knew little of the rest. Few of the associations to plants and incenses were familiar, though I possess magical reference books to look them up. I knew some of the suitable gods but not all, and would have made the connection to none of the gods. And yet again, I have other books which list such matches. A magician of my knowledge would turn to Starhawk's list and to other reference books when he had decided to do a ritual about the moon, or with the moon as the central symbolic focus, and if he needed suggestions for suitable incenses to burn and goddesses to invoke.

To move on to the tarot, tarot cards have been a part of European culture since at least the fourteenth century. As it has come to be established, the pack resembles common playing cards, with an additional court card and twenty-two further cards, the 'major arcana', or 'greater trumps'. These additional cards have images, elaborate pictures numbered sequentially from 0 to 21, which represent the panoply of human experience: they are the fool, the high priestess, the magician, death, justice, the sun, etc. The greater trumps are said to be the more important and significant of the cards, but all have divinatory value. Each of the seventy-eight cards has a 'meaning'; it is, in addition, associated with a planet, zodiacal sign, kabbalistic element, and the like. Magicians use them for divination and as a focus for meditation, and they say that the more meditation they do, the better the divination becomes.[9] (figures 8 and 9).

---

[8] Starhawk (1979: 204–8).
[9] There is no reference to European playing cards before 1377, where there are four – in Florence, Paris, Basle and Sienna. These, however, probably refer to the ordinary pack of playing cards, which came to Europe out of the Islamic world. Tarot cards themselves seem to have been a European invention (or so recent scholarship argues). Many books cite 1392 for the earliest

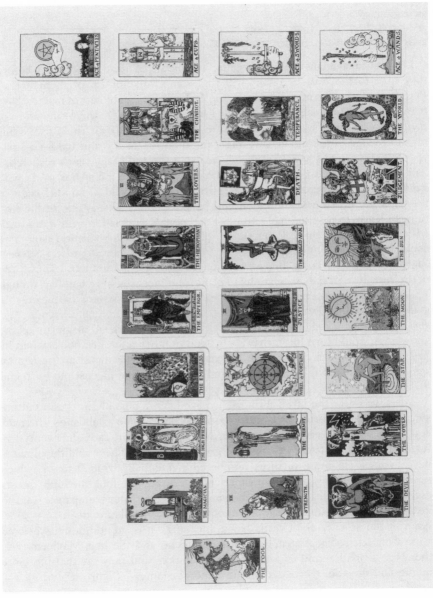

Figure 8   The major arcana and the four aces from the popular Rider-Waite tarot deck. The cards were designed by Pamela Coleman Smith under the direction of one of the Golden Dawn magicians, Arthur Edward Waite.

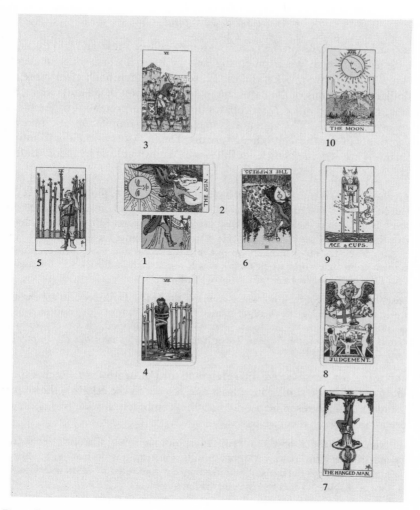

Figure 9 *There are many ways to spread and read tarot cards for the purposes of divination. The ten-card spread is particularly popular, and while each reader tends to have an idiosyncratic understanding of the proper way to read the individual positions, the following method is generally accepted. 1) This card represents the querent and the atmosphere in which he currently works and lives; 2) This, the 'block', reveals the obstacle or challenge with which the querent now struggles, or will shortly struggle; 3) This card represents either the final goal or destiny of the querent, or the 'gift' with which he was born; 4) If the third card is read as the gift, this card is interpreted as the final goal; if the third card is read as the final goal, this card is seen as the final past foundation of the querent's current situation; 5) This card represents recent past events which have a bearing on the current situation; 6) This card alludes to the influences which will shortly emerge to influence the querent's position. The first six cards are read as a set; the reader then turns to the last four for a more specific elaboration of the query posed. 7) This card represents the querent, revealed in his proper perspective with respect to his current circumstances; 8) This card displays the environmental factors which surround the querent – the way he affects and is affected by the people around him; 9) This card reveals the inner emotions of the querent, the emotional secrets he hides from others and perhaps even from himself; 10) The final result: the card displays the eventual result pertinent to the querent's concern, should his current circumstances remain unaltered.*

There are many books on the tarot. Beginners collect a few, and leaf through them, consulting them when practising and perhaps reading them in depth once they have a sense of what the cards are about. Each book gives more or less similar descriptions of the cards, but they will vary on detail and emphasis. One text, Butler's *Definitive Tarot* collates the basic interpretations of the more famous occult schools. The appended chart gives his compilation of (abbreviated) accounts of the thirteenth major arcana, Death. Most of the contributors and positions are – to the knowledgeable – well-known at least by name. Butler himself describes the Fool:

Among other legendary meanings he is the self at the beginning of the journey, he is the fool who has lost his wits, the fool who has, with divine wisdom, abandoned them for something better. He is the trickster whose practical jokes never quite come off, he is Punch or Reynard the Fox or Harlequin. He is the stupid brother (or sister) left at home in the ashes when his older brothers go out into the world and who must eventually rescue them from that world when their wit will not stretch as far as his cunning or kindness. Do you remember the fairy tales of the fool?

In a sense it is the spirit of the Fool which animates the entire Tarot deck. In the earliest deck he is shown towering over midget human figures, a Giant of Folly and of super-rational sanity. It is with his madness, that of the Fool of God, that the cards are illuminated; for in any reading of the Tarot it is the Fool who asks and the Fool who answers every question.[10]

The following list gives varied interpretations of the death card. Each expert gives accounts that are similar in at least one respect to the others – they have, as is said, a family resemblance – but they embrace a wide variation of interpretations among themselves:

Case: Nun, meaning fish. As a verb, to sprout or grow. Fertility, fecundity, productiveness, generative power. Motion, to walk. Change, transformation, modification, variation. Change as the basis of modification. Scorpio ruled by Mars with Uranus exalted. Greenish-blue, G natural. Imaginative intelligence.

Christian: Creation, destruction and renewal. The ascent of the spirit into the divine

mention of the tarot cards, a remark in Charles VI's account books that a man called Gringonneur had painted three packs of cards in gilt; a pack of tarot cards now in the Bibliothèque Nationale was thought to be the reference of the citation. However, these seem to be a fifteenth century pack of Italian workmanship. According to Dummett, the earliest reliable reference is in 1442, from the d'Este court at Ferrarra, in Italy. The most complete pack of these early hand-painted cards is the fifteenth century Visconti-Sforza pack, now divided between the Pierpont Morgan Library in New York, the Accademia Carrarra in Bergama and the private collection of the Colleoni family in the same city. Seventy four cards survive.

'Tarot' is the French adaptation of the Italian name of the cards – tarocchi, or (in the singular) tarocco. There is no known etymology for the term, although some (Kaplan 1972: 32) have suggested that it derives from the plaid backs of the early cards (tarotée).

The tarot became incorporated into occult practice in the nineteenth century with Éliphas Lévi's publications, occult works which claimed to see in the tarot the most primitive and profound sources of knowledge. There is no evidence for the gypsies' use of tarot cards for fortune-telling until the twentieth century; fortune-tellers they certainly were, but palmistry seems to have been their preferred medium. See Dummett (1980), a massive scholarly tome on the tarot as a card game; also Kaplan (1972) and Hargrave (1966 [1930]).

[10] Butler (1975: 109–10).

spheres. The transformation of human nature upon reaching the end of its organic period.

Crowley: Fish. Scorpio, water. Mars ruling water. Imaginative intelligence. Death. Green-blue. Typhon. Khephra. Kundalini. Ares. Mars, scorpion, beetle, lobster or crayfish, wolf. Cactus, snakestone. His magical weapon is the pain of the obligation. His perfumes are Siamese benzoin, opoponax. His magical power is necromancy. His geomantic sign is rubeus. The Child of the Great Transformers. The Lord of the Gates of Death. Transformation, change (voluntary or involuntary), logical development of existing condition, but perhaps sudden and unexpected. Apparent death or destruction.

Douglas: Major change, perhaps apparently by chance, which is the logical result of what has gone before. A clean sweep necessary for further growth.

Gray: Transformation, change, destruction followed by rebirth. Disaster, revolution, or other forms of violent change. Negative meanings imply stagnation, lack of change.

Golden Dawn: The sovereignty and result of victory. Sol acting through Scorpio upon Venus, Osiris under the destroying power of Typhon affecting Venus. The Child of the Great Transformers, Lord of the Gates of Death. Time, ages, transformation, change involuntary. Sometimes, but rarely, death and destruction.

Grimaud: Symbol of movement and steady advance. Death. The end of something. Illness or shock but a fatal outcome can be avoided. Can mean death whose effects do not stop at death alone, but continue beyond in evil deeds.

Huson: Death, literally. Profound change in the psyche. The initiate stripped of masks.

Kahn: Elements of sudden change common to other writers, but also the interpretation of escape from danger, escape from a tricky legal situation, escape from some kind of imprisonment, escape from the persecutions of parts of the Querent's unconscious mind. Change and liberation.

Kaplan: As Eden Gray plus the literal meaning of Death.

Knight: Literal plus regeneration of life force.

Lind: Death of the old, ridding oneself of fleshly desires.

Mathers: Death, change, transformation, alteration for the worse. Death just escaped, partial change, transformation for the better.

Mayananda: Transformation. Death and resurrection, reincarnation. The dark night of the soul.

Papus: Mem, a woman, the companion of man. Being in unlimited space. Destruction preceding or following regeneration.

Sadhu: Mem, a woman. No astrological sign. Immortality and permanency in the Essence (God). Transmutation of forces. Death and reincarnation.

Thierens: Saturn. Otherwise similar to Waite and Papus.

Ussher: The frontier between time and eternity, future and past. Mem, meaning water.

Waite: Change, transformation and passage from lower to higher. End, mortality, destruction, the loss of a benefactor for a man, many contrarieties for a woman, failure of marriage projects for a maid. Inertia, sleep, lethargy, petrification, somnambulism, hope destroyed.

Suggested [Butler]: Death in all forms. Resurrection is not in this card except in the sense. 'You die that you may live'. But if the resurrection comes at all it is in another card: perhaps Ace of Wands. The Fool, Judgement, Seven of Swords, Three, Six of Seven of Cups, Ace or Eight of Pentacles.[11]

The intriguing feature is the degree to which these apparently authoritative

[11]Butler (1975: 159–62).

interpretations differ, while yet remaining within limits. Death is always a card of transformation and change, even though to one authority the card means initiation and to another, a sudden stroke. With individuals, this diversity within constraints is even clearer.

Magicians do not randomly choose meanings for the cards. They read books and talk to other magicians and gradually develop the 'feel' of the cards. Then, they organize their own interpretations. They grasp what might best be called the 'sense' of the card, or the sense that it makes for them, and they interpret the pattern which they see in a spread of cards in some way that retains this sense. By 'sense' I mean a fuzzy, often unverbalized awareness of what the card 'means', how it can be used in giving an interpretation or reading to another person. That is, when magicians give a 'reading' – when they interpret ten cards placed in a set pattern by the person who wants their future told – they produce a coherent narration that draws upon some – but not all – of their multiple associations to each of the cards, in ways that do not violate the general thrust of those associations. Practitioners repeatedly tell you that only your own interpretation is valid for you: that you must learn to use the cards as a language to speak to your own unconscious, and whatever particular meaning that they have is valid if that meaning speaks to you. 'Don't worry if the symbols you choose are not to be found in any book, or do not seem to agree with written information. What feels right to you is best, no matter what anyone else may say'.[12]

The point is that these interpretations will stay within roughly demarcated boundaries. The magician feels comfortable with the card, feels as if he can recognize it hermeneutically, feels like a skilled interpreter of its meaning. These recognitions and the criteria on which he rests his skill evoke his former acquaintance with the card, and what others have said about it. Idiosyncrasy is possible only within convention. The shared conventions form the shadowy substance of this sense of meaning, and they are the common knowledge upon which interpretation rests.

These issues can be briefly illustrated by one of Knight's Greystone lectures on the tarot. In the 1983 December weekend people gathered for a series of lectures, pathworkings and rituals centered upon the tarot. In one of the early lectures, Knight discussed the historical background of the tarot trumps.

I think that [the trumps] were meditation symbols, because those of you who have read Francis Yates, talking about the interest that the Renaissance princes had in Hermetic literature and so on. It is thought that Botticelli, for instance, whose Primavera or Venus rising from the waves is in fact a meditation picture, that he was commissioned to do it for a magical society, for a group of nobles. Even the Pope was interested in magic, or at least one Pope. That's my view of them. Particularly as there are one or two paintings by Botticelli – there is one of Temperance, and I know that he was commissioned to do things like the Hanged Man. I don't think that the painting exists but I think it's on record that Botticelli was commissioned to do this. And it was actually the custom – this card is sometimes called, or originally called, the Traitor, because if you have been

[12] Green (1971: 43).

convicted of treachery against the state, or the city state, Florence and elsewhere, your effigy would be hung upside down from the city walls. And so that was one meaning of the Hanged Man. It certainly has other meanings as well. But we must not limit ourselves because we think that we have occult insight, and limit ourselves to our own favourite interpretation.

Court de Gebelin is quite amusing, because some Belgian card manufacturers got it wrong, and printed it that way up [i.e. upside down.] And Court de Gebelin said that that was the correct way, and that this card should be called Prudence, it's one of the virtues. It goes with three other cards, which includes Justice. This is Prudence, and he's about to put his foot in a puddle. (Laughter) So, someone capable of saying that, can you take him all that seriously when he says that it's an ancient hieroglyph? Well, this is the story of occultism through the ages, isn't it? It's a question of loonies, saying the right thing. (Laughter)

Lectures are a particularly good place to see the reliance upon common knowledge. Jokes are even better, for their force depends upon the unspoken. Here, Court de Gebelin's assertion that, in Knight's terms, the Hanged Man/ Prudence was about to step into a puddle was greeted with uproarious laughter because of the strength of the shared impression of the card's symbolic nature. To modern magicians and tarot-users, the card connotes learning through struggle, self-sacrifice, inner torment and possible self-defeat, Odin who hung himself from Yggdrasil for nine long nights and then received the wisdom of the runes. Odin is not coerced; his is a voluntary choice to undergo suffering in order to gain knowledge. While many tarot-users stress this interpretation, they often also cite the sense of failure in the card. The idea that the self-tortured figure should be about to step into a puddle seemed ludicrous in light of his solemnity and moreover violated the very point of the card: that the figure is bound, not free. The individual members of the lecture audience probably each treated the card differently in divination. Reading a meaning of initiation carries rather different meanings than one of struggle and defeat. But de Gebelin's interpretation is so far out that it became funny. It was particularly funny in light of Knight's admission of an early historical intepretation of the card, and his assertion that one's own interpretation is not necessarily correct. De Gebelin's was a reassuring example of an interpretation which is flagrantly wrong, because the anecdote reinforced the sense of a core meaning to the card.

The laughter at the end of the passage also drew upon this earlier joke. De Gebelin was defined as a 'loony': the Hanged Man is not Prudence, the tarot was created in medieval or Renaissance Europe, not in Egyptian antiquity. And yet, de Gebelin was not entirely foolish in his descriptions, and he recognized the tarot for what the audience thought it was: a repository of esoteric wisdom. The laughter sprang from the recognition of the central ambivalence of the magician's career, which is that non-magicians think them crazy, while they understand themselves to be gaining insight into hidden truths. Again, the laughter was reassuring: it was an acceptable admission of the knowledge that others think them foolish, and a denial of the importance of this fact. The jokes were only funny because of the audience's shared self-knowledge about their evaluation by non-magicians, about the connotations of the Hanged Man, and about the tacit boundaries which constrain the acceptable interpretations of the card.

Throughout his talk Knight constantly referred to scholarly authors and bibliographical information easily available to the audience. Most of the listeners knew who Frances Yates was, but few of them probably had read her books. The availability of her work was nevertheless important. The very existence of the scholarship provides the sense of historical depth that magicians find pleasing, as a later chapter details. The point of referring to them in a lecture is to identify and reiterate their existence as a resource for the magician. In fact, knowing that information is available is quite possibly considerably more important than having the correct information. The shared resources provide an external authority for Knight's account regardless of the validity of his attribution. The knowledge that information is available and has authority is as important as the information that is actually shared. It also provides for the magician a place to turn in order to describe tarot cards, develop pathworking, and write rituals. When the audience returned home at the end of the weekend, some of them would buy this material and use it for further reference.

What then is common knowledge? It seems to me that at least among magicians there are three components. What I have called common knowledge in this chapter involves shared knowledge of magic, shared knowledge of the resources from which one can find knowledge of magic, and shared acceptance of the tacit constraints within which personal knowledge of magic can claim an idiosyncratic realm.

Shared knowledge of magic is the shared information that one possesses about magic, and assumes that most other magicians will also possess. This includes the core pillars of the magical correspondences – the planets, the colours, the gods and goddesses – and knowledge of the structure of the correspondence charts, the sorts of things to which the core pillars are also compared – incense, days of the week, archangels. This is the basic knowledge of a given field, enough to give one the sense of its structure and to participate, minimally, in the conversations which inevitably arise about the subject. In astrology, this would mean knowing that planets, houses and zodiacal signs were used to 'draw up' a chart, and it would involve some notion of the significance of planets, signs and the like – enough to laugh when a friend is accused of being 'Scorpionic', although not necessarily enough to list the zodiacal signs in order. In tarot it would involve recognition of the tarot trumps and their crude meanings, the existence of the different suits and their associations, the way the cards are used for divination. This is part of the baggage that one acquires as a magician, the vocabulary terms of a conversation which no-one bothers to explain. They are, or are treated as, facts which most magicians are assumed to know.

Shared resources are also a feature of this commonality, one appreciated by a society overburdened with its own data, and the unchecked growth of computer-held knowledge. Few magicians memorize many of the elaborate sets of correspondences, the lists of incenses, god names and the like, and few know the lunar correspondences to the tarot pack, or its kabbalistic features. Yet all magicians use incenses and god-invocations in their rites, and search out 'correct' or 'valid' connections to their tarot spread. Knowing how to find such information quickly is far more efficient than learning it all in the first place, and magicians acquire correspondence charts and texts which list them easily, often at the back of the ritual text itself. This is an odd sort of knowledge, for people do not necessarily know such information, and yet it is so easily acquired that it works as if it were a shared body of information sufficiently structured to make its presence and nature easily and obviously available. It makes available so vastly greater an amount. The actual size and nature of this information resource seems better sketched than defined. For the general reader, the common knowledge available through shared resources is small enough to be quickly accessible to the newcomer, like the words contained in a dictionary (everyone knows that they should have a dictionary). It does not include articles in the newspaper because you are never sure that certain information will be there; nor does it include the books contained in the public library, for that pool is too large and its contents are too many. By this type of common knowledge, I mean to identify shared and simple access, the well-thumbed guides, the twenty books that magicians own or at least think that they 'ought' to own. These books change the context of knowledge by shaping the ease with which one moves around it.[13]

Shared constraints are much like shared information, but whereas the latter term implies content, the former term indicates category. Shared constraints are the sort of limits that would restrain a magician from understanding the Death card in the tarot deck as an embodiment of joy. A magician would have difficulty feeling skilled as a tarot card reader with such a definition, for it would violate many of the preconceptions, the shared information, which she would encounter upon entering. There is no logical reason for not deciding upon so idiosyncratic an interpretation, but it very rarely happens. The conventions are too strong, even though manuals explicitly demand idiosyncracy. Validity usually depends upon or at least is formed by convention to some extent, particularly when there are few other means to confirm the rightness of any interpretation. The tacit constraints of others tend to hold.

Through this common knowledge, magicians learn to discriminate between events in ways a non-magician cannot understand. When magicians speak within the territory bounded by shared knowledge, resources, and constraints, they sound foreign to those who have no sense of their subject because these things are assumed. The background of this common knowledge drops out of the conversation, and is not explained. Two magicians discussing whether Pluto has a Scorpionic impact when it appears opposite the ascendant do not bother to point out that planets can alter behaviour and that Scorpio is a zodiacal sign.

---

[13] Chapter 17 provides a list of such books.

After some reading and some preliminary conversations the newcomer starts to sound like a magician when he talks with them. He starts to use certain terms and make certain associations, to use common sources of information, to personalize his insights within certain boundaries. These books, terms and boundaries are not all explicitly taught. And different books have different information, and there are many interpretations of words like 'force'. But they share a crude commonality, rough contours of a mental geography, and while magicians may talk about the geography they rarely draw out a careful map.

The consequence is that magicians often make remarks and state propositions which are unsurprising or illuminating only to those who also inhabit this very specific realm of common knowledge. Those familiar with the domain can respond, but the outsider, unable to answer, may call the magician's language crazy. Remarks like 'I conjure thee, O Circle of Power' are bleak or embarrassing to the non-witch. To witches the statement does something. They may not agree about *what* it does, but the statement rests upon the convention that saying the words, under certain circumstances, makes the witch experience being inside a circle of power, whatever she imagines that circle to be. Remarks can be evaluated only upon the terrain marked out by magical knowledge. 'Thursday is a bad day for a love spell', 'sea rituals should be done only by the experienced'. These rituals presuppose a shared framework, in which love spells should be done under the influence of Venus (Friday) rather than Vulcan (Thursday), each of whom represents a way of feeling and is associated with a particular day, or a framework in which sea rituals are among the most dangerous or powerful of rites, in which rites and spells are certain sorts of things done in certain sorts of ways. A non-magician could argue that it is ridiculous to do spells; he could not argue that Thursday might be a good day for such a spell, on the grounds, say, that the day-associations are far less significant than the astrological associations in choosing a time for spell performances. To the extent that communication relies upon convention, the shifting set of common knowledge – and the shift in convention it entails – creates different possibilities for communicating, and to the extent that understanding depends upon knowledge, this common knowledge creates new possibilities for understanding.

12

Seeing patterns in the jumbled whole: becoming comfortable with new assumptions

S O FAR I have suggested that magicians experience two shifts in intellectual habits which alter the way they pay attention to events. One is that magicians begin to learn ways of identifying events as being connected to magical ritual, indeed as 'proof' that the ritual worked. The other is that they acquire the knowledge to allow them to discriminate between events in a 'magical' way. The third shift concerns the sort of assumptions with which people interpret their experience. Neophytes begin to rely on a set of rarely articulated and sometimes incoherent assumptions, assumptions that tend not to be challenged within magicians' discourse but might well be challenged outside. By this I do not mean clear premises, precise ontological propositions about the way magic works, but remarks made in conversation which imply some sort of uncommon assumption about the boundary between self and world. A magician will remark that your talisman will become charged with your power when you hold it during ritual. Learning how to become a magician involves taking that remark for granted. At some point the newcomer might find this magical discourse confusing, difficult to understand. By the time he becomes comfortable with it, he may forget why he found it initially confusing. His interpretive style has slowly shifted so that once meaningless remarks become sensible.

Such implicit assumptions are well worn channels, carved by training and experience, in the associative flow. They are habits of making connections and patterns in a jumbled world. Many of them are part of the theory of magic which magicians read about in books and occasionally discuss. But as they appear in magicians' conversations they are far looser than the word 'theory' seems to imply, and it is quite possible that they are not explicitly formulated in the magician's mind. It is more that by the time magicians think of themselves as 'understanding' magic, certain ways of drawing connections and talking about them are well-entrenched. Everything starts to 'make sense' from the magical point of view. It 'fits together', 'falls into place'. The magician now sounds like a magician when he talks to other practitioners, partly because these assumptions embedded in the discourse no longer trouble him.

In discussing assumptions in this way I am deliberately blurring the boundaries between rhetoric and ideology, and between implicit and explicit assumptions. I do so because I found it impossible to distinguish between the two; indeed I tried to write only on implicit assumptions but found that people too often slipped between talking as if something were so – although not perhaps 'really' intending to assert it – and articulating a conception. Sometimes magicians explicitly and deliberately listed what they called the 'theoretical assumptions' of their practice, as did the authors quoted at the end of the introduction to this section. Usually the people willing to make those assertions will also make remarks that imply that they held those assumptions. Co-practitioners listen to them and perhaps adopt the same style of description in their conversation: if they are forced to explain their views – by the inquisitive anthropologist, for example – they may produce the explicit assumption. But sometimes they do not. Nor is it clear that they would do so if not questioned. The tendency to talk as if a proposition were true, but nevertheless to deny it, becomes particularly prominent when magicians are confronted by the question whether they 'believe' in magic. Even with an explicit denial the fact that they talk in new ways implies that they notice and remark upon new aspects of events. Later chapters discuss the varying rationalizations which magicians make about the practice, and the metatheories used to justify their engagement. The point I am trying to make here is that after a series of conversations about magical ritual, the magician is often persuaded that the magical rituals have 'worked'; and this comes about partly because through his conversations he has begun to pay attention to some things and not to others. One of the elements instrumental in this changing focus of attention is that magicians usually talk as if they accepted certain assumptions about the world.

Because magicians move from initially being non-magicians into committed practice, they discuss the conceptions of their practice more readily than, say, a Christian might discuss the theoretical tenets of Christianity. Nevertheless, practitioners do not continually thrash out the assumptions which underlie their practice. They simply talk, and do not bother to explain the theoretical context of the discussion, which is in any event probably a little fuzzy in their minds. Even when discussing some magical tenets, they speak loosely in terms of others. As a result, to outsiders magical conversations can sometimes seem a little bizarre. This is apparent in the following discussion between practitioners – some novice, some very experienced – in a Western Mysteries meeting.[1] The discussion concerns the value of actually performing a ritual compared to merely imagining that it takes place, and the importance of 'sealing' it, doing a 'closing' ceremony at the end to mark its finish. This is called 'earthing': bringing the force, and its magicians, back into normal material reality. Participants argue vehemently, but while the argument seems to be about whether doing rituals is effective, most participants talk about the way that this

---

[1] This dialogue is taken from the same Western Mysteries meeting as described in the other two chapters. I am relying so heavily upon it because I have very few recorded sessions of conversation. This meeting was recorded for the group, which kindly allowed me to make use of the cassette.

takes place and speak as if they assume a layered universe filled with quasi-tangible forces. A discussion which seems to be about an axiom in fact does not challenge it.

Enoch: If you were purist about it, you'd say that on your own, there's really no justification for doing a physical ritual. You can do it on the astral, you can do it in your imagination, you can do it on the inner, why the dickens do you need to move the body if there's only one of you?

(Babble)

Martha: Yes, yes, it's the *earthing*.

Emma: That aspect.

Martha: The earthing, bringing it down. Bringing consciousness into this other place.

Emma: Otherwise it can stay on the astral. Yes. A talismanic earthing brings the forces of whatever the ritual was about, down to earth, and gives it a talismanic form. Makes it more actual.

Enoch: Even if it's only one person?

Martha/Emma: Yes. Certainly. Yes.

Martha: Enoch, if that wasn't so, then there's no purpose, for me, in having body. I started getting around this when I was about seventeen, because I couldn't understand this, why I'd got a body, because it seemed in the way, so I thought, well, if it's in the way there must be a damned good reason it's here. Which is another way of saying – that the purpose of the existence of all this – I've called it a lot of different things, actually, and I'll be quoting myself – is to make it all, to reconsecrate it all, to make it conscious, to spiritualize the physical, to bring what we perhaps rather crudely call higher levels of consciousness right through into the physical universe.

Philip: What is ritual? Surely if you seal, if you do a meditation, surely it would be advisable, I would think, to clean an area, to seal an area, and to do the med inside.

Enoch: Why do you think that?

Philip: Well, I think that it seals the area from outside influences. Some of us do tend to draw external influences towards us and –

Enoch: You're talking about unseen entities, and things like that.

Martha: Yes.

Philip: Yes, yes, there are bugs that crawl out on the astral plane and what-not.

Enoch: So you figure that going around and doing some pentagrams or a circle or something actually makes a difference to such entities, that –

Philip: Well, I don't know about that. What I would suggest is that if you do some pentagrams, similar as we use for sealing in the temple, and we open up – we clear a space for ourselves, and we do our meditation in that, I think that the meditation is more effective and I think that it has an effective earth in us, to get our concepts down from these – what's the word I want? abstract concepts into a physical earthing.

Enoch: You're talking about in some way anchoring the thing to your own physical nature. You're talking about earthing. Peter, what do you think about what he's saying?

Peter: Well, I don't know. I tend not to do any ritual [apart from the group]. I just do the meditation [the group leader suggests daily meditation], and the grounding, to me, is the writing of it down.

Enoch: Right.

Peter: But, I haven't tried the other way, and if I did, I might find, you know, that it was helpful.

Enoch: You think what they're saying is reasonably sensible? Does it seem real to you, this notion that, this earthing idea, that goes around and sort of –

Peter: Yes.

Enoch: Ritual gesture, you're earthing –

Peter: Some kind of earthing is necessary, but even just writing down is an earthing . . .

Nigel: [But] it's possible to do something wrong, to do the pentagram the wrong way round or something, by mistake.

Enoch: What would happen if you did a pentagram the wrong way around, d'you think?

Nigel: I don't know.

Daisy: Depends on what you expect, I suppose.

Philip: Banish one and invoke another.

Nigel: I was just thinking that if you did something without really fully understanding what you were doing, you might create some – patterns.

Enoch: You might create some unexpected results, you mean. You might get into trouble, or burn your finger, or pick up something you couldn't cope with.

Nigel: Yes.

Enoch: D'you really think so? I mean, just drawing a shape in the air the wrong way round?

Nigel: Well –

Philip: It's gotta be done with *intention*.

Daisy: Yes, exactly.

Enoch: But you would say that you'd be cautious. In other words, what he's saying is that he's regarding the – I think; correct me if I'm not right – is that you're regarding this pentagram as a tool, as a specialized device which you don't fully understand, and you're going to treat it with respect, and you're not going to risk misusing it through ignorance, that's what you're saying.

All participants seem to have somewhat different ideas about what rituals do and why, and their differences are not sufficiently troublesome to cause any member of the group much concern. They discuss the 'grounding' of the ritual, but take its 'earthing' for granted. They discuss the types of powers, or spirits, but the idea that spirits exist is not contested. It is foolish to think of members of these groups as individually maintaining some list of theoretical assumptions even when the assumptions seem to be explicit. They talk at some times as if one particular way of characterizing the world were correct, and within certain limits they are not severely challenged. But the assumptions which remarks imply are not always the exact form of the premises for which the magician would argue. People talk somewhat sloppily; here I focus, as it were, on the range of sloppiness, the sorts of remarks which magicians are unlikely to reject.

There are several reasons for drawing upon a book rather than upon direct quotation to illustrate this aspect of the practice. The range of my taped data is quite small: I had access to some tapes of the meetings in a Western Mysteries fraternity, and several tapes of one-on-one conversations. For this analysis, it seemed unsatisfactory to rely solely on reports of paraphrase. Also, I wanted to illustrate that the assumptions I am discussing arose in a magical context, rather than from the idiosyncratic psychologies of the particular magicians with whom I spoke. The best way to emphasize the importance and centrality of these assumptions within the subculture would be, I thought, to draw my examples from a very basic, very common text which explained magic to newcomers. There are of course differences in rhetorical stance between the written text and the spoken word. But the book I choose was relatively unsophisticated, close to conversational style, and the advantage of using it seemed to outweigh the disadvantages.

To detail these assumptions, then, I turn to a frequently used basic teaching text in the magical practice: Marion Green's *Magic in Principle and Practice*. The manual was the basis of Green's home study course, and was written for rank beginners by a woman who had had considerable experience in the Western Mysteries, in ritual magic, and on the edges of Gardnerian witchcraft. Many of my London friends had taken the course, and had learnt their magic through its pages. The text is typical of the conversations I had with magicians about magic, and of the remarks I had heard magicians make. The assumptions I extract from it are not the only ones to be found within the text, nor are they exclusive to magicians. They do, however, indicate elements of a 'style' of thought, common and applauded in magic but often frowned upon elsewhere.

I should explain that sometimes these quotations state quite clearly the sort of assumption I am discussing, and at other times the quotation is more obscure. The point is that magicians start to talk with these sorts of sentences and to respond to these sentences without being surprised or wondering whether they are valid. The sort of ideas that they defend in argument may, or may not, take the form that they do in these assumptions. It is as if these ways of talking are tools: they are acceptable ways of organizing and understanding events and ideas, and they do a job in talking about them and making sense of them. Tools change the ability of a tool-user to do certain tasks, and he uses different tools, in different contexts, for different tasks. But he need not develop elaborate theories about his tools, or make an effort to 'rationalize' the toolbox. I am interested in the sorts of tools the magician brings to his practice, and what can be said about them without presupposing very much about the organization of the toolbox.

There are three major groups of assumptions. The first involves the conflation of the self and the world, the collapse of the thin divide which separates subjectivity from an objective world. The second is an assumption that the world is non-random. It is patterned, meaningful and often intentionally compelled. The third assumes the inferential validity of analogy, that analogies provide not only insight, but also knowledge, of an unknown physical reality. These three primary assumptions percolate into more specific forms, not necessarily consistent or formally elaborated.

First, magicians talk as if they are deeply linked to the world. Their conversational style tends to be what a psychologist might call 'ego-centric', to have difficulty distinguishing between objective reality and subjective experience.[2]

---

[2] The terminology 'ego-centric' is used by Piaget, among others. In its weak sense it is often used to describe the subject's inability to speak to another, taking into account the limited information that the other may have. In its stronger sense, the term implies the inability to see oneself as one thing in a world of things.

They speak as if a change in their own inner perception of events changes (or is) the external reality. This assumption in fact is the lynchpin of magic: that mind and body are linked, so that in special circumstances the imaginative can shift the material. Magicians do not confuse their souls with their tables, nor do they act on the belief that a traffic light has changed if they only wished that it would have done so. However, they do talk about magic in ways that imply various versions of this sort of assumption. They change their names, their costumes and their bearing as if the adoption of a new identity will produce new abilities, a nominalist fallacy with a potent psychological force.

Magical practice often relies upon what some psychologists term 'participation', the sense that actions and objects remain associated with the person who has touched them, and that his thoughts influence the object from a distance.[3]

Once you have blessed your mirror [used for scrying, divination through vision] keep it dark or the power of vision which will gradually build up within it will be quickly dissipated.[4]

Once again it is the work of the wearer himself, for though suitable pendants may be bought they never have the same power and link with the magician as something which he has created.[5]

Magicians do not talk in this way about all objects with which they have come in contact. They describe contact as transmitting some sort of personal power when that contact has a magical form: magicians 'participate' in the objects they use in ritual – robes, wands, chalices – and in special objects, like statues of the Goddess. They also use this concept when they talk of using an ordinary object which belongs to someone to gain psychic knowledge of that person ('psychometry'), or to improve their contact with them in a ritual.

Within magical practice, there is often talk of 'linking'. A 'link' is an action which asserts that when the practitioner uses some object, mind and body, subjective imagination and objective reality, are not divorced.

The first part of any true dedication, of yourself or of anything used in magic, is the formation of a link between the seen, real, tangible world and that of the unseen, inner world where acts of magic become acts of reality.[6]

This interconnection is said to be particularly strong at certain times. When Green speaks of 'an unseen inner world where acts of magic become acts of reality', she implies that it is not always true that imagination affects the world. You need special circumstances, like ritual practice or the concentration of a highly trained mind, before the imagination can make its physical impression. The preparation for this process – and this is the point of her quotation – involves making a 'link' then used in magical practice. The 'dedication' of a magical sword is the announcement that the sword is not only physical but also

---

[3] Again, the term is Piagetian; however, it has a distinguished history, not the least through its association with Levy-Bruhl. The Piagetian phrase does not imply an adoption of Piagetian theory; the term in any event has a wide use in many psychological theories.

[4] Green (1971: 24).   [5] Green (1971: 13).   [6] Green (1971: 9).

magical. If used in magical ritual to draw the power of Hermes, say, that power will have a real effect on the physical world because the physical/magical sword 'links' the tangible world of physical materialism to the intangible world of imaginative thought.

This connection between magical intention, physical object and physical world lies behind Frazer's characterization of magic. Frazer reduced all magical practice to the extended application of two principles of similarity and contact:

If we analyze the principles of thought upon which magic is based, they will probably be found to resolve themselves into two: first, that like produces like, or that an effect resembles its cause; and second, that things which have once been in contact continue to act on each other at a distance after the physical contact has been severed.[7]

Frazer called magic based upon association by similarity 'homeopathic', and that based upon association by contact, 'contagious'. Both could be found together, and could be described as 'sympathetic': 'both assume that things act on each other at a distance through a secret sympathy'.[8] Homeopathic magic included damaging a waxen figure to damage the person upon whom it was modelled; when nail clippings were added the magic also became contagious.[9]

Frazer's similarity and contagion emerge in these two of Green's remarks:

If you wished to make a charm for good health you would probably find that the Sun relates to health and life in general, as well as the individual. It is usual to link the colour yellow or gold with this luminary . . . You may do all the work on a Sunday or consecrate the talisman at the hour of the Sun, or sunrise . . . [it] is best sewn up, as were very ancient charms and spells, in a bag of golden coloured silk . . .[10]

If you make a talisman for someone else you will need to link it with them, perhaps by enclosing a few hairs or their signature from a letter, so that it is associated with them.[11]

Starhawk's manual provides two other examples:

Homeopathic magic: enacting a representation of a desired end:
'Anger spell'

---

[7] Frazer (1922: 12). [8] Frazer (1922: 14).

[9] Most subsequent anthropologists have retained Frazer's description of magic and discarded his evolutionary polemic. Malinowski certainly accepted his description (1935: 11: 240) but defined religion functionally as 'a body of self-contained acts being themselves the fulfilment of their purpose' and magic as 'a practical art consisting of acts which are the only means to a definite end expected to follow later on' (1954: 88). Evans-Pritchard conceded the accurate picture of the 'magical association of ideas' (1965: 29) and defined magic for the purpose of his material as 'a technique that is supposed to achieve its purpose by the use of medicines' (1937: 9). Even Durkheim accepted that Frazer's categories were constitutive of magic, and argued that he could show how they were derived from collective experience (1915: 398ff).

However, not all magical acts seem to fall beneath a Frazerian rubric. The account of modern London magic clearly includes but also expands Frazer's analytic classifications. The most significant difference lies in the merging of the subjective and the objective, the conflation of self with the ordinary world. A notion of contagious magic implies such a conflation, but there are magical acts which use merely mental activity to generate their results: modern magic is a case in point, but Elizabethan magic (for example, Dee's and Fludd's kabbalistic alchemy) provides another. Insofar as Frazer did not specify the conflation of the objective and the subjective, his account is inadequate as a general definition of the practice.

[10] Green (1971: 44). [11] Green (1971: 44).

Visualize a circle of light around yourself. Cup a BLACK STONE in your hands and raise it to your forehead. Concentrate and project all your anger into the stone. With all your might, hurl it out of the circle into a lake, stream, river or ocean. Say:

> With this stone
> Anger be gone
> Water bind it
> No one find it

Earth the power. Release the circle.

Contagious magic: using a part to influence the whole:

'To attract money'
Use a square of green cloth, filled with borage, lavender, High Joan the Conqueress Root, and saffron (or any four appropriate herbs), a few crystals of rock salt, and three silver coins. (Dimes, although no longer solid silver, seem to work fine.) Tie with gold and silver thread in eight knots.[12]

The first spell actually contains elements of contagion, in making the stone make contact with the anger. Its central purpose, however, is to throw away anger in the same way that you threw away the stone. In the second ritual, the magician uses a small bit of money to attract more.

The second set of assumptions relies on various forms of the idea that the world is patterned and meaningful. The assumption takes at least three more specific forms: that events arrange themselves in interpretable patterns, that chance does not exist, and that all change is intentional, guided by a wiser being. The first of these – interpretability – is necessary to magic. One cannot practise magic without talking as if events form patterns which the magician can understand. The others are not. At least, they slide more easily in and out of magical discourse. Many magicians talk about pre-determined events, and events which arose because of God's intent. However, the same magician at other times, and other magicians at most times, speak of contingency and atheism. Certainly both of these tendencies underlie many passages of Green's manual.

Chance plays an ambiguous role in the magical universe. An interconnected whole leaves little space for aberration. Some magicians allow more room for randomness than others, and speak of chance, accidents and the bad luck that leads a man to sit under a rotten granary which falls and kills him. But even stochastically-inclined magicians treat simultaneity as significant and interpret apparent coincidences as causal connections. If two events coincide, it is because they are in some way related. This is called 'synchronicity', the term borrowed from Jung.[13]

Finding the real cause beneath apparent coincidence is the basic material of many magical conversations. The configuration of stars at your birth is said to be related to your behaviour this afternoon, the apparently accidental configuration of tarot cards is intimately linked to your future.

---

[12] Starhawk (1979: 116, 122).   [13] Cf. previous footnoted discussion. Ch. 10, n. 28.

Gradually you will find that random ideas, snippets from books read and dreams even will begin to form patterns, follow a certain line of study or subject material, then you will know that you are progressing.[14]

Magicians seem to enjoy interpreting patterned interconnections between events. Performing a ritual allows you to interpret any subsequent event as related to it. You 'work' a ritual to reunite Christian and pagan spiritual currents, and in it use imagery from the stories of Joseph of Arimathea and Bran's voyage to the Celtic underworld. All of these story elements have associations: Joseph of Arimathea is connected to Glastonbury, famous for its druids and its sacred well; the underworld is a place of darkness, of the unconscious; Christianity is about transcendence, Celtic religion about ancient wisdom. Any event subsequent to the ritual which somehow embodies one of these associations can be seen as related to the rite. A Walt Disney movie about Merlin (a druid, by these accounts), mistletoe hanging in the church (a pagan intrusion into Christianity), a flood of tears (the strong feelings of the unconscious) ending in an embrace (redemption) – all of these *could* be seen as offspring to the rite and presented as evidence that it raised power. Magicians try to avoid saying that some event occurred by chance. Evans-Pritchard describes the logic well: that the stump was in the path was an accident, but that this normally careful man should stub his toe against it must be a result of witchcraft. That the priest hangs mistletoe in the church *this* year, that you fought with your lover *this* week, that the Walt Disney film was in production just then – these things must have an explicable cause. Events need explanations, and magicians fit them into chance-free patterns which they can interpret to make sense of them.

Magicians often write and talk as if chance did not exist, that in energy's Saivite dance no action is truly random. For example, Green will say that:

Remember too, that magic is an art of causing changes, once you begin to use these skills you will discover a great number of changes in your life pattern, often unexpected and unsought. This will be a sure proof that you are working on the more subtle levels of your own sphere of existence, and having an effect![15]

As it says in 'A Wizard of Earthsea' . . . 'To light a candle is to cast a shadow . . .'. Every act has an opposite effect. In magic it is not immediately apparent what the recoil will be, that doesn't stop it happening though.[16]

Magicians argue for a philosophy of holism: the world is an interacting whole, no part independent and no element autonomous. An action one takes has far-reaching consequences, and any event which affects you emerges from a previously interconnected whole. Magicians often compare their natural philosophy with quantum mechanics in order to make the point that events which seem disconnected can in fact be interlocked. Starhawk explains the way spells work by writing of 'this view of the universe as an interplay of moving forces – which, incidentally, corresponds to an amazing degree with the views of

[14] Green (1971: 17).   [15] Green (1971: 25).   [16] Green (1971: 40).

modern physics'.[17] When I asked the leader of the Hornsey group about magical theory, he told me to read particle physics. The comparison runs rampant through the magical literature. But chance is a complex issue. Holism does not deny chance; indeed quantum mechanics depends upon an elaborate understanding of randomness.

Magicians need coincidence, and many of them talk at times of chance. Coincidence makes magic surprising, for if coincidences exist it is all the more impressive if you 'know' that some event was not coincidental. Coincidence also enables one to deride other magicians. Magicians talk about chance when they want to accuse other magicians of over-interpreting, or when they want to distinguish good rituals from bad. The cry of 'chance' is the easiest way to argue against another magician's claim to power. Also, magicians tend to use a concept of chance freely when they are not discussing magic, and then to talk about magical actions as if nothing happens by chance. And so magicians talk about chance in different, inconsistent ways. They make remarks which startle the observer because they suggest a strong commitment to non-randomness, and yet they often argue against such a view. Nevertheless, they become comfortable with statements that imply a nearly chance-free world.

The third version of this assumption of a patterned, often chance-free world, is that a higher being governs earthly events. However, it too falls prey to similar ambivalence. Certainly many magicians talk, quite explicitly, about the existence of a deity. 'The most important of these [magical tenets] is that there is a force or entity of greater power, knowledge or wisdom than Mankind.'[18] Such entities are often spoken of as guiding events on earth. Magicians appeal to them in ritual – although not all who appeal to them in ritual would argue that they exist – and often describe ritual 'consequences' in terms of some deity's deliberate action. I have heard people explain that they asked the Goddess for a better job, house or sex life, and that she decided otherwise. One Western Mysteries initiate told me that he initially became interested in magic to improve his acting career. 'But She thought I needed a few hard lessons first, a few hard knocks. Well, I got them.'

And yet magic by its title implies a more active control of the environment than simply requesting the deity to intercede. Magicians talk in terms of controlling a quite impersonal, amoral force. According to another manual author:

As a witch, you do not necessarily have to worship any complete and permanent hierarchy of supernatural beings if you don't want to. There simply exists power to be tapped – to do good or to do evil, both of which are remarkably relative concepts.[19]

Some magicians think of themselves as agnostic, even as atheists. Some assert that one's attitude towards the deity is irrelevant. A selection of 'god-invocations', designed for rituals or ritual-like settings and written by the couple who hosted the Monday workshop, begins with a remarkable description:

The group's Leader has everyone seated with closed eyes, and goes to each member in

---

[17] Starhawk (1979: 18).   [18] Green (1971: 1).   [19] Huson (1970: 32).

turn, burns before that person with the appropriate incense, and reads aloud the invocation, with maximum intention to communicate with and call forth that aspect of the person's higher nature which corresponds to the Divinity concerned. (Or, if you prefer it, to communicate with and call forth the Divinity Itself: the distinction is subtle and the results the same).[20]

The distinction between objective and subjective is unimportant, they say; what the magician would describe as their 'belief' in a god, and the truth of that belief, is irrelevant to the practice. What matters is the magician's decision to act, and if that decision must rest on a belief in the divine, then the belief in the divine is valuable. If not, then not. Action is prior to belief.

The third set of magical assumptions involves the assumption that analogistic thinking is effective, that drawing conclusions from analogies is a valid intellectual move. Magicians use analogy easily, not only to illustrate but to elucidate a theory of their environment and to conceptualize its nature. They do not behave as if the analogy is merely a bridge to knowledge, but as if it itself is a way of knowing.[21] Theirs is a conceptual world of images, myths, symbols and their associations, in which poetic evocation is more highly valued than analytic evaluation, and the force of a poetic analogy is strong.

In some sense, the entirety of pre-Christian mythology involves analogistic thinking, as magicians use it. Magicians often interpret some natural or political event – like a storm or a demonstration – in terms of the actions of deities, and explain the event on the basis of what that mythological character would do. Magicians understand that the world is alive, organic, person-like, and explain its events on the basis of a reasonable person's action. Green remarks,

Is it any wonder that we face droughts, earthquakes and other natural disasters? Nature has a will of her own, and once man oversteps what she is willing to allow then she can retaliate, just as the kindly mother will slap the erring child. Not in anger but because he must learn that there are things that are wrong, and overstep the mark.[22]

Natural events can be understood because they are like the intentional actions that a mothering woman would take: to give an explanation of the events, Green describes why such a woman would act in that way, not what reasons intrinsic to natural events would cause certain natural events to be mother-like.

Magicians often argue through analogy. They draw out the discussion through the imagery, rather than arguing independently for their claims. Green says also:

Much of ancient magic was a striving towards true equilibrium for the balanced Universe would travel more smoothly on its evolutionary journey, like a boat on a calm sea. If the world, its people and objectives are at cross purposes it sets up many ripples and even great waves, all of which prevent a smooth passage.[23]

Green does not go on to talk about 'true equilibrium'; she is content to explain it through the analogy with the sea, and explain the consequences of its

---

[20] Williams and Cox (n.d. 2).
[21] Lloyd (1966) discusses the use of analogy as a means to knowledge in the ancient world.
[22] Green (1971: 40).   [23] Green (1971: 40).

disturbance through the consquences of disturbing the sea. I was once present at a conversation about Paracelsus' doctrine of resemblance, which someone was advocating as a medical technique. The doctrine holds that if a plant resembles a part of the body, then it will be medically valuable for that part of the body, as the lung-shaped lungwort can be used for the care of human beings.

Magicians sometimes assume that two sets of objects used for similar ends will have similar structures.[24] I watched such a pattern emerge in a group discussion about incense. A group of magicians, most of whom had taken or were taking Green's course, sat around a London flat in a meeting designed to talk about herbs and their uses. Angel said that dragonsblood, an incense, 'was lovely, it came from Sumatra'. 'Wherever *that* is', said Emily. This led to a discussion of whether one should work magic only within one's own tradition, with the symbols and material with which one's ancestors had been familiar. 'Well' said Roger 'we'll have to find our own substitute for dragonsblood' and proceeded to talk on the assumption that different cultures had exactly the same concerns; it was merely their expressions which differed. Again, the assumption was that if two sets of objects served similar functions for two different cultures, the nature and function of the elements of those sets would be neatly correlated. That assumption is central to Jungian understanding: all religions symbolize common human concerns as 'archetypes', clothed differently for different cultures. Cultures describe the black goddess in various ways, but every culture has one. Magicians are very sympathetic to Jungian psychology and use his language of 'archetypes' and 'the collective unconscious' freely.

Assumptions often underlie the sorts of statements which magicians make, the sorts of arguments they find persuasive, and the sorts of links they draw between events. These assumptions are not necessarily systematized, but a few recur commonly. Some magicians tend to articulate them more readily than others. But for all, such assumptions are part of the linguistic and experiential package into which the magician becomes acculturated. Perhaps a little contradictory, a little incoherent, the assumptions are like a storehouse of tools suited for different jobs but all designed for gardening. Gardeners disagree about the usefulness of different tools, but they face similar problems and become accustomed to using the toolshed for their needs. Magicians learn to use these assumptions in arguing about their magical procedure and its justification; they use different assumptions to meet different ends, and they tend not to think about them self-consciously because other magicians see them as valid, persuasive moves in the discussion. The assumptions are, as it were, good to think.

---

[24] This psychological tendency has already been mentioned in this book: one judges the probability of something being x based on its resemblance to a stereotype that is x (Kahneman and Tversky, 1982). Magicians tend to be particularly free in relying upon symbolism and mythological narratives in constructing their stereotypes, a tendency not described here, particularly, but illustrated throughout this study.

PART III

Summoning the powers: the experience of involvement

13

Introduction: working intuitively

MARGARET, the truck-driving witch, found the summer of 1984 difficult. Her account of it illustrates a mixture of symbolism, phenomenology, intellectual habits and rationalization characteristic of magical involvement.

'I went away for this holiday, which was a pretty magical holiday, at Midsummer – which in the witch tradition is when the Grail makes itself manifest. And in the witch tradition it's also been a state of marriage, between sky and earth, light and darkness, and there is this English tradition of the Midsummer Marriage, which is the marriage with the fairy part of ourselves. Being in a magical place [Stonehenge], looking back I can see that a lot of magical things were beginning to happen, but I just thought that it was an overactive imagination at the time.

'. . . I'd been reading Jung, and Laurens van der Post . . . I started to have imaginative flashes. Just flashes, of being crusaders and knights, and Saracens and so on . . . I remember one woman at the fair saying, "There's something *noble* about John, isn't there? I mean, you could see him as a Crusader or something". I'd been seeing this all the way through – it was definitely a past life thing, but I didn't take it seriously because, in the Craft, I'm used to this sort of thing, in between imagination and vision. I just thought, I've got to be very down to earth about it. But when we drove through Glastonbury something went click. It's difficult to explain what that's about. It was as if it was a confirmation, but I didn't know what it was a confirmation of. And then we went to my parents, and washed and showered and had a meal.

'. . . Then we were driving up to come home, driving over the Severn bridge, talking about these ideas – romance, chivalry, sort of the glory of life, and I realized that I could *see* the air filled with golden specks. They weren't actually there, but it was as if they were there, and if I saw it, it was objective. I mean, I knew they weren't there, there was no confusion between vision and real world: they were separate. But I was actually able to see – I was actually able to hear the tinkling of tiny bells, corny as it sounds. Real, but on a different plane. It wasn't a trick of vision. It was seeing two realities at once, and being tuned in to the ideal reality . . . It was tremendously exciting and fulfilling. It was a revolution. Suddenly everything made sense on an emotional level. There was no propositional content, but suddenly there were no problems anymore. As if a veil had dropped, that previously the world had been covered by a veil. Of course there were problems – people in dire trouble and so on. But that was because we weren't really tuned in to the world as it really is.

'. . . (While having Grail visions) a lot of other things became clear. And this wasn't a set of visions, this was like memory. I say like memory because I don't know whether it was a true memory, but it came to me exactly as a memory does. They concerned this fourteenth century life. It works exactly like another memory. But it supposedly happened six hundred years ago! . . . I don't know quite whether I believe in past lives. I don't know whether they're a metaphor or a reality.

'. . . I take [magic] as something real, and I don't have a fixed system which explains it. I know lots of magical systems. They're all fascinating, and they explain different things. So I've experimented and worked out a system that suits me fairly well, but it's given to change.

'. . . Magic is the means to a religious end. When I discovered magic, magic was something I could do. It was fun, it was a hobby, it was like a philosophical theory, or – I've never written a word – it was like a train of thought. It was a personal statement. Now, it's more cosmic, if you like. It's more objective. So what matters now is not what happens materially, though materially I've got to get my act together to be of any use to anyone, to any cause. Now the goal is to bring out the hidden perception of human beings. That's the point. That's what magicians are here for.'

INTRODUCTION

We have seen that becoming a magician, becoming a specialist in magic, results in systematic changes in the structure of interpretation itself. A new definition of evidence, new assumptions, new common knowledge – these changes systematically alter the way yet-to-be-interpreted events are noticed, organized and analysed. But as, if not more, important are the unsystematic experiences which, although they may have little to do with intellectual analysis, make the magician want to justify the practice, and which motivate him in the end to rationalize his commitment. These are the experiences which create bias. New ways of feeling and imagining change the context in which the specialist makes assertions. They affect the practitioner's willingness to become further involved in the practice, they alter the importance that the practice assumes for the practitioner, and, in the end, they affect the vehemence with which the practitioner defends his involvement and argues that its theory is true. One thinks of truth as a property of propositions, which are true by virtue of their logical structure or which have truth in relation to the world. The image of the rational individual is of one who carefully and clearheadedly assembles all information to judge the truth of any sentence. But when a certain opinion or idea appears in a statement, someone's tendency to defend it, to call the statement 'true', depends on feelings, fantasies, the enjoyment associated with the practice – things which would seem irrelevant to an ideal notion of its truth.

We now turn to the activities of magical practice which make the magic exciting, challenging and deeply significant to its practitioners. Certain aspects of magical practice turn it into an engagement which many practitioners find compelling. They find the rituals deeply moving, the pre-ritual 'homework' engrossing, they dream with the images of magic's potent symbols. There are new, or at least noticeable, ways of feeling, and the magician often finds this pleasing. His practice also gives him an imaginatively stimulating secret world, ambiguously neither quite fantastic nor quite real. He has the excitement of learning about the magic, of gaining mastery over some body of knowledge, and he may feel the satisfaction of gaining some mastery of himself as the symbolism works its psychotherapeutic effects. These satisfactions make the practice compelling to practitioners, regardless of the referential truth of magic's theory. Certainly they may spur the magician to continue his practice and justify it, to himself and others, when he must.

One indication of the personal significance which the magic attains is that many magicians come to treat their magic as a religion. The line between magic and religion has always been uncertain. Anthropologists have treated magic both as religion's precursor and as the individualistic offspring of collective religious ecstacy.[1] My impression of modern magicians is that many of them began to understand their practice as a religion only after they had been practising for some time. How can one identify a religion? There are some famous definitions of the term.[2] Geertz's avoids the difficulty of demanding propositional belief:

[Religion is] a system of symbols which acts to establish powerful, pervasive and long-lasting moods and motivations in men by formulating conceptions of a general order of existence and clothing these conceptions with such an aura of factuality that the moods and motivations seem uniquely realistic.[3]

Certainly long-term magical practice produces these results: many symbols associated with feelings, motivations, and world-descriptive conceptions which seem real or true. My concern is not some theoretician's quarrel over the definition of religion and whether magic falls beneath its rubric. That debate seems somewhat pointless, language gone on holiday. Rather, the issue is that magicians themselves come to use the term 'religion' because they feel comfortable calling the feelings elicited in some meditations and rituals 'spiritual'. That, too, is a vague, contested term. But the term gains its value

---

[1] The uneasy intercourse of magic and religion in European civilization is particularly clear in the early Renaissance (Walker 1975; Thomas 1971); the anthropological these have been held most notably by Frazer (1922), Durkheim (1965 [1915]) and Mauss and Herbert (1972).

[2] Tylor's minimal definition of religion as a belief in spiritual beings (1970 [1871]: II: 8) is among them (see also Goody (1961)): Durkheim's – religion is a unified system of beliefs and practices relative to sacred things (1965 [1915]: 62) – is another. Frazer wisely pointed out that 'there is probably no subject in the world about which opinions differ so much as the nature of religion, and to frame a definition of it which would satisfy everyone must obviously be impossible' (1922: 57). He went on to define it as 'a propitiation or conciliation of powers superior to man which are believed to direct and control the course of nature and of human life' (1922: 57–8).

[3] Geertz (1973: 90).

because it is used to describe markedly distinctive ways of feeling. Magicians seem ready to use the word to describe the experience of magic, and – crucially – they do so not particularly because they are socialized into using the term, but because they are socialized into having certain experiences. Magicians entering magic are not simply acquiring a new vocabulary.

Engaging in certain activities – like the meditation and visualization used in magic – produces potent phenomenological results, of the type that people feel comfortable calling 'spiritual' or 'religious'. These techniques are hardly unique to magic: they are associated with religious practice throughout the world. It is probably true that in all cultures, humans have the psychological capacity to engender feelings of ecstacy, oneness and peace by certain methods. It is perhaps also true that different people possess this capacity to individually different degrees, like the capacity to paint or swim. The intriguing point is that the newly initiated magician may have entered magic with thoughts of power, of doing ritual merely as the means to wealth and glory. He quickly begins to have powerful personal experiences associated with moving symbols. And he finds these feelings and rituals pleasing in their own right, regardless of their 'magical' effects.

Ultimately, this involvement is probably the most important element of the magician's increasing commitment to his practice. In the last analysis, the magician is probably more concerned to repeat and to make sense of moving experience than to prove any 'theory' true. Claims about magical efficacy probably become more crucial as the means to identify and rationalize the intense involvement than as an elaborate testable theory which the magician demonstrates to hard-nosed satisfaction. One might imagine that merely having a spiritual response to a ritual should not commit one to any theory about divine existence or magical force. Just because you have a profound experience during prayer, it does not mean that God exists. But people often find the distinction hard to handle: they tend to accept the magical or theological ideas because the involvement – the spirituality, the group meetings, the moving symbols, the sheer fun of the practice – becomes so central to their lives. If they experience Lèvy-Bruhlian participation, they tend to explain it by adopting a Frazerian theory. Perhaps the difficulty of proving magic's efficacy in the physical world inadvertently pushes the magician's attention onto the inner psychological realms. Magical rituals rarely achieve their material goals with blatant, manifest success. Magicians make interpretative accommodations which give the rites more apparent validity, as the last section discussed. But magic is clearly a different sort of enterprise than firing a gun or moving a table, where the empirical consequences of action are obvious. This difference may inevitably place the emphasis upon some spiritual and psychological state said to be necessary to achieve the goals of ritual. This in turn may deflect the emotional attention of the participant on to the experience of the practice, rather than to its goal-oriented ends. In any event the spiritual, symbolic involvement becomes paramount in modern magic, and the magician's meditation and symbolism becomes an end in itself.

I have tried to dissect the various components of magical experience with care, and what I see as four distinctive categories of experiential response form the division into four chapters. The first, on meditation and visualization, explains the two techniques which magicians always learn upon becoming involved in practice. These are remarkable techniques: they change the practitioner's phenomenological experience in relatively well-understood ways, and magicians are notably affected by their use. The second, on magician's language, discusses the linguistic style with which magicians describe their rituals and meditations. This style evokes a significant imaginative involvement with the ritual's narrative and gives the magician concrete experience of the abstract terms of magical theory, like 'contact' or 'power'. At the same time, the magician is told that no understanding of magical theory is complete or accurate: she can have confidence that the term refers to something, but she need not state unequivocally what it is.

The third, on ritual, discusses the magician's strategies in constructing rituals. There are three, in particular: he is concerned to create a separate space and time, to exploit mind-altering techniques like chanting, and to alter the personality of the ritualist. All these techniques take their central task to be setting ritual apart as something different, to be experienced almost as if it involved a different reality superimposed on the everyday. The fourth chapter, the most complex, centres upon symbolism. The use of symbolism is the most important element of the magician's magical engagement. Symbolism plays many roles, and evokes many responses, and probably bears most responsibility for magic's excitement. Magicians invent a mythopoeic history, talk about intimate feelings in symbolic terms, therapeutically reorganize their lives with symbolic 'archetypes'. They also create a secrecy-shrouded mystery religion and talk of the 'esoteric knowledge' which their rites provide. Throughout all this, the implication should be clear: magic is far more than a theory, and the pleasures of these other aspects – difficult to verbalize, difficult to forget – wed the magician more strongly than any intellectual analysis to a commitment to the validity of his practice.

14

New experiences:
meditation and visualization

WORK TO DO

1 There are small illustrations on pages 7 and 31. Meditate on each of these for six days and write a brief report on your findings. Choose two sentences from Chapter V and meditate on them and report.

2 Try out the self-blessing ritual on pages 33/34 and explain what seemed to happen. If you don't like the words or gestures make up your own self-blessing and use that. Say what you experienced.

3 Briefly explain some traditional happening you have seen and say how you think it is continuing the old traditions of the Mysteries.

4 Select four sentences which you think are the keys to magical ritual and explain your choices.

5 Make up a short ceremony of consecration for two participants. If possible perform it with someone (or alone) and say what happened.

6 Have you ever been through a ceremony of initiation, in any life? What did you FEEL at the time?

7 When do you think you will be ready to perform the Self-Initiation Ceremony – or have you done it already?

8 Explain why you are responsible for the outcome of any magical work you have done.

9 List 8 Festival Occasions in the year. Choose a Natural Symbol for each and explain your choice. (Select something you could openly have around the house at that time!)

10 Design your own personal Magical Sign or Symbol which could be used, say, to identify your books or equipment, or embroidered on robes etc.

(lesson, home study course in Natural Magic by Marion Green)

When Simon was nine, he had an intense awareness of the unity of all creation, and fell off his bike. He has had other full blown mystical experiences since – experiences of ineffable transcendence which convey an absolute certainty of immortality and divine union, and which are utterly different from all other psychological states. Now, Simon leads the Hornsey group and is widely respected as an adept in the Western Mysteries. When I asked him why he was drawn to magic, and not to the Church, he said, 'I didn't want only to experience the spirituality. I wanted to know what I could do with it.'

To judge from the manuals and the practitioners' accounts, all magicians are supposed to meditate and to visualize, techniques used throughout all times and cultures in magico-religious activity. These techniques can have significant effects upon the practitioners, and magicians talk about them as if they do. Many magicians have had these phenomenologically dramatic mystical experiences that often leave their experiencer in a state of spiritual bliss. Sometimes such states can be elicited by meditation: practitioners of long experience, like Simon, seem able to elicit them almost at will. More often they are unelicited, and they seem to increase significantly the magician's commitment to his practice.

In magic, non-ordinary states have a practical, this-worldly purpose. Magical rituals are meant to concentrate forces and direct power. According to the theory, this happens only when magicians sink into altered states of consciousness in appropriate ritual conditions and visualize images with great intensity. In order to manipulate the subtle currents and interconnections of their world, magicians are said to need to step outside the normal ways people think and communicate, to step over the barrier which Western conceptions of subjectivity and objectivity place between self and world. They are trained in techniques intended to make this possible.

The remarkable feature of this training is that it works. That is, if you studiously undergo training, your awareness of your inner life changes, as does your experience of its isolation from an outer world. Your imaginative intensity increases, you begin to use the word 'spiritual' as the most appropriate way to describe your feelings during meditation, your dreams become more intense, and magical images like the moon, stag's antlers and Artemis fill your fantasies. I say this so boldly because I myself began to have these experiences, and because magicians both fresher and more seasoned than I spoke and acted as if they, too, had experienced such changes. Magicians are not simply learning a language with which to communicate with each other; they are learning (or possibly, relearning) ways of experiencing. These experiences become important in persuading magicians of the validity of their theory and its practice. They are new, or at least different, experiences. They need to be understood. And not unnaturally, magicians often turn to the ideas with which these experiences are associated in order to explain them.

Home study courses, advertised in books and magazines, offer the most structured forum for the training which most magicians assume a neophyte needs. Most of these courses are quite similar. They provide a series of fortnightly or monthly lessons for which the student does daily exercises, and writes short essays on assigned themes. Courses explain magical theory, and the nature and purpose of magical practice. They then teach the student to meditate and to visualize, guide him through the rudiments of ritual technique, and encourage him to develop an elaborate, personalized symbolism. They are structured like English university courses. There are Directors of Studies, and supervisors, and revision essays. Each 'student' is assigned to a supervisor who comments on the 'lessons'. And upon finishing the course, the student is often initiated as having attained the first 'degree'.

Many people take these courses just to learn more about magic, although many Western Mysteries fraternities actually require that potential initiates take the course offered by their particular group before they will agree to the initiation. In 1984, the largest organization was run by the Servants of the

Light, an offshoot of a Western Mysteries fraternity organized in the late sixties specifically to administrate a study course (it did not then offer initiation to its students). The student can take at least fifty month-long lessons from the 'SOL' – and indeed, I met people who had completed that course and other courses, repeating the training because they had so enjoyed the structured meditations and exercises which the courses demanded of them. In 1984 the SOL listed twelve hundred people as students; in 1987, twenty three hundred. The number seems larger than in all probability it was: many students were international,[1] and many had enrolled but had not completed, and had not announced their termination. Another course, Marion Green's Natural Magic Course had handled some six or seven hundred students in the five years (or so) of its existence. Green did not advertise her course as the precursor to initiation, but she sometimes wrote to promising students to invite them to join small 'working' groups. There were other courses, but they tended to be smaller in size. Most lasted for between one and five years. None of them were money-making institutions.[2] I paid twelve pounds for a one-year course of twelve lessons, and thirty pounds for a ten-month course of twenty lessons – each with considerable attention from my supervisors.

To the non-magician these lessons are remarkable because they seem so far removed from a layman's stereotype of wizardry-in-training. But they are seen as the royal road to magical success. Green's sample lesson, cited above, is typical in its amalgam of 'feeling' and 'explaining'. Here is another lesson, from another course, a published manual which offers a guide to the Western Way – 'a body of esoteric teaching and knowledge which constitutes a system of magical technique and belief, dating from the beginning of time'.[3] Each chapter of the course manual talks about different concepts – the 'old religion', the 'magic earth', 'meeting the gods' – and suggests meditations and imaginative exercises at the end to let the reader experience these things directly.

This is the Two Trees exercise. To do it properly, you would memorize the imagery or record it on cassette, and play it to yourself while you relaxed into a meditative state.

You are standing at the top of a low hill. Below you is a shallow valley at the centre of which lies a lake. Beside it are two trees – silver birches – which are reflected upside down in the water. Walk down from the hill and around the margin of the lake until you pass between the two trees. As you do so, focus your attention on the sky well above the horizon. There you will see either the sun or the moon: is it day or night? When you have established which, lower your gaze and see a figure approaching. It may be male or

---

[1] In 1987, three fifths of the students were British. It had been the case that the majority of the foreign students were Nigerian. However, around 1984 (or thereabouts) the SOL supervisor in Nigeria had advised the English leader that the Nigerian involvement was unwise (in fact, I was told that he was subsequently murdered).

[2] All the courses which I ran across in Britain were not financially exploitative. However, there was at least one American course (it offered the key to life with Rosicrucian knowledge) which seemed quite profitable to its organizers, and one group with whom I was familiar in Britain spoke of creating a similarly profitable course in the States.

[3] Matthews and Matthews (1985: 2).

female, veiled or unveiled. This is your guide. Follow the instructions he or she gives to you. Your guide may accompany you or appoint a companion, or you may be sent on alone. Remember that no actual harm can come to you. Follow the way laid down for you and seek the goal to which you will be led.[4]

The striking aspect of the lesson is the sense of reality which the authors clearly expect the exercitants to feel. And indeed with time the sense of reality does heighten. The depth of meditation increases, the imagery grows more intense.

But these remarks may sound strange to the reader. To unpack them, and give an impression of the often new and unusual experiences which the practitioner encounters in magic, it helps to describe the exercise's two central techniques of meditation and visualization and what they involve.

MEDITATION

'Meditation' is a word generally used to identify certain sorts of relaxation techniques which involve mental concentration. It does not really matter *what* one concentrates upon: it is the act of concentration, over a long period, which produces the desired results. Concentration techniques are widespread throughout very different cultures. Zen and Therevada Buddhism, Islamic Sufism, Bhakti yoga, Judaic kabbalism, Christian Hesychasm – all these involve the same basic technique of single-minded awareness,[5] and all produce the same effect: feelings and awareness recognized as spiritual, divine, or religious. There is a technology of the sacred, and it is accessible without dogma, doctrine or drugs.

There is also little doubt that meditation produces physiological effects, although it is not clear whether the physiology differs from the general physiological effects of relaxation. Beginners experience a lower metabolic rate, decreases in heart and respiratory rates, a lower blood lactate level (tension-related), higher skin resistance. The more advanced meditator may exhibit a greater number of slow alpha brain waves, followed by their inhibition and the increase of theta waves. Some researchers have described this as a 'wakeful, hypometabolic state'.[6] Some scientific inquiry has also suggested that the

---

[4] Matthews and Matthews (1985: 129–30).

[5] Actually, one may describe this single-minded awareness according to different rubrics. One psychologist distinguishes two types of mental devices used to halt thinking activity: meditation on an object or upon the mind itself (Goleman 1977: 108). He characterizes Bhakti yoga, Judaic kabbalah, Christian Hesychasm, Islamic Sufism, Raja Yoga, Transcendental Meditation, and Kundalini Yoga as object-dominated techniques. Gurdjieff and Krishnamurti he describes as mind-dominated, and Zen, Tibetan and Theravada Buddhism as integrated uses of the two (Goleman 1977: 110). Another psychologist casts four categories, four basic types of meditation schools: structured meditation upon intellectual matter (Habad Hasidism and Krishnamurti); emotional yearning (the Catholic monastic, the Hasidism of the Baal Shem Tov, the School of Meher Baba); dynamic meditation in which bodily activity completely absorbs attention (Sufi dancing, the followers of Bhagwan Shree Rajneesh); and the 'path of action', which similarly demand total concentration upon an activity (St Theresa's Little Ways, Zen tea ceremonies). He then describes a variety of other structured and unstructured meditations (Le Shan 1974). These are, however, distinctions within commonalities, despite the wide cultural dispersal of the practices.

[6] Wallace, Benson and Wilson (1971).

likelihood of apparently 'psychic' activity (i.e. telepathy, clairvoyance, pre-cognition, psychokinesis) is increased in meditative conditions and in dreams.[7]

Meditation is not an easy path to follow.[8] Most people take weeks or months of disciplined practice to notice any effect, and few achieve the transcendent state which is explicitly the goal. Most meditative practices involve concentrating upon a particular object – a flower, a matchbox, the sound of an endlessly repeated word, the number of inhalations – or upon the 'empty' mind itself. One example of this retraining of attention is what one author calls the 'Bubble Meditation'. As a practitioner, you would sit yourself in a comfortable position, shut your eyes, and draw deep, regular breaths.

Picture yourself sitting quietly and comfortably on the bottom of a clear lake. You know how slowly large bubbles rise through the water. Each thought, feeling or perception etc. is pictured as a bubble rising into the space you can observe, passing through and out of this space. It takes five to seven seconds to complete this process. When you have a thought or feeling, you simply observe it for this time period until it passes out of your visual space. Then you wait for the next one and observe it for the same amount of time, and so on. You do not explore, follow up or associate to the bubble, just observe it against the background of 'oh, that's what I'm thinking (or feeling or sensing) now. How interesting'. Then, as it passes out of visual space (as the imaginary bubble rises) you calmly wait for the next bubble.[9]

The point of such an exercise is to retrain your attention. Your mind is an unruly, skittish creature. Through meditation you teach it not to jump from thought to thought, not to respond to external stimuli, but to remain focused and aware.

Such concentration is hard to achieve, and hard to imagine for those who have not done it. Success, however, brings a palpable change in its wake. The term 'altered state of consciousness' is much abused, but one needs that sort of term to describe the altered perception of time, space and self as the

---

[7] Le Shan (1966); Ullman, Krippner and Feldstein (1966). Central studies of meditation include Bagchi and Wenger (1957); Wenger and Bagchi (1961); Anand, Chhina and Singh (1961); Wallace (1970); Wallace, Benson and Wilson (1971); Orme-Johnson (1973); Banquet (1973); Curtis and Wessberg (1976); Tebecis (1975); Kasamatsu and Hirai (1973); Deikman (1973). Shuman, in a review article, examines the thesis that 'psychophysiological effects are not merely correlated with altered states but are in some way necessary to their occurrence' (1980: 370). She points out that the physiological changes are associated with low arousal states, and that while there is a correlation between this state and the phenomenological description, the relation need not be causal. 'Psychophysiological processes appear to be involved in facilitating the emergence of certain psychological phenomena and/or making them accessible to being identified and labelled within awareness . . . meditation involves a process of learning to experience in a new way, and this learning is facilitated when the body is relaxed and the mind quiet' (1980: 370). She does not reject the notion of a neurochemical change in meditation; she is simply unsure of whether there is one specific correlate, or a shifting, interacting system which produces such a meditative state. Also see Naranjo and Ornstein (1971).

[8] As one knowledgeable writer says of the true altered state – 'a qualitative break with the normal range of one's consciousness' – 'these states are quite rare. They never happen to the majority of meditators' (Goleman 1977: xxiv).

[9] Le Shan (1974: 60–1).

practitioner becomes progressively more skilled.[10] At its most effective, this transformation involves profound mystical experience, where the body loses all sensory perception and rapturous feelings fill all conscious awareness. But long before that point is reached, the meditator will experience a sense of deep relaxation, with a fully relaxed but awake mind, which seems like a period of extended stillness, a sort of suspension in which one is aware of physical things but they also seem quite irrelevant – or, conversely, somehow more a part of oneself.[11] Time feels somehow stretched, as if one were within its interstices. One experienced initiate of the Western Mysteries, a librarian in her thirties, describes it: 'you know when you wake up at 7:00 and then fall asleep and dream the history of the world for hours and then the postman rings the bell at 7:05? It's like that.' One description glosses the early stages of meditation thus:

At the beginning you will find it extremely difficult to bring your mind to concentrate on your breathing. You will be astonished how your mind runs away. It does not stay. You begin to think of various things. You hear sounds outside. Your mind is disturbed and distracted. You may be dismayed and disappointed. But if you continue to practise this exercise [concentrating on your breathing] twice daily, morning and evening, for about five or ten minutes at a time, you will gradually, by and by, begin to concentrate your mind on your breathing. After a certain period, you will experience just that split second when your mind is fully concentrated on your breathing, when you will not even hear sounds nearby, when no external world exists for you. This slight moment is such a tremendous experience for you, full of joy, happiness, and tranquility, that you would like to continue it. But you cannot. Yet if you go on practising this regularly, you may repeat the experience again and again for longer and longer periods. That is the moment when you loose yourself completely in your mindfulness of breathing.[12]

Experienced meditators say that this intensity in suspension leaves one with a distinctive way of perceiving and experiencing in the deepest possible way because one loses the sense of being a self which is different from the world.

Meditation is the medium of magical practice because it is in this non-ordinary state that the intuitive impressions and responses thought necessary to practice are said to occur. As Green's course textbook warns:

Unless you are able to enter and hold the state of meditation you will be unable to use

[10] There have been philosophical attacks on the notion of a 'state of mind'; the term, however, is usefully deployed to describe experiential changes, and I use it loosely, as psychologists have done. Tart, an authority in this area, defines a 'discrete state of consciousness [as] a unique, dynamic, pattern or configuration of psychological structures; a discrete state of consciousness is an active system of psychological subsystems' (1977: 215). He gives this sentence some content in the article. The issue is that while sleep, dreaming and ordinary wakefulness are clearly different, deep meditation, and some drug-induced responses, seem distinctive enough to merit characterization as if they displayed a difference of the same degree.

[11] The sense of stretched time is very commonly reported. There are other perceptual changes: one psychiatrist attributes the marked alteration of the meditative state to the 'deautomatization' of ordinary perceptual processes: the subject, he says, is 'reinvesting actions and precepts with attention' (Deikman 1973: 221). Subjects meditating on a vase reported 1. increased vividness and richness of imagery: the vase became 'more vivid', 'luminous'; 2. animation in the vase, its acquisition of life-like characteristics; 3. a marked decrease in self–object distinction: 'I really began to feel, you know, almost as if the blue and I were perhaps merging, or that I and the vase were'; 4. syncretic thought, a fusing and alteration of normal perception: 'I began to feel this light going back and forth', 'When the vase changes shape I felt this in my body' (Deikman 1973: 223).

[12] Walpola Rahula in Ornstein (1973: 245).

the arts of divination, clairvoyance and inner perception when information is perceived from within.[13]

By 'information perceived from within', the author means any understanding which seems to arise spontaneously from within the mind, and not by conscious analysis of information derived from an external world. If there are 'messages' sent from 'contacts', this is the 'receptive' state in which they are likely to be received. Most magicians claim that relaxed states enhance psychic abilities. That state thus becomes the premier means to handle forces said to be somehow beyond ordinary perception. This is when psychic 'healing work' is meant to occur.

Meditation then is not merely a training technique to relax the neophyte, but in theory part of the basic equipment of magical practice, the technology through which it works. When in training, magicians are supposed to meditate once daily. After initiation, or on the completion of their training, they are often asked to meditate upon the group's symbols. This meditation has many functions. It is meant to give them an intuitive grasp of the nature of group symbols, to allow them to participate in a psychic network of all group members (known as the 'group mind'), and to enable them to sense external events which would not be accessible to the 'rational' mind – messages from contacts, awareness of important events, psychic communications, and the like. Magicians talk about 'doing work', usually for their group leader. By this they mean that they are meditating on a particular image – say, Isis – and that they will tell the other person what sort of image and thoughts arose in the meditation. If the magician is advanced, her impressions are thought to be externally inspired, although these external inspirations are always 'mediated' through the meditator's personality. (For example, if Ann wants children, and in her meditations perceives Isis to be pregnant, magicians are likely to call her meditation a 'projection', and not take it seriously.)

So magicians tend not to practise meditation extensively for the sole sake of attempting to attain an altered state of consciousness. For them it is a means to an end. They often learn to meditate by the time-honoured method of concentrating on their breathing, but soon move to meditating on certain images – a tarot trump, a kabbalistic sephiroth, and so forth. Some of them, particularly long time members of the Western Mysteries, clearly do experience significantly altered states in meditation. Many of the senior initiates I knew meditated every day. The woman who became my witchcraft high priestess certainly experienced altered states, and had developed the calm personality that often accompanies consistent meditation. Most magicians, however, probably only reach a state of deep relaxation – and not an altered state – through their meditations. One hastens to add that deep relaxation is not an insignificant experience: it often elicits a heightened visual sense and involvement with imagery and certainly leaves a deep impression upon the meditator. But the result is that magicians speak more often about a vivid involvement with a deity or a tarot image than about attaining samadhi, nirvana, or the other states described in the Western guides to Eastern meditation.

[13] Green (1971: 17).

MYSTICAL STATES

The real end of any meditative practice is a mystical experience. But few people get there by that hard climb. More often, if they have such an experience, they have sudden dramatic epiphanies which vanish almost immediately but may affect them for life. Very senior magicians have developed their meditative techniques to the point where they seem to be able to elicit mystical experience easily. Indeed, this seems to be the implicit definition of an 'adept'. Others cannot elicit them, but their meditation may make their occurrence more likely, and their experience of such states is profound.

The genuine mystical experience is of a particular type. James describes it as noetic, ineffable, transient and passive.[14] Another scholar includes the consciousness of unity, timelessness, and a transformation of the sense of self.[15] A psychiatrist identifies a sense of intense realness, unity, ineffability, unusual sensations and trans-sensate phenomena – experiences which 'go beyond the senses'.[16] The experiencer feels profoundly and with the utmost certainty that he and the universe are one, that the present is eternal, often that he is overwhelmed with light or love. Many writers ring changes on these remarks, and there do seem to be variations between different mystical states.[17] However, the common descriptions across cultures, both from within and without any mystical tradition, suggests that mystical states involve distinctive subjective experiences, probably the result of a particular biochemical event.[18]

Many examples could be quoted, most of them religious but some of them triggered by pain or by certain moods.[19] James' most hackneyed example captures many features commonly cited. The writer later produced a work entitled *Cosmic Consciousness*.

I had spent the evening in a great city, with two friends reading and discussing poetry and philosophy. We parted at midnight. I had a long drive in a hansom to my lodging.

---

[14] James (1902: 380–1).   [15] Happold (1963: 45–50).   [16] Deikman (1973).
[17] Wainwright (1981: 1–53).
[18] There are biological studies of this state. Mandell carefully examined the 'psychobiology of transcendence' and concluded that 'the neurochemical, neuropharmacological and neuro-physiological model constructed here suggests that within the continuum of slow waves to hypersynchronous seizures restricted to the hippocampal-septal-raphe circuit (without amygdala involvement) lies the essential neurological constellation underlying positive to ecstatic feelings, and that they can be induced by the use of techniques directed towards disinhibition of that circuit' (1980: 435). In other words, however it happens, biology has a role to play. These seizures are associated with ecstacy; the long after-discharge of the circuit, he suggests, produces the 'saintliness' which is often said to follow a mystical experience. The major source of information on this topic comes from clinical studies of temporal lobe epileptics, who often suffer from local disinhibition of this circuit. They often have multiple intense religious experiences: in a study of sixty-nine psychomotor epileptics, twenty-six reported 'mystical delusion' experiences (Mandell cites Beard 1963, Slates and Beard 1963, Dewhurst and Beard 1970, Geschwind 1964, Waxman and Geschwind 1974, 1975). The point is that the body manufactures its own morophine-like substances, the 'endorphins', whose release is inhibited. Activities which halt inhibiton include meditation, pain, and certain patterns of psychological discomfort. But this is not an established theory within the biological literature; I cite it here only to underline the biological involvement in the psychological state.
[19] E.g. Rousseau (1979: 39); see Laski (1981).

My mind, deeply under the influence of the ideas, images and emotions called up by the reading and talk, was calm and peaceful. I was in a state of quiet, almost passive enjoyment, not actually thinking, but letting ideas, images and emotions flow of themselves, as it were, through my mind. All at once, without warning of any kind, I found myself wrapped in a flame coloured cloud. For an instant I thought of fire, an immense conflagration somewhere close by in that great city; the next, I knew that the fire was within myself. Directly afterward there came upon me a sense of exultation, of immense joyousness accompanied or immediately followed by an intellectual illumination impossible to describe. Among other things, I did not merely come to believe, but I saw that the universe is not composed of dead matter, but is, on the contrary, a living Presence; I became conscious in myself of eternal life. It was not a conviction that I would have eternal life, but a consciousness that I possessed eternal life then; I saw that all men are immortal; that the cosmic order is such that without any peradventure all things work together for the good of each and all; that the foundation principle of the world, of all the worlds, is what we call love, and that the happiness of each and all is in the long run absolutely certain. The vision lasted a few seconds and was gone; but the memory of it and the sense of the reality which it taught has remained during the quarter of a century which has since elapsed.[20]

The intensity, the vividness, of the experience is common, as is the conviction of the insight. The sixteenth century contemplative, St. Theresa of Ávila, interpreted the state religiously. For her, these sensations were not accidental, but elicited through contemplation. This is her account of the 'Fourth Degree of Prayer':

Let us now come to the soul's inward sensations in this condition. These should be spoken of by those who know them; for as they are beyond understanding, so are they beyond description . . . [The soul] dissolves utterly . . . to rest more and more in [God]. It is no longer itself that lives . . . As it cannot comprehend what it understands, it understands by not understanding.

Anyone who has experienced this will to some extent understand. It cannot be expressed more clearly, since all that happens is so obscure. I can only say that the soul conceives itself to be near God, and that it is left with such a conviction that it cannot possibly help believing.[21]

These states are often called ineffable. Throughout the centuries mystics have written extensively of the state which is indescribable and the yearning which must bypass the intellect. The fourteenth century anonymous *Cloud of Unknowing* advises the seeker to struggle through a cloud of darkness, dark because the intellect cannot illuminate the way. 'For the love of God be careful, and do not attempt to achieve this experience intellectually. I tell you truly it cannot come this way . . .'[22]

In the Western Mysteries, leadership – adept status – seems to involve the adept's control over mystical states. It is said that initiation in the 'Greater Mysteries' cannot be conferred by ritual except in name; it must be achieved by the individual, and those who describe themselves as initiates depict their

---

[20] As quoted in James (1902: 399).   [21] Quoted in Happold (1963: 353–4).
[22] Wolters (1961: 66).

experiences in terms which are strongly reminiscent of mystical accounts. I met only three individuals who explicitly claimed such initiation and each led a group within the Western Mysteries. All three seemed to have had experiences similar to those that James describes. All in addition spoke of their Greater Mysteries experiences in terms of mystical states which were to some degree muted and contained.

Some time after his first, and then later, mystical experiences, Simon entered the central magical lodge in London in his early twenties. He has practised magic for thirty years and has described himself as a Greater Mysteries initiate for perhaps half that time. Now, in ritual conditions, he has a deep sense of 'timelessness': past, present and future are simultaneous. He feels that he has a greater, higher self, which is both more his true self and also more entirely in union with the universe. This feels like a state of knowledge. It also feels passive, and he considers these feelings to imply the existence of a greater, wiser being with whom he is in contact.

The striking feature of Simon's account is that this state of mind is somehow more durable than the transient mystical experience. Simon describes the difference between his earlier experiences and his adepthood as the distinction between falling in love and being in love. The mystical experience was the heady, dizzying experience of romantic intensity, he said. In contrast, the Greater Mysteries concretized those feelings into a more sustained state in which you retained access to the feelings but kept your feet firmly on the ground – love adapted to the reality of diapers. This state is not permanent; Simon and the other two adepts do not elicit it during their daily work; but it emerges in meditation and ritual.

I casually and unsystematically asked magicians whether they had had mystical experiences. Sometimes they did not know quite what I meant; others immediately understood and gave me an exact date for the event. I have no useful figures, but my impression is that many, but not most, magicians have had genuine mystical experiences. This may not be unusual.[23] Although practice and inclination may make these experiences more likely amongst magicians, magicians are probably not wildly different from the broader population. But magic may provide them with a means to interpret such events which a sceptical engineer might not possess. Let me offer some examples.

James is an initiate of the Western Mysteries in his late thirties (he teaches educationally subnormal students). He has been technically initiated into the

---

[23] Far more 'ordinary' people seem to have had profound spiritual experiences than intuition might suspect. Sixty-five per cent of the one hundred randomly chosen Nottingham education students answered 'yes' to the question 'Do you feel that you have ever been aware of or influenced by a presence or a power, whether you call it God or not, which is different from your everyday self?' (Hardy 1979: 126). A National Opinion Polls survey of 1865 people scored a 34 per cent positive response to the same question, with the older and more educated scoring somewhat higher. Obviously no genuine mystical experience is needed to answer the question affirmatively. Nevertheless, hundreds of the excerpts given in the report from the Oxford Religious Experience Research Unit are clearly of this nature. The author suggests that people are often chary of telling others of such odd experiences (Hardy 1979: 125).

Greater Mysteries (in other words, there had been a ritual to initiate him) but does not claim adepthood. Several years ago he celebrated his son's birthday – had kids over, cooked for them, took them out. By the time he tucked the child into bed he was exhausted. But he thought of how much he loved him, he said. He went to his own room, looked out the window, and – he remembers formulating the question – wondered whether God loved him as much as he loved his boy.[24] Suddenly he felt absolutely and completely sure that God did. He lay down on his bed, staring out the window, with this feeling 'like a warm glow' spreading through him, and he felt an intense sense of the interconnectedness of all things within God's love. He lay awake until dawn, but felt that only a minute had passed, that the night had been one suspended moment. He felt marvellous the next day, he said, although it was hard to return to the mundane world after the transformed vision of the evening. The experience had been intense, indescribable and unforgettable. He has had two other similar experiences since. None of them has been directly related to magic (this is probably why he does not consider himself an adept) but all occurred after he had been carefully trained. He felt that he had reached God (from agnosticism) only through magic and that the mystical experiences had deeply affirmed his faith.

Robert (the computer consultant-lecturer of the coven I joined) told me about his spontaneous mystical experience the night I was initiated: it was his way of explaining witchcraft. In 1958 he was walking home from a study group, about a year after his initiation. The moon was full. As he looked at it he mused about cosmology. It occurred to him that the revolutions of the planets were like the revolutions of the electron around the atomic nucleus, and he wondered – again, formulating the question – whether the atoms of our bodies were the solar systems of some smaller world, and whether our solar system was an atom in a larger. For some reason, the fleeting fancy triggered a mystical experience. He has written an account of his experience, which he sent to me.

Like Cocteau's Orphée, I suddenly walked through the mirror, out of space and time . . . I was the calm, placid, unchanging moon which I had been contemplating so intensely, the fiery furnace of the sun . . . I was every king and queen, general, priest, artisan and peasant since the dawn of history, and as well as every beast, bird and insect of the forest . . . I was the One Soul of the universe, the deepest part of all beings, that has always been and always will be, and survives the death of mortal bodies and egos, and even of the planet on which we live.

Then it ended. 'I was wholly back in space and time. Looking about to locate myself, I reckoned I could not have walked more than four paces during the entire experience. Dazed, I continued on my walk home.' This remains one of the most powerful events of Robert's life. Witchcraft, with its philosophy of an interconnected universe and its claims of magical efficacy, makes more sense than any other religion to Robert because it captures the sense of unity which he felt so intensely at this time.

[24] Questions often act as triggers in these spontaneous experiences.

Others have had experiences which are extremely important to them but whose mystical quality is unclear to me. In 1971 John, a graphic designer in his late thirties, smashed his legs in a motorcycle accident. 'When I regained consciousness, I looked at a tree in a certain way.' He became a pagan, and within five years had developed a 'language' with trees (this was a sort of divinatory system) and he founded a Druidic order which now has 150 members (by subscription), a journal with a circulation of 750, and an inner group. I suspect that his accident did involve a mystical experience: great pain can release the neurochemical response which may lie behind the phenomenology. In any event the event had been so convincing that he repeatedly explained the creation of his order as its direct result.

Magicians have an ambivalent attitude towards mysticism. On the one hand, authors clearly assert that genuine mystical experience is desirable. To Regardie, ex-member and chronicler of the major nineteenth century magical order, magic was 'a quest spiritual and divine'; 'the inevitable end of magic . . . is identical to that conceived in mysticism.'[25] Aleister Crowley, black sheep though he was, announced that 'the supreme and complete ritual is therefore the invocation of the Holy Guardian Angel, or in the language of mysticism, union with god'.[26] Dion Fortune entitled her magical training manual *The Mystical Qabalah* and opened the volume with a discussion of why magic was the mystical technique best suited for the West. Yet magicians differentiate themselves from mystics. In theory, meditation is a means to a practical end: a state of mind conducive to magical efficacy. Magical texts often read like manuals of Christian prayer but their authors quite clearly consider meditation and mysticism to be tools. Magicians seem to enjoy the involvement for its own sake, but explain it as serving particular ends.

VISUALIZATION

The second technique central to the magical practice is 'creative visualization' (their term), 'seeing' vivid mental images. Like the meditation, visualization is explicitly part of the magical technology, the means by which the magic works. The mental image is often thought to be the link between the subtle, ethereal energies of magical ritual and the physical world, so that the skill in 'bringing the power through' depends directly on the ability to visualize. When magicians learn how to visualize, they understand – or at least, their concepts allow them to understand – themselves to be learning to use the mechanism which makes the magic work. Every training manual emphasizes the need for imaging proficiency. There are even manuals devoted exclusively to its cultivation.[27] Most courses have daily imaginative exercises to improve concentration and detail.

It is essential to understand that visualization is a skill. Individuals vary widely

[25] Regardie (1969: 31); (1964: 41).   [26] Crowley (1929: 11).
[27] e.g. Ophiel (1967).

in their imaging ability, their ability to 'see' the image clearly. Indeed, the degree of variation probably fuels the active philosophical debate over the felicity of the term, 'mental image'. Mental images clearly do not have position, opacity, and the sorts of things commonly associated with 'images'. But the term is a useful metaphor because many people do feel as if they experience dream-like images when conscious, and in fact may behave as if they scanned those images (mentally 'rotating' them) for information. Practice can improve this mental-imaging ability: pictures become clearer, more detailed, more picture-like.[28]

Magicians quite specifically and systematically train this ability. Both of the correspondence courses I took began the training by having me look at my room, and then shut my eyes and replicate the surroundings in my imagination. The next step, for one of the courses, was to take a 'walk' in a place I knew well, and then one in an imaginary land. Then I was instructed to imagine a magical 'temple', a room to which I would imagine myself to travel each time I meditated. Over the next four months, during my daily practice, that imagined room became progressively more vivid, and I could 'remember' it more clearly each time I returned.

The exercise *par excellence* for visualization is a 'pathworking'. This is a guided fantasy, a story read slowly to allow a deeply relaxed audience to picture its images as they sit, eyes shut, in the darkness. This short example comes from one of the central texts in feminist witchcraft.

Marshland Ritual

Relax, deepen and protect yourself. Travel to a forest and wind your way through the forest, going deeper and deeper, down and down. And following along that forest path you notice the earth becoming softer beneath your feet. The air has grown cool and moist, the earth soft and spongy. Soon you have entered a marsh and this marshland awakens within you memories of a far distant past. Remember now, and this memory is vivid, this is the place where your sisters gathered each month when 'the moonswell fills to brimming'.

And they are here again tonight and you eagerly join them, moving swiftly into their circle. You enter their circle knowing that together you will participate in a ritual to gain knowledge. Together, hands joined, you circle, slowly at first, circling round and round. Swaying and circling in the moonlight, humming a quiet chant. Round and round you go as the circle begins to move faster and faster. Your whole body is in motion now, gentle, strong motion.

[28] Mental imagery is a hotly contested topic. An active philosophical debate addresses whether 'the inner representations involved in mental imagery are pictorial or representational' (Block, 1981: 9; the volume collects some important essays). (It may be the case that the most vehement philosophical opponent of mental imagery as a descriptive concept – Daniel Dennett – simply has very little mental imagery, as an empirical fact (see his essays in the Block collection). Psychologists are becoming increasingly interested in mental imagery, both as a means of memory (Yuille, 1983; Buzan, 1977; Paivio, 1971a and 1971b; Marks, 1972) and of physical and psychological therapy (Masters and Houston, 1972; Singer and Pope, 1978; Horowitz, 1983; Singer, 1974 and others). Mental imagery involves processes similar to vision (Neisser, 1973; Kosslyn, 1980; Shepard and Cooper, 1982). Individuals vary widely in their imaging ability – their ability to 'see' the image clearly (Galton, 1883; Ernest, 1983; Katz, 1983) but can also be trained to improve (Yuille, 1983). (Segal, 1971; Sheehan, 1972; Sheikh and Shaffer, 1979 provide further reading.)

Your voices chant full and rich. The chanting and dancing become stronger, louder and faster. The ritual of knowledge has begun. Knowledge, intuitive knowledge, will be gained in extraordinary ways.

And as you continue swirling and turning in the moonlight, your body begins to change. All the women's bodies are changing, changing into those of geese. And suddenly the flock of geese soars off into the night, off to gather knowledge. Upon returning to the marshland you will again assume your own body, but now in the bodies of geese you will gather knowledge. (Pause about ten minutes).

And now hearing my voice calling you back, back to the marshland, back to your own body, your own identity completely restored. And now return to this room, carrying with you the knowledge that is yours.[29]

Most pathworkings involve a descent, a journey, an encounter and a return. After the encounter the narrator breaks off to allow listeners to develop the story individually. Then he tells them that they are now to return to their 'normal, waking selves'. A good pathworking engages many senses. The narrator will say that the air smells autumnal, the grass feels cool, the water tastes fresh, and so forth.

Here, another example, is part of a pathworking Emily wrote for the Glittering Sword:

You are walking through a large plain. The ground is yellow. The grasses are changing colour ready for Autumn. The sky is blue and the lapwings are singing. You are walking towards the hills in the distance. On the other side of the hills is the sea. It is to the sea we are going . . . Shortly you are climbing the foothills, getting closer . . . and closer . . . and closer to the sea . . . We walk into the sea . . . the water deeper and deeper around us. We leave behind our fears of drowning . . . our fears of being out of our depth in water. We are now walking through magical water toward the horizon . . . The water is all around you . . . it is several feet over your head . . . all around you the lush green is seaweed instead of grass. You feel the sea is full of life. The anemones catch small fish . . . the crabs chase their prey sideways . . . The beauty of it is breathtaking . . . the shells . . . weeds . . . animals . . . all have more colour under water. The colours vibrate with life. There is a gap in the seaweed forest and we drop down towards it . . . spiralling . . . spiralling . . . spiralling down to the seabed . . . the floor of the sea is red . . . There is a strange light at the bottom of the sea and we notice that we are in a seaweed room . . . Sands of different colours make a spiral pattern on the floor. The spiral leads to a large cauldron in the centre. Standing around the cauldron are three women . . . the women of the waters . . . they speak together . . . 'This is the threshold between the worlds. We are your guides. We guide you from the conscious to the unconscious through your emotions . . . We are the guides to the Moon who will guide you around the phases . . .'

Again, listeners go on a journey, are taken 'down', and encounter a significant being who converses with them. This is an excellent pathworking, full of texture and colour, with hundreds of different images to see, and a new medium – being underwater – to experience. When Emily read the pathworking in a Glittering Sword ritual, I felt as if I were breathing water and looking at anemones through refracting sea.

[29] Mariechild (1981: 109).

Pathworking is centrally important for two rather different reasons. First, the technical theory of magic suggests that magical power is shaped and directed by the imagination. A pathworking is the paramount form through which power is supposedly generated, gathered and released as the story develops and climaxes. The standard explanation for a ritual is that as the story is being told, the power is flowing, stimulated by the participant's imaginations. At the climax of the story, the power is released through the final images in the rite. Many rituals use pathworking, or at least a version of pathworking, as their central ritual technique. Most training groups ended their sessions with pathworkings as the central activity of the evening.

The second reason for the importance of these exercises is that pathworkings are for some reason deeply satisfying and persuasive of the reality of the magic, or at least of the sorts of experience of which the magic speaks. Magicians obviously enjoy pathworking, and think of the experience as something of a treat – as well as granting it important status as effective action. For many of them, pathworking is a memorable experience. Afterwards, participants comment on how 'deep' they got and on what 'happened' as the story unfolded. Experienced magicians will often do unnarrated group pathworkings. The group will sit down together, and one member will take the lead in describing the images he sees. When he gets tired, or feels stuck, another member takes over.

The technique of visual imagery is especially important to magicians because it stimulates spiritual experience. For some reason, participants often describe these events – planned or unstructured – to be moving, or spiritual, in some way profound. This effect of imaging has been known for centuries. It is particularly vividly illustrated by the *Spiritual Exercises* of St. Ignatius. Magicians happily cite the similarity. 'St. Ignatius of Loyola certainly used the imagination in a magical fashion as preparation for personal prayer.'[30]

There are two central elements to the *Spiritual Exercises*: a remorseless, intense examination of the conscience and a highly structured meditation which uses the visual, sensual imagination as a focus for concentrated mental attention. The vivid mental image is always followed by colloquy (free and unstructured converse with God) and concluded with the traditional Our Father. Consider the exercise on hell.

Fifth exercise: a meditation on Hell

After the preparatory prayer and two preliminaries it consists of five headings and a colloquy. The preparatory prayer will be the usual one.

First preliminary. The picture. In this case it is a vivid portrayal in the imagination of the length, breadth and depth of Hell.

Second preliminary. Asking for what I want. Here it will be to obtain a deep-felt consciousness of the sufferings of those who are damned, so that, should my faults cause me to forget my love for the eternal Lord, at least the fear of these sufferings will help to keep me out of sin.

[30] Knight (1978: 205).

First heading. To see in the imagination those enormous fires, and the souls, as it were, with bodies of fire.

Second heading. To hear in imagination the shrieks and groans and the blasphemous shouts against Christ our Lord and all the saints.

Third heading. To smell in imagination the fumes of sulphur and the stench of filth and corruption.

Fourth heading. To taste in imagination all the bitterness of tears and melancholy and a gnawing conscience.

Fifth heading. To feel in imagination the heat of the flames that play on and burn the souls.

Colloquy. Talk to Christ our Lord. Remember that some souls are in Hell because they did not believe that He would come; others because, though they believed, they did not obey His commandments. They fall into three classes: (1) before His coming; (2) during His lifetime; (3) after His life on earth. Remembering this, I will thank him that he has not allowed me to die and so fall into one of these classes. I will also thank him for having shown me such tender mercy all my life long until now; and will close with an Our Father.[31]

Both Ignatian techniques and magical pathworking demand the concentrated attention upon visual imagery in which all senses are used to enhance the apparent reality of the imagined scene. Both techniques present a series of highly structured images to the participant who must give them personal form. Both demand a period of freedom in which personal fantasy can be developed and explored. Both preface their exercise with the injunction that it should reach into their inmost self. And both Catholic priest and apostate magician assert that these techniques are highly effective in creating profound spiritual experience. 'Their remarkable efficacy, their undoubted power – a new high-powered spiritual weapon capable of being applied with almost explosive results for use at all levels of spiritual need'.[32] The vivid imaginative experience is extremely persuasive of the shadowy otherworld about which the magic and the religion speak.

It is not clear to me why this intense imaginative involvement should be so potent. That it is potent, there is little doubt; one of the interesting lessons of this study is that people often describe their intense imaginative experiences as spiritual. Indeed many magicians describe themselves as being very involved in fictional, imaginative worlds as children, and as entering magical practice because it promises the return of what they call early religious experience. I myself remember becoming deeply involved with novels at the age of ten and that I would sometimes treat the books as if they were sacred. It is difficult to reconstruct what that felt like, but now when I read a novel in which I become deeply involved, the transition between the reading the novel and buying groceries has a distinctive tone: I feel somewhat suspended, as if I had to move into a mundane realm. Perhaps it is this sense of suspension itself, a remove from ordinary reality, whatever that is, which makes the experience seem spiritual.

---

[31] Loyola (1973: 35–7).   [32] Evennett (1965: 46).

Perhaps also the intensity and the sense of suspension arises from the involvement with externally provided imagery, and the personalization of public imagery. Reading a novel or attending a religious ceremony is neither an ordinary interaction with other people's conversation or an ordinary subjective experience: it is as if there is a third, liminal state, betwixt and between. In any event, part of the training in visualization involves personalizing images. The thrust of magical training is to have magicians make these magical images their own, to make conventional images deeply and personally significant. A subsequent chapter returns to this theme in its discussion of the symbolism's hermeneutic strength: here the point is that the mixture of private and public imagery may shape the phenomenological experience of the practice.[33]

An example may illustrate the attempt to give the imagery significance. This is the eleventh lesson of the Hornsey group course, their seventh on the kabbalah. The lesson itself is three pages long, and discusses the 'temples' of the kabbalistic sephiroth. Each of these symbols is represented as a place: the sephirah (singular) can be considered as a 'home' for a particular type of energy or mode of consciousness. The ten kabbalistic foci have each been created, according to the course text, by the many human minds which for centuries have used them in meditation and ritual. These forms are called Sephirotic Temples and they are understood to be complex three-dimensional glyphs, symbol-groups, into which the mind can walk. In other words, the course turns the abstract sephirah into a visual image which can be 'explored'. (See figure 5, p. 62) However, while the course describes the characteristics of each seiphirah, it demands that every student produce their own images for the sephiroth. The lesson gives an example in constructing the temple of Yesod. In magic, Yesod (the ninth sephirah) is associated with water and the moon. The two page description in the lesson includes the following:

The temple of Yesod is the temple of Levanah, the Moon, and it rests upon a small and perfectly flat plateau in the centre of the island . . . The interior is cool and dry and lit with a violet radiance which seems to emanate from the crystal walls. It is completely empty except for a black stone pillar exactly in the centre. This stone, which is the altar, is about a yard high and nine-sided like the walls of the temple. The top is perfectly flat and on it is a large moonstone supported on a silver stand. The air is fragrant with the smell of jasmine . . .

I quote the exercises for the fortnight's lesson in full:

Exercises on Chapter 7
Subjects for Contemplation
  1 Yesod (as the Foundation)
  2 Tiphareth (as the King)

---

[33] One could think of this in terms of performative efficacy. The sense that a ritual statement is effective depends on the conventional acceptance that it will be effective: that is the nature of performative statements. But magicians have little conventional foundation for their practice. Perhaps the interlocking of personal involvement and public convention progressively reinforces the conventions which makes the performative conventions seem valid, by making an otherwise weak convention seem personally relevant – but also not just a personal fantasy. Cf. Luhrmann (1985).

SEPHIROTIC IMAGE OF HOD

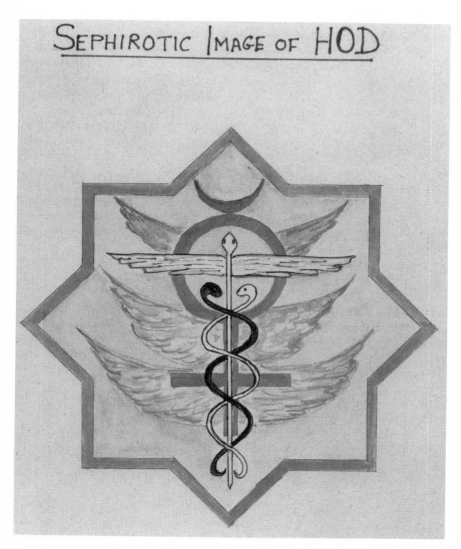

Figures 10, 11, 12, 13   Each student on the Hornsey group course creates suitable visual images for some of the kabbalistic sephiroth. One student has chosen to represent Hod through its associations with winged Mercury, with his caduceus; she represents Geburah as a vision of martial force. Geburah is also associated with justice, and an illustrator of a kabbalistic manual has chosen to represent this aspect of the sephirah. Here the illustrator relies on Egyptian imagery, representing Anubis and Horus, with the judgemental feather of Maat. Binah is a sephirah normally associated with women, the primordial and the womb.

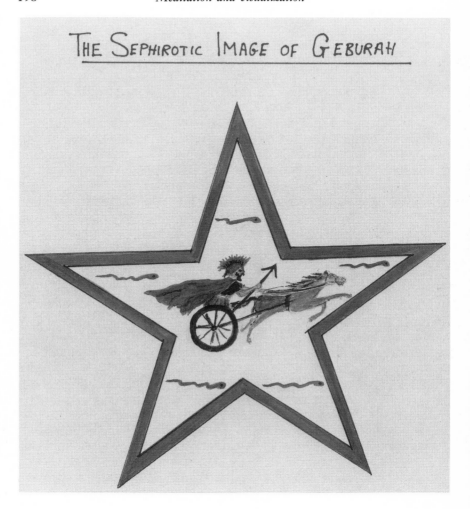

THE SEPHIROTIC IMAGE OF GEBURAH

3 Netzach (as Venus, the 'Star of the Morning')

Subjects for Image Building

1 Imagine yourself as in the sequence in the Sephirothic Temple exercise from standing on the slope overlooking the lake to entering the Temple of Yesod.

2 Continue the sequence and finish up back on the slope overlooking the lake.

N.B. Build carefully but remain relaxed. Attempt to 'feel', 'smell', and 'touch' as well as 'see'. Make sure that you visualize a proper return to Earth each time.

Test Paper

1 Design and describe a Sephirothic Temple for Netzach in roughly the same manner used for the Yesodic Temple described in this Chapter.

2 Comment on the phrase: 'by sympathetic induction the force can begin to flow through the image . . .'

Geburah

The point of the first two sets of exercises for this lesson is to continue practice in meditation (the course calls it 'contemplation') and visualization. The student should 'contemplate' and 'image build' daily and briefly record the experience. The two essays of the 'test paper' concern further training goals. The second essentially asks the student to rationalize a rather obscure account of magical theory, to explain the theory so that he finds it persuasive. The first asks that the student produce an account of a sephirothic temple which both adheres to the guideline of the course and yet is creatively personalized. By the time the student has reached this lesson, she has learnt a great deal about Netzach: it is associated with Venus, the colour green, and 'elemental force'. Its abstract 'meaning' has to do with relations, whether they be in love, work, or geometry. Netzach's name, she knows, is also 'Victory', and its 'spiritual

Binah

experience' is called 'a vision of beauty triumphant'. The student has learnt from this lesson's example that the number of temple walls should correspond to the sephirothic number, that the altar should display an appropriate stone, that a presence of a given archangel should be felt within the room. In her answer to the test question she should tell a conventionalized but creative story – a two-page story – about the temple (what it looks like, what it 'feels' like) so that she will remember it and find it evocative of that complex, abstract idea of relations. She might tell the story of a temple deep within an emerald mountain, its seven high walls hung with geometric signs. In the centre of the room stands a jade altar . . .

The interlocking of private and public is a common feature of magico-religious experience more generally. South American shamanism offers an arresting example of this balanced tension in the cultural use of visual imagery. Amongst the Bororo there is a standard sequence of imagined events for those who feel that they are 'chosen' to be shamans of a certain sort (the *bari*). The characteristic sequence involves a dream, in which the proto-shaman soars above the earth 'like a vulture'. Later in the jungle, he 'sees' an object move, 'talks' to the spirits (the *bope*), and finds certain bits of food. Then he is possessed in sleep, and leaps up, shouting wildly as the *bope* talk through his body. A mature shaman must come and talk with the *bope* at this point. Finally, the new shaman has a certain dream, in which a beautiful woman attempts to seduce him and he must refuse. And so on. There are other dreams in which he faces other tasks, all described as standard in his shamanic education.[34] And yet the conventional is clearly deeply personalized. 'Their detail and sequence are standardized almost to the point of collective representations, known by most adult nonshamans. Yet the three shamans I knew best spoke of them with vivid sincerity, adding variation and personal reactions at once idiosyncratic and consistent with the general pattern.'[35] The extremely private activity of dreaming is structured in defined ways. In Turkano shamanism the novice takes a narcotic drug in order to 'see' power objects.

Close by, the payé [shaman] is sitting. 'What do you see? Tell me, what do you see?' he will ask insistently, and the apprentice will try to find words to describe his visions. 'There is the bend of the river . . . a black rock . . . I can hear the water rushing . . .'. 'Go on, go on', the payé will insist, his ear close to the other's mouth. 'There are birds, red birds, sitting on the lower branches of a tree' . . . 'Are they sitting on your left or on your right?' the payé will ask. And so they continue, haltingly, at times in deep silence, until the older man knows what kinds of images and voices his pupil is perceiving and can now begin to interpret them for him.[36]

Again, the external authority helps to structure and order the novice's idiosyncratic imagery.

Visualization produces strong reactions in those trained in its use. They have spiritual experiences, find the images deeply moving, find them persuasive of the reality of the spiritual or magical realm. For these reasons at least, imaging techniques are widespread in religious practices. A knowledgeable survey concludes that 'the relationship between mental imagery cultivation and magico-religious tradition appears to hold regardless of societal complexity'.[37]

Magical training has a direct impact upon the magician in training. He learns to meditate, a practice among the most widespread of all religious techniques, and he learns to visualize, by a method akin to that called the militaristic training of the army of God. These are new or striking phenomenological

---

[34] Crocker (1985: 201–7).   [35] Crocker (1985: 206).
[36] Reichel-Dolmatoff (1975: 79).
[37] Noll (1985: 445). *Ethos* (*10*: 4, 1985) is devoted entirely to the discussion of shamans and endorphins. It discusses biological correlates – 'endogenously generated analgesia' (Prince, 1984: 420) – in terms which suggest an initially different biological phenomenon than the mystical or meditative state (though the end state may be in ways similar) which may be related to visualization. The discussions compare hypnotism and the analgesic effects in acupuncture and firewalking.

experiences. The magician needs to make sense of them in his understanding of himself. It would not be surprising if the experience were interpreted through, or understood within the context of, magical theory. That 'making sense' is likely to be anchored in the net of magical theory, and as these new experiences sink into the background of the magician's life to form the basis for his future action, they may take the theory with them. The process of coming to terms with the vivid phenomenological experience of magical practice may help to make magical ideas seem natural, unsurprising, unquestionable.

15

'Knowing of': language and imaginative involvement

THERE is a famous philosophical distinction between 'knowing that' and 'knowing how'.[1] To know that is to grasp explicit propositions: you know that the sky is blue, that the earth is round, that Monday precedes Tuesday in the order of the week. These are facts of the matter, clearly and specifically endorsed. Knowing that is a verbal acquisition, and to teach others, you tell them what they ought to know. To know how is to have a skill. You know how to row a boat, and you know how to draw. You teach others to know how by demonstrating, by showing what to do. Whether this know-how can always be verbalized is a deep question. A fine jockey who has great knowledge of his horses may find it difficult to explain his skills to the uninitiated, but it is not clear if his practical knowledge is inherently inarticulable. But for the most part the distinction is uncontentious.

Yet there is a different sort of knowledge. This is not a knowledge of 'fact', for few 'facts' are involved. Nor is it solely a knowledge of skill, for although there are few facts this knowledge is still concerned with something like information. It is, rather, an imaginative involvement with – a feeling of intuitively grasping the sense of, the ambience of, the nature of. It is the sort of understanding you gain of Hadrian by reading Yourcenar. This too is a type of knowledge, for through it one gains awareness of how to behave in different lives. I call this a 'knowing of'.

The key feature of 'knowing of' is the imaginative absorption with a different person or world view. You feel that you could imagine how an Egyptian priest might open his temple, how a Roman centurion might feel on the Danube, how a medieval scholastic might have lived his life. You will be wrong, at least in part: in the closest of intimacies one cannot climb inside another's skin. But the awareness of different possibilities and their constraints conveys an awareness of another way of being, tacked down haphazardly to realistic facts. What do you learn from *Antigone*? Not the truth about life in classical antiquity. But you learn what it might be to retain integrity in the teeth of a corrupted world. From James you learn that communication comes through silences, from Faulkner that the mad are wise. But you do not need to acquire propositions through

---

[1] Ryle (1949).

these authors: you learn what it might feel like with a different soul or body. You imagine other ways in which it might be possible to live. I call this knowledge because it involves an awareness, even if the details are false. It is this awareness which interests me, not some philosophical definition of knowledge; I use the philosophy to clarify why the people whom I study describe themselves as coming to a new and different way of knowing through their practice.

I suggest that magicians gain this fiction-like involvement with their practice through the linguistic rhetoric they adopt to describe their rituals, and that this has implications for the interpretation of their rites. When magicians describe their magic, their language has a remarkable style. They poeticize their speech with elliptical ambiguity and an enviable ease with analogy and association. They use grand phrases and picturesque terms, and, Colette-like, pepper their discourse with taste, smell and sensual imagery. In part they simply acquire a new vocabulary about myths, astrology and the tarot. But they also learn manners of handling speech which strip predictable reference from ordinary words, manners which undermine the precision of language in order to enhance the intensity of imaginative experience. This linguistic restructuring performs an important function: it allows magicians to gain an imaginative sense of the peculiar terms which are used in magical theory. At the same time it provides them with a means to avoid intellectual discomfort, by allowing them to avoid committing themselves to statements about magic which might clash with previously held beliefs. These linguistic transformations take two major forms.

First, magicians learn to use a literal language to describe events which have not occurred in reality but have been imagined, and they use a metaphorical language to describe actual events, feelings, and impressions. There are significant problems in distinguishing the metaphorical from the literal, in defining the difference between the two.[2] I use the distinction to indicate relative, not absolute, difference in the ease with which I can identify an obvious empirical reference for a word. When a magician says, 'Loki is loose tonight', I take this as a metaphorical manner of describing unruly behaviour because I could never point to the Nordic god although I can actually point to the behaviour. When a magician says after a ritual that 'I could taste the salt spray' and I can testify that she has been standing inside a Gloucestershire house for the entire time, I call this an unusual use of a literal language because I can normally identify events (being at the seashore, having a wave splash over the prow of a boat) which could lead one to say, 'I could taste the salt spray' but in this instance very few of them are present. All language is in some sense metaphorical.[3] The point, however, is that magicians have a remarkably free hand with reference when they talk about their rituals. They use words that have commonplace, in-the-world associations at times when those ordinary

[2] Black (1962), Ortony (1979), Hesse (1979, 1984), Davidson (1984).
[3] For an interesting if contentious argument to this effect see Hesse (1984).

associations are not there, and they use poetic diction to state the simple fact that they have meditated.[4]

Second, magicians have an explicit metatheory which claims that talk of magic bears an uneasy relation to its content. Magical forces exist, they say, but no-one can properly describe them, because no-one really understands how the magic works. It is possible – and common – for magicians to declare confidence in magic's efficacy, and indeed offer explanations for why the magic works, while disavowing any firm knowledge of its mechanism. And the blame is placed upon the nature of language and reality itself: words are mere conventions, chosen to describe a reality too complex to be captured in their distortions. Any description of magic will do, because no description is adequate.

The best way to grasp these linguistic somersaults is through example. The first is an account of a ritual and the ways its participants describe it later, an exemplary illustration of poeticizing language. The second is a transcript of a group discussion about magic in which the futility of language is underscored. Both descriptions are taken from the Western Mysteries, partly because the phenomenon is somewhat more characteristic of the Western Mysteries than it is of other forms of magic, but also because the quality of my tape-recorded data is far better for what participants call 'the Mysteries'.

THE RITUAL

The 1985 Western Mysteries weekend at Greystone was to adept Gareth Knight 'one of the highlights of my esoteric career'. Over forty people gathered for a three-day spring weekend ostensibly devoted to the works of C. S. Lewis. Greystone is a Wiltshire manor house converted into a residential study centre. Isolated, stunningly beautiful, Greystone heightens any sense of 'specialness'. More than thirty of those present had come on the earlier annual weekends. Seven were members of Knight's inner magical group and another five were close associates. This core, then, knew each other well. At Greystone there is no hierarchy *per se*, but newcomers tended to see this core as a prestigious clique who sat together at the communal meals and disappeared into corners to gossip. (Needless to say, members of the group saw themselves as very democratic and accessible.)

At Greystone days were a mixture of lectures, meals and walks in the countryside, followed by latenight parties with illicit liquor smuggled up to people's rooms. The lectures set the tone: Knight, with knotted scarf and tousled, silver hair, walked up and down before the group, reading passages

---

[4] I realize that this is terribly complicated philosophically. However, the present purpose is not to argue for a particular view of language or metaphor, but to identify what does seem to be a peculiarity in the magician's manner of describing his magical rites. Regardless of whether all language is metaphorical or not, magicians use descriptive terms which seem more self-consciously ambiguous than the rest of their speech, and I argue that its increased ambiguity serves a purpose.

from chosen books and talking about the weekend's goals. Before his first lecture, Knight remarked that there had been 'a lot of pressure'. By this he meant a feeling that some non-earthly being was watching and pushing him, the sort of being Western Mysteries initiates describe as a 'contact'. This description prepared listeners for a 'powerful' ritual on Sunday night. This was 'the big ritual' of the weekend, and many of those present had been nervously anticipating it. Stories of Greystone became legends in this subculture.

We came into the main room at 7:30 on Sunday night. The seats ringed the walls. A map was pinned to the easel at the back of the room. There was a table in the centre of the room with a covered drum. People sat down silently in the greying twilight. The adept walked in, brisk and striding. He cleared someone off the seat next to his in the east, so that he had two seats free on either side of his own. Then he stood behind the central seat, facing us from outside the circle, as though behind the helm of a boat. He told us that we would be 'working' with historical figures from Elizabethan England: this meant that he would tell a narrative based upon them, that they would be the imaginative vehicle for the rite through which the power would be released. Peter, in the west, would 'mediate' or 'carry' John Dee, and Jane, in the south, Queen Elizabeth. In the north Ted would carry Drake, and we would follow Drake's journey around the world. 'I myself', said Knight, 'am only the pilot'. Still standing, he walked to the map and spoke of Drake's journey, pointing out his ports of call around the world. He explained that we were now aboard the *Golden Hind*, and would set out from England.

Knight lit a candle near him, at the stern, he said, and then one at the equivalents of starboard, port and prow, setting the candles down abruptly on square mirrors. Then he took his seat, and told us in detail the story of Drake's voyage, of his trip around Cape Horn, and his discovery of passes that no Western man had ever known. He described Drake's trip up western North America, where ice had caked the mast-head and forced him back along the California coast. Drake and his shipmates were treated as gods when they landed, he said, and they named the land 'the new Albion', and put a brass plaque upon a tree with a sixpence behind it to dedicate it to the Queen.

Knight continued in this way for perhaps half an hour, the listeners sitting, eyes shut, in the dark. At the end, when he had spoken of Drake's death at sea, and the solemn burial, he read Newbolt's chestnut about Drake's drum: 'Take my drum to England / Hang it by the shore / Strike it when your powder's running low.' After a short silence he stood up, walked across the room, and beat a furious drumroll from the covered instrument. He drew the sword from the scabbard that was lying on the table (he had spoken of swords earlier, of Elizabeth knighting Drake, Dee hovering in the background) and held the sword aloft, saying 'let the sword that was broken be mended here on earth anew'. He replaced the sword on the table, resumed his seat, and faced us. There was a short silence. Then, in a throaty voice, he said, 'Ye can open the door, Mr. Duncan [Peter], and let 'em all ashore.'

What was happening in this ritual? Knight had been 'working' with Drake for months. His wife Abby explained this term afterwards. You begin with a structured meditation, she said. Their group was working on Astraea, the heavenly star maiden who represented Britain to them,[5] because ultimately they thought of themselves as helping, slightly, to bring heaven and earth together and to strengthen the inner life of their country. From one of your daily meditations, she said, an idea would emerge that you were sure was important. You would work around it, doing research, reading and meditation. Her husband had felt sure that Astraea had to do with geography, the earth, and maps. He had had maps up around the house for months. They had also 'needed', she said, to find a complete list of the English sovereigns.

During this preparatory period of several months, the group had been in frequent touch, telling each other about their dreams and meditations. The theory behind this is that a 'contact' reaches out to a number of people of the same interconnected group. Contacts are meant to be highly evolved human beings no longer encumbered by human bodies who, from their distant perspective, can give guidance and power to human beings. It is the magicians' job to 'bring them through', to understand this communication and act upon it. When the group uses their imagination collectively, great power can (in theory) be released in directions obliquely indicated by the symbolism.

The nature of this communication is unclear. On the one hand, communication can be direct. As Abby said, 'when you get a very strong insight, you call it communication, because you know that it was very different to anything you've thought of before'. All members of the groups were likely to ascribe creativity to the intervention of a contact. Once, for example, Ted had called Knight and Abby because he had had a disturbing dream. Afterwards Abby saw – her word; she 'saw' – a monk, who beckoned her into a church, where an abbot gave her advice for Ted. I asked her whether it might not have been her knowledge of Ted which led her to have that image and to offer that advice. 'No. When it happens you can't think with your conscious mind. If I'd stopped to think, I couldn't have heard the dictation.' She interpreted her psychological insight as a direct communication from another being.

On the other hand, the 'communication' is often just the sense that something is important. An adept might meditate on a cauldron, and have a mental image of an apple. He would then ask his group to meditate on cauldrons, and tell them about the apple. One group member might meditate on cauldrons and seem to see an apple tree growing through the cauldron, and see that the apple tree was hung with swords. The magical group would not conclude from this that their contact was a sword-strung apple tree sitting in a cauldron. They might, however, conclude that apples, swords and cauldrons were important symbols for some external contact, and that they ought to do a ritual which used all those three images to channel the magical force.

Because the spontaneous images are in theory externally inspired, there is

[5] See Yates (1975a) for a description of the Astraea figure in the Elizabethan era; Knight, and probably others in his group, was familiar with this text, which discusses Astraea as the name given to Elizabeth to glorify symbolically her reformed, just imperialism.

implicit social pressure to have personal experience which conforms to some common mould. When group members talk to each other about their dreams and images, they think of themselves as 'double-checking' the contact, making sure that their interpretation was reliable and their contact trustworthy, neither a personal fantasy nor an evil being masquerading as a benevolent contact. They talk to each other to establish whether their own images are collectively shared, and then they talk to each other to establish what characteristics this collectively shared being seems to have.

Before the Drake ritual, Knight's group had been reading about Drake and Elizabeth, meditating on maps, globes, ships and star maidens, calling each other to describe what seemed to be particularly important meditations, dreams and events. Sean became particularly involved in his meditations, and felt that he had a contact who had been a cabin boy on Drake's ship.[6] As the day of the ritual approached, Knight still felt that he was not entirely sure what the ritual was 'meant' to be about. Then Sean rang him up, to tell him about a book relevant to the weekend and to say that he had 'gotten some stuff through' which might interest Knight. This account – it is a description written during a meditation – begins,

They say that Drake's drum resounds in the world again, for in the times that are coming he, like Arthur before him, will be needed. The ancient trio of Arthur and Guineviere, balanced by Merlin, form a triangle. They are felt in the later images of Elizabeth, Drake and John Dee . . .

This is vague, poetic language whose only physical element is a drum. Knight decided – he would say, 'realized' – that they should use a drum. So he borrowed his daughter's set and took it off to Greystone. He felt when he left as if 'they' – the contacts – had been planning the ritual for eighteen months at least. It was then that he and Abby had gone to Greenwich, and been so unexpectedly moved that they had bought a picture of the palace and brought it home. They said that 'we didn't know why at the time'. Then Peter and his wife had quite unconnectedly gone to Plymouth. Knight told me that 'these things had been in the air'.

After the Sunday ritual the participants dispersed, wandering over the grounds. Knight and his officers hung around together, chatting. The woman who had been Elizabeth said that she had 'felt seasick', that 'my shoes were too tight', that 'lice crawled on my scalp'. Ted said that he had heard whistles blowing, and they all spoke of their sea legs. They made comments like, 'I felt the room rock'. Knight pointed over the valley at the lights of the town beneath us. 'It's remarkable how these things hang on – that looks like the lights of a

---

[6] Felt social status tends to influence reported status of contacts and reincarnations. Only people of Knight's stature are likely to claim important historical figures as personal contacts, or to describe themselves as a reincarnation of a powerful predecessor. I found very few reincarnated Dees or Elizabeths; I found quite a number of minor Egyptian temple priests and priestesses, many minor court figures, and the like. Acolytes, however, may share in often more glamorous contact of an adept.

float, bobbing in the water.' Here they use language as if it were describing events in the material world: they do so to indicate the vividness of their magical ritual experience and thus the efficacy of the rite.

A month later I spoke to Knight again. He described events in the aftermath of the rite that provided, for him, additional confirmation of the presence of magical power. Peter, he said, had had the 'archetype' of Dee around for a while and then that of Drake; Ted had felt Drake strongly, for a while, as had Knight; indeed, the archetype had been 'around' a good deal.[7] According to Knight, having an archetype around means that you look at the world in a new way, as if you were that character while also being yourself. With Drake, Knight said, he felt tactical and efficient. 'When you take the dog for a walk you check the terrain for strategic manoeuvres. Things in the house get mended when they've been waiting for months. Decisions get made fast. It's useful.'

Later I was sent a report on the meeting. It is customary, in a Western Mysteries group, that after the ritual, individuals write accounts of their experiences and send them to the presiding adept, who then compiles a general report. Knight illustrated his general report of the ritual with excerpts from participants' accounts. These individual reports were quite unlike common-place conversation. One said, about a morning lecture, that: 'I was aware of an Astraea figure in midnight blue robes, on which were the morning stars. The stars were metallic and twinkled, and slid from the folds of her gown as she moved. Small flurries of tiny metal starlets bounced up where she walked, and the floor was soon covered in a layer of stars from her gown. She circumambulated the hall, making no direct contact by word or by look, twirling gracefully at intervals, until, her circular dance completed, she walked back up the slope of the sky and disappeared'. The writer may have casually described this sense to others over the weekend: in the report Knight continues 'this stardust was very apparent to several of the officers and it felt almost as thick as the dry autumn leaves that one used to scuff through as a child'. Here Knight describes the opening of the ritual itself:

The power came in very strongly, even when the hall was being prepared for this working. As one who assisted reports, 'during the setting out of the room, the ship began to materialize, almost, and with the most unexpected power. So much so that I found it difficult to walk, and found myself swaying with a rolling gait'. [And another . . .] 'At tea time, I had a lot of stomach-ache, in anticipation of something. In fact, I got quite ill again. This was not improved as the boat got going in the next working. I don't usually get seasick, but this was an exception. Didn't they have stabilizers? Every time I looked across at Ted he was going up, and I was going down. And when I looked at Peter, he was going up. I came damn close to putting the port light out'. [And another:] 'The idea of the redemptive blood contained in the two martyrdoms of Aslan, with the two grieving women, the two Marys, continued into the evening, with Drake's ship the *Pelican*, later renamed the *Golden Hind*, a sort of pre-Christian sacrificial equivalent . . . The associations are endless . . . When we got ashore, into the Andes, I knew what I was after

---

[7] Archetypes are discussed briefly in chapter 17; see n. 4.

and what I was up to before anything was said. The worship of the sun, and the sun behind the sun . . .'. The journey had its more troublesome side, however, as might be expected with all the dimensions of relationships involved. The officer in the north reports, '. . . There were contending forces which were hard at times to balance. The Lemurian [chthonic, underworld forces supposedly pre-dating Atlantis] contact was clear, but I found it hard to assimilate, particularly with the Christian element. It can't have been easy for Drake, either. However, at the beating of the drum, the head of steam became colossal. I was overshadowed by the Drake archetype. I could smell and taste salt spray. I was aware of Sean as a shipmate. There were overtones of Arthur. Then, oddly, Perseus. Then the star form broke through, and I saw a great sword above the altar, point down . . .'

And so on. The language is striking. On the one hand there is literal language to describe a let's-pretend account: 'I saw a great sword', 'I found myself rolling'; 'didn't they have stabilizers?' On the other hand, language is also deliberately poetic, laced with mythology: 'the martyrdom of Aslan . . . continued into the evening'; 'the associations are endless . . . the worship of the sun, and the sun behind the sun'. This language is meant to indicate that the power did indeed 'come in very strongly'. The participants' impression that the sword or boat was real implies that the let's-pretend narration in the ritual was somehow as large as life, that it was different from ordinary narration, because the power flowed. Likewise, the poetic, symbolic responses are meant to identify a ritual so powerful that it elicited those associations. None of these reports lie, or consciously misrepresent the experience. The sense that there are 'contending forces' or a rocking ship was no doubt very 'real' and the experiential gist of these descriptions is no doubt accurate. And no doubt, the experiential intensity is heightened by the language.

Subtle pressure may bring about the conformity to this linguistic habit. Knight does not quote all, or even most, of the personal accounts. It seems highly unlikely that a participant would deliberately falsify his experience in order to be anonymously excerpted. Nevertheless there is pressure upon participants to be able to report such experiences and certainly to become one of Knight's henchman – a desirable, high prestige position – one must learn to be able to respond in this manner and learn this style of handling language. The eager neophyte is likely to accord a passing fancy more seriousness than he ordinarily would, and to elaborate it and remember it with vivid vagueness.

DISCUSSION GROUP

This next example illustrates the explicit theory of the futility of language. It is a transcription of a discussion meeting of another Western Mysteries fraternity, the Hornsey group.[8] These discussions were held perhaps four or five times a

---

[8] Although both examples have been taken from the Western Mysteries, illustrations from other magical groups could have been used to make these points. I use them only because my taped conversational data are richer for the Western Mysteries groups.

year, when the group assembled but instead of performing ritual, had a discussion under the adept's leadership. Here are excerpts from a transcript of an hour's talk, slightly altered to smooth out jocular conversational hiccups.

adept: Why do we do rituals?

member: It's a matter of correspondences, channelling forces; by using particular words we're giving the energy direction.

adept: Why can't we use wires? Like we do with electrical energy, or wave direction, like we do with radios?

same member: Because we're dealing with two different planes.

adept: What's a 'plane', in your definition?

same member: A different level of reality.

adept: You just defined the word by its synonym. You know we talk in a sort of gobbledy-gook in everyday language anyway. A plane is simply the appearance given to the universe at any different level. That's what a plane is.

The adept announces that language is limited, 'gobbledy-gook'. Nevertheless he provides a definition that will dominate the discussion, although he will adopt the words of a member's redescription of that definition.

different member: You mean it's a function of viewpoint?

adept: Yes, but because we are human, there's a sort of standardized coherence. The plane is simply the appearance given to the universe. If you look at the universe astrally, you see the astral plane. It's a question of viewpoint . . . We use all sorts of things to concentrate. Wires draw electrical energy, radios guide waves. Why ritual? Why could we not set up a machinery in this room to draw the forces? Is it because these forces are purely imaginary, in the usual sense?

second speaker: No. They come from inside.

adept: So you're saying that the entire universe is within you.

same member: Yes.

adept: Interesting viewpoint. Sarah?

The adept acknowledges an opinion about something which, to a magician, is extremely important, and (here I also interpret from his tone and smile) both approves it and seems to suggest that he cannot judge whether it is correct.

Sarah: The manifest universe has its sources – as far as I'm prepared to say at the moment – in human consciousness. There's something peculiar about human consciousness.

adept: Right. Okay.

Sarah: All ritual, any ritual object, is at a different level than my consciousness, but there are dynamics in my consciousness so that something perceived in one way on one level may be perceived on another. There's passage.

adept: Never embroider. Is there then a 'real' world, an external world?

Sarah: Yes, it exists, but it doesn't exist as it's normally supposed to do.

adept: You can't count on supposition.

Sarah: Okay, it exists, but it does not exist independent of human consciousness.

adept: Be careful of the 'human'.

The adept points out the difficulty of commonly used words. He will continue to do so.

Sarah: Yes. Exactly.

different member: Could we be careful of the word, 'external'?

adept: Yes, I was hoping that someone would explain that to me. Eleanor? Do you believe that there's an external world and an internal world, a world of imagination and a world out there?

Eleanor: There's a world, but how you see it is totally subjective. How you see it is your viewpoint.

adept: So if you were removed from it, would it still exist?

Eleanor: Yes, but for someone else, not for me.

adept: Does the outside have anything to do with the inside? Sarah was saying . . .

Eleanor: Yes, the actual reflection of it. But how you see the reflections depends on you.

adept: What do you think, Beth? In eleven words.

Beth: Eleven words. Well, I'm just going after this aspect of the energy – that human consciousness is the appropriate channel for the sorts of forces we're trying to bring through.

adept: I don't understand forces and channels and things like that. *He* [pointing to the second speaker] says that we cannot do it with a mechanism because it needs human beings, that it's all coming from within anyway.

Here the adept significantly challenges the sort of words magicians take for granted, saying that he doesn't know what they mean, doesn't know why they are even necessary. Simultaneously he is forcing participants to formulate a first-order theory of magic which they can defend.

Beth: It's as if we're all leaves on a tree. This group is a branch, and we're linked to a trunk.

still different member: That calls into question your whole nomenclature of inner and outer. [General yeses]

Beth: Again it's a point of view. The trunk is part of the leaf, but they're all part of a greater whole.

adept: Facile, facile.

Beth: Rubbish. [Laughter]

Again, he challenges the description, this time as being too simple and therefore probably not accurate. At the same time, Beth has acquired an explanatory analogy to which she can refer in the future.

fifth speaker: Let me add to Paul [the second speaker]. To follow this story of strings and wires, everything you'd attempt in that respect would be earthed, but [to Sarah] we can channel results.

Sarah: What I was saying was that the manifest universe is a result of consciousness. And I've got another bit.

fifth speaker: We're still on ritual, and what the purpose of ritual would be. If it can't be done with the bit around you, then you've only got yourself left, right? You can't use anything else.

Paul: We share the physical plane.

previous member: You can't rise above the physical, you're sort of forced.

Sarah: By what circumstances can't you?

previous member: There's a pressure upon you not to see anything else than what is – you can't see it from above because we're still moribund.

Sarah: Do you mean that my consciousness is irretrievably attached to the physical plane?

previous member: What would you say if I said yes?

Sarah: I'd say, *no.* [Laughter]

This is a matter upon which magicians should, one might think, have common views: after all, magical theory is often presented as a science-like theory which is applied, and the group members are discussing the supposedly theoretical basis on which the practice rests. Nevertheless, the point of this discussion has been to show how greatly members' interpretations differ.

adept: Functionally, for practical purposes, there's no difference between inside and outside. Read a decent book on particle physics. It's a question of viewpoint.

first speaker: Surely there's a difference of levels.

adept: No, not really. We make these mechanisms to get at something we can't actually grasp.

Paul: There's nothing in the physical plane that could contact the levels we get at.

adept: But there isn't any physical plane. There isn't any astral plane. There isn't any mental plane. There isn't any plane at all. All is consciousness. Or, looking at it as an old Buddhist saying, all is light. We can play with it, we can give it appearances and things, we can live inside it or outside it, it's all one, the whole thing.

Paul: And the forms we build are as this chair.

adept: It doesn't matter how you play this game, so long as you know what you're doing. And there *is* an astral plane, so long as you know what it is, what you're doing with it. But you've got to know what you're doing, and the whole structure of this esoteric group is to give you the means of grasping it and ultimately, within the Greater Mysteries, to build your own constructs within it. You don't play them by someone else's rules. *You* know the rules for making contacts – at least you think you do, the greatest joke of all which is a construct. You are a point. You have a Euclidean definition and position, but no dimension. You can be anywhere, but all the time. You can be the circle whose centre is everywhere. It's extremely valuable to read books about planes. Stretches the mind and so forth. But it also points out that it's all words, that one really doesn't know, that it's semantics, purely, but you have to use them . . . It's absolutely vital to have the structures and know how to use them. The fact that later they're discarded totally is neither here nor there, because without them you are incapable of grasping anything, you have nothing against which to kick, and if you have no boundaries you can raise no power. You have an open vessel; if there's steam rising from it, no work gets done. But if you put the lid on, there's an explosion. So we build forms and we have forms to concentrate power.

Both the method of the discussion and the final, summary speech are extremely interesting. The method the adept uses is to state a general position, then to involve different members by challenging them, showing them the difficulty of the verbal formulations which they are using. Then he provides words to describe what is under discussion. In the process, he forces members to articulate their own theory, and allows them to challenge each other's interpretations without allowing that scepticism to challenge the general validity of magical practice and efficacy. At that point – the central message of the talk – he announces that words cannot grasp what is the case, that any distinctions and divisions make a mockery of the interconnected whole. Words are essential tools but have no hold on truth. The game metaphor frequently appears in magical discourse: magic uses different rules from those of science, but neither has greater claim to reality. Language, it is said, is a tool used to structure something which is structureless and inherently unknowable, and performs a function in letting one work within it. So magic is semiotics with a vengeance. The doctrine says that the choosing and systematizing of signifiers yields great power, but that the content of what is signified is more or less irrelevant. If magical theory is disputed or if events cannot be explained, this is cast as the fault of the language. The magician will feel more free to use metaphorical, allusive terms both because that language use is encouraged and because a second-order theory – words are 'semantics, purely, but we have to use them' – explains that no words can grasp the true nature of things. In this discussion language was both retrained and undermined.

DISCUSSION

There have been many studies of magical language: such language is often stereotypical, formalized, repetitive; it allows participants to define what they are doing as something different, as a creative act somehow divorced from their ordinary use of language.[9] Malinowski even suggested that the child's first experience of language is magical. The child speaks, the world responds, and the child acquires a sense of power. Here I am not analysing the magical language particular to ritual, but modern magicians' language about magic, the way magicians frame their descriptions of their activities, describe their meditations and rituals, and evaluate the reference of their theories. Few studies have explored the significance of magicians' meta-magical language in conjunction with the language used in rituals, and the effect that the rhetorical style can have upon the practitioner. The lesson of the exploration is that the rhetorical style can affect the way the practice is experienced and understood.

I suggest that the imaginative rhetoric used to describe magical ritual may be instrumental in engendering the practitioner's confidence in the significance and validity of the practice. Establishing the validity of the practice is a problem in modern magic. People who once knew nothing of magic engage in rituals meant to produce results directly in the physical world. They have relatively little social support from the wider culture for engaging in the ritual, and the basic idea behind magical ritual is counter-intuitive to culturally commonsensical views. I would argue that the rhetoric of the practice may elicit an ease with the involvement by presenting the practice as non-ordinary but significant, and that it does so by giving the terms of the practice some ontological weight while leaving the reference of the terms vague, but simultaneously giving practitioners an experiential sense of that reference. This process rests upon the vivid,

[9] E.g. Ogden and Richards (1923), Malinowski (1935), Tambiah (1985).

ambiguous fiction-like rhetoric, and the type of understanding I call 'knowing of'.[10]

The critical term in magical practice is 'power'; others are 'force', 'plane', 'inner' and so forth. One might not, perhaps, expect such terms to be learnt by ostention, but one might expect that they would be associated with certain feelings and experiences repeated over subsequent rituals, and that the magician would learn to recognize power through his responses to the rite. In other words, power would have some recognizable attributes, at least in its effect upon the magician. To some extent, this supposition is valid: magicians do have striking experiential responses to the rituals, and they take those responses to indicate the power of the rite. As we have seen, magicians talk about 'feeling' the power in the rite. However, one magician does not necessarily experience the same feeling over a series of supposedly powerful rituals, and what he does experience is not necessarily unique to his magical involvement. Learning the reference to the word 'power' is not like learning the words 'pain', 'sadness', or 'joy'. Magicians do identify rituals as 'failing' because there was no power, and when they make such assertions they often mean that they have had no response to the ritual at all. However, it does not follow that they have a particular feeling which identifies the presence of power to them. A great variety of factors lead the magician to identify a rite as powerful: strong emotional responses, the authority of the ritual leader, the subsequent achievement of the goal, and so forth. 'Power' is neither uniquely nor consistently defined.

Indeed, the ambiguity is explicit. Words have no meaning, the adept says: they are only tools, handles to a complex world. In modern magic, the representation of complex magical categories – categories like the magical 'plane', magical 'force', or whatever it is that is the subject of a ritual – is self-consciously uncertain. Magicians are explicitly told of the ambiguity of language, and different magicians use different words and images in different ways to characterize the same event. In discussion of magical ideas, and descriptions of magical practice, the specific words seem almost irrelevant: it is as if the word-value dwindles to its phatic importance, so that magicians use their descriptions of the ritual to signal a sense of involvement and commitment instead of as a means to convey information. That of course is an exaggeration: when Sean says that the ancient trio of Arthur, Guinivere and Merlin is felt in the later images of Elizabeth, Drake and Dee, he is not simply trying to express his enthusiasm for Knight's ritual. But his language is no more precise than

---

[10] Recent discussion in the literature of concept acquisition and categorization has emphasized that prototype theory is inadequate to account for the acquisition of categories: the use of most categories implies a reliance upon idealized cognitive models, scripts, schemas, frames, affordances – upon something which enables the subject to draw inferences about the behavior or nature of the category concerned (e.g. Neisser, 1987). No adequate theory of categorization, it is said, can be based on characteristics of the categorized objects themselves. The thrust of the literature has been to stress that no category can be understood to be independent of some model or framework. It is as if the magician's rhetorical style provides something like an inferential or implicative model for the term *without* its more specific attributes, which remain explicitly ambiguous.

poetry: startling images, new juxtapositions which are evocative rather than exegetical. It is not clear – to speaker or listener – exactly what information is meant to be conveyed. It *is* clear that the ambiguous language signals an involvement in the ritual and is meant to signal that magical power was present and active; if a participant thought that power was not present, he never says anything that gives a realistic description of an imagined event. The most common thread to the identification of power's presence is the vivid imaginative language to describe one's experience of the ritual itself.

I suggest that the first role of the rhetoric is to give the involvement a special status and, in particular, a special truth status. The negative form of this suggestion is to say that referential ambiguity frees the practitioners from conflict with previously held commitments or beliefs. All magicians were once new to their practice, and all must learn to find it persuasive despite the seeming oddness of its theory and practice. In modern sceptical society, conscious of what Gellner calls a 'new cognitive ethic' that derides magic, lauds science and establishes rational canons of coherent consistency,[11] this might not seem easy. The style of the language helps these rationalistic practitioners to accept statements which if baldly claimed they might find difficult to sanction. Magical assertions hover between the fictional and the real, eluding clear declaration. The ambiguity grants the possibility that magic works, that the forces, like tables and chairs, are real. At the same time it sidesteps an empirical assertion of the dubious claim, for the practitioner is told that no statement is really valid. The language can be both persuasive, for the literalness asserts the reality, and incontestable, because its metaphoricity avoids making the direct assertions which *can* be attacked. The magician can have it both ways, with the freedom both to believe and not to believe, without ever making a decisive comment as to which of the two he endorses. Indeed, the adept's metatheory explicitly encourages this ambiguity, for it asserts that something like magic is at work in the universe, while also asserting that it is impossible to describe or explain whatever it happens to be. According to the metatheory, all statements about magic are false, and yet also true. No magical statement, then, can challenge long-held views in the same way that a strict dogmatism might. The ambiguity significantly eases the possible stress of cognitive dissonance by suspending the ordinary canons of truth.[12]

However, I suspect that the specialness is more significant than the avoidance of intellectual conflict, and that the poetic rhetoric, with its

---

[11] Gellner (1974).

[12] 'Cognitive dissonance' was a term developed by Festinger (1957) to describe the incompatibility of two 'elements' of one's mental universe. The desire to smoke, for example, is incompatible with the knowledge that smoking is bad for one's health. Festinger theorized that people would seek to reduce cognitive dissonance; the most interesting part of the theory is that people would use various irrational 'tricks' to avoid dissonance. Smokers, for example, would avoid information about smoking-induced lung cancer. Magicians use rhetorical strategy, among other strategies, to avoid the dissonance between the practice of magic and knowledge of the social disapprobation of magical practice. For a further discussion of mental tricks and dissonance, see Elster (1979, 1983). Luhrmann (1986) describes the use of morality in a similar manner to avoid intellectual discomfort. See also Chapter 18.

referential ambiguity, effectively marshalls commitment to the practice by this endowment of a special truth-status. The use of paradoxical language – literal statements used metaphorically, poetic statements to describe ordinary events, words which explicitly have no definition – indicates that the occasion described was extraordinary. It means that the statement has a truth-status apart from the everyday and, by implication, is as if not more significant than the ordinary. When a practitioner says, 'I could taste the salt spray', she means that she was so caught up in the imaginative narrative that she felt as if it were real. According to magical theory, this indicates that the power was flowing: the feeling of being caught up in the ritual is the feeling of magical force. Similarly, if a magician says, 'They say that Drake's drum sounds in the world again', he means that the meditation felt very powerful, and that he had a strong sense of his 'contact'. Again, this feeling indicates – to him – that the power was flowing and that the contact was there. A sceptic argues that the paradoxical nature of religious statements detracts from religion's appeal, and in fact many theologians have studiously devoted themselves to providing a logically coherent account of beliefs. Here it seems that the very paradoxical nature of religious and magical claim may give them their significance. They become special, and set apart.[13]

The second effect of this rhetoric is to create the awareness of the more specific elements of the inferential models behind the terms, the set of intuitive associations which help to govern the use and interpretation of a concept. The special truth-status is part of this inferential frame, but there is also far more, which differs for the individual and for the rite. The magician describes the rituals he thinks were important with a richly imaginative rhetoric. The particular description varies from ritual to ritual – some rituals are about Drake, others concern Apollo – but on each occasion, the imaginative evocation is great. I would argue that the rhetoric significantly increases the magician's tendency to treat the magic seriously, because it conveys an experiential 'knowing of' sense of magic's concepts despite the explanation that these terms have no established content. The magician imagines what it would be like to be Drake, or Apollo's priest, either 'being' a powerful person or wielding magical power directly. This involves identification with a being about whom relatively little information has been given; it is a leap of imaginative faith in which one 'feels like' the being described. The process demands a novel melange of a variety of associations: in the case of the Drake ritual, being on a boat, wearing a high collar, being very cold, discovering something new, being frightened, being excited. The more sensuously detailed the description, the richer the melange, and the richer the resulting inferential backdrop. By some process, the ritualist combines an imaginative context which momentarily overrides the mundane.

[13] Malinowski (1935) identified what he called the 'co-efficient of weirdness' in magical language. In his ethnographic material, magical chants were often extremely peculiar, fraught with gibberish and apparent nonsense. The point of the weirdness, he said, was to underscore the intentional difference in the purpose of magical words. Since then a body of literature has been built around the peculiarity of magical or sacred words.

'Power' becomes more vivid to the magician in each ritual because in the rites the magician creates a context in which power plays a part, and he can experience its use or manifestation, regardless of his intellectual understanding of what the power is. I knew Sean when his 'contact' was a cabin boy on Drake's ship. To him, the imaginative involvement was quite vivid, and while he might reiterate the adept's assertion that one could give no explicit characterization of what a 'contact' is, he himself had a powerful, hands-on sense of what one contact had been. From this, he could assume an ontological reality for the term's reference; and yet, because of the term's stressed ambiguity, he could not conceive of that reference as being an ordinary thing-in-the-world. He 'knew' what a contact was because he had imagined it to behave in certain ways. He could feel its presence, talk with it, experience its vicissitudes. Yet he would also explain that one knew very little about contacts. Indeed, he has said that they only reveal themselves through the imagination, adapting their appearances to the personal needs of those to whom they wish to appear, and thus, one can never know them in themselves. In modern magic, one becomes absorbed in the fictional narrative of any ritual, and through imagining oneself to be Drake, or Apollo's priest, or in contact with Drake's cabin boy, one gains a vivid experiential sense of the nature of power wielded or contacts met. And simultaneously, the ambiguity of the terms suggests that they refer to something real, but real is an unusual, special way.

It is like teaching someone about classical antiquity: one could read Rose, Jaeger, Cornford, but if you start with Mary Renault's novels, the dryer text springs to life. Any magician can offer a definition of an inner plane – it is an alternate way of viewing reality, as the adept says – and then assert that one can never be sure of its reference. The dodge avoids cognitive dissonance, but the description is hardly comprehensible. But to feel, vividly, that Astraea has entered the room, even though one cannot physically see her – that experience gives a 'knowing of' reality to the term, the magical 'plane', because supposedly one is on this plane when one sees her. Mary Renault's novels have an oblique relation to the truth: Theseus and Ariadne may have existed, but how and in what form we do not know. Nevertheless the stories make the myth-and-history combination memorable and engrossing in a way that the careful, fact-filled survey might not have done, and the adolescent who encounters the novel before the historical survey is more likely to read the survey, enjoy it, and remember it. Magical practice differs from this fictionalized history in suggesting the distinctive nature of the fiction's realistic template: as if one not only became absorbed by the novel of classical antiquity, but acquired the impression that the book described a sacred, separate realm.

There has been a recent focus on the way that the ambiguous categories of religion or other activities becomes pertinent because the individual is able to make the terms personally significant, by using them to refer to his personal experience in the rite, or to previous personal experience.[14] Apt metaphors in

[14] Fernandez (1982), Whitehead (1987).

Bwiti religiosity and key terms in Scientological discourse give content and shape to personal events and emotional feelings. This of course is relevant to modern magical practice: the magician knows that a term like 'contact' refers to something which is experienced during meditation, he has a memorable experience during meditation, and he learns to apply the term 'contact' to describe the source of that experience. However, in magic this fictional involvement does not necessarily reiterate a particular concept, or focus attention upon a particular term in any one given ritual or its interpretation. Rather, the participant becomes involved with a fictional world specific to that one ritual or meditation – it might be Drake, Arthurian romance, Atlantean priestship, Celtic journeying in the underworld – and if the fiction-like involvement was gripping, she later identifies the magic as powerful, or claims that she was 'contacted', with the same loose fictional style of language. Each ritual and meditation allows her to experience a particular instance of the power, the contact or the plane. She is able to build up an experience-based understanding of the general term, while still allowing its abstract definition to remain opaque. This may give the magician more confidence in the sorts of things magic is meant to concern.

'Knowing of' is the mechanism through which the ritualist acquires the associative context of a category while its reference remains self-consciously opaque; it is the imaginative, fiction-like, almost deliberately poetic description of an event, an evocation rather than a denotation, as thickly descriptive as an ethnographic text and for the same reason: one acquires the associative, inferential context that underlies interpretation in that very different world. There are two parts to this mechanism. The first is that the ambiguous, paradoxical nature of the rhetoric imputes a truth-status to magical statements which make its practice seem special and set apart. The second is that the combination of referential ambiguity and imaginative involvement gives the magician a way of understanding the crucial categories through experience. This understanding develops regardless of the specifics of the term, and in such a way that the knowledge need not violate commonsense knowledge of the world. It is a state of knowledge in which the magician is imaginatively caught up in the practice, is not committed to an ordinary truth-status assertion about its claims, and understands the crucial terms through experiential involvement, not clear definition. Imaginative language significantly increases the capacity to learn about and accept new and unusual ways of interpreting the world.

Many speculations on primitive society have assumed that early man lived in a world in which poetry and reality were not divorced, and that somehow this gave early society an experience radically divorced from our own and more deeply satisfying. Cassirer spoke of a mytho-poeic reality, Barfield of saving the appearances, Lévy-Bruhl of a mystical union with the natural world. Vico, among the earliest of these romantics, postulated three ages of man in which the first experienced a world of living metaphor. 'That first language, spoken by the theological poets, was not a language in accord with the things it dealt with . . . but was a fantastic speech making use of physical substances endowed with life and most of them imagined to be divine'[15] And Weber spoke of disenchantment, and the ruin of a world in which magic had its force. The speculations are historically dubious. However, they may be relevant to the didactic process of acquiring ritual knowledge. It may be that this imaginative 'knowing of' rhetoric is commonly used to give magical terms more persuasion, that this imaginative narratology creates the sense of 'living myth' so well depicted in, for example, Melanesian ethnography.[16] Modern magicians do not mistake the imagination for physical reality, the error Levy-Bruhl was meant to make. They neither trip over imagined tables nor open the door for Astraea when she circumambulates the room. Nevertheless, what Freud called the reality-testing of any particular magical statement is suspended, and this suspension has something of a cumulative effect, so that through this magicians become more deeply involved in their practice.

Anthropologists have paid relatively little attention to the imagination.[17] This is a mistake, because the neither-true-nor-false status of an imaginative, fiction-laden language can serve a vital role is making culturally peculiar remarks believable, by providing a way in which one can know of the terms and their reference without ever committing oneself to their truth or falsity. Contemporary magic re-enchants the world, filling it with myths and images, poetic resonance and imaginative ambiguity. These linguistic transformations – literal merged with metaphorical, language undermined – grant an imaginative richness because they allow one to respond to words not for their factual content but for the imaginative possibilities which they offer. They are remarkable transformations, because they create a vivid let's-pretend world which is neither purely fiction nor confused with a tables-and-chairs reality. Magicians, struggling within a sceptical modernity, are able to become comfortable with a magical practice which much of the culture disavows, and they are able to do so in part because of their language's rhetorical flexibilty.

---

[15] Vico (1961: r. 401).

[16] Young (1983), Leenhardt (1979).

[17] Needham (1978) has rightly observed this point, although his exploration of 'primordial characters' is not one which I would necessarily adopt.

16

Ritual: techniques for altering the everyday

C HANTING. Incense. Slow, rhythmic dancing. If the language describing magical ritual creates a suspension of disbelief, ritual itself involves a totality of word and action which magicians treat as, and seem to experience as, something wholly apart from ordinary reality. We have already seen that magicians learn special techniques of meditation and visualization, both used in ritual practice, which may have significant effects upon performers. We have seen that magicians experience unusual emotional, spiritual or physiological feelings in rituals, and that they identify those feelings as an indication of the ritual's 'power'. We have seen that the language to describe rituals suggests that magicians have an intense imaginative involvement in their rites, and that the narrative used with them may seem almost realistic. Magical rituals are deliberately constructed to have impact on their ritualists, and the tools of their construction often have a wide cultural dispersal. Again, there is something like a technology of the sacred, which these sophisticated magicians consciously exploit to affect the practitioners in the practice.

Many anthropologists have discussed the characteristic feature of ritual as formalized speech and action.[1] 'Rituals tend to be stylized, repetitive, stereo-typed, often but not always decorous, and they also tend to occur at special places and at times fixed by the clock, calendar or specified circumstances.'[2] These characteristics of redundancy, stereotypy, and regularity, allow the rituals to do certain sorts of socio-cultural jobs: to carry social codes, to convey analogical associations, to elicit emotional support for cultural canons. Ritual efficacy in this respect is enabled by the formality which sets these actions off as different, not to be evaluated as technical, instrumental acts but in some other way. Tambiah defines ritual words and acts as characterized, to different degrees, by 'formality (conventionality), stereotypy (rigidity), condensation (fusion), and redundancy (repetition)'.[3] He argues that these qualities distance the private emotions of the actors from the public morality expressed by ritual performance.[4]

Much of modern magical ritual is formalized, and the formality certainly

---

[1] Rappaport (1979), Tambiah (1985), Bloch (1974), Munn (1973b), Malinowski (1935), Bateson (1972), Moore and Myerhoff (1977).
[2] Rappaport (1979: 175–6).   [3] Tambiah (1985: 128).   [4] Tambiah (1985: 133).

serves to differentiate the engineer from the ritualist he becomes. However, some rituals are more formal than others. Some are performed once only; even these can be highly conventionalized – Moore and Myerhoff remark that newly invented rites are constructed with tradition-like conventions[5] – but others seem freely spontaneous. There is extraordinary range in the ritual practice of modern magic, and it may be more useful in this self-conscious context to describe the goals in a magician's construction of his ritual rather than the micro-characteristics of repetition or formality with which they can be achieved. These conscious goals provide an interesting perspective upon common ritual characteristics.

Most magicians say that the purpose of any ritual is to allow the ritualist to visualize with great concentration in an altered mental state. The manuals are full of this sort of exhortation. Knight says, for example:

> In magical ritual, however, all depends upon the state of mind of the operators, and unless they are well-trained in the techniques of concentration and creative visualization, the work will invariably prove abortive. The whole aim of occult ritual is in fact for it to be an aid to concentration and visualization.[6]

Perhaps curiously, this consciousness-changing rarely included drugs in the groups I attended. Participants never took drugs during rituals, or indeed outside them, although for some of them, youthful experience with consciousness changing drugs had lead them to magic because they realized, they said, that they could change their perception of reality.[7] Robert, member of the coven I joined, told me that taking drugs in rituals was like taking a helicopter to the top of Mount Everest. Part of the experience lay in the climb. Ritualists did, however, seem to have three general strategies to achieve their ends: they acted out and described an altered space and time, they used mind-altering techniques, and they went to elaborate efforts to construct a separate identity for the performers of the rites.

The greatest effort seems to go into the creation of a separate space and time, new Kantian categories for the inhabitants of what is meant to be a new noumenal reality. Separate space is defined rhetorically, and theatrically recreated in every rite. All rituals begin by creating a 'magic circle', an actual physical circle within which the rite takes place. Witchcraft's founder declared that 'the circle is "between the worlds", that is, between this world and the next, the dominion of the gods'.[8] Another witch says, 'in drawing the magical circle, man, in a sense, creates and defines his own little universe'.[9] A classic in the Western Mysteries claims that 'by definition, the [circle] implies a confining place, a limitation, separating that which is within from that which is without'.[10]

[5] Moore and Myerhoff (1977: 8–9).   [6] Knight (1976: 45–6).

[7] Beth had an intense religious experience on mescaline (under Huxley's guidance) which made her aware, she said, of the way in which altered perception could change one's reality, and of the limitations which everyday awareness places upon one's reality. This experience led her to seek other ways of experimenting with her perceptions; it was instrumental in leading her into magical practice. However, she did not use drugs within the magical practice, at least when I knew her.

[8] Gardner (1954: 26).

[9] Valiente (1970: 60).   [10] Regardie (1969: 111).

This word, the 'circle', is used to mean 'a ritual': all magicians talk of holding a circle, going to a friend's house for a circle, gathering at a circle, and so on.

In theory, a circle is a boundary to keep and concentrate the power within and to protect the magicians from any evil without.[11] All rituals begin by creating one within which the rite proceeds. This part of the ritual is called 'drawing' the circle. In witchcraft, it is rather elaborate. The coven I joined actually drew a chalk circle on the carpet before coven meetings began. It was always thirteen feet in diameter, and the chalk was always guided by a string held down by the high priestess' athame (ritual knife) in the circle's centre, an apt compass. To begin the meeting, the high priestess redrew the circle with ritual symbolism, over the chalk one on the floor. With her athame, starting in the place defined as the 'east', she walked around the circle, knife pointed at the chalk to inscribe a second circle in the air. Returning to the east, she kissed the knife and moved into the centre, to the altar. Then she purified the circle with the 'elements'. She consecrated water (water) and then salt (earth), and mixing them, sprinkled them around the circle. Her blessings are loosely modelled upon a famous early grimoire.[12] For example, over the salt she says:

Blessings upon this creature of salt. Let all malignity and hindrance be cast forth hencefrom, and let all good enter herein. Wherefore do I bless thee and invoke thee, that thou mayest aid me, in the names of Cernunnos and Aradia.[13]

The high priestess then draws pentagrams in the air at each 'quarter' (where the different directions are marked by tall candles) and summons the 'Old Ones' of that quarter 'to guard the circle and witness our rites'. She then puts incense (air) in the lit censer (fire) and presents it to the gods at the quarters.

---

[11] Among practitioners there is a controversy about what the magically created circle actually does. Gerald Gardner wrote that 'it is necessary to distinguish [the magical circle of the witches] from the work of the magician or sorcerer, who draws a circle on the ground and fortifies it with mighty words of power and summons (or attempts to summon) spirits and demons to do his bidding, and he dare not leave it. The witches' circle, on the other hand, is to keep in the power which they believe they can raise from their own bodies and to prevent it being dissipated before they can mould it to their own will' (1954: 26). Gardner's account seems a fair description of the way in which many witches seem to understand the function of the circle; it also seems a valid interpretation of the use of the magician's circle in the *Key of Solomon*, an early grimoire on which much current practice draws. However, most contemporary magicians use the circle as a symbolic representation of the magical working itself, that they are working upon the 'inner planes', rather than as a device for shielding or containing power. It is a way of asserting that the ritual has begun, and that those present are in ritual, magical conditions.

[12] Much of the actual working of the witchcraft opening is taken from the *Key of Solomon*, an early grimoire translated by Mathers (the creative force behind the nineteenth century Golden Dawn) from manuscripts in the British Library. The *Key* is the most famous of grimoires, 'grammars' of magical technique. The dating of the manuscripts is uncertain, but the kabbalistic invocations imply at least major alterations after the late fifteenth or early sixteenth century, when Christian kabbalistic magic was created in Italy and slowly made its way to England. As an example of Gardner's use of the *Key*, these are the words for the 'benediction' of the salt:

> The Blessing of the Father Almighty be upon this Creature of Salt, and let all malignity and hindrance be cast forth hencefrom, and let all good enter herein, for without Thee man cannot live, wherefore do I bless thee and invoke thee, that thou mayest aid me. (Mather, 1888: 91).

[13] Farrar and Farrar (1981: 37).

The circle is now created, but aside from her all participants are huddled at its edge. To allow them to enter, the high priestess 'slashes' the circle, in the air, to make a door. After they are in it, she walks around it with the athame, so that it is 'closed'. Vocabulary treats this circle in the air as a tangible thing: an 'open' circle is a ritually drawn circle that has been cut, and members can go to fetch food or use the lavatory. A 'closed' circle has been redrawn, and none are allowed to step outside it.

In the Western Mysteries – at least in the Hornsey Lodge, and at Greystone – the circle is not so literally defined. Hornsey Lodge members (the brethren) usually sit quietly in a circle of chairs in the temple before the rite begins, in an atmosphere of funereal sobriety. The adept enters and walks three times around the circle's interior. This is understood to 'draw' the circle; now, as in witchcraft, he summons forces and purifies the space. In the Hornsey Lodge, he performs the 'Lesser Banishing Ritual', a Golden Dawn legacy. In its original version, the ritualist faces east and draws the 'kabbalistic cross': he touches his forehead and says *ateh* (thou art), touches his breast and says *malkuth* (the kingdom), touches his right shoulder and says *ve-geburah* (and the Power), touches his left shoulder and says *ve-gedulah* (and the Glory), clasps his hands and says *le-olam* (forever) *amen*. Then he draws a pentagram in the air, points through it to the east, and intones the kabbalistic name of God in the east. Holding his hand steady he moves to the south, west and north, drawing pentagrams and intoning the appropriate God-name, and in the process drawing a circle in the air. (In most versions, the ritualist is also meant to visualize the right colour associated with that quarter.) Returning to the east, he stretches his hands out to his side, like a cross, and cries:

> Before me, Raphael
> Behind me, Gabriel
> At my right hand, Michael
> At my left hand, Auriel
> Before me flames the pentagram
> Behind me shines the six rayed star

The Lesser Banishing Ritual is sometimes called the foundation of all rituals. After its use, the temple is considered purified and ready for ritual work.

Ritual openings vary, but the basic idea formulated by the practitioners is always to inscribe a circle, to purify the space within and to summon forces to guard from without and grant their power to the work. There is always a ceremony at the end of the evening's main ritual to 'banish' the created boundary. The standard opening for the Glittering Sword rituals was written by the erstwhile Cambridge classicist. It began with the Lesser Banishing Ritual. Then candles were lit at each direction. Air and other elements were invoked at the quarters associated with them, and candles were lit to represent those quarters. This was done with suitably classical reference: 'Zephyros, Lord of the soft West Wind, waft thy breezes on us'. A 'Celtic' version of this opening involved laying a green cord around the group and invoking Celtic deities at the quarters: 'Epona, white mare of the hills, I bid thee welcome. Give a blessing to our work and keep us free from interruption during this night's work'. Not all openings were so elaborate. I attended a pagan gathering on Lammas (August 1) which drew the circle simply, with forty people who walked around dropping brown rice.

Even before the circle is drawn, the space of the ritual, the environment in which it takes place, is often defined as special. Magicians try to put aside a room in their house for a 'temple', dedicated to their gods. They use these rooms for their rituals, hanging odd symbols and paintings on the walls, and in time the walls grow thick with smoke and incense's reek. Such rooms are never meant to be used for anything but magic, although once a party was held in the Glittering Sword temple, to the horror of some of its members. The rooms are sometimes extravagantly arranged: the Hornsey group rebuilt a room in their collectively purchased house to make it exactly square, and built thrones and altars and ritual regalia. But not all people can manage a suitable, separate room. The coven I joined used a living room, but radically altered it, stripping the room of furniture and filling it with seasonal leaves and flowers.

One goal of all this effort is to create a separate place which is good, pure, and sacred. People talk about the circle being safe, about trusting other people in the group, about being able to weep without embarrassment. They become free with their immediate emotions, more able to transgress ordinary social boundaries. For example, a woman in the coven once asked us to 'do' something for her because, she said, she was terribly depressed. She was prodded with questions, and talked for perhaps twenty minutes about feeling uncreative, unfulfilled, unconfident. For the spell, the group put her into the centre of the circle, and gave her a sword to hold as a symbol of the successful warrior's struggle. They chanted around her, stopped, and held their hands high. At this point her husband put his arms around her neck. The high priestess whispered, 'Don't lean on her'. And at this the woman burst forth into a mixture of shouting and tears. 'Yes, that's it, you always lean on me, always protect me, never let me be myself.' When she seemed to finish, the high priestess – a woman of capable equanimity – said, 'do you dare to affirm to the Goddess that you can do what you want to do?' Silence. Then the woman took the sword, held it aloft, and said, 'I dare to do what I want to do.' 'Convince us.' And this time the woman spoke in clear and ringing tones. And each member of the group kissed her and said, 'we believe you'.[14]

[14] Theoretical accounts of secretive groups have discussed this creation of an intimate, protected world, though those accounts have not focused on the therapeutic value of this openness. Simmel's (1950) account is particularly elaborate. In the applicable elements of his theory, the secret society encourages members to trust one another, to treat each other as equals, and to develop affective bonds; the secret society tends to be highly self-conscious of its social life; and the secret society tends to present itself as a counter-image of the ordinary world, clearly set apart from it and organized along different lines. Bok stresses the affective component of the solidarity created by severe initiations (1982: 52; see also Aronson and Mills, 1951). She points out that secrecy creates a sense of shared privacy and trust because of the group's explicit acceptance of its members. The secret society 'offers the freedom to trust and to be creative, and the excitement of transcending ordinary limitations' (1982: 49). Groups encourage intimacy by removing social barriers. Trust is an emotional bond forged through the mutuality of sharing something private with others, and trusting them not to violate that privacy.

This woman, Kate, said that she could never have cried so openly except within the circle, a remark I often heard echoed. People felt safe in speaking openly within this protective, good enclosure. In addition, the very structure of spell-casting encouraged them to do so. To understand what imagery a spell should use, the group questions the person who requested it. In the coven I joined, many spells were psychological in nature: someone wanted a boost of energy, wanted to revive flagging spirits, wanted a sense of direction after forced unemployment. The requester would talk for up to half an hour before the spell was performed, about what he felt and why he felt that way.[15]

The freedom to break down, and the freedom to be healed. The magic circle chalks out space which magicians idealize as special and different, a mixture of the safe and the sacred. One manual speaks of the ancient stone circles – magic's paradigm for the ritual circle – as 'the sacred place where the life-force of the earth's energies was focused, and where those properly trained in the Mysteries could, for a time, become one with that vital essence'.[16] To understand that space, the authors say:

We have to reconstruct, within our own minds and with our own imagination, the landscape of the Foretime: filled with strange and frightening things, with a power that could as easily create or destroy – but every part of it uniquely holy.[17]

The magic circle is meant to recreate this sort of space. It is curiously like the imaginative sacrality of childhood, the special spot behind the armchair, under the desk, out in the woods, the secret place where fairy tales are almost true and adults are forbidden to enter.

Time is also said to alter in the circle. Part of the common knowledge holds that watches stop or speed up during ritual. I have already mentioned my first London meeting, where one participant boasted to me that he couldn't wear ordinary watches because they sped up too much, that even his (twelve-hour cycle) digital watch occasionally displayed thirteen in 'this sort' of atmosphere. In the Hornsey Lodge, in the coven, in the Glittering Sword – in all rituals, watches are meant to be removed. People notice this requirement. They check to see that they *have* taken off their watches and remind novices to do so.

Most magicians say that time itself moves slowly, if at all, in ritual. An experienced supervisor in the Servants of the Light remarked over dinner that 'when I teach I always explain that on the "inner", time is very different – it's not linear but cyclic, eternal and unchanging'. The high priest of the coven I joined claimed that to him, ritual's most dramatic difference from the everyday was the sense of a 'time that flows with a different current'. And he explained

---

[15] Psychoanalysts have long noted that small groups tend to encourage 'primary process' thinking – in psychoanalytic terms, wishful, non-logical, emotional thinking (Freud, 1965: 626–48) – and seemingly allow participants to lapse into patterns of behaviour exhibited in childhood (Bion, 1961; Slater, 1966; Colman and Bexton, 1975). Certainly it is the case that witches (who have the smallest, most intimate groups) allow themselves more emotional outbursts than they would do in public.

[16] Matthews and Matthews (1985: 50).

[17] Matthews and Matthews (1985: 50).

that 'through ritual, we break through to a different sensation of space and time'. Another witch explains in her manual that 'in witchcraft, we define a new space and a new time whenever we cast a circle'.[18] The theme constantly repeats itself. 'We were told by a medium that those involved in the ritual [Greystone, May 1983] would be dead within the year', one of Knight's students glumly announced. 'Of course we weren't. But then [this as an afterthought] time works differently on the inner.' Rituals are supposed to break watches and stretch time.[19]

The major mind-altering techniques have already been described. Magicians almost always include some period of quiet before a rite begins to allow the participants to sink into meditation, and throughout the rituals there are periods of meditative silence, or periods of pathworking to be experienced in a meditative state. In the Hornsey group, the meditation began in the changing room, before the ritual. After five minutes or so, participants went up to the temple, where they meditated some more. The ritual itself nearly always involved meditation, in which participants 'left' the room to go on a journey and 'returned' upon its completion. Participants kept their eyes shut for well over half the time they were in the temple, and they seemed to go to considerable efforts to relax into an altered state. Particularly after 'big' rituals – the Spring Equinox at the Hornsey group, or any of the meetings at Greystone – people seemed exhausted, elated, or somewhat out of touch, in some way affected by their struggle to dissociate themselves during the performance.

In addition, techniques like chanting or dancing are used to unsettle ordinary conscious awareness. When I joined the coven, the high priest told me to focus on the central candle on the altar when we performed a spell. The usual structure for a spell was to hold hands in a circle around the altar, and then begin to run, at first slowly and then more quickly, chanting a nonsense verse. The objective, he said, was to feel as if the altar was spinning wildly around the candle's flame. This was an effective disorienting technique. The group would run at full final speed for several minutes before suddenly stopping to visualize the ritual goal. I, for one, sometimes felt distinctly not-normal; not dizzy, but not myself. It would take a moment to readjust.

Chanting has appeared in many of the rituals described: most coven spells involve chanting, Emily used chanting in her Glittering Sword pathworking about the sea, the feminist women's mysteries group chanted at the Kentish barrow on Halloween night. The idea that chanting, or sound more generally, can be used to sever an ordinary relationship with reality is widespread in the subculture, and there have been a spate of lectures and workshops on sound's

---

[18] Starhawk (1979: 57).

[19] Many anthropologists have pointed to different time-reckoning within different cultures (Evans-Pritchard, 1940; Whorf, 1956; Leach, 1961; Goody, 1968; C. Hugh-Jones, 1979). The interesting point is that the possibility of varying time-reckoning provides a valuable means to distinguish experiences which the culture needs to distinguish. Space and time are fundamental categories. To show that they are not imperative is exciting: to claim that magic alters them is to shout about the difference – and the fundamental reality – of the magical world.

use.[20] Often, the chant can be a nonsense verse, as is the spell-chant in the coven I joined. Sometimes it is a rhyme, invented by members for a particular spell. Margaret's coven invented rhymes for each spell, and chanted them throughout the 'working'. The actual words never seem to matter very much: members vary the words, or chant the spell-subject's name, or join in with a sing-song harmony.

Starhawk's manual provides a number of seasonal chants. The 'Kore chant', for spring and fall equinox, represents the changing, transforming goddess:[21]

> She changes everything She touches
> And everything she touches, changes

She also gives instructions for creating a 'multi-voiced' chant, in which different people chant different lines or cycles of words; sometimes these seem far from any meaning. These chants include:

MOON Mother Bright Light of All Earth Sky We CALL You.
LUNA Momma Shiny Shine COME
HAIL Old Moon Secret WISE One HAIL Old Moon Secret WISE One
She SHINES For All She FLOWS Through All
All That Is WILD and Free All That Is WILD And Free
Green Bud Leaf/Bud Leaf Bright/Leaf Bright Flower/
Bright Flower Grow/Flower Grow Fruit/Grow Fruit Ripe/
Fruit Ripe Seed/Ripe Seed Die/Seed Die Earth/
Die Earth Dark/Earth Dark Waken/Dark Waken Green/
Waken green Bud . . .

Sumerian chant: half sung on two or three notes – repeat entire chant.

NAMmu NAMmu O NamMU AE EE AE AA O NamMU
NINmah NINmah O NinMAH AE EE AE EE O NinMAH
MAmi MAmi O MaMI AE EE AE EE O MaMI
MAma MAma O MaMA AE EE AE EE O MaMA
MAH MAH O MAH MAH AE EE AE EE O MAH MAH . . .[22]

The point of the chants is to shake off ordinary reality and allow the subject of the chant to affect the chanter in some unordinary state. Starhawk gives these instructions for their use: 'when you use the invocations given here, please play with them, experiment with melodies and plainsong incantings, rearrange them, combine them, interweave them, change them, and take inspiration from them to make them your own'.[23] The words do have value – they are the names of the Goddess, in different ways – but they are meant to form a texture of sound which involves and affects the magician in unordinary ways.

Another, similar technique is 'tuning'. The coven I joined used this technique occasionally, as did the workshop run by its high priestess. Essentially this is a technique of wordless chanting. One person begins by

---

[20] Jill Purce holds well-attended and well-respected workshops: Emily told me that they were among the most powerful experiences of her magical career. Purce's approach is described in *Resurgence* no. 115, March/April 1986.
[21] Starhawk (1979: 175).   [22] Starhawk (1979: 86).   [23] Starhawk (1979: 85).

humming or singing a single note, and the rest of the group members join in and begin to vary their pitch and intonation. The result has the odd eeriness of whale-song: it is music, but without the frame of melody. The sound can seem to have its own life, rising and falling, becoming stronger and weaker as the group continues. Tuning was thought to be particularly effective as a healing technique, and the occult workshop performed many healing rituals to which tuning was central.

Participants create different non-ordinary magical identities with a cornucopia of different methods: name changes, costume changes, a conscious theatricality. They speak and act differently. They use an archaic, otherworldly language – 'I conjure thee, O Circle of Power, that thou beest a meeting place . . .'. They walk more solemnly and gracefully (or with the graceless embarrassment of those under pressure to be graceful). They gesture slowly and dramatically. Elder, experienced magicians give advice about how to walk and act in ritual performance. 'Keep it slow. When you're new at it, you want to move too quickly.' The manuals advocate this conscious manipulation of the personality, and explicitly name it theatre.

In many ways [ritual] is a form of acting for you are playing the part of someone who is in touch with vast powers, and how convincingly you play the role will depend upon your natural and improved abilities. There is much to be said for following the production of a ritual as you would for a stage play. Each part requires its proper costume and props, it all needs rehearsals and practice of the actions, words and gestures.[24]

If you consciously treat magical ritual as a play in which you are a powerful magician, the manual says, your self-confidence in your magical abilities will dramatically improve. Again there is an element of the suspension of disbelief: create a fictional otherworld in which the magical power is present, and the power becomes more realistic in the process.[25]

Magicians rarely perform in ordinary dress. Witches dance nude around their circle, their nakedness supposedly representing freedom and equality: as the liturgy says, 'and ye shall be free from slavery, and as a sign that ye be really free, ye shall be naked in your rites'.[26] Whatever the reason for its introduction, it marks the rituals as different. The nudity is also usually well-contained within the circle. The coven I joined would disrobe just before the ritual, and another instituted separate 'changing rooms' for men and women to disrobe and robe before the ritual. Other magical practitioners also change costume. The Hornsey Lodge member dressed in black, with monk-like robes and Egyptian headdresses. The Glittering Sword asked each member to make their own robes, which appeared in rainbow shades. Gown patterns are simple, and often given in the manuals. The point is to wear something non-mundane. 'You will find that the very act of putting on a magical robe will make you feel different and it is in this way that it does help with magical work'.[27]

[24] Green (1971: 33).
[25] Theatre has always been an anthropological concern; some anthropologists are turning to it more explicitly as an explanation and understanding of ritual process e.g. Gregor (1977), Turner (1982). [26] Farrar and Farrar (1981: 43). [27] Green (1971: 12).

And this of course is a secret world, hidden behind closed doors and heavy curtains. Magicians often take a name in magic which they never use outside; it is a peculiarly persuasive means to assert a separate magical personality. Upon initiation a neophyte usually chooses a special name only to be used within the group. The Hornsey Lodge, for example, demanded that I choose a motto for a name. On the night, the adept read the initials of the phrase aloud, and placed the full name in a box then solemnly locked and stowed beneath the altar. So secret was the name that its full title was known only to myself, the adept, and the magus of my degree. In ritual, I was always addressed by these initials, though over tea we reverted to common names. During initiation I also learned that the fraternity had a new name, its 'true' name, different from the one which I had known, and I was told a secret 'word of power' which was the name of the greatest being who was thought to guide us.

The different name is sometimes described as the 'key' to power, because it helps move the participant into a magical practice marked by its separation from the everyday. A witchcraft manual remarks:

Having settled on your witch name, you must keep it very, very secret, as it will eventually be one of the keys to your deep mind. You will be using it whenever you wish to 'switch on' to perform a spell; this will be partly accomplished by pronouncing the name silently to yourself.[28]

To work effective magic, the manual says, you must consciously switch into another way of being, another personality style, where the 'deep mind' holds. By using a magical name, that switch is more easily enacted. Words, as Tambiah remarks, are an artificial creation, and their artificiality allows them to create the unreal.[29] A magical name is a potent aid to identity-creation.

The crucial feature of the secret name is that it not only separates two 'worlds' but allows magicians to move between them with ease. The straddled separation makes the magicians feel special. They acquire identities far more dramatic than those of their daily lives, identities in which they have great power and influence. Keeping the magical identity secret prevents it from being challenged by outsiders while retaining the sense of power and daring which makes it exciting. It seemed to me that participants quite liked the fact that their neighbours remained ignorant of their activities but would be shocked by them if only they knew. One woman who led an otherwise drab housewife's life spoke eloquently of feeling special and more alive through magic. It gave her something different from her husband. And when he drove me to the station he asked me what we did at meetings. 'She tells me very little.'

Inversion and the transformations of identity are standard fare for anthropologists: carnival, with its licensed ribaldry and rude mockery, its freedom to violate the ranks of the social hierarchy, came early to anthropological attention. So too did the transforming qualities of the liminal, the term fathered by Van Gennep but nurtured by Turner, in Turner's words 'that which is neither this nor that, and yet is both'.[30] Those in a liminal phase are

[28] Huson (1970: 39).   [29] Tambiah (1985: 53).   [30] Turner (1967: 99).

statusless, sexless, outside secular space and time. The liminal subject will experience *communitas*, comradeship between equals, with fellow participants, and she will feel discontinuous moments of sacred, suspended time. Magic, with its newly identitied practitioners bound with the family-like closeness of the coven, with its transformed space and time and altered state of awareness, probably qualifies as liminal – neither mundane nor entirely non-mundane, but an uneasy mixture of the two. The primary anthropological interest in these categories has been focused on their social function; Turner, for example, talks about its role in facilitating the flow between social categories, the movement between 'high and low, *communitas* and structure, homogeneity and differentiation, equality and inequality'.[31] These social capabilities are not very significant in magic. The real point of the creation of a difference, something outside the bounds of normal society, is to make the participants feel as if they are of another, different, sacred world. There has been perhaps too much analytical attention to liminality's success in effecting secular ends. The techniques of the liminal can be used to make the that-which-is-not seem persuasively more realistic.

Modern magicians strive to make magic realistic in an age of sceptical suspicion, and their strategies aim at making the rites seem different from the everyday. Published manuals and common knowledge stress the need to mark the ritual as different from the everyday, hidden from the outside world. Wear a magical robe you use only for ritual, and call yourself by a special, secret name; wrap your weapons in purple silk to hide them from the mundane; light candles and incense to transform the sitting room into Prospero's cave; draw the curtains, lock the door, take the phone off the hook, and the external world is quite literally excluded. Whatever it is that a magician does feel or experience in a rite, if the ritual is well-designed the feelings are at least unusual. In the end, it is these unusual qualities which the magician will find striking, and which he will need to understand.

[31] Turner (1969: 97).

17

The varied uses of symbolism

B EYOND all else, magicians' immersion in symbolism is perhaps the most compelling element of their involvement, and the experience which has the greatest impact upon them. Myths and images come to fill their dreams, dominate their fantasies, alter their self-awareness. Practitioners often find a particular myth or deity profoundly significant, and they draw pictures of it, write rituals about it, fill the room with its statues and symbolic associations. It would be hard to overemphasize the importance of myth and symbolism to magical practice. Magicians are often people who are temperamentally attracted toward myth; their involvement legitimates and intensifies their interest, and those who have warm memories of childhood tales often find themselves caught up in myths more strongly than before. One witch puts the transformation this way:

My friends and I [at age 12] lived through the battles of the *Iliad*; we read the historical novels of Mary Renault and Caroline Dale Snecker and took the parts of ancient heroes and heroines in plays and fantasy . . . In my deepest and most secret moments I daydreamed that I had become these beings, feeling what it would be like to be Artemis or Athena . . . As I grew up, I forced myself to deny these experiences of childhood . . . [then a witchcraft coven sent her a tape of the Charge] The contents of the tape had simply given me *permission* to accept a part of my own psyche that I had denied for years – and then extend it.[1]

This woman's experience is not unusual. Magic returned her to a childhood involvement with mythology that can grow more intense in this adult state, for magic justifies the intensity as a philosophy, a religion and a science. 'I had simply accepted, reaffirmed and extended a very old experience. I allowed certain kinds of feeling and ways of being back into my life.'[2]

Symbolism seems to appear everywhere in magic, and it plays many different roles. For one, magicians develop a personal mythology. That is, they collect an amalgam of the myths and images of other cultures, and weave them together in idiosyncratic ways. They specifically attempt to personalize their symbolism, so that their understanding of the tarot cards, for example, becomes a 'language' to talk to their own unconscious. They turn to history for its evocative, legitimating depth, but treat it like a myth whose claims of accuracy are irrelevant, a myth peculiarly suited to this fact-conscious age. They use symbolism to talk about

---

[1] Adler (1986: 15, 16, 20).   [2] Adler (1986: 20).

deeply personal experience, and because intimate feelings can be aired and reshaped within symbolic garb, involvement in myth and symbolism can be deeply therapeutic. The myths become a sort of image-based hermeneutics, a manner of interpreting experience which need not be directly captured in words. The practitioner also comes to experience magic as a mystery religion, rich with pregnant images and esoteric knowledge. This section examines these different symbolic involvements: the training which aims to create a phenomeno-logical awareness of the symbols, the creation of a myth-drenched history, the symbolism's capacity for personal self-description and its psychotherapeutic function, and the secrecy and secret-laden knowledge which is said to be magic's core.

THE PHENOMENOLOGY OF SYMBOLS

The central feature of a magician's training is his development of a creative, personalized symbolism to understand his magic, his personal life, and all aspects of his experience. Whether formally, through a correspondence course for the Western Mysteries, or informally, through reading and discussion, magicians begin to use particular symbols which they find personally salient. The importance of this personally relevant symbolism is widely recognized. This training is widely perceived to be effective. One course text announces:

The initiate of a genuine esoteric group begins to live, work and have his being within the symbol system of his tradition. He works with it daily, meditating upon it and interpreting his life in the light of its structure. It brings order to his inner life: both his dreams and his psychism will appear in terms of its symbolism, and the ritual workings of the group of which he is a member will be based upon it.[3]

Any group's symbolic system seems to become intensely important to the student who takes it seriously. In the Hornsey group, most of the rituals are based upon the kabbalah. I had the impression that the individual members found the arcane symbolism of the different sephiroth extremely potent. Certainly the symbolism entered both casual conversation and more solemn discussions about the ritual, and members seemed to dream and fantasize freely with them, hang symbolic representations of different kabbalistic sephiroth on their walls, and so forth.

The intensity is partly engineered by the way the formal course is taught. The course I completed before entering the Hornsey group seems standard for Western Mysteries courses: its goal was to teach the two central techniques of meditation and visualization, and to provide the student with an effective, personalized symbolism. The course seemed to expect that by the end of the training, the symbolism would be deeply significant for the student, and moreover, that the symbols might seem to have certain sorts of qualities. Witches, of course, did not have this formal training. However, the goals so

---

[3] Unpublished text for the Hornsey group.

clearly stated by the Hornsey group and the older manual which served as its foundation seem similar to remarks about symbolism made more widely by witches, pagans, and other magicians.

The Hornsey group course includes eight fortnightly lessons on the kabbalah, all of which involve meditation and visualization. The first four lessons ask the student to draw the tree of life (the kabbalistic glyph), and place correspondences upon it (the archangels, the planets, different names of god, the Egyptian gods, aspects of the Christian god). He is asked to meditate upon 'Netzach and Hod', on 'Yesod', on 'Tiphareth as the sun'. These four lessons provide you with the basis of kabbalistic symbolism. The next four lessons teach you to use that symbolism. They present more information, but repeatedly stress that traditional associations must be redrafted in terms appropriate to one's personal life.

A table of Primary Symbolism is included in the chapter, but the student should on no account accept it merely as something to be learnt and filed away . . . For no matter how much one may revere Qabalistic revelation in the past, human experience has been much enriched since then. More appropriate symbols may be found for archetypal ideas or old symbols may be interpreted in a new light. The serious student does not 'study' the Tree of Life as much as participate in it.

The theme repeats itself: history and tradition must be remoulded in one's image. In the last lessons, students fill the outline of kabbalistic symbolism with their own interpretations. Lesson five asks for an essay relating different 'archetypes'.[4] It asks for a magical image of Netzah, and asks the student to find Geburic and Chesedic incidents in the papers and Hod- and Netzach-type occupations. Lesson six involves creating magical images for eight of the sephiroth, and lesson seven presents a pathworking sequence in which these images can be used. Lesson eight presents an elaborate pathworking in which magicians use their visualization and meditation skills extensively with the symbols they have developed.

In other words, the course gives the student a complex visual map, and asks the student to develop its correspondence to his or her emotional life, to use it to define and differentiate aspects of his or her personal experience. There is a dual focus, then, upon the conventional and the personalized, upon the authoritatively defined, external, taught system and the private experience which one learns to identify as its 'meaning'. Symbolic meaning, the magician

---

[4] To teach the importance of symbolism and its role, the course introduces the notion of archetypes, the term and authority borrowed from Jung. Archetypes, it says, are specific areas of human experience, 'a complex of force of a specific type'. They are said to be deeply important to all people and to motivate human behaviour. Among the examples are the crucified god, the old wise woman or man, the hero, the king, and so on. All archetypes are significant to all people, but the particular significance varies with the individual. The course gives an example in the wise old man or woman who represents authority. All individuals must confront and make their peace with the authority of their society, but each does so in different ways and upon distinctive terms, and so the emotional resonance of the one archetype can vary widely. The point of the magician's discussion of archetypes is that each person experiences these archetypes in different ways, and as a magician you are meant to understand your response to any archetypes and 'work through' its experience, so that you no longer have an unhealthy or neurotic relationship to it, if you once did.

discovers, is the interpretation of a collective symbol in the context of your own life: 'the importance of a symbol lies in what you learn about it. You can learn much from reading books, but you can learn a great deal more by turning over in quiet and regular meditation the knowledge you have already acquired from sources external to yourself'.[5]

As a result, symbol-use has a creative, free associative nature. One is meant to think creatively about a symbol when it is used in meditation or in path-working; the aim of the magical teaching is to provide one part of the underlying framework which will guide one's associations. Personal, emotional significance is also meant to govern one's associations: the symbol should have a potent psychological force, according to explicit magical ideas. Magicians draw connections and comparisons, teaching strange symbologies and interpretations through more familiar structures. For example, Knight's *Practical Guide to Qabalistic Symbolism* (1965) describes one kabbalistic path thus:

It is like the hole in the earth into which Alice fell, leading to her strange adventures in Wonderland. It is also, on a mythological level, the way down to the Underworld, trod by Oedipus at Colonos, Orpheus in search of Eurydice, and many others; but primarily it is Persephone's descent to the King of the Underworld. Alice, indeed, might be said to be a modern version of Persephone.[6]

Magical texts are full of this sort of prose, linking one myth to the other and explaining them by a third. Magicians become skilled at constantly jostling and interrelating these different images, myths and stories, creatively re-organizing them and re-ordering them, linking them to the tarot, kabbalah and astrology and describing new events and concepts in strings of these other images and in ways relevant to their lives.

The most puzzling feature of this emphasis on symbol-acquisition is that magicians' symbols are meant to have certain qualities, and the magician is presented with definite criteria to establish whether he has acquired symbols properly. These criteria are most fully elaborated in the classic manual in the Western Mysteries, Fortune's *Mystical Qabalah*. Foundation for all Western Mysteries courses, it claims that magical symbolism involves a distinctive mental skill. This skill employs symbols as tools, and such symbols are intensely real, exact in their reference, and ineffable. The author also claims that the use of this skill should feel like a state of conscious dreaming and be spiritual in quality, and she compares the symbolism to a card index system. These are the markings of 'good' magical symbols, characteristics which students should strive to emulate, and manuals describe how they can be obtained. Let me emphasize that this account of symbolism as a skill is not ethnographic over-interpretation. The author asserts:

[5] FPD in Wilby (1968: 64). The initials are those of the magical motto of one of Fortune's closest associates, a man called Colonel Charles Seymour. The practice of referring to someone by the initials of their magical motto, often a Latin phrase of several words, is common in Western Mysteries fraternities.

[6] Knight (1965: 1).

The use of the Tree of Life is not merely an intellectual exercise; it is a creative act in the literal meaning of the words, and faculties have to be developed in the mind even as manual skill is acquired by sculptor or musician.[7]

Symbols are 'tools'; the magician yearns for mastery in their use in the same manner that a musician strives for 'the mastery of a virtuoso over his instrument'.[8] The characteristics which define good symbol-use in this manual are intriguing because they are not intuitively obvious. But they describe the way that the magician is meant to feel about his symbols once she is magically expert in their use, and they indicate how powerful indeed the symbolism becomes for her.

Ideal symbolic qualities

Ineffability The magician 'formulates a concrete symbol that the eye can see, and lets it represent the abstract reality that no human mind can grasp'.[9] Visual symbols transcend the limitation of the cerebral, analytic mind to seize the intellectually unthinkable. 'The mind can no more grasp transcendent philosophy than the eye can see music.'[10] Magicians repeatedly call this magic ineffable, and repeatedly say that visual imagery captures what cannot be caught in words.

Exactness The manual states:

An occult glyph is more akin to a coat of arms than anything else, and the person who builds up a glyph goes to work in the same way as a herald designing a coat of arms. For in heraldry every symbol has its exact meaning, and these are combined into the coat of arms that represents the family and affiliations of the man who bears it, and tells us his station in life. A magical figure is the coat of arms of the force it represents.[11]

Images may exceed words but they can still be sharply distinguished. The student learns to use the symbols to distinguish between ways of feeling and being. The magician uses a symbol system 'as an algebra by means of which he will read the secrets of unknown potencies'.[12] Magical training, then, involves learning to analyse different magical images and the interconnections between them: in what ways does the kabbalistic sephirah Hod oppose or relate to the sephirah Netzach? how does Tiphareth balance Malkuth and Kether?

Reality Magical figures 'are given names, and the initiate thinks of them as persons, not troubling himself about their metaphysical foundations. Consequently, for all practical purposes they are persons'.[13] It is a mark of magical proficiency that the symbols are experienced as ontic. A close associate of the manual's author gave this advice to the aspiring novice:

Act and react to these inner representations until you have lost all sense of the HOW, the WHEN and the WHERE in feeling spontaneously created within you by these

---

[7] Fortune (1935: 148).   [8] Fortune (1962: 2).   [9] Fortune (1935: 14).
[10] Fortune (1935: 29).   [11] Fortune (1935: 68).   [12] Fortune (1935: 15).
                             [13] Fortune (1935: 68).

visions which have been so often built up by daily mental toil. When this happens, a representation is not only just your subjective mental picture. It has become (for you) an entity which is not only objective but also vibrant with life, and it is real upon its own plane of being though that is not the material plane of physical sensation.[14]

This is a remarkable statement. Act as if the symbol is real, and it will be real for you. It may not be real the way tables and chairs are real, but it is nonetheless more genuine than a daydream. 'Whatever may be the rational foundations of the system, as an empirical method it yields results.'[15] The ambiguity is at the heart of magic and is explored in later chapters. Here the point is that the sense of reality is presented as a criterion of a skilled technique.

Oneiric intensity 'A vision provoked by the use of the Tree is, in fact, an artificially produced waking dream, deliberately motivated and consciously related to some chosen subject.'[16] The difference between the spontaneous dream and the magical symbol is that the magician uses a limited set of interrelated imagery. 'It is this peculiar power to turn the mind loose within determined limits which constitutes the technique of occult meditation.'[17] These limitations are meant to bite into the depths of one's psyche. 'If [the student] is working up the 32nd path of Saturn [a 'path' runs between two sephiroth] whose colours are all in the sombre hues of indigo, dark blue and black, he knows that something is amiss if a scarlet-robed figure presents itself.'[18] The idea is to make these symbolic distinctions so natural, so much a part of one's unconscious, that they appear in the 'right' combinations in dreams and visions.

Spirituality Magical kabbalah is 'a practical system of spiritual unfoldment; it is the Yoga of the West.'[19] This is a recurrent theme and an ultimate justification. 'The innermost spiritual essence of anything, whether man or world, is never in actual manifestation, but is always the underlying, behind-standing basis or root whence all springs belonging in fact to a different dimension, a different order of being. It is this concept of the different types of system which is fundamental to esoteric philosophy.'[20] The spiritual is not an 'aspect' of the symbol: it is rather that practitioners learn that magic is about spirituality because magic uses symbols to alter that fundamental reality and thus the material world which rests upon it. Conventional religions, they argue, simply do not admit that when they pray they put their worship to practical use.

Card index system 'No better simile [for magical symbolism] than that of the card index system could possibly have been formed.'[21] Any symbol is related to any other in a semantic organization. Mature development as a magician consists in furthering and elaborating the interrelations of the symbolism: 'of this gathering of correspondences there can be no end'.[22] The author exemplifies this systematic syncretism:

[14] FPD in Wilby (1968: 66).   [15] Fortune (1935: 68–9).   [16] Fortune (1935: 96).
[17] Fortune (1935: 96).   [18] Fortune (1935: 76–7).   [19] Fortune (1935: 20).
[20] Fortune (1935: 112).   [21] Fortune (1935: 65).   [22] Fortune (1935: 64).

Through its astrological associations [each kabbalistic sephirah] can be related to the gods of any pantheon, thus opening up vast new fields of implication in which the mind ranges endlessly, symbol leading on to symbol in an unbroken chain of associations; symbol confirming symbol as the many branching threads gather themselves together into a synthetic glyph once more.[23]

Highly ordered symbology enables anything and everything to be comprehended in its terms. This global capacity is consciously a goal of practice. The Hornsey group course is concise: 'there is no characteristic, influence or energy which is not capable of representation on the Tree [i.e. kabbalistically]'.

So: ineffability, exactitude, reality, oneiric intensity, and a card index system. These are the characteristics used to describe what the use of symbolism should feel like when the magician has been trained to use it. The interesting point for an anthropologist is that the manual's description includes semantic organization, 'meaning' structured by a set of categories; a sense that the symbol has a real, external being as one feels that dream-elements are real and external; and a feeling that this symbol transcends language, that there is something in it which is independent of and inexpressible in words.[24] Symbols are both like a language, organized to express certain ideas, and utterly unlike a language, indescribable objects-in-the-world.

THE CREATION OF MYTHO-POEIC HISTORY

Magic is a literary culture.[25] Potential magicians enter magic through browsing in its bookstores. They have often read fantasy and science fiction in armloads

---

[23] Fortune (1935: 16–17).

[24] Symbolism is a topic about which anthropologists have had many fruitful thoughts. However, there has been a tendency in the last two decades to interpret symbolism by means of an analogy with language, and in particular, to stress its semantic, organizational character. There seem to be four dominant approaches either relying upon or reacting to this linguistic analogy: symbolism is a message, or at least emerges through a communicative grid (Leach e.g. 1976; Douglas, 1966); symbols are the product of human classification (Levi-Strauss e.g. 1966, 1975, 1981); symbols are metaphors (Fernandez, 1982; Sapir and Crocker, 1977; Geertz, 1973; Rappaport, 1979 – actually, Rappaport stresses the canonical 'meaning' embedded in a rite, then acted out by players who *de facto* endorse it); symbolism is irrational, emotional, and precisely not a communicative message as clear-cut as language (Sperber, 1975, 1982; Turner – in ways – 1967, 1969; Barth, 1975; Lewis, 1980). The relevant point contributed to this discussion by modern magic is that visual symbolism is both highly semantic – organized by means of some structure – and, seemingly, unlike a language, or at least sufficiently unlike to draw attention to its differences. That is, there is a phenomenological immediacy to the mental image of a symbol which is not part of our ordinary language understanding of the use of words. Fortune's criteria define ideals, of course, and one could argue that there are specialist languages which have a particularistic phenomenological immediacy. However, this vividness is certainly part of what many anthropologists describe to be a part of symbol-use (e.g. Fernandez, 1982; Daniels, 1984) and I would suggest that interpreting symbolism as analogous to language detracts from our understanding of this feature.

[25] It is I suppose possible that there are illiterate magicians who practise this modern magic in London, but I doubt it. There are of course voodoo practitioners amongst the West Indian community, who may be less dependent upon the written word, but they stem from a very different background and engage in a quite distinctive practice. Most of the magicians I knew were avid readers: many of them, including the more technical, were science fiction fans. Certainly all seemed to depend upon books in some way for their magic.

before they enter, and their first year in involvement is likely to involve extensive further reading in magic, tarot, astrology and the like. After several years of practice, their libraries may extend above a hundred volumes. Indeed, one couple – Sean and Caryl, senior initiates in the Western Mysteries – had literally thousands of books, almost all about mythology, and the floorboards of their apartment were slowly giving way. And magicians write. Fraternities and societies produce journals for their initiates with articles, poems and philosophical discussions. The more enterprising edit publications for a larger public, and market them at occult fairs. Practitioners keep magical diaries, and record their rituals, dreams and meditations in words meant only for themselves. The experienced magician is known by his books.

The literature is extraordinarily rich. We have seen that there are novels written by magicians to evoke the sense of practice. There are manuals for feminist witches, for Gardnerians, Alexandrians, pagans, Western Mysteries initiates, and *ad hoc* magicians; theoretical discussions by practitioners; earlier texts of magical practice; histories of magical ritual by both practitioners and academics; published accounts of enacted rites. There are guides to magical herbalism, tarot or kabbalah, astrological almanacs, and specialities like 'candle magic'. And then there are books commonly found on the magician's shelf but never intended by their authors for that purpose: mythological anthologies, fantasy novels, children's stories, anthropological texts.[26]

The more amateur publications are equally abundant. There are over a hundred esoteric journals in Britain, of which thirty are specifically magical. Most, like *Round Merlin's Table, Isian News, The Kabbalist*, are associated with a particular study course or coven. They contain articles by members, news of the community, and the occasional poem. *Arachne*, published by the Matriarchy Network, is an excellent example. In the 1985 Candlemas (February) issue, the stapled sheaf of A4 mimeos displays an Etruscan goddess on the front and back covers. Throughout there are drawings of goddesses, spiders, moons and sacred sanctuaries. There are four historically oriented articles of one or two thousand words, some with footnotes and bibliographies: on Etruscan goddesses, Northern goddesses, the archaic significance of pigs, the varied representations of Lilith. There are two poems and a story set in a matriarchal past. Both the editorial and a political essay are about a 'woman's spirituality'. Another article contains magical and emotional advice about self-dependence – 'shielding' (the term refers to Native American medicine shields). There is an article entitled 'How to Recognize Patriarchal Magic.' The last two pages comprise a bibliography on women, goddesses and magic. The list includes Philip Slater, Sarah Pomeroy, Margaret Murray, Dion Fortune, and Homer. The journal is standard in mixing political and magical perspective, creative writing, quasi-scholarly research, and practical advice for a particular variant of a complex subcultural whole.

The most curious aspect of the literary abundance is its attitude towards

---

[26] See the appendix to this chapter.

the
Hermetic Journal

Issue Number 30   Winter 1985

Edited by *Adam McLean*

Felindenys, Silian, near Lampeter, Dyfed SA48 8LX. Wales.
Telephone 0570 423098

Figure 14   Most magicians are fascinated by the early history of magic and witchcraft. The
Hermetic Journal *delves into arcane historical esoterica; it not only presents knowledgeable*
research, but describes the symbolism as part of a still valid mystical system. The cover shown here
displays an illustration from Athanasius Kircher and represents Kircher's reworking (1652–54)
of John Dee's Hieroglyphic Monad *(1564).*

myth and history. Unlike Trobriand Island gardeners, magicians do not draw from a collective mythological corpus. Their literature seems to be part of a conscious attempt to provide a mythology for their practice in a myth-impoverished world, and they borrow lavishly from the myths of other times and cultures. Their magical practice becomes a loosely syncretic, freely inventive symbolism which uses the historical depth of myth and legend for its evocation, but freely adapts the myths to personal ends.[27] Magic is said to work through the imagination, and the more intensely you can imagine something, the more likely, it is said, that the magic will work. If you find your kabbalistic invocation more gripping when addressed to an Egyptian god, so be it. At the same time it is said that the real truths are not tied to any particular religion or mythology. Historical and cultural circumstance is but an ephemeral stain upon a deeper substrate. Thus history becomes the raw material out of which to craft a personal vision, and the role of tradition is to forge it anew, to suit your own particular symbolic needs. A famous magician, a kabbalist, says of her early kabbalistic texts that 'I use the work of my predecessors as a quarry whence I fetch the stone to build my city'.[28]

The most blatant invention of tradition can be found in the guides to magical practice. Such books deliberately teach a 'tradition' from scratch, with a lenient, creative eye. One recent example is a book entitled *Practical Egyptian Magic.*[29] The first section summarizes critical texts in the history of Egyptian magic: the *Book of the Dead*, the Hermetic Corpus, Iamblichus. Then it lists the gods, their myths, and their relative status and significance. There are charts of colour attributions and associated symbols. Then the author offers suggestions and exercises for practical ritual work, and presents possible invocations and ritual forms. She describes how to set up an Egyptian magical lodge. At the end there is a chronology of the Egyptian dynasties and a careful bibliography for further reading. There is a strong, clear emphasis on history and the age of the magical tradition: after all, the critical texts and their gods are historical facts. But the point of giving the reader such information is to enable him to create a magical practice no Pharaoh could have envisaged. Some of the colour attributions and associated symbols are historically dubious, and the suggested invocations certainly have no veridical ancestry.

In this context history can play the role of myth, the more effective for its ends because it carries an apparent validity which sheer invention lacks. Magicians are distinctly ambivalent about their historical claims. Most magical manuals assert the antiquity of magic and, more to the point, of the particular practice they endorse. They attribute the embarrassing paucity of the historical record to the self-protective secrecy in which the occult has been enshrouded.

---

[27] This is not to say that all cultures do not allow individuals to adapt myths to personal ends. Magicians are noticeably more flamboyant than most ethnographic examples, however. A Hindu may adapt one of the myths of Kali, an ascetic one of the myths of Siva, but a magician may adapt one of the myths of Isis, conflate it with a tale of Cerridwen, talk of the universal aspect of the black mother in Erishkigal, Hecate, Kali, and enact a 'traditional' ritual using the names and symbols of all five.

[28] Fortune (1935: 20).   [29] Hope (1984).

Historical associations are particularly evocative, particularly effective at creating the persuasive atmosphere that those newly fledged magicians inevitably need. However, magicians are also equipped with a metatheory which can explain why the accuracy of their claim is unimportant. The theory which legitimizes their syncretistic mythology also grants freedom to their use of history, because evocation is always more important than truth-tested fact. The past is treated as myth and, genuine or invented, it becomes the crude ore for symbolic creativity.

Among magicians, witches are particularly cavalier with historical accuracy – there is no good evidence for a history to their practice[30] – but are particularly addicted to its claims. As discussed earlier, modern witchcraft was actually invented in the twentieth century, but its founder deliberately falsified its recent origins. Margaret Murray's dubious scholarship announced in 1921 that the seventeenth-century witchcraft crazes were serious attempts to stamp out a thriving pre-Christian fertility religion. When the book inspired Gerald Gardner to create a contemporary practice, he wrote a fictional ethnography which claimed to have discovered a modern descent of these secretive covens that had survived persecution through the centuries. And he began initiating interested readers into covens. Each initiate copied out an extensive ritual manual written in a crabbed seventeenth-century style. I quote 'Tis sure, if steadfast you go to the pyre, drugs will help you; they will reach you and you will feel naught. An you go but to death, what lies beyond? the ecstacy of the Goddess'.

In seventeenth-century England, witches were never burnt, but hanged. Similar gross errors run throughout the text, which is blatantly not ancient. But the small magical journals still rage with debates over whether the civil servant had found a genuine but dying religion, or whether he struck his witchcraft anew with literary flint. There is a strong desire to attribute antiquity. Different witches draw the boundary between fact and fiction at different points. But most claim kinship with medieval witches even while admitting that the evidence for their existence is small. A recent witchcraft manual points out that Gardner's supposedly ancient text has nineteenth- and twentieth-century literary sources, and even cites those sources carefully. Then, it announces that 'for many centuries, [witchcraft] has been a personal or small group religion; and until our lifetime, it has survived those centuries by secrecy'.[31]

Some witches accept these invented historical claims easily. Others feel compelled to qualify their assertions as 'symbolic': one route is to assert the factual falsehood but to embrace the historical claim as a metaphorical truth. One manual opens with a seven-page account of the history of witchcraft, from the neolithic shaman, through the 'Burning Times', until today. Then it essentially says that the truth of the legend is irrelevant. To witches, the author says, the 'myths, legends and teachings are recognized as metaphors'.[32] In other words, the legends teach us about our culture and our human nature in the

---

[30] See chapter 4 on witchcraft.   [31] Farrar and Farrar (1984: 276).
[32] Starhawk (1979: 7).

same way that the *Odyssey* does, but they have a similarly vague relation to empirical reality. Invented history is satisfying myth. The high priest of the coven I joined wrote many of the group's seasonal rituals himself. As soon as he did so, he told me, he 'buried' his authorship: if you want the tradition to persist, he said, you must deny your intervention. 'That's good magic.'

The next step is to recreate the past. Miscegenated myth-making is particularly obvious among feminist witches, because to them creativity is a political responsibility. They declare that women have been damaged by a patriarchal Christianity, and that to regain their integrity women must actively construct a mythology more pertinent to their current lives. The manual just quoted continues, 'Today women are creating new myths, singing a new liturgy, painting our own icons, and drawing strength from the new-old symbols of the Goddess, of the "legitimacy and beneficience of female power" '.[33] Myths must be created anew from historical fragments, because no previous culture has given women due acknowledgement. Yet the 'new' myths retain the style of other, older myths. An example:

Creation

Alone, awesome, complete within Herself, the Goddess, She whose name cannot be spoken, floated in the abyss of the outer darkness, before the beginning of all things. And as She looked into the curved mirror of black space, She saw by her own light her radiant reflection, and fell in love with it. She drew it forth by the power that was in Her and made love to Herself, and called Her 'Miria, the Wonderful'. Their ecstacy burst forth in the single song of all that is, was, or shall ever be, and with the song came motion, waves that poured outward and became all the spheres and circles of the worlds. The Goddess became filled with love, swollen with love, and She gave birth to a rain of bright spirits that filled the worlds and became all beings. But in that great movement, Miria was swept away, and as She moved out from the Goddess She became more masculine. First She became the Blue God, the gentle, laughing God of love. Then She became the Green One, vine-covered, rooted in the earth, the spirit of all growing things. At last She became the Horned God, the Hunter whose face is the ruddy sun and yet dark as death. But always desire draws him back towards the Goddess, so that he circles Her eternally, seeking to return in love. All began in love; all seek to return to love. Love is the law, the teacher of eternal wisdom, and the great revealer of mysteries.[34]

The myth's following chapter explicates the Eleusinian, Biblical, shamanistic, palaeolithic, archetypal roots of the myth, the meaning of the Goddess, the significance of her separation into a duality. Male and female, it is said, are one force flowing in opposite directions, and the world is the spiral of this dynamic polarity.

Even those who think of themselves as carrying on ancient traditions freely combine different sources to create an undeniably new practice. Their rituals are historically indiscriminate conflations of older tales. Recall that the central liturgy opens thus: 'Listen to the words of the Great Mother; she who of old was called among men Artemis, Astarte, Athene, Dione, Melusine, Aphrodite, Cerridwen, Dana, Arianhod, Isis, Bride, and by many other names'.[35] Its poetic

---

[33] Starhawk (1979: 188).   [34] Starhawk (1979: 17–18).   [35] Farrar and Farrar (1981: 42).

symbolism romanticizes myth: '. . . I who am the beauty of the green earth, and the white Moon among the stars, and the mystery of the waters, and the desire at the heart of man, call unto thy soul.' Rituals meld Isis and Persephone, Cerridwen and Kali. A magician is learned in the lore of many different cultures.

Magicians are extremely self-conscious of their history: the Hornsey group actually recorded their bimonthly group discussions, and kept them in what were called the 'archives'. But self-consciousness does not lead them to exactitude, as least as far as their use of wider historical material is concerned. This is, perhaps, because of their particular social context. The rationalizing, secular society that strips away religious symbolism also heightens the sensitivity to abstract theorizing, and magicians develop an elaborate theory that justifies the use of myths of other cultures. The justification which allows them to borrow myths from others does so by arguing for the importance of personally evocative symbolism and the irrelevance of historical pertinence, and so they invent their myth and history from what historical material lies at hand, a sophisticated, self-conscious bricolage. This invented history makes excellent mythology in a sceptical modernity, for even when explicitly called myth, the invented history retains the aura of genuine history, meaningful within the authoritative canon of apparently objective science.

And so magicians have it both ways. They appeal to the past, and claim a distinguished blood-stained lineage with all the emotional depth which that entails. Thousands of years of magical practice imply a solidity against which contemporary scepticism seems a minor irritation. Yet magicians free themselves from the need to prove their historical accuracy and the cultural pertinence of the appropriate mythology by arguing that history can serve the role of personal metaphor or myth. Magicians make an effort to ground their myth and symbolism in history, and in the process they ascribe false depth to their practice, invent tradition, and freely draft their own mythology from myths whose historical accuracy they take the trouble to establish. Since Thucydides, history and myth have been separate categories. Magicians deliberately blur the distinction to make the practice more appealing and to legitimate their endeavour in a rationalistic world. They poach from the past in the interests of the present and plunder the world's mythology for their symbolic goods.[36]

SYMBOLISM AS A LANGUAGE OF SELFHOOD

Part of the reason people enjoy practising magic is that it becomes a vehicle for self-expression. Myths and symbols fill magicians' reading and infiltrate their

[36] The invention of tradition has recently become a focus of attention with Hobsbawm and Ranger's (1983) collection of essays; and the role of history and the historical in understanding society and societal change has emerged as one of the central issues in recent anthropological debate (Rosaldo, 1980; Comaroff, 1985; Sahlins, 1981 and 1985). Relatively little attention (apart from those interested in literacy, and then for different reasons) has been paid to the nature of history itself, as a manipulable category of cultural self-consciousness. This is an area that should be explored.

dreams; practitioners meditate extensively on Isis, Astarte, and end up writing long articles about their meaning. It is not surprising that these images become a complex hermeneutic, an interpretive, exegetical language to make sense of all possible events. The magician becomes skilled in seeing complex symbolic patterns, as he learns to see the pattern of events which served as evidence for the rite's power. It is as if magicians learn a new language in which to talk about their world, and gain a new set of possibilities for organizing it. The analogy to a language does not really work: symbolism is messy and complex, nothing like as ordered a system. But the analogy has heuristic value. Magicians use symbolism to capture, express or articulate their experience, and in its mixture of precision and evocation it becomes tremendously important to them. Ultimately, it can become a means of therapy.

One way that symbolism forms a magician's hermeneutic is by providing an apparently objective medium in which to talk about one's quite subjective self. An excellent example of this process can be found in astrology. The explicit intention of astrological talk is usually to work out interesting facts about astrology, but the latent purpose is often to talk about personal issues in an apparently objective frame. The abundance of astrological signifiers – houses, planets, signs, aspects – means that a chart provides endless scope for discussion.

I used to call this 'astro-speak': people would settle down over tea and biscuits and discuss why their twelfth house moon made them tidy or obsessed with work. Britain is a private culture which frowns on intimate discussion. Within an astrological vocabulary, the magician could talk openly about personal feelings under the guise of intellectual exploration. Most of my involvement in this sort of discussion took place in pubs or after meetings, and the memories of the dialogue recorded in my fieldnotes are not sufficiently rich to present. However, here in a rare taped interview, a witch (Mick, the Fenwoman) describes her chart. We had been talking about another person, and she had demonstrated her point with a trait given by his chart. I asked her if she had done her own. She launched into an account of it, and her description reveals exactly this brand of speaking personally as a legitimate illustration of objective law.

Of course I've done it. Well, it's quite interesting. I've got a lot of stuff under the horizon, mostly in the third house, like Mercury and the sun. Saturn. And that's all about the mentality, and if I didn't know it was mine I'd say I was clever, which I am. And a thinker, which I am. And one who investigates carefully, which I do. Y'know I don't take things for granted. I'm not in any way an emotional or hysterical person. I'm cold, emotionally. I really don't have much in the way of feeling. I'm not brilliant, obviously. I'm no great intellect. But I am clever. And that shows in my chart. And I'm lucky, and that shows in my chart. Not over lucky, but I've got Venus in the second house of gains, and if you've got Venus in the house of gains, in the second house, you ain't ever gonna starve, y'know. You're not going to have to beg for crusts at somebody else's table. And I've certainly never been rich, but on the other hand I've never been poor, or wanted for anything. I have Mars up at the mid-heaven in the tenth house, which makes me aggressive, which I am, and pushy, which I am. Dominating, which I am! And suited to positions of authority, which I've always had. Uranus in the sixth house of psychism is perfect for an astrologer, which I've got. Jupiter – I've got Jupiter in the ninth, which is to do with convention, and tradition. And I'm very hidebound. I'm very conventional. I mean, I may be odd, but I really am very conventional, in the sense that I'm very law abiding. I have a great respect for the law, and authority, and tradition. And I'm totally hooked on the past. Jupiter's all about the past, the right and proper way to do things. That's what I like, you know, about being British. All this tradition. And I love it – I love it! Weddings, and coronations, and the lord mayor's show, and banquets and anything, anything at all, to do with uniforms and splendour and show, just turns me on tremendously. And as a Capricorn, I'm hot anyway on the past. If everyone were a Capricorn, everything would be terribly organized, but there would be no progress. There would be no progress at all, because we would say, it was good enough for my father, it was good enough for my grandfather, and it's good enough for me. That's what Capricorn says. And it's perfectly true. I don't change things, I don't enjoy change. I like status quo. As long as it's fine, and it suits me, leave it alone, y'know? Don't make waves – because if you make waves, you might change things, which is not always for the best. But that, y'know, is Capricorn for you. True, blue, little Capricorn. Autocratic, bloody-minded, snobby, traditional, honourable . . .

And here a cat landed on her lap. People enjoy talking about themselves and explaining themselves to other people, but rarely get the chance to do so. Astrology provides this opportunity because it masks the discussion's content: the purpose of this conversation was to explain the planets, not the person.

The underlying assumption in astrology, that personal characteristics can be explained by the geometric relationship of the planets at one's birth not only allows magicians to talk about personal issues in public, but frees them from responsibility for their personalities and for any particular events. Here, in another example, an *ad hoc* magician uses his astrological knowledge to interpret his intense but unrequited attraction for another member of his group. Again, this is an excerpt from a tape. The language has the odd jumpiness of spontaneous musing.

I felt dissatisfied with the rationalist explanation, that I was just someone at a low point, and that was why I'd fallen for her. It was the uncanniness of it all. My dreams had sort of built up to meeting her. I had a dream, the interpretation of it was that I was going to link up with something from my past, which I'd lost, and then there was this business of going to a meeting, which there were all sorts of coincidences around. I saw her there and I'd seen her before. The first time she was in the audience of a talk I gave. I remember sitting there, watching the people come in, and the moment I saw her, instantly, I felt an affinity. It wasn't lust or anything, it was – if life had been a cocktail party, she was the person in the room I would have gone up to and felt at ease with, that sort of feeling. Then I saw her again, at the meeting, and thought, what a marvellous person. That's just the sort of person I would have wanted to have living next door. The images weren't sexual: it was more exploring life with someone, sharing cups of tea, reading books together.

It's hard to relate that instant of affinity to psychological complexes, and things like that. It's much easier to see in terms of astrology. When you look at our charts, she has so many planets aspecting her Saturn. All except two of them are in early degrees of signs – all close to five degrees. The fact that my Saturn is opposite hers, means that nearly all my planets are in aspect to her Saturn. And as Saturn's very much the point of weakness, the point of the air, in my case, sort of the point of self-doubt, false humility, things like that, it's like all those parts of her seemed to bear on that part of me, and make a tremendous impression. Liz Greene [a well known astrologer] says that when there's a lot of Saturn contact between charts, it tends to give a strong feeling of karma, and I think that I certainly felt that. She seemed like – she just seemed so important to me.

Rather than using astrology as a way to speak more personally and intimately, this magician uses the astrology to describe what could be seen as a personal failure in forging a sexual relationship as an inevitable consequence of knowing this woman. It is not that he failed, but that the sense of affinity and failure in connection to her was ordained by the constellation of their planets, by Saturn's heavy hand.

Learning to use symbolism in this manner is far more compelling, for the practitioner, than learning to speak another language. Far more is at stake than the power to express oneself to a new group of people. Magicians feel quite strongly about this symbolism; it comes to carry a good deal of emotional affect. People often asserted the sweeping nature of their symbolic involvement. For example, in each monthly meeting of the Kether Lodge of the International Order of Kabbalists, we explored one sephirah, in one of its 'aspects'. When I joined, the group was studying the sephiroth's astrological associations. One evening, the topic was Chesed and Jupiter. The meeting of fifteen people convened sharply at eight p.m. Six members had written papers on the subject, which they read out. They listed symbolic associations to the Jupiter – Chesed pairing and then gave interpretations of those associations. Members described the different sorts of people and spiritual feelings they would have associated with Jupiter's Chesed, and explained their emotional response to the symbol. In essence, they described and redescribed their own experience in kabbalistic terms. At times, the leader stopped a reader to comment (e.g. on why tin, as well as silver, was associated with that sephirah). Then, there was a short paper on Greek mythology and the kabbalah. A meditation followed the hour's discussion and finally, a kabbalistic ritual. 'It is the basis of *all* ritual.' Later I went to lunch with some of the members. Mary is a thirty-eight year old secretary who has been 'doing' the kabbalah for twenty years. 'The kabbalah' she told me 'becomes everything. It takes over.' She had brought along a friend, a twenty-eight year old secretary who got bored with typing and took over the management of a fast food store. Their remarks echo those of the fortyish housewife I also met at the Lodge. She said that the kabbalah had become 'everything', that she saw 'everything' in its terms. And she spoke glowingly of the meetings: 'you *need* the lodge, after a while. I miss it when I don't come. Everything gets so dull and uninspired.'

The power of this involvement has something to do with the therapeutic efficacy of the practice. For many people, this symbolic redescription becomes a therapy, a way of making sense of the facts of their experience and of learning how to alter their attitudes towards those experiences or their manner of handling them. Many magicians – though not all – think of their magic as having therapeutic qualities, and I suspect that most of them would think that their magical practice had led to a positive improvement in their sense of well-being. Therapeutic techniques of course are difficult to evaluate, but I had the impression that the magic could be beneficial for its practitioners, and I saw some people become happier and more confident through their practice.

Certainly there are many tales to tell of magic's therapeutic efficacy: the timid woman who grew more confident by identifying with Sehkmet, fiery Egyptian lion-goddess; the man who reforged his manhood through a dream-gift of a sword. I shall give only two brief accounts. Mary told me that it was only after she had become a witch that she was able to accept her womanhood with pleasure and pride. She is an unusual witch, a conventional housewife who believes that a woman's place is within the home. But when she was growing up she had difficulty seeing any woman's role as worthwhile. She said that she was a second child and was, as a girl, unwanted, and that her father felt that it was useless to educate a girl. At eighteen she came across a book about witchcraft and found it compelling, hunted around for a coven and got initiated. The witches' worship of a universal female deity made her feel creative and powerful. Indeed, when she had difficulty becoming pregnant with her first child, she said that reading the myths of the Goddess enabled her to become fertile.[37] The Sumerian myth of Erishkigal and Inanna was particularly important, as was the classical tale of Demeter and Persephone. 'I began to realize that a woman must face her dark side, a sort of death, and that this confrontation is the source of creativity.' Childbirth and witchcraft each taught Mary that the pain which accompanies menstruation and childbirth is a good pain, not some sign that women fail at their body's task of reproducing but an inevitable element of life. Women are the powerful centre of this life-giving process. Other female witches might use these lessons in a different way, but for Mary witchcraft legitimized her choice to be conventionally feminine because through it she gained a confidence in her womanhood that her childhood had not afforded, and it gave her that confidence without forcing her to confront directly her no doubt complex feelings about her father.

Ann, by contrast, is an ardent feminist and a successful commercial artist. She is a member of a pagan Women's Mysteries group, and sometimes describes herself as a feminist witch. At puberty she was a Christian, earnestly devout as adolescents sometimes are. But after a few years she left the Church because she could no longer tolerate the deification of a sexless woman. She felt that God was female, and that Christianity made her own sexuality seem filthy. She began to read about feminism, and about the goddesses of classical Greece and Egypt. She joined a study group on matriarchy, and then the Mysteries group. She finds different goddesses appealing, but when I knew she was

[37] In fact she said that it was one book in particular that made her fertile: *The Descent to the Goddess*, by a Jungian analyst (Perera, 1981), which contains the myth of Erishkigal described in chapter 8.

'working' with Sekhmet, a fire goddess represented as a lioness. Ann felt that she did not handle anger very well, and that she needed to be more confident and assertive. She also believed that this had to do with the mixed social messages that a British woman receives about her sexuality. Sekhmet embodied her ideals, and Ann read about her, wrote about her, and took her part in dramatic rituals. She became able to identify Sekhmet-type reactions, Sekhmet-type people, Sekhmet-type feelings. In the course of the year, she became more confident and self-determined.

Magical imagery probably does help magicians handle their irrationality, their fears, angers and strong emotion. One possible explanation for therapeutic efficacy is that the imagery becomes emotionally charged, and this emotional content is both sufficiently explicit to provide a useful model for emotional responses but also sufficiently masked so that this content is not denied or rejected out of fear. A man confused by conflicting feelings about his dragon-like mother does well to imagine himself as Perseus, for in such a guise he feels himself strong enough both to slay the dragon – which he can identify as evil – and to lust after women. Rather than having to express some deep hatred for his mother, he identifies with a being more powerful than women, and who both loves them and is harrassed by them. The feelings are there, and they acquire a label. But because the label is unrealistic, it does not force the individual to confront those feelings directly.

Therapy seems to work when someone externalizes, or labels, some internal feeling and then is able to transform it, though how and why that happens seems quite unclear. Narratives could be therapeutic because of the way in which someone finds a central character or symbol moving, the way in which they identify with it. The person would imagine herself as that character by using her own experience as the ground. This probably constitutes some sort of labelling process: you imagine what Demeter's grief must feel like because of the grief you have suffered yourself. If that character has emotions which you have repressed within you, your identification may help you to experience these feelings more directly. If the character undergoes some change you again imagine the change based on your own experience, and perhaps imagine yourself through some experiences you have not had, or not dealt with properly. The narrative then becomes a practice-ground, a dry-run to handle feelings and responses in new ways.[38]

---

[38] There have been a number of discussions of the therapeutic value of different forms of narrative. Among the many contributors, Singer (1974; also Singer and Pope, 1978), Masters and Houston (1972), Noll (1985) focus on daydreaming and mental imagery; Winnicott (1971) and Axline (1969) consider play; Bettleheim (1975) discusses the importance of fairy tales, the 'uses of enchantment'. Lévi-Strauss, in an essay that has launched many recent explorations, describes shamanic healing through narrated imagery (1967: 'The Effectiveness of Symbols'). The central thesis of that piece is that something of more or less the same nature is taking place (although in different ways) in psychoanalysis and in the shaman's use of symbolic imagery, a thesis which seems profoundly correct, in that people seem to have the ability to hook feelings and sensations on to symbols and words in particular contexts, and then to manipulate them. The precise nature of this process is in some ways the central mystery of psychoanalysis. Much recent work has been directed to this interconnection between symbolism and healing.

The important feature of the magical narrative is that the magician explicitly identifies the narrative as efficacious and empowering. Magic, the Western Mysteries say, is about regeneration. By this is meant that magic involves the evolution of the self and the planet, and in order to bring through and carry the force to change the planet, you yourself must become a fit vessel to channel the force. Magic, then, is seen as a series of confrontations with oneself, with different archetypes that represent different aspects of being. Through these symbolic confrontations, the magician's 'true' self is meant to emerge undeterred by any distortions acquired through the course of his life. The practice, then, is explicitly therapeutic. More than that, the reward of the transformation is power. As in all therapy – but whereas most therapy promises greater success in running one's life, this magical therapy almost treats self-transformation as the means to run the world. The point of magical practice is to identify with a narrative, to feel powerful in the course of the identification – in a ritual pathworking, ritualists talk literally about the power running through them – and by virtue of that powerful identification, to know that one has wielded power within the physical world. Magic is therapy without identifying the patient as sick, and the promised outcome of the process is a power far greater than a conscious therapy admits.

The issue of how imaginative involvement works therapeutically is deep and unsettled. It seems clear, however, that imaginative involvement with myths and images can be curative. Their curative properties have something to do with externalizing – providing a public label for – internal feelings, and with the ambiguity of the link between inner feeling and outer label. Magical symbolism is probably therapeutic because the magician can both identify his feelings and keep the identification hidden. Secretive esoteric knowledge – mythological self-knowledge – is in ways a key to this therapeutic efficacy, for that knowledge allows the magician both to gain the benefit of controlling his own self-knowedge, of holding a secret about himself, and of knowing truths which if phrased explicitly he might reject.

SECRET KNOWLEDGE

I, — , in the Presence of the Mighty Ones, do of my own free will and accord most solemnly swear that I will ever keep secret and never reveal the secrets of the Art . . . And may my weapons turn against me if I break this my solemn oath.[39]

Magic has always been steeped in secrecy. Secret words supposedly opened the doors to hidden treasure and remedied manifold ills; they were passed from ancient magician to magician, and competing practitioners contested the power of their hidden wares. But the nature and function of this secrecy has been little explored. In modern magic, secrecy supports the magician's commitment to his magical ideas, and gives him a sense of control over an uncertain, uncontrollable world.

[39] Initiation oath in witchcraft, Farrar and Farrar (1984: 19).

Magical practice is swathed in secrecy. There are secret words, secret societies, secret weapons. Initiates have secret names and use secret invocations. Manuals repeatedly stress the need to keep the practice secret, and even assert that the practice requires secrecy in order to be effective. Students in magical training are told never to show their tools or weapons to outsiders, never to reveal their magical diary to anyone at all. The reasoning behind this hinges on the partly unspoken assumption that power is a tangible emanation, somehow connected to oneself, which dissolves in the open, public air. Green's manual remarks: 'magical robes, equipment, and ritual books should always be kept under lock and key as power is built up around and in them and this becomes dissipated if things are just left about'.[40] Most of the magicians I knew wrapped their equipment in special clothes and kept it out of sight.[41]

Keeping the magic secret separates the magic from the non-magical, but still allows magicians to move between these disparate worlds with ease. Doing so allows magicians to insulate their claims from sceptical criticism – both other people's and their own. Magicians can hold their claims in secret without ever subjecting them to scoffing outsiders. They can think of themselves as believing in magic, and get on well both in a magical context and within their everyday world, without ever putting their secretively held ideas at risk.

An important psychological phenomenon might lie behind the effectiveness of this strategy. In order to commit yourself to a belief which you do not hold, there must be a time when you acknowledge the possibility of the view but have not yet accepted it. During that period, you must be able to toy with the idea of believing, and to imagine yourself as the sort of person who believes. It is then that the separateness of secrecy is instrumental. I was often told – by adepts, by witches, by most participants with whom I discussed it – that the suspension of disbelief was a necessary step towards committed, positive belief. To turn the possibility of belief into active commitment demands that the subject is comfortable with the 'let's pretend' position. Secrecy facilitates this comfort by removing the normal social barriers to socially unacceptable ideas. You might feel pretty foolish invoking Hecate in your living room. But if you light the room with candles and smoky incense, wear special clothes, and pretend that you are not yourself but someone different and more powerful, you might at least pretend that Hecate's power has begun to flow. If there is no-one there to ridicule you because no-one knows of your activities, and indeed if you have secret co-religionists who positively support your action and seem also to believe, then your belief will have a chance to grow. Embarrassment is a social

---

[40] Green (1983: 87).

[41] The primary theoretical authors here are Simmel (1950), Bok (1982), Tefft (1980) and Bellman (1984). There is a large literature on secrecy, but much of it – including Shils (1956) and much of Simmel and Tefft – focuses upon governmental secrecy. The important issue in the useful literature is that concealment creates property, something that is possessed, and the existence of this special property distinguishes possessor from non-possessor and affects the attitudes of both towards the thing possessed. Luhrmann (forthcoming) provides a further study of the role secrecy plays within magic.

disease. Secrecy can banish it and thus create the potential for private, idiosyncratic belief.

Secrecy also fosters a deferential attitude towards the contents of its secret knowledge.[42] The concealment of magical names, words, images and gestures heightens the value of what has been hidden by implying that it is too great to be shared lightly. Magicians make much of their moral responsibility in controlling access to magical knowledge. For example, the introductory pamphlet of one Western Mysteries fraternity asserts that magicians have especially stringent moral standards because of the importance of their work. To be a member of this fraternity, you must be a righteous, upstanding person. The founder justified secrecy as follows:

The knowledge guarded by the secret fraternities is too potent to be given out indiscriminately, and is guarded, not as a sordid trade secret, but as the power to dispense drugs is guarded – for the safety of the public.[43]

She goes on to say:

Can you, then, blame the guardians of this dangerous brightness if they use every precaution to ensure that it shall only find its way into clean and trusting hands? Be assured that the secrecy of the occult schools will never be relaxed til human nature is regenerated.[44]

These secrets are too powerful to share, claim the morally righteous. Maybe so: but by keeping them secret one needs never test their strength. To keep a secret creates the sense of the secret's power without the need for its demonstration.

Beyond deliberate concealment, the difficulty of obtaining magical knowledge also swathes it in secrecy and heightens the awe in which it is held. Magical knowledge is extremely elaborate. There are complex correlations between the Hebrew letters, astrological planets, tarot cards, gems, scents, colours and so forth. As we have seen, practitioners acquire hefty reference texts that match gems to planets and kabbalistic arcana to scents. To learn these associations properly is a lifetime's task. Not all magicians conquer such complexity and most say that book-studied knowledge is not essential to magical success. They assert that it is not what you say but how you say it that matters. Obviously this attitude is more defensible that the view that particular words bring results: the

---

[42] See particularly Barth (1975): in his study of a secretive men's initiation cult among the New Guinea Baktaman, seven slow stages of initiation reveal progressively deeper 'truths' which were deceptively inverted in earlier stages: the most impure animal is in fact the most pure, a lower house of initiation contains ossuaries unthinkable in those above. Because the deeper knowledge makes the early knowledge false – because no knowledge, then, is trustworthy – initiates treat all religious knowledge with ginger care. 'From that first, frightening morning when initiations started, and through a series of subsequent stages, the novice develops a fearful awareness of vital, unknowable and forbidden power behind secret and cryptic symbols' (1975: 219). Knowledge, they learn, is dangerous, inherently deceptive, and acquired in often painful rituals. Even so, initiates take pride in their new status. The confluence of pride in greater status, deceptive data, and pain of revelation forms their attitude towards this special ritual knowledge. The way knowledge is acquired affects the way you feel about it. When the knowledge is hidden, and revelation demands hard, painful work but brings status in its wake, one treats these secrets with overvaluing awe.

[43] Fortune (1967: 112).

[44] Fortune (1967: 113).

ritual didn't fail because you used the wrong invocation, but because you didn't use it properly. But whether scholarship or knowhow serves as the touchstone, magicians present magic as the consequence of long and patient learning. Entering magic is like entering a scholarly pursuit: the practitioner is impressed by the depth of knowledge, and dazzled by the learning of the leaders of the profession.

As a result, the magician can always explain failure by attributing it to insufficient learning while retaining the promise of potential success. The fantasy of a truly successful command of magic depends upon detailed symbolic knowledge and expertise in performance so complex that actual achievement is impossible. Power remains eternally the promised prize but the means to attain it eternally elusive, an infinite regress of symbolic complexity. The scholarship creates the secret of success as the unattainable end of eternal study.[45] The very act of hiding knowledge raises the value of what is written, both by lending it awe and by keeping it from public confrontation with potential rivals.

Secrecy plays another role in creating a certain type of symbol-centred knowledge. Contemporary magic presents itself as a mystery religion centred on a secretive knowledge of something inherent hidden and thus unknowable by ordinary means. This knowledge is called 'esoteric knowledge'. Practitioners describe esoteric knowledge as the 'deep secrets' of magic, and they say that it is these secrets which ultimately confer power.

To call esoteric knowledge 'secretive' is to use the word in a strained way: truths of the mysteries are intentionally hidden only if you think that there is a god who conceals them. But this is more or less what magicians do accept – or at least it is the myth-like account by which this knowledge is conceptualized. Magicians call esoteric knowledge secretive and speak about initiations through which deity-like initiators reveal knowledge which they have previously concealed. The real point seems to be that 'esoteric knowledge' is the name given to a certain sort of experience, and that access to the experience itself is restricted to the participants of secretive groups. Writing about the experience cannot give access to this knowledge: the experience must be experienced, and only the experiencer can lay claim to his own, unique and inherently hidden knowledge of what happened.

---

[45] Kermode points to the awe-inspiring secrecy which scholarship endows upon its subject. Interpretation lies between us and the original text like a plate of wavy glass, he says. 'Once a text is credited with high authority it is studied intensely; once it is so studied it acquires mystery or secrecy' (Kermode, 1979: 144). Creative intellectual scrutiny wraps a text in secrecy by the daunting expertise needed to unravel its hermeneutic strands. 'Like the scriptures, [Shakespeare] is open to all, but at the same time so dark that special 'training', organized by an institution of considerable size, is required for his interpretation' (Kermode 1979: 144). An insider to Bible studies must not only know the ancient languages, the compositional history, the massive texts themselves, but he must also be competent to judge what all others have said about his subject. And the more he knows, the more complex and difficult his questions will become. The barrage of scholarship demands ever greater mastery to understand, and its potential complexity is infinite because any narrative it tries to conquer eludes exhaustive explanation. To study any subject deeply is to invest it with secrecy and thus with the awe and deference the outsider accords to the knowledgeable initiate. The accessibility of knowledge alters one's evaluation of its worth.

What does it mean to call something a mystery religion? To magicians, the term implies that magic is about finding profound meaning in symbolism. For each magician certain symbols come to embody the intensity of meaning, feeling and emotion that the cross bears for the devout Catholic. When magicians enter magic they suddenly confront an enormous complexity of symbols: the kabbalah, tarot cards, mythologies of different cultures. As they 'progress', they meditate on certain symbols, read about them, perform rituals about them, talk about them with their companions. They talk about the mysteries of Isis, of Tiphareth, and the like: almost any symbol or image can be the centre of esoteric knowledge, although the inspiration behind the talk comes from the ancient mysteries of Eleusis, Egypt, Dionysus. When magicians say that their rituals are revelations of mysteries, they mean that through the ritual they come to understand a symbol or a set of symbols – Demeter with her pigs, her sheaf of wheat – more 'deeply', and either find this understanding difficult to articulate or its content impossible to comprehend rationally. They call this understanding a religion because their language talks about a transcendent spiritual reality which the images reflect and affect.

As understood by these magicians, this symbolic knowledge of the Mysteries is of a different kind from instrumental, scientific or factual knowledge. The initiate of the Mysteries learns few new facts, little information which could be conveyed to others. Nevertheless he feels that he has learnt something significant. The nature of this knowledge is ambiguous. There are, however, three recurring elements in the descriptions commonly given of it.

The first feature of this knowledge is that it is experiential and ineffable. When magicians describe themselves as obtaining knowledge through initiation in the Mysteries, they mean that they have an experience of certainty which makes them call their understanding knowledge, but that the object of this certainty cannot be communicated. Esoteric knowledge involves an understanding that bypasses rational cognition and can never be expressed in words. A pre-eminent text in witchcraft explains:

> When we speak of the 'secrets that cannot be told', we do not mean merely that rules prevent us from speaking freely. We mean that the inner knowledge literally *cannot* be expressed in words. It can only be conveyed through experience, and no-one can legislate what insight another person may draw from any given experience.[46]

The remark is constantly repeated. Two Western Mysteries initiates, with whom I have participated in many rites, make this assertion in their published guide to magic:

> The real secret of the mysteries is that *they cannot be communicated by one being to another;* the mystery guardian can only give guidelines and keys to knowledge, not the actual knowledge itself, which is revealed to the initiated by *personal experience and initiatory revelation.*[47]

Again, symbols are ineffable. Truths of the Mysteries slip through the web of

---

[46] Starhawk (1979: 7).   [47] Matthews and Matthews (1985: 37).

words like mist, and like mist they seem opaque and substantive but vanish when one comes close to capture them. It is not entirely clear what it means to say that truths cannot be communicated, and can be known only through experience. The remark sounds like a strategic way to assert the impregnability of what one chooses to call truth, by claiming that it cannot be rationally challenged. But it would be tendentious to see incommunicability as simply a retreat in the face of scepticism, a defensive reaction to doubt. People often say that religious truths are incommunicable, that mystical insight is ineffable. They may also say that the scent of ripe peaches or the sound of running water is impossible to describe (these are not usually called 'truths', however). Magic depends heavily on sensual and spiritual stimulation, and when people learn something through their practice it may be that they genuinely find that it is difficult to put into words. They do talk abut their experiences but they always say that words are finally inadequate. Esoteric knowledge seems inherently secretive because it can be partly shared – and thus concealed – but can never be fully communicated to others.

The second, related, feature of esoteric knowledge is that magicians often say that the truths of the Mysteries are conveyed through images. The classic training manual in the Western Mysteries grandly asserts that the mind cannot comprehend the truths of the Mysteries rationally, but that the human can understand them when they are couched in imagery. Witchcraft is said to engage a different mode of thought than analytic rationality. In that mode, 'verbal understanding is limited; [the mind] communicates through images, emotions, sensations, dreams, visions and physical symptoms'.[48] There is knowledge that has content, but is understood in terms of images and communicated neither verbally nor in rational terms.

The essence of this distinction between the experientially image-bound and the rationally verbalized seems to be the sort of recognition involved in saying, 'now I *really* know what love is'. The role played by the 'really' in that sentence seems to be the sort of deeper understanding described by esoteric knowledge. Greater acquaintance can always lead one to say, 'now I *really* know', but the intellectual content of the knowledge may remain more or less unchanged. Someone may be able to describe the Christian cross as the symbol of redemption through suffering. After a traumatic but successful trial, she may feel that she 'really' knows the meaning of the phrase, although she has not added substantially to her intellectual understanding of it, and she will associate that newer insight with the image. Magicians seem to use the category of esoteric knowledge to indicate experiential acquaintance rather than intellectual content, and use imagery as a mnemonic for their experiential insights.

The third quality often mentioned is that knowledge of the Mysteries seems also to involve knowledge about oneself. The emphasis of the self is part of the technical theory of how magic works. The magician is an instrument for the gods and must make that instrument effective for their use. A Western Mysteries adept gives this account:

[48] Starhawk (1979: 21).

The first part of occult work consists in fashioning yourself into an instrument worthy of use by the forces of light, and the second is the dedicated service to God and man that follows from this.[49]

Being able to change yourself in a particular manner requires that you know yourself well enough to effectuate that change, and this self-knowledge is understood as the necessary means to this end. ' "Knowing yourself" is the first, and one of the most important, steps in ritual.'[50]

Note that the emphasis upon self-knowledge and self-exploration person-alizes whatever is learnt, so that it is unique and specific to each. 'In witchcraft, each of us must reveal our own truths'.[51] There is no objective touchstone. Esoteric knowledge is private and individualized. A beginner's guide to magic advises:

From your own secret journal you will begin to discover patterns of your own emerging. This is the beginning of the magical journey of inner exploration. You are mapping an uncharted country which you alone can visit totally.[52]

Even if this esoteric knowledge were communicable, its communication would be meaningless. Book-learning is fine, but it is only your own interpretation which constitutes true knowledge to these magicians. Thus esoteric knowledge is secret in a double sense: you keep your journal intentionally hidden, and your experience is inherently hidden and personal, communicable to none.

The striking feature of this self-knowledge is that magicians assert that self-knowledge is the only way to gain knowledge of the external world. Another Western Mysteries initiate with whom I worked in ritual makes this remark:

There is a state of perception, of awareness . . . in which we are enabled to gain direct knowledge of hidden realities. This ability arises from our innermost knowledge, the heart of our being, our centre that is normally ignored or feared. In traditional magical or mystical vocabulary, this awareness is often called, 'the mediation of the Knower Within'.[53]

Magic is repeatedly said to involve knowledge of the 'inner realities'. When magicians practise magic – when they meditate, visualize, or participate in ritual – they are said to be 'working on the inner'. Sometimes the psychological emphasis is explicit: 'magic is a series of psychological techniques so devised as to enable us to probe more deeply into ourselves'.[54] But the more common assumption is that esoteric knowledge examines 'inner reality' to know about an outer world. Two high-ranking Western Mysteries initiates – members of my London circuit – have written a two-volume introduction to magic.[55] They immediately assume that the reader is about 'to explore your own *inner* landscape' in the 'quest for a transcendent reality'. Magic 'is a continual spiral of discovery: we go inward to come out again, and when the thread is wound out fully we must return inwards to take stock, to garner our findings, and to rest.

---

[49] Knight (1976: 71).   [50] Ashcroft-Novicki (1982: 12).   [51] Starhawk (1979: 9).
[52] Green (1983: 18).   [53] Stewart (1985: 49).   [54] Regardie (1964: 28).
[55] Matthews and Matthews (1985: 2).

This is the pattern we must follow, if we desire to learn.'[56] Knowledge of the world is indissoluble from a knowledge of one's self and from an ineffable knowledge of the divine.

The fundamental premise is that by understanding the self at its deepest level one not only acquires true knowledge of the world but – crucially – the power to control it.

Although the keys to the Mystery are given to the initiate of the Western Way, each must still find the way in darkness by the light of personal intuition . . . suffering and pain are only one feature: at the heart-chamber of the mystery maze is freedom and mastery over the elements of life.[57]

Mastery over life comes through self-mastery, a curious but pervasive theme in modern magic. Again a central witchcraft text:

The final price of freedom is the willingness to face that most frightening of all beings, one's own self. Starlight vision, 'the other way of knowing', is the mode of perception of the unconscious, rather than the conscious mind. The depths of our beings are not at all sunlit: to see clearly, we must be willing to dive into the dark, inner abyss and acknowledge the creatures that we may find there.[58]

To the author, freedom from constraint – freedom to act – arises from knowledge of the unconscious, what she calls the depths of her being, the dark. Her underlying assumption is that her awareness of unconscious motivation grants her the power to alter its constraints. Self-knowledge can lead to change.

So magical practice turns on the assumption that the ability to control the physical world arises through disciplined religious apprenticeship in which experiential, image-bound self-knowledge confers that power. This knowledge is not a body of objective facts but a process of understanding, a way of knowing. Many non-magicians think of magic as a science-like body of instrumental words and gestures, the false science Frazer canonized. But modern magic turns out to be a mystery religion in which the deepest truths are radically unlike scientific knowledge. Magic is an esoteric mystery rather than an instrumental science and symbolism is its religious heart. Why should this transformation occur?

There are strategic explanations, for creating esoteric knowledge helps to sidestep disconfirmation. The words 'open sesame' are not – or at least, not obviously – effective. The magician is in need of a theory which explains both why his rites have failed and how, if only he had greater expertise, the magic still could work. Esoteric knowledge neatly serves that purpose because by its nature it is incomplete. Scholarship creates an infinite regression of facts to be garnered and books to be read; esoteric knowledge creates an infinite regression because one can always have a deeper sense of self, or richer sorts of experiences. One can never grasp the totality of self-knowledge, let alone exhaust experiential self-awareness. Your knowledge of the 'meaning' of the moon can never be finite, as might be your knowledge of the rules of baseball. If

[56] Matthews and Matthews (1985: 4).   [57] Matthews and Matthews (1986: 3).
[58] Starhawk (1979: 19).

a spell fails, then, the failure can always be attributed to ignorance while retaining the possibility of a future success.

Another strategic explanation is that this slide of the secretive into the esoteric elevates worship and spiritual service above immediate instrumental efficacy. Devotion and dedication are more highly valued than the ability to conjure successfully. The rewards of this exchange are great. The elevation of worship values the thing which one can do over the thing which one cannot. Paradoxically, the student comes to feel himself to be a better and more powerful magician on the basis of practices which have little to do with instrumental magic directly.

But there is a more complex interpretation which arises from the nature of magic itself. Magic is the search for total control. 'As I do will, so mote it be', run the witchcraft spells. Yet people live in a world of uncertainty. They make choices within the constraints of insufficient information and their reasoning is hampered by their own irrationality. Esoteric knowledge makes the important uncertainties (like when one dies) inconsequential by mastering (or trying to master) our apparently irrational responses to them. As one manual says, 'the objective of all these practices is to get YOU in total control of your SELF'.[59] And perhaps not surprisingly, the practices work. That is, they provide, to some extent, a greater sense of self-control and personal competence.

Let me illustrate this point ethnographically, by describing the way esoteric knowledge is acquired. Death most vividly illustrates that humans are at the mercy of uncertainty. It is the most terrifying absolute of human life. Few people choose to die, and few choose the time at which death comes. And death is unknowable. Magicians place the knowledge and mastery of death at the centre of their practice. One adept gives the following account of the student's training:

During his process through the early grades he should be trained in emotional and mental control . . . After the individual has achieved the optimal mental, emotional and physical control over himself, which means control in function, not inhibition, it is his task to face the Dweller on the Threshold . . . [This involves] personal Agony in the Garden, Trial, Cruxifiction, Descent into Hell and eventual Ascension . . . Once the process has been gone through, the individual is in a position to look everything in the face, without distortion or delusion, and to accept full realization for all that he does or has done . . . And how does he work out his destiny? By being himself – literally. By acting within the centre of his being, his essential self. Not by acting according to the dictates of his mind, his emotions or his instincts, but by using them according to his and their needs.[60]

The message is fundamental: to achieve self-mastery one must face and surmount the possibility of annihilation. More specifically, the story of the initiate's training is that he first trains himself in self-control to the greatest possible degree. At this point he confronts his own death, emotionally experiencing death and his own redemption (this adept has cast the process in

---

[59] Green (1983: 12).   [60] Knight in Fortune (1979: 264–9).

Christian form). If this experience is sufficiently vivid the initiate will have lost all irrational constraints, for he will feel that he knows and has mastered this most terrifying of experiences. The initiate will fear no uncertainty; he will feel no hampering biases. He will be that ideal of a human being, a unique being who acts with unfettered rationality to enact his own particular desires.

The important point about the initiate's esoteric knowledge of his own death is that some process has enabled him to feel that he has attained a sense of insight into the unknowable and has experienced things – like death – into which no human can possibly have any insight. For the most part these insights come through magic's rituals. Ritual creates the sense of knowing the unknowable through the referential ambiguity of poetic dramatization, which permits a kind of experiential knowledge of the unknown. Halloween can serve as the best example of this process. It is a central ritual in witchcraft, and celebrates the turn in the year when the dead are said to walk abroad. And in the ritual, the witch meets and makes his peace with Death himself.

Halloween is a 'god' ritual in witchcraft. This means that it is the horned god, not the Goddess, who is incarnated in the circle, and thus it is the high priest who takes the central ritual role. He dons a set of antlers and walks around the circle, announcing that the year is dead and that a new one must begin. This, he says, is the night when the veil grows thin between the worlds of the dead and living, and as the dead come forth to feast with the living, so the living must confront the dead. And then Death (the high priest) gives his central speech:

> I am the God who waits
> In the dead of the year, in the dark of life
> In the depths of the wood where no birds sing
> There will you rest again in my hand
> Be fearless to look upon my death's head
> For I have other faces and another hand
> To give again that which I have taken . . .
>
> Remember you trusted me in the spring green child places
> Finding enchantment;
> Found me merry in summer attendance when you wed
> Feared not to meet me in the autumn forest hunts
> Shrink not from me now in the winter snow . . .
>
> As the great cycle of the year brings forth the time of my domain
> Take me into your hearts, as you have ever been in mine

All witches present salute Death in turn, and they share communion with him in his honour. Death has announced that he is integral to life, that he is but another form of being. Nevertheless participants are meant to confront, accept and incorporate death in his state of non-life which people commonly find terrifying. And the visual impact, as the firelight flickers over the horned, furred mask, the death's sword held aloft, is an easy mnemonic.

Poetry removes the everyday reference of words. Poetic remarks are neither true nor false, for their empirical base is ambiguous and their logical structure that of metaphor, where the listener draws insights to make sense of the sentence whose literal meaning is false. And so the poetry can move in two directions. It removes the obvious truth of a description and makes it mysterious and unknown, and it speaks of the unknown in a way that cannot be dismissed as false. It intentionally transforms the intolerably banal into the mysterious and the unknown into the imaginable. When magicians call esoteric knowledge a secretive knowledge, they exploit both of these directions. On the one hand, esoteric knowledge turns the obvious into the hidden. Death, for example, is rather ordinary. Flowers die. Worms die. To talk of the secrets of death is to assert that there are concealed truths behind the appearances. Yet on the other hand, the poetry turns the unknown into the imaginable. Your own death, once terrifying, is no more mysterious than the flower's. Magicians both make the mundane mysterious and provide a means to know the mystery.

Participating in rituals in which one meets death seems to provide an experiential awareness associated with those poetic images. Again, it is an experience of 'knowing of' death, although magicians tend to use the term 'esoteric knowledge' to refer only to concepts with primitive emotional intensity like death and fertility, rather than to the particular terms of magical theory. No magician can experience death, but it is precisely the nature of magical ritual that the magician begins to feel as if she does so through the story of death which she is told. This is the mechanism at work in theatre: the viewer feels that he comes to understand the experience of murder by identifying with the homicidal protagonist, even if he has never committed it himself. And this theatrical catharsis is esoteric knowledge par excellence: an experience couched in images which ultimately hangs on your personal identification with the actors.

Magic is about controlling the uncontrollable world. Esoteric knowledge serves a protective role: knowledge of the Mysteries offers an infinite regression of deeper truths whose total acquisition would make the magic work, and substitutes worship for efficacy as the highest form of practice. Even more centrally, esoteric knowledge handles the ways in which control is thwarted: the unknowable uncertainties, of which death is the most terrible and frightening, the irrational motivations which govern human decisions. By mystifying the ordinary processes and poetically dramatizing them, the magician can come to experience the unknown, to feel as if he knows it, and so for him the unknown loses some of its terror, while the poetic grandeur of the secret mystery justifies the awe which remains. The fantasy is that total control comes with mastery of the uncertain and irrational, and thus esoteric knowledge is the keystone on which the triumphal arch of power hangs.[61] It is deeply therapeutic, for it gives the magician some access to his private, perhaps frightening, inner life, offers

[61] Bok points to the individualizing function of secrecy as central to the young child's development. Learning that it is possible to keep a secret teaches child that he is an independent self who has some control over his world. His parents are not, after all, omnipotent thought readers. Secrecy functions 'as a safety value that allows partial control over privacy and human contact' (Bok, 1982: 37). To hold a secret is to assert your control over your private life, to choose what it is that you make public. It is this that makes secrecy therapeutic.

the hope of controlling those feelings rather than being controlled by them, and provides the symbolic forum through which those personal feelings can be confronted, identified and to some extent understood.

Any list would be incomplete but certain books are central. Established manuals include: for classical Western Mysteries ritual magic Dion Fortune *The Mystical Qabalah* (1935) and Gareth Knight *A Practical Guide to Qabalistic Symbolism* Vols. I and II (1965); for Christian-oriented classical ritual magic Gareth Knight *Experience of Inner Worlds* (1975); for feminist witchcraft Starhawk *The Spiral Dance* (1979), Z. Budapest *The Holy Book of Women's Mysteries Parts I and II* (1979), Diane Mariechild *Motherwit* (1981); for non-feminist witchcraft Doreen Valiente *Witchcraft for Tomorrow* (1978) and Paul Huson *Mastering Witchcraft* (1970); and for more general magical practice (this is sometimes called 'Aquarian'), Marian Green *Magic in Principle and Practice* (1971), *Magic for the Aquarian Age* (1983), Dolores Ashcroft-Novicki *First Steps in Ritual* (1982), and Francis King and Stephen Skinner *Techniques of High Magic* (1976). These are but a sampling of the manuals, the ones which magicians I met seemed most likely to have. In addition there are manuals of specific techniques, as Ophiel *Creative Visualization* (1967) and J. H. Brennan *Astral Doorways* (1971). Central 'theoretical' accounts include Israel Regardie *The Tree of Life* (1969), Aleister Crowley *Magic in Theory and Practice* (1929), W. E. Butler *The Magician: His Training and Work* (1959), and most of Dion Fortune's non fictional (i.e. non-novelistic) work, such as *The Cosmic Doctrine* (1966), *Sane Occultism* (1967), *Applied Magic* (1962). Also see Johnstone, *SSOTBME* (1979). Many more recent books on magical theory combine discussion with exercise; a recent example is Gareth Knight *The Rose Cross and the Goddess* (1985).

If magicians read the works of earlier practitioners, they would most likely include Francis Barrett *The Magus* (1801), Éliphas Lévi *Transcendental Magic* (1896), *The Key to the Mysteries* (1959), *The History of Magic* (1913), and possibly works by Agrippa, the Hermetic Corpus, and associated writings like the Tibetan Book of the Dead and all writings by E. Wallis Budge. Some magicians have works by Francis Yates on Renaissance magic.

The central text in the histories of magical practice is the Regardie compilation of the Golden Dawn papers in *The Golden Dawn* Vol. I and II (1937–40) and the associated publication of other Golden Dawn papers, as in King *Astral Projection, Magic and Alchemy* (1971), R. A. Gilbert, ed. *The Magical Mason* (1983), R. A. Gilbert, ed., *The Sorcerer and his Apprentice* (1984). Historical accounts of the Golden Dawn are Ellic Howe *The Magicians of the Golden Dawn* (1972), R. A. Gilbert *The Golden Dawn* (1983), and Francis King and Isabel Sutherland *The Rebirth of Magic* (1982). Gerald Gardner's books, *The Meaning of Witchcraft* (1959) and *Witchcraft Today* (1954) give a fictitious account of covens but are nevertheless read as a guide to the contemporary practice. There is an excellent survey of current practice in the States by a practitioner, Margot Adler *Drawing Down the Moon* (1986). These have already been mentioned; they are however among the books magicians are likely to own.

Published accounts of rituals apart from the Golden Dawn include Herman Slater *Pagan Rituals* (1978), W. E. Gray *The Rollright Ritual* (1975), Janet and Stewart Farrar *Eight Sabbats for Witches* (1981) and *The Witches' Way* (1984).

Novels include Aleister Crowley *Moonchild* (1970), Peter Valentine Timlett *The Twilight of the Serpent* (1977), Dion Fortune *The Sea Priestess* (1959), *Moon Magic* (1956), *The Secrets of Dr. Taverner* (1978), *The Demon Lover* (1957). A recently much praised revision of the Arthurian story which explicitly cites magical works in its introduction was read by most people I knew: Marion Zimmer Bradley *The Mists of Avalon* (1983). Ursula LeGuin's *Earthsea Trilogy* (1979) is often read, and Dennis Wheatley's books often form the background of someone's interest in the practice. Fantasy novels often encountered include works by Charles Williams, C. S. Lewis, J. R. R. Tolkien, and Alan Garner. A session at the 1984 Quest conference listed some twenty children's books thought appropriate to magic (not listed in bibliography); their 'esoteric in fiction' booklist was (in order) Rosemary Sutcliffe *Warrior Scarlett* (1968), Richard *Monaco Runes* (1984), Philip K. Dick *The Divine Invasion* (1982), Vera Chapman *The Three Damosels* (1978), C. S. Lewis *That Hideous Strength* (1945), Meriol Trevor *The Sparrow Child* (1967), Liz Greene *The Dreamer of the Vine* (1980), Rudyard Kipling *Puck of Pook's Hill* (1983), John Crowley *Little Big* (1983), Joy Chant *Red Moon, Black Mountain* (1982), Michael Ayrton *The Movie Maker* (1982), Steward Gordon *Suaine and the Crow God* (1975), Robert Nye *Merlin* (1978), Alan Garner *Elidor* (1975), Gillian Bradshaw *Hawk of May* (1981), Peter Vansittart *The Death of Robin Hood* (1981), Marion Campbell *The Dark Twin* (1973), George Mackay Brown *Greenvoe* (1982), Robert Graves *Seven Days in New Crete* (1983), John Cowper Powys *Porius* (1974), Kathleen Herbert *Lady of the Fountain* (1980), Marion Zimmer Bradley *The Mists of Avalon* (1983), Naomi Michison *Corn King and Spring Queen* (1983), Moyra Caldicott *The Stones Trilogy* (1977), Avram Davidson *The Island Under the Earth* (1975), Kathleen Kurtz *Lammas Option* (1983), Dorothy Dunnett *King Hereafter* (1982), John James *Not for all the Gold of Ireland* (1968), Hannah Closs *The Tarn Trilogy* (1968), Jacquetta Hawkes *A Quest of Love* (1980). The couple who provided this list were librarians, as well as well-known magicians. They were the ones with literally several thousand books. Magicians were also quite likely to have standard anthologies of Greek, Egyptian and Celtic books, and to possess Robert Graves' *White Goddess* (1948) and Frazer's *Golden Bough* (1922 abridged).

Popular books on the tarot include: a classic guide to the interpretation in A. E. Waite *The Pictorial Key to the Tarot* (1959). Other books include Gareth Knight *A Practical Guide to Qabalistic Symbolism Vol. II* (1965); Stuart R. Kaplan *Tarot Classic* (1972); Bill Butler *The Definitive Guide to the Tarot* (1975); Sasha Fenton *Fortune Telling by Tarot Cards* (1985); Paul Huson *The Devil's Picturebook*

(1971); Papus *The Tarot of the Bohemians* (n.d.); R. Gardner *The Tarot Speaks* (1971); F. Lionel *The Magic Tarot* (1982). The definitive scholarly text on tarot as a game is Michael Dummett's tome, *The Game of Tarot* (1980), but this has only a short, arch section on the occult tarot. Astrological systems of some sort have been common amongst a wide range of Indo-European, Semitic, Asian and other cultures. In this small area of the world Liz Greene's psychological astrology seems to be amongst the most highly regarded, and many magicians own her books (e.g. Greene, 1976). On kabbalah, Gersholm Scholem is the greatest scholar of Judaic mysticism. *Major Trends in Jewish Mysticism* (1941) discusses kabbalah in its historical context but relatively few magicians own this work. Francis Yates discusses the transformation of the kabbalah in the Renaissance in *The Occult Philosophy in the Elizabethan Age* (1979) and in *Giordano Bruno and the Hermetic Tradition* (1964); magicians may know of this work, even if they have not read it in full. The classic Western Mysteries work on the kabbalah (as above) is Fortune *The Mystical Qabalah* (1935).

PART IV

Justifying to the sceptics

18

Introduction: coping with the dissonance

DIALOGUE

Wendy: I was wondering just how people actually saw it when you *are* sealing a space around yourself. In the temple I can understand, because presumably what you're saying is that there are various forces and they've all been brought up. And if you sort of open the thing, they can sort of come down on you. And at the end you close them, and they can stay there until next time. And that I can understand. In the temple, I don't have any problems with that. I feel contradiction – and after we spoke, I still thought of that – if it's in a living room, because it's not like a temple. Things are going on, all the time. And therefore you don't want to, in fact, keep that particular otherworld place there. I don't want to keep it there, I want to get rid of it.

Enoch: You want to dismiss it, in a sense.

Wendy: Yes. I want to bring it to me and put it away, so you can do other things, like hoover. I mean, I know, ideally – you can do everything with certain intentions. But –

Saul: But that's exactly what happens. I can see where the confusion lies. At the beginning of the ritual, there is an opening seal, a seal at least done to open up, which seems – the space within the circle becomes more sensitive, it keeps everything there, within, so it doesn't go off flying into the atmosphere in all sorts of directions. And you use that time, and that space, as Enoch says 8 o'clock is the specific time, we don't do it at 10 past, we start at 8. And then when we finish with the working, there is the seal, which is done in a different way. It releases it, if you like. But it's been protecting what we've been doing within that atmosphere. Am I right or am I wrong?

Enoch: I think you're right as far as it goes. But she was saying that she didn't have a problem as regards the temple, but with other contexts. Rebecca, what were you going to say?

Rebecca: Well, if it's – referring to the temple's use, when it's called an opening, it's really an invoking of a circle, you're invoking the force of the name you're using, into the temple. And at the closing, the sealing at the end, the archangels sort of reverse themselves, and keep what's true, there, but stay for a limited period. It's rather like getting the tap turned off: you're not getting more in, you've turned off the mains. Which are 'up there', if you like, metaphorically speaking. Whereas if you're doing it individually, ordinarily people will be using a fairly general sort of god-name – the logos, or the solar logos – which is a generalized form, not something specific, like for example, a rite of Mars, which might lead to discord in the family, say, if you had too much of it. So if it's a generalized spiritual force, which you've invoked down into your sitting room, so if there's some of it left, although you've stopped the continuous bringing down, after you've done the sealing, well, you should be able to hoover *better*, with no contradiction whatsoever, if you've got spiritual forces in your sitting room, if they're of the balanced, Middle Pillar variety.[1]

Enoch: What do you think of that, Wendy?

Wendy: Yes. I can understand that. Thank you. I still feel, though, and maybe this is just a personal thing of mine, that there's more of an element of protection when you're sealing on your own, because it [the room] is used for so many different things. You're opening up one thing, and closing it off to others, and I think – you did mention this earlier – there's an important element of keeping things out.

Enoch: But when you finish, in that case, if your sealing discontinues that protection, I would have thought that that would run counter to your argument. That if it was a protective thing you'd be more likely to want to leave it there anyway, presumably, while you did your hoovering. You see, there's not – what are you really doing with this stuff? You're putting a bounded context, I suggest, in time and space. You're saying, *this* space, for this piece of time, is special. And while it's special, I have a belief system that I operate in this special space and time. There might be all sorts of nasty things that want to get in there, because I have just *ditched* all the defences of the common sense world that I normally live in, and therefore anything's possible. So I'm vulnerable, because all of a sudden I believe in Mickey Mouse and God Save the King and everything that ever was, y'know. Whereas, when you get rid of all that, you're back to a sort of common sense world reality. Nonsense, anyway. Nothing's *really* going to come through the wall and get at you. There are buses out there. I mean, you've shifted your reality.

Wendy: But in the everyday world, you're prepared to deal with all those things. In fact you have to, that's part of the process. But you don't want to be bothered with them when you're trying to do something else.

Enoch: The bounded context in space and time.

Amy: What is it that you want to keep away from what?

Mike: Dogs barking.

Amy: You want to keep the hoovering away from the meditation, or the meditation away from the hoovering? Cause I agree with – see, I'm not –

Barry: Difficult things, vacuum cleaners, aren't they.

Martha: One of the things I notice, I don't seal physically, actually, when I've been doing, despite what I said before, I visualize. And actually, what I usually do when I close, when I visualize, seal, whether it's a cone of light or four pentacles, is, I do the closing seal and then I visualize it being absorbed into my body. And for me, what that means is that I've assimilated it. And that means that that can then act – it just seems safe to me, that's all . . .

(a bit later on)

Rebecca: Is that not like dividing your life into two parts, like going to Church on Sunday and being somewhere else the other six days?

Enoch: But you divide it into more than two. You divide it into hundreds of pieces.

Wendy: The forces are always with you, what you're doing is always with you. What I would like to do is to get rid of most of it, and I don't think that's splitting me, because that bit about getting back to normal, everyday – what I've got from it is in me, and contracts around. But I don't want to live in a temple atmosphere. I want – I don't know.

[1] 'Middle Pillar' is a term used by Golden Dawn students (and their descendants) to describe the balanced use of the kabbalah, along the central core of the Tree of Life – Malkuth, Yesod, Tiphareth, Kether. The term is often shorthand for a balanced, integrated approach to life and its problems.

Enoch: But not only that. It's not only your mundane world that suffers. I suggest, it's your temple that suffers when you blur the edges. It's no longer a special place in the same sense. You are trying to create a *special* context, and if you blur the edges of that special context – I mean you wouldn't, for instance, you wouldn't walk into this temple up here and have a party in it, or something. Or come to that, you wouldn't even go and play a game of chess in it, probably because you've set it aside as something special. In that case you set a physical piece of space and time aside. What we're talking about now is a subjective piece of space and time, something that's projected out of you, wherever you happen to be. You say, I set my magical space about me here in this place, and when you do *that*, what you're laying on the line is your own secret, sacred innermost place, and when you do that, by God you don't want to leave it laying about for people to wipe their feet on.

Rebecca: I see what you're expressing now, Enoch. You're talking about, in a sense, making more of a subjective temple, relative to oneself. I was doing it as a much more objective thing, in which if you use one room and you keep on sealing it, you do build up an atmosphere, which I feel won't do any harm if the force is of a generalized, spiritual nature. And also, let me add the point, that all life can be considered as a ritual. Everything we do. And therefore I don't feel that one wants to make a separation between so-called temple things and so-called mundane things. That temple up there is supposed to be symbolic of life, really.

Enoch: But you can't *do* that, I mean really, because people are not at that level.

Amy (with general yeses): That's why we have a temple upstairs.

Enoch: They're not at that level. If you pretend that they are, all you do, in the end, is to dilute the effect of your form.

Amy: But I think there's something on both sides. I think it would be a pity to cut out that alternative altogether, because that cuts out the alternative of aspiring, of seeing that that is possible. I quite agree that that's the point, that is why we've got the temple, because we're not at that level, and we need to do it in a separated space.

As the above dialogue illustrates, magicians feel some tension between the magical and the everyday, the invocation and the hoovering (a hoover is a vacuum cleaner), the 'belief system' in magic and the buses in Hornsey. They often talk about the differences between the two and the conflict between the ideas found in magic and those of the everyday. For the most part, their arguments and explanations justify the difference between them rather than striving to knit them together into some integrated seamless whole. Wendy feels 'contradiction' when she performs her rituals in the living room, because she hoovers in the living room, and she wants advice about a ritual gesture that will set the living-room-as-temple apart from the commonplace mundanity. Rebecca recognizes the difference between the contradicting parts (magical forces, archangels and the like on the one hand, and the ordinariness of the vacuum cleaner on the other), but does not seem as troubled by their incongruity as Wendy. Enoch tries to clarify the issue by which he too is clearly troubled. Magic, he says, involves creating a 'bounded context in space and time'. In that context, you have a special 'belief' system. 'I have just *ditched* all the defences of the commonsense world I normally live in . . . when you get rid of all that, you're back to a sort of common sense reality.' Rebecca objects: it sounds too much 'like dividing your life into two parts'. But Amy, Wendy,

Enoch and the others think that the division is necessary and normal. You need to keep the distance, Enoch says, and he seems to think that one can maintain that distance with ritual gestures or, even better, a spatial separation of the magical and the mundane. 'You say, I set my magical space about me in this place and when you do *that*, what you're laying on the line is your own secret, sacred, innermost place, and when you do that, by God you don't want to leave it laying about for people to wipe their feet on.'

People who are not questioned need not develop answers. Magicians live in a society in which their magic is intellectually rejected and socially disavowed – it is one thing to read your horoscope, it is another thing to have your boss stand naked in his living room and invoke Hermes for a more efficient secretary – and yet they make a conscious choice to practise magic. The last two parts of the book have illustrated the ways in which magical practice, and the ideas behind it, becomes persuasive. Systematic changes in the style of intellectual interpretation make the ideas seem more believable; the satisfactions of involvement make the desire to justify the involvement even greater. Nevertheless, despite magic's growing appeal, at some point in their practice – for some, throughout their practice – magicians confront scepticism, other people's or their own. For the most part, they hold on to their views, and respond by justifying the apparent contradictions or discrepancies between magical ideas and commonplace conceptions rather than carefully testing their new views within the ordinary criteria they use to evaluate ideas. And they develop a host of ideas, strategies and arguments which allow them to move back and forth between different ways of explaining their magic in the face of different challenges.

Upon reflection this accommodation is surprising. We live in a highly bureaucratized, rationalized, world, with a misty ideal of the theory-laden Westerner – Taylor's rich rationalist, Gellner's cognitively consistent capitalist. One knows nevertheless that human animals are not syllogism-solving maximizers. But given the self-consciousness of these sophisticated, educated Londoners, one might have thought that they would be anxious to defend magical practice as an activity as rational and as acceptable as, say, modern medicine. Often they do not. Magicians do not search, exhaustively, to prove an elaborate theory true, nor do they abandon their claims when they find it difficult to convince sceptical outsiders within conventional intellectual canons. They adjust the canons to adapt to the unusual claims – they say that all truths are relative, or that science is valid only in a mundane context – and explain why their belief is personally fulfilling for spiritual, psychological or aesthetic reasons. They describe the claims and the practice as different from ordinary endeavours, set apart as separate and thus not amenable to critique. This ability to set the practice apart, to compartmentalize it, is crucial. It allows magicians to explain their involvement without having to defend the magic directly and to defend the magic without having to abandon previously held intellectual commitments. Their explanation becomes a patchwork job. Magicians adjust their assertions depending on the audience, explain that the ideas are true but on a different plane, or that truth is relative, according to the occasion and the need. To the outsider, it seems as if they have an ambivalent, shifting attitude towards their magical ideas. But it may be that they simply explain in different ways to different people, with the intellectual tools that come to hand.

This patchwork rationalization can be clarified through the concept of cognitive dissonance – an old-fashioned term in psychological circles, but one that captures well the intellectual uneasiness created through the adherence to magic, and the attempts to alleviate it. In the fifties, Leon Festinger (and others) developed a sociological theory of 'cognitive dissonance' to understand intellectual discomfort. Its most famous application concerned an American flying saucer cult which predicted that the world would end on 21 December. On 22 December – *after* the prophetic failure – the adherents began to proselytize, for the first time, claiming that the world had been miraculously redeemed. Festinger interpreted this as an attempt to reconcile their considerable commitment to their belief with the embarrassing evidence of its falsity by creating social support for a somewhat transformed version of it.[2]

In Festinger's more general theory, dissonance, roughly, is the ill fit between intellectual concepts and actual behaviour, incompatible 'elements' of one person's mental universe. 'Two elements are in a dissonant relation if, considering these two alone, the obverse of one element would follow from the other'.[3] Dissonant elements are manifest in logical inconsistency, poor manners (given an awareness of polite behaviour), conflict between a specific and more general opinion (voting Tory in one election, while thinking of oneself as a Labour supporter), and all decisions: if one ever considered choosing one alternative over another, the memory of that consideration is dissonant with the subsequent decision.

The central tenet of Festinger's theory is that individuals strive to reduce dissonance. 'The reality which impinges upon a person will exert changes in the direction of bringing the appropriate cognitve elements into correspondence with that reality'.[4] Dissonance can be avoided, he points out, by either altering one of the clashing elements – changing behaviour, changing the environment so that it fits with behaviour, adding new cognitive elements – or by avoiding the clash in the first place. For example (his examples) a smoker will search out material that points out weaknesses in the experiments which attest to tobacco's harm, but avoid discussion with articulate oncologists. A man who has carefully avoided a spot on the floor for no apparently rational reason – he 'knows' that the floor is as sturdy in that spot as at any other – might drill a hole in it to justify the avoidance. The Ifaluk, who believe that all people are good, attribute their

---

[2] Festinger (1956) The case study was challenged, on the pleasing grounds that there were more investigators than subjects and as the investigators pretended to be convinced believers they may have altered the experimental situation by producing considerable social support at a crucial time. This criticism, among others, is voiced by otherwise laudatory early reviews (e.g. Hughes, 1958). Alison Lurie wrote a novel on this theme of observer effects and the consequential effects of the observed, the sociologist-turned-extraterrestrial-avatar (Lurie, *Imaginary Friends*, 1967).

[3] Festinger (1957: 13).

[4] Festinger (1957: 11).

children's nastiness to malevolent ghosts, who possess them.[5] Cognitive dissonance theory is loose, but exegetically fruitful, and it illuminates some features of magicians' behaviour.

The important feature of this theory is that the effort to straighten out inconsistencies in experience-and-belief resemble an odd-job-man's repairs. If people notice a mismatch of ideas and experience, they do something to make them fit. The key point is that they have to notice the mismatch, and after noticing they act to relieve the discomfort generated by their observation. If they can arrange to ignore the observation or explain it away without making major readjustments in ways of acting or thinking about things, they will do so. Festinger's subjects do not act to promote long-term consistency or even long-term self-interest; they act to avoid current cognitive embarrassment, and they do so in ways which are sometimes quite damaging to long-term interest. For example, the smoker has considerable self-interest in survival, and would probably claim that more knowledge is always better. By avoiding information about tobacco's harms, he acts against his own interests and beliefs, but avoids undermining his self-confidence the next time he pulls out a cigarette. It involves far more work, one might think, to drill a hole in the floor than to step on it. And drilling a hole for the sake of preserving appearances would run against the man's belief that he should act rationally. But once the hole is there, it is rational to avoid the spot.[6]

In a society that values cognitive consistency and goal-directed action, magicians often feel pressure – internal or external – to justify their involvement.[7] This is particularly a problem of modern magic: simple, straightforward explanations of the causal effects of magic are rejected by their social environment, and they feel the need to produce others. Magical theory may be dissonant with the magician's empirical reality, though the magician's methods of interpreting evidence and explaining failure may reduce that misfit; magical practice is certainly dissonant with general social expectations, and with what is rather grandly conceived as 'science'. But magicians do not produce an elaborate philosophy which would describe all their beliefs, actions and desires as consistent, and substantively rational – oriented towards a genuinely

[5] See Festinger (1957: 1–31); examples pp. 20–4.

[6] The theory of cognitive dissonance became a major focus of psychological research in the fifteen years following its publication. Some of the developments and critical assessments are collected in Abelson et al. (eds., 1968), and Feldman (ed., 1966). The theory has now fallen out of favour, because it was difficult to define precisely within an experimental paradigm, and there were great difficulties in interpreting what any given experiment might 'mean'. Elster's more recent discomfort with cognitive dissonance lies in what he sees as the paradoxicality of the subject's desire to avoid knowledge which he must know is there in order to avoid. The paradoxicality was in fact a part of Festinger's point; however, Elster may have a valid critique insofar as this activity was not experimentally described as self-deception, but as the selective assimilation of information.

[7] Gellner (1974), following on from Weber, addresses the increasing importance of this 'new cognitive ethic' in modern society in which justification by reasoned argument becomes socially important. Attribution theorists have examined the phenomenon that the functional value of explaining events in particular ways will influence the explanation given by a subject. Hewstone (1983) provides a helpful introduction; see pp. 15ff for a discussion of causal attribution. See also Jaspars, Fincham and Hewstone (1983) for an introduction to other work.

desirable goal in the most effective manner possible. Instead, they justify the inconsistency with a range of arguments and make efforts to separate magic off from the mundane by ritual and metaphor. Through practice, theory and styles of arguments, magicians insulate their magic from hostile criticism, real or imagined, and they acquire reasons to explain this separation. This is a powerful protective device, hardly unique to magic but well exemplified within it. People rationalize rather than acting rationally, and strive for local consistency with a patchwork job of *post hoc* rationalization. The following two chapters describe, first, an intellectual metaphor which magicians adopt in order to separate magic from the non-magical, and second, the magician's styles of rationalizing arguments, the ways in which magicians self-consciously learn to order their dissonant reality by disassembling it into separate boxes identified by different claims.

19

The magical plane: the emergence of a protective metaphor

MAGICIANS make use of a metaphor which suggests that magic is a sort of reality different from the mundane physical world – magical forces can affect the physical world, but they exist as a different level of being. Magic is on a different 'plane' or 'level'. Recall the first of magic's 'four fundamental theoretical assumptions' given in a popular manual: 'that the universe of the physical scientist is only a part, and by no means the most important part, of total reality'.[1] The authors explain that assumption in the following way:

> Most magicians believe as firmly in the existence of matter as any Marxist, but they regard it as only the 'densest' of a number of different types of existence, usually referred to as 'worlds' or 'planes'. The last mentioned term is an unfortunate one, for it often leads those unfamiliar with occult terminology to conceive of the planes as being one above the other, rather like geological strata. The magician does not look upon them in this way; instead he regards them as interpenetrating and co-existing with one another – the so-called 'astral plane', for example, having the same spatial co-ordinates as the physical plane but nevertheless remaining quite separate from it and obeying its own natural laws.[2]

The basic idea is that there are many different kinds of matter-like substances. Among them are psychic forces, granite rocks, imagined objects, spiritual essences and so forth. All of these substances interact with each other, but granite-like objects and spirit-like objects are governed by different natural laws. The point is that things which are normally thought not to exist (like a mental image of a polar bear, outside the imaging subject's mind) *do* exist, but in a different way, and under different laws, than do tables and chairs. Golden-hearted dragons are real, but not like brown-eyed anthropologists.

Many magicians hold different versions of this general idea, and use it at different times and in different ways to explain their practice. However, most of them view things imagined as a sort of stuff, which has an impact upon a tables-and-chairs reality. The imagination carries and directs the magical force in this understanding, and magicians use a term like 'plane' to confer a separate but equal status upon this imaginative world. They also speak of the 'inner plane' and shorten the phrase to 'the inner'. 'Inner' is a disingenuous term. It does not

---

[1] King and Skinner (1979: 9).   [2] King and Skinner (1976: 10).

mean 'merely' imaginative or emotional or internal, although that is what it seems to imply; the entire thrust of magical ideas is to assert how much more the term includes. Somehow, the 'inner' has links to the physical. The notion of a real-but-different magical reality is central for a modern magician, for it allows him both to assert the magic and to block it off from the sceptic's probing stare. The protection is considerably bolstered by psychoanalysis, which magicians invoke (as will be described) to explain that not all mental activity is rational or logical, and indeed that the irrational is powerful, effective (in that it alters behaviour), and inaccessible to conscious analysis.

The best illustrations of the metaphor of a separate 'plane' can be found in magicians' writings, where authors boldly assert claims while wooing the sceptics among their readership – and the sceptic within themselves. In one of the earliest texts of modern magic, an elder statesman of the Golden Dawn says this to his students:

> The uninitiated interpret Imagination as something 'imaginary' in the popular sense of the term, i.e. something unreal. But the imagination is a reality. When a man imagines, he actually creates a form on the Astral or some higher plane; and this form is as real and objective to intelligent beings on that plane, as our earthly surroundings are to us.[3]

For the author the astral world is objectively real. Imaginary forms are not kickable, like Johnson's rock; they are objective only to other beings also 'on that plane'. But that is not to say that they are not real. His colleague says, 'it is an ancient Hermetic dogma that any idea may be made manifest externally if only, by culture, the art of concentration be obtained'.[4] That is, if you think or concentrate properly, the imagined will come to physically exist. That is how the imagination can have dramatic impact under conditions of magical ritual.

To Crowley reality is mutable, and best understood as a mixture of co-existing separate planes. It is not exactly clear what he means by 'plane': he says that a plane is an imaginative construct built of associated symbols. There are Celtic planes, Nordic planes, spiritual planes. 'In short, every country, creed and literature has given its characteristic mode of presentation to some 'plane' or another'.[5] What he seems to mean is that any elaborate fantasy can be called a 'plane', and that – the important point – these planes become real, in some more-than-imagined sense, to the magician. However, the reality is not an ordinary reality: by calling that unordinary reality a 'plane', Crowley asserts that the reality is of a different sort.

> Now this interior body of the magician . . . does exist, and can exert certain powers which his natural body cannot do. It can, for example, pass through 'matter' and it can move freely in every direction through space. But this is because 'matter' in the sense in which we commonly use the word, is on another plane.[6]

Magic is effective because the magician can alter a tables-and-chairs reality by moving around in a fantasy world, and because the fantasy can have this effect,

---

[3] Berridge, in King (1972: 33).
[5] Crowley (1929: 250).

[4] Westcott in King (1972: 37).
[6] Crowley (1929: 144).

it must somehow be real. The term 'plane' simply serves to give that other reality a name.

For Crowley, the metaphor of a separate plane also becomes a way of reconciling magic and science, two apparently different interpretations and explanations of reality. He commends a book by Éliphas Lévi, a magician who treats magic as a form of religion and presents the scientific scepticism of magic as part of the conflict between religious faith and scientific knowledge. Crowley introduces the English translation, his translation, of Lévi's work:

> The volume represents the high water mark of the thought of Éliphas Lévi. He is no longer talking of things as if their sense was fixed and universal. He is beginning to see some of the contradiction inherent in the nature of things or, at any rate, he constantly illustrates the fact that the planes are to be kept separate for practical purposes, although in the final analysis they turn out to be one.[7]

Render unto science that which is science's, and treat religion and magic as if they were apart, even though you know them ultimately to be parts of a whole. The metaphor of a 'plane' is more than a description; its purpose lies in keeping unhappy bedfellows apart.

Throughout his writing, Israel Regardie – Crowley's secretary, Golden Dawn initiate and author of classical magical tomes – speaks here as the sceptical psychologist and there as the committed spell-caster. He too speaks of a different 'plane', and it serves him in both roles. To him it is 'of the utmost importance in magical work' that the magician assumes that 'symbols represent, on the astral plane, real and tangible realities'. These symbols 'are not intellectual conventions, nor even arbitrary representations of universal ideas and natural forms. They are absolute living entities'.[8] Yet at times he seems to regard magic as no more than a system of psychology. Regardie's magician consciously manipulates powerful symbols to gain direct access to his unconscious feelings, and the reality of the symbols is neither here nor there. A 'series of psychological techniques',[9] magical methods 'reveal our secret selves more directly, and unlock the vast store of wisdom and power within our souls, showing us how to control them in ways that neither psychoanalysis nor modern science has succeeded'.[10] But Regardie ultimately comes down on the side of magic. That magic seems unprovable or unreasonable is reason's failure, not magic's. The mind is far greater, far more complex, than human reason could ever comprehend. Rational thought could never grasp the whole. Magical methods 'may appear irrational to us. They certainly are irrational. But that is no argument for rejecting them summarily. A great deal of life itself *is* irrational.'[11]

As magic has expanded in the twentieth century this geometric metaphor has coloured all practitioners' writings on the theory of magic. The director of the largest correspondence course describes a ritual which 'touches a level far deeper and higher than the most elaborate ceremonies can ever do'.[12] The

---

[7] Levi (1959: 7).   [8] Regardie (1969: 65).   [9] Regardie (1964: 28).
[10] Regardie (1964: 26).   [11] Regardie (1964: 14).   [12] Ashcroft-Novicki (1982: 50).

'higher' spiritual levels of an external world are fused with the 'depths' of the psyche. The symmetry of inner and outer experience – and its reality, even though non-physical – likewise surface in Gareth Knight: 'to the trained occultist who is "on his contacts", the unconscious is merely a magic mirror in which are reflected objective, though non-physical, realities'.[13] The unseen layers within the self reflect the unseen layers of the universe, and by manipulating the inner unconscious, one affects the outer non-physical entities which occupy a 'higher' level within the world than the physical. 'Such is magic, working from one level of existence to another'.[14]

One of the interesting features of this metaphor is that it has been in existence for years, but its use has changed substantially, from moral injunction to cognitive insulator. The moral hierarchy which separated an impure materiality from the spiritually divine now distinguishes between what are perceived to be two modes of thought, two ways of carrying on, between magic and its sceptics. The advent of psychoanalysis gave particular force to this metaphor; indeed psychoanalysis gave significant credibility to magic in magicians' eyes. To explain this, I shall quickly sketch the roots of the geometric magical metaphor.

The metaphor of a separate-but-connected plane derives in part from the early Hermetic philosophy, which has two central claims: that man reflects in his microcosm the complexity of the macrocosm, and that the universe's macrocosm has many tiers. The Hermetic Corpus is a compendium of second century philosophy and magic, a collection of scattered works by many hands on metaphysics, astrology, spell-casting and mythology. The philosophical dialogues echo Plato, Genesis and the Christian teachings; those who thought them ancient documents must have read them with delighted awe. The dialogues speak of a gnostic, dualistic world in which the divine has split asunder from the material. Humans straddled the two. 'Thus man was formed from a double origin, so that he could both admire and adore celestial things, and take care of terrestrial things and govern them.'[15] In 1460 the *Corpus Hermeticum*, the Greek manuscript nearly complete, reached Florence, where the works of Plato were awaiting translation. The early Church Fathers acclaimed its supposed author, Hermes Trismegistus, as Moses' contemporary, and the hieratic Egyptian source from whom Plato himself derived his

---

[13] Knight (1976: 9).

[14] Gray in Wilby (1968: 2). The notion of a separate 'plane' to identify things spiritual seems quite pervasive, though the job it does in modern magic is quite specific. The ancient Maya conceived of the sky as divided into thirteen layers, with an underworld similarly tiered (Thompson 1954; Vogt 1976 describes its transformations in their Zinacantecan descendants). The Hugh-Joneses describe the ordered cosmos of the Amazonian Barasana as divided into layers transmigrated by their shamans (e.g. S. Hugh-Jones, 1979: 248). When men participate in male initiation *he wi*, they become 'people of another layer (*gahe tutiana*)' (C. Hugh-Jones, 1979: 148). Among shamanic cultures generally, but also among the Nuer, the Dinka and other traditional religions, the spatial metaphor becomes a fundamental means to articulate conceptions of the spiritual world, as it is in Judaeo-Christianity. It may be that this sort of metaphor provides a manner of representing a concept whose intellectual context is hard to grasp, without in some manner defining it.

[15] The Asclepius: quoted in Yates (1964: 36).

teachings. Cosimo de' Medici yearned to read this work before he died, and the translator, Ficino, put aside his Plato and turned to them.

A Neoplatonic magical philosophy emerged, fostered by these documents, and had a remarkable impact on its times.[16] That philosophy interpreted the Platonic triplicity of body, soul and spirit through the Hermetic writings, and incorporated a Christianized kabbalah to purify and exalt its power. In the early sixteenth century Agrippa popularized this magic in a clear text which outlined the heavenly hierarchy that served as magic's base. There are three worlds in this account: the elemental (the base material world), the celestial (the heavenly world, contacted by astrological means) and the intellectual (the Godly world, contacted by the kabbalistic names of God), each influenced directly by the one which supersedes it. Their domains map on to one another, and with the knowledge of their interconnections, man – who spans all worlds – may call upon the higher to influence the lower.

For so inferiors are successively joined to their superiors, that there proceeds an influence from their head; of the First Cause, as a certain string stretched out to the lowermost thing of all, which string, if one end be touched the whole does presently shake, and such a touch doth sound to the other end; and at the motion of an inferior the superior also is moved, to which the other doth answer, as strings in a lute well tuned.[17]

As God's influence descends through the world, so man's can ascend, and by manipulating chains of interconnections, alter the flow of influence. 'It should be possible for us to ascend by the same degrees through each World [. . . and . . .] to draw new virtues from above.'[18]

The hierarchy teaches a moral lesson. The purity of the world increases in its higher reaches and those who wish to reach there must match its standards. 'By how much the more noble the form of any thing is, by so much the more prone and apt it is to receive, and powerful to act.'[19] To fully exercise his magical ability the magician must become a fit vehicle for a power and a pure form for its attraction.

No one has such powers but he who has cohabited with the heavens, vanquished the elements, mounted higher than the heavens, elevating himself above the angels to the archetype itself, with whom he becomes co-operator and can do all things.[20]

This demand for the magician's purity grows particularly strong in alchemy and in the subtle philosophical magic of Elizabethan men like John Dee and Robert Fludd. The universe is a complex, interdependent hierarchy in which higher beings directly control lower in a descending chain of command. Through his

---

[16] The major sources here, as throughout, are Yates (1964) and Walker (1975); works by Gombrich (1972), Panofsky (1968) and Wind (1980: [1958]) are relevant to the historical interpretation of imagination's power and the nature of art and ideas. The more recent history of imagination's power as understood by Hume, Kant, Coleridge, Wordsworth and Sartre can be found in Warnock (1976) and Abrams (1971).

[17] Agrippa (1974: 125).   [18] Agrippa (1974: 37–8).
[19] Agrippa (1974: 121).   [20] Arippa quoted in Yates (1964: 136).

purity the magician rises in the hierarchy – or at least becomes fit to exercise higher powers – and influences that which is below.[21]

There is no suggestion in Neoplatonic philosophy that different rules of rationality govern mundane, celestial and spiritual. If anything, reason increases with ascent on to higher planes. The advent of psychoanalysis and the emergence of a scientific scepticism altered this understanding of other 'planes'. Now, magic became different by virtue of the different laws its forces follow, and the geometric metaphor differentiates between different laws, not different states of heavenly purity. The Renaissance conception separated different worlds and saw magic as the means to use the one to influence the other, and the magician made great moral and spiritual efforts to gain access to the higher realms for tools to manipulate the lower. Modern magic separates different types of stuff, or worlds, which run by different rules, and to acquire magical power the magician must lose hold of his rational mind. The goals have shifted dramatically: to gain essentially the same powers, the Renaissance mage strove for moral purity but the modern magician embraces the non-rational.

Modern magic first emerged in a world torn by the struggles between science and religion. Many of the thinking population wanted to preserve the claims of religion within the guise of science. This produced a curious interpretation of spiritual and psychological experience. In the 1840s and 1850s the Anglo-American world had seen an occult wave of astonishing proportions. There was a 'mesmeric mania' which spoke of 'electro-biology' and 'odyllic force', terms for mysterious magnetic forces which could be altered by human will. Seven years after the Fox sisters heard the peculiar rappings of the communicative dead, a Catholic convention estimated eleven million American spiritualists, a staggering number even if exaggerated.[22] Theosophy gained world wide support in the 1870s with its mixture of spiritualism, evolutionary biology, and Indian philosophy and it claimed to be a 'scientific' spirituality directly correlated with Darwinian theory. In 1882 the Society for Psychical Research was formed with a most prestigious initial membership.[23] For these men their project, if achieved, would be the ideal solution to their dilemma: the reality of the religious substance and the immorality of the soul, proved by means of the experiments and logic of the scientific canon.

The psychology of the day walked a tightrope between materialism and speculative metaphysics in its sweeping vision of nature as a vast mechanism run by evolution. In this 'psychophysical parallelism', as they called it, complex thoughts and feelings emerged from the association of simple ideas, in turn derived from physiological constraints. Bain, commonly described as psychology's

---

[21] This emphasis upon purity continues throughout the literature into the present day. Even Crowley (1929: 182) reveals 'the most important of all magical secrets that ever were or are or can be' as this:

> The magician becomes filled with God, fed upon God, intoxicated with God. Little by little his body will become purified by the internal lustration of God; day by day his mortal frame, shedding its earthly elements, will become in very truth the Temple of the Holy Ghost. Day by day matter is replaced by spirit, the human by the divine; ultimately the change will be complete; God manifest in flesh will be his name.

[22] Gauld (1968: 29).

[23] Gauld (1968: 40).

founder, remarked: 'the mind is completely at the mercy of bodily conditions; there is no trace of a separate, independent, self-supporting spiritual agent, rising above the fluctuations of the corporeal frame'.[24] Mind and body were experientially separate but ultimately one.

The doctrine of two substances – a material united with an immaterial in a certain vague undefined relationship – which has prevailed from the time of Thomas Aquinas to the present day is now in the course of being modified . . . The only tenable supposition is that mental and physical proceed together, as individual twins.[25]

But this view that the mental depends upon the physical was challenged by other psychologists, James Ward, Sidgwick's pupil, among them. He claimed that action altered cognition, that perception is not a physical given. 'The steel worker sees half a dozen tints where others see only a uniform glow.'[26] Mind alters the world one sees.

Into this charged atmosphere arose the Golden Dawn, founded in 1887, with its doctrine that imagination was a reality and that it could affect the material world. The different 'plane' that these magical writers present is not defined by different rules – that conception emerges somewhat later – but is rather composed of different materials, one apparently unsubstantial, the other substantive, but both ultimately interdependent. As in the psychology of the day there seems to have been some confusion in understanding how the mental alters the physical: magicians held, for instance, that to make something occur one must both imagine it and will it, and while they insisted upon the willing they rarely explained why their theory required it. But there was no elaborate account of the inherent difference between mental and physical in the way that shortly followed.

By 1920 English translations of Freud and Jung stirred much public interest. (Freud was actually first introduced in England in the Society for Psychical Research in 1893 by Myers, three months after the first Freud-Breuer paper on hysteria.)[27] Psychoanalytic theory, emerging in a society increasingly secular and sceptical of magical claims, had a profound effect upon magical practice. Under its influence, the symbolic images of magic were no longer associated directly with an external reality, but became the language of the unconscious, which in turn became the channel through which the magical power flowed. Magicians began to speak of the tremendous power 'beneath' the imagination which magical rituals could access.

A concept of the unconscious was important for magicians because the unconscious was powerful and irrational, and was said to 'think' with emotionally primitive, mythic images of the sort used in magical ritual. Jung's formulation of the unconscious appealed particularly strongly to magicians for two reasons. First, he stressed the limits of the rational comprehension of the unconscious and its symbolism. 'As the mind explores the symbol, it is led to ideas which lie beyond the grasp of reason.'[28] True reality, represented in the

---

[24] Bain quoted in Hearnshaw (1968: 12).   [25] Bain (1873: 129–30, 131).
[26] Ward (1886: 45).   [27] Jones (1961: 324).   [28] Jung (1968: 4).

symbol, escapes the conscious mind; humanity 'never perceives anything fully or comprehends anything completely'.[29] Second, Jung spoke of a collective unconscious which all people, particularly those of the same race, share. On this account, humans inherit instinctive tendencies to use particular images or motifs – 'archetypes' – which Jung denotes as the 'collective unconscious', and describes as a 'layer' beneath the psyche.[30] Because of this primordial layer, people are meant to find certain stories and symbols deeply significant, but cannot respond to others. So rather than writing as if the unconscious were the source of mankind's trouble, Jung presented the irrational as a shared and potent human foundation.

Magicians somewhat misrepresented Jung's admittedly enigmatic account, and reified his collective unconscious. In magicians' writings, the collective unconscious practically became a place, to which magical ritual could be a map which magicians used to travel in the collective human soul. By the third decade of the twentieth century, magicians were writing as if the individual's unconscious was not his personal problem but his connection to his race:

A man's soul is like a lagoon connected with the sea by a submerged channel; although to all outward seeming it is landlocked, nevertheless its water level rises and falls with the tides of the sea because of the hidden connection. So it is with human consciousness, there is a subconscious connection between each individual soul and the World-soul deep hidden in the most primitive depths of subconsciousness.[31]

Even though a person seems isolated, unto himself, in fact his mind is linked with others. Jung gave powerful support to magical theory, for his work was used to claim that the individual could affect the culture by manipulating his own unconscious depths. Magicians use this sort of lagoon-imagery freely: they affect the racial whole by affecting their own subjectivity. They talk about 'dropping' a symbol into the collective unconscious by performing rituals in which certain symbols become emotionally fraught for them personally. They also speak of holding back their own rationality as if it were a gate, to let these symbols pass beneath it.

The crucial feature of this new unconscious was that it obeyed alien, irrational laws. Magicians used this characterization in their explanations: you use symbols in ritual to stir the unconscious depths, which then affect the world by affecting other people and – a key move – you cannot rationally comprehend the irrational mechanisms that make this work. This adaptation of the new psychology allowed magicians to claim that magical laws are necessarily incomprehensible. Magic is true on its level, but it cannot be understood by the rational – 'scientific' – mind. In a novel famous in magical circles, the protagonist remarks:

Sometimes I think one thing about myself and sometimes I think another. As long as I believe in myself I find that I can do certain things. If I ceased to believe in myself, I think I should just crumble into dust, like an unwrapped mummy. There is more than

---

[29] Jung (1968: 4).   [30] Jung (1965: 163).   [31] Fortune (1935: 17).

one kind of truth. A thing that does not exist in our three dimensional world may exist in the fourth dimension and be true in its way.[32]

This complicated statement asserts the reality of implicitly contradictory truths, and separates them by claiming that they belong to different dimensions. That other dimension is true, but one cannot know it rationally; one can have faith in its existence. And only if one has faith in oneself as being able to work effectively in that other dimension will one be able to do so. The protagonist seems to think that the most difficult part of magical practice is maintaining the psychological security to allow oneself to accept these complex views about truth. Agrippa's hierarchy separated angels from impure humanity. Fortune's 'dimensions' separate the magical priestess from the English housewife. The religious hierarchy has shifted into a division between intellectual commitments.

The psychological transformation of magic serves two quite different ends. On the one hand, it allows magicians to argue that magical symbols have a real, therapeutic effect on the individual, regardless of any theory of magical impact. That is, magical practice has a valuable function even if its theory is false. On the other hand, it allows magicians to give a technical explanation for magical efficacy which actually entails the impossibility of full rational understanding of its ritual. The unconscious is irrational, and magic lies in its domain. Magic becomes part of a different context, something separate from a rationally comprehended materialism. The term 'inner plane' carries with it this freedom, this sense that it is not important to give a rational explanation of the magic. Rationality, after all, is what the conscious mind is good at. Linked to psychology and its authoritative figures, the metaphor of a separate plane is a magician's intellectual resource that dispenses with ordinary canons of truth.

[32] Fortune (1957: 201).

20

In defence of magic: philosophical and theological rationalization

MAGICIANS need to rationalize their magic, to give reasons for their involvement which they think that the outsider should at least accept as reasons, because they live in a society in which magic is not taken for granted. Different magicians follow different routes to justify their practice. However, a common tendency emerges. Magicians often argue indirectly for the value of believing in magic, rather than for the truth of magical ideas. That is, rather than arguing for magic as a persuasive account of physical reality, magicians tend to explain why the normal criteria of truth-testing do not apply to magic. Then, they justify their involvement on the grounds of its spirituality, its freedom, its aesthetic beauty and so forth. Despite the difficulty of arguing by the normal rules, magicians are not willing to abandon their claims. That, one might imagine, would be the simplest solution to cognitive dissonance. But magicians seem to need their claims; the magical claims seem too important as the means to identify and legitimize an activity deeply significant to the practitioners.

Let me quickly reiterate what I mean by the term, 'claims'. The most basic understanding of magic is that doing a magical ritual has an effect which is not due to commonly accepted psychological consequences. Magicians can usually give some account of the way the ritual should work, with the body of ideas described earlier. There are a host of more specific ideas about astrology, tarot, divination and the like, with which the magician is also probably comfortable. I doubt very much that a magician is always fully conscious of an abstract list of relevant propositions which he calls his 'theory'; nor do I think he formulates a propositional assertion about the efficacy of ritual when he performs his rite. However, he probably does think of the ritual as being effective while performing it. And certainly there are times when he explicitly defends the idea that magical rituals can be effective, and asserts what he calls his belief about the rite's power. This commitment to the view that the rituals do produce results, which usually includes some rather fuzzy explanation of why these results occur, is what I mean to identify by the term 'claims'.

There seem to be four primary rationalizations of magical claims themselves, four different ways of intellectualizing the idea that rituals produce results. I call these approaches realist, two worlds, relativist, and metaphorical. The realist position says that the magician's claims are of the same status as those of 'science'; the two worlds position says that they are true, but cannot be evaluated by rational means; the relativist position says that it is impossible even to ask questions about their 'objective' status; and the metaphorical position asserts that the claims themselves are objectively false but valid as myth. In essence these are different positions about the truth-standards applied to ordinary discourse and about whether magic fits within them. The first position asserts that there is an objective reality and that magic is valid in its terms; the second asserts the possibility of an objectively true referent for the magical talk of other planes and forces but says that the claims are rationally indeterminable, not evaluable by ordinary means; the third also claims that ordinary truth-standards do not apply to magic, but not so much because magic is different but because the very idea of truth-standards is itself an illusion; and the fourth, that objective reality is knowable but that the magical claims are false descriptions of it, failed by a justifiable test. As theories based on different conceptions of objective truth, these positions are incompatible, but as means of asserting commitment they are often employed in tandem.

My sense is that most magicians will give most of these arguments at some time during their magical career. The metaphorical position, probably the most sophisticated philosophical view, is the least frequently used. This may be because it is intellectually comfortable to abandon truth-claims only if there is another very obvious reason for commitment to the practice – and I heard the metaphorical argument almost exclusively from women who were drawn to Goddess worship with political concerns. However, it is not at all uncommon for someone to argue both realist and two worlds of relativist positions together, a commitment to the reality of magic along with an explanation of why magical claims seem inconsistent or false. In essence, arguing both that magic is real and that truths are relative, amounts to an argument for relativism; however, I am not convinced that the magicians who gave me these arguments were genuinely convinced that the non-magical Christian had as clear a perspective on the truth as a magician. A relativist should think that anyone's views are as valid as his own. But when a magician argues for relativism, he seems to want to justify a view about magic to which he is already committed, and the argument for relativism is a way to end the disagreement with a sceptic. The magician does not arrive at his magical claims by way of philosophical argument. He justifies a position already taken. And yet, there was sometimes a genuine hesitation, and a sense that all knowledge was freely chosen, that there was no final 'truth'.

This chapter presents the four common positions illustrated through case examples. Then it compares them with the recent arguments in British theology to illustrate the common strategy in this type of defensive argument. Magicians will assert that objective reality is partially or completely unknowable, and that in consequence magical ideas cannot be challenged under truth's banner. They treat magic as set apart, and offer reasons independent of its truth for engaging in its practice. These are the tactics of the modern theologian: the divine is different, it cannot be tarnished by your rational scepticism. The similarity between the two, magic and Christian religion, might not be so obvious – after all, one might initially think of magic more as a pseudo-science of occult vibrations rather than as a religion focused on a transcendent reality. But the thrust of the previous part of the book was to illustrate the spiritual, other-worldly feelings conjured by the practice. Dependent as they are upon ideas of a spiritual reality, magical ideas are hard to defend in the same way that God's existence is difficult to demonstrate. There may be good reasons for that difficulty: claims about transcendent reality are inherently difficult to prove, while claims about racial supremacy may be hard to defend because they are wrong. In any event, the similarities between magicians' arguments and theologians' arguments identify common tactics in defending the unprovable.

THE REALIST POSITION

Magicians who hold a realist position think that there is a knowable objective reality and that magic reveals more of it than science. There are controllable forces, they say, that escape the scientific purview. The magicians who say this might not be too concerned with the accuracy with which they can describe these forces: where they come from, what they are, how they can be directed. They still think that the forces exist on some other 'plane', and they still describe them as spiritual. But they rely on accounts of that spiritual plane as being a type of reality which is integrated with material reality. They *will* say that they know that the forces are real in the same ways that they know that tables and chairs are real. You kick chairs to see if they are really there; you do rituals to see if the forces are really there. They might also say that they do not 'believe' in magic. They practise, sceptical and intrigued, until they 'know' through personal experience that magical power genuinely exists.

*   *   *   *

Emily had been reading about magic for five years – mostly astrology, herbs and tarot – when she decided to enter magic practice in earnest. She took a home study course advertised in a magical journal which she found in an occult bookstore, and became involved in discussion groups. She joined the Glittering Sword shortly before I did, and then joined a 'women's mysteries' group – the one that performed the Halloween ritual described earlier. During the year in the *ad hoc* group, she performed rituals which she 'knew' were powerful. She said about one which she wrote that, 'I couldn't remember reading more than a third of it. Something else took over.' That ritual was about water: later, she remarked: 'and the results have been amazing. For a week everyone around me was bursting into tears or anger, and then it rained. There was water everywhere.' When she went to study groups on divination, she was delighted with the high rate of her predictive success. It was she who thought that a Greystone ritual was powerful, but that the leader's 'direction' of the power was wrong because her images were so different from the ones he described. Soon afterwards, alone in her room, she had a vision of the Goddess. It was, she said, very much her own view of the goddess, a woman with stars around her head. 'But I saw her the way I see you now.'

By the end of that year Emily was quite sure that magic had practical effects and that magical forces were part of physical reality. When I told her that some of my academic colleagues had asked if magic was only a hobby, like stamp collecting, she laughed. 'They're afraid. And if they only knew that we could really do things, they'd *really* be afraid.'

* * * *

Tom was raised a Catholic. He now gives lectures on computers. Although he says that he was always drawn to religion – 'I had a contact and had made a dedication before I knew who or what it was to' – he dropped out of the conventional church in adolescence and became involved with a theosophical group with spiritualist leanings. His marriage ended his occult involvement, but after a divorce, he came to England from his native midwestern America and picked up Knight's mystical, magical training manual in a bookshop. The book contained a leaflet describing the correspondence course. 'I knew, when I started it, that it was me. It was exactly right.' That was seven years ago; Tom is among a few who have attended every Greystone weekend. He has dropped the course – he got 'stuck' – but it has provided his primary esoteric orientation.

When he drove me back to central London from the study group he ran with his magical partner – that night he had lectured on the kabbalistic sephirah Yesod – he said that after the powerful Greystone ritual in May 1983 he had switched from 'the necessary suspension of disbelief' to a state of 'knowledge'. That Greystone meeting was the Atlantean ritual, the culmination of a six year series of annual ritual workings. The weekend has been described as exciting, upsetting and extremely powerful by most of its participants. 'I'm not sure that even [Knight] was aware of everything that happened.' Tom's vivid experience of the ritual power convinced him of the absolute, objective reality of magical forces. He was always predisposed to that conviction – 'I always "believed" in my "belief" ' – but now, he said, 'I've had experience, I *know*.'

* * * *

Tom and Emily assert that they know that the magic works, and that the forces are part of a physical reality. This, they think, is objectively true. They have been convinced by the results of their ritual practice. They still rely on experiential, emotional response for the evidence of the rite's success, but they find this evidence compelling: it is, for them, a clear indication of the external magical force. They even distinguish between 'knowledge' and 'belief' because the latter, they say, implies uncertainty. Knowledge is acquired through experimental practice; belief in faith is something which never can be fully known. Emily uses 'knowledge' to indicate her certainty. Tom exaggerates the uncertainty by speaking of the 'suspension of disbelief': to experience magic, one must quell a natural scepticism, but after enough experience, one knows. In the philosophical literature, one common definition of knowledge is that it is 'justified true belief': knowledge must be true, be believed, and be justified by adequate grounds.[1] Knowledge is more certain than belief. However, the certainty arises because knowledge comprises true statements. These magicians use the conventional distinction between religious belief and scientific knowledge to assert a claim about the ontological status of magical forces.

TWO WORLDS

Those magicians who take what I call the 'two worlds' approach talk explicitly about a 'suspension of disbelief' in magic, and assert that the objective referent of magical claims is unknowable within the terms of an ordinary, scientific world. No explanation which captured the essence of magic could be comprehended by the rational mind. In this explanation, magicians say that they leave their analytic minds behind them when they step into the magical circle. The experience of magic, they say, stands outside the limitations of the analytic mind and cannot be conceived by it. Whereas Tom and Emily seem convinced that magical forces are real, these magicians are more convinced when they are practising magic than when they are not. They intuitively feel that magical claims are correct, but they do not think that their truth can be rationally verified. This is not quite a relativist position: subscribers stress an incompatibility between magic and science, both of which they see as somehow 'true' but also mutually inconsistent. They do not make an effort to debunk the source of the inconsistency itself, or to take the further step and cast aspersions upon rational analysis. In other words, they do not provide an overarching account of this incompatibility. Indeed, the unprovability of the magic sometimes seems to make them nervous.

* * * *

Jan and Philip met ten years ago at university and married; he is now a physician and she, an officer of a pension scheme. They entered magic through an occult Workshop, where they met a fellow participant with witchcraft contacts. They became fascinated by witchcraft, with its paganism and magic, and through the occult exercises they began to understand the inner imaginative experience of what was called the 'psychic plane': an intuitive, associative use of imagery. Four years ago they found a coven with which they felt comfortable and were initiated.

To Jan the 'gut-interpretation' makes the magic real and effective. 'In the circle I refuse to ask, "is this rational?" '. And you cannot challenge or question the circle from outside. 'The point is just to let it happen.' Philip stressed that this was not a psychological trick, a self-conscious psychotherapy. Magic differs from psychotherapy because the latter works on the self and assumes that the outside world does not change. Within the magical circle you must feel as if you

[1] E.g. Ayer (1956: 35).

know that your inner imaginative world affects a physical reality. You do not 'try' to change an outer world: you assume that you can, and this assumption, if it is genuine, distinguishes the circle from mere theatre and makes the magic work. Inside the circle, the magic is fundamentally real. Outside it, in the mundane world, you acknowledge the possible consequences of the ritual but retain a healthy scepticism.

*   *   *   *

To Jan and Philip the abandonment of the analytic, critical mind is the most difficult step in entering the circle, but it is central to the magical experience.

*   *   *   *

Paul is a witch of some five years' standing. He introduced Jan and Philip to their coven's high priestess and is a primary organizing force behind the sabbat gatherings of some four or five covens in the local countryside. We met weekly in the same study group. Sometimes Paul would lead one of the evening sessions. Once he interpreted the myth of Osiris as creative expansion constricted by form, Osiris locked into a coffin by his malicious brother Set. As we stood in the darkness Paul told us to imagine ourselves as Osiris, toasting the success of our creation and then ensnared by Set. Then we imagined that our spinal column had become the leaden coffin and we were told that throughout our lives action and constraint must be in perfect balance.

A librarian, Paul worked nearby and occasionally we lunched together. When a 'textbook' on witchcraft was published he was scornful and indignant. The authors had presented a kind of dogma, with short essays on witchcraft ethics, symbolism, nudity and so forth. To Paul the book was idealized and intellectual. The circle is a whole experience, he said, an intuitive merging of action and belief. The very point of the witchcraft was not to analyse. After coven meetings Paul tries to forget about them, to keep the experience undissected and self-contained. 'It's the only way I can hold it. When I intellectualize, it disappears'. On the evening he had talked to the exercise group about Osiris, he presented ideas from Egyptian, Indian and Greek mythology through a medium of Jungian and humanistic psychology. His narrative style is intellectually demanding and complex. In the library he is surrounded by books and catalogues. With the witchcraft he feels that he escapes the intellectual strictures which his personality and his chosen work impose upon him. He still writes intellectual pathworkings, but for the most part he feels as if he simply experiences within the circle. But while he thinks that witchcraft is psychologically good for him, he does not think that magic is 'only' psychotherapy. He thinks that the rituals work. But he would prefer not to mix his views about magic with commonplace understanding.

*   *   *   *

When Maria entered magic (she is the pre-doctoral biochemist who was a member of the Glittering Sword) she came to magic, with trepidation, because she could not explain the strange happenings that suddenly seemed to fill her life. There were odd events, usually during her menstrual period, that she interpreted as paranormal: curtains she had drawn at night stood open in the morning, her dreams had become peculiarly clairvoyant. Most traumatically, she could no longer reproduce a published chemical reaction central to the thesis. Neither her supervisor nor her colleagues understood why the procedure failed, again and again, in different laboratories and in different circumstances.

Maria now thinks that perhaps she has a scientific insight into the nature of the reaction. But in spring 1983 she found it inexplicable and coupled with the paranormal experience it lead her, she said, to casual reading in magic, a correspondence course in natural magic (one I took), and thence to practice. I have seen her develop from a frightened novice into a learned practitioner. We become involved in the same study groups – herbalism, dream interpretation – and were initiated on the same night into the Glittering Sword. We went to Greystone together, socialized together, and together jumped over festival fires in various London parks.

One year after our first encounter, over tea at the Glittering Sword, Maria said that she kept her magical and scientific worlds very separate. 'I don't do this with my rational mind.' She was not sure whether the forces we invoked were objective or subjective – she could not decide. But the magic worked; the rituals gave results. If a magical rite was performed it would have consequences, she said, and while at first she had struggled with that notion she had accepted it by then. Ritual sets things in motion that could not be stopped, and the ritualist must pay careful heed to the words and symbols which he chooses. 'The important thing is to define magic by results.' She does not find this uncertainty about the objective nature of magical forces irrelevant, as some magicians claim, but because her trained scientific mind cannot accept her magic she keeps the two distinct. 'It's harder for me, you see, because I'm a scientist and agnostic.' The original motivation for her involvement has vanished, but she has become progressively more active and interested.

* * * *

To these magicians, magic violates the acceptable canons of their logical minds. Indeed that may be why Jan, Philip and Paul find it so enjoyable and so profound. Magic provides a type of experience which their intellectual minds ordinarily deny to them. The attitude is not dissimilar from that of the countercultural sixties: in that discourse, the analytic mind was said to alienate the soul from true experience, suffocating it within rigid, conventional constraints. However, these three magicians express a quite significant difference from the countercultural rhetoric. They did not search out the witchcraft with the specific goal of 'dismissing' their analytic minds. That they could have done with LSD. Rather, they say that they became involved in magic and subsequently discovered that involvement demanded abandoning rational analysis. For Jan, Philip and Paul, it seems more accurate to say that witchcraft may only be experienced outside of barriers of rational scepticism than to say that the removal of those barriers is their conscious aspiration. Nevertheless that aspect of magic may make it deeply satisfying to them.

Maria did not initially see the abandonment of her cautious scientific assumptions as good in itself. Rather, she found it a necessary step in her determination to comprehend her strange experiences. After considerable involvement she decided that the two sets of assumptions, those of magic and science, were not compatible. In her magical work she does not employ her scientific rationality – and thus, cannot provide a 'rational', 'scientific' explanation for magical efficacy. That it does work, she is convinced. But rather than interpreting her conventional scientific assumptions as wrong, she simply defines them as inapplicable.

The point is that the 'two worlds' approach asserts the objective truth of the magical claim while simultaneously expressing its scientific dubiety, and without giving some relativist theory to justify it. Maria felt that she could not explain the magic, but she did feel that it worked, that it gave tangible results. Jan, Philip and Paul also found it impossible – even self-defeating – to explain the magic by what they call 'rationality'. Within the circle, at least they assume their claims to be correct. They act effectively on that basis and enjoy the non-analytic experience which this demands. They assume that magical theory is valid; in fact, they assume that the magic will work only if they assume that it works; and certainly, it provides them with the non-analytic involvement which they enjoy.

RELATIVIST

Relativism is a common approach. Rather than arguing that magical claims are not rationally determinable, this argument rests on an overarching philosophy which defines all truth as relative and contingent. Where the two worlds position describes magic as incompatible with scientific norms, this position goes beyond to attack the very notion of those norms. Here magicians say that all people create their own realities, that no knowledge can be certain. Subjective and objective can never truly be unravelled. The magical world of the practising magician is as true to him as is the traffic light to the man in the Clapham omnibus.

*   *   *   *

Mick is the witch who lives alone with ten cats in a Jacobean cottage at the edge of the desolate Fens. She calls herself a witch and treats the witchcraft seriously: she casts spells and claims very tangible results. But she also qualifies her claims. In one of my rare taped sessions, she declared: [the statement is slightly abridged]: 'Descartes says, I think, therefore I am. Maybe it is, I believe, therefore it is. And if you believe something enough, maybe you make it happen. Maybe I created the witchcraft. But I know that it works, for me. I can't prove it one way or the other. It is only what I believe, and my truth is as valid as anybody else's. I mean, truth is like beauty, it's in the eye of the beholder, isn't it? And therefore I haven't got any answers, I haven't got any explanations. I only have my faith and my beliefs, which may or may not be right. But it really doesn't matter, because it's what I believe that matters to me. So I am. *I* am. I occupy a little bit of space in a little bit of time, and I am a witch, and whether this is all nonsense or not is totally unimportant. Because if it's true for me then it's *true*. If it's true for me, that's my truth, and my truth is really all that matters to me.

Mick is making two sorts of claims with her notion of truth. The stronger claim is that no absolute truth can be known by man, as implied in her statement that 'truth is in the eye of the beholder'. The weaker claim asserts that she can't tell if her interpretations are 'right' – whether she, in some unknowable empirical context, has the powers that she claims – but that she finds it psychologically helpful to maintain her claims to witchhood. No human, she says, can truly know. 'Mankind's got a tiny brain.' Although she may not in actuality be a witch, neither she nor anyone else has legitimate authority to dispute a claim which in her own experience she finds bountifully confirmed.

* * * *

Like Mick, Gareth Knight, the adept, has performed rituals which he 'knows' have worked. His goals are always lofty – revitalizing England, uniting Christian and pagan spiritual currents – but he has convinced himself of magical efficacy through the 'coincidences' that follow the rites and through his sense of power within the ritual performance itself. Magical power, he says, is real. But he has a sophisticated notion of that reality. In lectures, articles, and in private conversation he attacks the Cartesian split of inner subjectivity and an outer subjective world. (As quoted before) 'the most glaring assumption upon which all modern science is based . . . is that there is an absolute dichotomy between mind and matter, subjective and objective, observer and observed'.[2] Whether or not his characterization of science is accurate, his point is that there are no objective foundations, that subjectivity presents the only truth. He told me that this split is philosophically naive, that observation itself alters the observed and thus renders any concept of objectivity fatuous. Reality, he says, does not lie behind the appearances. It is the appearances – imaginative or otherwise – themselves.

In ways Knight's position is not dissimilar to the realist claim. But where Tom and the others felt they had demonstrated the empirical reality of the spells, Knight does not distinguish between subjective and objective and would be less likely to use the term 'empirical'. The inner world profoundly alters the interpretation of an unknowable external reality; thus, the magician lives in a

[2] Knight (1981: II: 20).

different reality from that of the engineer, and his 'truth' is bound to differ. His students reiterate this position. 'The critical point is when you accept that the imagination *can* be a reality.' The speaker is a professional actor. 'For me, it's been gradual – but oh yes, the magical forces are real.'

*   *   *   *

Enoch was initiated into Gardner's original coven over twenty five years ago and is a person of seniority and status in the magical subculture. He is also a talented computer software analyst, and analogies of rules and patterning permeate his conversation. All life situations, he says, are determined by 'game conditions'. They are governed by particular rules, circumstances and assumptions which constrain the actor's creativity and behaviour within ordered structures. Daily work provides one set of game conditions, magic, another. In daily work we experience one 'map' of time and space. In ritual that map alters, and indeed one of the most valuable lessons magic teaches is that experiential maps are underdetermined. The raw data of life can be surveyed and mapped in various ways. The magical 'adept' can transcend a particular map and see the whole. In that sense there can be no true adepts, for as humans we remain within a given map at any time. But the ideal of omniscient, unfettered comprehension and control is at the heart of magic.

I have heard Enoch play with the metaphor of a plum pudding to suggest the rich diversity of our lives. To bring order into chaos each individual cuts his pudding and draws connections between the random fruits which that slice reveals. The world is infinitely complex, and its interrelations infinitely inter-referential; each map is bound to be good and explanatory. But if you had cut a different slice your map would differ. Sometimes otherwise unconnected maps intersect; they create 'synchronicities' in which an event interpreted by one set of assumptions is differently expounded by another. No hermeneutic system can give justice to the whole, and because humans demand structure they may never perceive reality as it is. Meaning emerges through the interstices of the mapped and structured framework. Magic is simply a particular set of maps, an heretical exegesis which heeds different events and has distinctive axioms.

*   *   *   *

Mick, Knight and Enoch have different philosophical positions, but each handles cultural scepticism by describing it as a different but not superior account of an unknowable reality. Mick asserts that absolute reality is inaccessible. There is, she says, no privileged viewpoint. Therefore, all viewpoints must be seen as equally valid. Enoch holds a similar but involuted position. Interpretation, he says, relies upon ordered maps based upon adventitious circumstance, drawn with common human standards of coherence and explanatory power. No human is independent of his map, and magicians simply use a different one. Knight asseverates that the distinction between subjective and objective experience is invalid. Perception arises through imaginative apprehension and is transformed by the creative imagination. True reality lies in our awareness, and through our awareness we shape our world in interaction with it. They all state, in different ways, that humans have a limited, subjective perception of the world, and they give this account to explain why this unusual view is valid, and cannot be dismissed.

METAPHORICAL

Magicians of the metaphorical position argue that it *is* possible to know an objective reality, and that the claims of magical theory are probably false. But magic is about personal development, spiritual experience and so forth, and to think in terms of an efficacious magic facilitates these ends. The claims of magic may be false, but claiming them does something which is satisfying and creative in itself. In the magical literature, this is a position largely taken by those who have come to magical practice largely through political concerns. I have heard it argued by practitioners far less often than the other approaches.

* * * *

Angel had come to magic through her interest in goddess worship and described herself as a committed feminist. She told me that she could not see what ritual magicians spoke about when they talked of 'contacts' and 'Masters' and 'disincarnate entities'. To her, 'that's like a low-grade spiritualism'. Magic had to do with 'spiritual experiences and the imagination, and how you conceive of yourself'. Once, after a winebar discussion of various magical groups, I asked her if she believed in the magical claims of efficacy. 'Belief – that's a loaded term.' It was hard not to be sceptical in the ordinary world, she said. But the brain is remarkably complex. Who knows? 'We do work for ourselves in the group, but the world is changing for women. I'd like to think that there's a chance that all the goddess groups did something.' She's seen things she finds it difficult to explain; she would like to think that there's something in it even though she often suspects that there is not.

In any event, it is the pleasure in the practical involvement which drew her into practice.

* * * *

Celine, an expatriate American in her thirties, runs a (different) feminist coven in London. She lives in a beautiful house on Hampstead Heath, with wide kitchen counters and soft cushions in the sitting room; as I left her after morning coffee she went out with a friend from the BBC for pasta. She told me that she become involved in magic through her political commitments to ecology and to the women's movement, and more specifically through feminist political theatre and its relation to ritual. She talked about the complexity of her religion and how different it was from Judaeo-Christianity. She was raised in the Jewish faith but became agnostic. Now, she describes herself as 'believing' in the Goddess, but talks about the 'duality' in her belief. On the one hand, she thinks of the Goddess simply as a personification of the natural world. On the other hand, 'She *is* there. I can talk to her.' The difference from Judaeo-Christianity is that 'the Christian god is always out there. He can be in your heart, but he is not you'. In witchcraft, she said, there was no goddess apart from the natural world, but you could treat her as a being, and she described this as using 'mythology, not rationality' to describe the world. Magic in this setting plays an ambiguous role for her. She performs spells and experiences the rise and fall of the 'power', but treats the spells as ways of expressing her feelings about the Goddess. Spells are creative, expressive, and they contain a sense of the holy.

*   *   *   *

Celine and Angel then were both drawn to the practice for political reasons, and both treat the magic primarily as a myth, a way of expressing rather than of doing. Angel would like to retain the possibility that the magic is instrumentally effective, and Celine would also probably concur, but their primary emphasis is upon ritual practice as expression, not as practical act based upon intellectual claims. Yet even though they both recognize that magic may not be real, they are reluctant to admit this.

The striking feature of these four sets of rationalizations is that even though most arguments recognize the doubtfulness of the arguments for magic's validity, magicians are noticeably reluctant to abandon them. Few magicians adopt the position that 'magic' is really only a metaphor for very ordinary experiences. Three of the four positions argue about how one can accept the claims, not why they should be accepted – even the realists give personal, inaccessible experience to explain their convictions. The magician does not conclude from a philosophical argument that magical claims could be valid; she gets involved with magic, and argues for the validity of the apparent inconsistency, on the grounds that the outsider's critique relies on misguided standards of truth and objectivity. I am sure that Knight thinks that his views are fundamentally more valid than his neighbour's; however, I am equally sure that he is doubtful that he could convince his neighbour through appealing to what he would see as evidence.

Having explained why the magic is immune from criticism, magicians proceed to justify their practice by other means, with second-order explanations that talk about the value of holding magical ideas to be true, not about whether the ideas are in fact true. For the most part these arguments rest on grounds of morality, spirituality, aesthetics or psychology. Some of these we have already seen: magicians recognize many of the benefits of the practice, and use these to justify their engagement with it. For example, Fortune remarks that ritual is a system of 'pure psychology'[3] and many other magicians describe magic as a psychological practice. Green depicts magic as a psychotherapy: 'how can you expect to change the world around you when you aren't even concerned with

---

[3] Fortune (1935: 306).

changing yourself?' An initiate of the Western Mysteries said that 'magic is really about coming to terms with yourself: first you work on yourself, and then you become a fit channel for the forces'. A witch explained to me that magic drew him because it combined creativity and mystery (he is a professional artist, a painter). He told me (twice) of his trip to Japan and his question to a Japanese potter about what made one pot worth four hundred and fifty pounds and another pot worthless. 'He essentially said that if I did the tea ceremony for twenty years, I would begin to understand.' Magic, to him, involved that trained intuitive sense of the aesthetic. Another witch spent her adolescence searching for a powerful goddess in the Virgin Mary and entered witchcraft for its spiritual depth for women; in my encounter with the group of women with whom she was associated, it was clear that this was a common theme. Others felt that magic was morally justifiable, that it forced you to grow up and take responsibility for your actions. Two members of Knight's group told me that the Greater Mysteries – in other words, the 'real' magic – was about taking responsibility; it involved spirituality, but it was justified by 'the work that must be done'. Magic required you to take on adult morality and commitments. Magicians of the two worlds, relativist or metaphorical positions are arguing that there are alternative reasons besides the 'proof' of magical claims that leads them to defend those claims, and they will put forward more reasons along these lines.

These sorts of explanations are used in addition to accounts of how one can accept the magical claims, and as magicians slip from the realist to the relativist position they rely on the second-order justifications as demonstrations of magic's value within the terms of the sceptic's language. They can move back and forth, from one account to another, so that they need never violate their intellectual integrity. They are able to maintain their commitment, without necessarily being sure of the epistemological status of the commitment.

For example, it is common for a magician to offer a second-order justification for the practice, and then a first-order account to whose validity he refuses to commit himself. He explains first why accepting the theory is a good thing to do, and then offers an account of how the theory might be true. One manual, Starhawk's manual, gives this account of spell-casting:

Spells work in two basic ways. The first, which even the most confirmed sceptics will have no trouble accepting, is through suggestion. Symbols and images implant certain ideas in Younger Self, in the unconscious mind. We are then influenced to actualize those ideas. Obviously, psychological spells and many healing spells work on this principle. It functions in other spells, too. For example, a woman casts a spell to get a job. Afterward, she is filled with new self-confidence, approaches her interviewer with assurance, and creates such a good impression that she is hired.

However, spells can also influence the external world. Perhaps the job hunter 'just happens' to walk into the right office at the right time. The cancer patient, without knowing that a healing spell was cast, has a spontaneous remission. This aspect of magic is more difficult to accept. The theoretical model that Witches use to explain the workings of magic is a clear one and coincides in many ways with the 'new' physics. But I do not offer it as 'proof' that magic works – nor do I wish anyone to drop their doubts. (Skeptics make better magicians). It is simply an elaborate – but extremely useful – metaphor.

. . . When our own energy is concentrated and channelled, it can move the broader energy currents. The images and objects used in spells are the channels, the vessels through which our power is poured and by which it is shaped. When energy is directed into the images we visualize, it gradually manifests physical form and takes shape in the material world.[4]

The 'real' explanation of magic – magic affecting the physical world – is difficult and a little unclear. You can't give a completely convincing explanation, the author implies: all you can do is to suggest how the magic seems to work, and be convinced, by your results, that it does. In the meantime, even die-hard sceptics must admit that magic does some good. The invocation of psychology assures that even if magic's theory is not acceptable, its practice is vindicated as a worthwhile pursuit. This assurance is terribly important in a sceptical society. It gives sceptics an entry into a practice whose theory they need not endorse until later, and still not think of themselves as wasting time. Magicians often shift back and forth between these first and second order explanations, between claims that magic works, and claims that whether or not it works, it is beneficial in some way.

THEOLOGY

Modern theologians face similar difficulties: they must explain and justify their understanding of God to a secular community. Many do so with the same sorts of arguments that magicians use, often asserting that ordinary judgements of truth or objective reality cannot apply to religion, and mixing the defence of the theology's validity with the satisfaction of the theology's practice. Like the magicians, they argue that spiritual reality is somehow different from ordinary reality, and argue for their practice on the basis of its ethical or spiritual value. Theologians are responding to an age-old authoritative tradition. Magicians fly in the face not only of modern science, but of traditional religious beliefs as well. Unlike many theologians, they claim that their rituals have a physical effect. But as we have seen, magicians accommodate to the difficulty of achieving their goals by interpreting spiritual and emotional response as positive evidence and firmly establishing themselves as arguing about spiritual matters. Both modern magic and theology make claims abut their different realities which are difficult either to prove or to disprove. That they share similar strategies suggests that the magician's style of argument springs not from his idiosyncracy but from the general nature of his difficulty – defending a hard-to-defend belief in a sceptical society.

To illustrate the similarity in theological and magical arguments, I turn to

[4] Starhawk (1979: 111–12).

some British Protestant theologians of the last two decades. They are not the theological giants of their age – neither are the magicians – but they emerge from a similar social context, and they write books, like the magicians, partly targeted at a secular audience and partly toward those of their persuasion.[5] I cannot claim to have given an exhaustive or even representative survey of theologians; however, those authors that I have encountered argue in ways that resemble these magicians' approaches.

One position, a realist view similar to the knowledge-not-belief position sketched above, argues that the intellectual claims of religion are of the same nature as the intellectual claims of science. They are true statements about an objective reality and those people that do not share them are profoundly mistaken. One recent examplar remarks:

The intellectual credentials of thorough-going Christianity are very strong, much stronger than is often allowed . . . Scepticism, solipsism and nihilism, being philosophies of ultimate negation, cannot be refuted in the ordinary way, but can yet be shown to be paradoxical and unnecessary, while affirmation of alternative absolutes, Marxist, humanist, Freudian or whatever, prove on inspection to be inadequate to fit all the facts.[6]

Another says that a Christian explanation of cosmology is essential because a non-deistic description is simply 'inadequate'. In his *Existence of God* Swinburne examines the various arguments about the existence of God and concludes that, all things considered, existence is more probable than not. This is an assessment of truth, of things-as-they-are in the world, and his discussion of probability is actually presented in mathematical symbols.

The only plausible alternative to theism is the supposition that the world with all the characteristics which have I described just is, with no explanation. That however is not a very palatable alternative. We expect all things to have explanations. Above all . . . it is probable that things which are inert, diverse, complex and yet show manifold correlations, have explanations.[7]

That there is something, rather than nothing, must be explained. The existence of God is induced from the facts, as an objective rational statement about what is the case. God exists, and he made the world.

Other theologians hold that faith is for the most part a practical experience. Like the two worlds position, this argument contends that the believer must evaluate his faith by experience and not worry too much about its rational inconsistency. The metaphysical claims are still said to be objectively true, but they are not judged as the claims of science or philosophy would be judged – they are not evaluated by intellectual means – but rather by an appeal to the quality of life lived through accepting those metaphysical claims. Some theologians acknowledge the doubtfulness of the claims in a commonsensical world; they still assert the importance of the claims. The magicians who take

---

[5] There are other authors, with somewhat different and quite sophisticated theologies, within the Roman Catholic church: e.g. F. Kerr and H. McCabe.

[6] Packer in Stacey (1981: 65).   [7] Swinburne (1979: 287–8).

the two worlds position sometimes say they believe in magic within the magical circle, and tend towards scepticism outside. Nevertheless, their arguments resemble those of these theologians because neither doubts the general validity of real-world, science-validated canons. It is simply that they do not accept that those canons can judge the claims of a spiritual reality.

To Baelz, intellectual doubt is an almost necessary component of faith in contemporary English society. 'Once the intellectual difficulties inherent in [the Christian's] belief have been fully drawn to his attention, especially in a culture in which alternative if equally problematic beliefs are widely held by persons whose integrity, insight and understanding he respects, the believer must accept the inevitability of doubt within himself'.[8] One possible solution might be to say that the religion does not demand theoretical belief, but is merely a 'way of living'. Baelz acknowledges but rejects this solution. 'I must simply affirm my own opinion that [the solution] fails to do justice to the theoretical and explanatory functions which belief in God has more commonly been thought to include . . . Belief in God is theory as well as practice, even if the theory cannot be fully understood apart from the practice'.[9] But, he asserts, 'there is a sense in which practice may be allowed priority over theory'.[10] Baelz articulates this as the 'justification by response', and claims that the commitment to faith is a moral choice. What may the doubt-inflicted half-believer believe with integrity?

The half-believer, disposed to follow the Christian way because he acknowledges in Jesus a manner of life which engages his deepest response, may, I suggest, without dishonesty act on the *assumption* that the basic Church affirmation concerning the way of God is true. To assume that this affirmation is true is not the same as to believe that it is true. It is to accept it as a fundamental working hypothesis . . . It is an experiment with life.[11]

Neither demonstrable proof nor indisputable answers are forthcoming to assert the truth of these metaphysical beliefs and if this is the basis of the belief then belief *per se* must be tentative. Nevertheless, these claims can also not be disproved, and when the rationally inquiring mind cannot judge the answer the potential Christian must assert his choice on the basis of these different factors. Moral idealism, the restructuring of his human experience, the vision and hope of the Christian message, may be allowed to persuade him to accept the claims as a 'working hypothesis', and this is the basis for his commitment.

Drury takes a similar if oblique line of argument. Theologians, he says, must tolerate uncertainty. 'Life with God, the concern of theology and prayer, is . . . a game of hide and seek which is enacted on the brink of the precipice of tragedy with masks and disguises concealing the participants from one another'.[12] It is the metaphysical claims themselves which are incomprehensible to the religious individual. He cannot understand them, and therefore must be content to accept that they surpass his rational comprehension.

---

[8] Baelz (1975: 134).   [9] Baelz (1975: 137).   [10] Baelz (1975: 137).
[11] Baelz (1975: 138–9).   [12] Drury (1972: 138–9).

The material of theology is the mystery of the intersection of two worlds, so that it too 'must contain something incomprehensible'. It therefore expresses itself in hints, points and even jokes ... It never reaches the level of comprehension which amounts to mastery over its subject by the abolition of its mysterious material.[13]

In order to understand religion, one must relinquish the demand for objective, delineable metaphysical reality. 'Success consists in an alliance of overcoming and letting be, which gives birth to something new, indefinable, and real.'[14] It is because there is something new and 'real' that the demand to ignore paradox is worthwhile. Again, it is an argument from the quality of life and from the apparent truths that this life reveals. Christians 'thread their way through the labyrinth to the source or *datum* of the one who was there all the time, revealing himself and making himself clear in a thousand ways which all added up to something unified and real which they cannot pin down'.[15] Baelz stresses the moral satisfaction and quality of life which faith will bring, Drury, the incomprehensibility of its claims. To both, the claims are confirmed through the experience of accepting them, and cannot even be comprehended by rational analysis.

A somewhat different line is taken by theologians who claim Wittgenstein as their philosophical fountainhead. These theologians, like relativist magicians, say that questions of objectivity cannot even be broached. Metaphysical faith in God is enmeshed in religious language, and one cannot step outside the limits of language to ask if its tenets are true. It is not that the metaphysical beliefs are true but indeterminable, as in the two worlds position; it is that the question of their truth, in relation to the truth of scientific claims, cannot be posed.

For Rhees there can be no 'proof' about whether God exists as an object. Being religious depends upon using language in a certain way. The use of language in this particular way involves and indeed constitutes religion, and it is not the expression of something distinct which can be articulated. He speaks to the sceptic thus: 'you still seem to want to think of the language of religion as though it were in some way comparable with the language in which one describes matters of fact'.[16] The language of religion is not the language of matters of fact and cannot be understood as a claim about objective reality. In fact, 'objective reality' cannot be conceived at all.

You say that I 'deny that the term "God" stands for any objective reality in the literal sense'. I cannot have said just that, because the phrase 'objective reality' is one which I can almost never understand, and I try to avoid it.[17]

'Objectivity' is not one of the things which life provides. One has faith, one is committed to the religion, but the religion can only be understood by, with, and in the language which constitutes it. 'There could not be religion without the language of religion'.[18]

Phillips, Rhees' student, presents his persuasion similarly. Religious faith is not about the issue of whether or not something is the case. 'The point is not

---

[13] Drury (1972: 94–5).   [14] Drury (1972: 94).   [15] Drury (1972: 96).
[16] Rhees (1969: 120).   [17] Rhees (1969: 114).   [18] Rhees (1969: 121).

that *as a matter of fact* God will always exist, but that it *makes no sense* to say that God might not exist'.[19] Like Rhees, Phillips is not making a claim about an 'objective' reality. He is rather concerned to emphasize that people who talk about God talk in a context. 'If the philosopher wishes to give an account of religious beliefs he must begin with the contexts in which these concepts have their life'.[20] Through these contexts particular concepts find their meaning, but without them such meaning does not exist and it is nonsensical to attribute any to them.

> The philosopher is guilty of a deep misunderstanding if he thinks that his task in discussing prayer is to try to determine whether contact is made with God; to understand prayer *is* to understand what it means to talk to God.[21]

Religion cannot be understood outside of the language which envelops it. The religious have faith in certain ideas, but one cannot examine their faith in relation to scientific claims, for to do so would be to step outside the texture of religious language and one cannot do that without destroying the nature of its thought.[22]

Still other theologians wish to preserve religion while simultaneously denying its metaphysical claims. They specifically reject the realist conception of a God who exists in an objective physical sense. Religious language has a function as a myth used to talk creatively about the religious life, as an expression and ideal of its aims. The human animal, they say, is a myth-maker, and its myths are quite important. But the language should be recognized as myth, not metaphysic.

Cupitt specifically denies the realist concept of a God who exists in an objective physical sense.

> God is the pearl of great price, the treasure hidden at the centre of the religious life. The religious claim and demand upon us is God's will, the drama of the religious life within us is God's activity, and the goal of the religious life before us is God's nature. But we should not suppose God to be a substance, an independently-existing being which can be spoken of in a descriptive and non-religious way. Religious language is not in the business of describing really-existing super-sensible objects and their activities.[23]

Religious language does not prevent us from asking the question of God's existence; the metaphysical claim can be denied but the language has a function as myth. Such myths are essential to humans as myth-makers, but they cannot be considered as rational claims.

> I continue to speak of God and to pray to God. God is the mythical embodiment of all that one is concerned with in the spiritual life. He is the religious demand and ideal, the pearl of great wisdom and the enshriner of values. He is needed – but as a myth.[24]

This myth enables one to talk creatively about the nature of the religious life. But it would be foolhardy to make the claim greater than this, for it is not.

---

[19] Phillips (1965: 14).   [20] Phillips (1965: 27).   [21] Phillips (1965: 38).
[22] Hesse made a similar point, more closely argued with respect to recent accounts of metaphor and critical theory, in the 1979 and 1980 Stanton lectures, which exist only in typescript, and in a more recent article on metaphor (1984).
[23] Cupitt (1980: 164).   [24] Cupitt (1980: 166).

Kee subtitled a book 'Faith without Belief in God'. He proposes 'an understanding of Christian faith, appropriate to our secular age, which does not require belief in God as its prior condition'.[25] This is not, for him, an attack upon faith in God, but rather an understanding of what faith would be without such a metaphysical claim. He attempts to offer an exploration of faith which does not involve a claim about God. This he describes as the 'Way of Transcendence', the comprehension of that which is beyond the human. 'There is a life which is natural to man, and there is another kind of life for which he must consciously decide . . . paradoxically, we may discover later that the life which transcends our "nature" may ultimately prove more natural, since in it we find fulfillment.'[26] To Kee, the justification of that life by its quality is sufficient unto itself, and the metaphysical claim is explicitly acknowledged as irrelevant. 'The mystery is that secular faith in the way of transcendence *is* confirmed by subsequent experience'.[27] Religion is justified by morality, by the qualities of life, and evaluated through personal experience.

The most significant difference between the theological texts and the magician's arguments is that theologians rely more heavily upon justification from morality. Magicians seem to expend more effort in explaining why magical theory is impervious to sceptical doubt, whereas these theologians seem to focus more closely on the moral, spiritual gains to be had from the practice. There are good reasons for the difference: theologians write within a dense tradition in which spiritual life is possessed of moral value and in which the ethical worth of the religious life is widely credited. Magicians, by contrast, do not have such a culturally approbated tradition, nor is the moral worth of their undertaking immediately obvious. Their practice, moreover, is associated with a particular set of ideas about the physical world which is widely perceived to be false, and they struggle for intellectual legitimacy without the benefit of traditional cultural acceptance. It is also less obvious that the magician's claims are unprovable than the theologian's: certainly the magician is more likely to compare her practice to a science than is the theologian, and it is characteristic of a science that its ideas are meant to be testable. However, the magician does use many theological strategies, marking off the magical as insulated from sceptical attack but valid for the benefits of engaging in its activity.

The similarity between theological and magical arguments highlights an important characteristic: that the claims of both enterprises, difficult to defend as they are, are seen as central by the practitioners, and once practitioners are deeply involved in the practice they use a variety of different methods to patch together the apparent rift between the practice and an outsider's scepticism of its conceptual frame. It is surprising that the magical concepts *are* so important to its practitioners. To the observers, it seems that magicians cling to their magic ideas – that rituals affect reality – and assert the possibility of their truth more to mark off and legitimize a set of practices than for their content. Magicians do not exclusively, or even primarily, attempt to prove a theory within

[25] Kee (1985: 20).　　[26] Kee (1985: 37).　　[27] Kee (1985: 270–1).

an established intellectual realm: they are willing to argue in ways that stretch the conventional criteria of intellectual validity. Somehow, the claims are sufficiently important to the practitioners that they will not abandon the possibility of their truth, even if that truth seems difficult to demonstrate in a conventional, reliable manner.

Magicians use a variety of odd-job methods to argue for their practice. Rather than arguing for the theory directly, testing it by methods that seem satisfactory when arguing about whether the house has termites, they explain that magic is different, that it does not interfere with other claims (two worlds), is of the same status as all other claims (relativist), is not science-like but myth-like (metaphorical). Then, they justify holding it. These justifications by morality, aesthetic pleasure, therapeutic efficacy, allow the magician to make sense of his practice with justifications shared by the wider society without sacrificing the magical theory that the society would reject, or even holding that claim up for scrutiny. Magicians can shift back and forth between first-order and second-order claims, between justifications by truth-testing and justification by effect of faith, depending on their audience and their needs.

To reach this *modus vivendi*, the magician must be able to abstract his magic, to treat it as a way of thinking different from other ways. He must be able to understand what it is about it to which the sceptic objects. He meets the sceptic's argument by asserting that it is irrelevant; he transcends the conflict of particular claims by giving a meta-argument, explaining why holding those claims is personally valuable, whether or not they are true in the disbeliever's eyes. This calls for a high degree of abstraction, and a marked ability to move conceptually between being involved, and referring to your involvement. Magicians develop this skill of distancing themselves from an activity which they care for deeply, and doing so in a way that justifies their involvement without calling it into jeopardy. They are aided by conceptual 'tricks' to underline a difference between the magical and the mundane: special names, clothes, space, a metaphor of separation, tricks which enable them to treat the magical involvement as something set apart.

Magic leads its magicians into a world of symbolism and fantasy which is hard to talk about but which becomes quite important to its practitioners, and its personal significance forces them to make sense of it in terms which at least relate to those of the wider society. They rely on this claim of efficacy: they are not willing to abandon it if it seems unacceptable within conventional canons; they adjust their view of the canons in order to make it fit. Then, by marking off their magic with elaborate theatre and metaphor, they can defend their involvement in ways which they think that the wider society can also understand. This is no different from the theologian's defence of his faith. But it does present an image of human as tool-user rather than as coherent rationalist: if a practice is important to someone, he will explain away its intellectual disjunctions when he must – locally, haphazardly, with the intellectual tools that come to hand – rather than evaluating its claims as intellectual end in themselves.

There is an important concluding remark. Most magicians take their claims and practices seriously and when they give relativist or two-worlds arguments, they seem to be defending their practice using the best means available to them. However, their wavering to and fro, this shifting of positions and defences, is not without its effect. Most practitioners do question the rational canons that seem to undermine their practice, and while they are committed to their practice, they are also aware of the idiosyncratic, personally relevant manner in which they have constructed their interpretations. I think that many of them are genuinely aware of being in a paradoxical intellectual position, in which they both adhere to a set of ideas, and are also conscious that their adherence owes as much to choice and circumstance as it does to any 'truth'. This seems to be an intellectual attitude endemic at least to modern magic: that magicians affirm their practice and its claims by attacking the notion of rational standards, and while they take their claims to be valid, they are sometimes painfully aware of the limited nature of any claim to 'truth'.

PART V

Belief and action

21

Interpretive drift: the slow shift towards belief

IMAGINE yourself suddenly set down – Malinowski's famous phrase[1] – in a society of whose ways you know nothing, but which you must describe to the culture from which you come. This, more or less what anthropologists do, magnifies the day to day encounter between two strangers. From a small number of remarks and gestures, one person builds up a sense of what the other person is like, which affects the way he responds to her and describes her to his friends. For the most part, perhaps for good reasons, people assume that the other people they meet are like themselves except in the obvious differences. They assume that they share the same attitudes, customs, ways of being in the world. Only when it is forced upon them that the others are different do they change their commonplace assumptions, like Jamesian heroes whose American naivety is forced aside by Europe's subtle complexity.

The difficulty is that people tend to interpret the behaviour of other people on the basis of the ideal models that they have of themselves, which are far from empirical reality. That is, people tend to conceptualize themselves as unitary selves, coherent and all-of-a-piece. In order to understand their actions as part of that self, directed towards an end suitable to that self, they talk about 'beliefs' and 'attitudes' and 'desires', proposition-like assertions which explain why someone performs an action. If you see an aborigine eating grubs, you assume that he believes that the grub is nourishing, delicious, or imbued with sacral power. Long before we meet the great white whale, we ascribe the belief in its existence to Captain Ahab. Indeed it is the bizarre nature of the beliefs and desires we attribute to him in order to make his actions consistent which gives Melville's novel its peculiar force.

In order to function effectively, humans – these interpreters of culture – must act as if humans do not act randomly, but in a way they can learn to anticipate and to which they can learn to respond. This involves attributing to them a set of proposition-like assertions about the state of the world – he is carrying an umbrella, he must believe that it will rain this afternoon – which they maintain over time. Davidson has pointed out, in a different context, that to hold a conversation you must treat most of another person's remarks as true, at least initially, and to do so, you must assume that the person shares roughly the same world and the same beliefs, making adjustments in your assumptions when you

---

[1] He used it to introduce his understanding and explanation of fieldwork (1922: 4).

are forced to do so. Beliefs are used to describe the intentional consistency of the believer and as such they are an invaluable tool in the interpreter's kit. We know that at least to some extent the mind directs our action and mediates between body and world, and it is simple and more pleasing – a convenient shorthand – to describe an action as directed by a belief rather than by a complex, perpetually changing set of environmental cues.

Particularly in post-Enlightenment culture, enriched by the legacy of Kantian epistemology and Weberian sociology, we assume that a person's beliefs should be consistent. Gellner calls this a cognitive ethic: that we examine our claims to knowledge with canons of consistency, efficacy, the sorts of appeal to logical coherence and verification that gave science its authoritative hegemony.[2] Our notions of rationality, variegated though they may be, hinge upon the consistency of our beliefs: that they are consistent with each other, with certain ends, with advancing our satisfaction. The very term 'belief system' underlines the hold which the assumption of cognitive consistency has upon the culture. Indeed it leads people to rationalize their behaviour beyond any call of reason: the post-hypnotic subject explains that he *wanted* to walk to the back of the room before resuming his seat. In making sense of other people's behaviour, charitably attributing rationality to them, we treat people as if they have a more or less coherent set of proposition-like beliefs to which they adhere, by which they organize their life and for which they would argue.

But there are problems, even from within philosophy. One could argue that many beliefs are logically inconsisent, that people manipulate their own beliefs, and that the manipulation and inconsistency may be useful. If the fox cannot get the grapes he desires, he calls them sour. If you believe that a project should take a good deal of time, but also believe that you should complete the project quickly, the inconsistency explains away potential failure (I performed too quickly for a good project) and increases self-confidence after success (despite the speed, the project was good). 'If thou hate me, take care of hating me', Donne says: the hater needs the object to maintain his own identity, though that identity is founded on the hope of the object's annihilation.[3] The master needs both the slave's total, non-human subjugation and another human equal's recognition of his mastery. 'If a mode of consciousness is defined through the negation of another object, then consciousness depends upon that object in its very being.'[4]

Consider the attempt to achieve certain desirable states: being spontaneous, being emotionally overwhelmed, deciding – clearly and consciously – to believe.[5] Trying to be spontaneous – acting on the belief that one should try to

---

[2] Gellner (1974: 205).   [3] Elster (1979: 161).   [4] Elster (1979: 162).

[5] Elster (1979: 50). There are difficulties with this notion. Pascal takes one view, Williams another. Elster sides with Williams to explain induced belief. He states: 'Williams has argued convincingly that even if it is possible to believe *p*, one cannot both believe *p* and believe that the belief that *p* stems from a decision to believe *p*. If the decision to believe *p* is carried out successfully, it must also obliterate itself from the memory of the believer . . . The loss of the critical faculty is not simply a *by-product* of self-induced faith, but an essential *condition* for that faith to be held seriously.' One can however, use action to generate conviction.

emulate that desired quality – is a psychological paradox. Further, beliefs may emerge to adapt the believer to difficult circumstances, but be inconsistent with the believer's overall goals. If the fox preferred not to eat the grapes, then the utilitarian could justifiably exclude them from his consumption. But as Elster remarks, because the cause of his preference was his conviction that he would be excluded from their consumption, one cannot justify the allocation by invoking his preferences.[6] And in any event the ascription of belief-consistency is not straight-forward. Elster repeats the story that Neils Bohr, on being asked whether he really believed that the horseshoe hanging above his door would bring him good luck, replied: 'no, but I understand that it works even for those who do not believe'. The statements that 'The horseshoe will not bring me luck' and 'The horseshoe brings luck to those who do not believe that it will bring them luck', are not inconsistent, but it is at least paradoxical to admit to believing both.[7]

One needs a concept of belief, although it has been emphatically (and wrongly) argued that the word should be expunged.[8] People do think of themselves as 'believing' in propositions about God, the weatherman's forecast, and the value of the Conservative policy on education. But the ethnography presented on modern magic and the persuasiveness which the practice obtains elicits three observations about belief. Let me summarize.

First, it is optimistic to think that people have an ordered set of beliefs about a particular endeavour which forms a consistent set with other beliefs which together describe the totality of thought and action. People are much fuzzier, and more complex, than that. The ethnographer can legitimately identify something like a belief when someone argues for a proposition, at least during the period when they are doing the arguing. But magicians argue in different ways at different times; some of them claim to believe one thing when practising magic, and another thing when not practising magic; others seem to be firmly committed to their practice, and produce arguments about relativism which do not seem entirely plausible in the face of their behaviour. They perform spells which they talk about as effective, joke about them as ineffective, and give several interpretations of their ends. When they 'know' that magic is valid, they rely on feelings, senses – subjective experiences which might be 'merely' psychological. They give nested explanations which may contradict each other or which imply contradictory beliefs: I believe that magic works, I believe

---

[6] Elster (1983: 109).   [7] Elster (1983: 5).

[8] Needham (1972) has argued this in a learned, intelligent book. Its strategy rests upon a curiously fundamental error: he invokes Wittgenstein as a philosophical messiah who argues that concepts like belief are not well-defined and should be discarded. This is probably an inaccurate representation of Wittgenstein. The philosopher in fact argued that most language – ordinary language – had an ambiguous, meaning-lies-in-use-rather-than-in-definition quality, and although one might find some support in his work for a commendation to stop talking entirely, his primary intention seems to have been to use this linguistic ambiguity to challenge notions of epistemological foundations. Needham's point is nevertheless important: that the word is referentially too vague to be useful. However, I would argue that the term is entrenched in our language and in our perception of ourselves, and is probably no more vague than other self-descriptive concepts – love, desire, and the like. The challenge is to describe what the term does, given its ambiguity.

in magic but all truth is relative, the reason I believe has nothing to do with whether magic works. An observer often interprets 'belief' by examining behaviour. But the beliefs one might infer from a magician's behaviour are sometimes belied by what he says about his belief.

Second, it is hubris – and bad ethnography – to assume that people act first and foremost because they are motivated by belief. The material on modern magic suggests particularly clearly that people often argue for a belief as a means to legitimize, and even to understand – to rationalize – the practice in which they have been involved. If someone enjoys a political party gathering for its manifold social and intellectual pleasures, she is not unlikely to assent to its assertions. If someone goes to church as a regular part of his life, he is likely to argue for a belief in God. If he feels deeply spiritual when praying to God, he is more likely to be persuaded that God exists, for the religious framework provides a way to interpret that unusual feeling. When someone enters magic, she begins to have many hard-to-interpret, often novel experiences. Magical ideas give a meaning and a provenance to those experiences which they might otherwise lack. Obviously action can be guided by belief. What tends to be less recognized – and cuts against the common stereotype – is that belief can be guided by action.

Third, magicians *have* beliefs; it is not true that becoming a magician simply involves learning to speak a new 'language'. Some scholars use such a depiction to account for apparently strange beliefs and behaviours.[9] That is more than a bow towards relativism: the assertion claims that apparently strange beliefs say nothing startling, but simply express conventional beliefs in new and surprising ways. Or, the assertion can be that in becoming a shaman, a Scientologist, a believer in something, someone is simply acquiring new terms to describe new experiences. Magicians seem to be doing something more than that: they make assertions about the state of the world which are more complex, and acquire more bite, than the phrase, 'acquiring a language' would imply. The term 'belief' might be somewhat vague, but it identifies something which involves some sort of commitment to an assertion, and which most people acquire when they become practitioners. If one takes belief loosely to be a willingness to make certain assertions and to act as if those assertions are true, then magicians have beliefs – particularly if they are not concerned with being criticized by a sceptic.

What happens as the newcomer, not yet fully persuaded, becomes a magical practitioner? The astonishing fact about magic is how routine its practice becomes, with what little effort. These are, after all, pension plan managers, industrial engineers, and teachers. They meet every few weeks to call upon the 'Horned One' while standing naked in an Islington sitting room, and they talk

---

[9] I am thinking here of scholars influenced by a relativist interpretation of Wittgenstein and by some of the modern and post-modern theoretical work on language: Winch (1970), and Beattie (1970) in his wilder moments, adopts this interpretation; Silverman's (1975) account of cultural experience; Leach's (1976) more extreme understanding of cultural process; and, more generally, the accounts of cross-cultural or conversion experiences which emphasize a shift in symbolic 'language' as the most central transformation in the adoption of a new cultural understanding. Elements of this approach crop up in Fischer and Marcus (1986) and Clifford and Marcus (1986).

about contacting Isis, evoking dragon-power, and receiving a message for a friend from a hallucinated monk. Even in tolerant London this is not commonplace. Yet it becomes quite normal for the practitioners. Magicians talk about different planes and separate worlds, and they seem to try to maintain the aura of mystery around their practice, but the therapist who sets aside Friday evening for her ritual group is on Friday morning more likely to be worried about roasting the group's supper chicken than about entering the magic circle. And she is not at all flummoxed by a conversation about generating power with a tarot card.

No dramatic moment pivots this shift into another sort of normalcy. From the outside it seems as if new magical practitioners accept a set of beliefs, and a set of practices based upon those beliefs, which is significantly at odds with conventionally assumed ideas and actions. But there is no clearly marked threshold, no singly persuasive incident, no new explanation of anomalous events, that catalyses the movement away from some more commonly acceptable manner of viewing the world. Kuhn describes scientific 'revolutions' in which one scientist suddenly experiences a Gestalt-shift and is able to see his results with almost literally new eyes. Indeed the suddenness of the scientific insight has been documented from Archimedean times: at least in some cases, the puzzled scientist experiences a sudden insight, and the structure of his interpretation rapidly transforms.[10] Religious conversations are sometimes similarly deep and sudden – though, as with many scientific accounts, one suspects that a long preparatory period leads up to the moment of epiphany.[11] James, for example, speaks of 'those striking instantaneous instances of which Saint Paul's is the most eminent, and in which, often amid tremendous emotional excitement or perturbation of the senses, a complete division is established in the twinkling of the eye between the old life and the new'.[12] The scientist and, sometimes, the pre-convert, are faced with a puzzle, and sometimes the solutions seem suddenly to appear. A swift realization shatters the previous intellectual world.

Magical practice simply is not like that. In my experience, people did not suddenly adopt magical 'beliefs', and they did not explain their practice as the result of sudden insight or (as a rule) a sudden transcendental experience.

---

[10] Stories of sudden realization, as with Einstein's understanding of special relativity and Kekulé's insight into the benzene ring, are often told, and certainly many scientists report sudden flashes of puzzle-solving insight. Whether sudden insight into deep problems is characteristic of scientific research is more difficult; Lakatos and Holton describe the slow process in which a particular problem comes to be understood with a new theory. However, the experience of puzzle-solving is unlike the magician's involvement; the closest comparison would be the sense of uncanny coincidence, as when some particularly significant event follows closely upon a ritual.

[11] Cardinal Newman apparently wrote that there are no sudden conversions. The appearance of one was merely a sudden realization that one had already become a believer, through hard work. The same has been said about the awareness of a new historical paradigm: the historian labours, and may experience a moment of insight, but it is more a matter of recognizing what one already knows, than dramatically altering what one thinks.

[12] James (1902: 217). James also discusses more gradual transformations of belief which he calls, borrowing the term, 'volitional' (1902: 206ff). However, he finds them less interesting than the instantaneous conversations, and spends more time discussing the latter.

There are few puzzles that could be immediately solved by adopting magical ideas, and little moral or cultural demand for the ideas to be adopted. There is no authoritative demand for belief upon joining a group: indeed, apart from vague ideas about the imagination and the physical world, it is not clear what the collective belief *is*. People do not talk about their 'beliefs' very frequently – they are far more likely to argue over the interpretation of a tarot card. Nor do they carefully test assertions about the material and immaterial worlds. No one in the coven kept score of the unsuccessful spells. No-one carefully checked hypotheses to see if they were disconfirmed by the ritual and whether, in fact, they were disconfirmable. Some people anguished over whether magical ideas were in fact valid, and they sometimes concluded – like Maria, the postdoctoral biochemist – that the ideas were valid, but that they could not explain why. But this was a realization achieved slowly. Magical ideas begin to seem normal in the process of becoming a magician: in this way, the involvement is more similar to becoming a certain sort of specialist than to producing a new theory. Magicians may identify significant events in retrospect, or be struck by startling instances, but there does not seem to be any experience comparable to a sudden conversation to a different way of thinking.

I call this 'interpretive drift' – the slow, often unacknowledged shift in someone's manner of interpreting events as they become involved with a particular activity. As the newcomer begins to practice, he becomes progressively more skilled at seeing new patterns in events, seeing new sorts of events as significant, paying attention to new patterns. On one level this is simply a well-recognized shift in the sorts of events that become noticeable: the neurologist sees a patient exhibit a strange nervous activity which, like hysteria, was meant to have disappeared, and the next afternoon he walks in mid-town Manhattan and sees three cases in an hour. You hear the word 'catachresis' in a seminar, and it soon springs out from every other page. But interpretive drift involves a shift in what one wants to call belief – at least, a shift in the types of assertions about the world which a practitioner will defend, and the assertions the observer might infer from practice and conversation. By the concept of interpretive drift, I mean to identify the adoption of something like a theory, or a least a significant shift in the interpretation of events. Developing faith in God after atheism is an instance of interpretive drift; falling in love is not. Once-non-magicians begin to practise magic, sceptical and intrigued by the ideas. Several years later, they act, talk and argue as if they accepted the bold claims of magical practice. I use the term 'drift' because the transformation seems accidental, unintended. The once-non-magician certainly intends to become a magician and to practise magic. But that is very different from intending to believe. Rather: the once-non-magician begins to do what magicians do, and begins to find magical ideas persuasive because he begins to notice and respond to events in different ways.

What elements contribute to this drift? This material has suggested that there are three loosely interlocked transformations which together propel change from one manner of understanding to another: interpretation, experience and rationalization. There are systematic changes in the very structure of interpretation, in the sort of analysis which the magician brings to bear in making sense of any particular event. The new magician learns to identify evidence for magic's power, to see patterns in events, to explain the success or failure of the rites. She acquires a host of knowledge, which enables her to distinguish between events and to associate them to other events in ways not done earlier. She becomes accustomed to particular assumptions about the constitution of her world. These are changes which affect the structure of her intellectual analysis, the form of the arguments she finds appealing. They are learnt, often informally, either through conversations or books. (It is easy to forget that books are important socializing influences, if not more important than people in this literary world. The new magician meets relatively few other magicians, but he reads very many books.) As a result, the ideas of magical practice make progressively more sense, and seem progressively more natural; the magician becomes more likely to 'believe' in their truth, by acting as if they were true and defending them in conversation.

Beginnings are always difficult. The newcomer to magic struggles to learn about the arcane, clumsy kabbalah and the intricately complex astrology. As he learns more, he acquires a hermeneutic structure in which later knowledge finds a place. The patterns he sees in events have progressively more resonance in his increasing breadth of intellectual knowledge – and at the same time the richness of these categories allows more subtle discrimination. With greater involvement comes greater knowledge, and magical ideas gain still greater structure and cogency. Using that knowledge is fun: it is like arguing about politics as an inveterate news reader, or writing a novel on Gnosticism after reading Hans Jonas's scholarly text. The magician slowly gains a sense of mastery over the material, and with that sense comes a sense of naturalness and pleasure in using the ideas to interpret one's world. Use is more important than testability. As this material makes clear, confirmation and disconfirmation are fairly unimportant parts of most people's lives.

Then there are experiential changes, which are not so systematic. The magician becomes immersed in new experiences – new phenomenological experiences, a vivid imaginative engagement, a world awash with personally powerful symbolism. She participates in rituals that are designed to make her feel quite unlike her normal self. And her fantasies change, her dreams become intense, she reads novels in new ways. There are four distinctively different types of experience, with different effects: there are the new feelings and responses, which need to be comprehended; imaginative intensity which gives experiential content to otherwise contentless words; self-manipulation in ritual practice which makes that other world realistic; and symbolism, which dominates the magician's imagination, surrounds his practice with secretive mystery, and provides a mythology when one seems lacking. Symbolism is the most diversely slippery of these different involvements. But they all make the magic dramatic, exciting, appealing.

The point about these experiential involvements is that they must be interpreted and rationalized. They become deeply pleasing to the participants, the participants associate them with magical practice, and they remember and justify the experiences through the ideas with which they are associated. The involvements are personal and private: they become intrinsic to the way the individual experiences and conceptualizes his inner life. They are also hard to explain and to explain away in words, hard to describe to another person or to abstract in ways that make them seem independent of the particular engagement with which they are associated. The way magicians argue about their practice suggests that magical ideas make sense of those experiences for them, and that when they argue for the practice, in part they are defending the ideas because those ideas can interpret their experience. To believe in God because one has had a spiritual experience is quite unnecessary; one could, and on the grounds of parsimony, should, explain the experience by commonplace physiology. But people find it unsatisfactory to interpret spirituality as a biophysical capacity, elicited by technique, with God as a metaphor for certain ways of thinking and acting. The British theologian Cupitt is vilified because he takes this stance. The claim to a God makes a sense of the spirituality, justifies it, makes it seem important to its practitioners.

Finally, there are rationalizations. Intellectual habits and experiences are interdependent. The magician makes sense of a powerful experience in ritual by searching for evidence that it has worked; that gives him confidence in further involvement in the practice, and his experiences intensify. But the ideas associated with the practice not only come to seem more reasonable through the practice; they also serve to justify the practice, and if forced, practitioners will go to lengths to maintain them as a means of defending their involvement, even if this is not logically necessary to explain their feelings. They produce some kind of intellectual account, suitable to their socio-intellectual context, which allows them self-consciously to assert and argue for the ideas they identify with the practice. Rationalization is particularly important in a modern context, where critical outsiders possess a culturally given language to accuse magic of irrationality. Modern magicians are forced to argue for their practice; having argued, they learn to talk about the practice in ways that make sense of and reinforce their own commitment to it.[13]

The experiences give the magical ideas content:[14] the magical ideas make

[13] G. E. R. Lloyd (1979) has suggested that in the ancient world, the fact that medical practitioners were forced to argue and persuade other people of their skills led to the emergence of that pattern of description and practice we call science. Being forced to persuade others of a particular viewpoint may not only alter one's commitment to it, but ultimately one's manner of conceptualizing and articulating ideas.

[14] Whitehead's ethnography of Scientology describes this experiential transformation slightly differently, as 'renunciation and reformulation'. The idea is that becoming a practitioner involves abandoning old ways of contextualizing experience for new; by this she means 'a movement away from and dissolution of a set of [mental] structures, and the construction and movement into another set' (1987: 247). Scientology is an extraordinary enterprise: a richly descriptive philosophy of mental life, cast in a peculiar mentalistic vocabulary, with a practice involving extensive self-revelation and fantasy before an 'auditor' who judges its value by the subject's metered skin-resistance (and thus, emotional stimulation). The subject talks through emotionally charged events

sense of the experience. Intellectual and experiential changes shift in tandem, a ragged co-evolution of intellectual habits and phenomenological involvement. Magicians demonstrate the rite's efficacy by their experiential response; they interpret their dreams with altered intellectual habits. And the more the rituals are confirmed and the dreams interpreted, the more sensible the magic becomes. Magicians can understand the newness of the experience, the pleasing quality of the involvement, most easily if they understand that quality as part of the magical way of looking at the world, a package with the intellectual habits they acquire. The form of life which is magic comprises both intellect and involvement, and the vividness of the one reinforces the authority of the other. Learning about magic, becoming a magician, is a messy whole.

This is not, quite, a socialization process. The term 'socialization' implies a process in which the practice of socializing itself produces the primary effects. Much of this study has been an effort to point out how solitary the magical involvement can be, and how much of it happens within the private self – albeit inner personal experience depends upon external social interaction. The spirituality, the vivid imaginative experience – these feelings and experiences are extremely significant in persuading magicians of the worth and power of their magical involvement. Talking to other magicians certainly helps to make the new magician comfortable with the language of magical practice and helps him to identify personal experience as having to do with the term of magical ideas. However, the crucial element of the persuasiveness of magical ideas is the private phenomenological experience within the practice of magic. Except insofar that all involvement with ideas and language are mediated through language, socialization is not the primary feature of this interpretive drift, in the same way that one might describe the process of learning to talk like an adolescent as a socialization process. It is more that a transformation of experience leads magicians to have ever more faith and ease in certain ways of talking about their world.

Anthropologists celebrate the collective, and their study of ritual – *communitas*, conflict resolution, social reaffirmation – has concentrated upon the collective. But becoming a magician has much to do with privacy. As magicians read myths and participate in imaginative exercises, they develop a rich inner life of visual imagery which dominates their inner life and is inaccessible to others. They specifically say that symbols transcend verbal

until the constrictive 'bank' of obstructive psychological tendencies has been emptied. By Whitehead's account, the practitioner begins to have intensely personal experiences which he makes sense of with the symbolism and the language of the practice, and begins to redescribe past life events in its terms. The evocative power of symbolism – the 'meaning' of the rite – is important, but even more important is 'the interpretive function of the symbolism in handling the unusual experiential world called into being by the practice' (1987: 284). Personal experience is understood by the terms dictated by the practice. Similar analyses – similar to the extent that they describe the symbolic description of experience as the means by which a particular symbolic system becomes effective and personally persuasive – include: Lévi-Strauss's comparison of shamanism and psychoanalysis (1967), Kakar's analysis of indigenous medical techniques (1982), Harding's study of fundamental Baptist conversion (1987) and so forth.

limitations, that they engage the psyche's pre-verbal core, that the 'secrets of the Mysteries' lie in experience, not intellectual knowledge, and cannot be communicated because the words cannot encase them. The same rich solitude, I suspect, is developed in the young Baktaman boys who go through extensive initiations; in Trobriand islanders told endless myths and who learn to tell their own; in Amazonian Indians who listen to myths and take hallucinogens in which the mythic characters take on realistic form. The internal tapestry of mental imagery is intensely solitary; there is a 'privacy and exclusiveness of the mental imagery in which each of us has his being'.[15]

The nature and use of private experience no doubt depends upon social interaction.[16] There is, as one argument declares, no private language and the argument must extend in some sense to all experience. (If all experience is to some, perhaps very limited, extent mediated through language – one may not be able to describe pain, but one calls it by its name – then even very private experience has a social dimension.) But made possible, the world of mental imagery and fantasy becomes personally secluded, private to the extent that a language would be private if a person lived for a short time among people and then retreated, hermit-like, to a mountainside to live in solitude, muttering to himself in half-finished sentences with ellipses. It may be the case that a particular image is not unique to one individual, or that imaging ability is highly dependent upon language. But because the imagery is rarely described to others, the magician's perception – what the magician experiences – is that the imagery is intensely personal and unshared. After all, when these magicians participate in the Durkheimian collectivity of a ritual, they do so by sitting in the dark with their eyes shut. When Baktaman boys begin their first degree initiation, they sit in silence for hours in the jungle's night, and they do not (Barth says) ask questions afterwards. When the Bororo shaman has his initiatory encounter with the *bope* spirits, he is walking through the jungle by himself. Of course there is a feeling of *communitas*, of shared siblingship with other participants. But actual participation is solipsistic. The interpretive drift which relies upon the individual's dreams and life cannot be understood as a pale variant of a socialized language.

In fact, the interesting observation is how little verbalization enters into the interpretive drift at all. Most of the intellectual habits are not self-consciously introduced into magician's conversations. They are often not recognized by the magicians themselves. They happen, so to speak, below the tidal mark of verbal articulation, as the newcomer becomes comfortable with his practice. The new magician is rarely told that thinking by analogy is intellectually valid, or told that it is acceptable or valid to make a theory – practice distinction and invalidate a ritual performance on its basis. Rather, as he begins to talk to other magicians and read magicians' books, these shifts in evidence-seeking, implicit assumptions and common knowledge simply become part of the magician's statements,

[15] Gordon (1972: 65).
[16] The interdependency of mental imagery and language is a matter of considerable debate; the references that define the topic are identified in chapter 14 of this volume.

the grammar of his remarks. Very few of the implicit assumptions need to be stated directly; little theory must be clearly stated and offered before a sceptical audience. But the newcomer begins to see the patterned connections between events that these shifts describe. At the same time, these specialists-to-be become involved in significant symbolism and phenomenological experience that is captured rather badly, if at all, in words. Magicians repeatedly assert the ineffable, inchoate quality of their involvement. Their sense of this inarticul- ableness is explicitly enshrined in discussion of meditations, and of the esoteric symbolism. More subtly, they begin to have private experiences – events – which are salient within the context of magical ideas but hard to account for outside. They begin to have spiritual experiences which they find quite important. They have dreams with strange imagery. They begin to represent people and events in terms of complex images: such-and-such a person is Dionysiac, or like the tarot's Fool. They exercise new skills with pleasure as their powers of visualization and meditation increase. Magicians are very verbal people. But this shift from one manner of understanding to another rests to a large measure upon events and involvements which they do not consciously articulate, and which they often call 'ineffable' when they do.

Magicians enter magic with a vague notion that the practice is based on the claim that the mind can directly affect the outer world. They then get involved in the practice, immersing themselves in books and rituals, dreams and meditations and learning about the tarot. The magic becomes a mixture of inventive scholarship and mystical religion, a surfeit of ideas and feelings which are hard to articulate and to understand apart from the practice. Part of learning to be a magician involves changing the implicit assumptions, pattern-finding and knowledge-defining habits which make magical ideas seem plausible, and in the process magicians simply get on with gathering firewood for Beltane fires, doing the tarot reading, learning the kabbalistic invocation. But if they are challenged to demonstrate the magical claim in terms which the non-magician will accept, and fail to do so, they balk. The whole enterprise of being a magus has become deeply important to them, and whether or not it is justified in a more general context magicians do not want to relinquish it. Magicians build an edifice upon a simple premise of magic's efficacy: they often ignore the premise in the proceedings, but it becomes more crucial to them as time goes by. When challenged, they argue that the premise is justified, and rationalize the involvement, in part because they need to defend the practice in which they have been engaged.

The role of belief in this picture is not obvious. Certainly magicians, after they get involved in practice, after their interpretations begin to drift away from their initial style, are more likely to assent to statements that magical rituals affect the physical world, even if they qualify that statement. Certainly they talk and act as if they assented to the statement. But they tend to make complex belief statements when challenged on their practice; they give different arguments, at different times, to different people; they assert their claims even knowing that they cannot argue within the conventional intellectual canons of their interlocutors. It is as if these belief statements do a specific job, of justifying an engagement which is a changing mixture of feelings and images and social encounters. Asserting a belief makes sense of the activity with which the belief is associated, even though there need be no necessary connection between the activity and the claim. James' Isabel Archer argues vehemently for her independence, not particularly because she wants it, but because she likes the personality with which it is associated. Academic professionals sometimes argue for claims at variance with the claims of a seminar paper because they find the paper-giver's style offensive. People argue for claims for many different reasons. But when a way of talking, behaving and expressing is concerned, people tend to argue for the validity of the ideas behind the involvement because the personal nature of the involvement seems so vital. Magicians do have beliefs, in the conventional sense of a commitment to an assertion about the world which they publicly defend and which could be inferred from their action. But it is not obvious, when talking to magicians and observing their practice, when they have consistent, articulate views about their practice, and when they do not. Belief, in terms of overt commitment to a proposition, depends far more on the intellectual and social context, and the constraints which its peculiarities impose.

Perhaps my own history might make this interpretive drift and the constraints upon belief more concrete. I met my first magicians with little idea that magic involved spiritual, meditative experiences; indeed I scarcely had a sense of the sorts of experiences to which those words referred. I found magical novels quite difficult to read. Somehow, I could not quite catch hold of the thread. But I began to read widely about magic, and tried to understand it as a magician would. Certain early experiences gave me a sense of the referential content of magical talk. For example, some months after I met my first London magicians I read a magical text on the train from Cambridge, and felt that I was beginning to understand magical power. Indeed I imagined the force flowing through me and felt electrically vital, as if the magical current were pulsing through my body. In the midst of the phenomenological fantasy, a bicycle battery in the satchel next to me melted, with a crisp singed smell, and while no doubt coincidental it was disconcerting at the time. Later I jogged around Regent's Park after a Greystone ritual, and visualized white kabbalistic light flowing off Knight's arm in ritual. Again I felt vital and electric, 'filled with force', as some of the manuals said. I also happened to be wearing a watch, which stopped. It was not a fine watch. I had bought it several weeks earlier for two pounds in a street market, and its longevity had already surprised me. Nevertheless, watches are said to stop in ritual, and that this watch stopped while I was imagining ritual experience – that was startling. With the watch and the battery, I had ready-made, non-magical, culturally laudable explanations of both events: they were coincidental, and had I not been involved in magic they would have been unsurprising. But I had been thinking about magic, trying to 'think like' a magician, and these events were striking because they made the alternative way of looking at the world seem viable.

By May, about a year into the study, I could use tarot cards, analyse horoscopes, discuss the kabbalah. In fact I would use tarot cards whenever I wanted to think about a complex relationship or a difficult choice. I 'knew' that I turned up the cards in an arbitrary pattern. Nevertheless, that arbitrary pattern could help me impose structure upon the slippery ambiguity of my particular problem, and by so doing, help me interpret it. And even though I knew, intellectually, that the cards that appeared were random, I was repeatedly astonished by their pertinence. I kept a dream diary to record my dreams, and my dreams became vivid, filled with magical ideas and symbolism, often myth-like; far from a tapestry of the day's events.[17] By the end of the first year I read magical novels avidly in the way that one should read magical novels, with an uncritical child-like absorption in the story. In the midst of a novel on Arthurian Britain I woke early one morning to see six druids beckoning to me from the window. This was not a dream, but a hypnopompic vision.[18] I saw the druids as I see my desk. And while the momentary vision frightened me, it also pleased me deeply, because it taught me experientially what I had learnt intellectually: that when people said that they 'saw' Christ, or the Goddess, they were not necessarily speaking metaphorically. In May, at Greystone, I became first nauseous in the ritual, then unutterably sad, then joyous, as if I felt the power but was too raw to handle it with skill. In London I participated in a ritual as the priestess of Bast, Egyptian cat goddess, and as I prepared in the darkness I tried to 'push out' the me-ness, and 'pull in' the catness, and when I rose to take my throne amid the chanting I felt feline.

By the end of the year some rituals still seemed theatrical, performed to a watching audience rather than events in which I participated. Others did not. I began to feel force whirling around the magical circle as I had felt it on the train. I had increasingly vivid imaginative experience in ordinary pathworkings and in rituals. Perhaps most importantly – certainly with respect to my own maturing understanding – I began to use the word 'spiritual' to describe a fuzzy set of relatively new phenomenological states, experiences and responses. In my

---

[17] Example from my dream diary 21.6.84: 'I was taking my sister to Beth's workshop. We had to walk across the path to Granchester [in Cambridge, not London] to get there. First we were going to walk in a slightly different way – this would have required going across a running stream. I held my sister by a string tied around her neck. She dove off the bank, and swam to the centre, but the waters were high and there was no way I could cross without getting very wet. So I pulled her back, and she lay for a moment, on the grass, looking drowned. But this was a passing thought. Then suddenly the sky looked *very* dark (instead of the summer day it had been) and a wind began to blow, and I thought that we should take the bus – but my sister wanted to walk. I was a bit nervous because there was no shelter once you got out on the path, but I too wanted to walk, and we set out, up the small rise away from the stream, over a path. But as we passed the farm house (Wizard of Oz?) the sky became *very black* and the wind whipped up ferociously – and I woke up when the lightning cracked, a very white, loud bolt that lit up the earth.' The imagery had the Jungian tilt with which I had come to be familiar in magic, and used all sorts of symbols – the sibling as a way to represent the self, the dangers of crossing running water, the storm as the symbol of emotional chaos – which I had encountered in magical sessions.

[18] In other words, a vision on the borders of sleep and awareness – not quite a dream, but not reality.

magical training I had, in essence, spent long periods in prayer, with intense solitary meditation and collective concentration on recited liturgy. I had read myths and scholarly texts about the deities, and could give to these once cardbound characters a local habitation and a name. I felt as if I were becoming religious. Perhaps there is something like a spiritual capacity which, like the capacity to swim or draw, all people possess to some degree but which few of them exercise and train. Certainly I felt as if I had developed a capacity weakened from disuse.

As Evans-Pritchard had done among the Azande, I had little difficulty running my life in accordance with magical techniques, by tarot cards, astrological charts and the like – though I rarely allowed them to violate my common sense perceptions of a situation. I enjoyed the practice. Writing rituals and pathworkings was certainly creative. And it is always stimulating to learn about something new, to read books about the kabbalah and see its dry complexities spring into life. The spirituality, the dreams, the intense mental imagery enriched my world, and the ebullient symbolism of the practice imbued all events with associations, interconnections, even 'meaning': whatever event occurred, it always *could* be understood as relevant to some significantly potent symbolism.

The only reason I continued to think of myself as an anthropologist, rather than as a witch, was that I had a strong disincentive against asserting that rituals had an effect upon the material world. The anthropologist is meant to become involved, but not native. The very purpose of my involvement – to write an observer's text – would have been undermined by my assent to the truth of magical ideas. Favret-Saada declared that to understand witchcraft you must be entangled in its practice as a speaker of its sentences. She herself became deeply involved in the witchcraft of Normandy's Bocage. The rural villagers explained misfortune as the consequence of witchcraft, and 'un-bewitchers' were used to protect the victim of a curse. To acquire information, Favret-Saada announced that she had been bewitched, and was counselled by a local 'un-bewitcher', and in the course of fieldwork she became terrified of witchcraft and wrote a book about her fear.[19] Entanglement is indeed necessary. But Favret-Saada studied a community in which no-one would talk of witchcraft except to the bewitched, and when she called herself bewitched she was told that she might die of the curse if she took no precaution – and she then narrowly escaped her death upon the road. Pascal's wager was weighed quite differently for her. If the 'unbewitcher's' claims were right, Favret-Saada risked her life by refusing to believe them and gained it – and a novel ethnography – by accepting that they were true (most ethnographers do not admit to a fearful belief in their ethnographic subject's ideas about witchcraft and so forth; fewer claim that such belief is essential to the project). I stood to gain nothing by belief except power which I was told that I could exercise unconsciously even if I made no explicit acceptance, but I stood to lose

[19] Favret-Saada (1980).

credibility and career by adherence. Throughout my time in magic, whenever I felt magical power inside the circle or wanted to say that a ritual had 'worked', I chalked up the event as an insight into the field.

In other words, the process of becoming involved in magic makes the magic believable, and makes explicit belief in magical theory quite tempting unless there is a strong disincentive against it. Learning about magic *means* acquiring the knowledge, assumptions, ways of identifying evidence that make the ideas seem reasonable – but one does not recognize this in the process of the practice. Being involved with magic usually leads to the experience which gives the terms content and the practice a persuasive reality. It is natural and exciting to explain these experiences in terms of the ideas associated directly with their acquisition. An explicit commitment to magical ideas is then a likely, though not inevitable, not quite intentional result of its practice. In a way, Favret-Saada is correct: if one really understands the practice, one is at a point where the ideas seem quite natural, unless some other factor intervenes to alter one's belief. However, the complexity of belief within this modern social context affects the ease and consistency with which magical ideas are defended.

The specific form of the explicit commitment to belief takes a particular shape in modern society. Interpretive drift is characteristic of many cultural processes, where ideas about the world becomes persuasive as a by-product of a practice. The willingness to assert that the ideas are unambiguously correct, and the arguments used to justify the commitment, will depend on other factors – namely, the intellectual and social context in which the practitioner finds herself. Magicians practise magic in an intellectually sophisticated context. While that context tends in general to be tolerant of idiosyncracy, it also tends to be secular and sceptical. We turn below to the particular ways in which the magician's understanding of her practice have been shaped.

But first, to reiterate the general conclusions of this chapter, this material challenges three widely held assumptions. First, it challenges the assumption that people have coherent, clear-cut sets of beliefs. People often talk as if they had a particular set of beliefs which is ordered and coherent: this is often the assumption behind talk of 'rationality'. Yet as this material amply demonstrates, people argue for different visions at different times, or their views can be inconsistent with other views, and they themselves are uneasy about what it means to 'believe'. Second, it undermines the assumption that people act on their beliefs, that beliefs are prior to action. This material also suggests that people invoke beliefs to justify their action, that they rationalize previous action by referring to rationales which they describe as beliefs. Third, this material also attacks a common loose relativist argument advanced by some anthropologists, that when people adopt a strange practice, they are not so much acquiring beliefs but language, simply a different way of expressing views about the world. This is clearly not the case. Magicians are acquiring new assumptions, new ways of viewing the world; although the term 'belief' is not crystalline, the point of the word is that it involves some commitment to an assertion about the world. Becoming a magician is not like learning French.[20]

Interpretive drift is the slow slide from one form of explanation to another, partially propelled by the dynamics of unverbalized experience. As an anthropologist one can point to the noticeable elements of the transformation: ways of identifying evidence, seeing patterns between events, noticing significant events, parameters of shared knowledge, ways of using language to create effects, practical techniques, a symbol-inundated world. It may be that the magician notices none of these new changes in herself; it may be that she is self-conscious of the changes. In either case the form of the practice prompts further involvement, and the more that the magician learns and experiences, the more sensible and unquestionable the magic becomes, and the more altered her interpretive style becomes. Magicians do not live in a world in which every ritual affronts commonsense reality, and in which they desperately avoid the disconfirmation which constantly undermines their beliefs. Given this drift, magic seems practical, reasonable, commonsensical, and the experience of engaging in magic an enjoyable part of their life.

Durkheim felt that his sociology could complete the job Kant had begun, that he could explain why people were constrained in the ways Kant had described. Individuals in groups, he argued, generated intense emotion. This emotion was identified and represented as religion: 'religious beliefs rest upon a specific experience'.[21] From the identification derived universal categories of time, space, causality, logical class and moral imperative. Durkheim described the origin of religion amongst the Australian Arunta (his test case for primitive man) thus:

> The dispersed condition in which society finds itself [when gathering and hunting] results in making its life uniform, languishing and dull. But when a corrobori [ritual gathering] takes place, everything changes . . . When they are at once come together, a sort of electricity is formed by their collecting which at once transports them to an extraordinary degree of exaltation . . . as such active passions, so free from all control, could not fail to burst out, on every side one hears nothing but violent gestures, cries, veritable howls, and deafening noises of every sort, which aid in intensifying still more the state of mind which they manifest . . . How could such experiences as these, especially when they are repeated every day for weeks, fail to leave in him the conviction that there really exist two heterogeneous and mutually incompatible worlds?[22]

There is a profound experience – for Durkheim's Arunta, ecstatic experience within a group – difficult to verbalize by pre-existing context. The memory of the experience can be intellectually handled, he suggested, by redescribing it as part of a separate context and identifying it as incompatible with, separate from and superior to human knowledge.

Magic seems at least superficially to turn this on its head. People come to

---

[20] The criticism attacks a tight analogy between language and culture. In some loose sense in which the term 'language' implies a set of attitudes and conceptualizations, the magician *is* learning a new language. This is a view of language not uncommon in Continental philosophy. It has emerged in some works of American anthropology, as in Crapanzano *Waiting* (1985).

[21] Durkheim (1915: 465).   [22] Durkheim (1965: 246–7; 250).

magic with the idea that it concerns a particular theory, one generally unacceptable in their social context (in its strong form of ritual efficacy, rather than in its weak form of there being 'something to' astrology). They are taught to develop a rich experiential involvement in their training and practice. The experiential involvement of course confirms the theory directly: strange feelings in rites are said to indicate magical power. But, more profoundly, magicians have odd, moving experiences which they make sense of in magical terms. Their imaginative world becomes filled with vivid magical images. Like the Arunta in this model, magicians identify that newness as separate, aided by the theatrical separation of the magical in ritual and by the intellectual separation that describes the magic as being upon a different plane. Once conceptualized as separate, by virtue of its different feelings, the claims become protected, true but uncontestable, not amenable to sceptical inquiry. It is as if magicians take a pseudo-scientific theory and create a religion on Durkheim's model to protect its scientific status.

22

Serious play: the fantasy of truth

A S we have seen, the basic strategy magicians use to argue for their practice is to underline the difference between magic and the mundane, and then to justify engaging in it. Many practitioners would heartily protest at the notion that magic is separated from the world: as self-conscious Christians stress the religious nature of everyday action, so magicians stress the ritualistic, spiritual nature of the most ordinary activity and the holistic nature of their world. The material and the spiritual, they say, are elements of a whole: 'one of the foremost aspects of Neo-Paganism is the return to the ancient idea that there is no distinction between spiritual and material, sacred and secular'.[1] But the general view that the world is one does not preclude the interpretation that it has many aspects, and magicians talk of different realities, different spaces and times, different planes, different states of consciousness and so forth. Interpretive drift makes the magical ideas which articulate the difference seem normal and persuasive. But how the sense of normalcy is explained and justified – how magicians explain their belief in their ideas and their commitment to the practice – that is something quite different. Indeed, magicians seem to tolerate a very wide range of justifications for practising magic, to the extent that being a magician does not seem to involve a commitment to a particular assertion about the world, but a commitment to the idea that magical practice is important – an assertion that can be defended in a great diversity of ways. In order to explore the nature of this commitment to belief in this particular social context, we turn first to the sense of difference.

This separateness is both deliberately evoked, and unintentionally created. Magicians consciously set out to build a practice which they understand to create a different perception of reality. Their rituals are designed to induce an altered state of awareness, with meditation, chanting, visualization and other tricks of psychological self-manipulation. They perform elaborate sequences to establish the separate, sacred nature of the space inside the magical circle, and they describe it with the rhetoric of a different space and time. They use linguistic techniques to heighten their awareness of this separate reality, and a battery of methods to give symbolism a sense of vivid realness. Likewise, the rhetorical descriptions of magical reality emphasize that it is different, set apart, not like an ordinary world: it is described with fluid, poetic prose, defined as a

[1] Adler (1986: 12).

different plane, explained by some of the participants as another kind of world.

But the sense of difference also seems to be inherent to the practice itself. Magicians have a deep-rooted supposition that the nature of magical practice cannot be put into words. Practitioners find it extremely difficult to verbalize what magic feels like and to identify the reasons for which they cannot communicate to others. Authors even use this difficulty to justify breaking the apparent bonds of secrecy through publication. 'It is the *process*, and the *experience*, not the secrets, that are the mystery of the Mysteries';[2] 'the mysteries of the absolute can never be explained – only felt or intuited'.[3] The most frequent response to my own account of my project was: 'but how can you ever do it? How can you say it in words?' The symbols, the rituals, the theories can be revealed, they say: it is the experience of the involvement which is at the heart of magic, and its secrecy arises simply because it can never be communicated. This sense of incommunicability has a certain pragmatic validity. To outsiders magicians' talk may seem crazy or irrational. Magicians chat about sacrificing to Isis and listening to the Goddess, and because they are rarely aware how much of their conversation depends upon the implicit assumptions, knowledge, experience and so forth of their practice they rarely fill in the gaps for outsiders. The non-magician feels confused, even angry, when listening to a magician, because the conversation violates his common sense, his taken-for-granted, non-specialist way of understanding events. However, when the magician talks about the difficulty of explaining magic, she points primarily to the difficulties in conveying the experience of meditations and rituals to those who have done neither.

Kuhn introduced the term 'incommensurability' into the philosophy of science to explain that, as he saw it, proponents of different scientific theories, competing paradigms, failed to understand one another. Paradigms were on the one hand the 'entire constellation' of beliefs, values and techniques shared by the community and on the other the concrete and exemplary puzzle-solving solutions which served the world as the model for future work. The understanding of the latter had to some extent a tacit, intuitive quality, embedded in the shared exemplars. Incommensurability arose, he said, because scientists of different paradigms might disagree about the importance of particular problems or the standards by which to judge them; they might use the same terms and experimental approaches in different ways; most importantly, to the extent that theory and data are not entirely independent they lived in different 'worlds'. In other words perception itself is an interpretive process conditioned by education. 'What perception leaves for interpretation to complete depends drastically upon the nature and amount of prior experience and training.'[4] Feyerabend, a more radical disciple, stressed the untranslatability from one scheme to another, the mutual inexpressibility of the two systems.

Magicians often talk as if magic and the mundane were incommensurable. At least they stress that the experience of magic is ineffable, and beyond the non-

---

[2] Adler (1986: 442).   [3] Starhawk (1979: 7).   [4] Kuhn (1970: 198).

practitioner's conception. Certainly they talk in ways that confuse outsiders, with idiosyncratic methods of problem-identifying, problem-solving and word-use which they may not even realize that they have adopted.[5] The intuitive appeal of Kuhn's analysis has been the sense that two groups of people – be they Azande diviners or Cambridge biologists – may be separately 'rational' but mutually incomprehensible because their assumptions, interpretations and goals differ.[6] But incommensurability becomes more perplexing in under-standing contemporary magicians, because the witchdoctor and scientist co-exist, as it were, within them. This sense of incommensurability is significant, because it is a clue to the nature of magical involvement and to what I see as the ambivalence of the magician's belief.

One source of what magicians perceive to be incommensurability seems to lie in the different imaginative fabrics associated with magical practice and the mundane. 'Imaginative fabric' is a vague term. But it helps to identify a significant difference between the magical and the non-magical. The process of switching back and forth between witchcraft and engineering, kabbalism and the civil service, involves a switch of different fantasy worlds, the magical fantasy constituted by its practice and the everyday world of role-models and self-images constituted by one's working world. The magician has acquired rich experiential imagery in her practice, has learnt to have profound feelings associated with it, has used it to interpret a good deal of life-experience. Magic re-enchants the world, filling it with myths and images, poetic resonance and imaginative ambiguity. The magician develops an extensive set of magical symbols. The semantic grid of the kabbalah, the tarot, the gods, the elements, are used to re-label and redescribe the most personal parts of one's life. The gods and figures are embedded in narrative and myths, and magicians are taught how to reconstruct those narratives and repeatedly placed in situations – pathworkings, rituals – where they need to re-enact the narrative frame. They identify particular gods and goddesses as especially pertinent, as beings which represent their own inner nature particularly well. They read endless accounts of wizards and witches, LeGuin and Tolkien giving depth to culturally skeletal stereotypes.

These images, symbols, myths significantly affect the magician's interpretation of events around him. Previous chapters have discussed the therapeutic function of the imagery, that the magician somehow re-labels aspects of his inner life with imagery then used in repetitive narratives, and that the re-labelling process and the manipulation of the imagery in narrative seem to have genuine, frequently reported, sometimes observed therapeutic effects. Previous chapters have also indicated that magicians see patterns in events according to

---

[5] There are no 'problems' in magic the way there are 'problems' in scientific research; the comparable situation might be the interpretation of a tarot spread, or the evaluation of a specific ritual situation.

[6] This has been much criticized, of course; but Kuhn has had an astonishing appeal to professionals within the social sciences and humanities, where he is usually seen as describing a relativism at the heart of rationalist science, a view which he now says that he never intended.

symbolic associations: if you do a ritual about water, you notice subsequent events in the news about floods, rain, emotional disturbance, unconscious expressions and the like. Magicians experience strange states in which they see the symbols of their training and reading, and enter vivid imaginative states in which they imagine those images to appear. The structure of their common knowledge, knowledge they assume shared by all practitioners, is based on sets of images and symbols. The semantic structure of their symbolic imagination affects their perception of significance, of association, and, at times in the most literal manner, of what they see.

There are times in which magical images and symbolism – pervasive as they are – become more salient than they are at other times. Most people, for many activities, have role models, images of practitioners whom they wish to emulate. The sense of good fatherhood is an imaginative sense, based on an idealized role model of the good father. When acting as a father, one just acts: one doesn't, normally, think of the ideal model. But behind the action lies the imaginative stereotype which partly guides the action. It may be that the ability to move between two different involvements demands a shift of different thematic sets of representing images, of which the most important is the imaginative representative of the self.[7] When playing music, one is a musician, when drinking beer in a pub one is a pub-goer, when defending an academic paper one is an academic. The role models, the imagined settings, the theatrical sets of anticipated responses change. The magician may think about the kabbalah day and night, but it is immediately relevant to a ritual or a social encounter with a magician, and not immediately relevant to the pension-plan office.[8]

All this is pertinent to an understanding of belief in magic, because magic is about turning a let's-pretend fantasy of being a witch or wizard into a serious assertion about the world. Magical practice is understood to be different from the everyday: the task of the magical practice is to make that different engagement seem persuasively real. Much of the book has been devoted to explaining how that happens. The point here is that part of taking magic seriously involves granting an importance to a complex set of imaginative

[7] Cognitive psychologists have developed the idea of a 'script' which governs the perception and memory of particular actions. These scripts are best understood in relation to simple, often repeated action: going to a restaurant is a favourite example. People seem to anticipate a certain set sequence of actions, to remember unusual alterations, and to understand the actions in a manner dependent upon previous experience. Some authors speak of a 'script-based theory of understanding' which has far-reaching implications: 'in order to understand the actions that are going on in a given situation, a person must have been in that situation before' (Schank and Abelson, 1977: 67; see also Graesser et al. 1979, 1980).

[8] Borrowing metaphors from linguistics, one might think of the imaginative associations as 'marked' in relation to certain social contexts. Certain sorts of contexts call for generalized social responses; some social contexts, which are more unusual, call for a particular set of responses which are 'marked' in relation to the more general. Another way to describe this would be to say that certain encounters elicit remarks which are indexical of the range of magical associations: when one encounters a magician, he will say things that allow one to infer his comfort with certain ways of talking about and conceptualizing experience, and those ways will then become pertinent to the conversation.

fantasies. Many commentators have noted that a narrative, metaphor or central image usually underlies a scholar's understanding.[9] However, it is not often appreciated how pervasive this imaginative construction of reality can be, the degree to which it alters the way one perceives and responds to events. Taking magic seriously involves accepting this imaginative set as important: this can feel as if it is very different from the everyday, so that the magician may sense that his experience in magic is incomprehensible to the non-magician.

In support of the importance of this fantasy world, one should notice that magicians often define their commitment through their imaginative involvement. When they describe how they become committed to magic, they talk about imaginative experience – dreams and novels, books that they read as children. They are not explaining some psychological predisposition to be involved with a magical group. It simply happens that when one asks how they got involved in magic, many of them begin their account with childhood novels and fantasies of playing Artemis and Apollo in Central Park. Magic seems to have deepened their involvement with that imaginative encounter.

For example, the first item Enoch described as significant to his involvement was a book he encountered at thirteen in which a sorcerer was introduced in the first chapter.[10] About the same time, his schoolmaster talked about Neoplatonism as a religious system centred on the idea that everything was crystallized thought. Enoch decided to be a Neoplatonist; he says that this, coupled with a conversation with a friend about spiritualism, helped him to get out of a 'terrible paradox' that either you accept what your (Baptist) parents say about God, or you die in hell. He attended some talks at the Theosophical Society, and borrowed some of their books; once he went to gain recruits for a political party – the Independent Democratic Party – and met someone who gave him a book written by Crowley. When he read the hymn to Pan, he says, he 'woke up' – he read it once, then twice, and then, he said, the whole page felt like it was blazing with light. The poem has an unusual combination of delicacy and excess: it reads in part:

> To watch thy wantonness weeping through
> The tangled grove, the gnarled hole
> Of the living tree that is spirit and soul
> And body and brain – come over the sea,
> (Io Pan! Io Pan!)
> Devil or god, to me, to me . . .
> Io Pan! Io Pan! I am awake
> In the grip of the snake.
> The eagle slashes with beak and claw;
> The gods withdraw:
> The great beasts come, Io Pan! I am borne
> To death on the horn
> Of the Unicorn.
> I am Pan! Io Pan! Io Pan Pan! Pan!

---

[9] E.g. White (1978: 110); Lovejoy (1936) is another example; there are many others.
[10] This was Rafael Sabatini's *The Banner of the Bull.*

Later, he married. His wife was involved with spiritualism, and they attended the Liberal Catholic Church (a theosophical version of Catholicism). He read Gardner's novel about witchcraft, saw Gardner on television, and began to wonder about witchcraft, and eventually saw a gutterpress scandal about a coven, wrote off to defend it, was invited to a social evening, and ended up as an initiate. The point is that he identifies the novel and, particularly, the poem, as crucial in understanding his movement into practice.

The emphasis on fiction, imagery and fantasy becomes particularly intriguing when magicians explain the evolution of their belief. Sometimes magicians feel that there is one particular period when they 'really' commit themselves. This can take the form of an initiatory dream. I learnt of a number of these through the Green Circle study group on dreams. For example, Helga, from the Glittering Sword, discovered Wodan and the 'Nordic Tradition' in the course of my fieldwork. This Germanic god became extremely important to her, and shortly after the following dream, she described herself as his 'shaman', by virtue of the following 'initiatory' dream.

She jumped into a well, intending to be a sacrifice to Wodan. At the bottom she found driftwood, and when she floated to the surface she was encased in wood. She lay on the grass asleep. A man came up to her and put three fingers into her handbag, whereupon she lept up and hit him over the head with it. The police arrived, and her lover told them to 'piss off'.

The sexual interpretation was not lost on Helga. But to her the dream 'meant' that she was reborn (Osiris-like) through Wodan, and that through the rebirth she became sexually and emotionally confident enough to stand up for herself. The dream persuaded her that she was, on the 'deepest' level, the god's chosen initiate. Soon she would dream that Wodan had given her an animal familiar.

Another woman – Maria, the pre-doctoral biochemist – had a sequence of dreams shortly before her initiation into the Glittering Sword. At this point she had been doing Green's Natural Magic course for nine months. She was extremely nervous about her initiation into the group. These dreams helped convince her that her involvement was not only a good thing, but somehow intrinsic to her nature.

dream 1: She was holding cats, and saw a black cat and talked to it – 'Come and be stroked'. It turned around and with a shock she realized that it had human eyes. But it was friendly; and she knew that it knew everything about her.

dream 2: She was climbing a mountain with her sister and her sister's friend. She knew that there was a witch on this mountain, and she found the witch's bag, full of light-and-grey rings in pairs. They came to an old, derelict house, and she knew that the witch was inside. Maria gave her sister and the friend some rings to protect them, but the most powerful ring, the ring of power, she kept within the bag. The witch asked for the bag back, but Maria wouldn't give it to her, for she mistrusted her. When some miners walked by she went out to talk to them, ostensibly to say hello but really to let them know where she was.

dream 3: She saw bonfires, garlanded with flowers, which she thought extremely beautiful. They were there for St. John's Eve [Midsummer]. Then she led a group up the mountain, the night lit by the light shining from her forehead.

Maria by this point had begun to think of herself as a witch. She had struggled to think that the claims of magic were valid; she presented these dreams as a sign of her progress and of her acceptance of magic on a 'subconscious level'. In other words, she saw the dreams as asserting her 'true' witch nature, and her conviction that the magical path was the right one for her to tread, regardless of her intellectual qualms about its claims.

Another member of the Glittering Sword also dreamt vividly before her initiation. Emily was deeply pleased with her dream, because she 'got the entire ritual'. She dreamt that she was taken into a courtyard, where a circle of people were waiting, and was shown a shining disc and a variety of other objects which were used in the ritual (but whose descriptions she preferred to remain unpublished). Then, the woman in charge had placed tarot cards out in a row on the table before her. Emily understood the dream to be not only clairvoyant, but magical: it was an initiation on the 'inner' before the initiation in the outer world. Around that time, she also had another striking dream. She attended a dinner party in which all the guests were asked to sit at the table as if they were seated upon the sephiroth of the Tree of Life (there were two tables, interconnected to resemble the kabbalistic glyph). Emily sat at Tiphareth: the place of deep initiation, of self-actualization, of personal balance. After dinner, the guests went to the garden to meet the Queen Mother, who was also the Queen of the Fairies. These dreams gave Emily a sort of symbolic surety, a confidence that her magical involvement was appropriate and effective.

The shift to commitment is often emotional, not based on intellectual analysis but upon gut response. A witch wrote the following passage three weeks after having received the highest of the three 'degrees' in witchcraft. She describes her transition from philosophical acceptance to gut-level commitment as common for many magicians, although not necessarily conscious.

A change of perception has come over me in the previous week. It seemed to me that although I had worked much magic, had many premonitions and dreams etc., I had never committed myself to the reality behind them. Although I had believed in magic and the mystical/magical world, I had never been willing to commit myself to accepting and acting upon the fact that it *was so* rather than it *might be so*. Certainty rather than intellectual acceptance. A willingness to live by the belief rather than just accepting it philosophically. One must be prepared to act upon it without any reservations and to strike boldly out into the depths rather than staying safely in the shallows.

The significant remark in the quotation is the assertion of 'a willingness to live by the belief rather than just accepting it philosophically'. There is no longer an issue of intellectual evaluation. The witch is simply a witch. This is also the nature of the dreams: the dreamer sees herself as being a witch, initiate or magician. Many magicians told me that they had longed to be witches or wizards when they were young. At some point, they take that fantasy seriously. This sort of non-intellectual commitment has to do with the imagination, with whom one imagines oneself to be rather than the theories to which one gives assent; it involves self-image rather than proposition. I suspect that the committed believer no longer thinks in terms of particular claims – if he ever did so – but in terms of what being a magician is like.

I understand this talk of imagery, fantasy and acting by one's guts through the model of play, that for many magicians, magic, and believing in magic, is analogous to a sort of play, and that the involvement in magic retains the ambiguity of the play world while also allowing for it to be understood as serious. This is not to imply that people move into playful magic from solemn civil service – that magic is like collecting bottlecaps or model airplanes. Rather, I suggest that the shift from interpreting like a civil servant to interpreting like a magician may be similar in type to the shift in and out of 'let's pretend' play – except that some of the play-claims are also serious assertions about the world. I also suggest that this comparison illuminates the particular characteristics of belief in modern magic: magical claims are neither ordinary assertions, nor false assertions, and their ambiguity is best described through the ambiguity of play. It is an ambiguity particularly suited to the ambiguity of this self-conscious, rationality-conscious, technologically complex world.

The important feature of play is that it is distinct from the non-play world. While players have no difficulty identifying its differences, they often do not articulate the nature of that shift. Play theorists, however, have made singular efforts to do so. The most famous definitions of play describe it as a bounded context defined by rules, identified as the product of the metacommunication, 'this is play'. Huizinga defined the formal characteristics of play as 'a free activity standing quite consciously outside "ordinary" life as being "not serious", but at the same time absorbing the player intensely and utterly . . . It proceeds within its own proper boundaries of time and space according to fixed rules and in an orderly manner'.[11] Caillois expanded and generalized the definition of a 'rule' to include 'let's-pretend' games, the sorts of games that are closest to magicians' activities:

Many games do not imply rules. No fixed or rigid rules exist for playing with dolls, for playing soldiers, cops and robbers, horses, locomotives, and airplanes-games, in general, which presuppose free improvisation, and the chief attraction of which lies in the pleasure of playing a role, of acting as if one were someone or something else, a machine for example. Despite the assertion's paradoxical character, I will state that in these instances the fiction, the sentiment of *as if* replaces and performs the same function as do rules.[12]

Players play locomotive by creatively imitating locomotives. That they fail completely at imitating the locomotive sound is irrelevant: let's-pretend games do not have rules in so strict a sense, though the other children can accuse the little girl who acted as if the train could fly of 'not playing' properly. Caillois emphasized that the central feature of her play is her ability to recognize its unreality. But this does not mean that it is not serious: as Huizinga points out,

[11] Huizinga (1950: 13).   [12] Caillois (1962: 8).

the play can be tense, gripping, seem profoundly significant. And Huizinga remarks upon play's ambiguity: 'in play as we conceive it, the distinction between belief and make-believe breaks down'.[13] Bateson describes play as framed, paradoxical behaviour. In play, a gesture does not mean what it would ordinarily communicate because of the framing metacommunication, 'this is play'. When two monkeys play at combat, these communicative actions are in some sense untrue, used for some purpose other than the conventional one.[14]

One could recast this description as follows: when someone engages in let's-pretend play, she adopts a vague role-model or self-image, and behaving 'as if' she were that model defines the rule-bound context of her play. There is something like a core image in her play-imagination, the being that she is trying to be, something like the supreme fiction, in Wallace Stevens's sense, of the practice. But there are also the images and narrative sequences that flesh out the narrative form, the formulaic structures which associate narrative elements, the imaginative accoutrements that make an 'as if' story persuasive. Whether taken from fiction or from idealized fact, there is something like a set of narratives about the role model or sets of role models which the subject knows and creatively acts within – 'playing at' being a doctor, a lawyer, or a magus. While playing, the imaginative fabric provides the 'as-if' context which is the play-context, different from the real, bounded and all-encompassing and at times, intensely serious. If it is a serious play, the nature of that bounded context and its rules becomes opaque: the play is not 'only' play, but somehow also a real commitment to a particular understanding of the world.

All people move between different contexts, but few notice the clash between the different frames. Magicians do, for social scepticism forces it upon them. Whether magical ideas do or ought to conflict with the ideas of a non-magical mundanity, magicians are conscious that they are often thought to do so. And in their self-consciousness, the bounded context of play-like activity serves a crucial role because its ambiguity is the ambiguity of claims that are held, but defended with shifting arguments and complex strategies. The magical ideas of modern, sophisticated magicians do at least three things. First, the claims are concrete claims about an external physical world and are the basis for the science-like assertion that magic reveals a greater portion of the world than does ordinary science. Second, they are the descriptive statements associated with the odd, inarticulable experiences of the practice and become the markers through which these experiences are identified and explained. Third, they act like the framing, boundary 'as if' rules of play in which the practitioner imagines himself to be his idea of an effective magician in the rite.

The crucial part of magical practice is that the play-claim of being a powerful, efficacious magician is also a reality-claim, a science-like assertion

---

[13] Huizinga (1950: 25).

[14] Bateson (1972). To psychologists like Winnicott (1971), Axline (1969), Vygotsky (1978) and Piaget (1951), playing is a means of growth and development. Its central feature is the ambiguity between personal subjectivity and the experience of objective reality. The precariousness of that boundary makes play exciting, and Winnicott says that this is 'the precariousness of magic itself' (1971: 47).

about the objective instrumental efficacy of magic within the physical world. Performing efficacious magic is part of what it means to be a magician. It is a game condition that witches cast spells that work. Magic involves and encourages the imaginative identification in which the practitioner 'plays at' being a ritual magician or a witch; the theatrical setting and dramatic invocations are directed at evoking precisely that sort of complete identification with what one imagines the magician to be. Here the role models are taken from fiction: the magician fantasizes about being Gandalf, not about being his coven's high priest. He obviously is not Gandalf and he knows that fire will never leap from his staff. Yet magicians are not 'just' playing: they argue for the truth of their beliefs and look for confirming proof of practice.

The ambiguity gives magicians freedom. In modern magic the fact that the same assertion is both play-claim (context-defining claim) and reality-claim (claimed true for the larger context of 'ordinary' reality) can allow magicians to waver between the literal and the metaphorical when casting a spell: literal, in that the spell is thought to do what the first order theory says that it will do, and metaphorical, in that the spell is thought to do something else justified by the second order theory – spiritual, psychotherapeutic, expressive or creative – by representing an inner state in figurative form. This grants ambiguity, an ambiguity quite important for the magician. The seriousness of the claim of magical efficacy makes their practice seem serious and important. Yet the play-claim allows the magician to justify the magic on other grounds. Regardless of the veracity of its claims, they argue, magical practice is worthwhile because the experiential involvement is spiritually, morally, aesthetically or psychologically uplifting. Through this process magicians both confirm their claims and become admirably well-equipped with second-order theories to justify their first-order theory if they are pressed to do so. The claims are simultaneously reinforced and emasculated. The practitioner becomes more committed: but he can explain that commitment away, justify it in terms independent of the validity of the claim. The rationalizing process depends on the ambiguity of the relationship between these apparently different contexts, and the ability to identify them as different, so that magical claims are both like and unlike 'ordinary' claims.

All ritual activity involves play, because ritual involves a not-quite-ordinary reality, a creation of something different from the non-ritualistic. The wafer is the body and the wine the blood, the crown the embodiment of divine kingship. Huizinga indeed argues that religion, and particularly archaic ritual, emerges as sacred play: 'in the form and function of play, itself an independent entity which is senseless and irrational, man's consciousness that he is embedded in a sacred order of things finds its first, highest and holiest expression. Gradually the significance of a sacred act permeates the playing. Ritual grafts itself upon it; but the primary thing is and remains play'.[15] Sacred play is let's-pretend play experienced as divine, sacred, as if pertaining to another real but not-ordinary

[15] Huizinga (1950: 17–18).

world: it can be the state of becoming the gods, or interacting with the gods, in which pretence passes the threshold into vivid reality, the 'really real'. One knows that the masks and bull-roarers are only make-believe; and yet one is frightened of these impersonated ghosts, finds them awe-full, experiences ecstasy. 'The disguised or masked individual "plays" another part, another being. He *is* another being. The terrors of childhood, open-hearted gaiety, mystic fantasy and sacred awe are all inextricably entangled in this strange business of masks and disguises.'[16]

The play element in the rites of many pre-literate societies is clear: the indigenous carnival, the mock kingship, the enactment of natural seasons and human development – Richards' *chisungu*, Turner's *ihamba*, Bateson's *naven*, Frazer's king-killing, harvest-insuring, fertility rites. Perhaps some of this play disappears from modern Judaeo-Christian ritual, with its symbol-stripped solemnity. In modern magic there is something of this sacred play. 'Religions that combine humour, play and seriousness are a rare species', Adler says[17]; this is a world of creative, syncretic, theatrical performance. The businessman becomes Horus, the computer consultant Cerridwen, the engineer writes long rituals about Zeus, Isis, and the sacred Eleusinian Mysteries. Modern magicians talk of sacred play and the ecstasy of becoming other, the intense absorption into the fantasy realm which becomes a sacred reality. A long passage from Starhawk's manual describes the emergence of sacred play, the 'secret smiles . . . of archaic Greek statues, hinting at the highest and most humorous of the Mysteries'. Other coven members may or may not have shared this particular impression, but the mixture of play and sacrality which she describes have often been described to me as one of the most attractive features of the practice.

Humour and play awaken the sense of wonder, the basic attitudes that Witchcraft takes to the world. For example, last night my coven held a May Eve ritual, the central action of which involved winding a 'Maypole', and weaving into it those things we wish to weave into our lives. Instead of a pole, we used a central cord, and instead of ribbons we had strings of colored yarn, anchored to a central hook on the ceiling of our meeting room. We also had eleven people in the circle. Of course, we knew perfectly well that it is impossible to wind a Maypole with an odd number of people, but we did not want to leave anybody out. So, with a cavalier disregard for ordinary reality, we went right ahead.

The result, to begin with, was chaos and confusion. Everyone was laughing as we dodged in and out, creating a tangled knot of yarn. It was scarcely a scene of mystical power; a ritual magician would have blanched pale and turned in his wand on the spot. But an odd thing began to happen as we continued. The laughter began to build a strange atmosphere, as if ordinary reality was fading away. Nothing existed but the interplay of colored cords and moving bodies. The smiles on faces that flashed in and out of sight began to resemble the secret smiles of archaic Greek statues, hinting at the highest and most humourous of Mysteries. We began to sing; we moved in rhythm and a pattern evolved in the dance – nothing that could ever be mapped or plotted rationally; it was a pattern with an extra element that always and inevitably would defy explanation.

---

[16] Huizinga (1950: 13).   [17] Adler (1986: 319).

The snarl of yarn resolved itself into an intricately woven cord. The song became a chant; the room glowed, and the cord pulsed with power like a live thing, an umbilicus linking us to all that is within and beyond. At last the chant peaked and died; we dropped into trance. When we awoke, all together, at the same moment, we faced each other with wonder.[18]

For the modern urbanite, one of thousands on the city pavement, the sense of archaic sacred play in modern ritual may be central to her own explanation and understanding of her practice.

But if modern magicians understand themselves to return to an ancient sacrality in play and drama, they also take with them a highly modern, sophisticated explanation of their action. Most magicians take magic seriously, most are committed in some way to the ideas on which the practice relies. Most are willing to at least argue in support of those ideas. However, there is a noticeable nonchalance about the sorts of arguments they use, and a remarkable toleration of diversity both in the practice and in the views practitioners take towards the practice. There are witches, kabbalists, Western Mysteries initiates, some who are all three and some who call themselves Egyptian priestesses to Isis and the like. There are those who seem to accept strange magical forces as a literal part of the physical world, and others who claim that the concept is a useful metaphor. A magical group may contain people with both these views. Until some event forces those views into the open, no-one need know of the divergence, and that they diverge would in any case probably be thought irrelevant. 'While most Neo-Pagans disagree on almost everything, one of their most important principles is polytheism . . . polytheism has allowed a multitude of distinct groups to exist more or less in harmony, despite a great divergence in beliefs and practices'.[19] There are no established rules, or gods, or forms of worship: while these groups all encourage an imaginative participation in the divine, the nature of the divine and its interpretation are matters of seemingly little consequence.

This is a very self-conscious awareness of the multiplicity of interpretation. Any modern magical ritual can be understood by its participants as a manipulation of supra-physical force, a religious invocation of the transcendent, a poetically expressive metaphor, a therapeutic encounter, a political rebellion against convention. It can be all of these or any of these, and the magician knows it. What concerns him is that the 'as if' engagement of practising magic seems to be important to the practitioners he respects, and that he can argue for its importance to the sceptic within himself and in the wider society. There is a scientized explanation of the reality of magical forces, supported by references to modern physics, research on physical events, and the like. There are articulate explanations of the nature of truth and the epistemological access to a noumenal reality. There are justifications for the psychological, spiritual aesthetic value of the engagement.

Most emblematic of the ambiguity is that 'belief' is not a term with which

---

[18] Starhawk (1979: 23–4).   [19] Adler (1986: 24–5).

magicians feel comfortable. 'The magician does not believe: he knows that his prayers can be answered. He has seen or sensed the presence of angels or the gods, and he has had a variety of real personal experiences'.[20] 'Belief has never seemed very relevant to the experience and processes of the groups that call themselves, collectively, the Neo-Pagan movement.'[21] There were similar remarks quoted in an earlier chapter about the difference between knowledge and belief. The disavowal of belief is quite interesting, because it is both a way of affirming commitment – asserting that understanding in magic is not about the hypothetical but about the known – and yet also a manner of rejecting overt commitment to any set of principles. Saying that one does not believe in magic permits an ambiguity between commitment so deep it is thought to be knowledge, and a lack of any commitment at all. The ambiguity depends upon a self-consciousness of belief-statements which are ratified by rational canons in order to become knowledge, and identified as 'beliefs' if they cannot be so proved. It also expresses doubt about those canons: 'spirituality leaps where science cannot yet follow, because science must always test and measure, and much of reality and human experience is immeasurable. Without discarding science, we can recognize its limitations. There are many modes of consciousness that have not been validated by Western scientific rationalism . . .'[22] The mind is limited, the soul is infinite. Rationality is not enough, I was informed. It fails to satisfy because it cannot answer the really important questions.

Magical practice is specially structured so as to evoke the ambiguity in which, as Huizinga remarks, belief and make-believe are intertwined. The mark of the magician's modernity is that the complex, many-layered sophistication of his explanation allows him to remain committed to the practice while recognizing that it might violate well-established rationalistic principles; he does so by providing a coherent explanation of why those principles are inapplicable or limited. He plays at magic and understands the play as serious, and the truth of magical theory hovers in limbo between reality and fantasy. Magic is a modernist religion: it challenges the validity of religious dogmatism, authoritative symbology, and intellectual analysis, while gaining its inspiration from archaic primitive forms; and its structured ambiguity rests upon a deconstructed notion of belief.

[20] Green (1983: 61).   [21] Adler (1986: 20).   [22] Starhawk (1979: 191).

23

Final Thoughts

Why, in the end, do magicians practise magic? My findings suggest that the people who turn to modern magic are searching for powerful emotional and imaginative religious experience, but not for a religion *per se*. Magic is replete with psychologically powerful images of death, fertility and regeneration, moulded in the symbolism of earlier cultures. The magician makes the ancient imagery personally relevant through meditation, story-telling, and theatrical enactment, and his involvement with the imagery seems to provide him with intense religious experience. Yet magical practice lacks the institutional structure that demands a commitment to a particular belief. Unlike the vast majority of other sects, cults and devotions it is clear that magic does not require an explicit endorsement of a specific creed, or of the teachings of a particular teacher, or indeed – since the occult so often presents itself as avant-garde science – of a hypothesis of the divine at all. Magical practice does not obviously call itself a religion, nor does it command adherence to a set of propositions as a prerequisite for the practice – despite the fact that many practitioners eventually describe their practice as religious and produce similar accounts of spiritual and physical reality. The imaginative attraction of magic lies in its talk of ancient tradition, old ways, unknown powers buried in the earth, strange forces accessible to the gifted, and in the appeal of the forbidden, mysterious and beyond. The practice may promise spiritual enlightenment through the Goddess, or a new understanding of the divine, with the meditative and pop psychological practices in current vogue, but it does so without violating an intellectual distrust of religious belief, both because of the emphasis upon occult 'technology' and because of the magicians' self-conscious doubt of faith itself. That combination – the emotional and imaginative intensity, with the solemnity of religion but without an explicit demand to adopt some authority's belief – is, I suggest, what makes modern magic compelling.

Interest in the occult waxes and wanes within England and the United States. Spiritualism, psychical research, ouija boards and general occult activity exploded in Victorian and Edwardian times. Scholarly opinion attributes that period's marked interest in the occult to the ascendance of science and the apparent demise of religion.[1] Spiritualists and psychical researchers tried to show scientifically that the claims of religion – the immortality of the soul, for example – were true.[2] Interest in the occult began to blossom again during the 1960s.[3] Some scholars argue that this modern magic provides 'meaning' for youths who are alienated from a scientific-rationalist society.[4] The occult gives them a sense of vitality and involvement in a society dominated by scientific progress. Others explain the occult as the response to social crisis and its psychological impact, 'the consequence of rapid social and technological change, which leads to the dislocation of values, uncertainty about traditional authorities and roles, alienation, anxiety, deprivation, tension and anomie'.[5] This theme of alienation from the culture has been the dominant chord in understanding many new religious movements.[6] One line of argument sees the occult revival as narcissistic, a retreat from commitment, a regression to a childhood state in a refusal to cope with urban commitments.[7] Others remark that the occult is a 'cocoon', both a rite of passage which transforms an emergent individual and an attempt to reform the social order, with both of which the occultist is dissatisfied.[8] Some claim that it is a response to pervasive social disorganization.[9] One sociologist asserts that the occult is a 'seedbed' for cultural change, and that 'in the historical unfolding of Western civilization, occult revivals have attended such crucial periods of transition from one cultural matrix to another.'[10] These explanations seem too general. It is difficult to conceive of an historical period that is not, in some sense, in crisis and of an adolescence that is not in need of meaning.

Another reason often given to explain the occult renaissance is the recent surge of religious enthusiasm. It is widely claimed that the last decades have been a period of religious reawakening, in which many people have found themselves following what they call a spiritual or religious quest. This sense of a religious revitalization is corroborated by media attention to religion. The last twenty years have seen the emergence of the great media evangelists, the 'televangelists', a rise in Christian fundamentalism, the flowering of authoritarian cults and bizarre sects, of Eastern gurus, urban American shamans, and Latin American voodoo queens. If there is indeed an awakening, the reasons for it are not entirely clear. We live, of course in a technological society commonly stereotyped as sterile, cold, bureaucratic, in want of spiritual values and in need

---

[1] See Turner (1974), Gauld (1968), Brandon (1983), Oppenheim (1985).

[2] Science and religion were also mixed in the Renaissance, but in a different recipe. The scholarly debate concerns whether the rise of Hermetic-kabbalistic magic, with its vision of man at the controlling centre of his universe, contributed to the scientific revolution. See, for example, Yates (1964, 1972, 1979), Vickers (1984).

[3] A spate of books published after the period pressed the interrelation between quantum mechanics and mysticism, and the former's proof of the truth of the latter (LeShan 1966, Capra 1975, and others). On the other hand, some of the occult-oriented New Age literature stresses the need for spiritualism in the face of science's hard reality.

[4] Greeley (1974). [5] Galbreath (1983: 23).

[6] E.g. G. K. Nelson (1969) on spiritualism, McLoughlin (1978). Also cf. Jahoda (1974) on superstition.

[7] Lasch (1979). [8] Prince (1974). [9] Wallace (1970). [10] Tiryakian (1974: 274).

of humanizing. We also live in an increasingly tolerant world, tolerant at least of religious practice, and this unprecedented religious freedom has been coupled with the media exposure which brings these unusual practices into the houses of religious consumers. The possibilities for religious diversity and involvement have never before existed in quite this way. However, we should be wary of this assertion of a general religious awakening. Religion has earned publicity in recent decades, but it is not clear whether individuals have become more religious. Church attendance in England, for example, has fallen[11]. Involvement in the occult, then, is difficult to attribute to the rise of interest in religion more generally.

Part of the explanation is simple. The 'occult revival' has more to do with a commercial success story than an alienated or religiously enthused society, a fad which was able to pass some threshold of visibility and now appeals to people because it meets some basic need for spiritual, imaginative, emotional play in a remarkably tolerant cultural milieu. The countercultural 1960s turned to occultism – to astrology, tarot, and alternative healing and eating – because they were alternatives to the established culture: many people discovered tarot cards at about the same time they discovered beansprouts. The period after the sixties saw different cults and new religious movements born into a society marked by tolerance. The occult acquired a countercultural chic, and many people came across it in an atmosphere of religious diversity. More newspapers have carried horoscopes, and yet more even now begin to do so. More occult stores have been and continue to be opened. And in the last twenty years the detective novel has been replaced by fantasy and science fiction as the light fiction of majority choice. Fantasy fiction can be a powerful inducement to magical practice, because, as we have seen, the fiction and the practice share many characters, themes and ideals. In the last five or ten years most readers of Tolkien, C. S. Lewis, or Ursula LeGuin have been able to find a local bookstore with instruction books on how to recreate the sort of magico-religious practice characteristic of this fiction, and there quite likely see an advertisement for a coven or a magical course. These bookstores, and the sections on the occult and mythology in old bookstores, have appeared for the most part within the last ten years. To some extent the interest in magic has grown because the perennial interest in fantasy, recently stimulated by genre fiction, has now been provided with an arena for practical exploration. Adolescents who thirty years ago would not have heard of the tarot might now have seen a witch on television and realized they have the option of joining an occult group.

Magical practice does seems to strike some religious nerve in the lives of its practitioners, to provide the intense imaginative and emotional involvement with symbolism that we associate with a religion. This claim demands a sympathetic interpretation of the category of 'religious experience' and to define that term by criterial attributes would be a dubious exercise. Never-

---

[11] In fact, church attendance has decreased since the fifties, although televised church services cast doubt upon the importance of those statistics. See Malise Ruthven 'Rapture and the New American Right'. *The Times Literary Supplement*, January 29–February 4, 1988.

theless, as we have seen, the particular phenomenologies and symbolic involvements that we are prompted to call 'religious' are found in modern magic, and form indeed the core of the practice. In magic, ancient images of Persephone, Cerridwen, Osiris and so forth directly confront powerful psychological issues – death, pain, maturation, a mother's grief at the loss of a daughter to marriage, a son's rebellion at a father's command. They cast individual traumas of death, separation, and love into the dramatic themes of romantic fantasy. Through the practice, the magician loads these mythologically redolent images with personal relevance and feeling. Potent images like the sickle-wielding crone, the destiny-spinners, the elderly guide, mischievous youth, or virgin huntress come to represent attitudes and events; dragons, moons, sacred chalices and magical stones embody personal fantasy. Imagination provides a route into the feelings associated with a religion, through Ignatian meditation, shamanic training, magical pathworking, parable or myth. Devotion and worship are linked to and intermingled with imaginative fantasy. And through the practice, the individual magician comes to experience what he calls spiritual responses, transcendent epiphanies, and he gains gods who become confidants and sources of moral wisdom. He may have feelings of mystic absorption into another, higher 'plane'. He has moments of great solemnity and sacred ceremonial. These are sensations that tend to be associated with a religion, and magic provides them in abundance.

More specific to magic than to conventional religion is the *frisson* of secrecy, mystery and the forbidden. However, it would be dangerous to link the almost morbid elements of the fantasy with a general theme in modern culture – spiritual corruption or moral depravation – and thus to explain magic's appeal by the prevalence of that theme. Magical imagery does contain overtones of decay and despair, with ideas of death, darkness, and the deep. Fascination with the macabre is, however, fairly commonplace. Modern magic caters to this fascination by offering a safely packaged context for it. Magic is full of blasted heaths, illicit sexuality, daggers, darkness and archaic symbols. But the practice is usually organized so that these wild fantasies are stimulated in a context in which they can be kept well in hand. Witchcraft, for instance, uses a symbolism of fertility, pagan sexuality and death, and it enacts its rites in the nude. Yet the witches' circle is presented almost as a child's playground: the magical circle is good, protective, safe, and its members feel that they are 'like a family'. While magicians may say that sexuality and morbidity were factors that attracted them to magic, the explanation they give for remaining practitioners has more to do with spiritual and emotional experience. Magical enthusiasm cannot be explained by the appeal of the perverse to the peculiar in a tolerant society. A more satisfactory approach is to consider whether the general conditions of self-conscious modernity may make the practice attractive.

We live in a tolerant society with communications media capable of bringing the unusual into the most commonplace home: as we have seen, magic offers the vivid religious experience that many people enjoy. A further factor in its appeal lies in the scepticism of contemporary culture. Magic – oddly enough –

offers imaginative and emotional involvement without the normal costs of irrational belief demanded by a society concerned with demonstrable, objective, coherent truths. Magicians are so aware of the difficulties of rationalizing, of producing a universally acceptable account of their involvement, and of the many possibilities of explanation that they tend not to demand the adoption of a particular viewpoint or the assertion of a particular creed. Becoming involved with magic is like entering a world of 'let's pretend' fantastic ideas which might or might not be true, to which one does not immediately commit oneself, and with which one can experiment and play before becoming gradually persuaded of their value. The practice allows its practitioners to be ironic: to be committed to their practice and yet prepared to disclaim the apparent truths on which it rests.

Magic has as much to do with the rejection of traditional religion as with its provision of religious experience. These days the word 'religion', for many intellectuals, is a difficult, suspicious term. Some people associate it with personal constraints and institutional demands; others define it as a commitment to an unprovable metaphysical assertion about a strangely different reality. The nature of modern magic allows such wary outsiders to sidestep their intellectual hesitation. Being involved with magic is not like converting to a new religion; involvement is not so much a conscious decision to adopt a belief and then a practice as a slow persuasion of the value of the practice. Initiation into a Western Mysteries fraternity does not seem to be like joining a religion. The word 'religion' is mentioned cautiously, although there is talk of spirituality and gods: the magician claims that he uses those feelings for a pragmatic, even scientific, physical end. Even witchcraft, which explicitly calls itself a religion, focuses as much upon the efficacy of spell-casting as upon worship, and the talk is about planes, vibrations and Jungian symbolism rather than about a separate god. The hard-to-believe ideas in magic are theories about the physical world, not about a divinity existing in some real but otherworldly form. To an outsider, magic presents itself more like a fantasy science fiction than a religious odyssey, an extension of mundane scientific assumptions rather than a wholly new hypothesis about the existence of a divine being utterly distinct from the material world. A member of an intellectually secular, sceptical society may find in magic a less improbable account of the world than he would in mainstream religion: many may find that attractive. Despite appearances magic is the romantic intellectual's religion, a religion demanding no explicit belief but ripe with symbolic and experiential fruits.

I have suggested that magicians may rationalize their involvement by means of an intellectual strategy that allows them to remain ambivalent about their commitment, and further that this style of rationalization is shared by some modern Christian theologians, and probably by other practitioners of hard-to-defend involvements. This intellectual strategy of ambivalence seems common in our self-conscious, rationalistic society: it seems not unlikely that magic is appealing partly because it so evidently relies upon this sort of intellectual strategy. The first books that newcomers will buy are full of intellectual vacillation, asserting the claim that the magical forces are clear and effective alongside a justification of the practice even if the claims should prove to be false. As the newcomer becomes more involved, he will develop his own manner of explaining away the apparent intellectual difficulties of a practice that has become of increasing emotional importance to him. But the possibility of explaining them away may attract him from the start.

Magicians are remarkably self-conscious about their practice, and their self-consciousness gives them freedom. They are aware of themselves as people born into one form of life among others, but able to choose and change the social and intellectual constraints under which they live. They lead lives within a highly complex world which they are sufficiently educated to appreciate in its ethnic, ideological and moral diversity, and they are remarkably aware of having chosen one path from a multitude of choices. What does it mean to be a pagan and a polytheist? – a witch gave this answer:

> To some people, it seems like a contradiction to say that I have a certain subjective truth; I have experienced the Goddess, and this is my total reality. And yet I do not believe that I have the one, true, right and only way.
>
> Many people cannot understand how I find Her a part of my reality and accept the fact that your reality might be something else. But for me, this is in no way a contradiction, because I am aware that my reality and my conclusions are the result of my unique genetic structure, my life experience and my subjective feelings; and you are a different person, whose same experience of what may or may not be out there will be translated in your nervous system into something different. And I can learn from that.
>
> I can extend my own reality by sharing that and grow. This recognition that everyone has different experiences is a fundamental keystone to Paganism; it's the fundamental premise that whatever is going on out there is infinitely more complex than I can ever understand. And that makes me feel very good.[12]

This is a remarkable statement. It nearly endorses intellectual anarchy, for it seems to say that truth and reality are for the individual to choose. Throughout this book magicians have spoken of choosing the rules of the game, adopting the truth that is valid for them, seeing the world in a way others might not. Most say that they exercise some choice in the rules, beliefs, and perspectives which govern their understanding; all accept, as this witch has done, that an unalterable legacy of parentage and culture also determines their understanding. Magicians pride themselves on toleration and diversity and many take pleasure in their own limited subjectivity, because their own limitation, they think, implies the world's iridian variety. Magic seems more suitable to Melanesia than to Swaffham Bulbeck, and practitioners tend to wonder about what life would be like in Papua New Guinea. But they repeatedly assert their right to choose to be magicians in modern England.

Many magicians will say that objective truth is not accessible, because it must always be understood by people and through people, and people have limited perceptual tools. Words are tools to put a handle to reality; gods are

---

[12] Alison Harlow; quoted in Adler (1986: 36).

psychological constructs, no more than archetypes; truth is relative to the believer – these remarks are as commonplace to the magician's conversation as is his reference to science's hegemony. These remarks are paradoxically the result of the reflexive self-awareness, for their consciousness of rational canons allows them to argue that the canons are misguided. Magicians' denial of the rational foundations is most clear in the literature of 'chaos magic', which asserts that the point of the practice is to free oneself from the intellectual and social constraints which bind one's thoughts. The mind, it says, is a trap of structure, building endless categories, playing with itself, to try to gain a hold upon and power over reality. True power comes of letting go, of freeing oneself from the distorting shackles of the categorizing mind, to relax into primordial chaotic power. One manual advises an exercise called 'random belief': it lists what it calls stages in the belief cycle – paganism, monotheism, atheism, nihilism, chaosism, superstition – and suggests that the student believe in each of them for a week, month, or year at a time. It calls these beliefs 'dice-options'.[13] The point, supposedly, is that believing different things will cause belief itself to lose its power.[14] There are no absolutes, no foundations, no ultimate truths or moral dictates: the dogma is repeated throughout the literature.

Ours is a culture of supposedly self-confident rationalism, in which clear thinking delivers ever greater certainty of the truth. And our reliable knowledge of the external world does undeniably mount. But the very clarity of these intellectual standards has produced an uncertainty of their value. Gellner describes modernity as an ironic culture – that we take rational canons and scientific enterprise as the serious business of thinking, and that this gives freedom to that part of life which lies outside them.[15] Religious and leisure activities flourish and multiply in a world which tolerates them because they do not really matter. The very emphasis upon the validity of certain claims to knowledge – like scientific research – frees other engagements from that demand to be rational. My analysis is somewhat different. The larger cultural order probably tolerates magical practice because it seems unthreatening – foolish perhaps, but not genuinely heretical. Magicians may be drawn to the practice because they see the freedom with which they can believe, rationalize and interpret their involvement. But I suspect that many of them are also confused about the so-called serious intellectual standards of logic, objectivity and demonstrability, and that their magic is an expression of their ambivalence. They are as hesitant about the value of scientific insight and rationalism as they are about the magic.

Relativism is something of an intellectual's philosophy of the age. Rorty, Habermas, Gadamer, Derrida, Kuhn – not that they are all relativists, but they

---

[13] Carroll (n.d.a: 64 ff).

[14] This is a fairly popular manual used by the largest mail-order outlet in England (the one with 25,000 listed customers who had made at least two purchases) and was used in the introductory stages of a home study course. Three thousand copies of a similar volume have been sold by the store.

[15] Gellner (1974).

struggle to avoid the label – have probably arisen out of a similar trans-cultural self-consciousness, a reflexive questioning of an intellectual style which is obviously accepted. That style need not be well-defined: it is sometimes called rationality, and often associated with science, logic and experimental rigour. The awareness of the intellectual style in a multi-faceted, many-textured world generates an anxious fear of its power. Many magicians are rebelling against the very idea of an objective truth. They deride science, and they not only explain why a personal truth can be prior to an apparently objective understanding, but also assert that true knowledge lies beyond 'mere' intellectual understanding. When they explain why they practise magic they give a variety of answers, which both deny and accept the irrationality of magic. Relativism is not unique to modern culture; many preliterate cultures, even some Eastern cultures, accept a notion of a malleable truth. However, the particular form of self-conscious relativism which deliberately undermines rational foundations by articulating and rejecting them is a modern characteristic, what Cummings called the cordial revelation of the fatal reflexive turned upon itself. It may be that this sort of relativistic concern arises from the platform of a confident faith in scientific validity. It is nevertheless seriously distressing to its individual adherents.

Certainly magicians are themselves evidence of the limitations of reason's scope. Their understanding is shaped by complex constraints, within which they are clear-thinking but which give them no guarantee of access to some putatively objective truth. This examination of the practice suggests that the truth of any claim can be irrelevant to the persuasiveness of its theory or to its coherence with the other kinds of claims that people tend to make. Magicians probably cling to their magical ideas more because of the unverbalized part of the practice rather than because of verifiable knowledge, experimentally tested claims and the like: the associated experiences have become so fundamental to their lives. Over time the practice elicits the gut sense that it is correct. Yet magicians are aware that they look out of a warped window upon the world, and see it in blurred focus, and that all people have but a limited purchase upon the world. One most basic lesson of the modernity of magic is not merely the emergence of intellectual self-reflection – the activity to which most scholars point – but the attenuated appreciation of rational absolutes engendered in its wake.

Magicians seem radically unlike the rest of English culture, an enclave of Azande on the Hornsey Rise. But they are simply a more flamboyant instance of the conceptual cacophony of contemporary culture, of the scientist who spends Sunday in the church and weekdays in the lab, the moralist who preaches to his children but poaches from his boss. The flamboyant talk and action of the magicians illustrate what many people prefer to ignore – the ease with which we all come to see a given view as valid, and the skills we gain in explaining it so that its limitations, biases, and contradictions with other views need never seem apparent.

WHAT WE LEARN: ANTHROPOLOGICAL APPROACHES

Odd beliefs and peculiar practices are the dhal of the anthropological diet. The unnatural and non-obvious are the stuff of human culture and it is to explain them that the discipline was born. Over the years a certain gestalt has emerged. As I see it, two basic preconceptions have coloured the understanding of magic and ritual, and though there have been efforts to overturn them they still underlie much anthropological thought. The first is that magic, and rituals with intentions, must be understood as based on a theory, upon which the ritualist acts to achieve certain goals. To explain apparently bizarre action, one looks first to belief – and then to experience. The other preconception, in tension with the first, is that rituals should be explained through their impact on the social system, and the way the rite supports, maintains and expresses the cultural order. Here ritual is exegetically prior to belief. But still the experience of involvement is shoved aside. Where the one assumption lays the stress upon cultural ideas, the other emphasizes social organization.

These concerns have been crystallized in what to most anthropologists is known as the rationality debate. A brief history of that debate will adumbrate the concerns which have been uppermost in the arguments. It is only a map, compressed, telegraphic, schematic. My intention, however, is not to discuss particular theorists but an overall approach. Ultimately I shall suggest that much of the discussion has missed the point – at least, it has been based upon counterproductive assumptions. More fruitful work is now emerging from within the discipline, but its concerns need to be clarified and its tools sharpened.

The immediate precursor of what came to be known as the 'rationality debate' is one monograph: Evans-Pritchard's account of Azande witchcraft.[16] Scholars had speculated on the difference between the minds of primitives and our own at least since Vico. 'Let us suppose a Montesquieu, Buffon, Diderot . . . travelling in order to inform their compatriots, observing and describing . . . we ourselves would see a new world come from their pens, and we would thus learn to know our own.'[17] Evans-Pritchard was among the first to address this problem of primitive mentality directly from a mass of careful ethnological description, and the monograph became and has continued to be the focus of considerable argument.

The Azande live in the savannah forest of the southern Sudan, where they are agricultural and cattle-less. Their ethnographic fame arises from the witchcraft, *mangu*, which pervades their understanding of their world. Essentially, the Azande hold that some people are witches, which means that they have the power to affect others in unfortunate ways. This is often considered to be an unconscious power – witchcraft is inherited, and the witch exercises his or her powers psychically, without rite or speech, and often

---

[16] Evans-Pritchard (1937).   [17] Rousseau (1964: 212–13).

without conscious intention (there are also sorcerers, who deliberately perform malevolent rites). When a misfortune occurs, the Azande often attribute it to witchcraft. If it is a significant misfortune from whose consequences the victim is still suffering, he looks around for neighbours who might bear a grudge against him and have bewitched him, and he consults a 'poison oracle' to determine whom it is. (He also consults the poison oracle to know whether misfortune will occur if he embarks upon some venture.) This poison oracle is a chicken, which is fed a quantity of poison, *benge*. Whether the chicken – in fact, two or more chickens – lives or dies provides the answer to the consulter's question. Having determined the witch, an intermediary (if necessary) approaches the accused aggressor, who will then 'blow water' over the chicken wing that has died in naming him witch, and assert his good intentions towards the harmed man and his determination to 'cool' the witchcraft in his belly.

Witchcraft appears in every aspect of Zande life, where Evans-Pritchard says that it plays the role that chance or luck plays in our own. It explains the particularity of events. The man died when the rotten granary fell upon him: he died because of the granary's rottenness, but why he should have the rotten luck to be there when it fell – that is witchcraft. A skilled woodcarver splits the wood during his work, despite his expert knowledge of his craft. He is not maladroit, and thus attributes the split to witchcraft. Misfortune is not ascribed to witchcraft if it can be demonstrated that it is due to sorcery (again, this can be determined through the poison oracle, along with more general evidence) or to incompetence or suspect behaviour, such a taboo-breaking or immorality. Those misfortunes can be otherwise explained.

In the study, Evans-Pritchard was implicitly attacking the theories of Lévy-Bruhl, whom he discussed explicitly elsewhere.[18] That philosopher was intrigued by the reports of primitive beliefs then arousing much Parisian interest, accounts of totemism and peculiar rituals, of apparently contradictory beliefs and incoherent ideas. He argued that the thought of primitive man was different not in degree but in quality from his civilized counterpart. The primitive did not think less well or less reasonably: he started from different assumptions, noticed different things about the world, and was untroubled by the contradictions in some of the conclusions to which this led him. Above all he experienced his environment by 'participation', subtitled mystical drunkenness, an affective bond with the natural world around him. 'His mind does more than present his object to him: it possesses it and is possessed by it. It communes with it and participates in it, not only in the ideological, but also in the physical and mystic sense of the word.'[19] To Lévy-Bruhl primitive man had

---

[18] Initially these articles were published in the Bulletin of the Faculty of the Arts, Faud I University (1933, 1934). The primary material on Lévy-Bruhl was then later republished in the *Journal of the Anthropology Society of Oxford* (1970). Anthropologists and philosophers hoarded xerox copies for some years. Now the text seems to have been mostly reprinted in the posthumous *History of Anthropological Thought* (1981).

[19] Lévy-Bruhl (1979 [1926]: 362).

a 'pre-logical and mystic' mentality, governed by the law of participation, which paid little heed to contradiction.[20]

The thrust of Evans-Pritchard's attack was to take Lévy-Bruhl seriously – he claimed that he was one of few Anglo-Saxons to do so – and to demonstrate that the difference between civilized and primitive lay not in some qualitative distinction but in the different intellectual context in which their thought occurred. Evans-Pritchard agreed with Lévy-Bruhl that the pattern of thought within any society must be explained as part of the culture; he agreed that the apparent strangeness of primitive customs became meaningful when understood within the overall pattern of ideas and behaviour. But he fundamentally disagreed that the Azande were somehow radically different from Westerners in the way they understood and experienced their world. Their apparent differences had to do with differences in the social context of their intellectual analysis. They failed to notice contradictions in their system of thought because they never abstracted across contexts, but asked about witchcraft in specific situations. They asked why this particular man fell ill, not whether the logical implications of a series of witchcraft attributions were consistent. Preliterate Africans might be unscientific, Evans-Pritchard said, but not illogical, and he went on to describe how the system did not contradict experience, that for (twenty-two) various reasons the Azande did not notice the futility of the oracle's performance, and that the practice was in fact a quite reasonable one to adopt if one lived within the society.

Evans-Pritchard's brilliance lay in arguing that the strange statements made by members of a different culture did not imply that their mental capacities were similarly strange. Subsequent anthropologists have tended to follow this route with increasing sophistication, explaining that if one understood the social context in which people spoke, then their magical and ritual remarks would no longer seem irrational. Two poles of debate were established: the intellectualist, which explained magic as based upon mistaken belief, and the symbolist, which explained away the magic by showing how it had little to do with belief. The debate has been also described as between Enlightenment theory and its romantic rebellion: the philosophers demonstrate progress, science and the triumph of reason, the romantic rebels describe the creativity, emotion, and imaginative activity which can be called neither rational nor irrational.[21]

Tylor and Frazer are claimed, *post hoc*, as the canonical intellectualists: they held that magic arose out of natural thought processes and observation, and differed from science primarily in being wrong. Tylor spoke of a primitive man who 'having come to associate in thought those things which he found by experience to be connected in fact, proceeded erroneously to invert this action, and he concluded that association in thought must involve similar connection in

---

[20] See (in English translation) *How Natives Think* (1926) and *Primitive Mentality* (1923). Lévy-Bruhl's later views, in which he considerably modifies his views and talks instead of the variable interaction of logic and affect and the different types of representation developed in the face of different needs, are found in his: *The Notebooks on Primitive Mentality* (1975). Needham (1972: 160–75) provides a useful account which is weighted slightly differently than Evans-Pritchard's.
[21] Shweder (1984).

reality'.[22] Frazer asserted that 'the analogy between the magic and scientific conceptions of the world is close. In both of them, the succession of events is assumed to be perfectly regular and certain, being determined by immutable laws, the operation of which can be foreseen and calculated perfectly'.[23] Nearly a century after Tylor, Horton argued that African traditional thought served as a theory of the natural world which acquired magic-like characteristics because it was, as it were, the only system available. Those holding it were afraid to abandon it in the absence of a Popperian 'open society' of competing theories, and surrounded it with taboos and sacrality. Horton's primary aim was to demonstrate that magic – or, more generally, 'traditional thinking' was an explanation of the physical world (although not necessarily aimed at controlling the physical world). 'In treating traditional African religious systems as theoretical models akin to those of the sciences, I have really done little more than to take them at their face value'.[24] Horton somewhat qualified his concern in later works but the theoretical nature of traditional thinking, hemmed in by its lack of competition, remained his primary concern.[25]

The symbolist approach is usually attributed to Durkheim and, as Skorupski explains, it has three significant differences from intellectualism.[26] Science is sharply distinguished from magic or religion; that difference lies in the latter's being a symbolic system (often, to express something about the social order); this difference demands that one distinguish between the literal meaning and the symbolic meaning of magico-religious remarks, which are aesthetic, expressive uses of metaphor and analogy and are not true or false.

Most anthropological work in magic, ritual and religion has adopted some broad variant of this position, although the ethnographer also often feels compelled to describe the 'theory' behind any particular rite. Leach pressed hard the expressive, symbolic dimensions of all action, particularly of ritual. 'Ritual action and belief are alike to be understood as forms of symbolic statements about the social order'.[27] Douglas asserted that rituals and symbols gained their force from the strain within the natural and social classificatory order. Dirt is matter out of place, and rituals and beliefs emerge to handle the anxiety created by these inevitable violations of the ordered schemes through which the world is understood.[28] Beattie announced that magic and religion did have instrumental purposes, but that they were better understood through comparison to art than to physics. He contrasted symbolic, expressive behaviour, like ritual, with practical, instrumental science, and claimed that whereas hypothesis-testing was basic to the second, it was irrelevant to the first. Purported claims are not claims in the ordinary sense – or, while practitioners may think them to be instrumental, they are not actually judged as if they were instrumental.[29] Lewis is perhaps the best example of the view that magical rituals are about sheer phenomenological experience, and can be interpreted

---

[22] Tylor (1871: 116).   [23] Frazer (1922: 56).   [24] Horton (1970: 152).
[25] Horton (1982).   [26] Skorupski (1976: 18).
[27] Leach (1954: 14); see also (1968, 1976).   [28] Douglas (1966, 1975).
            [29] Beattie (1964, 1970, 1984).

neither for their communicative nor instrumental value. When the anthropologist approaches magic, he fails to see it in its sensual, experiential context, and his failure to see that context makes it seem strange; he imputes belief to those who practice which they may not have; he fails to see the mixture of metaphorical and literal interpretation in the words. Anthropologists, then, are responsible for the seeming strangeness of many magical claims.[30] Sperber argued that symbolism and apparently irrational beliefs arise when the individual confronts information which cannot be processed in the usual manner. 'The symbolic mechanism has as its input the defective output of the conceptual mechanism.'[31] Tambiah adapted Austin's linguistic philosophy to assert that magical acts are 'performative' in nature. The performative utterance does not assert a proposition that can be judged true or false; rather, the utterance itself did something, was intended to act in some way in the world. Tambiah argued that magical statements should be understood as performative actions rather than as scientifically instrumental actions, and be judged accordingly.[32] There are other examples.[33]

Skorupski, who made a detailed and philosophically acute exploration of these different positions, argued for a realist literalism: for an interpretation of ritual in which the statements are taken at face value and assumed to reflect a belief in the divine beings they describe.[34] His strategy in arguing for this position was to identify three theses which might be tenable symbolist

---

[30] Lewis (1980, 1985).

[31] Sperber (1975: 41); see also (1982). The argument gains complexity in the later essay, where he distinguishes between propositional and semi-propositional representations. A propositional representation identifies one and only one proposition: a semi-propositional representation fails to do so. 'Shakespeare wrote Hamlet' is a propositional representation. If one did not know what 'stagflation' meant, one might be willing to accept an economist's statement that it was an economic problem, but one would treat it as a vague, unclear, semi-propositional remark. The vagueness serves a function: to let us cope with difficult-to-cope-with information. 'Our capacity to form semi-propositional representations gives us the means to process information – and in particular verbal information – which exceeds our conceptual capacities' (1982: 170).

[32] Tambiah (1985).

[33] One delightful version speaks to the mask of meaning. The author of an account of the Scottish wedding cake recently argued that a ritual might depend upon the fact that the performers did not know what was at least arguably its original meaning. Scottish wedding cakes have hard, nearly impenetrable icings which the bride and groom must cut through together at the wedding. The ethnographer reported having a dream-like impression of the bride and cake as one, which inspired his understanding of the custom, and cited as evidence that one couple who had mentioned this interpretation (indigenous exegesis of any symbolic meaning was apparently thin) rejected the custom as 'a horrible idea' (Charsley, 1987: 107). He pointed out that he realized the validity of his interpretation when the natives rejected the custom on this basis. Truth's kerygmatic power, as it were.

[34] He makes a number of arguments, one of which is that the use of a generic term for ritual does not capture the diversity of activities which it involves, and tends to collapse different activities into the same category 'symbolic-expressive'. He challenges this easy collapse in order to examine claims about ritual more carefully. He then characterizes religious action as involving more or less direct reference to religious beings in which he believes (this is not that far from Tylor's 'minimal' definition of religion as a belief in spiritual beings (1871: II: 8)), and magic as an action whose efficacy is rationalized according to a particular pattern of thought, usually in which the action is selected by symbolic identification or contagious transfer. Ceremonial action he describes as formal action used to mark out or highlight some action (1976: 161–73).

arguments, and then to explain what philosophical positions would reject them and whether the rejection would be valid.[35] The first was that the real meaning of the ritual – what the anthropologist would pinpoint – was not what the traditional religious doctrine would say. This he rejects, as a literalist: 'It strains credulity to suppose that the Trobriander is unconsciously coping with his lack of analytical concepts while at the conscious level he thinks himself to be talking about the causal antecendents of procreation'.[36] The second was that traditional belief, properly understood, does not imply the real existence of imperceptible beings like gods. This he rejects, as a realist, because it makes sense neither of the ritual – if the gods are only metaphors, what is the point of invoking them in a rite? – nor of the strong religious feelings that do exist toward these gods. The third symbolist thesis is that traditional religion and modern science are comparable neither in logic nor function. This, he says, the intellectualist would reject. Skorupski does not. He argues that there is some validity in a Lévy-Bruhlian description of traditional religion and that the more suitable comparison to traditional religion is modern religion – say, Catholicism.[37]

Philosophers like Skorupski became interested in Evans-Pritchard and the subsequent debate because the material seemed relevant to the analysis of 'meaning': the issue was how far any belief or concept was dependent upon its social context, and whether an outsider, then, could grasp it.[38] Winch argued that when Evans-Pritchard described Azande beliefs as false and unscientific, he failed to understand his own material. The very concept of science, Winch claimed, was culture-bound. There is, he said, no access to an objective, knowable reality. The European cannot claim himself 'right' and the Azande 'wrong': they are playing different language games.[39] MacIntyre attacked by

[35] Skorupski (1976: 174–5). In fact, he explains these theses as determining the compatibility of a certain version of symbolism with intellectualism, a version which he describes as anti-realist. However, he rests the weight of his position on the fate of these three theses, because they determine what positions must be taken within a symbolist or intellectualist account.

[36] Skorupski (1976: 41); general discussion 36–52.

[37] Horton recognizes Lévy-Bruhlian characteristics in traditional religion, but explicated their only 'apparent' paradoxical character by comparing them to scientific concepts in which he saw similar characteristics. 'The sciences are full of Lévy-Bruhlian associations of unity-in-duality and identity of discernibles . . . I shall argue, not only that they are irreducibly paradoxical, but also that their paradoxicality is integral to their role in the process of explanation' (1973a: 232).

[38] Actually, the philosophical inspiration was genuine, but the anthropological content became somewhat garbled. Soon after Evans-Pritchard published the Azande material, he also published an ethnographic account of the Nuer, a pastoral Nilotic people whose interest in cattle is such that they have several thousand terms to refer to different types of animals. Gellner recounts that Winch and MacIntyre began a heated exchange on the meaning of cattle to the Azande and even held a public debate on this subject, to which they invited Evans-Pritchard. At the debate's conclusion, Evans-Pritchard apparently remarked that he had little to add to the philosophical subtlety of the exchange, but that he wished to point out that there were no cattle amongst the Azande. In fact, if one looks up 'cattle' in the index of the 1937 volume, it is listed as 'cattle, absence of'.

[39] Winch was much influenced by Wittgenstein, but there is some doubt as to whether this fervent relativism would have won Wittgenstein's approval. Wittgenstein's position on this sort of full-blooded relativism is notoriously unclear. In *On Certainty*, Wittgenstein seems to seek to show that the search for independent foundations is misguided, but that this does not entail that no beliefs are contestable. Rather, he seems to say, there are beliefs which, pragmatically, are

announcing that our ability to communicate with the Azande implied a shared human framework within which Westerners could assert a more 'rational' interpretation of the physical world. Statements have meaning within a context, but one can understand that context and evaluate it accordingly. 'Beliefs and concepts are not merely to be evaluated by the criteria implicit in the practice of those who hold and use them'.[40]

Several volumes of collected essays appeared,[41] some of the contributions by anthropologists but the lion's share by professional philosophers. These were dominated by two separate but interrelated issues: first, could Westerners claim to translate accurately the thought of another culture, and if so, could they claim a superior rationality? Rephrased, the second issue took science as its icon. Was magic an attempt at being science, and was it just less good, or was it a different kind of enterprise, with different goals to manage?[42]

Many of these essays drew upon a larger background of philosophical discourse. Much of the powerful and significant philosophy of the recent twentieth century has had to do with belief, interpretation and meaning: Davidson's radical interpretation, Putnam's accounts of meaning and rationality, Quine's two dogmas and the indeterminancy of translation, Wittgenstein's slowly influential account of meaning and the use of words. These arguments were essentially the template for the philosophical work in the volumes on rationality. Hacking, for example, speaks of learning from Davidson in order to argue that in translating from another culture, the possibility of a proposition's truth or falsity might depend on whether the translator had suitable ways to reason about it; Lukes takes Davidson on directly for his 'method' of translation.[43] Most of the argument specifically addressed the interpretation of alien cultures, the Azande in particular but also European societies. The

fundamental to our way of deciding about other beliefs, beliefs which are part of the river bed and beliefs which are like the quickly flowing river. There is no clear way to determine the difference between the two, but there is a difference (1969: n. 96, 97). One might then have some legitimacy in arguing that some particular belief in another society was mistaken. G. E. M. Anscombe remarked once that when discussing certainty she asked Wittgenstein how he would respond to an Azande's decision to return from, say, a year in Cambridge to learn to become a witchdoctor. Would he think that good? Wittgenstein apparently walked on in silence for a few minutes, and then responded, 'No. But I do not know why' (in lecture 20.2.86). However, the *Remarks on Frazer's 'Golden Bough'* are primarily concerned with the unsatisfactory characterization of primitive magical practices as 'mistakes'. One need not move from the discussion there to Winch's position, but it is one possible, if tendentious, interpretation of the text.

[40] MacIntyre (1970: 67).

[41] Wilson *Rationality* (1970), Horton and Finnegan *Modes of Thought* (1973), Hollis and Lukes *Rationality and Relativism* (1982), Brown *Objectivity and Cultural Divergence* (1984), Overing *Reason and Morality* (1985).

[42] Many of the contributors did rephrase the question in this way. Overing's volume, however, at least in the introduction, tries to attack the anti-relativistic tendency of the previous volume by asserting that one cannot rank cultures if one takes into account their moral weight, a true but not particularly startling conclusion. The interesting question which that primarily anthropological volume raises is the interdependency of moral understanding and the conception of rationality; this interdependency has been given considerable philosophical play, as in Putnam's understanding of rationality (1981). However, much of the discussion in the rationality volumes concerned the difference between the reasoning in science and that in a pre-science-dominated culture.

[43] Lukes (1982: 263).

mixture of professional philosophy, historical speculation (about what the Paracelsian, pre-Galilean, or Herschelian man had in mind) and ethnographic interpretation led to interdisciplinary confusions between translation as the paradigm of understanding and translation as what the ethnographer or historian does, between meaning as a symbolic aphasia or as an explicit communication to other people, and between intention, reference and truth more generally.[44]

The primary difficulty with the rationality debate is that much of it has assumed the existence of clear cut, coherent beliefs. As a result, it has prejudged the issues, and the basic conception of the problem of irrational action has been ill-formed. At least, the arguments over interpretation and meaning have often been framed around the wrong question. In its crude form the symbolist – intellectualist debate sets up two straw men, the one with his articulate theory like a banner before him, and the other with no beliefs at all but an emotive, expressive, socially apt poesis. On the one side there is the pseudo-scientist, clear, intellectually coherent, acting on the basis of prior beliefs. On the other, there is the intellectually vacuous but metaphorically rich emoter, whose actions carry no cognitive relevance. The debate, then, has centred around the explanation of the apparent belief in magical efficacy. These were the obvious terms in which to set the initial terms of the debate, and it is only by virtue of the strenuous argument about the nature of belief, the role beliefs might play in ritual practice and about other explanations for a seemingly result-oriented ritual practice, that the problems in the argument have emerged. Because the debate was framed in an almost binary fashion – either magic has mostly to do with belief, or it has little to do with belief – the difficulty in arguing about belief has become apparent.

The phenomenon of middle-class magic is not the same as that of magic in pre-literate communities. These are people self-conscious in their rejection, at

---

[44] Somewhat outside the rationality debate proper, other anthropologists addressed the empirical question of how different the human mind can be. Around the late sixties and early seventies, a series of studies attacked the Whorf-Sapir conception of total linguistic relativity and cognitive anthropology emerged. Berlin and Kay (1969) demonstrated the remarkably systematic manner in which cultures acquired basic colour terms; Rosch (1972), from work among the Melanesian Danai, developed the concept of the 'prototype' in category construction. Hallpike (1979), much criticized (see Jahoda, 1982; Shweder, 1982; Lave, 1984) used a Piagetian framework to interpret some of the more marked characteristics of preliterate society, and claimed that primitive thought did indeed differ cognitively from that of educated Westerners, and that the difference could be attributed to the limited possibilities for abstraction and self-referentiality to develop amongst the preliterate. Other mainstream theorists have sought to explain what is colloquially called the 'great divide', the gulf that seems to stretch between the modern West and the preliterate population. Goody (1977) argued tht literacy provided a decisive distinction between primitive and modern by making available a new intellectual technology. Writing altered the cognitive capacities available to a society and enabled changes in the nature of conceptualization itself. The thesis has been challenged (e.g. Eisenstein, 1979; Stock, 1983; Street, 1984; Parry, 1985) but the debate seems to be not yet resolved (e.g. Goody, 1986). Gellner is another major voice in the discussion. The difference, he says, lies in the new ethic of cognitive consistency that dominates modern discourse and development. He identifies the ethic through Kant and Weber: each saw mankind in an ordered world, the one because of the rules of perceptual structure and logical consistency, the other because of the pressures and accidents of human history.

least to some extent, of conventional ideals. Thus they are likely to be more aware of and ambivalent about terms like 'belief' which signal a public commitment to a particular view. Nevertheless I would hope that this book might suggest a productive approach to the study of apparently irrational belief in any culture, because it argues that the ethnographer should look at the reported experience and interpretation of events and the manner in which they influence each other. In this way, the nature and function of magical actions and statements about them may become more clear. This work on magic has suggested that beliefs are not the sorts of things they are stereotypically assumed to be: propositional commitments held consciously and claimed consistently and in a logical relationship to other such commitments. At least in the case of modern magicians, the ideas associated with their practice become persuasive because people rationalize an imaginative, emotional involvement. Their beliefs are not fixed or consistent, for they are often presented to justify some action. Beliefs do a job; they are not always disinterestedly asserted because they are felt to be true in themselves. Ideas and beliefs drift, in a complex interdependency of concept and experience. This interdependency is often given passing acceptance as a cliché, but it is rarely genuinely appreciated when people settle down to analyse the nature of apparently irrational ideas and action. This book has been an attempt to describe the way in which the interpretive drift may take place.

The debate between symbolists and intellectualists has cleared the path for a new sort of discussion, and a new form of ethnographic writing. We need ethnographies that describe the cognitive impact of cultural experience in its natural setting, rich, detailed accounts that are sensitive to psychological theories and philosophical problems but which are neither experimentally based nor speculatively abstract. Above all, we need ethnographies that take the multifarious mind as their topic, but do not take the existence of beliefs, desires, thoughts and the like for granted. The ordinary language categories of mental action are ideal constructions. They presuppose too much about human thought. To guard against these preconceptions but yet to analyse the activity to which they refer demands a careful attention to the terms of ethnographic reference – a hesitation to use words like belief, theory and meaning – and a concerted attempt to avoid folk models of the mind.

The real questions behind most anthropological work on ritual are old philosophical questions on the nature of mind. What is knowledge; what role do intention and intellectual commitment play in public performance; how does one think about the imagination, and about the individuals who tell myths and invent stories? These things are basic to the human psyche, and they are perennially intriguing. I strongly suspect that curiosity in the inexplicable permutations of human thronght attracts most anthropologists to their discipline. What constitutes feeling, memory and fantasy? Why do people dream, create and philosophize? Why should they engage in rituals that seem to serve no overt purpose, practise magic that seems to work no effect, tell myths and legends which they claim to have some eternal verity, assert faith in a being who is insubstantial, indeterminable and capricious? The large questions are the elusive sylphs that tempt us into fieldwork.

Anthropologists can work towards the answers to these questions in ways a philosopher cannot. Professional philosophers struggle to define certain events, like understanding a sentence, in a manner defined by the canons of their scholarly world. Their arguments centre on clarifying messy intellectual concepts: what it means to believe, to know, to state. Many of them have thought of their project as an attempt to give a description of the world which builds up from first principles and clear definitions a portrait of reality. In recent years a Wittgensteinian enthusiasm has led many of these professionals to question whether any such ground rules for articulating concepts can in fact be established, whether there can be rational foundations for our understanding of the world. Words, they say, are necessarily loose and undefinable. These philosophers are attacking a philosophical method that has held sway for many years. They have not in general described the way an understanding of the world can be built up from loose, fuzzy words and concepts: that is perhaps an empiricist's job, something towards which observations of the diversity of human culture may point the way. Geertz remarks that philosophers seem to like anthropology because it provides them with a source of sublunary Martians.[45] Certainly their focus has been upon the coherence of the arguments about their world, rather than on the empirical description of that world, their challenge to analyse a concept of knowledge rather than to determine the empirical correlate to the term's reference. Anthropology has tended in the opposite direction, and while its accounts may provide examples for philosophical argument, the two disciplines are engaged in essentially different projects.

Anthropologists may also contribute in ways that psychologists do not. Cognitive psychologists have studied mental processes through experiment, placing people in artificial conditions to perform what to them are atypical tasks. The testing reveals a considerable amount about the tendencies and capacities of the experimental subject. These experiments are crucial for formulating and examining basic theories of mental heuristics and cognitive capability. But the danger is that one learns about the behaviour of the animal in caged conditions. There has been a recent call for an 'ecological' approach to cognitive psychology, for watching the human mind at play in its natural environment.[46] Even so experiments have been the spine of the research, and the mainstay of much psychological theory: attribution theory, thematic apperception, cognitive dissonance theory and the like. Psychoanalytic work rests for the most part upon individual case analysis, a unit smaller than the one anthropology would consider; it draws its interpretation, moreover, from a base not all anthropologists would accept, though many find its insights useful. But the notable difference between psychological and anthropological approaches is, for better or worse, anthropology's theoretical freedom. Anthropologists tend to value

----

[45] Geertz (1986: 267).   [46] E.g. Neisser (1982).

description highly, and to be suspicious of psychological theories which they fear to have been forged in a Western foundry. The emphasis upon the account of cultural difference and loose anchoring to a particular analytic theory may free anthropologists to observe what psychologists might not.[47]

Anthropology as a discipline rests upon the careful study of societies in their natural surroundings. It is an attempt to give a detailed account of the behaviour of an aggregate of individuals through which we can examine our basic assumptions about human activity. A good ethnography within psychological or symbolic anthropology – the two seem to be different, but to overlap – should be alert to the multiple manifestations of thought and action while assuming as little as possible of the mental baggage which lies behind them. For this, it can be helpful to be aware of some philosophical distinctions, and of psychological experiments and theories, for those tools help to discriminate within the amorphous mass of observed events. But the ethnographer should not necessarily adopt a particular psychological or philosophical approach: the goal is to provide a model to elucidate the fieldwork experience, and the approaches from other disciplines aid a distinctively anthropological enterprise. The basic challenge is to describe what is experienced, how it is interpreted, and how it is rationalized.

There has been a move within anthropological writing to pay increasingly detailed attention to the experience of such events like ritual, and the impact of that experience upon the ritualist. Works by Whitehead, Fernandez, Daniel, Obeyesekere, Crapanzano suggest that experience is prior to belief, for reasons very different than those assumed in a crude Durkheimianism. These anthropologists are more aware of the rationalizing human, that each individual makes sense of his personal past with the tools his psychological capacities and his socialization have given him, that each individual gropes towards the accommodation of powerful instinctual desires and compensation within a world of competing personal and socio-economic demands. They point to the need for detailed description of particular experiences, of styles of paying attention and of rationalization. One of the most pertinent lessons of this ethnography on magic is that involvement entails very particular sorts of

---

[47] Recently, cognitive anthropologists have addressed issues previously within the domain of cognitive psychology. Most of those have focused upon the nature of the category, the linguistic manner in which we carve up the world; participants have discussed intension and extension, propositional networks, inferential patterns, and the like (e.g. Cole and Scribner, 1974; D'Andrade, 1981; Shweder and Levine, 1984; Dougherty, 1985; Lave, 1986; Boyer, 1986; Holland and Quinn, 1987). Some of the recent concerns have been to understand how to characterize aspects of 'traditional thought': what is happening when you ask someone why he performs a particular ritual, and he answers that his ancestors have always done it – and gives no further justification. Others have been to pinpoint the cognitive process behind the everyday activities like shopping or the use of terms like 'mana' or 'good'. Participants have talked of 'maps' and 'schemas' and 'cultural models', terms inspired by current work in cognitive psychology and sometimes adapted in a more speculative manner in the anthropological work. The research has established itself as a vital subdiscipline. Nevertheless it remains for the most part a subdiscipline, isolated from mainstream anthropologists and not mentioned in their work. Moreover, the participants still tend to frame their work in terms of experiments and have rarely used their knowledge more speculatively to produce general ethnographies.

experience, and that these can be identified and described. The material suggests that there are certain basic human experiences which are often associated with magical and religious practice. They are discrete, describable, and – crucially – accessible to any human, regardless of her civilization. Some religions cultivate them deliberately. Others do not. But that these experiences are vivid, and that the experiencer needs to make sense of them in order to make sense of himself – that brute reality is central to any explanation of magical practice. Out-of-body experience, mystical transcendence, meditative peace, visions, hallucinations, oneiric fantasies, imaginative intensity, spiritual unfolding, the excitement of costumes, incenses, chanting, dance, impersonation – all these have a significant impact upon the performer. That they affect the practitioner, and that through his understanding and analysis of them his interpretative style drifts away from its previous moorings, is the most general point of this book; its more specific discovery is the ironic, refracted, play-like belief that seems particular to a self-conscious, modern context.

That anthropologists interpret cultures is a social fact. But it is possible to become complacent in the indulgence of critical skills. The purpose of the discipline is not only to understand individual cultures, unravelled in their idiosyncrasy as the kernel dynamic of a text can be revealed. It is also an attempt to answer compelling questions about the nature of human knowledge and understanding, which it works towards through describing particular instances which challenge comfortable assumptions and which reveal human under-standing in an unexpected light. The questions are large, and the answers can be only partial, suggestive models to account for behaviour. Understanding the difference between cultures and within them brings us moral humility in the face of human adaptation. It also brings us closer to the Delphic imperative under which we struggle.

Bibliography

BOOKS AND ARTICLES

Abelson, R. P. et al. (eds) 1968: *Theories of Cognitive Consistency: A Sourcebook*. Chicago: Rand McNally.

Abrams, M. H. 1971: *Natural Supernaturalism*. New York: Norton.

Adler, M. 1986: *Drawing Down the Moon*. Boston: Beacon.

Agrippa, H. C. 1974: *The Philosophy of Natural Magic* Secausus, N.J.: University Books.

Anand, B. K., G. S. Chhina, and B. Singh 1961: 'Some aspects of electroencephalographic studies in yogis'. *Electroencephalography and Clinical Neurophysiology*, 9, pp. 132–49.

Appel, W. 1983: *Cults in America*. New York: Holt, Rinehart and Winston.

Aronson, E. and J. Mills 1951: 'The Effect of Severity of Initiation on Liking for a Group'. *Journal of Abnormal and Normal Psychology*, 59, pp. 177–81.

Ashcroft–Novicki, D. 1982: *First Steps in Ritual*. Wellingborough, Northamptonshire: Aquarian.

—— 1983: *The Shining Paths*. Wellingborough, Northamptonshire: Aquarian.

Axline, V. 1969: *Play Therapy*. New York: Ballantine.

Ayer, A. J. 1956: *The Problem of Knowledge*. London: Macmillan.

Baelz, P. 1975: *The Forgotten Dream*. London: Mowbrays.

Bagchi, B. and M. Wenger 1957: 'Electrophysiological correlates of some Yogic exercises'. *Electroencephalography and Clinical Neurophysiology*, 7, pp. 132–49.

Bain, A. 1973: *Mind and Body*. London: H. S. King.

Bainbridge, W. S. 1978: *Satan's Power: A Deviant Psychotherapy Cult*. Berkeley: University of California Press.

Banquet, J. P. 1973: 'Spectral Analysis of the EEG in meditation'. *Electroencephalography and Clinical Neurophysiology*, 35, pp. 143–51.

Barker, E. 1984: *The Making of a Moonie*. Oxford: Basil Blackwell.

Barrett, F. 1967 [1801]: *The Magus*. Intro. T. d'arch Smith. Secausus, N.J.: Citadel Press.

Barth, F. 1975: *Ritual and Knowledge among the Baktaman of New Guinea*. Oslo: Universitatsforlaget.

Bartlett, F. C. 1932: *Remembering: A Study in Experimental and Social Psychology*. Cambridge: Cambridge University Press.

Batcheldor, K. J. 1966: 'Report on a case of table levitation and associated phenomena'. *Journal of the Society of Psychical Research*, 43, pp. 339–56.

—— 1982/4: 'Contributions to the theory of PK induction from sitter-group work'. *Journal of the American Society of Psychical Research*, 78, pp. 105–22.

Bateson, G. 1937: *Naven*. Cambridge: Cambridge University Press.

—— 1972: *Steps Towards an Ecology of Mind.* New York: Ballantine.

Beattie, J. 1964: *Other Cultures.* London: Routledge and Kegan Paul.

—— 1970: 'On Understanding Ritual'. In Wilson 1970b: pp. 240–68.

—— 1984: 'Objectivity and Social Anthropology'. In Brown 1984: pp. 1–20.

Becker, H. S. 1963: *Outsiders: Studies in the Sociology of Deviance.* New York: The Free Press.

Beckford, J. 1975: *The Trumpet of Prophecy.* Oxford: Basil Blackwell.

Bellman, B. L. 1984: *The language of secrecy: symbols and metaphors in Poro ritual.* New Brunswick: Rutgers University Press.

Ben-Yehuda, N. 1980: 'The European Witch-craze of the 14th to 17th Centuries: A Sociologist's Perspective'. *American Journal of Sociology*, 86(1), pp. 1–31.

Berger, P. and T. Luckman 1967: *The Social Construction of Reality.* New York: Anchor.

Berkhofer, R. F. 1978: *The White Man's Indian.* New York: Vintage.

Berlin, B. and P. Kay 1969: *Basic Colour Terms.* Berkeley: University of California Press.

Bettleheim, B. 1975: *The Uses of Enchantment.* New York: Random.

Beyer, S. 1973: *The Cult of Tara: Magic and Ritual in Tibet.* Berkeley: University of California Press.

Bion, W. 1961: *Experiences in Groups.* New York: Basic Books.

Black, M. 1962: *Models and Metaphors.* Ithaca: Cornell University Press.

Blackmore, S. J. 1982: *Beyond the Body: An Investigation of Out-of-the-Body Experiences.* London: Heinemann.

Blavatsky, H. P. 1960 [1877]: *Isis Unveiled.* Vols. I and II. Pasadena: Theosophical University Press.

Bledsoe, C. H. and K. M. Robey 1986: 'Arabic literacy and secrecy among the Mende of Sierra Leone'. *Man*, n.s. 21(2), June, pp. 202–26.

Block, M. 1974: 'Symbols, Song, Dance and Features of Articulation'. *Archives Européennes de Sociologie*, xv, pp. 55–81.

Block, N. (ed.) 1981: *Imagery.* Cambridge: Massachusetts Institute of Technology Press.

Bok, S. 1982: *Secrets.* Oxford: Oxford University Press.

Bourguignon, E. 1974: 'Cross Cultural Perspectives on the Religious Uses of Consciousness'. In Zareksky and Leone 1974: pp. 228–243.

Boyer, P. 1986: 'The "empty" concepts of traditional thinking: a semantic and pragmatic description'. *Man*, 21(1), pp. 50–64.

Boyer, P. and S. Nissenbaum 1974: *Salem Possessed.* Cambridge: Harvard University Press.

Bradley, M. Z. 1982: *The Mists of Avalon.* London: Sphere.

Brandon, R. 1983: *The Spiritualists.* London: Weidenfeld and Nicholson.

Brennan, J. H. 1971: *Astral Doorways.* Wellingborough, Northamptonshire: Aquarian.

Brown, S. C. (ed.) 1984: *Objectivity and Cultural Divergence.* Cambridge: Cambridge University Press.

Bruner, J. S., A. Jolly and K. Sylva (eds) 1976: *Play.* Harmondsworth: Penguin.

Budapest, Z. 1979: *The Holy Book of Women's Mysteries.* Parts I and II. Oakland, Cal.: Susan B. Anthony Coven.

Burrow, J. W. 1966: *Evolution and Society.* Cambridge: Cambridge University Press.

Butler, B. 1975: *The Definitive Tarot.* London: Rider.

Butler, W. E. 1959: *The Magician: His Training and Work.* North Hollywood, California: Melvin Powers Wilshire Book Co.

Buzan, T. 1977: *Make the Most of Your Mind.* New York: Simon and Schuster.

Caillois, R. 1962: *Man, Play and Games*. Trans. M. Barash. London: Thames and Hudson.

Capra, F. 1975: *The Tao of Physics*. London: Wildwood.

Carroll, P. n.d.a: *Liber Null*. Leeds: The Sorcerer's Apprentice Press.

—— n.d.b: *Psychonaut*. Leeds: The Sorcerer's Apprentice Press.

Charlsey, S. 1987: 'Interpretation and custom: the case of the wedding cake'. *Man*, 22(1), pp. 93–110.

Chomsky, N. 1968: *Language and Mind*. New York: Harcourt, Brace and World.

Clifford, J. and G. Marcus (eds) 1986: *Writing Culture*. Berkeley: University of California Press.

Cohn, N. 1975: *Europe's Inner Demons*. New York: New American Library.

Cole, M. and S. Scribner 1974: *Culture and Thought*. New York: Wiley.

Colman, A. D. and W. H. Bexton (eds) 1975: *Group Relations Reader*. (A. K. Rice Institute Series), Sausalito, Ca.: Grex.

Comaroff, J. 1985: *Body of Power, Spirit of Resistance: the Culture and History of a South African People*. Chicago: Chicago University Press.

Crapanzano, V. 1973: *The Hamadsha*. Berkeley: University of California Press.

—— 1978: *Tuhami*. Chicago: Chicago University Press.

—— 1985: *Waiting*. London: Paladin.

Crocker, C. 1985: *Vital Souls*: Bororo Cosmology, Natural Symbolism, and Shamanism. Tucson: University of Arizona Press.

Crowley, A. 1976 [1929]: *Magick in Theory and Practice*. New York: Dover.

—— 1970: *Moonchild*. New York: Samuel Weiser.

Cumont, F. 1960 [1912]: *Astrology and Religion among the Greeks and Romans*. New York: Dover.

Cupitt, D. 1976: *The Worlds of Science and Religion*. London: Sheldon.

—— 1980: *Taking Leave of God*. London: SCM Press.

Curtis, W. D. and H. W. Wessberg 1976: 'A comparison of heartrate, respiration, and galvanic skin response among meditators, relaxers and controls'. *Journal of Altered States of Consciousness*, 2(4), pp. 31–7.

D'Andrade, R. G. 1981: 'The Cultural Part of Cognition'. *Cognitive Science*, 5, pp. 179–95.

Daniel, E. V. 1984: *Fluid Signs*. Berkeley: University of California Press.

David, R. (ed.) 1981: *Hakluyt's Voyages*. London: Chatto and Windus.

Davidson, D. 1980: *Essays on Actions and Events*. Oxford: Oxford University Press.

—— 1984: *Inquiries into Truth and Meaning*. Oxford: Oxford University Press.

Davidson, J. M. and R. J. Davidson (eds) 1980: *The Psychobiology of Consciousness*. New York: Plenum.

Deikman, A. 1973: 'Deautomatization and the Mystic Experience'. In Ornstein 1971: pp. 216–33.

—— 1982: *The Observing Self: Mysticism and Psychotherapy*. Boston: Beacon.

Demerath, N. J. and P. Hammond 1969: *Religion in a Social Context*. New York: Random House.

Demos, J. 1982: *Entertaining Satan*. Oxford: Oxford University Press.

Department of Health and Social Security. Mental Health Statistics for England 1984. Booklet One.

Douglas, M. 1966: *Purity and Danger*. Harmondsworth: Penguin.

—— (ed.) 1970: *Witchcraft: Confessions and Accusations*. London: Tavistock.

—— 1975: *Implicit Meanings*. London: Routledge and Kegan Paul.

Dougherty, J. W. D. 1985: *Directions in Cognitive Anthropology.* Urbana: University of Illinois Press.

Drury, J. 1972: *Angels and Dirt.* London: Darton, Longman and Todd.

Dummett, M. 1980: *The Game of Tarot.* London: Duckworth.

Durkheim, E. 1965 [1915]: *The Elementary Forms of the Religious Life.* Trans. J. Swain. New York: The Free Press.

Eisenstein, E. 1979: *The Printing Press as an agent of change.* Cambridge: Cambridge University Press.

Eister, A. W. 1950: *Drawing Room Conversion.* Durham, N.C.: Duke University Press.

—— 1972: 'Outline of a Structural Theory of Cults'. *Journal for the Scientific Study of Religion,* 11(4), pp. 319–33.

Eliade, M. 1964: *Shamanism.* Princeton: Princeton University Press.

Ellwood, R. S. 1978: 'Emergent Religion in America: A Historical Perspective'. In Needleman and Baker 1978: pp. 267–84.

Elster, J. 1979: *Ulysses and the Sirens.* Cambridge: Cambridge University Press.

—— 1983: *Sour Grapes.* Cambridge: Cambridge University Press.

Ernest, C. H. 1983: 'Spatial-imaging Ability, Sex Differences, and Hemispheric Functioning'. In Yuille 1983: pp. 1–38.

Estes, L. 1983: 'The Medical Origins of the European Witch-Craze'. *Journal of Social History,* 17, Winter, pp. 271–84.

Evans-Pritchard, E. E. 1937: *Witchcraft, Oracles and Magic among the Azande.* Oxford: Oxford University Press.

—— 1940: *The Nuer.* Oxford: Oxford University Press.

—— 1956: *Nuer Religion.* Oxford; Oxford University Press.

—— 1965: *Theories of Primitive Religion.* Oxford: Oxford University Press.

—— 1981: *A History of Anthropological Thought.* London: Faber.

Evans-Wentz, E. 1911: *The Fairy Faith in Celtic Countries.* Oxford: Oxford University Press.

Evennett, H. O. 1965: *The Spirit of the Counter-Reformation.* Cambridge: Cambridge University Press.

Farrar, J. and S. Farrar 1981: *Eight Sabbats for Witches.* London: Robert Hale.

—— 1984: *The Witches' Way.* London: Robert Hale.

Favret-Saada, J. 1981: *Deadly Words.* Trans. C. Cullen. Cambridge: Cambridge University Press.

Feldman, S. (ed.) 1966: *Cognitive Consistency.* New York: Academic Press.

Fenton, S. 1985: *Fortune Telling by Tarot Cards.* Wellingborough, Northamptonshire: Aquarian.

Fernandez, J. W. 1977: 'The Performance of Ritual Metaphors'. In Sapir and Crocker 1977: pp. 100–32.

—— 1982: *Bwiti: An Ethnography of the Religious Imagination in Africa.* Princeton: Princeton University Press.

Festinger, L., H. W. Riecken and S. Schachter 1956: *When Prophecy Fails.* New York: Harper and Row.

—— 1957: *A Theory of Cognitive Dissonance.* Stanford: Stanford University Press.

Feyerabend, P. 1978: *Science in a Free Society.* London: New Left Books.

Fischer, M. and G. Marcus 1986: *Anthropology as Cultural Critique.* Chicago: Chicago University Press.

Fortes, M. 1962: 'Installation to High Office'. In Gluckman 1962: pp. 53–89.

—— 1966: 'Religious Premises and Logical Technique in Divinatory Ritual'. In Huxley 1966: pp. 409–22.

Fortune, D. 1979 [1926]: *The Secrets of Dr. Taverner.* Saint Paul, Minn.: Llewellyn.

—— 1934: *Avalon of the Heart.* London: Aquarian.

—— 1935: *The Mystical Qabalah.* London: Ernest Benn.

—— 1985 [1956]: *Moon Magic.* York Beach, Maine: Samuel Weiser.

—— 1957: *The Demon Lover.* London: Aquarian.

—— 1985 [1959]: *The Sea Priestess.* York Beach, Maine: Samuel Weiser.

—— 1960: *The Goatfoot God.* London: Aquarian.

—— 1981 [1962]: *Applied Magic.* Wellingborough, Northamptonshire: Aquarian.

—— 1966: *The Cosmic Doctrine.* Toddington, Glos.: Helios.

—— 1967: *Sane Occultism.* London: Aquarian.

Frazer, Sir J. G. 1922: *The Golden Bough.* Abridged version. London: Macmillan.

French, P. J. 1972: *John Dee.* London: Routledge and Kegan Paul.

Freud, S. 1965 [1900]: *The Interpretation of Dreams.* Trans. J. Strachey. New York: Pocket.

Friedman, C. T. H. and R. A. Faguet (eds) 1982: *Extraordinary Disorders of Human Behavior.* New York: Plenum.

Galbreath, R. (ed) 1972: *The Occult: Studies and Evaluations.* Bowling Green, Ohio: Bowling Green University Popular Press.

—— 1983: 'Explaining Modern Occultism'. In Kerr and Crow 1983: pp. 11–37.

Galton, F. 1983: *Inquiries into Human Faculty.* London.

Gardner, G. B. 1982 [1954]: *Witchcraft Today.* New York: Magickal Childe.

—— 1982 [1959]: *The Meaning of Witchcraft.* New York: Magickal Childe.

Gardner, H. 1987: *The Mind's New Science.* New York: Basic Books.

Gardner, R. 1971: *The Tarot Speaks.* London: Tandem.

Gauld, A. 1968: *The Founders of Psychical Research.* London: Routledge and Kegan Paul.

Geertz, C. (ed.) 1971: *Myth, Symbol and Culture.* New York: Norton.

—— 1973: *The Interpretation of Cultures.* New York: Basic Books.

—— 1983: *Local Knowledge.* New York: Basic Books.

—— 1984: 'Anti- Anti-Relativism'. *American Anthropologist,* 86(2): pp. 263–78.

—— 1986: 'The Uses of Diversity'. The Tanner Lecture, in McMurrin 1986: pp. 251–76.

Gellner, E. 1974: *Legitimation of Belief.* Cambridge: Cambridge University Press.

Gilbert, R. A. 1983a: *The Golden Dawn: Twilight of the Magicians.* Wellingborough, Northamptonshire: Aquarian.

—— (ed.) 1983b: *The Magical Mason.* Wellingborough, Northamptonshire: Aquarian.

—— (ed.) 1983c: *The Sorcerer and his Apprentice.* Wellingborough, Northamptonshire: Aquarian.

Ginzburg, C. 1983 [Italian 1966]: *The Night Battles.* Trans J. and A. Tedeschi. Baltimore, Md.: Johns Hopkins University Press.

Girouard, M. 1981: *The Return to Camelot.* New Haven: Yale University Press.

Glock, C. Y. 1964: 'The Role of Deprivation in the Origin and Evolution of Religious Groups'. In Lee and Marty 1964: pp. 24–36.

Gluckman, M. 1955: *Custom and Conflict in Africa.* Oxford: Blackwell.

—— 1962: *Essays on the Ritual of Social Relations.* Manchester: Manchester University Press.

Goleman, D. 1977: *The Varieties of the Mystical Experience.* New York: Irvington.

Gombrich, E. H. 1972: *Symbolic Images.* Oxford: Phaidon.

Gombrich, R. 1971: *Precept and Practice.* Oxford: Clarendon.

Goodman, N. 1983: *Fact, Fiction and Forecast.* Cambridge: Harvard University Press.

Goody, J. 1961: 'Religion and Ritual: the Definitional Problem'. *The British Journal of Sociology*, 12, pp. 142–64.

—— 1968: 'Time: social organization'. *International Encyclopaedia of the Social Sciences*, volume 6, New York: Macmillan.

—— 1977: *The Domestication of the Savage Mind.* Cambridge: Cambridge University Press.

—— 1986: *The Logic of Writing and the Organization of Society.* Cambridge: Cambridge University Press.

Gordon R. 1972: 'A Very Private World'. In Sheehan, 1972: pp. 64–82.

Gosse, E. 1982 [1907]: *Father and Son.* Harmondsworth: Penguin.

Gould, J. and W. L. Kolb (eds) 1964: *A Dictionary of the Social Sciences.* London: Tavistock.

Graesser, A. C. et al. 1979: 'Memory for Typical and A-Typical Actions: Test of a Script-Pointer and Tag Hypothesis'. *Journal of Verbal Learning and Verbal Behavior*, 18, pp. 319–32.

—— 1980: 'Memory for Typical and A-Typical Actions in Scripted Activities'. *Journal of Experimental Psychology–Human Learning and Memory*, 6, pp. 503–15.

Graves, R. 1968 [1948]: *The White Goddess.* New York: Farrar, Strauss and Giroux.

Gray, W. E. 1975: *The Rollright Ritual.* Cheltenham: Helios.

Greeley, A. M. 1974: 'Implications for the Sociology of Religion of Occult Behavior in the Youth Culture'. In Tiryakian 1974: pp. 295–303.

Green, M. 1971: *Magic In Principle and Practice.* London: Quest.

—— 1983a: *Magic for the Aquarian Age.* Wellingborough, Northamptonshire: Aquarian.

—— 1983b: *Quest List of Esoteric Sources.* London: Quest.

Greene, L. 1976: *Saturn.* New York: Samuel Weiser.

Gregor, T. 1977: *Mehinaku.* Chicago: Chicago University Press.

Griffiths, A. P. (ed.) 1967: *Knowledge and Belief.* Oxford: Oxford University Press.

Hacking, I. 1982: 'Language, Truth and Reason'. In Hollis and Lukes 1982: pp. 48–26.

Hallpike, C. R. 1979: *The Foundations of Primitive Thought.* Oxford: Oxford University Press.

Happold, F. C. (ed.) 1963: *Mysticism: A Study and an Anthology.* Harmondsworth: Penguin.

Harding, S. F. (forthcoming). 'Convicted by the Holy Spirit: the Rhetoric of Fundamental Baptist Conversion'. *American Ethnologist.*

Hardy, A. 1979: *The Spiritual Nature of Man.* Oxford: Oxford University Press.

Harner, M. 1980. *The Way of the Shaman.* New York: Harper and Row.

Hargrave, C. P. 1966 [1930]: *A History of Playing Cards.* New York: Dover.

Harper, G. M. 1974: *Yeat's Golden Dawn.* London: Macmillan.

Haynes, R. 1982: *The Society for Psychical Research.* London: MacDonald.

Hearnshaw, L. S. 1964: *A Short History of British Psychology 1840–1940.* London: Methuen.

Henningsen, G. 1980: *The Witches' Advocate: Basque Witchcraft and the Spanish Inquisition (1609–1614).* Reno: University of Nevada Press.

Herdt, G. H. 1981: *The Guardians of the Flutes.* New York: McGraw Hill.

Hesse, M. B. 1979, 1980: The Stanton Lectures. Unpublished text. Cambridge, Whipple Library.

—— 1984: 'The Cognitive Claims of Metaphor'. In von Noppen 1984: pp. 27–45.

Hewstone, M. (ed.) 1983: *Attribution Theory*. Oxford: Basil Blackwell.

Hobsbawn, E. and T. Ranger (eds) 1983: *The Invention of Tradition*. Cambridge: Cambridge University Press.

Hodgen, M. T. 1964: *Early Anthropology in the Sixteenth and Seventeenth Centuries*. Philadelphia: University of Pennsylvania Press.

Holland, D. and N. Quinn (eds) 1987: *Cultural Models in Language and Thought*. Cambridge: Cambridge University Press.

Hollis, M. and S. Lukes (eds) 1982: *Rationality and Relativism*. Oxford: Blackwell.

Honigman, J. (ed.) 1973: *Handbook of Social and Cultural Anthropology*. Chicago: Rand McNally.

Hope, M. 1984: *Practical Egyptian Magic*. Wellingborough, Northamptonshire: Aquarian.

Horowitz, M. J. 1983: *Image Formation and Psychotherapy*. New York: Jason Aronson.

Horton, R. 1967: 'African Traditional Thought and Western Science'; Part I: 'From Tradition to Science'. Part II: 'The "Closed" and "Open" Predicaments'. *Africa*, 37, (1) and (2) (January and April), pp. 50–71 and 155–87.

—— 1970: 'African Traditional Thought and Western Sciences'. In Wilson 1970b: 131–71.

—— 1982: 'Tradition and Modernity Revisited'. In Hollis and Lukes 1982: 201–61.

Horton, R. and R. Finnegan (eds) 1973: *Modes of Thought*. London: Faber.

Hough, G. 1984: *The Mystery Religion of W. B. Yeats*. Sussex: Harvester Press.

Howe, E. 1972: *The Magicians of the Golden Dawn*. London: Routledge and Kegan Paul.

—— (ed.) 1985: *The Alchemist of the Golden Dawn: the letter of the Revd. W. A. Ayton to F. L. Gardner and others 1886–1905*. Wellingborough, Northamptonshire: Aquarian.

Hugh-Jones, C. 1979: *From the Milk River: Spatial and Temporal Processes in Northwest Amazonia*. Cambridge: Cambridge University Press.

Hugh-Jones, S. 1979: *The Palm and the Pleides: Initiation and Cosmology in Northwest Amazonia*. Cambridge: Cambridge University Press.

Hughes, E. C. 1958: Review of *Why Prophecy Fails*. In *American Journal of Sociology*, 63(4), January, pp. 437–8.

Huizinga, J. 1949: *Homo Ludens*. Trans. R. Hull. London: International Library of Sociology and Social Reconstruction.

Huson, P. 1970: *Mastering Witchcraft*. New York: Perigree.

—— 1971: *The Devil's Picturebook*. London: Abacus.

Huxley, J. (ed.) 1966: *A Discussion of Ritualization of Behavior in Animals and Man*. Philosophical Transactions of the Royal Society. Series B. No. 772. Vol. 251. London: Royal Society.

Jahoda, G. 1982: *Psychology and Anthropology: A Psychological Perspective*. New York: Academic Press.

James, W. 1902: *The Varieties of the Religious Experience*. London: Longman, Green and Co.

Jaspars, J., F. D. Fincham, and M. Hewstone (eds.) 1983: *Attribution Theory and Research: Conceptual, Developmental and Social Dimensions*. New York: Academic Press.

Johnson-Laird, P. N. and P. C. Wason (eds) 1977: *Thinking*. Cambridge: Cambridge University Press.

Johnstone 1979: *SSOTBME*. Petersham, Surrey: Nigel Grey-Turner.

Jones, E. 1961 [1953–7]: *The Life and Work of Sigmund Freud*. Abridged. Harmondsworth: Penguin.

Jones, M. 1977 [1941]: *How to Learn Astrology*. London: Routledge and Kegan Paul.

Jorgensen, D. L. and L. 1982: 'Social Meaning of the Occult'. *The Sociological Quarterly*, 23, pp. 373–89.

Josten, C. H. 1964: 'A Translation of John Dee's "Monas Hieroglyphica" (Antwerp 1564) with an Introduction and Annotations'. *Ambix* xii, pp. 84–221.

Jung, C. G. 1916: *Collected Papers on Analytical Psychology*. Trans. C. E. Long. London: Baillière and Co.

—— 1953: *Psychology and Alchemy*. London: Routledge and Kegan Paul.

—— 1959: *The Archetypes and the Collective Unconscious*. New York: Pantheon.

—— 1965: *Memories, Dreams and Reflections*. Trans. R. and C. Winston. New York: Vintage Books.

—— 1972: *Synchronicity: an acausal connecting principle*. Trans. R. Hall. London: Routledge and Kegan Paul.

—— (ed.) 1968. *Man and His Symbols*. New York: Dell Publishing.

Kahneman, D., P. Slovic, and A. Tversky (eds) 1982: *Judgement Under Uncertainty: Heuristics and Biases*. Cambridge: Cambridge University Press.

Kahneman, D. and A. Tversky 1982: 'Judgement under Uncertainty: Heuristics and Biases'. In Kahneman et al. 1982: pp. 3–22.

Kakar, S. 1982: *Shamans, Mystics and Doctors*. London: Urwin.

Kaplan, S. 1972: *Tarot Classic*. New York: Grosset and Dunlop.

Kasamatsu, A. and T. Hirai 1973: 'An Electroencephalographic Study on the Zen Meditation (Zazen)'. In Ornstein 1973: pp. 269–70.

Katz, A. N. 1983: 'What does it mean to be a High Imager?' In Yuille (ed.) 1983: pp. 39–64.

Kee, A. 1985: *The Way of Transcendence*. London: SCM Press.

Kermode, F. 1979: *The Genesis of Secrecy*. Cambridge: Harvard University Press.

Kerr, H. and C. L. Crow (eds) 1983: *The Occult in America*. Urbana: University of Illinois Press.

King, F. (ed.) 1972: *Astral Projection, Ritual Magic and Alchemy*. New York: Samuel Weiser.

King, F. and S. Skinner 1976: *Techniques of High Magic*. New York: Destiny Books.

King, F. and I. Sutherland 1982: *The Rebirth of Magic*. London: Corgi.

Kirkpatrick, R. G. 1984: 'Feminist Witchcraft and Pagan Peace Protest: Sociology of Religious Counter-Cultures and Social Movement Intersections'. Paper read at the meetings of the American Sociological Association, 24 August 1984, San Antonio, Texas.

Knight, G. 1965: *A Practical Guide to Qabalistic Symbolism*. Vol. II. Cheltenham: Helios.

—— 1975: *Experience of Inner Worlds*. Toddington, Glos.: Helios Books.

—— 1976: *The Practice of Ritual Magic*. Wellingborough, Northamptonshire: Aquarian.

——1978: *A History of White Magic*. London: Mowbrays.

—— 1981: 'The Importance of Coleridge'. *Quadriga*. Part I: no. 17, Spring, pp. 3–13; Part II: no. 18, Summer, pp. 14–22; Part III: no. 20, Winter, pp. 13–15.

—— 1985: *The Rose Cross and the Goddess*. Wellingborough, Northamptonshire: Aquarian.

Kosslyn, S. M. 1980: *Imagery and Mind*. Cambridge: Harvard University Press.

Kuhn, T. S. 1970: *The Structure of Scientific Revolutions*. Chicago: Chicago University Press.

Lakatos, I. and A. Musgrave (eds) 1970: *Criticism and the Growth of Knowledge*. Cambridge: Cambridge University Press.

Larner, C. 1981: *Enemies of God.* Oxford: Basil Blackwell.
—— 1984: *Witchcraft and Religion.* Oxford: Basil Blackwell.
Lasch, C. 1979: *The Culture of Narcissism.* London: Abacus.
Laski, M. 1961: *Ecstasy: a study of some secular and religious experiences.* London.
—— 1981: *Everyday Ecstasy.* London: Thames and Hudson.
Lave, J. 1979: 'How They Think'. Review of Hallpike 1979. *Contemporary Psychology*, 26(10), pp. 788–9.
—— 1986: 'The Values of Quantification'. In Law 1986: pp. 88–111.
Law, J. (ed.) 1986: *Power, Action and Belief.* London: Routledge and Kegan Paul.
Le Shan, L. 1966: *The Medium, the Mystic and the Physicist.* New York: Ballantine.
—— 1974: *How to Meditate.* New York: Bantam.
Leach, E. 1954: *Political Systems of Highland Burma.* London: Athlone.
—— 1961: *Rethinking Anthropology.* London: Athlone.
—— 1967: 'Magical Hair'. In Middleton 1967: pp. 77–108.
—— 1976: *Culture and Communication.* Cambridge: Cambridge University Press.
Lee, R. and M. E. Marty (eds) 1964: *Religion and Social Conflict.* Oxford: Oxford University Press.
Leenhardt, M. 1979 [1949]: *Da Kamo: Person and Myth in the Melanesian World.* Trans. B. M. Gulats. Chicago: Chicago University Press.
Leland, C. 1974 [1889]: *Aradia: Gospel of the Witches.* New York: Samuel Weiser.
Le Roy Ladurie, E. 1987: *Jasmin's Witch.* Aldershot: Scolar Press.
Lévi, E. 1968 [1896]: *Transcendental Magic.* Trans. A. E. Waite. London: Rider.
—— 1959: *The Key of the Mysteries.* Trans. A. Crowley. London: Rider.
—— 1969: *The History of Magic.* Trans. A. E. Waite. London: Rider.
Lévi-Strauss, C. 1963. *Totemism.* Trans. R. Needham. Boston: Beacon.
—— 1966: *The Savage Mind.* Chicago: Chicago University Press.
—— 1967: *Structural Anthropology.* Trans. C. Jakobson and B. G. Schoef. London: Cape.
—— 1975: *The Raw and the Cooked.* Trans. J. and D. Weightman. Harper and Row.
—— 1981: *The Naked Man.* Trans. J. and D. Weightman. London: Cape.
Lévy-Bruhl, L. 1923: *Primitive Mentality* Trans. L. A. Clare. London.
—— 1979 [1926]: *How Natives Think.* New York: Arno.
—— 1975 [1949]: *The Notebooks on Primitive Mentality.* Trans. Peter Riviere. New York: Harper and Row.
Lewis, G. 1980: *Day of Shining Red.* Cambridge: Cambridge University Press.
—— 1985: 'The look of magic'. *Man*, 21(3), pp. 414–37.
Lienhardt, G. 1961: *Divinity and Experience.* Oxford: Oxford University Press.
Lionel, F. 1982: *The Magic Tarot.* London: Routledge and Kegan Paul.
Lloyd, G. E. R. 1966: *Polarity and Analogy.* Cambridge: Cambridge University Press.
—— 1979: *Magic, Reason and Experiences.* Cambridge: Cambridge University Press.
Lofland, J. 1969: *Deviance.* Englewood Cliffs, N.J.: Prentice Hall.
Lofland, J. and R. Stark 1965: 'Becoming a World Saver: A Theory of Conversion to a Deviant Perspective'. *American Sociological Review*, 30 (6), pp. 862–75.
Long, J. K. 1985: 'Psycho-dynamics of PK (Psychokinesis) in Jamaica'. Unpublished paper delivered at the American Anthropological Association meetings in Washington, 4–8 December.
Lord, A. 1960: *The Singer of Tales.* Cambridge: Harvard University Press.
Lowes, J. L. 1927: *The Road to Xanadu.* London: Constable.
Lovejoy, A. 1936: *The Great Chain of Being.* Cambridge: Harvard University Press.

Loyola, I. 1973: *The Spiritual Exercises of Ignatius Loyola*. Trans. T. Corbishey. Wheathampstead, Hertfordshire: Anthony Clarke.

Luhrmann, T. M. 1985: 'Persuasive Ritual: the Role of the Imagination in Occult Witchcraft'. *Archives de Sciences Social des Religions*, 60, 1, pp. 151–70.

—— 1986: 'Witchcraft, Morality and Magic in Contemporary England'. *International Journal of Moral and Social Studies*, 1(1), pp. 77–94.

—— 1986: Scions of Prospero: Ritual Magic and Witchcraft in Present-day England. Unpublished doctoral dissertation. Department of Social Anthropology, University of Cambridge.

—— (forthcoming): 'The Magic of Secrecy'. *Ethos*.

Lukes, S. 1982 'Relativism in its Place'. In Hollis and Lukes, 1982: pp. 261–305.

Lurie, A. 1967: *Imaginary Friends*, Harmondsworth: Penguin.

MacAvoy, R. A. 1983: *Tea with the Black Dragon*. New York: Bantam.

Macfarlane, A. 1970: *Witchcraft in Tudor and Stuart England*. New York: Harper and Row.

MacIntyre, A. 1970: 'Is Understanding Religion Compatible with Believing?' In Wilson 1970b: pp. 62–77.

Mackenzie, K. 1987: *The Royal Masonic Cyclopedia*. Wellingborough, Northamptonshire: Aquarian.

McLoughlin, W. B. 1978: *Revivals, Awakenings and Return: An Essay on Religious and Social Change in America*. Chicago: University of Chicago Press.

McMurrin, S. M. (ed.) 1986: *The Tanner Lectures on Human Values*. London: Cambridge University Press.

Mahathera, P. V. 1962: *Buddhist Meditation in Theory and Practice*. Colombo, Ceylon: Gunaseca.

Malinowski, B. 1961 [1922]: *Argonauts of the Western Pacific*. New York: Dutton.

—— 1978 [1935]: *Coral Gardens and their Magic*. Two volumes, bound as one. New York: Dover.

—— 1954: *Magic, Science and Religion and Other Essays*. Garden City, New York: Doubleday.

Mandell, A. J. 1980: 'Toward a Psychobiology of Transcendence: God in the Brain'. In Davidson and Davidson 1980: pp. 379–464.

Mariechild, D. 1981: *Motherwit*. Trumansberg, New York: The Crossing Press.

Marks, D. F. 1972: 'Individual Differences in the Vividness of Visual Imagery and their Effect on Function'. In Sheehan 1972: pp. 83–108.

Marwick, M. (ed.) 1970: *Witchcraft and Sorcery*. Harmondsworth: Penguin.

Maslow, A. 1964: *Religion, Values and Peak Experience*. Columbus: University of Ohio Press.

Masters, R. and J. Houston. 1972: *Mind Games*. New York: Dell.

Mathers, S. L. MacGregor 1968 [1887]: *The Kabbalah Unveiled*. New York: Samuel Weiser.

—— 1972 [1888]: *The Key of Solomon the King*. London: Routledge and Kegan Paul.

Matthews, C. and J. 1985: *The Western Way*. London: Arkana.

—— 1986: *The Hermetic Tradition*. London: Arkana.

Mauss, M. 1972: *A General Theory of Magic*. Trans. R. Brain. New York: Norton.

Middleton, J. (ed.) 1967: *Myth and Cosmos*. Austin: University of Texas Press.

—— (ed.) 1967: *Magic, Witchcraft and Curing*. Austin: University of Texas Press.

Middleton, J. and E. H. Winter (eds) 1963: *Witchcraft and Sorcery in East Africa*. London: Routledge and Kegan Paul.

Mitchell, J. L. 1981: *Out-of-body Experiences: a Handbook*. London: MacFarland.

Moody, E. J. 1974a: 'Urban Witches'. In Tiryakian 1974: pp. 223–36.

—— 1974b: 'Magical Therapy: An Anthropological Investigation of Contemporary Satanism'. In Zaretsky and Leone 1974: pp. 355–83.

Moon Walker 1987: 'Preparing for Aquarius'. *Quest*, 71, pp. 23–4.

Moore, S. F. and B. Myerhoff (eds) 1977: *Secular Ritual*. Assen: Van Gorum.

Muldoon, S. 1936: *The Case for Astral Projection*. Chicago: Aries.

Muldoon, S. and H. Carrington 1929: *The Projection of the Astral Body*. London: Rider.

Munn, N. D. 1973: 'Symbolism in a Ritual Context: Aspects of Symbolic Action'. In Honigman 1973: pp. 579–612.

Murray, M. 1921: *The Witchcult in Western Europe*. Oxford: Oxford University Press.

Naranjo, C. and R. E. Ornstein 1971: *On the Psychobiology of Meditation*. London: George Allen and Unwin.

Needham, R. 1972: *Belief, Language and Experience*. Chicago: Chicago University Press.

—— 1978: *Primordial Characters*. Charlottesville: University Press of Virginia.

Needleman, J. and G. Baker (eds) 1978: *Understanding the New Religions*. New York: Seabury.

Neisser, U. 1967: *Cognitive Psychology*. New York: Appleton-Century-Crofts.

—— 1973: 'The Processes of Vision'. In Ornstein 1973: pp. 195–210.

—— (ed.) 1982: *Memory Observed: Remembering in Natural Contexts*. San Francisco: Freeman.

—— (ed.) 1987: *Concepts and Conceptual Development*. Cambridge: Cambridge University Press.

Nelson, G. K. 1968: 'The Concept of a Cult'. *Sociological Review*, n.s., 16(13), pp. 351–62.

—— 1969: 'The Spiritualistic Movement and a Need for a Redefinition of Cult'. *Journal for the Scientific Study of Religion*, 8(1), pp. 152–60.

Niebuhr, H. R. 1929: *The Social Sources of Denominationalism*. Cleveland: Meridian Books.

Nisbett, R. E. *et al.* 1982: 'Popular Induction: Information is not Necessarily Informative'. In Kahneman et al. 1982: pp. 101–16.

Noll, R. 1985: 'Mental Imagery Cultivation as a Cultural Phenomenon: the Role of Visions in Shamanism'. *Current Anthropology*, 26(49), pp. 443–61.

Obeyesekere, G. 1981: *Medusa's Hair*. Chicago: Chicago University Press.

O'Dea, T. 1968: 'Cults and Sects'. In Sills 1968: pp. 130–5.

—— and J. O. Ariad 1983 [1966]: *The Sociology of Religion*. Englewood Cliffs, N.J.: Prentice Hall.

Ogden, C. K. and I. A. Richards 1923: *The Meaning of Meaning*. New York: Harcourt, Brace and Co.

O'Keefe, D. L. 1982: *Stolen Lightning: the Social Theory of Magic*. New York: Continuum.

Ophiel 1967: *The Art and Practice of Getting Material Things Through Creative Visualization*. New York: Samuel Weiser.

Oppenheim, J. 1985: *The Other World*. Cambridge: Cambridge University Press.

Orme-Johnson, D. W. 1973: 'Autonomic stability and transcendental meditation'. *Psychosomatic Medicine*, 35, pp. 341–9.

Ornstein, R. E. (ed.) 1973: *The Nature of Human Consciousness*. New York: Viking.

Ortner, S. B. 1978: *Sherpas Through their Rituals.* Cambridge: Cambridge University Press.

Ortony, A. (ed.) 1979: *Metaphor and Thought.* Cambridge: Cambridge University Press.

Oskamp, S. 1982: 'Over-confidence in Case-Study Judgements'. In Kahneman et al. 1982: pp. 287–393.

Otto, R. 1958: *The Idea of the Holy.* Oxford: Oxford University Press.

Overing, J. (ed.) 1985: *Reason and Morality.* London: Tavistock.

Pagden, A. 1982: *The Fall of Natural Man.* Cambridge: Cambridge University Press.

Paivio, A. 1971a: 'Imagery and Language'. In Segal 1971: pp. 7–32.

—— 1971b: *Imagery and Verbal Processes.* New York: Academic.

Panofsky, E. 1983 [1955]: *Meaning in the Visual Arts.* Harmondsworth: Penguin.

—— 1968 [1924]: *Idea: A Concept in Art Theory.* New York: Harper and Row.

Papus n.d.: *The Tarot of the Bohemians.* North Hollywood, Cal.: Melvin Powers.

Paracelsus 1894: *Hermetic and Alchmeical Writings.* A. E. Waite. (ed.) and trans. London.

Parry, J. 1985: 'The Brahmanical Tradition and the Technology of the Intellect'. In Overing 1985: pp. 200–25.

Phillips, D. Z. 1965: *The Concept of Prayer.* London: Routledge and Kegan Paul.

Piaget, J. 1930: *The Child's Conception of Physical Reality.* London: Routledge and Kegan Paul.

—— 1951: 'Mastery Play'. In Bruner, Jolly and Sylva 1976: pp. 166–71.

—— 1966: 'Necessité et signification des recherches comparatives en psychologie génétique'. *International Journal of Psychology*, 1, pp. 3–13.

—— 1972: 'Intellectual evolution from adolescence to adulthood'. *Human Development*, 15, pp. 1–12.

—— 1977: *The Essential Piaget.* H. E. Gruber and J. J. Voneche (eds). London: Routledge and Kegan Paul.

Popper, Sir K. 1959: *The Logic of Scientific Discovery.* New York: Harper and Row.

Price, H. H. and R. B. Braithwaite 1964: 'Half-Belief'. *Proceedings of the Aristotelian Society*, XXXVIII, pp. 149–74.

Prince, R. 1974: 'Cocoon Work: An Interpretation of the Concern of Contemporary Youth with the Mystical'. In Zaretsky and Leone 1974: pp. 255–71.

—— 1982: 'Shamans and endorphins: hypotheses for a synthesis'. In *Ethos*, 10(4), pp. 409–23.

—— (ed.) 1982: Shamans and Endorphins. *Ethos*, special issue 10(4).

Putnam, H. 1981: *Reason, Truth and History.* Cambridge: Cambridge University Press.

Quine, W. V. O. 1960: *Word and Object.* New York: Technology Press.

Radcliff-Brown, A. R 1922: *The Andaman Islanders.* New York: The Free Press.

Rappaport, R. 1979: *Ecology, Meaning and Religion.* Chicago: Chicago University Press.

Regardie, I. 1970 [1937–40]: *The Golden Dawn.* Four volumes. River Falls, Wisconsin: Hazel Hills Co.

—— 1964: *Art and Meaning of Magic.* Toddington, Glos.: Helios.

—— 1969: *The Tree of Life.* Wellingborough, Northamptonshire: Aquarian.

Reichel-Dolmatoff, G. 1975: *The Shaman and the Jaguar.* Philadelphia: Temple University Press.

Rhees, R. 1969: *Without Answers.* London: Routledge and Kegan Paul.

Richards, A. 1956: *Chisungu.* London: Faber.

Richardson, A. 1972: 'Voluntary Control of the Memory Image'. In Sheehan 1972: pp. 109–31.

—— 1985: *Dancers to the Gods: the Magical Records of Charles Seymour and Christine Hartley 1937–39.* Wellingborough, Northamptonshire: Aquarian.

—— 1987: *Priestess: the Life and Magic of Dion Fortune.* Wellingborough, Northampton-shire: Aquarian.

Rorty, R. 1979: *Philosophy and the Mirror of Nature.* Princeton: Princeton University Press.

Rosaldo, R. 1980: *Ilongot Headhunting 1883–1874.* Stanford: Stanford University Press.

Rosch, E. [E. R. Heider] 1972: 'Universals in Color Naming and Memory'. *Journal of Experimental Psychology*, 93, pp. 10–20.

Rosch, E. and B. B. Lloyd 1978: *Cognition and Categorization.* Hillsdale, N.J.: Lawrence Erlbaum.

Rousseau, J. J. 1964: *The First and Second Discourses.* R. D. Masters (ed.), trans. R. D. and J. R. Masters. New York: St. Martin's Press.

—— 1979: *Reveries of the Solitary Walker.* Harmondsworth: Penguin.

Runciman, W. 1966: *Relative Deprivation and Social Justice.* London: Routledge and Kegan Paul.

Russell, B. 1912: *The Problems of Philosophy.* London.

Ruthuen, M. 1988: 'Rapture and the New American Right'. *The Times Literary Supplement*, 29 January – 4 February.

Ryle, G. 1949: *The Concept of Mind.* London: Hutchinson.

Sahlins, M. 1981: *Historical Metaphors and Mythical Realities.* Ann Arbor: University of Michigan Press.

—— 1985: *Islands of History.* Chicago: Chicago University Press.

Sapir, J. D. and J. C. Crocker (eds.) 1977: *The Social Use of Metaphor.* Philadelphia: University of Pennsylvania Press.

Schank, R. C. and R. P. Abelson 1977: *Scripts, Plans, Goals and Understanding.* Hillsdale, New Jersey: Lawrence Erlbaum.

Scholem, G. 1941: *Major Trends in Jewish Mysticism.* New York: Schocken.

—— 1974: *Kabbalah.* New York: Quadrangle/The New York Times Book Company.

Scott, G. G. 1980: *Cult and Countercult: A Study of a Spiritual Growth Group and a Witch-craft Order.* San Francisco: Greenwood Press.

—— 1982: *The Magicians: A Study of the Uses of Power in a Black Magic Group.* New York: Irvington.

Scott, W. G. 1982: *Hermetica.* Boulder, Colorado: Hermes House.

Segal, S. J. (ed.) 1971: *Imagery.* New York: Academic.

Seligman, K. 1971 [1948]: *Magic, Supernaturalism and Religion.* New York: Pantheon.

Sheehan, P. W. (ed.) 1972: *The Function and Nature of Imagery.* New York: Academic Press.

Sheikh, A. A. and T. T. Shaffer (eds) 1979: *The Potential of Fantasy and Imagination.* New York: Brandon House.

Shepard, R. N. and L. A. Cooper 1982: *Mental Images and their Transformations.* Cambridge: MIT Press.

Shils, E. 1956: *The Torment of Secrecy.* New York: Free Press.

Shuman, M. 1980: 'The Psychophysiological Model of Meditation and Altered States of Consciousness: A Critical Review'. In Davidson and Davidson 1980: pp. 333–78.

Shweder, R. 1977: 'Likeness and likelihood in everyday thought: magical thinking and everyday judgements about personality'. In Johnson-Laird and Wason 1977: pp. 446–67.

—— 1982: 'On Savages and Other Children'. Review of Hallpike 1979. *American Anthropologist*, 84, pp. 354–66.

Shweder, R. A. and R. A. Levine (eds) 1984: *Culture Theory*. Cambridge: Cambridge University Press.

Sills, D. L. (ed.) 1968: *International Encyclopedia of the Social Sciences*. New York: Macmillan.

Silverman, D. 1975: *Reading Castenada*. London: Routledge and Kegan Paul.

Simmel, G. 1950: *The Sociology of Georg Simmel*. K. Wolff (ed.) and trans. New York: Free Press.

Singer, J. L. 1974: *Imagery and Daydreams: Methods in Psychotheraphy and Behavior Modification*. New York: Academic Press.

—— and K. S. Pope 1978: *The Power of Human Imagination: New Methods in Psychotherapy*. New York: Plenum.

Skorupski, J. 1976: *Symbol and Theory*. Cambridge: Cambridge University Press.

Slater, H. 1978: *Pagan Rituals*. New York: The Magickal Childe.

Slater, P. 1966: *Microcosm*. New York: Wiley.

Spencer, H. 1887: *The Principles of Psychology*. Vol. 1. New York: Appleton.

Spencer, J. 1983: *The Memory Palace of Matteo Ricci*. Harmondsworth: Penguin.

Sperber, D. 1975: *Rethinking Symbolism*. Cambridge: Cambridge University Press.

—— 1982: 'Apparently Irrational Beliefs'. In Hollis and Lukes 1982: pp. 149–80.

—— 1985: *On Anthropological Knowledge*. Cambridge: Cambridge University Press.

Stace, W. J. 1960: *Mysticism and Philosophy*. London: Macmillan.

Stacey, D. (ed.) 1981: *Is Christianity Credible?* London: Epworth.

Starhawk 1979: *The Spiral Dance*. New York: Harper and Row.

—— 1982: *Dreaming the Dark*. Boston: Beacon.

Stewart, R. A. 1985: *The Underworld Initiation*. Wellingborough, Northamptonshire: Aquarian.

Street, B. V. 1984: *Literacy in theory and practice*. Cambridge: Cambridge University Press.

Stock, B. 1983: *The Implications of Literacy*. Princeton: Princeton University Press.

Summers, M. 1974 [1946]: *Witchcraft and Black Magic*. London: Arrow Books.

Swinburne, R. 1979: *The Existence of God*. Oxford: Clarendon.

—— 1981: *Faith and Reason*. Oxford: Clarendon.

Tambiah, S. J. 1985: *Culture, Thought and Social Action*. Cambridge: Harvard University Press.

Tart, C. (ed.) 1969: *Altered States of Consciousness*. New York: Wiley.

—— 1977: 'Putting the Pieces Together: A Conceptual Framework for Understanding Discrete States of Consciousness. In Zinberg 1977: pp. 158–219.

Taylor, C. 1982: 'Rationality'. In Hollis and Lukes 1982: pp. 87–105.

Tebecis, A. K. 1975: 'A controlled study of EEG during transcendental meditation: a comparison with hypnosis'. *Folio Psychiatrica et Neurologica Japonica*, 29(4), pp. 305–13.

Teffts, S. (ed.) 1980: *Secrecy: A Cross-Cultural Perspective*. New York: Human Sciences Press.

Thomas, K. 1971: *Religion and the Decline of Magic*. New York: Scribner's.

Thompson, J. E. S. 1954: *The Rise and fall of Maya Civilization*. Norman: University of Oklahoma Press.

Thorsson, E. 1984: *Futhark: A Handbook of Rune Magic*. York Beach, Maine: Samuel Weiser.

Timlett, P. V. 1977: *The Twilight of the Serpent.* London: Corgi.

Tiryakian, E. (ed.) 1974: *On the margin of the visible: sociology, the esoteric, and the occult.* Englewood Cliffs, New Jersey: Prentice Hall.

Tiryakian, E. A. 1974: 'Toward the Sociology of Occult Culture'. In Tiryakian 1974: pp. 257–80.

Tolkien, J. R. R. 1965: *The Lord of the Rings.* Three volumes. New York: Houghton Mifflin.

Trevor-Roper, H. R. 1956: *The European Witchcraze.* New York: Harper and Row.

Troelstch, E. 1912: *Protestantism and Progress.* Trans. W. Montgomery. London: Crown.

Truzzi, M. 1974: 'Definition and Dimensions of the Occult: Towards a Sociological Perspective'. In Tiryakian 1974: pp. 243–57.

—— 1974 'Towards a Sociology of the Occult: Notes on Modern Witchcraft'. In Zaretsky and Leone 1974: pp. 628–45.

Tulving, E. 1983: *Elements of Episodic Memory.* Oxford: Clarendon.

Turkle, S. 1984: *The Second Self: Computers and the Human Spirit.* Cambridge, Mass.: The Massachusetts Institute of Technology Press.

Turner, F. M. 1974: *Between Science and Religion: the Reaction to Scientific Naturalism in Late Victorian England.* New Haven: Yale University Press.

Turner, R. (ed.) 1986: *The Heptarchia Mystica of John Dee.* Wellingborough, Northamptonshire: Aquarian.

Turner, V. 1967: *The Forest of Symbols.* Ithaca: Cornell University Press.

—— 1968: *The Drums of Affliction.* London: International African Institute.

—— 1969: *The Ritual Process.* Ithaca: Cornell University Press.

—— 1982: *From Ritual to Theatre: the Human Seriousness of Play.* New York: Performing Arts Publications.

Tversky, A. and D. Kahneman 1983: 'Extensional vs. Intuitive Reasoning. The Conjunction Fallacy in Probability Judgement'. *Psychological Review,* 90, pp. 293–315.

Tylor, E. B. 1871: *Primitive Culture.* Two volumes. Gloucester, Mass.: Peter Smith.

Ullman, M., S. Krippner and S. Feldstein. 1966: 'Experimentally induced telepathic dreams'. *International Journal of Neuropsychiatry,* 2, pp. 420–37.

Valiente, D. 1978: *Witchcraft for Tomorrow.* London: Robert Hale.

Van Blerkom, L. M. 1985: 'The Goddess movement: revitalization among middle class women'. Unpublished paper presented at the 1985 American Anthropological Association meetings in Washington, 4–8 December.

Van Gennep, A. 1960: *The Rites of Passage.* Trans. M. B. Vizedom and G. L. Chaffee. London: Routledge and Kegan Paul.

Vickers, B. (ed.) 1984: *Occult and Scientific Mentalities in the Renaissance.* Cambridge: Cambridge University Press.

Vico, G. 1961: *The New Science of Giambattista Vico.* Trans. T. G. Bergin and M. H. Fisch. London: Cornell University Press.

Vogt, E. Z. 1976: *Tortillas for the Gods.* Cambridge: Harvard University Press.

Von Noppen, J. P. (ed.) 1984: *Metaphor and Religion: Theolinguistics.* Vol. II. Brussels.

Vygotsky, L. S. 1978: *Mind in Society.* Cambridge: Harvard University Press.

Wainwright, W. J. 1981: *Mysticism.* Brighton: Harvester.

Waite, A. E. 1959: *The Pictorial Key to the Tarot.* New York: University Books.

Walker, D. P. 1975 [1958]: *Spiritual and Demonic Magic.* London: University of Notre Dame Press.

Wallace, A. C. 1970: *Culture and Personality.* New York: Random House.

Wallace, R. K. 1970: 'Physiological Effects of Transcendental Meditation'. *Science*, 167, pp. 1751–4.

Wallace, R. K. and H. Benson. 1973: 'The Physiology of Meditation'. In Ornstein 1973: pp. 255–68.

Wallace, R. K., H. Benson and A. F. Wilson, 1971: 'A wakeful hypometabolic physiologic state'. *American Journal of Physiology*, 221(3), pp. 795–9.

Ward, J. 1886: 'Psychology'. *Encyclopaedia Britannica*, Ninth edition. New York, pp. 40–8.

Warnock, M. 1976: *Imagination*. London: Faber.

Waugh, L. 1982: 'Marked and Unmarked: A Choice Between Unequals in Semiotic Structure'. *Semiotica* 38(3/4), pp. 299–318.

Webb, J. 1974: *The Occult Underground*. La Salle, Ill.: Open Court.

Weber, M. 1963 [1922]: *The Sociology of Religion*. Trans. by Ephraim Fischoff. Boston: Beacon.

—— 1976 [1930]: *The Protestant Ethic and the Spirit of Capitalism*. London: George Allen and Unwin.

Wenger, M. A. and B. K. Bagchi 1961: 'Studies of autonomic functions in practitioners of yoga in India'. *Behavioral Science*, 6, pp. 312–23.

Werner, H. 1961 [1948]: *Comparative psychology of mental development*. New York: Science Division.

Westcott, W. W. 1983: *The Magical Mason: Forgotten Hermetic Writings*. Ed. and intro. R. A. Gilbert. Wellingborough, Northamptonshire: Aquarian.

Weston, J. 1920: *From Ritual to Romance*. Cambridge: Cambridge University Press.

Wheatley, D. 1954: *The Devil Rides Out*. New York: Arrow Books.

White, H. 1978: *Tropics of Discourse*. London: Johns Hopkins University Press.

Whitehead, H. 1987: *Renunciation and Reformation*. Ithaca: Cornell University Press.

Whorf, B. 1956: *Language, Thought and Reality*. Cambridge, Mass.: Massachusetts Institute of Technology Press.

Wilby, B. (ed.) 1968: *New Dimensions Redbook*. Cheltenham: Helios Books.

Wilde, J. n.d.: *Grimoire of Chaos Magick*. Leeds: Sorcerer's Apprentice Press.

Williams, J. 1978: *Herbs, Incense and Candle Magic*. London: Aquariana.

—— and Z. Cox. 1979: *The Pagan Pathfinders Book of God Evocations*. London: Pallas Aquariana.

Wilson, B. R. 1970a: *Religious Sects*. London: Weidenfeld and Nicholson.

—— (ed.) 1970b: *Rationality*. Oxford: Basil Blackwell.

Winch, P. 1970: 'The Idea of a Social Science'; 'Understanding a Primitive Society'. In Wilson 1970: pp. 1–17; 78–111.

Wind, E. 1980 [1958]: *Pagan Mysteries in the Renaissance*. Oxford: Oxford University Press.

Winkleman, M. 1982: 'Magic: A Theoretical Assessment'. *Current Anthropology*, 23(1), pp. 37–66.

Winnicott, D. W. 1971: *Playing and Reality*. London: Tavistock.

Wittgenstein, L. 1958: *Philosophical Investigations*. Trans. G. E. M. Anscombe. Third edition. New York: Macmillan.

—— 1979: *On Certainty*. Trans. Denis Paul and G. E. M. Anscombe. Oxford: Basil Blackwell.

—— 1979: *Remarks on Frazer's 'Golden Bough'*. Trans. A. C. Miles, R. Rhees. Retford: Brymill.

Wolters, C. 1961: *The Cloud of Unknowing*. Trans. and intro. Harmondsworth: Penguin.

Yates, Frances 1964: *Giordano Bruno and the Hermetic Tradition*. London: Routledge and Kegan Paul.

—— 1984 [1966]: *The Art of Memory*. London: ARK (Routledge and Kegan Paul).

—— 1975 [1972]: *The Rosicrucian Enlightenment*. Frogmore, St. Albans, Herts: Paladin.

—— 1975a: *Astraea: the Imperial Theme in the Sixteenth Century*. London: Routledge and Kegan Paul.

—— 1975b: *Shakespeare's Last Plays*. London: Routledge and Kegan Paul.

—— 1979: *The Occult Philosophy in the Elizabethan Age*. London: Routledge and Kegan Paul.

Yinger, A. 1970 [1949]: *The Scientific Study of Religion*. New York: Macmillan.

Young, M. 1983: *Magicians of Manumanva: Living Myth in Kalauna*. Berkeley: University of California Press.

Yuille, J. C. (ed.) 1983: *Imagery, Memory and Cognition*. Hillsdale, N.J.: Lawrence Erlbaum.

Zaehner, R. C. 1961: *Mysticism*. Oxford: Oxford University Press.

Zaretsky, I. and M. P. Leone (eds) 1974: *Religious Movements in Contemporary America*. Princeton: Princeton University Press.

Zinberg, N. E. (ed.) 1977: *Alternative States of Consciousness*. New York: Free Press.

PERIODICALS

The Boston Globe 24 March 1984

The Cambridge Evening News 23 October 1982

The Guardian 28 February 1983, 6 March 1983

Isian News No. 40 1986 Enniscolthy: Cysara Publications

The New York Post 7 July 1984

The Pipes of Pan No. 15, Beltane 1984

Resurgence No. 115 March/April 1986

The Sunday Times 21 August 1983

Time Out 3–9 November 1983

Index